COMPARATIVE GOVERNMENT AND POLITICS

Published

Rudy Andeweg and Galen A. Irwin
Governance and Politics of the Netherlands (2nd edition)

Tim Bale
European Politics: A Comparative Introduction (2nd edition)

Nigel Bowles
Government and Politics of the United States (2nd edition)

Paul Brooker
Non-Democratic Regimes: Theory, Government and Politics

Robert Elgie
Political Leadership in Liberal Democracies

Rod Hague and Martin Harrop
* **Comparative Government and Politics: An Introduction (7th edition)**

Paul Heywood
The Government and Politics of Spain

B. Guy Peters
Comparative Politics: Theories and Methods
[*Rights: World excluding North America*]

Tony Saich
Governance and Politics of China (2nd edition)

Anne Stevens
The Government and Politics of France (3rd edition)

Ramesh Thakur
The Government and Politics of India

Forthcoming

Tim Haughton and Darina Malová
Government and Politics in Central and Eastern Europe

Xiaoming Huang
Politics in Pacific Asia

Robert Leonardi
Government and Politics in Italy

* Published in North America as **Political Science: A Comparative Introduction** (5th edition)

Comparative Government and Politics
Series Standing Order
ISBN 0–333–71693–0 hardback
ISBN 0–333–69335–3 paperback
(*outside North America only*)

You can receive future titles in this series as they are published by placing a standing order. Please contact your bookseller or, in the case of difficulty, write to us at the address below with your name and address, the title of the series and one of the ISBNs quoted above.

Customer Services Department, Macmillan Distribution Ltd
Houndmills, Basingstoke, Hampshire RG21 6XS, England

Also by Tim Bale

IMMIGRATION AND INTEGRATION POLICY IN EUROPE:
Why Politics – and the Centre-Right – Matter (*editor*)

This book is dedicated to
Jackie, Javier, Belén and Jack

2nd Edition

European Politics

A COMPARATIVE INTRODUCTION

TIM BALE

palgrave
macmillan

First edition 2005
Second edition 2008

Published by
PALGRAVE MACMILLAN
Houndmills, Basingstoke, Hampshire RG21 6XS and
175 Fifth Avenue, New York, N.Y. 10010
Companies and representatives throughout the world

PALGRAVE MACMILLAN is the global academic imprint of the Palgrave Macmillan division of St. Martin's Press, LLC and of Palgrave Macmillan Ltd. Macmillan® is a registered trademark in the United States, United Kingdom and other countries. Palgrave is a registered trademark in the European Union and other countries.

ISBN-13: 978–0–230–57378–9 hardback
ISBN-10: 0–230–57378–9 hardback
ISBN-13: 978–0–230–57379–6 paperback
ISBN-10: 0–230–57379–7 paperback

This book is printed on paper suitable for recycling and made from fully managed and sustained forest sources. Logging, pulping and manufacturing processes are expected to conform to the environmental regulations of the country of origin.

A catalogue record for this book is available from the British Library.

A catalog record for this book is available from the Library of Congress.

10 9 8 7 6 5 4 3 2 1
17 16 15 14 13 12 11 10 09 08

Printed and bound in China

Contents

List of Illustrative Material viii
List of Abbreviations and Acronyms xiii

Introduction 1
Why European politics? 1
Why this book? 2
Keeping it real – and up to date 3
Where is it going? 4
Getting started 5

1 **Europe – A Continent in the Making** 7
People into empires 9
Empires into nations 10
Nations into states 10
States into blocs 12
The new Europe 16
Europe's economy – rich in variation 17
Regions 19
'Postindustrialism'? 20
Transition 21
Globalization and/or Europeanization? 22
National and patterned variation 23
Whatever happened to 'the classless society'? 26
Women – working but not yet winning? 29
In theory if not in practice – religion in Europe 32
Composition and identity – multi-ethnic, multinational – and European? 35
Learning resources 38
On the web 38
Discussion questions 39

2 **The End of the Nation State?** 40
Stateless nations 40
Belgium – federal solution or slippery slope? 44
'Asymmetrical' federalism – Spain 46
The UK – another hybrid 49
France – no longer quite so indivisible 52
The EU and the end of sovereignty? 54
Origins, enlargement and institutions 55
Integration via economics and law 63
A constitution in all but name? The Lisbon Treaty 64
The end of the nation state? 66
Learning resources 69
On the web 69
Discussion questions 70

3 **From Government to Governance – Running the State, Making Policy and Policing the Constitution** 71
Passing power downwards – decentralization 72
'More control over less' – central government reform 77
Policy-making – sectors and styles 84
The booming third branch of government – the judicialization of politics 90
Learning resources 98
On the web 98
Discussion questions 99

4 **Governments and Parliaments – A Long Way from Equality** 100
The head of state 101
Prime minister, cabinet and parliamentary government 102
Permutations of parliamentary government in multiparty systems 105
Minimal (connected) winning coalitions 105
Minority governments 106
Oversized or surplus majority coalitions 109
Government duration and stability 110
Dividing the spoils – portfolio allocation 110
Governing 111
Parliaments – one house or two? 115

Parliaments – hiring and firing 117
Parliaments and the production of law 118
Parliaments – scrutiny and oversight 122
Parliament and government – the European level 124
Parliament, power and parties 125
Learning resources 129
On the web 129
Discussion questions 130

5 Parties – How the Past Affects the Present, and an Uncertain Future 131
What are parties, and what are they for? 131
Organization 132
Party systems and party families 135
The bases of party systems – social and institutional, luck and skill 150
Party system change? 153
Are parties in decline? 158
The Europeanization of parties and party systems? 162
Learning resources 165
On the web 165
Discussion questions 166

6 Elections, Voting and Referendums – Systems, Turnout, Preferences and Unpredictability 167
Europe's myriad electoral systems 167
Turnout – decline and variation 175
Volatile voting 179
Preferences – what makes people vote the way they do? 180
EP elections 191
Direct democracy – useful tool or dangerous panacea? 192
Learning resources 198
On the web 198
Discussion questions 199

7 The Media – Player and Recorder 200
Variations in usage and style 201
Structure and regulation 204
State and public service broadcasting 208
The connection between media systems and political systems 210
The changing coverage of politics 212
Bias and its effects 220
Pressure groups and populists 226
The impact of ICT – cyber-optimism or cyber-scepticism? 227
The media and 'Europe' 230
'Overseas' news 233
Learning resources 236
On the web 236
Discussion questions 237

8 Participation and Pressure Politics – Civil Society, Organized Interests and Social Movements 238
Participation – the expanding but not necessarily alternative repertoire 240
Pressure groups – different types, different opportunities 245
Pluralism, corporatism and policy networks – some cases in point 247
Rebels with a cause? NGOs and (new) social movements 255
'Venue shopping' and the Europeanization of pressure politics 263
Learning resources 269
On the web 269
Discussion questions 270

9 Politics over Markets – Enduring Differences between Left and Right 271
Has politics ever really mattered? 272
Drifting to the right? The centre-left in Europe 274
Party positions on the welfare state – words and deeds 275
Privatization 283
Flexible labour markets? 288
The EU – deadweight or driving force? 289
The end of the welfare and regulatory state? Separating the facts from the hype 293
Why it still makes sense to be different 295
No easy explanations – the rise of the far right 299
Learning resources 301
On the web 301
Discussion questions 302

10 Not Wanted but Needed – Migrants and Minorities 303
Migration into Europe – then and now 304
Europe's immigrants – grim realities and perceptions 307
Asylum-seeking 310
Encore le plombier polonais! Intra-EU migration since enlargement 314
The new stereotype – migrants and minorities as terrorists 315
Political responses – populism, priming and 'catch-22s' 315
Integrating and protecting migrants and minorities 323
Policy responses – towards 'Fortress Europe'? 326
The Roma – Europe's oldest ethnic minority 330
Learning resources 334
On the web 334
Discussion questions 335

11 Protecting and Promoting – Europe's International Politics 336
Security and defence – the background 337
'Old' and 'New' Europe 339
Still 'the German Question' 342
Russia – Eurasia's (ex-?) superpower 344
Europe's Mediterranean 'neighbours' 348
Towards a European army? 350
Foreign policy 352
Europe in the developing countries 357
Europe and the global environment 361
Europe as a global trader 362
Lest we forget – the enlargement and domestication of international politics 365
Learning resources 369
On the web 370
Discussion questions 371

References 372
Index 400

List of Illustrative Material

Country Profiles

Germany 60
France 88
United Kingdom 112
Italy 186
Spain 218
Poland 258
The Netherlands 296
The Czech Republic 320
Sweden 354

Debates

2.1 Is EU membership a good idea? 68
3.1 Would rule by judges be better than rule by politicians? 97
5.1 Are political parties doomed to extinction? 161
6.1 Should we have more referendums? 195
8.1 Are pressure groups good for democracy? 262
10.1 Should immigration be stopped? 327
11.1 Should Turkey join the EU? 367

Maps

1.1 Europe c. 1500 – on the eve of two centuries of religious wars 11
1.2 Europe during the Cold War 15
2.1 Spain's autonomous communities 47
2.2 The British Isles – the UK and Ireland 50
2.3 France 53
2.4 From the EEC Six to the EU-27 – enlargement, 1957–2007 57
11.1 Europe's Mediterranean neighbourhood 349

Boxes

1.1 Globalization or globaloney? 8
1.2 The Soviet Union and communism 13
1.3 Fascism and socialism 14
1.4 The postwar boom – east and west 16
1.5 Poverty amid plenty – Europe's huge regional variation in wealth 20
1.6 Europe's various welfare state regimes 24
1.7 Births, deaths – and a lot more in between 26
1.8 Politically significant ethnonational minorities in Europe 36
2.1 Break-up in the Balkans 43
2.2 Padania? 44
2.3 Multiple identities: the evidence – and the way forward? 48
2.4 Catalunya – nationality and nation 49
2.5 The hardliners share power at Stormont 51
2.6 The Scottish Executive and/or Government 52
2.7 A dangerous comparison – Quebec and Corsica 54
2.8 Balancing the intergovernmental and the supranational 56
2.9 The EU's supranational institutions 58
2.10 The EU's intergovernmental institutions 62
2.11 Cyprus – where the EU and minority nationalism meet 67
3.1 Separation of powers 72
3.2 Alpine exceptionalism – the Swiss confederation 73
3.3 Germany's *Länder* – not quite as autonomous as they look 74
3.4 The trend towards direct election in European local government 78
3.5 France: *plus ça change* – perhaps not 79
3.6 Neither new nor neo-liberal – government agencies in Sweden 80
3.7 Living up to the stereotype – the civil service in Italy 81
3.8 What, no constitutional court? 91
4.1 *Monsieur le President* – France's executive head of state 101
4.2 The Netherlands' non-parliamentary executive 105
4.3 The Italian *Senato* – powerful or pointless? 116

4.4 The upper house with the upper hand? The German *Bundesrat* 118
4.5 How long does law-making take? 119
4.6 France's feeble parliament 120
4.7 Power outside the plenary – Danish parliamentary committees 121
4.8 Europe's unrepresentative representatives? 127
5.1 The evolution of party political organization 133
5.2 Michels' iron law of oligarchy 134
5.3 Modernization over Marxism – two social democratic parties 139
5.4 Fighting in the centre-ground? – three conservative parties 141
5.5 Crossing classes and denominations – Christian Democratic parties 143
5.6 Two liberal parties; one country 144
5.7 The difficult art of compromise – two Green parties 145
5.8 Different, but all here to stay? Three far-right parties 147
5.9 Making the best of a bad job? Four 'former' communist parties 148
5.10 Insiders and outsiders – two successful regionalist parties 149
5.11 Two farmers' parties – 'ecohumanists' and populists 151
6.1 The timing of elections 168
6.2 'I-voting' in Estonia 168
6.3 The uncertain science of electoral engineering – Italy and Poland 172
6.4 PR or plurality – for and against 176
6.5 Why people's class might no longer predict their vote 183
6.6 The home of direct democracy 193
7.1 Going, going, gone? Age and the decline in newspaper reading in Europe 202
7.2 The agenda-setting Cinderella – radio and politics 204
7.3 Defending whose interests? Ownership and the French press 205
7.4 Poland and political interference 206
7.5 The EU as protector of public service broadcasting 208
7.6 It's not what you do, it's the way that you do it – protecting public decency 209
7.7 People power and Czech public broadcasting 210
7.8 Greece – the battle against government control 211
7.9 Ads and debates 214
7.10 Mars or Venus? Head-to-head debates in France and Germany 215
7.11 Silvio Berlusconi – *il cavaliere* 222
7.12 Other influences 223
7.13 Priming '*l'insécurité*' in the French presidential election 225
7.14 Legislators 2.0? 229
8.1 What is civil society, is it a good thing, and how much does each country have? 239
8.2 New social movements 241
8.3 The F-15 anti-war demo, 2003 243
8.4 The church – sectional or cause group, insider or outsider? 246
8.5 Sweden – the coexistence of corporatism and parliamentary democracy 248
8.6 Poland's trade union movement – defeat from the jaws of victory 253
8.7 Rational choice 256
8.8 Different aims, similar tactics – direct action, old and new, in Germany 257
8.9 Functions of a campaigning group 261
8.10 REACH and the Services Directive 265
9.1 Manifesto tracking 275
9.2 East is east? Left and right in the Czech Republic 278
9.3 A clear choice – the French elections of 2007 280
9.4 Finally, an honest politician? Who's to blame in Hungary? 282
9.5 Does globalization render politics powerless and pointless? 284
9.6 Privatization as politics 286
9.7 Supply-side social democracy in Sweden 289
9.8 EU competition and de-regulation – good for business or good for people? 291
9.9 Big stick or big joke? The EU's SGP 292
9.10 *Vive le plombier polonais*! The EU's Services Directive 293
10.1 Out of Africa, but not necessarily everywhere else – European decolonization 305
10.2 Immigration types and terms 306
10.3 Spain – from sender to receiver 308
10.4 Islamophobia 316

10.5 Too many black sheep? Switzerland's immigration debate 318
10.6 Sweden – still immune? 322
10.7 Determined integration or indefensible discrimination? Bans on religious dress 324
10.8 The EU's Schengen Agreement 326
10.9 Immigration regimes – still path dependent? 329
10.10 Bottom of the heap – Roma in the Czech and Slovak Republics 332
11.1 Europe's traditional democracy promoters – the CoE and OSCE 338
11.2 European Security and Defence Policy – key dates and events 341
11.3 Europe's 'meagre' defence spending 343
11.4 Europe and the aftermath of the 2006 war in Lebanon 344
11.5 Poland and Russia (and Germany) 347

Figures

1.1 GDP, 2005 17
1.2 GDP *per capita*, 2005 – Europe's range and its competitors 18
1.3 The shape of unemployment in Europe, 1961–2006 19
1.4 CO_2 emissions *per capita*, 2004 21
1.5 Public social expenditure as a proportion of GDP, 1983–2003 25
1.6 Changes in inequality, late 1970s/early 1980s to late 1990s/early 2000s 27
1.7 Inequality in Europe compared 28
1.8 More and more women in the (paid) workforce, 1960–2006 30
1.9 Male and female labour force activity rates – towards convergence, 1960–2003 30
1.10 The end of traditional gender roles? 31
1.11 Europe's persistent gender pay gap, 1995 and 2005 31
1.12 The west European decline in church attendance, 1973–98 33
1.13 People thinking that 'the place of religion in our society is too important' 34
1.14 Mixed feelings – European and national identity 37
2.1 EU budget, 2006 63
4.1 Single-party majority government – Greece, 2007 105
4.2 A minimal connected winning coalition – Hungary, 2006 107
4.3 A minority government – Denmark, 2007 108
4.4 An oversized or surplus majority government – France, 2007 109
4.5 A 'grand coalition' – Germany, 2005 109
4.6 European parliaments – the strong and the weak 120
4.7 How much influence European parliaments have over government budgets 123
4.8 EP party groups, 2008 125
5.1 (Lack of) trust in political parties 132
5.2 Party system classification, by fragmentation and polarization 136
5.3 The evolution of Europe's party families, from the nineteenth to the twenty-first century 137
5.4 The German party system after 2005 153
5.5 Eight contemporary European party systems 154
5.6 Party membership, c. 1980 and 2000 158
6.1 The mismatch between votes and seats at the most recent election 174
6.2 The effective number of parliamentary parties at the most recent election 174
6.3 Record lows in turnout – when have they occurred? 177
6.4 Turnout in two postcommunist democracies, 1990–2007 178
6.5 Record-breaking volatility – when has it occurred? 179
7.1 Appetite for news in Europe, 2006 203
7.2 TV as the main source of news 223
7.3 Trust in the media 224
7.4 Penetration of ICT in the EU and US 229
8.1 Variations in associative activity in selected European countries 240
8.2 Patterns of protest in 'western' and postcommunist Europe, 1999–2002 243
8.3 Percentage of people who engaged in at least one 'protest activity' 244
8.4 The gap between less and more active 'protesters' 244

9.1 Average annual growth in public spending on health, 1997–2002 280
10.1 The jobs gap between natives and immigrants in Europe, 2005 309
10.2 Do immigrants make things better or worse? 310
10.3 Perception is reality? The gap between how many 'foreigners' people think there are and how many there really are 310
10.4 Total asylum applications, 1998–2006 313
10.5 Annual asylum applications, per 1,000 inhabitants, 2003–6 313
10.6 Rise and fall in applications in the EU-27, 1998–2006 313
10.7 Proportion of people disagreeing that 'immigrants contribute a lot' to their country, 2006 (and 2003) 316
11.1 Europeans' 'favourable' attitudes to the US (and its rivals) 339
11.2 Europeans' favourable views on Americans, their culture and their ideas 340
11.3 Fighting terrorism – a collaborative effort 348
11.4 'Should decisions on defence and foreign affairs be made by national government or jointly within the EU?' 351
11.5 'Do you think that, fifty years from now, the EU will have its own army?' 352
11.6 'Are you for or against a common foreign policy among the Member States of the EU towards other countries?' 353
11.7 Where ODA channelled through the EU goes 359
11.8 Other countries' views of the EU 361
11.9 'Should decisions on protecting the environment be made by the national government or jointly within the EU?' 362
11.10 Varying attitudes on future EU enlargement 366
11.11 'Do you think that, fifty years from now, the EU will be a leading diplomatic power in the world?' 366

Tables

1.1 Towards the postindustrial economy in Europe? 21
1.2 The growth and current importance of intra-European trade 23
1.3 International poverty rates from the mid-1980s to the most recent year available 27
1.4 Religious adherents in Europe in the twenty-first century 32
1.5 Muslims in the wider Europe 35
2.1 Multiple identities 48
3.1 Levels of government – three examples 75
3.2 The central/regional/local split of taxation, 1995 and 2005 76
3.3 Joined-up government – compartmentalized civil services 82
3.4 Policy styles and their institutional and normative influences 86
3.5 Europe's constitutional courts 92
3.6 New actions taken by the ECJ for the failure of a member state to fulfil its obligations 95
3.7 'Trust' in the legal system, government and parliament 96
4.1 Which type of government occurs most often in which country, 1945–2007? 106
4.2 The upper house – who decides who sits there? 116
4.3 Hours to pass a bill through parliament 119
4.4 Women lose out? 127
5.1 Party family and bloc performance across sixteen European democracies since 1950 156
5.2 No longer beyond the pale – west European radical parties in or supporting governments after 1989 157
5.3 Party funding 159
5.4 Feelings towards political parties – not close but necessary 160
5.5 Transnational party federations 163
6.1 Who uses which electoral system? 168
6.2 PR electoral formulas and the parties they favour 173

6.3 Turnout in selected European countries, 1945–2007 – long-term decline or trendless fluctuation? 177
6.4 The European turnout league table, 1961–99 178
6.5 Switching votes and deciding later, 1970s–1990s 180
6.6 The historical importance of class voting 182
6.7 Turnout in EP elections, 1979–2004 191
6.8 Types of referendums and where they can be used 194
7.1 Percentage of people regularly reading a newspaper 202
7.2 What the media provide at elections 214
7.3 Support for EU membership and self-perceived knowledge about the EU 233
8.1 The rise of 'elite challenging' participation in Europe, 1974–2000 242
8.2 Group and party membership in selected European countries, 1981–2000 245
8.3 Which wage deals are done where? 251
8.4 Unions in Europe 252
8.5 Bird protection societies 261
8.6 Who they like to see most – EU institutions and corporate lobbying 266
9.1 Total tax revenue as a percentage of GDP, 1973–2004 282
9.2 Government expenditure as a percentage of GDP, 1961–2006 283
10.1 Where they are – foreign population as a percentage of total population, 2005 307
10.2 Growth in employment, 1995–2005, foreign-born compared with total population 309
10.3 Top five countries of origin for asylum seekers in the EU-27, 2006 311
10.4 Country capacity and contributions, 2001–5 312
10.5 Where the Polish went 314
10.6 'Successful' populist radical right parties in Europe – electoral performance and parliamentary/government status 317
10.7 The granting of citizenship, 2002–5 325
10.8 Systems addressing racial or ethnic discrimination, 2005–6 325
10.9 Where most Roma live in Europe 331
11.1 EU and US defence spending, 2005 343
11.2 Who spends how much on aid, and where and how they spend it 358

List of Abbreviations and Acronyms

General terms

A-2	Bulgaria and Romania
A-8	Eight CEE states joining EU in 2004
ACP	African, Caribbean and Pacific
ADB	*algemene bestuursdienst* (Netherlands)
AMS	Alternative member system
AMM	(EU) Aceh Monitoring Mission
ASEAN	Association of South East Asian Nations
ASEM	Asia-Europe Meeting
BBC	British Broadcasting Corporation
BME	Black and minority ethnic
CAP	Common Agricultural Policy (EU)
CEE	Central and Eastern Europe
CEEP	European Centre of Enterprises with Public Participation and of Enterprises of General Economic Interest
cefic	European Chemical Industry Council
CET	Common external tariff
CFSP	Common Foreign and Security Policy
CH	*Confoederatis Helvetica* (Switzerland)
CIA	Central Intelligence Agency (US)
CIS	Commonwealth of Independent States
CoE	Council of Europe
CoR	Committee of the Regions
COPA	Committee of Agricultural Organizations
COREPER	Committee of Permanent Representatives (EU)
COSAC	Conference of Community and European Affairs Committees
CPHR	*See* ECHR
CSTO	Collective Security Treaty Organization
DDR	German Democratic Republic – (Communist) East Germany
DG	Directorate General (of the European Commission)
DOM	*Département d'Outre-Mer* (French Overseas Department)
EAJ-PNV	*Eusko Alderdi Jeltzalea – Partido Nacionalista Vasco*
EBA	'Everything but Arms'
EC	European Community
ECB	European Central Bank
ECHR or CPHR	European Convention for the Protection of Human Rights and Fundamental Freedoms (European Convention on Human Rights)
ECJ	European Court of Justice
ECOFIN	Economic and Financial Affairs Council
ECSC	European Coal and Steel Community
EDC	European Defence Community
EDF	European Defence Fund
EEA	European Environmental Agency
EEAS	European Economic External Action Service
EEC	European Economic Community
EFPIA	European Federation of Pharmaceutical Industries and Associations
EFTA	European Free Trade Area
EMU	European Monetary Union
ENP	European Neighbourhood Policy
ENPP	Effective number of parliamentary parties
EP	European Parliament
EPC	European Political Co-operation
ESDP	European Security and Defence Policy
ETA	*Euskadi Ta Azkatasuna* (Basque Homeland and Liberty – paramilitary organization)
ETUC	European Trade Union Confederation
EU	European Union
EUFOR-RDCongo	European Union Force – Democratic Republic of Congo
EUMS	EU military staff
EU-3	France, UK and Germany
EU-15	European Union of fifteen member states (1995–2004)
EU-25	European Union of twenty-five member states (2004–7)
EU-27	European Union of twenty-seven member states (2007–)
EVS	European Values Survey
FDI	Foreign direct investment
FRG	Federal Republic of Germany (West Germany)

FPP	First-past-the-post
FRP	*Framskrittsparteit*
FSU	Former Soviet Union
FYROM	Former Yugoslav Republic of Macedonia
G-8	Group of the world's richest industrialized countries (Britain, Canada, France, Germany, Italy, Japan, Russia, US)
GATT	General Agreement on Tariffs and Trade
GDP	Gross domestic product
GDR	German Democratic Republic (Communist East Germany)
GHGs	Greenhouse gases
GM	Genetically modified/modification
GNI	Gross national income
GNP	Gross national product
ICT	Information and communication technology
ID	Party ID (party identification)
IGC	Intergovernmental conference
IMF	International Monetary Fund
IRA	Irish Republican Army
IRU	International Romani Union
IT	Information technology
JHA	Justice and Home Affairs
JNA	Yugoslav Army
LDC	Less-developed country
LIS	Luxembourg Income Study
M&As	Mergers and acquisitions
MEDEF	*Mouvement des Entreprises de France* (French employers' organization)
MEP	Member of the European Parliament
MMP	Mixed member proportional
MP	Member of Parliament
NATO	North Atlantic Treaty Organization
NELF	New European Left Forum
NFU	National Farmers' Union (UK)
NGO	Non-governmental organization
NI	Northern Ireland
NIC	Newly industrializing country
NIS	Newly independent states
NPM	New public management
ODA	Overseas development assistance
ODS	*Občanské demokratické strany* (civil democratic party)
OECD	Organisation for Economic Co-operation and Development
OPZZ	*Ogólnopolskie Porozumienie Związków Zawodowych* (All-Polish Alliance of Trade Unions)
OSCE	Organization for Security and Co-operation in Europe
p.a.	per annum
PCA	(EU–Russia) Partnership and Cooperation Agreement
PFI	Private Finance Initiative
PPC	Permanent Partnership Council (EU and Russia)
PPP	Purchasing power parity
PR	Proportional representation
QMV	Qualified majority voting
R&D	Research and development
RRF	Rapid Reaction Force
RSPB	Royal Society for the Protection of Birds
SEA	Single European Act
SEM	Single European Market
SGP	Stability and Growth Pact
SIS	Schengen information system
SME	Small and medium-sized enterprises
SOE	State-owned enterprize
SSA	Sub-Saharan Africa
STV	Single transferable vote
TACIS	Technical Assistance to the CIS (EU)
TEU	Treaty on European Union (Maastricht Treaty)
TOM	*Territoire d'Outre-Mer* (French overseas territory)
TRNC	Turkish Republic of Northern Cyprus
UK	United Kingdom
UN	United Nations
UNHCR	United Nations High Commissioner for Refugees
UNICE	Union of Industrial and Employers Confederations of Europe (from 2007, *BusinessEurope*)
US	United States
USSR	(Union of Soviet Socialist Republics) Soviet Union
VAT	Value added tax (sales tax)
WEU	West European Union
WMD	Weapons of mass destruction
WTO	World Trade Organization

Political parties

AKEL *Anorthotikon komma Ergazemenou Laou* (Progressive Party of Working People – Cyprus)
ALDE Alliance of Liberals and Democrats for Europe (European Parliament)
AN *Alleanza Nazionale* (Italy)
AOV *Algemeen Ouderen Vorbond* (Pensioners' Party – Netherlands)
AP *Alianza Popular* (Popular Alliance – Spain)
ATAKA *Ataka* (Attack Coalition – Bulgaria)
AWS *Akcja WyborczaSolidarność* (Solidarity Electoral Action – Poland)
BNP British National Party
BZO Alliance for the Future of Austria
C *Centerpartiet* (Centre Party – Sweden)
CDA *Christen Democratisch Appèl* (Christian Democratic Appeal – Netherlands)
CDC *Convergència Democrática de Catalunya* (Democratic Convergence of Catalunya – Spain)
CDS/PP *Centro Democrático Social/Partido Popular* (Social Democratic Centre/ Popular Party – Portugal)
CDU *Christlich-Demokratische Union* (Christian Democratic Union – Germany)
CiU *Convergència i Unió* (Convergence and Union – Catalunya, Spain)
CSSD *Česká strana sociálné demokratická* (Czech Social Democratic Party)
CSU *Christlich Soziale Union in Bayern* (Bavarian Christian Social Union – Germany)
CU *Christen Unie* (Christian Union – Netherlands)
D66 *Democraten 66* (Democrats 66 – Netherlands)
DC *Democrazia Cristiana* (Christian Democracy – Italy)
DF *Dansk Folkeparti* (Danish People's Party)
DS *Democratici di Sinistra* (Democrats of the Left – Italy)
DUP *Democratic Unionist Party* (Northern Ireland)
FDP *Freie Demokratische Partei* (Free Democratic Party – Germany)
FLNC-UC National Liberation Front for the Liberation of Corsica – Union of Fighters
FN *Front National* (National Front – France)
FpL *Folkpartiet Liberalerna* (People's Party Liberals – Sweden)
FPÖ *Freiheitliche Partei Österreichs* (Austrian Freedom Party)
FrP *Fremskrittspartiet* (Progress Party – Norway)
GL *Groen Links* (Green Left – Netherlands)
IU United Left (Spain)
K *Kristdemokraterna* (Christian Democrats – Sweden)
KESK *Suomen Keskusta* (Finnish Centre)
KSČM *Komunistická Strana Čech a Morava* (Communist Party of Bohemia and Moravia – Czech Republic)
LAOS Laīkós Orthódoxos Synagermós (People's Orthodox Rally–Greece)
LN *Lega Nord* (Italy)
LPF *Lijst Pim Fortuyn* (Pim Fortuyn List – Netherlands)
LPR *Liga Polskich Rodzin* (League of Polish Families)
M *Moderata Samlingspartiet* (Moderate Rally Party Sweden)
MP *Mijöpartiet de Gröna* (Green Environmental Party – Sweden)
ÖVP *Österreichische Volkspartei* (Austrian People's Party)
PASOK *Panellīnio Sosialistikó Kinīma* – Greek Socialist Movement – Greece
PCF *Parti Communiste Français* (French Communist Party)
PCI *Partito Comunista Italiano* (Italian Communist Party)
PDS *Partito Democratico della Sinistra* (Democratic Party of the Left – Italy) or *Partei des Demokratischen Sozialismus* (Party of Democratic Socialism – Germany)
PiS *Prawo i Sprawiedliwość* (Law and Justice – Poland)
PP *Partido Popular* (Popular Party – Spain)
PRM *Partidul Rômania Mara* (Greater Romania Party)

PS	*Parti Socialiste* (Socialist Party – France)
PSL	*Polskie Stronnictwo Ludowe* (Polish Peasants' Party)
PSOE	*Partido Socialista Obrero Español* (Spanish Socialist Workers Party)
PvdA	*Partij van de Arbeid* (Labour Party – Netherlands)
PVV	*Partij voor de Vrijheid* (Freedom Party – Netherlands)
SAP	*Arbetarepartiet-Socialdemokraterna* (Social Democratic Labour Party – Sweden)
SDLP	*Social Democratic and Labour Party* (Northern Ireland)
SGP	*Staatkundig Gereformeerde Partij* (Political Reformed Party – Netherlands)
SLD	*Sojusz Lewicy Demokralycznej* (Democratic Left Alliance – Poland)
SNP	Scottish National Party
SNS	*Slovenská narodná strana* (Slovakia)
SP	*Socialistische Partij* (Socialist Party – Netherlands)
SPD	*Sozialdemokratische Partei Deutschlands* (German Social Democratic Party)
SPR-RSČ	*Sdružení pro republiku* (Czech Republican Party)
SVP	*Schweizerische Volkspartei* (Swiss People's Party)
UCD	*Unión Centro Democrático* (Union of the Democratic Centre – Spain)
UDF	*Union pour la Démocratie Française* (Union for French Democracy)
UKIP	United Kingdom Independence Party
UMP	*Union pour un Mouvement Populaire* (Union for a Popular Movement – France)
V	*Vänsterpartiet* (Left Party – Sweden)
VB	*Vlaams Blok*, now *Vlaams Belang* (Belgium)
VVD	*Volkspartij voor Vrijheid en Democratie* (People's Party for Freedom and Democracy – Netherlands)
WASG	Electoral Alternative for Labour and Social Justice (Germany)

Introduction

Why European politics?	1
Why this book?	2
Keeping it real – and up to date	3
Where is it going?	4
Getting started	5

It is perhaps ironic that a book introducing you to the politics and governance of Europe was conceived as far away from the place as anyone can get. While teaching European politics in New Zealand between 1998 and 2003, I was never quite happy with the textbooks I was using. Basically, there were two types to choose from. The first was the country-by-country approach. As a student, this arrangement has the merit of teaching you a great deal about a few very important countries. But even the best of such books (and there are some very good ones) sometimes leave you not knowing that much about how politics works in the continent as a whole. The approach makes it hard to compare and contrast because it cannot help but stress particularity. The second kind of textbook on offer, organized not by country but by theme, gets over this problem by being explicitly comparative. But this can leave you feeling both overloaded and a little detached from the living, breathing Europe that less abstract country-by-country texts are better able to evoke and convey.

What was needed, I thought, was something that combined the strengths of both approaches – something which did not lose sight of the wood for the trees or the trees for the wood; something that captured *commonality* but also diversity. The time had also come, I thought, to treat both the European Union (EU) and Central and Eastern Europe (CEE) as integral, rather than stranding them in separate chapters from those on the west European Countries. This book is the product of that critique and that thinking.

Why European politics?

This book is intended to be user-friendly enough for the general reader but is aimed at those studying politics for their degree or as part of their degree. Anyone doing that needs to be able (as specifically required in the UK but equally important elsewhere) to 'demonstrate knowledge and understanding of different political systems, the nature and distribution of power in them; the social, economic, historical and cultural contexts within which they operate, and the relationships between them' (QAA, 2000). Studying European politics is clearly one way of doing this. Europe also provides us with comparative material on political institutions, processes and issues – the kind of things that anybody with an interest in politics *per se* is naturally going to be keen to find out more about. Even if you are primarily interested in your own country, you can hardly avoid making comparisons, even if you do it only implicitly. Political science is inherently comparative because it has pretensions to building and testing theories (if not laws) that work *across time and space*; even when its focus is the unique, it attempts generalizable (and therefore) comparative explanations.

But the rationale for studying European politics goes wider than the intellectual. It may, for instance, be quite practical: even those readers who do not currently live or work in Europe may well do so at some time in the future. At the very least, they may pursue careers that involve some passing contact either with European companies or even European governments and the EU. Knowing what makes the continent tick politically, and having some handle on the social and economic issues that preoccupy it, is culturally and practically useful. Nor should we necessarily play down the emotional reasons. Having lived and taught outside Europe for five years, I am as aware as anyone that more and more of us are born and/or brought up outside our family's 'country of origin'. If that country is European, then studying the continent helps achieve a sense of connection to your roots. This obviously applies to students in the so-called 'settler societies' – the US and Canada, Australia and New Zealand, Israel, and South Africa. But it can just as easily apply if, say, you were born and brought up in one European country but your family (or a part of it) has its origins or still lives in another.

There is also a democratic and, if you like, political purpose to studying the politics of other countries. Wherever we live, we are generally given to believe by our own politicians that the way things are done in our country is either in tune with what goes on elsewhere, or probably even better. But when we look abroad we soon realize several things. The first is that 'it doesn't have to be this way': governments that do things differently to the way your own government does them do not necessarily go to hell in a handcart. Second, many of the challenges faced and the solutions offered by the politicians you voted (or did not vote) for bear a remarkably strong (and only sometimes depressing) resemblance to the challenges faced and the solutions offered by their European counterparts. And, third, wherever you are, the picture of European and EU politics painted by the media is almost guaranteed to be highly partial – in both senses of the word. Ample reason, then, to dig a little deeper.

Why this book?

Persuading you that European politics is something worth studying in general is one thing. Persuading you that this book in particular is worth using is another. One reason why it might be is because it is founded on experience in the classroom and is therefore based on what works. What works is providing you with a good balance of breadth and depth, simplicity and complexity, overview and detail. In other words, providing you with a book that will tell you not only what you need to know but also introduce you to issues that you might like to find out more about. A book that communicates the enthusiasm of the author but does not blithely assume you share it – at least at the outset, anyway! A book that you can understand but refuses to talk down to you. A book that avoids jargon when it is unnecessary but is not afraid to use it and explain it (either in the text or in the definitions emboldened in the text) when it is. A book that does not pretend that absolutely everything can be broken down into predigested, bite-sized chunks, but which also realizes that it needs to be accessible. A book that uses bang-up-to-date examples from the real world of European politics, allowing and encouraging you to make connections between what you study in the classroom or the library and what you watch, listen to and read in the media. A book that realizes that, unless it helps you better understand and function in the world as you perceive it, then education – an increasingly expensive commodity – is pretty pointless.

The media has a considerable advantage over an academic work, of course. It may be more simplistic and one-sided, but it is a good deal less time-consuming and even less time-bound. It rarely tells us more than we need to know – even if sometimes that is not quite enough. It is almost always well crafted and presented, with the accent on the visual and a style that aims to grab the attention of busy people who, by and large, can take it or leave it. Paradoxically, the media may also be quite influential: it helps to construct a common wisdom that by definition many of us buy into whatever our political convictions – assuming we have any in the first place. This book is unapologetic about seeking to question at least some of that common wisdom. Part of its point, without trying to sell you a particular world view, is to interrogate some of the popular assumptions – be they conservative or right-on and radical – about European politics and Europe's politicians. That will almost certainly include some of the truths you yourself hold to be self-evident, whether they concern, for instance, the supposed iniquity, inevitability and impact of globalization, the apparently all-pervading electoral power of the media, or the much-trumpeted shortcomings and sell-outs of self-interested politicians.

You should expect, then, to disagree – and anyone who is teaching you to disagree – with quite a bit of what this book says. Some of those disputes, indeed, are crystallised for you in a new 'Debate' feature in some chapters. At the very least, this book may make you think twice. Even if you do not change your mind, your opinions are likely to be the stronger for being tested. Maybe – indeed, probably – you can prove me wrong. Time itself might well do so, too. Part of the mix of fascination and frustration of studying politics is that things never stand still, hence the need for a new edition now and then. A new edition also allows an author to do some of the things he or she realized should have been done before. This time, for example, I have beefed up Chapter 8 so that it includes much more on political participation more generally, but all chapters have been extensively revised in the light of new research.

Keeping it real – and up to date

This book is full of tables and figures that, hopefully, will give you some helpful facts at your fingertips. Even though each chapter mentions all sorts of countries, focusing here and there on particular states that seem particularly relevant to the discussion in hand, I have made the decision to concentrate in the tables and figures on just nine countries. These run from the north through Sweden, down through the UK, the Netherlands, France, and Spain, then over, via Italy, to Germany, and east through the Czech Republic and Poland. Each country is given its own profile, providing an overview of its history, economy and society, governance, foreign policy, and contemporary challenges it faces, along with some further reading and – because it can give an insight into a nation's self-image – a bit of information on its national anthem. Some headline statistics are also provided but, since absolute numbers for things like area, population and GDP can easily be found elsewhere, I have tried to add comparative value by expressing each as a share of the EU total.

These countries are chosen because they are some of the biggest and because they represent variety. They can never, of course, represent every country in Europe. But there is always a trade-off in terms of focusing on a manageable core and doing everything. I have chosen the former, well aware that in so doing I am bound to disappoint some people who hoped to see more of their favourite countries – or at least the ones on which they had decided (or been asked) to write an essay or term paper. Not everybody who seeks to improve European understanding is faced with such a choice. Each of the seven banknotes that make up Europe's single currency, the euro (€), contains a picture of a bridge. Like the bridges on the front cover of this book, the intention is to emphasize links and communication between the different countries of Europe and between the continent and the rest of the world. Unlike those on the front cover, however, the banknote bridges, though apparently prompted by actually existing structures, are imaginary. They represent, if you like, an attempt to inspire without offending those who are left out. On the other hand, they avoid the sometimes messy reality which this book – admittedly a slightly lesser project than the epoch-making switchover to the euro! – tries to encompass and make sense of.

To that end, this book is also full of boxes. They are not there just to break up the text, though if they help do that, all well and good. They are there to provide you with vignettes designed to provide (hopefully) vivid examples of the points the surrounding paragraphs are trying to make. You do not actually have to look at them if you do not want to. But if you do, they should add a lot not just to your enjoyment, but also to your understanding and your ability to recall what you have read – something that can make all the difference when you are in the exam room or trying to pull that paper, essay or dissertation together from scratch. Think of the boxes like hyperlinks on a webpage. You do not have to click on them but it is often worth it when you do; and even when it turns out not to be, you can get back to where you were by hitting the Back button, or in this case just by turning over the page.

These boxes, as well as the book's tables and figures, have been brought up to date for this second edition – and many are brand-new. Of course there are other ways of keeping things current namely, the use of the web and other electronic and print media. This book refers to websites and has one of its own (www.palgrave.com/politics/bale) which will provide selective update material and function as a gateway to other websites. Some of them may be academic: indeed, it never ceases to amaze me how much time we all waste on search engines when a quick look at the electronic contents pages of a few politics journals (many of which offer free, downloadable articles via libraries) would get us what we need much quicker (and with more quality control). With the electronic subscriptions so many campus libraries now hold, many of the journals mentioned in the References are as easy to access as the internet itself. One way to find them is via the databases that most of the same libraries subscribe; another is via Google Scholar. Using these utilities, you can often search all the journals at once, get the citations and very often click straight on to what you want to read, normally in pdf, should you want to print it off and maybe write all over it.

Many websites will, of course, be run by media organizations who make it their business to keep us informed and are becoming increasingly good at providing searchable archives: the BBC's is an excellent example. Other sites, it is true, shut you out just when things get interesting. If you are studying at a university or college, however, you are very likely to find that your library actually gives you free and full access to the premium content that others who are less fortunate would have to pay for. Again, if you use a database (*LexisNexsis* is one, but there are others) you can search many newspapers and news magazines at once and save time doing it. Even if you are not at college or university right now and cannot take advantage of the reduced prices often offered to students, you might want to think about a trial subscription to a news magazine like *The Economist.* Notwithstanding its slightly off-putting title (and, for some, its off-putting editorial line!), it has to be one of the best (and definitely the best-written) concise sources on European (and indeed global) political developments. Subscribing also gives you access to its very useful archive on the web. *Time Magazine,* which is also a good source for in-depth articles on aspects of European society and politics, has a similarly useful searchable archive online – again, a subscription (or campus access) helps. You can, though, get news and opinion free at sites like europeunie.com, euractiv.com, and openDemocracy.net. I should also, of course, mention Wikipedia, regarded by some as a blessing and others as a curse. On balance, I fall into the former group – it is a great source for politics facts, figures and history, and for more besides: I would certainly like to acknowledge here and now the assistance given me by its backgrounders on national anthems.

Where is it going?

Having explained this book's rationale and suggested other places you can go to supplement its content, it is time to give you a broad overview of how the book is organized and to explain why it is done the way it is. What is needed is a route-map, a rationale and a taster all rolled into one.

This text does not assume any prior knowledge of European history. Rather, it starts by providing a brief but systematic overview intended to help both the novice and the person who just needs to fill in a few gaps to appreciate how we got where we are today. It also stresses the need to get to grips with contemporary Europe economically, demographically and sociologically – and with where it might be heading on all three counts.

Once it gets into the politics, this book takes a distinctive approach. Most textbooks begin, very democratically but perhaps rather idealistically, with citizens and then take readers on up through groups, parties, elections, parliaments, governments until they reach the top, the state itself. This book, however, begins at the top. After all, before there were citizens who could vote and groups they could belong to and parties they could vote for, before there were parliaments those parties could sit in and elected governments they could hold to account, there was the state. So, the state – historically if not always logically prior to other democratic institutions – is our starting point. As we show, though, it is an increasingly problematic one, under attack, as some would have it, both from below and from 'above' in the shape of the EU – a body we introduce early on but whose institutions and influence are deliberately woven throughout the chapters on the grounds that they are now woven throughout European politics. This **Europeanization** is an overarching theme and persistent concern in this book.

Europeanization is an observable process – ongoing and contested, more or less voluntary, but neither inevitable nor uniform – by which the policies, institutions, norms, goals and actors of the EU and/or other European countries have a perceptible and significant impact on those of individual European countries; policies, institutions, norms, goals and actors can be 'uploaded' to Europe, just as those from Europe are 'downloaded' to and by individual countries.

Europeanization is a recent and much contested field of enquiry in political science, and there are ongoing arguments concerning its definition and scope (for a recent review, see Graziano and Vink, 2006). Consonant with the working definition supplied above, the following chapters look not for convergence on some imagined 'European model', although many of them find evidence of patterned variation which often allows us usefully to group states. Rather, they look for evidence (and sometimes explanations) of this process of incremental and interactive influence – a process that is always mediated by national variations in political economy (Chapters 1 and 9), public policy (Chapter 3) and, of course, politics, be they bureaucratic politics (Chapter 3), parliamentary politics (Chapter 4), party politics (Chapter 5), mediated politics (Chapter 7), participation and pressure group politics (Chapter 8), or international politics (Chapter 11). The same interactive influence can be seen in the two chapters that concentrate on particular issues: one (Chapter 9) on the oft-noted (but not always accurate) extent to which left and right in Europe are becoming so similar that politics no longer really matters; the other (Chapter 10) on what the media often see as one of the biggest concerns facing European politics – immigration.

The way politicians are handling these and other issues, and the way the institutions they work within and create seem to be moving, involves what is sometimes called **multilevel governance.** This, like Europeanization, is also a persistent theme in this book. The idea of multilevel governance originated

Multilevel governance refers to the fact that the allocation of resources, the delivery of services, and the making of law and policy in Europe is characterized – perhaps increasingly so – by a dispersal or diffusion of power, a multiplication of (sometimes overlapping) sites of authority and policy competence, as well as a mixture of co-operation and contestation between tiers of government that would formerly have been considered more separate and hierarchically ordered.

in academic work on European integration (see Hooghe and Marks, 2001). It combines two things. First, it comprises criticism of academic work that explains integration as the product either of bargaining between self-interested governments or, in contrast, the role of EU institutions. Second, it contains insights derived from research into individual states on the fragmentation of formerly top-down government. Like Europeanization, multilevel governance is thus a portmanteau – and not altogether uncontested – term, but one that arguably describes – and perhaps even helps to explain – the complex reality created by decentralization and the impact of the EU. Unlike Europeanization, the extent of which perhaps varies much more according to the institutions and issues under discussion (indeed, part of understanding European politics nowadays is about getting some idea of where the EU matters more and where it matters less), we are likely to see multilevel governance in evidence in almost all the areas that we explore.

Getting started

Every chapter, then, is self-contained, but – to the extent that they are relevant in each case – each one touches on Europeanization and multilevel governance. Also, every chapter hopefully follows its predecessor in a more or less logical manner. Each one also contains lots of references to the other chapters so you can (to pursue the hyperlink metaphor one more time) click (or in this case flick) from one to the other. In other words, this is a book that can be read cover-to-cover, but one that realizes this is not normally the way things work. If you, or your lecturers, instructors and tutors are anything like me, you are pretty much guaranteed to create your own order to fit either the way your particular course runs or the way your own mind works. Use the contents pages, the definitions, tables, figures, boxes, as well as the index, and the sub-headings, the key points and the summaries contained at the beginning and end of the chapters, to help you 'pick and mix'. Take a look, too, at some of the suggestions in the Learning Resources section which concludes every chapter. And maybe check out some of the citations in the references in the back of the book: most of them are there not just to acknowledge the author (although that is always important in academic work, including student essays and term papers!), but also because I think they are worth chasing up. The web is all very well, but it cannot give you the depth and range provided by the experts who commit their words to the printed page (even if that printed page is available electronically, too). Much of what I cite is chosen with an eye to approachability.

So, there you have it. A book that tries to be a one-stop shop if that is all you want it to be, but also one that provides you with a gateway to other, more detailed and sophisticated takes on European politics. You can use it just for self-directed study. But more likely you will use it as part of a course that someone else has designed. If so, it hopes to sit neatly between the general overview that lectures are normally intended to give you and the more detailed stuff you will discuss in small group classes and read in the library. Hopefully, it will give you enough of what you need, something you might even like and, if you are of an argumentative cast of mind, something you can disagree with as well. If so, neither my time nor your time will have been entirely wasted. And nor will the time of all those whose work, support and generosity has helped me over the years.

Any writer of a textbook inevitably depends, like Blanche DuBois in Tennessee Williams' play, on 'the kindness of strangers' and there are way too many people who have responded to my requests for help – often by way of an email out of the blue – to mention by name. Most will, I hope, see their work cited in the References. Special thanks, though, should go to those who helped me refresh the country profiles, to my Sussex colleagues and students, to the near-legendary Steven Kennedy and his assistant Stephen Wenham at Palgrave Macmillan, and, most of all of course, to my family. This second edition is dedicated, once again and as always, to them.

Chapter 1

Europe – a continent in the making

People into empires	9
Empires into nations	10
Nations into states	10
States into blocs	12
The new Europe	16
Europe's economy – rich in variation	17
Regions	19
'Postindustrialism'?	20
Transition	21
Globalization and/or Europeanization?	22
National and patterned variation	23
Whatever happened to 'the classless society'?	26
Women – working but not yet winning?	29
In theory if not in practice – religion in Europe	32
Composition and identity: multi-ethnic, multinational – and European?	35

Covering around 10 million square kilometres or just under 4 million square miles, Europe is the second smallest of the world's seven continents. But it is number three in terms of population: over 725 million people live there, some thinly spread in the cold of the far north or the heat of the far south, but most packed closely together in towns and cities. That population density, combined with centuries of international trade and the fact that it was the home of the industrial revolution, has made Europe one of the richest and most powerful parts of the globe. In times past, it was also one of the most violent. Its turbulent history was crowned in the twentieth century by two world wars, after which it was divided during nearly fifty years of Cold War into the capitalist 'West' and the communist 'East'. With the collapse of the latter, however, Europe now contains more genuinely democratic states than any other continent on earth.

But Europe, like most continents, is not just a place, a geographical container for those states. It is also an *idea* and an *identity* (see Pagden, 2002). Indeed, because of this, it is actually quite difficult to define it as a place. Our notions of where it begins and ends are fuzzy: they change to suit our conceptions of who should be in and who should be out. The Europe covered in this book is as much of a conventional and convenient fiction as any other. For instance, it excludes some states like Russia, Ukraine, Georgia and indeed Turkey, despite the fact that all of them pop up in the European section of newspapers and news magazines and despite the fact that they could claim (and in the case of Turkey are claiming) to be sufficiently European to join the EU. The Europe covered here basically encompasses those states located between the Mediterranean in the south and Arctic in the north, and between the Atlantic in the west and the Urals and the Caspian Sea in the east. Most of our focus will be on the twenty-seven states that make up the EU, as well as inveterate non-joiners like Norway and Switzerland. This means there is less focus on the Balkan countries of the former Yugoslavia – although, as we shall see below, they have played a dynamic part in European history and provide an extreme example of what can happen when, as is the case in several European countries, multiple nations and/or ethnicities are obliged to live together in just one state.

The first aim of this chapter, however, is to provide some historical background to those concerns. It hopes to show not only how Europe got where it is today, but also how some of what happened to it along the way still resonates with and helps to structure the contemporary continent. The latter then becomes the chapter's main focus as it explores what Europe looks like now and how is it changing – economically, demographically and sociologically. All three aspects play a huge part in political processes, preoccupations and possibilities, not least because they help structure what political scientists call **cleavages**.

> **Cleavages** are splits or divisions in a society that give rise to conflicts that may well be expressed in political form – often, though not necessarily, via the formation of opposing parties representing people on either side of the split.

Exploring the 'then and now', and indeed the 'where next?' helps us to question and qualify some of the common wisdom surrounding social and economic (and so, perhaps, political) change. For instance, the welfare state appears to be alive and well but neither it nor mass education have brought about a classless society – social mobility and equality may even be decreasing. Certainly, women are not doing as well as some of their mothers and grandmothers might have hoped – a continued inequality that is remarkable not just because (as we shall see in, say, Chapter 4) it is reflected in a similar lack of progress in political institutions, but also because (unlike class inequality which continues to some extent to mobilise voters and parties) it does not seem to lead to much political discontent or expression on the part of those who suffer it (see Chapters 5 and 6). Conversely, a phenomenon that, as we note in this chapter, is often assumed to be on the wane – namely, religion – would still appear, at least in some countries, to help structure, say, the party systems and voting behaviour we examine in Chapters 5 and 6. Meanwhile, the ethnic minorities and identities we also deal with below not only have an impact on representative politics but, as we will see in Chapter 2, can threaten the integrity of states in which that representative politics largely takes place, as well as (see Chapter 10) creating political tensions between those living in them.

More generally, the chapter shows that European countries, and the people who live in them, may be growing a little less unlike each other. But it also gives us little reason to think that either Europeanization (which we defined in the Introduction) or *globalization* (discussed in Box 1.1), necessarily entail convergence, let alone homogenization. Europe may be coming together literally as well as figuratively in the guise and under the umbrella of

BOX 1.1

Globalization or globaloney?

Globalization has got to be the biggest buzzword of the twenty-first century so far. But like many buzzwords its meaning is a little fuzzy and the evidence for it not always as solid as those who bandy it about often assume. In short, the fact that the concept is used so often – as well as blamed or praised for almost all the woes and the wonders of contemporary life – does not make it true or mean that it explains that much.

As far as meaning goes, there are many versions (see Scholte, 2001 and Zolo, 2007). But the most popular ones are encapsulated in the following definitions:

> The intensification of worldwide social relations which link distant localities in such a way that local happenings are shaped by events occurring many miles away and vice versa. (Giddens, 1990: 64)

> A process (or set of processes) which embodies a transformation in the spatial organization of social relations and transactions – assessed in terms of their extensity, intensity, velocity and impact – generating transcontinental or interregional flows and networks of activity. (Held *et al.*, 1999: 16)

> A social process in which the constraints of geography on economic, political, social and cultural arrangements recede, in which people become increasingly aware that they are receding and in which they act accordingly. (Waters, 2001: 5)

Apart from this apparent collapse of time, space and national and regional difference, other writers see globalization as western capitalist imperialism by another name (see Hardt and Negri, 2000) and/or as heralding the end of the nation state and the rise of transnational states (see Sklair, 2000).

As far as evidence goes, there are, however, many analysts who are sceptical, claiming the rhetoric surrounding globalization may be more important than the reality, which is nowhere near as all-encompassing and transformative as many of us now routinely and casually assume (see Hay, 2000; Hirst and Thompson, 1999; and Mann, 1997).

the EU. As a result, it is already more than simply the sum of its parts. But, at the beginning of the twenty-first century, the contrasts and contradictions between those parts – contrasts and contradictions that emerged over hundreds and thousands of years of often overlapping development – are not disappearing quite as fast as we might think.

This chapter, then, provides the context for what we find in later chapters whose focus is more expressly political; namely, some shared (but rarely identical) challenges faced by countries with sometimes remarkably different cultures, conflicts and bureaucratic and representative arrangements (see Chapters 3, 4 and 6). By recounting in some detail the continent's sometimes bloody history and economic variation that led to such differences, it also indicates why a European integration project that seems to hold out peace and prosperity (see Chapter 2) has proved so attractive to so many countries. At the same time, it hints at why such a project may be more popular with the citizens of some countries than with those of others, as well as at the continued challenges faced on the foreign policy front by both individual countries and the EU acting collectively – challenges we deal with in Chapter 11.

People into empires

People have been around in Europe since the first Stone Age. From around 6000 BC, nomadic hunter-gathering began to give way to farming. And by the time the first Indo-Europeans began arriving in the southern and western part of the continent after 2500 BC, people were already working bronze, trading, and practising religious rites. Early civilizations included the Minoans of Crete and the Indo-European Mycenaeans, who by 1500 BC not only controlled most of Greece but had also supplanted the Minoans. In more central parts of Europe, a rapidly expanding population was beginning to work iron and had already begun to form (language) groups with which we are still familiar today. Celts lived at the western borders of the continent, Slavs in the east and the Germanic peoples in the north. In the south, the Greeks had recovered from the decay of the Mycenaean culture and now formed a number of powerful city-states. They were also expanding into what we now call southern Italy – a land whose northern half was peopled by the Villanovans and then the Etruscans, who, soon after it was founded, took control of Rome.

KEY POINT

The continent's early history was characterized by pan-European enterprises, like the Roman Empire, that rose to prominence and then, unable to maintain a grip on their far-flung territories, fell into disrepair.

In the fifth century BC, however, it was the city-state of Athens which, after fighting off Persia (modern-day Iran), was the foremost power in Europe. It was also home to many of the classical political philosophers, such as Aristotle and Plato, whom we read even today. Its ambitions proved too strong for its own good, however. Greece descended into a series of wars between the various cities, the devastating consequences of which made it relatively easy prey for Macedonia, to the north. Macedonia's Alexander the Great then proceeded to forge an empire from both Greece and Persia. By the middle of the second century BC, however, that empire was controlled by the Romans. Previously, they had taken not only all of Italy but also that part of Europe that bordered the Mediterranean sea, as well as much of North Africa and the Middle East. Although Greek culture was allowed to thrive by the Romans, they insisted that all those living under their protection become citizens of Rome and encouraged the use of the Latin language. This, and their commitment to building a transport infrastructure, facilitated trading and other contacts among the peoples of Europe (and North Africa and the Middle East). This helped usher in a period of prosperity and economic development throughout the continent.

Despite a series of civil wars, the Roman Empire persisted into the fourth century AD. By then, Christianity had become what amounted to its 'official religion', and the political and administrative centre of gravity had shifted east to Constantinople (now Istanbul). By the fifth century, however, Germanic peoples such as the Franks, the Visigoths and the Vandals (famous for their sackings of Rome) had first undermined and then destroyed the western part of the empire. What they did not undo, though, was the wide-spread use of Latinate languages and Christianity, with the latter increasingly under the sway of the head of the Roman Catholic church, the Pope. By the beginning of the ninth century AD, this religious power combined to mutual advantage with the military and political power of the Franks to form what became known as the 'Holy Roman Empire', under Charlemagne.

Empires into nations

This new empire, however, was a rather loosely coupled affair with overlapping authority exercised by various kings and princes. It also proved no more immune to invasion and division than its Greek and Roman predecessors. The Vikings came from Scandinavia and settled in mainland Europe, including the northernmost part of France, eventually producing a duke, William of Normandy, who became the conqueror of England in 1066. Elsewhere, too, monarchs other than the emperor, as well as lesser nobles, monastic orders such as the Benedictines, and eventually the papacy itself, dominated their own territories, wherein the 'feudal system' (the granting, from the king downwards, of land and rights in exchange for military and political support) gradually took hold. At the same time, Europe's economy and population expanded prodigiously, as did the towns and cities which, despite the power of the feudal nobility who often continued to live in less urban areas, became centres of commerce, religion and education. These developments provided the resources and the rationale for the Christian Crusades in the Holy Land (now the Middle East) of the eleventh, twelfth and thirteenth centuries. They also financed the overseas voyages of exploration to more far-flung continents, all of which were to provide new sources of wealth and raw materials and eventually empire and colonies.

KEY POINT

Later pan-European empires, such as the Holy Roman Empire, were even more loosely coupled and gave way to smaller nations run more effectively by monarchs. Some of these – with Spain in the vanguard but Britain not far behind – began to seek their own empires in the New Worlds of America and India.

The earliest beneficiaries of overseas expansion were Portugal and, in particular, Spain. Since the expulsion of the Moors of North Africa in the late fifteenth century and the subordination of the country's component kingdoms to that of Castile, Spain had become a firmly Christian country. It also became the foremost upholder of Roman Catholicism against the threat posed to it by what became known as Protestantism. This dissenting movement – aided by the invention of the printing press and the ambitions of German princes who chafed against the Holy Roman Empire – had grown up in central and northern parts of Europe at the beginning of the sixteenth century in both spiritual and political opposition to what it saw as the corrupt papacy. This role as defender of the faith helped put Spain on a collision course with its commercial rival, England which, after breaking with Rome over the Pope's refusal to acquiesce in its king's divorce plans, had adopted a non-Roman Catholic hybrid known as Anglicanism as a state religion. Spain's Armada, a sea-led invasion fleet, was defeated, and the country slipped into its long-term decline, its apparently endless access to the gold of South America stymieing economic dynamism. The religious question in the British Isles, however, was by no means decided and, as it did all over Europe, played a part in politics in the run up to and long after the country's civil war in the 1640s (see Map 1.1).

Nations into states

In fact, religious conflict and political self-interest and expression combined to cause wars not only between but also within countries throughout late sixteenth- and early seventeenth-century Europe – and not just in the west. Hungary, for example, had

KEY POINT

Competition between Europe's monarchies, and conflicts over religion, encouraged warfare that needed to be paid for, leading to greater centralization and to international treaties that established some if not all the borders we know today.

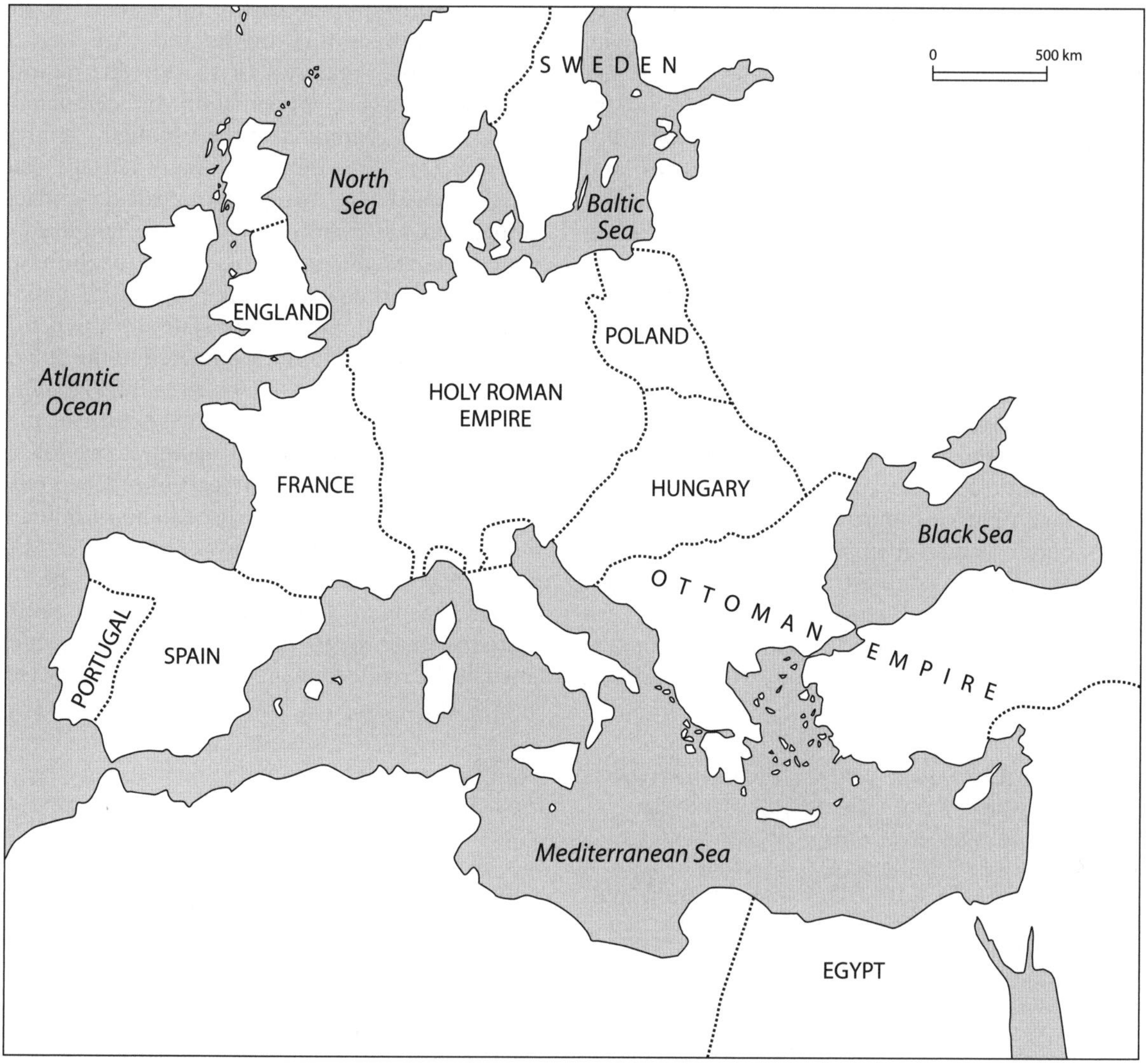

Map 1.1 Europe *c.* 1500 – on the eve of two centuries of religious wars

been one of central Europe's strongest powers but spent much of its strength on successive wars against the Islamic Ottoman empire, centred in what we now call Turkey. By the sixteenth century, however, its former rulers, the Habsburg dynasty of Austria, who also held the crown of the rather fragmented Holy Roman Empire, took advantage of Hungary's weakness to restore Roman Catholicism to a country that had – officially anyway – become Protestant. Struggles such as this culminated in the so-called Thirty Years' War. Fought between 1618 and 1648, it brought the Scandinavian countries into a prolonged armed conflict that also involved the kings and princes of central and western Europe. It also saw France emerge not just as mainland Europe's strongest rival to British power, but also as a centralized state with a large bureaucracy and a military maintained to fight wars, many of them aggressive rather than defensive, in what was supposedly the national interest.

This model was copied by other European states, so France's pioneering role did not grant it predominance for long. By the late eighteenth century, Europe was characterized not by one 'hegemonic' (all powerful) nation but by a so-called **balance of power** between countries such as France, Britain, Austria (and its unstable empire in Hungary and elsewhere) and Prussia, part of what we now know as Germany. By the nineteenth century, Europe was also characterized by a mixture of monarchies and republics. France had become the most famous of the latter, with its revolution acting as a shining example to some and a dire warning to others of the possibilities and the risks inherent in turning political ideals into reality. After what amounted to ten years of permanent upheaval from 1789 onwards, that revolution succumbed to the dictatorship of Napoleon Bonaparte. Napoleon declared himself emperor and proceeded to centralize the French state even further. He also unleashed a succession of aggressive military campaigns against other countries, onto which he attempted, quite successfully, to graft the French administrative model. That was until he overreached himself in Russia and was defeated by the combined might of Britain and Prussia at the battle of Waterloo in 1815, in what is now Belgium.

The **balance of power** is an equilibrium existing between states (or groups of states) when resources – especially military resources – are sufficiently evenly distributed to ensure that no single state can dominate the others. The concept was an essential part (and, indeed, aim) of European diplomacy and warfare from at least the seventeenth century onwards.

Nationalism, in part inspired by the Napoleonic wars, spread throughout Europe. Hungary continually chafed at its Austrian domination; Bulgaria tried (with the help of Russia) to break free of the Ottoman empire; and Romania actually succeeded in winning its independence from not just the Ottoman but also the Russian empire. Nationalism was soon competing, however, with demands on the part of the public of many European countries for political participation commensurate with what liberals suggested were their rights and what they themselves argued was their economic contribution. Such demands grew stronger among workers to whom industrialization and urbanization now afforded the concentrated power to organize collectively to press their case. In continental Europe, a series of failed proto-socialist revolutions in the mid-nineteenth century in the end gave way to politically more successful (if socially less radical) efforts to achieve representation by democratic means. By the beginning of the twentieth century, universal (or near-universal) male suffrage had been adopted in many European countries. Nationalism, however, continued apace, and Europe entered the twentieth century with the hitherto fragmented Germany and Italy now unified nation states, bringing the number of states on the continent to around twenty-five, compared to the 500 or more that had existed in 1500 (see Tilly, 1975). To a greater or lesser degree, all these turn-of-the-century states assumed an increasingly active role in their national economies, not least in order to raise the tax revenue that could be used to boost military strength, as well as to improve control over the increasingly industrialized population, be it through coercion through an expanded police apparatus or through education, much of which aimed at the reinforcement of national identity (see Tilly, 1993).

States into blocs

As Germany began to use its new-found unity to claim an overseas empire, Europe's always fragile balance of power began to harden into the military alliances that ended up driving the continent into the First World War. Germany's ambitions were opposed by its imperial rivals, France and Great Britain. They allied with Russia, a country whose association with Slavic national independence movements in Serbia set it on a collision course with Germany's ally, Austria-Hungary. Other countries were sucked into the war once it broke out in 1914: Italy, Japan and,

KEY POINT

With the coming of industry (and industrialized warfare) the tendency of states to seek protective alliances combined with the ideological struggle between capitalism and socialism to produce the Cold War – a stand-off between blocs led by the USA and the USSR that split Europe between a Soviet-ruled east and a west that sought peace and prosperity through European integration.

eventually, the US on the side of the self-styled 'Allies' (Britain, France and Russia); Bulgaria, and Turkey's Ottoman empire, on the side of Germany and Austria-Hungary. Only Scandinavia, Spain and Portugal, and Switzerland (which had pursued a policy of neutrality since it came together as a confederation in the early sixteenth century) escaped involvement. For most of the four years which followed, the combatants fought each other to a standstill at the cost of millions of human lives lost or blighted. But such a war of attrition eventually favoured the side with the greatest resources in terms of men and *materiel*. True, the Allies suffered a loss when, in 1917, Russia was seized by Communist revolutionaries under Lenin, who saw the war as benefiting only the old ruling class and its capitalist allies and ended Russia's participation accordingly (Box 1.2). Nevertheless, in the autumn of 1918, Germany and Austria-Hungary were basically starved into signing an armistice.

After the World War, the map of Europe was literally redrawn. First, came the creation of the *Soviet Union* (or USSR), through which Russia extended its empire (Box 1.2). Second came the Treaties of Versailles and Trianon. The Austro-Hungarian and Ottoman empires were broken up and Turkey forced out of Europe. Hungary lost territory to the new countries created for Slavic peoples in the artificially constructed states of Czechoslovakia and Yugoslavia, the latter created not just at the behest of Slav nationalists, but also to provide Serbian protection to small countries such as Slovenia and Croatia against larger powers such as Italy (which despite territorial gains continued to believe it had been short-changed). Further north, Germany – now a republic – lost territory to France and Poland and was forced not only to admit guilt for the war but also to pay financial compensation ('reparations') to France. The resentment thus created was cleverly exploited by nationalistic, fascist dictators, such as Hitler and Mussolini (see Box 1.3).

Other states, also coping with the economic depression, proved unable or unwilling to quash fascism's territorial ambitions, despite the existence of the 'League of Nations' (the forerunner of the postwar United Nations). Emboldened by its success in grabbing back Austria and much of Czechoslovakia, and determined to act before potential enemies such as Great Britain and France could fully prepare themselves, Germany signed a non-aggression pact with the Soviet Union. This pact basically delivered the Baltic republics of Estonia, Latvia and Lithuania to Russia, along with half of Poland. In September 1939, Germany invaded Poland to take its half, thereby provoking war with Britain, France and, in the end, also the Soviet Union. The US, which was attacked by Germany's ally, Japan, at Pearl Harbor in 1941, joined the fight against the so-called 'Axis' powers (Germany, Japan and a not altogether enthusiastic Italy) in the same year.

BOX 1.2

The Soviet Union and communism

The Union of Soviet Socialist Republics (USSR) was established in 1922 by the *Bolshevik* regime that came to power under its first leader, Lenin, during the Russian revolution of 1917. The Bolsheviks were communists, believing in a state supposedly run on behalf of the working class and with equality and social justice for all. It was dominated by Russia, but also came to include the republics to Russia's south, including Georgia and Ukraine, and the Baltic states of Latvia, Lithuania and Estonia (now EU members). Under the leadership of Lenin's successor, Stalin, it undertook the industrialization of vast swathes of eastern Europe, as well as the collectivization of its agriculture – projects that delivered economic growth but at a terribly high price: tens of millions died, most from starvation but also as a result of forced labour and the political repression needed to maintain the dictatorial regime. Millions of people also lost their lives during the desperate fight against Germany in the Second World War. The postwar period, during which the nuclear-armed Soviet Union faced off but never actually fought against the capitalist West, offered some respite, though the communist regime remained essentially intact until the late 1980s. With its collapse came the collapse of the Soviet Union, and its population of nearly 300 million people found themselves living in either Russia (population 145 million) or what are sometimes referred to as the newly independent states (NIS).

BOX 1.3

Fascism and socialism

European fascism of the 1920s and 1930s was in many ways defined by its opposition to communism, and to socialism or 'social democracy', which believed in achieving public ownership and redistributionary policies and seemed destined to win over many working-class voters. Although fascism was also about the supremacy of the ethnically exclusive state over the interests and rights of individuals, the private sector was allowed to profit from its activities. Fascist leaders promised easy solutions to the worldwide economic depression of the 1930s – solutions based not just on totalitarian politics and increasingly racist, anti-Semitic policies, but also on the sort of military rearmament and an aggressive, expansionist foreign policy that socialists and social democrats (some of them pacifists as well as 'internationalists') abhorred.

It took the use of nuclear weapons to bring Japan to surrender in the summer of 1945. But the Second World War ended in Europe with the occupation of first Italy and then Germany in the spring of that year. However, if anyone thought that the continent's problems were solved, they were sadly mistaken. Although spared a re-run of the postwar influenza outbreak that had killed millions in the aftermath of the 1914–18 conflict, Europe was on its knees. Millions of Jews, as well as political opponents, Roma (gypsies) and other minorities, had been put or worked to death by the Nazis – a tragedy now known as the Holocaust. In addition, the physical destruction and economic misery wrought by six years of total war involving civilian populations as well as armed forces was calamitous.

Any chance that the victorious Allies would continue their co-operation in peacetime was quickly dashed. The Soviet Union was determined to maintain a military presence in the eastern part of the continent and used its occupation to facilitate the seizure of power by Communist parties in Poland, Czechoslovakia, Hungary, Romania and Bulgaria. Only Finland was allowed to remain free, and over time it became a fully integrated part of a Scandinavia that included neutral Sweden as well as Denmark and Norway, occupied in the war by Germany. In the face of the developments in central Europe, the US quickly reverted to the strongly anti-communist stance that it had pursued since the Russian revolution and had softened only during the war. It took steps to ensure that the Soviet 'sphere of influence' (the area where its dominance could not be challenged) would not expand to include the western part of Germany, which was now divided into two states: the liberal capitalist Federal Republic of Germany (FRG), which most outsiders called West Germany, and the communist German Democratic Republic (GDR), routinely labelled East Germany. By the same token, the US put considerable effort (and cash) into ensuring that the home-grown (but Soviet-aided) Communist parties did not take power, even by ostensibly democratic means, in Italy and Greece (which endured a short civil war) (Map 1.2).

The other side of this anti-communist, anti-Soviet 'containment' strategy included the establishment of NATO and the stationing of American military capability throughout Europe. This included bases in Spain, which, like Portugal, had succumbed to right-wing authoritarian dictatorship in the interwar period but had remained neutral between 1939 and 1945. Another important part of the strategy was economic, with the US 'Marshall Plan' (named after the former general who initiated it) providing much-needed aid to most countries in its sphere of influence. European democracies spent it not just on American goods, but also on redeveloping their industrial base, on establishing welfare states and, in time, participating in the consumer booms of the 1950s and 1960s.

US efforts to secure a peaceful western Europe as a bulwark against Communist expansion and as a prosperous trading partner also led it to support moves among some European governments to create a mechanism for increasing interstate co-operation that would lock in their economic interdependence and, along with unity in the face of the Soviet Union, make war between western European powers a thing of the past. These moves began in 1952 with the European Coal and Steel Community (ECSC) and eventuated in the founding of the European Economic Community (EEC) by the Treaty of Rome in 1957. Having played a massive

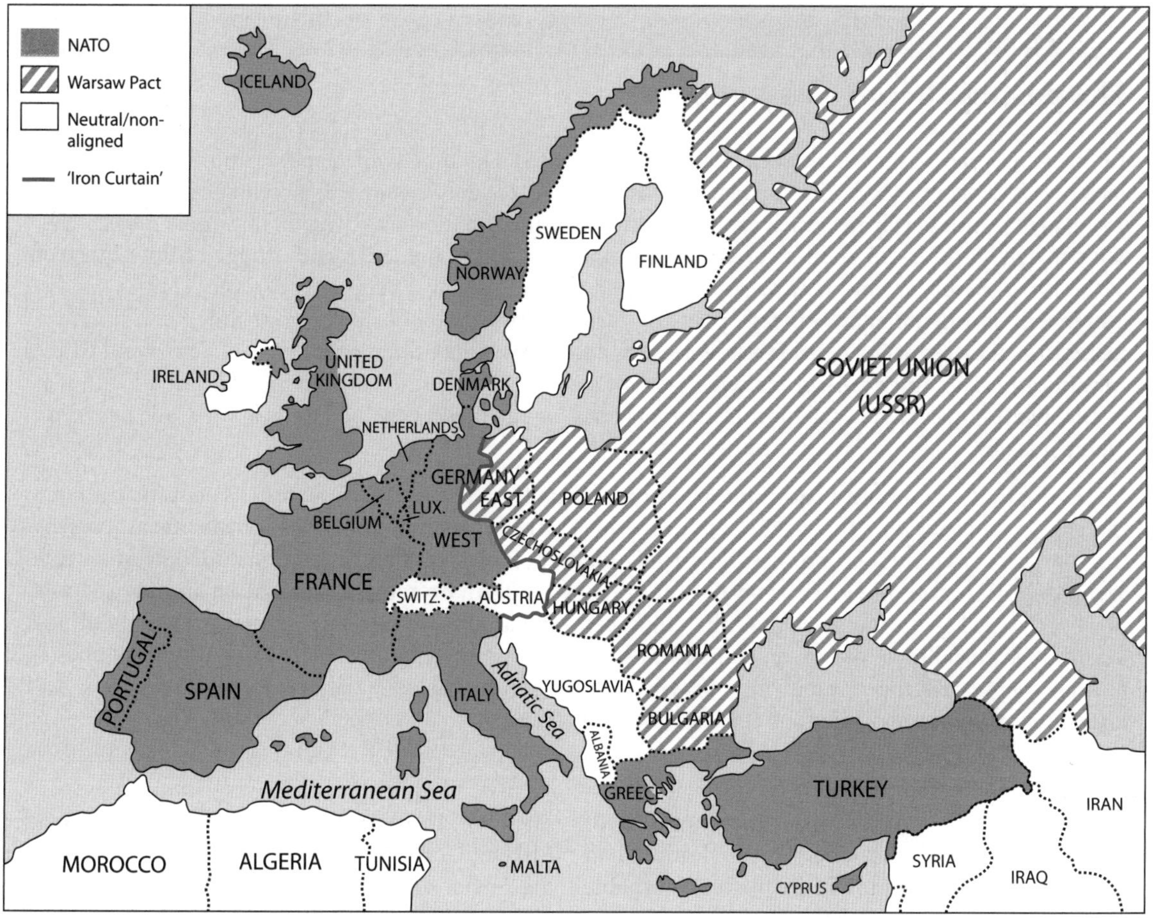

Map 1.2 Europe during the Cold War

part in helping to preserve peace and, for the most part, prosperity, it has since relabelled itself the European Union, commonly known as the EU. In 2004 and 2007, it expanded to take in a total of twenty-seven members, including former dictatorships in Southern and Central and Eastern Europe that are now functioning market democracies (see Map 2.4.

Notwithstanding the EU's importance, it was by no means the only thing that helped western Europe become such a secure and prosperous place. Other factors helped, too. A generation of politicians was determined not just to avoid the mistakes of the interwar period but also to prove that liberal capitalism was better than communism. They also presided over a withdrawal from what had become costly overseas entanglements, with Britain, France and smaller countries such as Belgium, the Netherlands and Portugal letting go of the bulk of their colonial empires (see Chapter 10). The American-led postwar boom (Box 1.4), and the fact that consumers were kept spending both by vastly expanded leisure and mass media markets and the extension of the welfare state, meant that, compared to the prewar period, even the bad times were good. Nor, as Box 1.4 also shows, were they as bad as we might think (at least when it came to the essentials) in what became known as the 'Soviet Bloc'.

CEE countries, in fact, were transformed during the postwar period from agricultural backwaters into modern industrial economies in which income inequalities were narrow and access to health, welfare and education was impressively wide. For all

BOX 1.4

The postwar boom – east and west

To many in western Europe, the years 1950–73 represented a kind of 'golden age'. Economic growth averaged over 4 per cent a year, with catch-up countries such as West Germany, Spain and Greece making up for relatively poor performers such as the UK and Belgium. Inflation was present, but rarely rose above 3–4 per cent. Europe's unemployment rate was only 3 per cent in the 1950s and dropped below 2 per cent in the 1960s. European countries began to catch up technologically. Energy was also very cheap. Moreover, consumer demand, already pent-up during the war, was boosted by governments willing to spend to avoid a return to 1930s-style depression and to meet the military challenge of Soviet and Chinese communism. The American-supervised system of stable exchange rates also provided liquidity within a secure institutional framework for international trade, while the EEC helped to facilitate trade between member states.

Interestingly, the economy of Communist Europe actually grew even more rapidly (7 per cent p.a.) in the 1950s and 1960s than that of the capitalist west. As the Soviet bloc countries transformed themselves from largely agricultural economies to basically modern, industrial nations, national income quadrupled and industrial output in 1970 was seven times that of 1950! An overemphasis on heavy industry, however, as well as the inefficiencies inherent in central planning, meant a poor environmental outlook, a continued curtailment of human rights, and only a very poor range and quality of consumer goods. However, eastern Europeans did enjoy heavily subsidized housing, essential foods and other goods. And unemployment was 'abolished', or at least heavily disguised.

this, however, it remains true that instead of 'burying' capitalism, as one Soviet leader had famously promised, communism proved incapable of matching either the technological progress, the prosperity or the freedom enjoyed by those living under liberal capitalism in 'the West' – an 'imagined community' (Anderson, 1991: 5–7) which seemed to stretch beyond western Europe through North America and down to Australia and New Zealand. The problem was there seemed to be nothing that those who lived in Eastern and Central Europe could do about it. Any time they came close to trying to liberalize their regimes, reformists were crushed by Soviet tanks.

The new Europe

Yet at the same time as it looked as if things would never change in Europe, something had to give. The Soviet Union found itself financially unable both to deliver its population a basic standard of living and to compete with the Americans militarily – particularly if it meant holding on as firmly as ever to its satellites in eastern Europe. This analysis persuaded Mikhail Gorbachev, who took over the leadership of the Soviet Communist Party in 1985, to signal to those countries that they could pursue their own course without fearing military action on his part. Gorbachev clearly hoped that this would mean merely a reform of the existing system, in whose basic principles he still believed. But it rapidly became clear that his famous policies of *glasnost* (openness) and *perestroika* (restructuring) gave the CEE populations the green light to overthrow Communist dictatorships in favour of democracy and market-based economies.

The year 1989 saw revolutions all over Eastern Europe, symbolized for many by the fall of the Berlin Wall that had for so long and so cruelly kept

KEY POINT

With the collapse of the Soviet Union, CEE countries were free to determine their own destiny and overwhelmingly plumped for liberal capitalism. Many of them also joined what has become the European Union (EU).

apart those living in the capitalist and communist halves of the city. Fortunately, most of these revolutions, barring the one in Romania and the events which followed the break up of Yugoslavia (see Chapter 2), were mercifully peaceful. Yugoslavia aside, border changes in what was now post-Cold War Europe were limited to the surprisingly swift reunification of Germany in 1990, and the slightly more drawn out and not entirely amicable 'velvet divorce' of the Czech and Slovak republics. The biggest changes on the map actually occurred in the former Soviet Union, which itself dissolved in 1991, after a failed coup by Communist hardliners. What became the Russian Federation, under Boris Yeltsin, initially tried to hold onto its regional hegemony by getting even large former Soviet republics like Georgia and Ukraine to join the so-called 'Commonwealth of Independent States' (CIS), although it soon became clear that the CIS would not allow it to exert anything like the control Russia had in the Soviet era (see Malgin, 2002 and Olcott, *et al.*, 2000). Moreover, Russia failed to exert any control whatsoever over the former Soviet republics of Estonia, Latvia and Lithuania, all of which joined the EU and NATO in 2004 (see Map 2.4).

To those so-called 'Baltic states', and to the other CEE postcommunist countries that joined the EU (and NATO) alongside them, accession was a symbolic 'coming home'. As we have seen, for centuries up until the end of the Second World War they were intimately connected to those countries which, as the Cold War wore on, sometimes forgot that they were part of the same continent. Now that they have assumed their rightful place, Europe has in effect reassumed the shape it had for hundreds, even thousands, of years. And it has done so in a manner that seems likely to forestall the kind of intra-European (and indeed intercontinental) warfare that characterized so much of its history, but also helped make it what it is today. It is to the task of describing this current reality – economic, demographic and sociological – that we now turn.

Europe's economy – rich in variation

KEY POINT

European economies vary according to size, resources and history: size isn't everything but the richest countries tend to be bigger, to have industrialized relatively earlier and to have escaped communism. Although most European countries are richer than they have ever been, unemployment has returned to haunt them.

Europe is the home of most of the world's great trading nations. As the industrial revolution that began in the UK in the late eighteenth century gained momentum all over Europe, these nations imported raw materials from the rest of the world in order to manufacture finished goods for export, as well as for the burgeoning home market. Yet Europe is by no means devoid of natural resources of its own. Norway, Finland and Sweden all have large forests. France and Sweden were traditional sources of iron ore. Coal could be found in quantity in

Figure 1.1 GDP ($US billion), 2005 (adjusted for PPP)

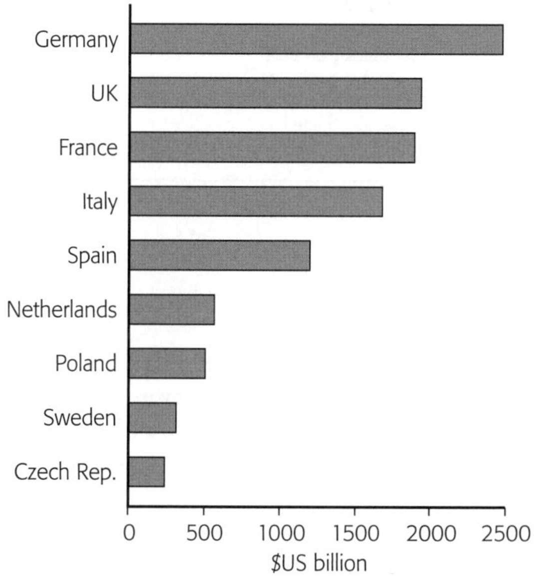

Note: GDP is the overall market value of goods and services produced in a country during the year. It comprises the country's consumer, investment and government spending, along with the value of everything the country exports, minus the value of what it imports. It is the generally accepted measure of a country's economic worth. All figures use purchasing power parity (PPP), which takes into account what money can buy in each country in order to make a more meaningful comparison.

Source: Data from *OECD Factbook 2007*.

Figure 1.2 GDP (adjusted for PPP) *per capita* ($US), 2005 – Europe's range and its competitors

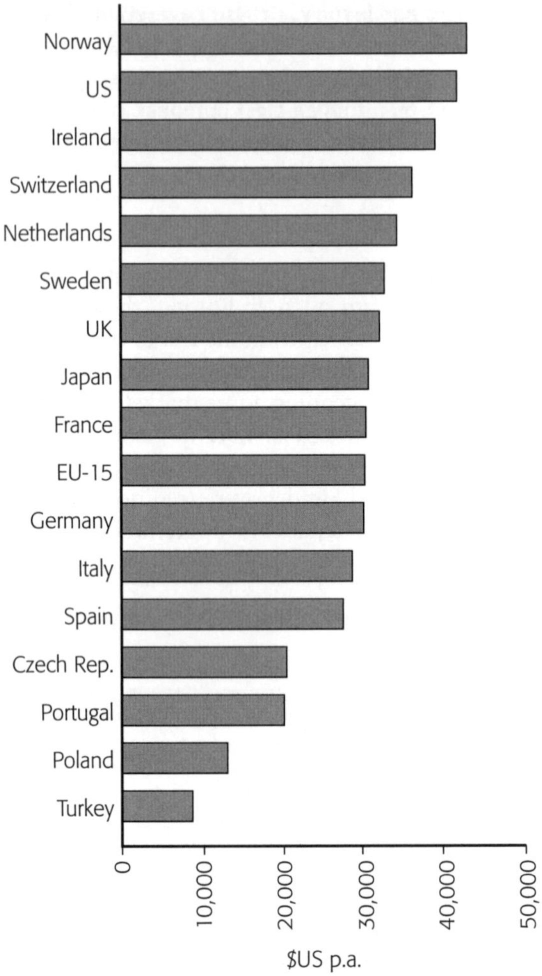

Source: Data from *OECD Factbook 2007*

Britain, Germany, Poland and even Spain. The North Sea between the UK and Scandinavia contains oil and natural gas fields. Europe has also been more than self-sufficient in most agricultural products for many decades. Although mixed farming predominates, the further north one goes, the more meat and dairy feature; the further south, the more citrus, olives and grapes one finds; the further east, the more cereal and other arable crops there are.

The differing extent to which Europe's states are blessed with access to this or that natural resource, however, combines with differing access to international trade routes and areas of expertise and comparative advantage, to make for a great deal of economic variation between their economies. Size matters, too. A quick glance at Figure 1.1 shows us that Germany's gross domestic product (GDP) dwarfs not only that of the neighbouring Czech Republic (as one would expect) but is also nearly twice the size of Spain's. To some extent, a country's wealth is a function of its population: Germany's population is currently twice that of Spain. But size isn't everything, as we can see if we control for population size by looking at wealth per person – or, to use the jargon, *per capita* (Figure 1.2). By dividing wealth by population, we can see that people in some countries are considerably better off than others, even if we take into account the cost of living.

At one end of the scale are the postcommunist countries whose *per capita* wealth means that, while they are clearly much richer than those living in developing or 'Third World' nations (or for that matter an EU candidate country like Turkey), they do not enjoy anything like the living standards of many of their fellow Europeans. Certainly the gap between the richest and the poorest European states is considerably greater than is the gap between, say, the richest and the poorest states of the US: Mississippi's *per capita* income is around half of Connecticut's, but Poland's is less than a third of, say, Norway's (which incidentally is greater than that of the US). For the most part, this relative poverty is a characteristic of former communist countries, particularly Bulgaria and Romania which, due in part to their comparative backwardness, did not join the EU until 2007. However, there are also differences between traditionally 'western' countries, with Portugal lagging some way behind the other pre-accession EU members (the so-called EU-15) and now 'overtaken' by a postcommunist country, the Czech Republic. Note also that Turkey, now a candidate to join the EU, lags some way behind current member states.

Behind the figures, however, lie all sorts of other measures of how well or badly a country is doing, many of which impact more directly on the public, who will be only dimly aware of things like GDP. The most obvious of these are *inflation* (a measure of rising prices, normally expressed as an annual percentage) and of course *unemployment* (Figure 1.3). During most of the postwar period, European (and American and Australasian) governments operated on the assumption (labelled 'Keynesian' after British economist John Maynard Keynes) that there was a trade-off between the two. In other words, if economic demand outstripped supply, then there would probably be plenty of jobs around (so-called 'full employment') but inflation would rise; if, however, government acted to reduce demand (by, say, reducing its own spending or that of consumers and business by raising taxes or the interest rates at which banks charged people for borrowing money) then inflation would fall but unemployment would rise. But, in the late 1960s-early 1970s, many advanced industrial economies began to suffer 'stagflation' – high inflation (i.e. rising prices) *and* higher unemployment.

From the late 1960s onwards, a number of influential 'neo-liberal' or 'monetarist' economists persuaded many governments that trying to boost demand to tackle unemployment was making the situation worse. Their answer was to stop allowing trade unions to use full employment to bid up wages, to stop subsidizing loss-making industries and generally to leave things like monetary policy (i.e. interest rates) to the free market. As governments moved towards these policies, there was what was euphemistically called a 'shake-out' of inefficient manufacturing firms (especially those involved in or connected to 'heavy industries' such as steel, shipbuilding, mining, etc.). This accelerated the end of the postwar boom and heralded the return of the kind of mass unemployment that postwar generations had assumed was a thing of the past. This unemployment is 'structural' as much as 'cyclical' (i.e. it will not completely disappear in times of economic growth), and is still relatively high in many European countries today – in marked contrast to the so called 'golden age' of the 1960s (see Figure 1.3). GDP figures, then, do not tell the whole story.

Figure 1.3 The shape of unemployment in Europe, 1961–2006

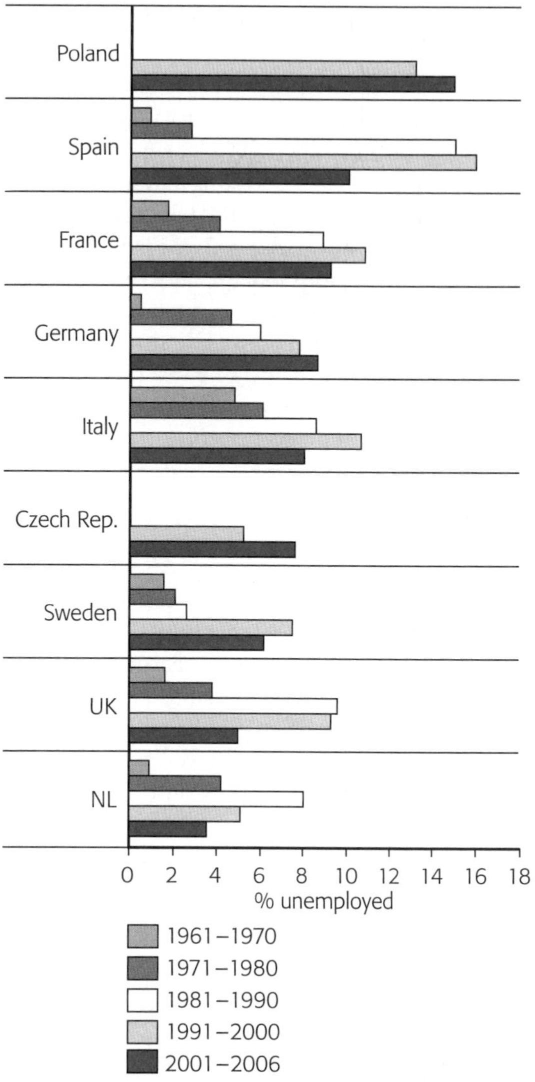

Sources: Data from European Commission, *The EU Economy: 2003 Review* and Eurostat, EU *Economic Data Pocketbook, 1–2007.*

Regions

Just as importantly, there are big regional variations between different parts of the same country (see Box 1.5). Germany, for instance, contains some of the richest regions of Europe; but, having absorbed the formerly Communist East Germany (GDR) in 1990, it also contains some of the poorest. It is by no means alone in this, for these national and regional variations are inherent in the very different ways in which the economies of European states are structured. Traditionally, wealth and development were associated with industrialization which, after

KEY POINT

There are also big disparities *within* nations as well as *between* them.

BOX 1.5

Poverty amid plenty – Europe's huge regional variations in wealth

Before the accession of twelve new member states in 2004 and 2007 there were, according to Eurostat (the EU's statistical division), just under fifty regions in EU member states whose per capita GDP was below 75 per cent of the EU average. Not surprisingly, nearly all the regions of Greece, Spain and Portugal were among them, as were the regions that made up the former East Germany. Also included were southern regions of Italy, and three in the UK. Taken as a whole, just under 70 million people (nearly 20 per cent) of the total population of the EU-15 (the EU of fifteen countries prior to 2004) live there. Yet they live alongside other regions that are far wealthier than the average. Indeed, many of the larger western European countries outside Scandinavia show huge regional disparities. In seven of the former EU-15 states, including Germany, the UK and Italy, the highest regional GDP per capita is more than double the lowest. Estimates for the EU's newest members show fewer regional differences within countries, though a great deal of poverty compared to the West. One of only two regions above an EU average recalculated to include the new members was the Czech capital, Prague. But the rest of the country was not much better off than other CEE regions: the regional GDP of Prague, indeed, was 2.5 times higher than the poorest region of the Czech Republic.

the Second World War, was concentrated in Southern Scandinavia (Gothenburg, Malmö and Copenhagen), England, Eastern France, Northern Italy, Belgium and the Netherlands, Germany, the Czech and Slovak Republics and Poland. In the latter half of the twentieth century, however, this relationship began to break down as wealth became more closely connected with services.

'Postindustrialism'?

Most European states, such as the UK and other advanced countries, can be labelled 'postindustrial' because the service sector has overtaken the manufacturing sector as the biggest employer in the economy, with agriculture shrinking still further (Table 1.1). This is not, however, to deny that the label may be a little misleading in view of the fact that many so-called 'service jobs' are no less routinized, low-status, low-skilled and low-paid than the production-line jobs traditionally associated with industrialization (see Wilensky, 2002: 186–90). Nor should we forget, that some European nations still have large farming sectors. In the west, over 10 per cent of Greeks and Portuguese, for instance, are employed in agriculture, forestry and fishing, but this is nothing compared to the situation in some of the continent's more easterly, often postcommunist states. Some of these resemble their counterparts in western Europe: the Czech Republic, Hungary, Slovakia, Slovenia and Estonia all have under 10 per cent of their workforce employed in agriculture. But in Romania, for example, over a third of the population still work in that sector. Poland, may not lag quite so badly, but a figure of 17 per cent of such a large population represents a lot of farmers! This was a major issue in negotiations to join the EU, since the then fifteen member states could not countenance extending the financial assistance afforded by the EU's Common Agricultural Policy (CAP) to so many marginal producers. For one thing, it would have breached their commitment to do no more than maintain the absolute level of agricultural spending, which takes up almost half the EU's total (see Chapter 2), thereby reducing it over time. For another, it would have involved subsidizing (and perhaps ensuring the continuation of) an industry badly in need of rationalization. Although there are exceptions, a large agricultural

KEY POINT

The relationship between industrialization and wealth no longer holds – Europe's future lies in the service economy.

Table 1.1 Towards the postindustrial economy in Europe?

	Agriculture, forestry and fishing (%)		Industry (%)		Services (%)	
	1995	2005	1995	2005	1995	2005
US	2.9	1.6	24.0	19.8	73.1	78.6
Netherlands	3.7	3.1	22.6	20.3	73.7	76.6
UK	2.1	1.4	27.3	22.1	70.7	76.5
Sweden	3.1	2.0	25.9	22.0	71.0	76.0
France	4.6	3.5	26.3	22.6	69.1	73.9
EU-15	5.1	3.7	30.4	26.5	64.5	69.8
Germany	3.1	2.4	36.3	30.0	60.5	67.6
Spain	8.9	5.3	30.2	29.9	60.9	64.8
Italy	6.7	4.2	34.1	31.1	59.2	64.6
Czech Rep.	6.6	4.0	42.2	39.6	51.1	56.4
Poland	22.6	17.4	32.0	29.2	45.4	53.4
Turkey	44.1	29.5	22.0	24.7	33.9	45.8

Source: Data from *OECD Factbook* 2007.

(or primary goods) sector tends to be associated with poorer states. All this makes it easy to see why concerns about the possible EU accession of Turkey (included in Table 1.1) are in part economic and financial

In the decades following the Second World War, there was also a strong association in Europe between wealth and industrial development. With the rise of the service sector in most advanced economies, however, this relationship began to break down. Nowadays, with the exception of Germany, which still benefits from its traditionally high-quality industrial base, Europe's wealthiest countries are those in which services – be they predominantly private (and profit-generating) or public (and welfare-creating) – are strongest.

Transition

One factor, then, in the disparity between western Europe, where two thirds now work in services, and CEE, where fewer of the workforce are similarly employed, is the fact that much of the latter has yet to move into the postindustrial age. At a regional level in the west, it is those parts of a country historically associated with primary production, mining and/or heavy industries such as steel-making or shipbuilding which, after the agricultural regions, are least prosperous. This means that CEE, where these sectors were key to Communist postwar modernization right up until the late 1980s, are at a big disadvantage. That industrialization – and the lack of attention paid to its environmental consequences – also explains why the region's relatively backward economies are no less polluting than their more developed western counterparts (see Figure 1.4).

The economic backwardness associated with communism is not a disadvantage that can be overcome overnight. It will take decades – at least. Nevertheless, the so-called 'transition' economies of postcommunist Europe have made considerable progress.

KEY POINT

Europe's postcommunist countries have made huge – if not always unfaltering or even – strides towards catching up with their western counterparts economically, although it will still be a long haul.

Figure 1.4 CO_2 emissions *per capita*, 2004

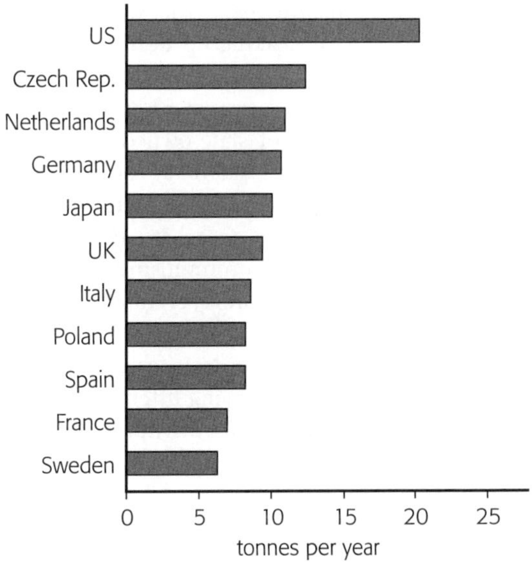

Source: Data from UN Development Goals Indicators, available at http://mdgs.un.org/usd/mdg/Data.aspx

That progress has not, of course, been even. Some countries were already closer to the West to begin with. And, although most decided early on that capitalism, and the privatization of the massive state sector, was where they wanted to go, there has been considerable variation in the route chosen to get there. Hungary, for instance, which actually had already begun market-style reforms under its communist regime, pursued a fairly cautious strategy. Poland, and to a lesser extent the Czech Republic, chose to move more quickly: both devalued their currencies to a realistic level, removed price subsidies and tolerated a degree of unemployment and (what they hoped would be) short-term contraction in order to achieve manageable inflation and respectable growth in the long term.

Privatization proceeded in different ways and at a varying pace (see, for example, Hopkins, 1998; and Klich, 1998). Generally speaking, however, with the exception of Romania and Bulgaria, most CEE countries largely managed to avoid the overnight creation of a semi-criminal oligarchy that occurred in Russia. Still, the process was not without its problems (see Iatridis and Hopps, 1998). Governments did little to dampen expectations early on and, especially in Poland, they suffered a backlash as the public caught on to the fact that privatization would make very few people wealthy and a lot of people unemployed. They were also so keen to get rid of state assets that they not only failed to realize their true value, but, in selling off rather than breaking up dominant firms, they also failed to create truly competitive markets. There were undoubtedly cases where entrepreneurs obtained profitable parts of state-owned enterprises (SOEs) with large market share at knock-down, never-to-be-repeated prices. And legitimate criticisms can be made of the extent to which the 'creative destruction' of some of communism's industrial inheritance was really that creative, even (and perhaps especially) in East Germany.

Generally, however, to have transferred so much in so short a time without causing utterly unbridled corruption, mass poverty or disruption to the supply of goods and services has to be seen as a major achievement. Given that speed and the creation of a viable market economy were by far the most important priorities of early postcommunist governments (much more so than preserving a relatively equitable distribution of wealth, for instance), then privatization in the region has to be judged a success on its own terms. In the Czech Republic, Poland and Hungary, by far the bulk of the economy is now in private hands. Because there is a lot of catching-up to do (and a relatively large amount of foreign direct investment (FDI) coming in) growth is, or is likely to be, slightly higher than in the former West. Inflation is similarly low. Unemployment, however, remains a persistent problem, especially in Poland, Slovakia and (to a lesser extent) the Baltic states (Latvia, Lithuania and Estonia). Meanwhile, Slovenia, formerly part of Yugoslavia – always rather closer to the West than countries in the Soviet bloc – boasts the best-performing economy of all the postcommunist states and is the only one of them so far to have joined the 'eurozone' – the group of EU members with the euro as their single currency. The wooden spoon goes to Bulgaria and Romania, where reform was slow until economic crisis finally galvanized change in the latter half of the 1990s.

Globalization and/or Europeanization?

The economic picture in Europe, then, is complex, and even in some cases quite negative, at least in the short term. Some accounts make it seem even bleaker by suggesting that jobs in manufacturing and even services are leaking away to developing countries, leaving Europe destined to be 'overtaken' by growth economies such as China and other East and South Asian economies. According to this view, Europe's corporates will, like their American counterparts, benefit from globalization, but its population will end up as victims. In fact, there is as little evidence to support this pessimistic view, however fashionable, as there is to support some of the more ambitious versions of globalization itself. Both of them buy too heavily into the idea that things are fast changing beyond recognition and that space, time, existing patterns and cultural inertia may not matter much any more. Arguably, however, they do. Even if we ignore the obvious argument that a great deal of European countries' economic activity is (as it is in the US) domestic, and concentrate on the international sector, it is (a) not clear that European countries are doing badly; and (b) obvious that all

KEY POINT

Globalization does not spell doom for European economies, although some are adjusting better than others.

of them spend more and more time and more and more money with each other than with anyone else.

Take, for instance, the argument that industry, and therefore jobs, will abandon Europe in favour of the 'Tiger' economies of South East Asia. Statistics do show that, like the US, some European nations (often traditional trading nations such as the UK and the Netherlands) seem to be running large deficits in manufacturing trade with newly industrializing countries (NICs) such as Korea and Taiwan. But they also show that others, notably Italy and Sweden, export far more goods (at least in terms of value) to those countries than they import from them. And, bluntly, none of this may matter if a country's 'comparative advantage' is in services rather than in manufacturing (as is undoubtedly the case with the UK). Moreover, despite the common fallacy, there is no finite number of jobs out there in the world that means if one country loses them, it cannot grow them again: a high- or low-tech plant in Shanghai or yet another call-centre in Mumbai does not spell the end of the road for Europe. In any case, rising trade with the rest of the world – which, if it were done fairly, should help all concerned – is not half so important as the steady rise in the extent to which European countries trade with each other, even if the figures for each country vary, with countries that are traditionally more wary about European integration (like Sweden and the UK) doing relatively less intra-EU trade (Table 1.2). The myriad connections this trade is built on are long-standing (centuries old, indeed) and increasingly institutionalized by EU membership and co-operation. At the very least, then, 'Europeanization is sufficiently deeply embedded to act as a filter for globalization' (Wallace, 2000: 381).

Table 1.2 The growth and current importance of intra-European trade

	Percentage growth in trade (1960–2000)		Intra-EU trade as percentage of total trade (2004)	
	Rest of World	Intra-EU	Exports	Imports
Czech Rep.	n/a	n/a	86	79
France	743	1666	65	69
Germany	755	902	63	65
Italy	1166	1720	59	60
Netherlands	862	1485	80	53
Poland	n/a	n/a	79	75
Spain	1909	2591	74	68
Sweden	1043	711	59	72
UK	342	1000	58	56
EU	734	1221	n/a	n/a

Sources: Data from Badinger and Breuss (2003); Eurostat (2005).

National and patterned variation

But just because European countries trade with each other and are all moving towards postindustrial economies, albeit at varying rates, we should not take Europeanization to mean some kind of uniformity. History matters in economics as much as it does in politics and policy. Obviously, there are some basic similarities. Notwithstanding some of the postcommunist outliers, European countries have relatively advanced and – compared with, say, the US – relatively 'mixed' economies. Within a largely capitalist framework that sees most goods and services produced by the private sector, there is public sector involvement in areas such as defence and law and order, education and welfare provision and, not uncommonly, in the ownership of utilities and other industries. Even where state involvement is relatively low, it is probably crucial to the continued health of a nation's economy. The state, whether

KEY POINT

Europe's economies and its welfare states can be more or less neatly divided up according to the extent to which government plays an active role and the extent to which welfare is intended as living expression of egalitarian solidarity or a form of social insurance or merely a safety net.

local or national, is a big customer for many private firms. Moreover, by maintaining transport and networks, and building and staffing schools and hospitals, it helps supply the infrastructure and the human resources those firms need. Its welfare payments help to ensure that as many consumers as possible have money to buy the goods and services produced by the private sector. Its stewardship of the economy, via tax and spending decisions and the legal and regulatory framework it maintains, contribute to the creation of an environment in which, hopefully, business will thrive.

But the distinctions between Europe's mixed economies are arguably every bit as important as the similarities. This need not mean we give up the search for some kind of patterned variation, however. Hall and Soskice (2001), for instance, put together a stimulating case that (west) European countries' economies can be characterized as 'liberal' (UK, Ireland) or 'co-ordinated' (Germany, Scandinavia and Benelux) or hybrids where the state is still quite a prominent actor (France, Greece, Italy, Portugal and Spain). Analysts also routinely draw distinctions between Europe's welfare state regimes, with the 'three worlds' typology pioneered by Gøsta Esping-Andersen (1990) the most popular – if no longer undisputed (see Scruggs and Allan, 2006a) – choice (see Box 1.6).

It is still too soon to place Europe's postcommunist countries precisely and firmly into such schemas. But the early signs are there. After seeming to take their initial inspiration from the US, via the recommendations of the International Monetary Fund (IMF) and the World Bank (see Ferge, 2001) many of them (notably the Czech Republic) are moving toward models that provide more than simply a residual safety net and which are highly regulated – often one which seems to pick and mix elements of both the social democratic and the 'corporatist' or 'conservative' model (see Cook, 2007b, Deacon, 2000 and Keune, 2006; see also Chapter 9). As one observer, after judiciously sifting through the impassioned arguments and the mixed evidence concerning postcommunist social policy, concludes, any border that still exists between Western and Central and Eastern Europe is most definitely not one that demarcates 'two essentially different types of welfare regime', not least because there are so many types in each region. In short, 'East-Central European welfare regimes are muddling through to achieve some degree of normalcy by an average of Western standards' (see Kovács, 2002: 176, 196). As Wagener (2002: 170) points out, it is crucial to remember this lest we allow '[a]ll the horror stories about transformation-induced alcoholism, falling life expectancy, deteriorating health status and appalling income inequalities' – phenomena that in the main affect the former Soviet Union (and therefore to some extent the Baltic states) – to give us a

BOX 1.6

Europe's various welfare state regimes

Stressing variations in the extent to which political and trade union representatives of ordinary working people were able to wring concessions from states that were essentially pro-capitalist, Swedish expert, Gøsta Esping-Andersen (1990) posited the existence of the following three 'worlds of welfare':

- *Social-democratic*: Extensive high-quality services, open to all irrespective of income; generous (and income-related) transfer payments to those out of or unable or too old to work; strong public support; exemplified by Scandinavian countries such as **Sweden**.
- *Liberal*, Anglo-Saxon: Basic services, many available only via means-testing; limited transfer payments; safety net for the poor so middle-class use and support is limited; both the **UK** and Ireland are examples, but (compared to, say, the US) only imperfect ones because they have been influenced by the other traditions.
- *Conservative*, corporatist: Insurance-based welfare schemes, many of which are administered by unions and employers; strong bias towards support for traditional family structures; Austria, **Germany**, **the Netherlands** and the other Benelux countries fit neatly into this category, though **France** and **Italy** (and rather less easily **Spain**, Portugal and Greece) can also be included.

totally misleading view of welfare in the mainly Central European states that joined the EU in 2004 and 2007.

The fact that some of Europe's postcommunist states are tending toward at least some aspects of Esping-Andersen's conservative or corporate welfare regimes, relying as they do on social insurance rather than tax-funded welfare, might not be a good thing for their populations, especially those who are unemployed. In Spring 2007, for instance, only one in ten Poles was unemployed but the figure for under-25s was nearly three out of ten. Rhodes (2002) notes that in west European countries whose welfare states rely on social insurance paid by employers and, to a lesser extent, employees (such as France, Germany, Italy and Spain), employers are reluctant to take on new (and that often means young) workers when the costs to them are so high, especially if what they see as 'red-tape' (but others see as worker protection) makes them difficult to offload if things do not work out. At the same time, as Rhodes also notes, their relative generosity to pensioners places a much greater burden on those in work than is the case in other countries. These residual 'Anglo-Saxon' welfare states, such as the UK or egalitarian 'Scandinavian' welfare states such as Sweden, are not only a little less generous to pensioners but load more of the burden of taxation onto the individual (via income tax) and their consumption, since they regard insurance-based levies as 'a tax on jobs' which hurts those looking for one.

If Europe's new democracies do adopt this insurance aspect of the conservative or corporatist (some use the term 'Bismarckian' after the founder of the system in Germany) welfare regime (see Wagener, 2002), it might mean that once the comparative advantage they enjoy over western economies in terms of cheap labour wears off they, too, run into some of the same problems. On the other hand, because that advantage is likely to last for at least a decade or more, they have plenty of time to adjust, and adjustment clearly is possible. Given a certain amount of political will (and perhaps a perceived 'fiscal crisis'), European states can and have moved from one category to the other or at least turned themselves into hybrids. The restructuring of social security in the Netherlands, which in the 1980s seemed to be trending to the 'welfare without work'

Figure 1.5 Public social expenditure as a proportion of GDP, 1983–2003

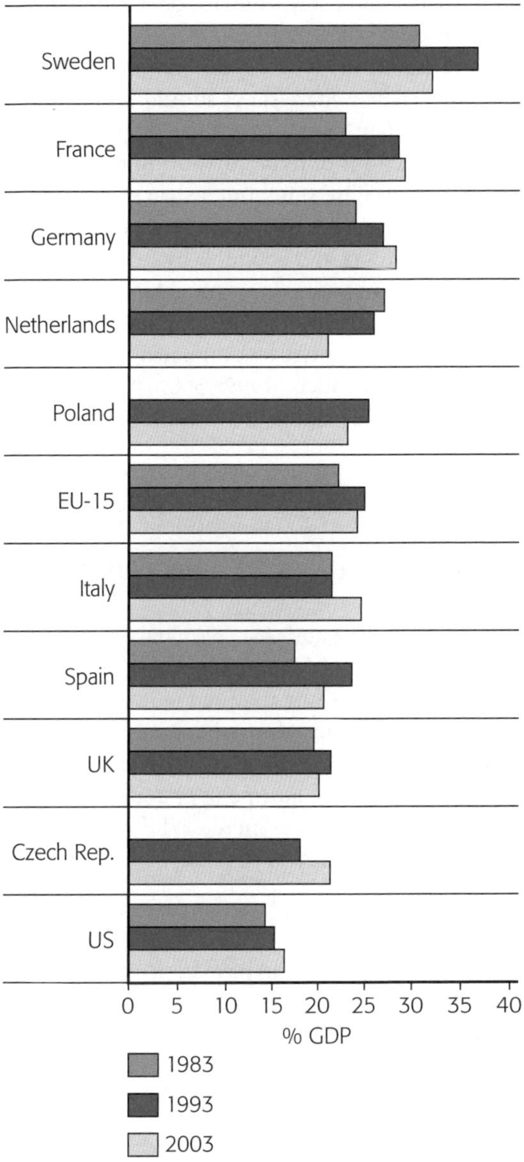

Source: Data from *OECD Factbook 2007*. Spending comprises cash benefits, direct provision of goods and services, and tax breaks with social goals. Benefits may be targeted at low-income households, but they may also be for the elderly, disabled, sick, unemployed, or young persons.

model, shows that, even faced with public opposition (over one million joined street protests in 1991), politicians are capable of turning things around (Green-Pedersen, 2001; and see van

Kersbergen *et al.*, 2000). Whether they have turned them round enough – and whether the so-called 'Dutch model' is really one to be followed – is another matter (see Keman, 2003).

Debates about *how* European countries should best finance their welfare states should not, however, obscure the main point that they do still finance them. There is a lot of hype surrounding 'the end of the European welfare state', but, as we show in more detail in Chapter 9, it is not well supported by the facts: the era of 'tax and spend' is by no means over, even if some European governments don't like to admit it. Certainly, they do not appear to be spending any (or much) less on social policies (see Figure 1.5 and Crouch, 1999: 368–74), with only slight (though not altogether insignificant) variations in what each country spends its money on. For instance, France and Germany spend (per capita) a little more than most on health, but Sweden spends (per capita) more than other countries on education; postcommunist countries do not spend significantly more or less (at least per capita) than the rest; all spend a good deal on the elderly – and will continue to do so (see Box 1.7).

Whatever happened to 'the classless society'?

In both the former West and East, however, there are systematic differences in the distribution of employ-

BOX 1.7

Births, deaths – and a lot more in between

Europe – both west and east (see Chawla *et al.*, 2007) – has probably reached its peak as far as population is concerned. This is primarily because, after a postwar boom, its birth rate has declined markedly below the 2.2 replacement rate required to keep numbers stable. In Poland, Spain, the Netherlands and Germany, for instance, women in 2006 were on average having one or even two babies less than they would have done in 1960. In 1950, 548 million people lived in Europe and this increased to 727 million by 2000. But by 2050, Europe's population will have declined to 580 million. On the other hand, life expectancy is expected to increase. Life expectancy at birth in Europe between 1995 and 2000 stood at 73.2; by 2045–50 it will be 80.8.

Putting these two things together leads to the obvious conclusion that Europe has an 'ageing population'. Take the median age – the age you would pick in order to divide a country's population into two equal halves. In 1950, this would have been 29.2, in 2000 it would have been 37.7 and in 2050 it is expected to be 49.5! In fact, Japan aside, it is in Europe where population ageing is at its most advanced. The proportion of children in Europe, for instance, is projected to decline from 17 per cent in 2000 to 14 per cent in 2050, while the proportion of older people (those over 60) will increase from 20 per cent in 1998 to 37 per cent in 2050. By then, there will be 2.6 older people for every child and more than one in every three people will be aged 60 years or over.

Italy, Switzerland, Germany and Sweden currently have median ages of 40 years each. But in 2050, Spain is projected to have the oldest population, with a median age of 55 years. Italy, Slovenia and Austria (54 years), will not be far behind. In Germany, Greece and Italy, there are already at least 1.5 people aged 60 or over for every child, and by 2050 Italy and Spain are each expected to have nearly four older people for every child. The old are also getting older! In 2050, Austria, Belgium, Finland, France, Germany, Greece, Italy, the Netherlands, Norway, Slovenia, Spain, Sweden, Switzerland and the UK are all projected to have at least 10 per cent of their population aged 80 years or over.

Sources: Data from UN Population Division, Eurostat, *Population and Social Conditions 2007* and Crouch (1999).

KEY POINT

While their governments are still committed to relatively high social spending and poverty is decreasing, most European countries are far from being classless societies – indeed, inequality and social mobility may well be increasing rather than decreasing in some of them. Education is certainly no panacea.

Figure 1.6 Changes in inequality, late 1970s/early 1980s to late 1990s/early 2000s

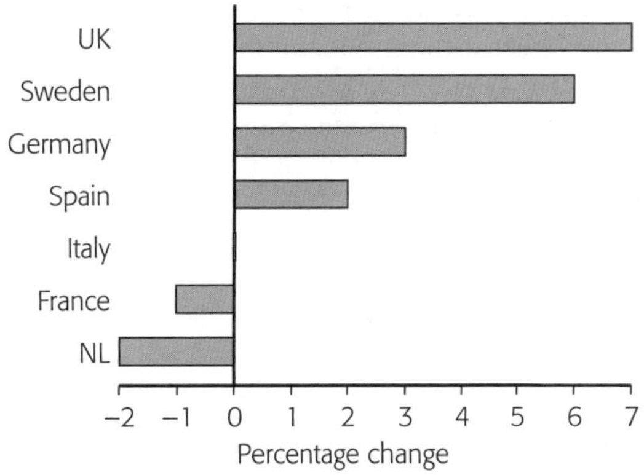

Note: Measured by Gini coefficient from Luxembourg Income Study (LIS).

Source: Data from Harjes (2007).

ment, income and wealth. This, many analysts would suggest, is because European societies remain (or in the case of postcommunist countries are becoming) 'class societies'. There is plenty of room for argument about the precise make-up of these classes. Sociologists disagree and different countries employ different means of categorization, and it may be true that the traditional categories are becoming somewhat blurred (see Crouch, 1999: Chapter 5). There is also considerable dispute, as we shall see in Chapter 6, about the precise and changing impact of class on political behaviour. However, it is difficult to refute the general proposition that the circumstances into which a child is born and the work an adult finds him or herself doing (or, in the case of the unemployed, not doing) strongly influence his or her income, life-style and life-chances.

In Europe, the manual working class – at nearly a third to almost a half of European countries' populations – is still the largest group (especially if we were to confine our figures to men). It is, though, in decline as jobs in manufacturing and mining decrease relative to jobs in the often non-manual service sector. Because many of the jobs in the latter are not necessarily well paid (especially if they are occupied by women), the so-called 'growth of the middle class' has not, however, been accompanied by a trend toward growing equality of incomes or wealth. Indeed, in some countries, it is quite the opposite (see Figure 1.6).

In many – though not all – European countries, including the postcommunist states and the UK (which along with Italy, Ireland, Spain and France was historically one of the continent's most unequal societies), inequality actually increased from the early 1980s onwards (see Figure 1.6). In East Central Europe, this increase began slightly later and occurred because of the collapse of the communist economic system and the move toward marketization; it has, however, been notably less extreme than in the countries of the former Soviet Union (see Heyns, 2005), and at least some governments – and here the Czech Republic would seem to be in advance of its counterparts in Hungary and Poland (see Ferge, 2001) – are taking the problem of poverty seriously.

Table 1.3 International poverty rates from the mid-1980s to the most recent year available

	Relative poverty rate		Absolute poverty rate[1]	
	Start	**End**	**Start**	**End**
France (1984–94)	6.3	3.3	13.8	10.0
Germany (1984–2000)	2.9	4.2	11.3	7.0
Italy (1966–2000)	5.5	7.3	21.6	18.8
Netherlands (1987–99)	1.7	4.5	22.3	7.4
Spain (1980–90)	6.7	5.2	n/a	n/a
Sweden (1987–2000)	4.2	3.6	13.9	7.9
UK (1986–99)	3.7	5.4	17.1	11.8
USA (1986–2000)	12.2	10.7	12.2	8.7

Notes: 1. Absolute poverty is 40 per cent of US median in 1986 adjusted for inflation and prices.
2. n/a = not available

Source: Data from Scruggs and Allen (2006b: 884). No comparable data for Poland and Czech Republic.

In the west, the increase in inequality was largely because (with the exception of the late 1980s/early 1990s when some workers lost out as unemployment affected them directly or indirectly by lowering wages), the rich got richer (as they benefited from more deregulated economies) rather than because the poor got poorer, at least in absolute terms (see Table 1.3). The rise in inequality even occurred in egalitarian bastions like Sweden, although that country, with its Nordic neighbours, nevertheless remains one of the most equal in Europe. Nowhere in Europe, however, is inequality as evident as it is in the US or, closer to home, Russia (see Figure 1.7).

The extent and growth of income inequality differs between European countries. But its continued existence would seem to contradict the claim that the so-called 'classless society' has finally arrived, brought about, ironically, not by communism but by the capitalism it set out to destroy. But inequality does not stop at income. Take education, which is said by many to be one of the factors contributing to the blurring of class distinctions. Throughout Europe, an individual's progress and performance is influenced most not by the school she attends but by the educational attainment (and to a lesser extent the socio-economic position) of her parents. Like the US, though later on, Europe has seen a massive expansion in university and other tertiary education provision. But research suggests that across the continent the main – or at least the first – beneficiaries were those sorts of families who were already consumers of such provision. Rather than many more working-class children going on to university, for example, places have been found for the siblings whose gender or limited ability would have ruled them out in the more sexist and selective days of old. In the UK, for instance, '[y]oung people from the poorest income groups have increased their [university] graduation rate by just 3 percentage points between 1981 and the late 1990s, compared with a rise in graduation rates of 26 percentage points for those with the richest 20 percent of parents' (Blanden *et al.*, 2005: 11).

In short, while there has been a considerable closing of the gender gap (and in many European countries the opening of a new one as more women gain degrees than men) education is as much influenced by class distinctions as ever. It is therefore

Figure 1.7 Inequality in Europe compared

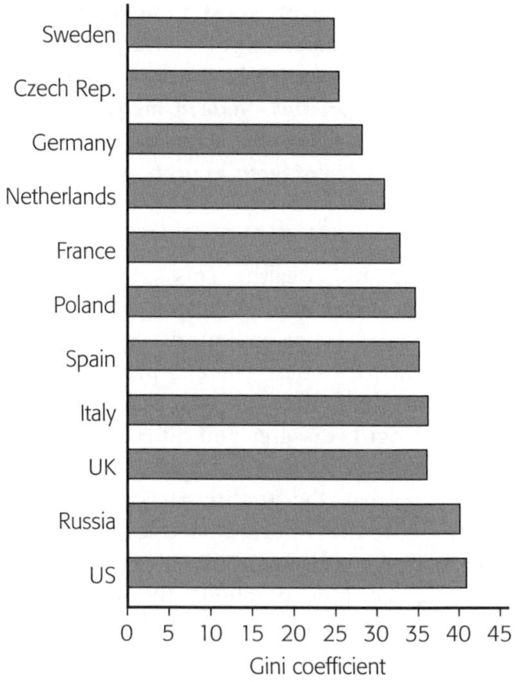

Note: The Gini coefficient is a standardized measure of income inequality, with zero being complete equality and 100 its opposite: a good example of a high-scoring, highly unequal country is Brazil (60), while Scandinavian countries (and, interestingly, Japan) score low on inequality.

Source: Data from United Nations, *World Development Report, 2006* (http://hdr.undp.org/reports/).

unlikely to have as big an impact on eroding such distinctions as some optimistic advocates suggest (see Crouch, 1999: 238–41). In fact, it may well be making things worse: social mobility in some European countries (see Breen, 2004) may even be declining because of the increasing relationship between educational achievement (now more vital than ever in the labour market) and family income.

Nor should too great a faith be placed in the capacity of social policy more generally to reduce inequality. There is some evidence to support the idea that reductions in inequality in former dictatorships such as Spain, Portugal and Greece may have had something to do with big increases in social spending (particularly in the last two countries). We can also say that efforts to curb welfare spending in the UK, which in the 1980s saw it swing toward the 'Anglo-Saxon' model and away from the social democratic one, probably exacerbated its relatively high level of poverty. At the other end of the scale, however, the Scandinavian countries that consistently emerge as having the most equal societies do so not just after, but also before we take taxation and transfers into account – though this is not to discount completely the redistributionary effect of their welfare states. Interestingly (and perhaps surprisingly to those who argue that, as in the US, inequality and national wealth go hand-in-hand), this is a reminder that in Europe there appears to be a positive correlation between how rich and how equal a country is (see Conceição *et al.*, 2001; see also Kenworthy, 2004 and Pontusson, 2005).

Glib predictions about the coming of the classless society, then, are at the very least premature. On the other hand, this should not prevent us from acknowledging that the proportion of the population that can be called, or calls itself, working class is on the decline. In short, while there are just as many workers on wages or salaries out there, far fewer of them are wearing blue collars and far more are wearing white. This is partly because, as we go on to discuss, more of them are wearing skirts, too. But it is also because of a move away from large-scale extraction and industrial production and into services. Fewer mines and large factory settings means fewer places where large numbers of (traditionally) male manual workers work, live and play together and in so doing sustain a sense of themselves as having different (and competing) interests to those who employ them. As we shall see in Chapters 5 and 6, this has had a major impact on voting and party politics, posing particular problems for parties of the left, for whom such people were historically their core supporters.

Women – working but not yet winning?

If class remains an important source of differences between people, so too does gender. This is despite the fact that one of the clearest European social trends of the latter half of the twentieth century was a move into the paid workforce by women, particularly married (or, increasingly, cohabiting) women. As we can see from Figure 1.8, the rate at which this move has occurred actually varied between countries. Some western European nations, particularly those such as Italy and Spain, in which the Roman Catholic church exercised a strong influence, historically had low levels of female participation in the paid workforce: the increase in the latter may seem impressive, but rates overall are still lower. Although comparable figures are not available, former communist countries deliberately and successfully encouraged women to enter the workforce by providing easily accessible childcare and promoting gender equality as official policy. But they, like other European states, are now well behind Scandinavian countries, which seem to have achieved a permanent culture-shift to which feminists in other countries can, for the moment at least, only aspire.

KEY POINT

Gender inequality continues to be the norm in Europe, although Nordic countries have made more progress on this score than most. Despite increased participation in education and in the workplace, women earn less and do more unpaid domestic work – possibly because of childbirth and childcare. Progress is partly dependent on political action but, remarkably, there is little demand for it.

Note, though that culture shifts are built on and backed up by political action: in January 2006, for instance, Norway's equality minister announced that, following the failure of a voluntary scheme, she would be bringing in legislation to oblige the 500 companies listed on the Oslo stock exchange to ensure at least four out of ten people in their boardrooms were women. At the time, only between one and two out of ten board members were female in the private sector; state-owned companies already adhere to a 45 per cent rule. Those companies which did not meet the target, she announced, would face winding-up. Interestingly, Spain is bringing in similar measures. Given women in general do far less well in the workplace than in Scandinavia (just 4 per cent of top company board members are female compared with 29 per cent in Norway (European Women's Professional Network, 2006)), it will be interesting to see how much of a difference a political change like this will make to an entrenched cultural reality.

The so-called 'feminization' of the workforce is relative as well as absolute. The increase in female

Figure 1.8 More and more women in the (paid) workforce, 1960–2006

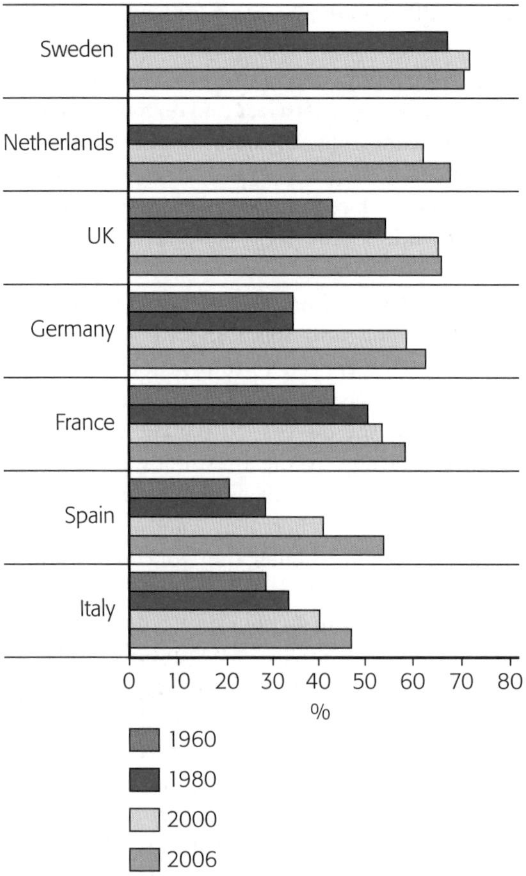

Sources: Data from 1960–2000 from Pissarides *et al.* (2004). Data for 2006 from Eurostat.

participation in paid employment has occurred alongside a decrease in the proportion of men working (see Figure 1.9). This decrease is mainly explained by the steep rise in unemployment experienced by almost all European countries as the 'long' or 'postwar' boom came to an end at the same time as technological advance really began to impact on jobs. Much of this unemployment is long-term, affects the less skilled, is often geographically concentrated and occurs in the manufacturing sector. The service sector, however, has remained very much a growth area, and it is clearly this sector that has provided the bulk of the jobs that women, in increasing numbers, have moved into. Many of these jobs are part-time. There are, though, considerable national variations in the supply of, and demand for, this kind of work: it is popular in the Netherlands, Norway, Denmark and the UK, for instance, but less so in, say, France and Southern Europe. Perhaps as a result women in these countries are more likely to be unemployed than men.

In some European countries, most notably in the Nordic countries, many of these jobs are also in the public sector, particularly in welfare (although men, it should be noted, continue to dominate the higher grades even here). There, so many women work that their need for childcare – a responsibility few European men seem willing to take on – cannot be met informally (through family or friends) and instead is met by the state. Those whom the state employs to perform that and other tasks (such as looking after the elderly) are mainly women. More women therefore work, and so on in circular fashion. Whether this circle is 'vicious' or 'virtuous' is a moot point. Some see emancipation and empowerment. Others see the traditional segregation of male and female roles simply transferred from the domestic to the paid economy, with Europe's women no less exploited. And, although there is evidence that Europeans are moving away from traditional attitudes about gender roles at the level of rhetoric (see from MacInnes, 2006), working women still do far more domestically than working men, and are therefore weighed down by the 'dual burden' or 'double shift' of work and family (see Figure 1.10).

Figure 1.9 Male and female labour force activity rates – towards convergence, 1960–2003

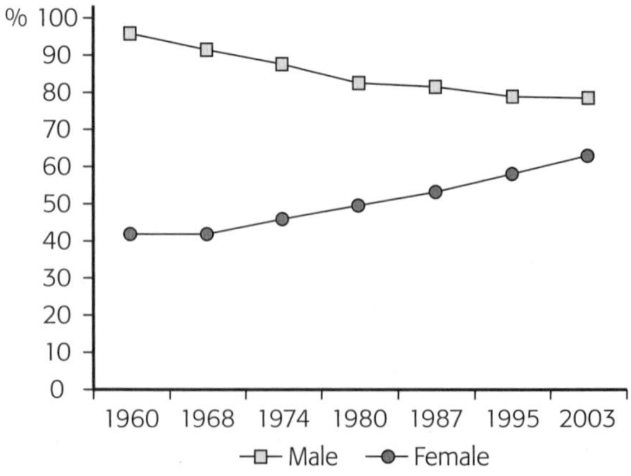

Source: Data from MacInnes (2006: 229).

Whether any real difference will occur as the result, for example, of a change made in 2005 to the civil marriage contract in Spain that obliges men to do their fair share of housework and childcare (failure to do so being taken into account in any subsequent divorce settlement) will, however, be interesting to watch. As with the same government's action on boosting women's presence in the boardroom – and its explicit promotion of women into the cabinet (see Chapter 4) – the measure represents a conscious attempt to achieve cultural change through political means. What is remarkable, however, is the fact that in most countries, there is the absence of organized pressure, either through groups or party politics (see Chapters 5 and 8) to emulate such measures.

Responses to this burden vary, but they seem to be more personal than political. Most obvious is the avoidance or at least the postponement of marriage and of childbearing and/or childrearing – activities that interrupt careers and account for a significant proportion of the persistent pay gap between men and women (see Figure 1.11). Certainly, there are strong trends in European countries (trends often led by Scandinavia and picked up last in Southern Europe) toward having fewer children and having them later on in life and toward later marriage or no marriage at all (though headline figures here can be misleading because of the rise of cohabitation). Divorce is also on the rise in Europe, although, outside the UK and Scandinavia, it is nowhere near the levels seen in the US. Indeed, in countries with a Roman Catholic (and Orthodox) tradition, it is still low, internationally speaking. This, though, may begin to change as religious constraints on the legal (i.e. divorce) regime, as well as on the thinking and behaviour of the population begin to decline.

Clearly, however, there are areas in which papal prohibitions on contraception have long since lost their influence. Roman Catholic countries like Spain, Italy and Poland have the some of the lowest

Figure 1.10 The end of traditional gender roles? Time spent on domestic chores by twenty-first century working men and women in Europe

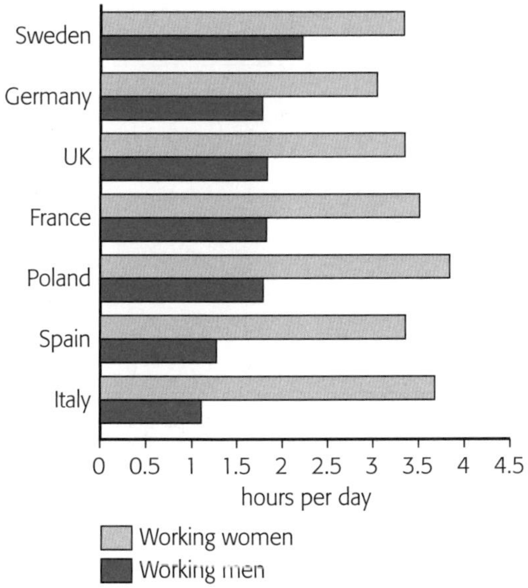

Source: Data from Eurostat, *Statistics in Focus, 4/2006*.

Figure 1.11 Europe's persistent gender pay gap, 1995 and 2005

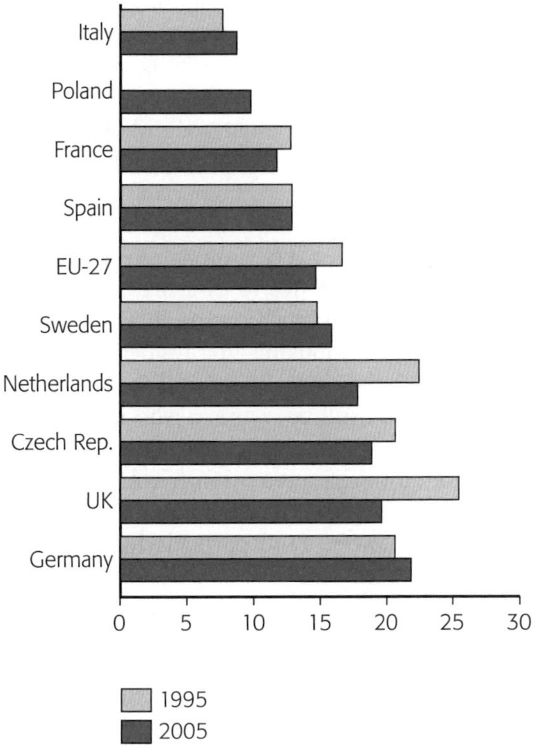

Source: Data from European Commission, *Tackling the Pay Gap between Women and Men*, 2007 (available at http://ec.europa.eu/employment_social/news/2007/jul/genderpaygap_en.pdf). The pay gap is the difference between men's and women's gross earnings as a percentage of male earnings.

birth rates in Europe (and indeed the world), and are therefore doing nothing to prevent the remorseless ageing of Europe's population (see Box 1.7) Interestingly, birth rates in the Nordic countries, where women participate more fully in the labour force, are nearer (though not at) replacement level. This is possibly because childcare and other welfare provision is easily accessed by working women in Scandinavia. It may also be because, as surveys consistently show, people in Southern Europe continue to place a higher priority on family obligations. Since they are committed to carrying out what they see as their duties (which, more often than in the north, also include looking after resident elderly relatives as well), they are more careful about adding to them. There are still few women who have no children, but many more who have just one. On a lighter (but by no means entirely frivolous) note, the low birth rate may also be a function of the fact that in Southern Europe (and particularly in Italy and Spain), adult children increasingly live with their parents far longer (i.e. well into their late twenties and thirties) than would be deemed 'normal' or even 'healthy' in other European countries. But whatever the reasons, such rates, when combined with greater longevity, are going to pose problems for Europe's welfare states (see Chapter 9).

In theory if not in practice – religion in Europe

Even this brief excursion into European demography reveals the extent to which some of the broad distinctions we can make between countries, or groups of countries, are influenced by religion. Since, as later chapters show, democracy would appear to be similarly influenced, no survey of Europe would be complete without exploring the continent's religious life a little more deeply. First and foremost, until very recently at least, Europe has been a bastion of Christianity. Yet the history of each country has been profoundly shaped according to which branch or branches of the Christian faith were important within its territory (see Table 1.4). The earliest divide in the Christian church was the eleventh-century breach between Roman Catholicism and the Orthodox church, which split Europe in an east–west fashion from (Catholic) Poland in the North down to (Orthodox) Greece in the South. This split left most modern states on one side or the other. In the sixteenth and seventeenth centuries, Protestantism either overcame (as in Lutheran Scandinavia) or (as in the UK, Germany, Switzerland and the Netherlands) came to exist alongside Roman Catholicism. The latter continued to dominate the Irish Republic, Belgium, Austria, France and, of course, Italy, Spain and Portugal.

In some countries, the influence of the dominant branch of Christianity went beyond society and was reflected at the level of the state. In the postwar period, of course, things changed, especially in the east where communist states displayed various

KEY POINT

Europe is not quite as Godless as some people assume: large numbers still profess to believe and, although, fewer people attend places of worship regularly, many still use them to mark births, marriages and deaths, etc. Christianity is still dominant, but Muslims (and Jews) make up an important part of Europe's religious identity.

Table 1.4 Religious adherents in Europe in the twenty-first century

	Percentage[1] of country's population who are:			
	Catholic	**Protestant[2]**	**Jewish**	**Muslim**
Czech Rep.	40	3	–	–
France	82	2	1	7
Germany	35	37	–	4
Italy	97	1	–	1
Netherlands	35	27	–	4
Poland	92	1	–	–
Spain	98	0	–	1
Sweden	2	95	–	2
UK	10	53	1	2

Notes: 1. Percentages are given only if the proportion of the population identifying with a particular religion reaches 1 per cent; the absence of a figure does not mean the total absence of a community (the Jewish community is a good example).
2. Note also that, because of the methodology used, Protestants in predominantly Catholic countries may be slightly underrepresented. The figure for Protestants in the UK includes Anglicans.

Source: Data from Barrett *et al.*, (2001).

levels of hostility towards organized religion, ranging from the obstructive (Bulgaria, Hungary, Romania and Poland) to the overtly antagonistic (Czechoslovakia). In the west, however, most states continued to provide subsidies to churches, whether direct or indirect (for example, by funding faith-based schools and hospitals).

In the middle of the twentieth century, Europe still seemed to be a religious place. Although regular attendance could be patchy, the church continued to play a part in the life of most Europeans as the place where rites of passage – births, marriages and deaths – were marked. As the new millennium approached, things had changed, but perhaps less than might be imagined. Research (see, for example, Halman and Riis, 2002; and Norris and Inglehart, 2004) suggests that the numbers of people who in censuses and surveys declare themselves adherents of no religion has increased, particularly in France and Belgium (where Roman Catholicism has been the big loser) and in the Netherlands (where Protestantism lost even more heavily than Catholicism). In addition, although religious baptism and marriage are still the norm for most western Europeans, there has been a continental decline in the former and a decidedly mixed picture as regards the latter. Eight out of ten couples still have a church wedding in Italy, Spain, Portugal, Greece and Finland – the 'western' states which historically took longest to move from the agricultural into the industrial age. But only around half of couples in other western states do the same. Moreover, while there is still a tendency to 'marry in' rather than 'marry out', it is very small – far smaller than among, for instance, some of Europe's non-Christian ethnic communities.

As for church attendance, problems with obtaining accurate information from either churches or their parishioners make it difficult to say anything conclusive or precise about change over time. However, the evidence we do have both from World Values Surveys and the big opinion polls regularly conducted by the EU known as *Eurobarometer* surveys suggests a general decline in western Europe (see Figure 1.12). Until recently we might have had the confidence to say that Roman Catholics, at least outside France, were much better at actually going to the church than Protestants, particularly those Protestants belonging to the official state churches of the UK and Scandinavia. Recently, however, there are reports that attendance even in bastions of Roman Catholicism such as Ireland and Italy, though still relatively high, is in rapid decline. On the other hand, participation in the EU members like Malta and Poland seems not to have dropped off, and in some CEE countries, attendance seems to be on the increase now that the state does nothing to discourage it. Interestingly, judging by surveys, years of communist anti-clericalism seems to have had only limited impact on a tendency for most people to believe in some kind of higher power. Outside the former East Germany, atheism (believing that no spirit or God or life force beyond mankind exists) is not noticeably higher than in 'western' countries such as Denmark. Similarly, agnosticism (not knowing either way) would appear from surveys to be widespread. Generally, however, there appears to be no evidence that either atheism or agnosticism is

Figure 1.12 The west European decline in church attendance, 1973–98

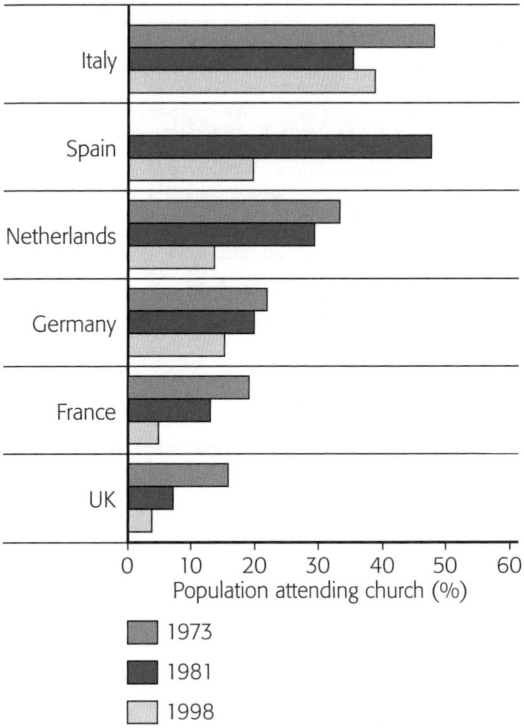

Note: UK excludes Northern Ireland where attendance is much higher (46 per cent in 1998).

Source: *Eurobarometer* data from Norris and Inglehart (2004: table 3.5).

Figure 1.13 People thinking that 'the place of religion in our society is too important'

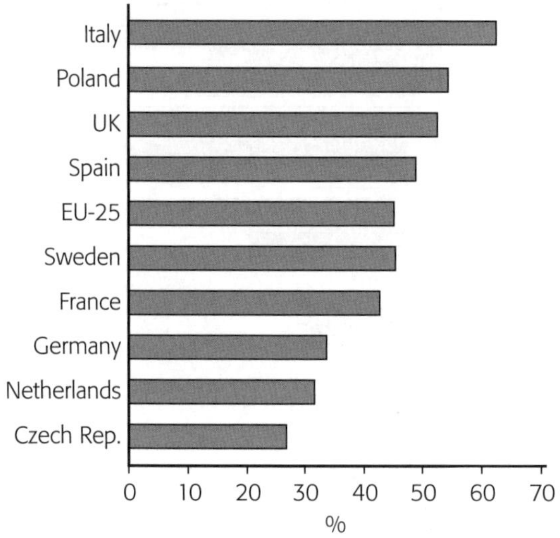

Source: Data from *Eurobarometer, 66* (2006).

on the rise, although these attitudes are much more openly admitted to – even by public figures (including politicians) – than they are in the US. And, despite all the above, the number of people still identifying with one religion or another is still significant (see Table 1.4), although there are large minorities and even majorities – particularly where one church occupies a privileged position – who worry that religion is accorded too much importance (see Figure 1.13).

What some label 'secularization', then, is real, but it can be overstated or misunderstood: not least because the number of people still believing in God, even if they do not attend religious services, is still considerable, even if it pales in comparison with the figure in the US. What cannot be overstated, however, are the considerable similarities between Europeans (east and west) on religion, and on its role in society and politics. These are neatly summed up by one researcher, who concludes (Laitin, 2002: 77) that:

> there is an EU-wide consensus in support of a secular Christianity, a respect for national churches that do not meddle in political life, and a recognition as well of minority religious groups as long as the religious expression of these groups is contained within that community.

This last aspect of the 'consensus', however, may lead to problems, not least because of the growth and increasing visibility of the continent's other main religion, Islam. Most estimates (and that is all they are) suggest up to 15 million people in Europe are Muslim, with various (and sometimes widely varying) figures given for each country (see Table 1.5). Unlike most of their Christian compatriots, many of them are relatively new immigrants and members of ethnic minorities. This makes them far more prone to discrimination, as well as to poverty. Many European towns and cities, however, contain mosques, and it does seem as if more Muslims attend worship than their Christian counterparts: Klausen (2005: 138, 142) calculates that around nine out of ten people who are nominally Muslim profess a belief in God (as opposed to between six and eight nominally Protestant Christians and seven and nine Catholics), and although only three in ten attend Mosque this is higher than the two in ten who go to church anything like regularly. However, the stereotype of non-integration in the face of supposedly decadent western values, on the one hand, and reactionary moral and doctrinal conservatism, on the other, is just that – a stereotype (see al-Azmeh and Fokas, 2007; and Klausen, 2005). That the stereotype is stronger than ever, however, is clearly one of the consequences of the terrorist attacks in New York, Madrid and London. But it merely builds on what one writer, in view of the crusades and expulsions touched on above, justifiably calls 'a thousand years of myth making in Europe' (see Reeves, 2003).

On the other hand, there are increasing media reports of European Muslim involvement in an apparent rise in anti-Semitic attacks – attacks on Jews or Jewish property – especially in France, which along with the UK has Europe's largest Jewish community. There are Jewish communities in other countries but, as Table 1.4, indicates, they are very small relative to the population. In absolute terms, of course, there are large numbers of Jewish people living in Germany (96,000) Italy (34,000), the Netherlands (25,000), Sweden (16,000) and Spain (13,000). In Poland and the Czech Republic, the population is no more than a few thousand, due mainly to the Holocaust. To give some idea of scale, the Jewish community of the US is five times bigger than the Jewish community of all the countries listed in Table 1.4. In contrast, the Muslim commu-

Table 1.5 Muslims in the wider Europe

	Estimated Muslim pop.	% of total pop.
Turkey	68m	99.0
Kosovo	1.8m	90.0
Albania	2.2m	70.0
Bosnia-Herzegovina	1.5m	40.0
Macedonia	630k	30.0
France	5–6m[1]	8.0–9.6
Netherlands	945k	5.8
Denmark	270k	5.0
Serbia + Montenegro	405k	5.0
Switzerland	311k	4.2
Austria	339k	4.0
Belgium	400k	4.0
Germany	3m	3.6
Sweden	300k	3.0
UK	1.6m	2.8
Spain	1m	2.3
Italy	825k	1.4

Note: 1 The figure for France is high compared to most estimates: Klausen (2005:6) notes that even the commonly-cited figure of 4 million has been calculated by some demographers as an overestimate of a million or more.

Source: Data from BBC News, *Muslims in Europe: Country guide* (December 2005), available at http://news.bbc.co.uk/1/hi/world/europe/4385768.stm#uk

nity in the US is only just over a third of that living in the European countries listed. This may or may not help explain some of the foreign policy differences we explore in Chapter 11.

Composition and identity: multi-ethnic, multi-national – and European?

But if the proportion of people in European countries who can be clearly and conventionally identified as religious, or working class, is shrinking, there seem to be increasing numbers whose self-definition now includes some element of nationality and/or ethnicity (distinctive group characteristics rooted in history and/or race). In fact, Europe provides plenty of opportunity for people to feel and claim multiple and divided loyalties because, as we explore in more detail in Chapters 2 and 10, the continent contains far more ethnic groups than states. Many people, even those who could be officially classified as citizens of one or other country, think of themselves as belonging (either solely or simultaneously) to some other entity or identity. Because of the way the map of Europe has been drawn and redrawn over the centuries, and because of migration, there is almost no country that is completely unaffected by such currents, or by the backlash against them. But some are more affected than others (see Box 1.8 and Chapter 2).

KEY POINT

Many European states contain ethnic and national minorities. This means a large number of people have multiple attachments. There is also some, albeit limited, evidence of the emergence of a European identity, although this varies between countries. The basic values that many deem necessary for the survival of capitalist liberal democracy, however, seem to be present in almost all countries, whatever their history.

While outright hostility to the EU is low in member states, there is limited evidence that the populations of the continent's various countries are developing an explicitly (let alone an exclusively) European identity. On the other hand, many people seem comfortable with both national and European identity. *Eurobarometer* surveys consistently suggest that just over half of people in the EU member states are happy to describe themselves both as a national of a particular country and European, while under half identify exclusively with their own country. The demographic analyses show that people who left full-time education at the age of twenty or older, those who are still studying and managers are most likely to feel European as well. They are also most likely to feel 'proud to be European'. Retired people and people who look after the home are most likely to identify with their own nationality only. In other words, education, class (and age) make quite a difference. Breaking things down by country, however, reveals even bigger differences, with the British standing out as less 'European' than their counterparts in other

BOX 1.8

Politically significant ethnonational minorities in Europe

Belgium	60 per cent Dutch-speaking Flemish in the north; 30 per cent French-speaking Walloons in the south: considerable rivalry (see Chapter 2).
Bulgaria	10 per cent Turkish; 8.5 per cent Roma (gypsies).
Czech Rep.	Moravians (13 per cent), but most identify as Czech; 2 per cent Roma.
Cyprus	12 per cent Turkish minority, living in officially unrecognized independent state.
Estonia	Formerly part of the Soviet Union: 30 per cent Russians, 4 per cent Ukrainian and Belarusian.
Finland	6 per cent Swedish.
France	Mediterranean island of Corsica. On mainland, sizable ethnic and racial minorities from former African colonies, many of whom are of Arab descent and practising Muslims.
Germany	Some regional identity in former East Germany. Large immigrant community, made up of various European groups plus Turks (2.5 per cent).
Hungary	4.5 per cent Roma, 2.5 per cent German, 2 per cent Serb, 1 per cent Slovakian.
Italy	Two small linguistic minorities: German-speaking *Alto Adige*, and French-speaking *Valle d'Aosta*. Significant North v. South divide.
Latvia	Formerly part of the Soviet Union: 30 per cent Russian, 7 per cent Ukrainian and Belarusian.
Romania	Collection of very small minorities from surrounding states, plus 6.5 per cent Roma, as well as 7 per cent Hungarian concentrated in Transylvania.
Slovakia	10 per cent Hungarian, 9.5 per cent Roma.
Spain	Several more or less self-conscious regions, two of which (Catalunya and *Euzkadi* or the Basque country) see themselves as separate nations (see Chapter 2). Small Roma population.
Switzerland	Patchwork of largely German-speaking and French-speaking areas, but no separatism.
UK	Sizable national minorities in Scotland and Wales, though separatism is non-violent and not as intense as in Northern Ireland where a large proportion identify with the Irish Republic to the south (see Chapter 2). Significant ethnic minorities from former colonial possessions in the Indian subcontinent (4.4 per cent) and the West Indies (2 per cent).

Sources: Data from CIA *World Factbook* and Barany (2002: 160).

countries (see Figure 1.14). There seems, however, to be no correlation between pride in one's own country and not feeling so European: according to Eurobarometer 66 (conducted in 2006), national pride is high (80–90 per cent) all around Europe (outside Germany, where it still seems to be associated with excessive nationalism) and the British do not stand out on this score.

People in some countries are clearly much more willing than others to identify with something called 'Europe'. The fact that some people are quite reluctant Europeans while others are comfortable with

Figure 1.14 Mixed feelings – European and national identity

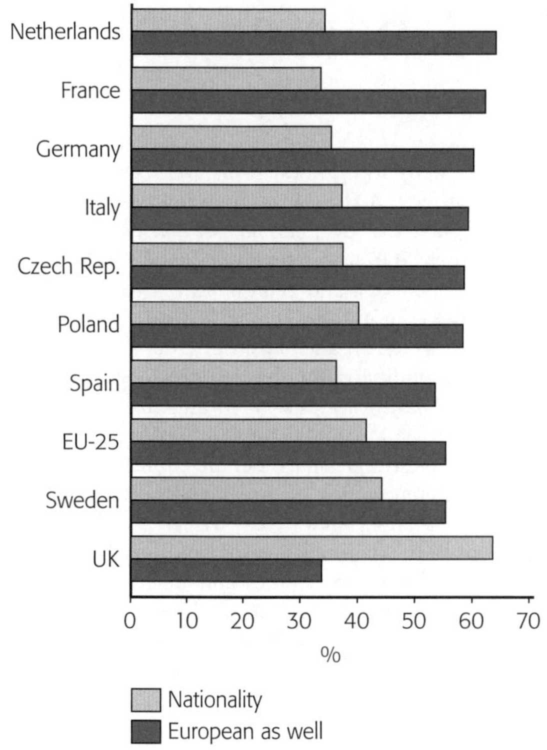

Sources: Data from *Eurobarometer, 64* (2005). Question asks if people see themselves as a national of their country only or as European as well.

multiple or 'nested' identities (local, regional, national and supranational) is interesting. But it could also prove politically problematic: it may divide an educated cosmopolitan elite from an undereducated parochial mass. There are clearly national differences which may have their origins in the extent to which European identity is portrayed in public debate as a threat or a complement to national identity (see Díez Medrano and Gutiérrez, 2001; and Smith, 1992). However, there are very tangible symbols of greater integration – travel, a common passport, a flag, a currency, for instance – that now exist independent of that debate and may over time be contributing to what some analysts clearly believe is 'the emergence of a mass European identity', even if it is stronger in those nations that first established the EU than in those who joined it later (see Bruter, 2005). Certainly, as the same analysts show, using survey and focus group evidence, there is no simple 'zero-sum' game between Europe and the nation: sometimes they are seen as opposed; in other places the one is constitutive of the other (see Kriesi *et al.*, 2003; and Stråth, 2001). This interaction and debate is destined to continue. As we suggest in Chapter 2, 'Europe' can no longer be thought of as existing outside or even above the state, while state and nation are no longer as commensurate as some countries tried to pretend they were.

But we need to be careful not to think that limited, or at least variable, levels of identification with an abstract called 'Europe' means that Europeans do not share some – or at least enough – attributes in common. In fact, recent research suggests that they do (see Fuchs and Klingemann, 2002). It is true that one can draw systematic distinctions between groups of European countries with regard to democratic and liberal values (e.g. self-responsibility and work ethic, solidarity with the disadvantaged and trust in others, ethnic tolerance, support for and confidence in democracy and the political system, rejection of violence). And it is true that these differences may be traceable to countries' religious and imperial histories, as well as their level of economic development. But it is also true that there seem to be systematic differences between (broadly speaking) the countries that currently make up the EU-25 and, on the one hand, the US and, on the other, countries further to the east (i.e. the Former Soviet Union, FSU). And it is true that the differences between the old and new member states of the EU are nowhere near as significant as we sometimes think. Indeed, in the realms of religion, ability to speak English as a *lingua franca,* and popular culture, there are often more differences between the fifteen member states that made up the EU before 2004 than there are between those fifteen and the states that joined in that year (see Laitin, 2002). As Fuchs and Klingemann (2002: 52) put it, 'Between the countries of Europe there is little difference in the political values and behaviours that are essential to a democracy.'

Learning Resources for Chapter 1

Further reading

Contemporary histories of Europe abound: the best reads are Mazower (1998), *Dark Continent* and Judt (2007), *Postwar: A History of Europe Since 1945*. See also Gaddis (2007), *The Cold War* and Davies (2007), *Europe East and West*. There are also plenty of reference works: Turner (2007), *Statesman's Yearbook 2008* is a good one. By far the best work on the sociology and economics of western Europe remains Crouch (1999), *Social Change in Western Europe*, but see also the introduction to the collection edited by Hall and Soskice (2001), *Varieties of Capitalism*. On (the lack of) social mobility or 'fluidity' in Europe, see the collection edited by Breen (2004), *Social Mobility in Europe*. A stimulating – and stimulatingly short! – essay on 'Europeanization and Globalization' is provided by Wallace (2000), in the journal *New Political Economy*. On the ethnic minorities of Europe, by far the best up-to-date reference book is Cordell and Wolff (2004), *The Ethnopolitical Encyclopaedia of Europe*. On values, see Arts *et al.*, (2004), *The Cultural Diversity of European Unity*. On religion, see Norris and Inglehart (2004), *Sacred and Secular*, and the volumes edited by Byrnes and Katzenstein (2006), *Religion in an Expanding Europe*, and edited by al-Azmeh and Fokas (2007), *Islam in Europe*. An informative, non-academic guide to the state of the Christian religion in Europe is Jeff Chu's article in *Time Magazine* (June 2003).

On the web

www.worldatlas.com – maps and basic country information

www.odci.gov/cia/publications/factbook – detailed country information

hdr.undp.org – country facts and figures from the UN

www.nationmaster.com – make your own charts and tables

epp.eurostat.ec.europa.eu and **www.oecd.org** – country and EU statistics

ec.europa.eu/public_opinion – Europe-wide survey research

www.pbs.org/wgbh/peoplescentury and **www.historyteacher.net** – European history

www.cnn.com/SPECIALS/cold.war – all things Cold War

www.palgrave.com
Companion Website
Visit the Companion Website to 'click and go'
www.palgrave.com/politics/bale

Discussion questions

1. Different countries have risen and fallen in pre-eminence in Europe over the last five hundred years. Pick one or two examples: why and how do you think status was gained and then lost?
2. What do you think drove Europe toward two world wars in the first half of the twentieth century? And how, in your opinion, has it managed to avoid something similar happening since then?
3. There may have been no world war after 1945 but there was a Cold War. Was such a conflict inevitable and why do you think did it came to an end?
4. Why is there so much economic variation between, but also within, European countries? And what does it mean to say that they are almost all 'post-industrial'?
5. The new democracies of Central and Eastern Europe (CEE) have had to adapt to life after communism: can you point to particular successes and failures?
6. How would you define globalization and what impact, if any, is it having on Europe? If you are opposed to it, why?
7. Europeanization doesn't mean that all the continent's countries are becoming more like each other. How does the organization and extent of welfare in different states, for instance, illustrate this point?
8. It's often assumed that Europe is becoming more classless, gender-blind, and secular. Do you think that's the case?
9. Why do some inequalities seem to mobilize people politically and others, which are just as glaring and have political ramifications, apparently excite little interest?
10. Why might it be unrealistic to talk about Europeans, or, for that matter, about, say, Britons or Spaniards or Belgians or Cypriots or Slovaks or Estonians or Latvians?

Chapter 2

The end of the nation state?

Stateless nations 40
Belgium – federal solution or slippery slope? 44
'Asymmetrical' federalism – Spain 46
The UK – another hybrid 49
France – no longer quite so indivisible 52
The EU and the end of sovereignty? 54
Origins, enlargement and institutions 55
Integration via economics and law 63
A constitution in all but name? The Lisbon Treaty 64
The end of the nation state? 66

A **nation state** is a country where the boundaries of the political and administrative system are presumed – rightly or wrongly – to coincide with those that contain a population with a supposedly shared culture, history and (probably) language.

The possession of **sovereignty** implies the ultimate right, free from external hindrance, to decide and control how a state will be run and the direction it will take.

As we saw in Chapter 1, the late nineteenth and early twentieth century confirmed Europe as a continent of states. These were constructed on the basis – sometimes firm, sometimes more fictional – that they were the institutional embodiment of a nation, of a community living (and in most cases born) in a territory and amongst other people with whom they felt a binding affinity. These **nation states** were presumed to be *sovereign* in the sense of exercising supreme political authority within their territorial boundaries and remaining free from hindrance from outside bodies.

In fact, the reality has rarely matched the presumption. There are two reasons for this. First, many European countries contain 'stateless nations' (Keating, 2001). These are minorities that consider themselves to be, or to belong to, nations other than that on which the state claims to be founded. In recent years, many have become politicized and, as we shall see below, have obliged states to respond to their demands. Second, few states could claim complete freedom from outside 'interference' Those in CEE formerly (if not formally) controlled by the Soviet Union are only the most blatant example. Many of their western counterparts, by joining what is now the EU, have also pooled (some would say) or (according to others) compromised their **sovereignty**.

This chapter explores, in turn, both facets of what some are bemoaning as the end of the nation state in Europe. It begins, first, by looking at how the phenomenon of **minority nationalism** is helping to make historically unitary states (in which sub-national government traditionally enjoyed no real power) look more like those federal states where (as we shall see in Chapter 3) local autonomy has long been important. And it asks whether the hybrid forms that they have taken on will be enough to save them from eventual break-up. Second, it looks at how the nation state is apparently being undermined both 'from above' and even 'from within' by the European Union.

Stateless nations

Some Europeans have an emotional attachment – sometimes only latent or dormant, sometimes vociferously and even violently manifest – to a nation

Minority nationalism is the feeling on the part of one community within a state that they belong to a separate nation that should therefore be accorded some kind of autonomy, special rights or even independence.

that is different from the state in which, officially, they live. In some European countries there is a clear territorial, as well as historical, cultural (and possibly linguistic) demarcation between these 'national minorities' and the majority population, even if the minority is effectively surrounded in its 'enclave' (a smaller territory within, yet distinct from, a larger territory) by the majority. In other places, the minority may assert there is a clear territorial demarcation, but so many people from the majority live inside what they claim to be their 'borders' that the pattern is in fact complex and confused. Complexity and confusion can also arise when a minority in one state sees itself as part of a nation, but the majority of their fellow 'nationals' live in a neighbouring state – a situation which can give rise to 'irredentism' (the pursuit of reunification with the homeland). This situation occurs (outside Northern Ireland, anyway) far more frequently in CEE than in the west: the Hungarian populations of Slovakia, Serbia and Romania mentioned in Chapter 1 are obvious examples (see Csergo and Goldgeier, 2004). In the west (again, with the exception of Ireland), states that could have laid claim to some common identity showed no interest in interfering in the politics of their neighbours: examples include the Swedish with Swedish-speaking Finns, or the Austrians with German-speaking Italians, or the Netherlands with Dutch-speaking Belgians.

That said, European history provides plenty of examples of the bloody consequences of minority nationalism. As we saw in Chapter 1, the First World War itself was sparked by Serbian nationalists anxious to throw off what they saw as the yoke of the Austro-Hungarian empire. Ironically, however, the treaties that followed the war were so intent on dismembering the latter that they established artificial borders which, in CEE, often left linguistic minorities stranded in a state they did not regard as their own. This was not something the architects of the peace after the Second World War did much about, the exception being their complicity in the forcible repatriation of the (Sudenten) German minority in Czechoslovakia, one of the many 'artificial' states created in the aftermath of the 1914–18 conflict. After 1945, an already broad consensus on borders in western Europe was effectively locked into place by the need for collective solidarity against the threat from the Soviet Union. This threat also ensured that Spanish dictator Francisco Franco would be given free rein to suppress those Spaniards who insisted on asserting the ancient autonomy of their regions. Moreover, the rush to join in the consumerist prosperity that seemed to be the natural accompaniment to peace and democracy also seemed to have helped reconcile minorities to living alongside the similarly materially preoccupied majority. Meanwhile in the east, communist regimes that were widely thought of as permanent seemed to have effectively kept the lid on, and perhaps extinguished, any lingering disputes between and within the member states of what became the Warsaw Pact (see Chapter 1).

Partly as a result, few texts on European politics written in the three decades following the Second World War considered 'minority nationalism' of sufficient contemporary interest to bother affording it much, if any, space. As a cleavage it was a has-been, a relic of a bygone age. Like that other formerly important cleavage, religion, it would supposedly slip into history. Yet the loyalty and identity we call nationalism, the need to belong to an 'imagined community' with whom we feel meaningfully connected (Anderson, 1991: 5–7), only appeared to have burned itself out. In fact, the embers could quite easily be fanned into life. Whatever states did to 'deal with' such loyalties – trying to ignore them (France), gradually acknowledging them (the UK and Belgium), or forcibly repressing them (Spain) – clearly did not deprive them of the oxygen they needed to exist, even if only in latent rather than in manifest form.

KEY POINT

Some states contain people who feel either that the territory they occupy should be part of a neighbouring country or that they are a nation that deserves a state of its own. This combination of grievance and aspiration was previously suppressed by dictatorship or lay dormant under wider concerns to secure material well-being. This changed with the coming of democracy, with socio-economic development and with a trend toward decentralization. Outside the Balkans, fears that the rise of minority nationalism may spark calls for radical revisions of borders and widespread abuses of human rights have not been realized.

The transition of minority nationalism from latency to relevancy seems to have resulted, in the main, from two developments. First, the concept of democracy itself seems to have undergone considerable stretching from the 1960s onwards. It began to include notions of 'subsidiarity' (decisions being taken at the lowest appropriate level) and participation, not least as a response to the idea that 'big government' was bad government and that the political system was suffering from 'overload' (see Chapter 3). Instead of trying and failing to keep up with and balance too many demands by too many people wanting too much money (especially in 'lame duck' peripheral regions), states would be better advised to let them get on with it themselves. Such advice applied as much to their treatment of national minorities as any other group. Second, democracy, or voting at least, seemed less hung up on class (see Chapter 6): clearly, there is no necessary trade-off between class and ethnic and/or regional identity, but as the intensity of one declined, the intensity of the other seems to have increased.

This is partly explained by politics and economics as much as by sociology. For instance, in the UK the Scots' increased sense of themselves as distinct is likely to have been influenced by the imposition of unpopular policies by a largely English Conservative government during the 1980s. That decade saw 'London' widely blamed for an economic recession that hit Scotland's heavy manufacturing base hard – and all this as nationalists (increasingly prepared to stand candidates in all electoral contests) were claiming that Scotland's oil wealth, among other things, could make it a viable independent state within the EU. In Spain and Belgium, too, the desire for more autonomy on the part of at least some of the nations that made up those states was likewise driven by a mixture of politics and economics. And it, too, developed in a context where European integration seemed to offer the chance for small states to prosper.

But material interests and institutions do not explain everything. Nowadays, only the most antediluvian Marxist or 'institutionalist' zealot would claim that people's identity, political or otherwise, can be 'read off' from their position in the market place or the political structures in which they are embedded. Clearly, we are all social and emotional as well as economic actors and are capable of storing, accessing and displaying multiple loyalties – not necessarily at will, but certainly when inspired by events, or at least the construction put on those events by inspirational and/or demagogic leaders. And the consequences of such politicization can be tragic. In the early 1990s, in the former Yugoslavia, latent minority nationalism was so whipped up by gangster politicians that it spilled over into civil war and the murder and forcible removal that was euphemistically labelled 'ethnic cleansing' (Box 2.1).

The terrible events in the Balkans in the early 1990s seemed to provide proof of this tendency, and heightened fears that in CEE states might celebrate their release from imperial bonds by attempting the kind of centralizing, majority 'nation-building' that characterized western Europe in the nineteenth century. The kind of nation-building, in other words, that ignored the wishes of often quite substantial minorities by privileging 'ethnic nationalism' over the sort of 'civic nationalism' that may have originated with a dominant ethnic core but saw it more or less peacefully co-opt, first, the elites and, then, the people of more peripheral regions (see Péteri, 2000; Schöpflin, 1995; and Smith, 1991). Fortunately, such fears were not in the main borne out.

There were certainly some concerns, especially in the early 1990s, about the Baltic states (Estonia, Lithuania and especially Latvia). They were understandably reluctant, after winning their freedom from the Soviet empire by precipitating its collapse, to think much about the rights of the many Russians that had settled there during the previous half-century. Attempts to restrict their rights – particularly in the field of language and education – did not, however, survive a combination of pressure from the newly-formed Russian federation and the EU, which made it crystal clear that any state with a poor record on minority rights might as well forget trying to join. In central Europe, individual politicians and parties have tried to make capital by harking back to a time when all their 'countrymen' were united in the one homeland, particularly in Hungary. Politicians in Slovakia (where many ethnic Hungarians live) also began the 1990s with a line in both exclusionary rhetoric and public policy decisions, though, as in the Baltic states, such populism was forced to soften in the face of their own possible exclusion from the EU (see Kelley, 2004; and Tesser,

BOX 2.1

Break-up in the Balkans

Yugoslavia was created by the victorious powers of the First World War not only to finish off the Austro-Hungarian empire, but also to contain those Balkan nations whose rebellion against the empire had helped spark the conflict in the first place. Though a Communist country from the end of the Second World War, Yugoslavia maintained its independence from the Soviet empire. It was also a federal state consisting of six republics. These were Bosnia and Herzegovina, Croatia, Macedonia, Montenegro, Slovenia and Serbia, which also contained two autonomous provinces (Kosovo and Vojvodina) with non-Serb populations (Albanian and Hungarian respectively). After the end of the Cold War, multiparty elections were held in the republics in 1990. They were all won by non-communist nationalist parties, except in Serbia and Montenegro where the Socialist Party (the successor to the communists) was elected on an aggressively nationalistic platform. Slobodan Milošević, the Serbian leader, had already withdrawn the autonomous status of Kosovo and Vojvodina, thus raising fears that Serbia would move to stamp its authority on the other republics.

Sensing a window of opportunity, Slovenia and Croatia declared independence in June 1991, followed by Macedonia in November. In Slovenia and Macedonia, the Yugoslav army (the JNA) made little or no attempt to stop them. Croatia, however, descended into a six-month civil war, during which Serbs living in Croatia, supported by the JNA, achieved control of around a third of the fledgling state. Early the following year (in March 1992), Bosnia and Herzegovina declared independence, an act that led to a three-way civil war between Bosnian Serbs and Bosnian Croats (both backed by the armies of their respective states) and Bosnian Muslims. Even though they asked the US to let them come up with a solution, European states were, from the outset, split over what to do. None of them was keen to get involved, and many even blamed Germany's recognition of Croatia for sparking the war in the first place. Because they could not (or would not) back up diplomatic initiatives with military force (particularly against Serbia), such initiatives proved fruitless. Fighting came to an end only in 1995 after the credible threat of US armed intervention, by which time hundreds of thousands were dead or wounded and millions made refugees. Many were the victims of what became known as 'ethnic cleansing' – the forcible removal (and, in some cases, the systematic rape, assault and murder) of populations in order to ensure areas were purely Serb (or, to a lesser extent, Croat and, to a much lesser extent, Muslim).

The Dayton Peace Accord brokered by the US did little more than recognize the situation on the ground in Bosnia. The republic is now split into three largely ethnically homogeneous sections, with the Serbs the biggest winners and the Muslims the biggest losers. When, however, the Milošević regime attempted, four years later, the 'ethnic cleansing' in Kosovo of its Albanian population, the Americans and the Europeans – working together as NATO – acted rather more rapidly, bringing the Serbian campaign to a halt by aerial bombardment between March and June 1999. Their action also hastened the fall of the Milošević regime, which was replaced in 2000 by politicians keen to end their country's isolation. However, it left Europeans with another, very serious headache; namely, what to do about the desire of Kosovo's Albanian majority to turn their province into an independent country – a desire attracting sympathy from the Americans but provoking alarm in China and Russia which understandably fear the precedent such an action would set.

2003). Just as importantly, perhaps, most of Europe's newest democracies could see for themselves that their western counterparts were beginning to accommodate rather than ignore or suppress what seemed to be a resurgence of minority nationalism from the 1960s onwards. This 'territorial management strategy' (Keating, 2006) is one that we now go on to explore in more detail.

Belgium – federal solution or slippery slope?

It used to be easy to sort European states into two categories. The majority were centralized, **unitary** states – a category which included, first, former imperial powers and their ex-colonies; second, the then communist countries; and third, Scandinavian states. Traditionally, only a handful of European states were **federal** states (Germany, Austria and Switzerland) although such a bald distinction always had its critics, not least because the federalism of Germany is very different to the federalism of, say, the US and also different to the federalism of Switzerland (see Chapter 3). But recently, the distinction has become even more blurred as some former unitary states under pressure from minority nationalism, even where the justification and support for it is weak (see Box 2.2), are adopting federal or quasi-federal forms in response. The question is, in the long term, whether this will save them from break-up.

In one former unitary state, Belgium, federalism is now fully fledged, even if (as in other federal states in Europe) it is not federalism US-style. Ever since it was, to all intents and purposes, conjured up by foreign powers in 1830, the country was linguistically divided between the Walloon, French-speaking, south and the Flemish, Dutch-speaking, north. However, well into the postwar period its government and administration was conducted in French, even if many of those who ran it were from Flanders, their main link with their Walloon counterparts being Roman Catholicism. The capital, Brussels, although located in the Flemish region was (and continues to be) predominantly French-speaking. This French-speaking control was facili-

KEY POINT

Belgium – arguably something of an artificial nineteenth-century creation – has adopted a federal structure in order to accommodate the demands for autonomy of its most assertive, Dutch-speaking linguistic community. But this seems to not to have halted but rather to have fuelled calls for more (or even complete) independence.

Unitary states are those in which regional government is really only local administration of centrally determined (and often financed) services, and where any power exercised by regional government is ultimately dependent on the consent of the central state.

Federal states are those in which territorial sub-national government enjoys constitutionally guaranteed autonomy and functional competence – in other words; regional government really is government and is not simply administration under delegated authority from the centre.

BOX 2.2

Padania?

Italy's *Lega Nord* (Northern League) is a political party that has been in centre-right national governments and is also renowned for its xenophobic rhetoric. For almost a quarter of a century, its leaders have been arguing for increased autonomy for some of the richest of Italy's regions, such as Lombardy, Piedmont and Veneto. Although the grounds for their claim to independence seem in the main to be economic (resentment at the supposed drain on dynamism caused by the South's relative poverty), they have tried to bolster it by dreaming-up a nation, *Padania,* that is supposedly united by history and culture. Few seem persuaded by such claims: they certainly seem less genuine than those of Italy's five existing 'special regions' (Sardinia, Sicily, Val d'Aosta, Trentino-Alto Adige and Friuli-Venezia) that have been accorded a degree of autonomy since the 1970s. But the *Lega*'s usefulness as a coalition partner, and the threat it poses to the votes and ability to govern of other political parties, has lent momentum to a rather less ambitious campaign for a federal Italy – a state which, after all, did not exist until 1861. In response, successive Italian governments have, since 2002, passed measures devolving power, although many of them are contested and remain to be implemented. *Padania* may be more fiction than fact, and Italy is, in reality, far from being a federal country yet. But it might be moving, albeit haltingly, in that direction.

tated not just by an essentially Francophone monarchy, but also by the fact that the more industrialised Wallonia provided the greater part of the nation's wealth. But the decline of heavy industry from the 1950s onwards reversed the situation and turned the political tide: as the Flemish north began to outstrip the French-speaking south economically, its people and their representatives began to demand autonomy from a community that, in their view, had not only dominated them unfairly for over a hundred years but was now also a drain on their resources. They were not, however, alone: a number of Walloon politicians believed their region would be better off without the Flemish. By 1993, this push for autonomy resulted in Belgium becoming a federal state, albeit one rendered unconventional because the ensuing **devolution** involved the transfer of powers not just to three geographical regions – *Wallonie, Vlaams* and *Brussel* or *Bruxelles*) but also to three 'communities' – French-, Dutch- and German-speaking.

What is significant is that when the process of disaggregation began as far back as the early 1960s, it started out as a way of defusing tensions, not as a conscious first step on the road to federalism. Yet Belgium seemed to slide inexorably towards the latter. Laws passed in 1962 and 1963 defined the boundaries of the linguistic groups. Constitutional reform in 1970 set up linguistically based communities with responsibilities in 'cultural' areas such as broadcasting and education. Further constitutional reform in 1980 not only granted executive status to these communities (which were given additional responsibilities in health and welfare), but also gave executive and legislative powers to the regions of Wallonia and Flanders in economic planning, environment and transport, as well as setting up a court to arbitrate disputes between the regions, the communities and central government. More reforms in 1988 and 1989 added to the powers and responsibilities already devolved, and granted the same to Brussels.

Literally, **devolution** is the transfer of competences from national to sub-national government. However, it has taken on a particular meaning in the UK where it is used in order to make it clear that the transfer of powers is not the forerunner of federalism, let alone complete independence for Scotland and Wales.

Equally significant is the fact that 1993 did not bring an end to the process. The so-called 'Lambermont Accord' of June 2001 saw even more devolution of powers to the regions and the latter now have the right, where they have such powers, to negotiate with other member states in the EU instead of leaving it up to the federal government. Indeed, beyond taxation, social security, the monarchy, sports and the location of Brussels in Dutch-speaking Flanders, there seems to be little holding the country together. Belgian parties have long since split into Dutch- and French-speaking organizations. An agreement that the federal government should be linguistically balanced makes government formation (see Chapter 4) possible but sometimes very tricky. After the general election of June 2007 the parliamentary arithmetic made things so complicated that it took until 2008 to form a coalition government bridging the linguistic divide – a divide that in the meantime grew wider as parties on both sides made seemingly irreconcilable demands concerning even greater devolution of power to Flanders. Not for the first time, people began openly to discuss the possibility of a split. Whether such a move would have public support, however much people grumble, is debateable. Polls taken after a French-speaking TV station mischievously ran a hoax news item in December 2006 on the supposed unilateral declaration of independence by the Flemish parliament showed majority opposition to a split on both sides of the linguistic divide. On the other hand, polls taken during the hiatus after the general election of 2007 suggested support for independence growing in Flanders.

In fact, there is a recent European precedent for a state splitting in two. In 1993, the Czech Republic and Slovakia underwent a largely uncontested, 'velvet divorce', ending a federation that had first been put into place in 1969, some fifty years after the state's creation after the First World War. The divorce came about more as the result of the people accommodating the politicians rather than the latter finally agreeing to give the former what they appeared to want, whereas in Belgium politicians have arguably reflected popular will as much as they have shaped it. Also, things were made easier for the erstwhile Czechoslovaks than they would be for the disgruntled Belgians because each region had its own recognized capital: it is hard to see Flanders breaking away and leaving Brussels (which may be French-speaking but which is located firmly in Flanders) to Wallonia. Another difference with the Belgian case lies in the fact that the main impetus for the break-up of the state came from the smaller, poorer and economically backward region, Slovakia, where politicians did their best to whip up fears over (among other things) language concessions to its Hungarian-speaking minority. By and large, Czech politicians were initially reluctant to dissolve the federation and consented only when it became clear that progress on other fronts would be blocked by the Slovaks until they did so. Given the often turbulent nature of politics in Slovakia in the 1990s, and the much slower economic progress it made relative to the Czech Republic, it seems clear who got the best of the deal.

'Asymmetrical' federalism – Spain

The lesson from Belgium, surely, is that decentralization, rather than satisfying calls for more autonomy, can whet the appetite for even more. Yet this has not discouraged politicians in other European states – most notably in Spain, the UK and more recently Italy (see Box 2.2) – proffering devolution as some kind of 'solution' to the 'problem' of minority nationalism (Map 2.1).

Since its emergence from authoritarian dictatorship at the end of the 1980s, Spain has transferred increased powers and competences to its *Comunidades Autónomas* (literally, autonomous communities or regions). Many of these continued, as historic kingdoms, to maintain a sense of themselves as distinct, despite forming part of what for hundreds of years was one of the most centralized unitary states in Europe. However, this transfer of powers has proceeded on an incremental basis depending on negotiations between the central government and each of the seventeen autonomous communities established under the 1978 constitution, all of which now have an elected assembly and government. According to the statutory agreement each community has made with the state, each has a unique range of powers on issues excepting defence and foreign policy, key aspects of social security and macroeconomics, all of which are reserved for the centre. They can exercise these powers in any way they see fit provided they do not conflict with the constitution which, although it created what some see as a hostage to fortune by acknowledging and guaranteeing 'the right to autonomy for the *nationalities* and regions' (author's italics), also committed itself to 'the indivisible unity of the Spanish Nation'.

KEY POINT

Spain is a state composed of several historic kingdoms, some of which have never been entirely reconciled to rule from Madrid. Since its return to democracy in the mid-1970s, it has accordingly granted some of its regions extra autonomy. Whether this flexible response can save Spain from separatist violence or even eventual break-up remains to be seen.

However, not all of Spain's autonomous communities have chosen (or been able) to assert their autonomy to the extent seen in, say, the Basque country and Catalunya. This has led to Spain being labelled as a practitioner of 'differentiated' or 'asymmetrical' federalism (see Agranoff, 1996). Under this hybrid system, most of the country still seems to operate as a unitary state, albeit with some devolution to the regions. But at the same time, there are parts of the country that look, to all intents and purposes, as if they are part of a federal state, or even independent nations. Theoretically (that is to say, constitutionally) Spain is not a federal state – the powers enjoyed by some of its regions, some might argue, are not defined as such by the constitution. But the idea that they can be taken back or that, as far as many in the regions are concerned, they are not actually inalienable rights, is fanciful to say the least. The question now is not so much whether Spain is or is not federal or on the way to federalism, but whether the latter – hybrid or pure – will be enough to prevent its eventual break-up.

In the three and a half decades since the Basque separatist organization, *Euskadi Ta Azkatasuna* (ETA), first began its campaign of violence against the Franco dictatorship, over 800 people have been killed. Millions of euros have also been paid out by businesses in what is one of Spain's wealthiest regions in protection money, extorted as a 'revolutionary tax' by an organization whose less high-profile *kale borroka* (or 'street struggle') has also caused millions of euros' worth of damage to prop-

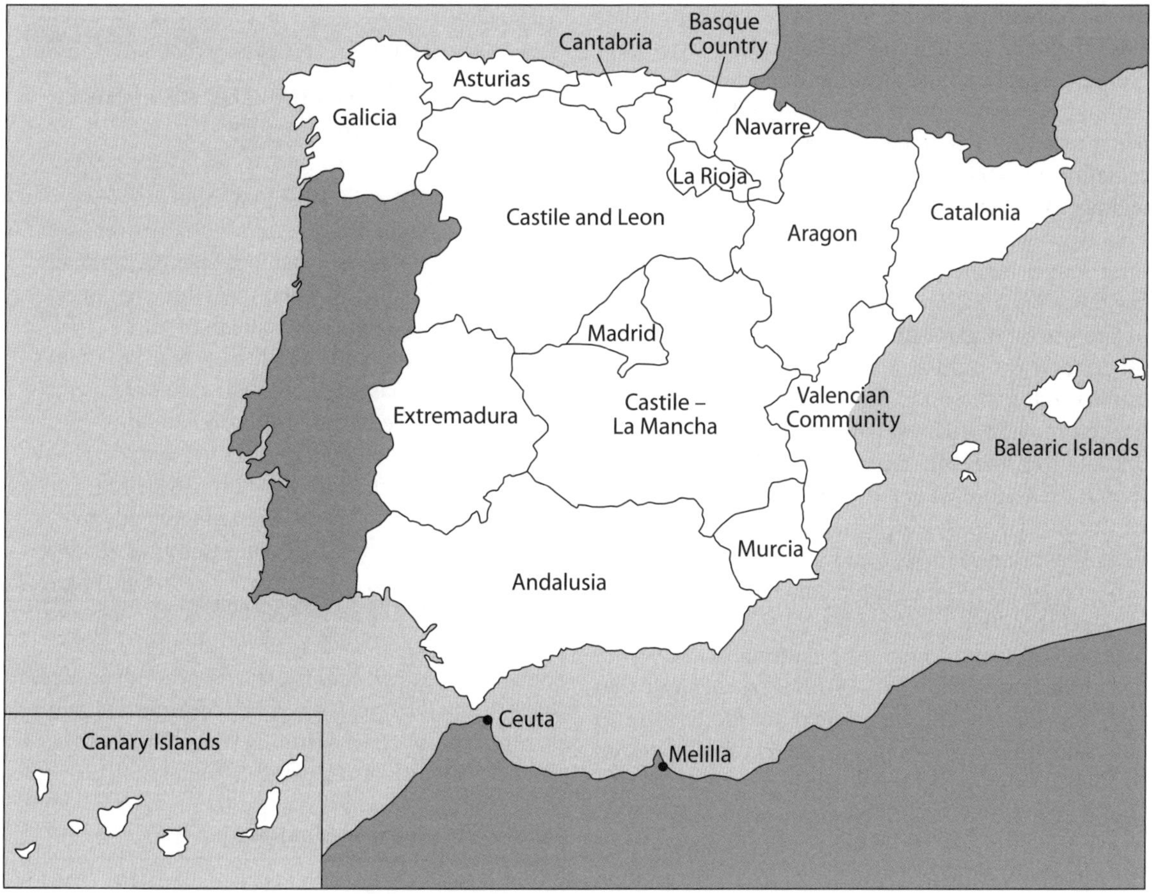

Map 2.1 Spain's autonomous communities

erty. ETA demands the independence of what Basque speakers call *Euskadi* and Spanish speakers call *el País Vasco,* with its most ardent supporters subscribing to a 'catastrophist' belief that unless it is achieved, the Basque 'race' will be wiped off the face of the earth by a 'genocidal' Spanish government. This has conditioned a revolutionary strategy, whereby terrorism will supposedly tempt the authorities into repression that will engender support for more violence until eventually the cost to Spain becomes too great to bear. Accordingly, the hope that the coming of democracy would see the end of ETA was a pipe-dream. The Basque country may have its own parliament and police force, it may control education and even taxation, but in relative and not just absolute terms, far more terrorism has gone on since Franco's death than before it, and in recent years has included 'soft targets' such as local politicians and foreign holiday-makers.

To the Spanish government, however, secession is not an option. The region may be an autonomous community with a unique cultural heritage, but it is home to hundreds of thousands of people who identify themselves either solely or (like the majority of the region's population) jointly as Spanish (see Box 2.3) – something that would make a Czechoslovak-style 'velvet divorce' impossible. The Basque country is also, Madrid maintains, but one part of an indissoluble state – notwithstanding the fact that the 1978 constitution failed to achieve majority support in the Basque country after calls for a boycott by peaceful nationalist parties. These parties – notably the Eusko *Alderdi Jeltzalea-Partido Nacionalista Vasco* (EAJ-PNV) – continue to do much better than the extremists in regional elections and to prevent candidates from the local branches of the national parties governing the region, much to their irritation. That irritation, not to say outrage, was rendered even greater when moderate nationalists, during a short-lived ceasefire in 1998 and 1999, showed themselves willing to contemplate negotiations with ETA and even work with its political wing, *Batasuna* – a party that is now banned in Spain under a controversial law passed in 2002 and which is also on the EU's list of proscribed organizations (see Bale, 2007). On the other hand, it would be a mistake to see 'Madrid' as a unitary actor: there are serious differences between the centre-right *Partido Popular*, which takes a hardline stance, and the centre-left PSOE, which has shown itself more willing to talk. ETA, too, of course, has its own factions, which may explain why negotiations that seemed to be going somewhere were suddenly ended by a bomb explosion at Madrid airport in December 2006.

Meanwhile, more moderate nationalists have not been idle. Since 2003, the EAJ-PNV has been flirting with the idea of an amendment to the 'statute of Guernica' (the law governing the relations between the Basque region and the Spanish government) that would create 'a free state associated with Spain'. This would then supposedly be presented for approval by the Spanish parliament and then, in a referendum, by the Basque region's voters. Despite polls suggesting that such a referendum would be popular but would not necessarily produce a vote for more independence, Madrid continues to remind the Basque government that there is no chance of any Spanish parliament accepting such an amendment and that the Constitutional Court (see Chapter 3) would be asked to (and in all likelihood would) annul it. Outrage was not the only emotion, however. Some saw Madrid's rejection of these calls for 'shared sovereignty' as hypocritical given that this is precisely the solution it currently favours for the British colony of Gibraltar on the Southern coast of Spain – a territory it continues to lay claim to in spite of the clear preferences of its population to remain British – and, at the same time, Spain insists it has every right to maintain its own possessions (Ceuta and Melilla) in Morocco.

An additional difficulty for the Spanish government is that any accession to the demands of those who want more autonomy for one region will be

BOX 2.3

Multiple identities: the evidence – and the way forward?

Research seems to suggest that fewer and fewer people in Spain's most autonomous 'nations' see themselves as Spanish or 'more Spanish' than, say, Catalan or Basque. In Catalunya, there has been growth in those who feel Catalan or 'more Catalan', and the number of those who see themselves as both has stayed the same. In the Basque country, it is the number of Basque or 'more Basque' identifiers that appears to have remained constant, while the number of those feeling equally Basque and Spanish has increased, presumably because fewer see themselves as Spanish or 'more Spanish'. Interestingly, the detailed figures vary considerably from year to year. For instance, 1992 (the year of the Barcelona Olympics, the Sevilla World Fair and the five hundredth anniversary of the European discovery of America) saw a temporary increase in those claiming to feel equally Spanish and Basque or Catalan.

Table 2.1 Multiple identities

	1979 (%)	2001 (%)
I feel:		
Only Basque or more Basque than Spanish	50	50
Equally Basque and Spanish	25	35
More Spanish than Basque or only Spanish	25	10

	1979 (%)	2001 (%)
I feel:		
Only Catalan or more Catalan than Spanish	25	40
Equally Catalan and Spanish	35	35
More Spanish than Catalan or only Spanish	35	20

Source: Adapted from Martinez-Herrera (2002), percentages rounded to nearest 5 per cent.

pounced on by those who want it for their own. In the wake of moderate Basque nationalists' demands for a referendum on shared sovereignty, their Catalan counterparts called again for Catalunya to be recognized as 'a nation' and for a single administration in Catalunya which, in addition to the control it already enjoyed over education, culture, health and policing, would have the final say on public finances and be represented separately from Spain in the EU and at other international bodies. The centre-right government in Madrid immediately rejected this idea, pointing out once again that Spain was indivisible and that there were millions of people living in Catalunya who considered themselves (at least partly) Spanish. However, the centre-left PSOE government elected in 2004, partly because it was a minority government (see Chapter 4) reliant on the support of some nationalist parties, proved more accommodating (see Box 2.4).

But whatever the ideological complexion of the government in Madrid, it has to face the fact that further privileges handed to so-called 'fast-track' autonomous communities (the 'nationalities' of Catalunya, the Basque Country and Galicia) will prompt further demands for equal treatment by what were originally considered mere 'regions' (such as the Canary Islands and Andalusia). If these demands are acceded to, then (a) Spain could end up fully federal; and/or (b) the 'nationalities' may, in the event that they enjoy no more autonomy than the 'regions', demand independence. On the other hand, given the numbers of people living in the 'nationalities' who are clearly comfortable with being Spanish as well as Basque or Catalan, and so on (see Núñez, 2001: 22–5), there is no reason to suppose support for independence would be sufficient to secure it even if a vote were allowed.

BOX 2.4

Catalunya – nationality and nation

Along with the Basque country, Catalunya, whose capital, Barcelona, is one of Europe's most widely admired cities, is at the forefront of claiming and exercising its rights as an autonomous community. Its wealth, linguistic differences (6 million speak Catalan as well as Spanish) and history of independence give it a good claim to nationhood – or at least to special treatment compared with other autonomous communities whose poverty, history, and the fact that they speak *Castellano* (the Spanish spoken all over the country) mean they are far more dependent on Madrid. Catalan nationalism may not have taken a violent turn, but it has profound ethno-linguistic roots (Miley, 2007) and has to be taken every bit as seriously as its Basque counterpart. Catalunya takes its independence very seriously: the *Generalitat* – its government – not only promotes the Catalan language and negotiates some agreements direct with the EU (see Roller, 2004), it also conducts its own 'foreign relations' with other governments. Catalan parties have achieved this by lending the support of the elected representatives they send to the national parliament in Madrid to governments of both right and left. Cynical or skilful, the strategy has been successful to the point that Catalunya enjoys more power and prestige than many regions in formally federal states, especially in the light of the new *Estatut d'autonomia* – a revision of the charter establishing the rights and powers of the region *vis-à-vis* central government in Madrid that (notwithstanding legal challenges by the centre-right *Partido Popular*) was ratified in a referendum in June 2006. On a practical level, the statute saw Catalunya gain more control over taxation and justice and home affairs, and even its ports and airports. But while its preamble referred to the fact that Catalans saw themselves as a *nation*, its second article only went as far as recognizing the reality of Catalunya as a *nationality* – five extra words that avoided a conflict with the Spanish constitution. Whether such a conflict is, in the end, inevitable remains to be seen.

The UK – another hybrid

The only European country outside the Balkans that rivals Spain in terms of the potential for violence associated with minority nationalism is the UK, and in particular Northern Ireland. It, too, has taken considerable steps towards a quasi-federal solution under which different regions are accorded different rights. We deal with Scotland and Wales below, but begin with Northern Ireland (Map 2.2).

The UK province of Northern Ireland (or Ulster) came into being because, although Ireland achieved independence from Great Britain in the 1920s, the majority Protestant population of the north-easternmost six counties of the island remained committed to the Union. Northern Ireland had its own government and parliament but, its largely Protestant 'unionist' population insisted, it was nevertheless very much part of the UK. Only a small minority of Roman Catholics thought the same way, with most looking forward, as 'nationalists', to 'a united Ireland' in the long term. The pursuit of this goal by violent means by the Irish Republican Army (IRA), however, attracted little support until the late 1960s and early 1970s when, following sectarian violence triggered by attempts to address the civil rights grievances of Catholics, the British government initially sent in troops and then imposed direct rule from London. There followed two decades of high-profile terrorist attacks in the province and on the mainland (in part funded by republican sympathizers in the USA), as well as lower-profile (but seemingly relentless) sectarian 'tit-for-tat' killings, not only by the IRA but also by Protestant paramilitary organizations – some allegedly with the collusion of the official security forces.

By the mid-1980s, it had become clear to many republicans that, despite the huge cost to the UK in terms of loss of life, security and, above all, taxpayers' money, the 'armed struggle' was not going to kick the 'Brits' out of Northern Ireland as long as the majority of its population remained committed to the Union. Meanwhile, the commitment of the Irish Republic and the UK to put an end to violence resulted first in the 'Anglo-Irish Agreement' (1985) and then in the 'Downing Street Declaration' (December 1993), which sought to institutionalize intergovernmental and cross-border co-operation, and created a new *quid pro quo*. London (declaring it had 'no selfish strategic or economic interest in Northern Ireland') now recognized the possibility of a united Ireland, while Dublin acknowledged that this could come about only with the consent of the majority in the North. These confidence-building measures, although they alarmed hard-line unionists, were enough to tempt the what is widely regarded as the political wing of the IRA, Sinn Féin, into talks with the British – talks that eventually led to a ceasefire and to the creation (backed up by a referendum, by the release of paramilitary prisoners and by a promise on the part of the IRA and others that they would 'decommission' their weapons) of an elected Northern Ireland Assembly and an executive on which all parties would serve depending on their share of the vote.

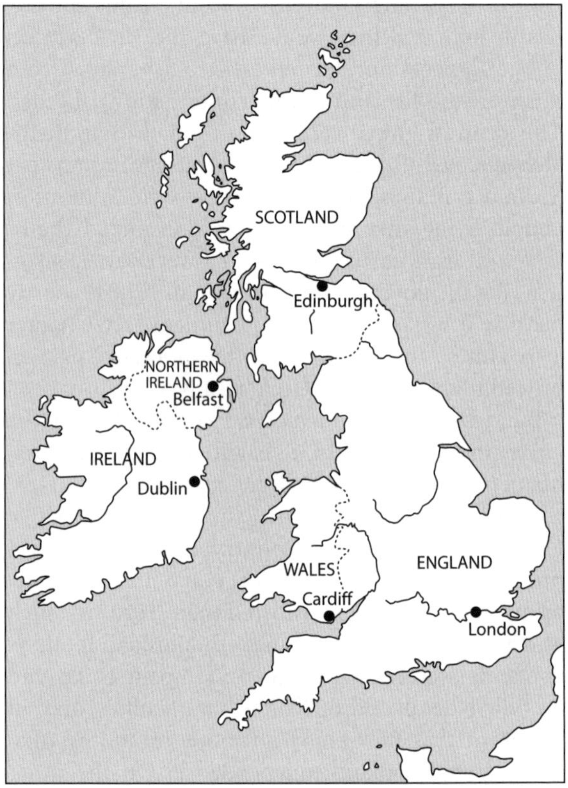

Map 2.2 The British Isles – the UK and Ireland

KEY POINT

The UK has, like Spain, offered its component countries varying levels of autonomy in order to contain minority nationalism. Its situation is rather more complicated because some in Northern Ireland would like to see the province absorbed into the Irish Republic and have taken up arms to achieve this outcome. This violent conflict, however, appears to be over, but it is by no means certain that in the long term the UK will retain its present shape.

To some this political progress looked ephemeral. The parties could not, it seemed, work together and, in October 2002, the power-sharing Northern Ireland Executive at Stormont was suspended and direct rule from Westminster re-imposed by a frustrated British government. Equally depressingly, but not perhaps surprisingly, the day-to-day sectarian divide between Protestants and Catholics – always a matter not so much of doctrinal nitpicking as cultural identity and social networks – seemed if anything to have deepened, reinforced by the long-term decline of mixed neighbourhoods and intermarriage. This deepening of, rather than decrease in, hostility between the two communities was also reflected at the political level. In November 2003, support for the more hard-line Democratic Unionist Party (DUP) and Sinn Féin growing at the expense of the official Ulster Unionists and Social Democratic and Liberal Party (SDLP), respectively. The moderates, it appeared were losing out, to the extremists. Yet there was another, more optimistic, way of looking at it: if a deal were to be secured, it would be more likely to hold if it were done by parties who could claim to be truly representative – either of the unionism that understandably fears being 'sold-out' by the British and losing its majority status to the expanding Catholic population, or of the republicanism intent both on defending Catholics from Protestant attacks and bringing about a united Ireland sooner rather than later. This analysis, it seems, was correct (see Box 2.5)

Interestingly, 'the troubles' in Northern Ireland have clearly taken a toll on the UK population outside the province, too. If opinion polls are to be believed, the majority blames both sides of the sectarian divide for the problem, and support for a united Ireland, while not quite reaching a majority, is considerably higher than that favouring keeping the province part of the UK indefinitely. Such views are not replicated, however, when it comes to Scotland, which was granted a parliament in 1997 – partly, some argue, in order to head off calls by nationalists for an end to the 1707 Act of Union. Support for independence in Wales (which was absorbed much earlier and which could never really establish such a clear claim for itself as a self-governing nation) has always been much lower, evidenced by the very narrow majority (on a very low turnout) that, in 1997, approved the setting up of an assembly without the tax-varying powers granted to Scotland's new legislature. Interestingly, there is as yet little evidence (certainly when compared to Belgium and Spain) that these measures represent a 'slippery slope' toward a more thorough-going federalism and possible threat to the British state itself. There have been calls for the devolved legislatures and the executives to be given more powers – particularly in Wales, where politicians at least would like

BOX 2.5

From sworn enemies to swapping smiles – the hardliners share power at Stormont, 8 May 2007

By 2004, however, things did not look hopeful for the Northern Ireland peace process. The power sharing government at Stormont remained suspended, with agreement between the parties elected to the Assembly foundering on the refusal of the IRA to allow release of photographic evidence of arms decommissioning. Worse was to come when the organization was widely blamed for a multi-million pound bank robbery towards the end of the year. Things looked up, however, towards the end of 2005, when the body in charge of decommissioning concluded the IRA had indeed put its weapons beyond use – a conclusion it confirmed in October 2006. Meanwhile, the British and Irish governments decided it was time to try and force the parties back into talks, and also (successfully, it turned out) put pressure on Sinn Féin to declare its support for the Northern Ireland police and criminal justice system. Fresh elections held in the spring of 2007 confirmed the leading role of Sinn Féin on the nationalist side and the DUP on the loyalist side, while a deadline imposed by the British government for the formation of a power-sharing executive seemed to concentrate minds. In May 2007, finally convinced that the nationalists were serious about never returning to violence and that a place in history was his, the DUP leader, the octogenarian Ian Paisley, took up the post of First Minister with Martin McGuinness, a former IRA commander, as his Sinn Féin Deputy.

to see themselves on a par with their Scottish counterparts. The latter, for example, have primary legislative powers for most bread-and-butter matters including health, education, social services and transport, as well as the right to vary taxation. Wales has recently added to its powers but would like to emulate Scotland.

The parties in both Scotland and Wales have also been keen to distance themselves from their counterparts at Westminster. But these developments have arguably been overshadowed – at least in the media – by concerns about public apathy and the excessive costs of constructing the new parliament and government buildings. Moreover, if the purpose of devolution from the Labour Party's point of view was to stop nationalist parties like the Scottish Nationalists and the Welsh *Plaid Cymru* from 'stealing' votes from it at Westminster elections, so far it seems to have worked. True, both parties have done much better in elections to their respective devolved legislatures – so well, indeed, that 2007 saw the nationalists in power in both Wales and Scotland (see Box 2.6). But support for nationalist parties at UK general elections has indeed declined. Meanwhile, fears that devolving power to Scotland and Wales would spark a serious 'English backlash' – perhaps in protest at Scottish (and Welsh) MPs at Westminster voting on legislation that did not actually affect their own constituents – do not seem (outside the Conservative Party at least) to have been born out in practice, although a much publicized poll in November 2006 suggested that English voters were even keener on Scottish independence than their Scots counterparts!

The prospect, then, of a fully federal Britain with separate parliaments for each of the nations currently seems a long way off – especially given the absence in the UK of a written constitution (and pressure for one) that could guarantee the existence and rights of those parliaments. On the other hand, as in Spain, it would be equally far-fetched to think that, merely because the national parliament (i.e. Westminster) is still technically sovereign and therefore able to take back any rights and powers it has granted to sub-national legislatures and executives, it would be politically feasible for it to do so except (as with the deadlocked Northern Ireland Assembly) from those devolved bodies that are so divided amongst themselves that they cannot function. Given this, it is not surprising that some constitutional experts argue that the UK is now a quasi-federal system (albeit one operating Spanish-style 'differentiated' or 'asymmetrical' federalism) and may eventually 'go all the way'. And if it did, there is no guarantee – especially in Scotland where comparisons with Catalunya can fruitfully be drawn (Greer, 2007) – that such a move would be the end of the process.

BOX 2.6

What's in a name? The Scottish Executive and/or Government

One of the first official moves of the Scottish National Party (SNP), once it had formed an administration after the elections of 2007, was to declare that the Scottish Executive would henceforth be called the Scottish Government – a move that, some alleged, would cost a small fortune as letterheads, publicity, documents and signs would all need to be changed. But the re-branding, some noted, was only skin deep. The government's legal name would continue to be the Scottish Executive, in order to escape the need to amend the Scotland Act that first established devolution. This may have been difficult because the SNP took power as a minority administration (see Chapter 4), meaning it would find it difficult to legislate on anything too contentious. One measure falling into the last category is likely to be its cherished ambition of holding a referendum on what the SNP leader calls 'the restoration of an independent Scotland'. His promise to hold 'a national conversation' over the country's constitutional future is an interesting one: if he doesn't like what he hears, will he press for a vote anyway?

France – no longer quite so indivisible

In view of this risk, those who wish to preserve the nation state intact sometimes look to France – supposedly *une et indivisible* (one and indivisible) – for inspiration. Despite movements for more independence for historic nations such as *Bretagne* (Brittany) in the west, *Occitanie* (modern-day Languedoc) in the south and *Pays-Basque* (Basque Country) in the south west (see Map 2.3), France continues to protest its indivisibility – even to the extent of preserving the myth that its overseas possessions (in, for example, the South Pacific) are simply extensions of mainland France. Closer to home, however, France has recently had to be rather more flexible. Nationalists on the Mediterranean island of Corsica (population just over 250,000) have not resorted to large-scale violence to anything like the same extent as their Irish and Basque counterparts, although empty holiday homes on the island are often fire-bombed. This reluctance to take life (and scare off the two million people who visit the island as tourists rather than as 'colonisers') possibly accounts for the relatively low profile of their struggle. The latter may also have something to do with the fact that in Corsica the relationship between nationalist terrorism and organized crime, by no means unimportant in Northern Ireland and Euskadi, is so close: violence there tends to be more surgical than spectacular, with hundreds of small incendiary explosions a year damaging (mainlanders') property and the line between mafia-style and apparently political assassinations very blurred. Due to this, perhaps,

Map 2.3 France

KEY POINT

France has never been quite as united as it likes to think of itself and has taken its first faltering steps towards granting additional autonomy to its island province of Corsica in order to respond to separatist feeling there.

and to the awareness that the island depends economically on the mainland for tourism and aid, there would appear to be rather less support for full-blown independence among Corsica's quarter of a million inhabitants than in, say, the Basque country. Certainly, peaceful nationalist parties do less well in elections than their Basque counterparts.

Yet following the murder of its prefect (local governor) in 1999, the French government made a bold move to break with its self-image as 'one and indivisible', putting together a staged autonomy package known as the 'Matignon Accords'. The island would be granted greater self-government and allowed to place greater emphasis on the teaching and use of its own language in return for progress on law and order that, if secured, would see a constitutional revision allowing for proportional representation (PR) elections and an assembly and executive with (albeit limited) law-making powers. Predictably, critics on the nationalist side declared that the Accords had not gone far enough, while critics in Paris declared it could be a Pandora's box that would not just lead to independence for Corsica, but also encourage claims for more autonomy by mainland regions. Nevertheless, the plan was adopted by the Corsican Assembly in July 2000 and given an initial green light by the National Assembly in May 2001. Notwithstanding a truce declared by the Corsican National Liberation Front, the murderous feuding between separatist organizations continued. Opinion polls also seemed to suggest that far from dampening enthusiasm for independence, the Matignon Accords may well have encouraged it and, as in the case of British attitudes to Northern Ireland, the number of 'mainlanders' happy to see the back of the island is also rising.

With the election of a centre-right government in 2002, hopes of action on the Accords looked as if they had been dashed, as the new government's rhetoric suggested a reassertion of the Gaullist unitary state tradition. But while the new prime minister withdrew his predecessor's promises of a tailor-made autonomy package for Corsica, he sweetened the pill considerably, first, by making it clear that Corsica could be at the cutting edge of plans for limited decentralization throughout France and, second, by not reneging on the previous government's promise of almost €2 billion in development aid over the next decade-and-a-half. By July 2003, the government's devolution plans – which centred on a merger of the island's multiple elected bodies into one in return for enhanced powers – were ready to put to the islands voters in a referendum. Some of the largest separatist parties, such as *Corsica Nazione,* were prepared to go along with the plan as the first step; others rejected it as inadequate. Frustratingly for the French government, and those prepared to give it a chance, the plan was narrowly rejected.

There seemed to be no 'Plan B' and the situation was made even more tense in April 2004 by the arrest, on racketeering charges, of Jean-Guy Talamoni, leader of the pro-independence party *Unione Nazionale.* He was acquitted but another nationalist Charles Pieri of the National Liberation Front for the Liberation of Corsica-Union of Fighters (FLNC-UC) was jailed on similar charges in the spring of 2005, upon which the organization broke off a ceasefire it had declared two years earlier. Later on that year, nationalist feeling was further inflamed by the decision of the French government to privatize the island's loss-making ferry service – and to send in troops to remove unions who were blockading the country's main port and effectively holding thousands of tourists to ransom. Things then quietened down but January 2007 saw small bombs go off in the Corsican port of Ajaccio. Nicholas Sarkozy, beginning his successful run for the Presidency, visited the island and argued that the way out of violence was to expand opportunities for the young: to this end he promised another billion euro investment programme in the island's economy, suggesting once again that throwing money at the problem rather than granting greater autonomy would continue to be the main strategy. Whether his socialist opponent agreed him was a moot point (see Box 2.7)

The EU and the end of sovereignty?

An argument put forward by those campaigning for the independence of nations with aspirations to statehood in twenty-first-century Europe is that (arguably anyway) it is rendered more feasible than ever by the existence of the EU (see McGarry and Keating, 2006). It may have been true, once upon a time, runs the argument, that Scotland or Catalunya (to take two of the most obvious examples) would have found it difficult to survive, given the costs of

BOX 2.7

A dangerous comparison – Quebec and Corsica

Socialist candidate Ségolène Royal's unsuccessful campaign for the French Presidency in 2007 was marked, especially in its early stages, by a series of 'gaffes' – mistakes that the media loves to pick up on. One made headline news in Canada as well as France when, after meeting the leader of the pro-independence *Parti Québecois,* Ms Royal said they shared a common position on 'the sovereignty and freedom of Quebec'. This led the Canadian Prime Minister to note acerbically that 'Experience teaches that it is highly inappropriate for a foreign leader to interfere in the democratic affairs of another country.' But the gaffe was compounded a few days later when a famous French hoaxer called Ms Royal pretending to be the premier of Quebec. When he suggested that her comments were akin to Canadians suggesting Corsica should be independent, a laughing Ms Royal (who clearly thought she was conducting a light-hearted – and private – conversation) replied that not all French people would disagree, but then quickly asked him not to repeat that lest it cause another row. The inevitable release of the tape prompted the Head of Corsica's legislature to observe that, even if her words were said in jest, they weren't funny. And Nicholas Sarkozy got the chance to intone presidentially: 'For me, Corsica isn't a joke . . . it is the Republic.'

mounting, for instance, an independent foreign and trade policy. Now, the argument continues, so many of these expensive tasks can, in effect, be 'contracted out' to the EU. To some observers, the latter already promotes a degree of autonomy, via a 'Committee of the Regions' (COR), which advises (though it cannot compel) other EU institutions on policy and legislation that affect local or regional government. More importantly, the EU operates an 'internal market' which supposedly guarantees that even the smallest state (Malta, Cyprus or Luxembourg, for example) can survive economically.

The irony is, of course, that while some who aspire to independence look to the EU to underwrite it, many of the latter's existing member states worry about the EU undermining the independence they currently enjoy. This final part of the chapter explores the extent to which the EU in general and some of its institutions, policies and processes in particular, may be impacting negatively on the sovereignty of its member states.

Origins, enlargement and institutions

The forerunner of the EU, the European Economic Community (EEC), began life in 1958 after the signing of the Treaty of Rome by six western European nations: France, Germany, Italy, the Netherlands, Belgium and Luxembourg. All had been co-operating with each other since the US had encouraged them in the late 1940s to work together to make the most of the aid granted to the continent by what became known as the Marshall Plan. The 1950s had seen that co-operation reinforced by the formation in 1952 of the European Coal and Steel Community (ECSC) – a project which aimed, by locking together those industries across the different member countries, not only to boost their economic fortunes but to tie them together in the hope that this might prevent yet another European war. Success in the economic and industrial realm contrasted with the failure of an ambitious attempt to bring together former enemies in defence co-operation. Economic co-operation was also limited somewhat by the reluctance of the UK to become involved on the basis of its perception that its interests were global rather than regional and that both its sovereignty and freedom of action might be put at risk. Joining the EEC committed 'the six' to very practical measures such as a customs union with a 'common external tariff' (CET), and a 'common agricultural policy' (the now infamously expensive CAP) to ensure both plentiful food and a reasonable standard of living for farmers by providing them with a mixture of subsidies, protective tariffs and guaranteed prices.

KEY POINT

What has become known as the European Union has expanded since its birth in the late 1950s to include most of the continent's states. Since, in large part, they wish to combine continued sovereignty with collective action and a common market, the EU experiences a more or less creative tension between intergovernmental and supranational impulses – impulses that are embodied by its component institutions. So far, this has not prevented increased integration, even if the latter (and the alteration in decision-making rules it has required) has proceeded in fits and starts.

The Treaty of Rome, building on ECSC structures, also set up the *European Commission* and the *European Court of Justice* (ECJ) (see Box 2.9). Both were supranational rather than intergovernmental institutions (see Box 2.8) and, as such, were to prove instrumental in the drive to what the Treaty called 'ever closer union.' This notwithstanding, the UK soon changed its mind about joining, realizing quite quickly that it would suffer economically if it stayed out. After the failure of two applications in the 1960s, it became a member in 1973, along with Denmark and Ireland. Although global recession in the early 1970s took some of the shine off the initially impressive economic performance of the EEC, further expansion followed, most recently with the admission of eight former Communist countries (see Map 2.4). The political security reasons behind expansion are dealt with in more detail in Chapter 11. The economic arguments are also important. A bigger union provides a bigger and, over time, a wealthier market for European goods and services; it should also encourage the kind of mergers and acquisitions (M&As), and economies of scale, that will allow European business to compete more effectively across the globe.

BOX 2.8

Balancing the intergovernmental and the supranational

Most international organizations are *intergovernmental*: those states that belong to them co-operate in search of better outcomes but reserve the right and maintain the power to block, or at least ignore, decisions that they feel are contrary to their interests. Such intergovernmentalism has always been one side of the story of European integration. But there is another, *supranational* side. This is the agreement on the part of member states, on some matters at least, to forgo the right to a veto and be bound by decisions with which they do not always agree. Arguably, the history of the EU is the history of the tension between *intergovernmentalism* and *supranationalism*. It is also a tension embodied in (if not always effectively tamed by) its institutional structure. No EU body is completely and utterly intergovernmental or supranational in both composition and role, but (as Boxes 2.9 and 2.10 suggest) all display a bias one way or the other.

The EU also provides a limited degree of redistribution from Europe's richer to Europe's poorer states. It gets approximately 15 per cent of its revenue from tariffs and duties, 35 per cent from a share of the value added tax (VAT) receipts of member states, and 50 per cent of it from member states who contribute a fixed proportion of their GNP. The EU then spends this money (equivalent to only around 1.1 per cent of the GNP of all its members or less than 5 per cent of all their government spending put together) on, among other things agricultural support (which accounts for around 45 per cent of spending) and structural funding (help for poorer regions, which takes up about 35 per cent of spending). This spending, particularly on poorer regions (see Chapters 1 and 3), as well as spending on countries that are hoping to join the EU, effectively takes money from the richer parts of the Union and gives it to their poorer counterparts. This is clearly not simply an act of generosity: in the longer term, making the backward regions better off should provide those that currently help fund them with more lucrative markets for their goods and services.

After a decade of relative inactivity after the recession of the mid-1970s, European integration got going again in the 1980s. The case law of the ECJ, the activism of the Commission and fears that, without an end to intra-European trade barriers and the encouragement of bigger companies, Europe would lose out to Japan and America, all combined to produce the Single European Act (SEA) of 1986. The SEA was an intergovernmental treaty which committed what became known as the European Community (EC), and then (after 1991) the EU, to further legislation enshrining the 'four freedoms' of goods, services, capital and labour.

The European project aimed from the outset to give its member states access to a common market. Member states also become part of a customs union, charging a CET on goods coming from outside the EU, although these are often moderated or even removed as a result of trade deals, most obviously with those countries belonging to the European Free Trade Association (or EFTA); namely, Iceland, Liechtenstein, Norway and Switzerland, which are unwilling to join the EU on the grounds that the political integration entailed by full economic integration is too much for them. Not joining may not mean much of a loss in trade terms, but it does mean that they are unable to take advantage of any of the financial support on offer from the EU for things such as farming or the development of poorer regions. On the other hand, EFTA members, as relatively well-off countries, would in all likelihood join the ranks of the EU's net contributors (see Figure 2.1), so it is understandable if such incentives pale beside the costs of membership. These are not only financial but logistical, legal and political. For instance, as the 2004 accession states found, any state wishing to join has to bring its administrative and legal system into what is known as the ***acquis communautaire*** – the corpus of legislation in force in the EU that is binding on member states, either directly or indirectly, via national laws that must be passed to give it expression. Largely because of the renewed push by the EU to make the common (or single) market a reality, the number of laws making up the *acquis* doubled between 1983 and 1998 (see Maurer *et al.*, 2003: 57).

- Founding members (1952 ECSC; 1958 EEC and Euratom): Belgium, France, (West) Germany, Italy, Luxembourg, Netherlands. The territory of the German Democratic Republic (East Germany) was incorporated into a united Germany in 1990.
- First enlargement (1973): Denmark, Ireland, United Kingdom.
- Mediterranean enlargement: Greece (1981); Portugal, Spain (1986).
- EFTA enlargement (1995): Austria, Finland, Sweden.
- 2004 enlargement: Cyprus, Czech Republic, Estonia, Hungary, Latvia, Lithuania, Malta, Poland, Slovakia, Slovenia.
- 2007: Bulgaria, Romania.

Key
1 Croatia
2 Bosnia and Herzegovina
3 Serbia
4 Montenegro
5 Former Yugoslav Republic of Macedonia
6 Albania
7 Switzerland
8 Moldova
9 Slovenia

Source: Adapted from Nugent (2006) p. xxiv.

Map 2.4 From the EEC Six to the EU-27 – enlargement, 1957–2007

BOX 2.9

The EU's supranational institutions

These bodies may be appointed by governments or elected by their voters, but those who are chosen go on to work for the EU, not for member states. They include:

European Commission

Based in Brussels, with a staff of some 27,000 people, the Commission is headed by a President and Commissioners appointed by member states. It is made up of over twenty Directorate Generals (DGs) which report to those commissioners and are charged with preparing and administering policy in a particular area – agriculture, environment, internal market, regional policy, etc. Most EU law is based on proposals from the Commission, which are then discussed and adopted (or not!) by the Council of Ministers (see Box 2.10), and increasingly the European Parliament (EP), too (see below). The Commission is also involved in overseeing the implementation of laws and ensuring that they (and the Treaties more generally) are obeyed in and by member states. This task sometimes involves the Commission in initiating legal proceedings against states, and sometimes commercial concerns as well, for non-compliance. It has a particularly strong role in competition policy where it can investigate, decide on guilt and levy fines without recourse to courts. As a result, the Commission is often in the news and, despite the fact that it is headed up by politicians from different countries and different parties and therefore lacks a degree of coherence, is often accused by politicians and the media of unwarranted interference. Less often commented on, but just as important (see Chapter 11), is the Commission's role as the sole trade negotiator for all EU states at the World Trade Organization (WTO).

European Court of Justice (ECJ)

Based in Luxembourg, the ECJ is staffed by judges appointed by member states. It hears cases involving disputes between member states and the Commission and also cases referred to it by domestic courts for clarification of European law which may or may not be relevant to cases those courts are trying. Early on its life, the ECJ successfully persuaded member states (or, at least, their courts) that European law was supreme and could enjoy 'direct effect' within them. This led to a body of case law that has had important ramifications within member states, most obviously with regard to the free movement of goods, services and labour, and sex discrimination. As with the Commission, the ECJ is often in the news because it says things that companies and governments do not want to hear. Even worse, because there is no higher court, it can legally oblige them to go along with its rulings. Not surprisingly, then, the ECJ is seen as one of the EU's most supranational institutions. Its critics argue that, because it has to adjudicate disputes in the light of treaties designed to promote 'ever closer union', it has a built-in bias toward integration. They also complain that this bias, along with the fact that it often has to operate where no court has gone

The EU's ***acquis communautaire*** is the body of accumulated law currently in force that must apply in every member state if the EU is to function properly as a legally based and regulated community. Laws include **directives** (rules that must be turned into, or 'transposed' into, domestic law in national parliaments), **regulations** (which are automatically binding on all member states without any parliamentary discretion on their part as to their precise form) and the case law of the ECJ.

Just as importantly, the SEA introduced procedural changes, such as the expansion of Qualified Majority Voting (or QMV) in one of the EU's most important and most intergovernmental institutions, the *Council of Ministers* (see Box 2.10). If every piece of European legislation required unanimity, it would be continually prone to deadlock or blackmail as member states exercised or threatened to exercise their veto. On the other hand, simple majority voting – where each member state was accorded one before, leads it not so much to interpret as actually make law. As we see in Chapter 3, however, this accusation is increasingly levelled against national courts as well.

European Parliament (EP)

Since it was first directly elected by voters in member states in 1979, the EP (which meets in both Brussels and Strasbourg, France) has been transformed from a body that was merely consulted to one that – at least, in certain circumstances – really counts. Its approval is required for the EU's budget and accounts, and under the 'co-decision' procedure it now has equal say with the Council of Ministers on most legislation, although it has very little impact on areas where the EU is most powerful, namely trade, agriculture and competition policy. The Commission has to pass an investiture vote in the EP and this is no longer a forgone conclusion. In September 2004, objections to a conservative Catholic nominee from Italy forced him to stand down and delayed matters considerably. The EP also has the power to dismiss the entire Commission – a possibility that prompted that body's resignation in 1999 after corruption allegations. Individual commissioners, the European Central Bank (ECB) and the European Council have to appear before and report to the EP, although practically there is little it can do if it dislikes what it hears. The EP tends to be seen as a supranational institution for three reasons: most of those who work in it are broadly in favour of European integration; they do not continually seek to uphold the views of the states from which they come; and they have an institutional interest in seeking to reduce (or at least match) the power of the body that most obviously represents those member states, the Council of Ministers. Members of the European Parliament (MEPs) are elected country-by-country (see Chapter 6), but they sit (and, for the most part, vote) in party groups based on ideology not nationality: the Party of European Socialists, for instance, contains members from all Europe's socialist and social democratic parties; the European People's Party is its centre-right equivalent (see Chapter 4). On the other hand, much of the real work done by MEPs is done in over twenty subject-specific committees where there is a premium put on cross-party cooperation. The problem all MEPs face, however, is that, despite their getting more and more power, those whom they claim to represent – the citizens of Europe – are less and less interested in them: turnout at European elections is at spectacularly low levels and has declined over time (see Chapter 6).

European Central Bank (ECB)

The ECB, based in Germany's financial capital, Frankfurt, is possibly the EU's most supranational institution. It sets an interest rate which applies across the member states that operate with the Euro, irrespective of whether it is as high or as low as they or their populations would like or need it to be. But the ECB is, to all intents and purposes, beyond the reach of individual member states: they may appoint its president and executive board and the national central bank presidents that make up its governing council, but that council is not practically accountable to them or to any other European institution.

vote – would risk the possibility of legislation being passed against the wishes of governments representing the bulk of Europe's population. Under QMV, therefore, voting strength is adjusted according to the size of the state. It was adjusted (largely at the expense of medium-sized countries) by the Nice Treaty of 2000 in order to reassure larger member states that they would not be overwhelmed by the increased number of small states after the accessions of 2004 and 2007. And larger member states stand to do even better out of the Lisbon Treaty (see below) – at least, when it comes to getting legislation they want passed. Blocking legislation, however, could be more difficult. The ostensible aim of such changes may have been to ensure the swifter passage of that legislation. But they have also had the effect of undermining the ability of individual member states (at least on topics where QMV applies) to veto proposals that they object to. According to 'Eurosceptics' – the nickname given to

COUNTRY PROFILE

GERMANY (Deutschland)

Area: 349,300 km^2 (8.3% of EU-27)

Population: 82.4 million (16.7% of EU-27)

Religious heritage: Roman Catholic and Protestant

GDP (2006): €2,323 billion (20% of EU-27)

GDP *per capita* as percentage of EU-27 average (2006): 114

Female representation in parliament and cabinet (end 2007): 32% and 40%

Joined EU: founder member, 1957

Top 3 cities: Berlin – capital city (3.4 million), Hamburg (1.7 million); Munich (1.3 million).

History: Present-day Germany has its origins in the Holy Roman Empire that, a thousand years ago, covered much of central Europe. It developed into a loose collection of principalities that, in the sixteenth century, spawned the religious break-away from Roman Catholicism that became known as Protestantism. These small states, plus the much larger states of Prussia and Austria, were melded into the German Confederation in the early nineteenth century and finally united, minus Austria, as one country (initially known as the German Empire) in 1871. Germany became a constitutional monarchy with a parliament under Bismarck, a statesman famous for building the first welfare state and maintaining a European balance of power that, for a few years at least, delayed all-encompassing war.

With its large population and industrializing economy, Germany rapidly threatened to overtake the UK and France – a challenge that helped to usher in the First World War (1914–18). The harsh peace settlement embodied in the Treaty of Versailles, along with the rise, rearmament programme and imperial dreams of Adolf Hitler's dictatorial *Nazi* regime, precipitated the Second World War just two decades later. Once again, the Germans (in alliance this time with the Italians and the Japanese) were pitted against the French, the British and, in time, the Americans. As well as inflicting (and suffering) enormous casualties in what became known as 'total war' (especially on the 'Eastern front' with Russia), Germany shocked the world by systematically putting to death some 6 million Jews across occupied Europe in what became known as the *Holocaust*.

The country's total defeat in 1945 saw it divided into the liberal capitalist Federal Republic (FRG, known as West Germany and the communist Democratic Republic (GDR, known as East Germany). The latter was easily eclipsed by the 'economic miracle' that saw its much bigger western counterpart become the powerhouse of the European economy from the 1960s onwards. In 1990, just a year after the fall of the communist constructed wall that had separated them for decades, the two states were reunified – or more, accurately, East Germany was re-absorbed by the Federal Republic. This new Germany was governed by the centre-right Christian Democrats, under Helmut Kohl, until 1998, and then by a 'Red–Green' coalition led by the centre-left SPD. The 2005 election saw the formation of a 'grand coalition' between the SPD and the Christian Democrats under Germany's first woman Chancellor (Prime Minister) Angela Merkel.

Economy and society: Since reunification, western Germany has not only extended its very generous welfare state to the east, but poured billions of euros into its economic development. Yet the east still remains comparatively depressed, with very high unemployment. Germany as a whole saw its

WHAT'S IN AN ANTHEM?

Das Deutschlandlied has the distinction of a score written by classical composer, Joseph Haydn, who penned it as the anthem for the old Austrian empire at the end of the eighteenth century. The current lyrics were supplied in the middle of the nineteenth century and it was officially endorsed as the German national anthem in the 1920s. During the Nazi period, the stress was very much on the stirring (but in hindsight rather menacing) first verse – 'Germany above everything in the world . . . Standing together as brothers for protection' etc. After that, the more idealistic – and less bombastic – third verse became the official version: it still mentions that staple of many an anthem, 'the Fatherland', but the emphasis is on striving 'with heart and hand' for 'unity, law and freedom', which are apparently the foundation for 'the glow of happiness'.

formerly world-beating economy run into trouble during the 1990s but it has begun to recover, mainly through its high quality manufacturing exports. It remains one of Europe's richest countries: in 2006 its 82 million people (nearly 2 million of whom are Turks drawn into the country during the boom years) enjoyed a standard of living a significant notch above the EU-27 average. Some regionalist sentiment is evident in eastern Germany, as well as in the predominantly Roman Catholic region of Bavaria in the south.

Governance: Germany is a parliamentary democracy, elected under proportional representation (PR). It is also a federal system, with considerable autonomy granted to its regions or states (called *Länder)* by the constitution, which is policed by a powerful federal constitutional court. The federal government is presided over by a prime minister (called the Chancellor), elected by a majority in parliament. The latter, which also elects a president as a ceremonial head of state, is divided into two houses: the popularly elected *Bundestag* and a second chamber, the *Bundesrat*, made up of *Länder* representatives, which (unusually in Europe) has the power to make or break a large (though now declining) proportion of legislation. Outside parliament, there is an extensive network of consultative bodies – involving regional government, employers and trade unions – that regulate the social and economic life of the country

Foreign policy: Germany spent most of the second half of the twentieth century persuading its neighbours that they had no need to fear a repeat of the first half. It placed a great deal of emphasis on the country's membership of multilateral organizations such as the UN and NATO and, until the latter's military intervention to remove Serbian troops from Kosovo in 1999, was very reluctant to send its armed forces abroad, even on peacekeeping missions. Also, crucially important to Germany's rehabilitation was its membership of what is now the EU, in which the country effectively ceded political leadership to France in exchange for the right to be able to rebuild economically. This fraying 'Franco-German axis' was somewhat revived by the two countries' shared opposition to the US invasion of Iraq in 2003. Germany has recently upped its involvement in EU peacekeeping without attracting too much controversy at home. It has also attempted to play a positive role in Europe's relations with Russia, though this has meant criticism from those – especially in Poland – who think it is placing economic advantage above geopolitical risks.

A KEY CONTEMPORARY CHALLENGE

INCORPORATING THE FORMER EAST GERMANY

The absorption of the formerly Communist German Democratic Republic (DDR) by what had come to be known as West Germany was a triumph of hope and aspiration. Underneath it lay a grim reality of huge disparities in wealth and (to a lesser extent) values. After nearly twenty years, and despite massive transfers of taxpayers' money, later these disparities remain – and in some cases are glaring: the Oberbayern region in Bavaria has a GDP *per capita* rate as much as 70 per cent above the EU average and Mecklenburg-Vorpommen in the former DDR around 20 per cent below it. And the disparities appear to be having serious demographic consequences which politics seems to be powerless to offset. A disproportionate number of women, enabled by their superior educational performance to find jobs more easily than their male counterparts, have gone west, raising fears of an Eastern underclass of jobless and alienated men and a shrinking population for whom it is hard to justify continued government investment in infrastructure and housing. This at a time when Germany's wealthier states are arguing that they should not have to pay so much in fiscal transfers to their poorer eastern counterparts.

Contemporary challenges

- Settling on a naturalization and citizenship regime that will allow the country's large foreign (mainly Turkish) population to feel fully integrated
- Incorporating the former East Germany so that the Federal Republic is genuinely socially, economically and psychologically united (see box above)
- Re-tooling the 'social market' model so that it provides jobs and helps pay for a welfare state facing pressure from an ageing (and falling) population
- Pursuing a bigger role in global affairs without alarming either pacifists at home or friends abroad.

Learning resources. For an overview, go for Green *et al.* (2007), *The Politics of the New Germany*. For something a little more advanced, try the collection cited by Green and Paterson (2005), *Governance in Contemporary Germany*. For a range of perspectives, see Padgett *et al.*, (2003), *Developments in German Politics, 3*. For native insight into the mores and psyche of their nation, try Zeidenitz and Barkow (1999), *The Xenophobe's Guide to the Germans*. Keep up to date with the news at http://www.dw-world.de/dw/0,2142,1432,00.htm

BOX 2.10

The EU's intergovernmental institutions

These bodies, in which member states are directly represented by national governments and civil servants, exist to ensure that the interests of those states play an important role in the decisions and direction of the EU.

Council of Ministers

Rather confusingly, the Council of the European Union (to give it its formal title) is, in fact, made up of a number of different councils, each dealing with a particular portfolio and each of which is attended by the relevant minister from each member state: hence transport, for instance, is dealt with by the transport ministers who meet regularly (around five times per year) in Brussels with their counterparts. Some sets of ministers meet much more regularly than others: for instance, those in charge of foreign affairs (the so-called 'General Affairs and External Relations' Council and Economics and Financial Affairs Council (dubbed ECOFIN) meet thirteen or fourteen times a year, whereas those in charge of education and health (subjects the EU is largely kept out of) meet only two or three times. At council meetings, ministers debate and amend, approve or reject proposed legislation from the European Commission, although often this is done on the nod after agreement has already been reached in the Committee of Permanent Representatives (COREPER), the committee made up of each member state's permanent representative (a senior diplomat each appoints) to the EU. The Council is, then, the EU's legislature. Although this is increasingly a role it shares with the EP under the co-decision procedure, the Council remains more powerful because it grants final approval on legislation under other procedures in which Parliament's wishes can be overridden. It also plays an influential role in initiating proposals, even in those areas for which the Commission supposedly has the sole right of initiation. The Council is often thought of as a bastion of intergovernmentalism, although recent developments in voting procedures (see Box 2.9) mean that member states are not always in a position to block unwelcome developments.

European Council

Although it got going only in the early 1970s, this originally informal meeting of heads of government and foreign ministers from the member states can lay claim to being the most powerful body in the EU. It is, for instance, free from any of the quasi-constitutional checks and balances that, because they were set up by treaties, constrain the other institutions. Over the years, the European Council has developed into an institution that sets the overall political direction of the EU, determining, for instance, that there should be monetary union and enlargement, or deciding that, for example, migration and the promotion of deregulation and economic dynamism should be key goals. Its summit meetings (which occur at least twice a year) also deal (though not always satisfactorily) with those issues that have proved too difficult to solve within the EU's formal structure, such as CAP and constitutional reform. The power of the European Council symbolizes to some the fact that, ultimately, the member states control the EU rather than the other way around.

those who want to reverse or slow the pace of integration (see Hooghe and Marks, 2007) – this seriously, even fatally, undermines or, at the very least, compromises state sovereignty.

Some member states, notably (but not exclusively) the UK and Denmark, were sensitive to what they saw as a diminution of their sovereignty. Their concerns fed into the agreement which turned the EC into the EU – the Maastricht Treaty (or 'Treaty on European Union', (TEU)) signed in 1991. Maastricht narrowed the range of topics on which a state could veto a proposal from the Commission. But it also attempted to 'ring fence' those issues that most directly touched on sovereignty. It did this by

Figure 2.1 EU budget – net contributors and recipients *per capita*, 2006

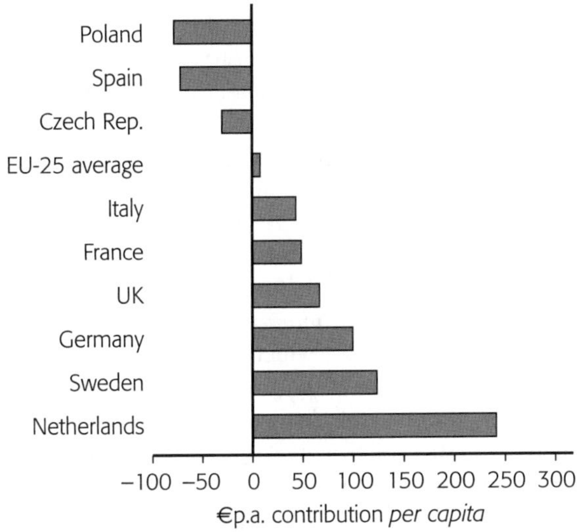

Note: EU revenue comes from 'own sources' (customs duties plus 0.5 per cent of member state's VAT receipts) and from a levy on member states' GNP. Countries benefit most directly from agricultural support and structural funds for deprived regions.

Source: Population data from Eurostat and expenditure and revenue data from European Commission, *EU budget 2006 – Financial Report.*

assigning them to the second and third of what was to become known as the 'three-pillar' structure. Broadly speaking, the first 'European Community' (or EC) pillar would include economics and trade and be subject to 'community procedures' that in the main ruled out a veto; the second ('Common Foreign and Security Policy', CFSP) and third ('Justice and Home Affairs', JHA) pillars would remain intergovernmental rather than supranational. This would allow any single member state to prevent progress on an issue if it objected. Matters deemed to be part of the second and third pillars would also be excluded from the jurisdiction of the ECJ. This lessened the chance that member states would see their preferences and their domestic legislation, on those matters at least, overridden by European law.

These concessions to intergovernmentalism were, however, somewhat balanced by Maastricht giving the supposedly more supranational *European Parliament* (see Box 2.9) much more say in law-making. Previously it had been very much the inferior of the Council of Ministers, in which each member state was represented equally and that alone could pass or block new laws proposed by the Commission. Henceforth (at least in some areas), the EP would have the right of 'co-decision' with the Council of Ministers. The EP was further empowered a few years later when, in 1997, the Amsterdam Treaty (much of which was an attempt to codify and simplify previous treaties) expanded the range of issues to which the co-decision procedure would apply.

Integration via economics and law

The EU has long encouraged integration by offering its member states not just security but also prosperity. True, only some member states benefit directly in net terms from its spending (see Figure 2.1). But all get to sell into and buy from a single market that massively expands opportunities and cuts transaction costs for business – and is therefore capable of delivering tangible benefits to ordinary citizens, with cheap flights, so-called 'health-tourism' (the ability to seek treatment in other countries but paid for by one's domestic provider), and the freedom to live and work 'abroad' only some of the most trumpeted achievements of recent years.

Another tangible benefit – at least, for holiday-makers and businesses trading in other countries – was added to the list in 2002 when twelve of the then fifteen member states gave up their separate currencies in favour of a single currency, the euro (€). The economic arguments for the move were not necessarily clear cut (see Chapter 9), but the political rationale and ramifications are clearer (see Jones, 2002). First and foremost, Germany gave up its

KEY POINT

Although they originated in political decisions, two of the key drivers of European integration are not overtly political. The euro is both the culmination and the spur to completion of a single market that locks member states into 'an ever closer union' – one that is underpinned and constantly reinforced not only by the supremacy of EU law but also by the fact that it is directly applicable by domestic courts.

currency, the *Deutsche Mark* – at the time, by far the strongest and most stable currency on the continent – for the cause of integration. This acted to calm concerns (especially in France) that it would demand a role in European and global affairs to match its increased size after unification in 1990 (see Chapter 11).

The coming of the euro, then, is not only an economic but also a huge political development. EU member states had agreed not only to a symbolic but also to a very substantial loss of political control over their economies – and arguably their destinies. True, control of interest rates had often been a matter for central banks in each member state. But governments had ways of exerting leverage over their decisions. The *European Central Bank* (ECB) (see Box 2.9), however, is presumed to be immune to political pressure – certainly from individual member states, for whom the Europe-wide interest rate may be so low it encourages inflation or so high that it chokes off growth and (by making the euro too strong against, say, the US dollar) renders exports uncompetitive. Individual governments can (and, as we see in Chapter 9, do) still employ fiscal measures (tax and spending) to help control their economies. But some observers argue that such measures need to be co-ordinated with other member states, creating a pressure for the Europeanization of fiscal policy (tax and spending) as well as monetary (mainly interest rate) policy.

Given all this, it is hardly surprising that those states traditionally less enthusiastic about further integration have chosen not to participate. Denmark, Sweden and the UK have strong traditions of parliamentary sovereignty and (in the case of the latter) governments that do not wish to surrender any more control of their economies than some argue they already have done (see Chapter 9). Their self-imposed exclusion, however, poses a problem for the EU as a whole. Most obviously, they are in a position to veto progress toward the kind of co-ordinated fiscal policy (beginning with, for example, the harmonization of taxation regimes) that some argue is necessary. Moreover, the fact that they have been allowed to 'opt out' and have not suffered economically as a result sends a message to the EU's newest member states that they can – and perhaps would be well advised to – do the same. Clearly, some of the latter will want to, and be allowed to, adopt the single currency: Slovenia, one of the strongest (though also one of the smallest) postcommunist economies is a case in point. But if some do not, it may prevent the euro becoming quite as much of a force for political and economic integration as many of its advocates – more or less openly – expected it to be.

Europe's newest member states already had first-hand knowledge of the extent to which the EU could override domestic practices and preferences even before they joined. In order to do so, after all, each had to demonstrate that they were capable of adopting the *acquis communautaire*. Indeed, inasmuch as there is clear evidence of Europeanization anywhere, it is the way candidate countries are obliged – though not always unwillingly – to bring their domestic policies into line, and not necessarily just in those areas (such as the environment) in which the EU has competence (see Börzel and Sedelmeier, 2006). This 'conditionality' does not, of course, apply to states once they have joined. But the legal implications of joining are never over. Since the 1960s, the Court's decisions not only have 'direct effect' (i.e. they do not need to be embodied in domestic legislation before being enforced by government and the courts) but are also 'supreme'. This means that in the event of a conflict between the existing law of a member state and European law, the latter will be upheld. Moreover, domestic courts, even at a low level, can go direct to the ECJ for a ruling, effectively bypassing the normal national hierarchy of courts and courts of appeal. Even more so than in the economic sphere, then, it is obvious that the sovereignty of member states, inasmuch as it involves the right to make the ultimate decision (via parliament) on its own laws, has been compromised. Moreover, the ability to use European law to achieve a desired outcome against either local or national government, or, for instance, employers and other businesses, provides another tangible benefit of European integration for its citizens.

A constitution in all but name? The Lisbon Treaty

In June 2004, the member states, following tough negotiations on a draft produced by a Convention including national delegations and EU institutions, finally agreed on the 66,000 word text of a *Treaty Establishing a Constitution for Europe*. Their ostensible aim was to provide a single document to replace the various treaties (Rome, the SEA, Maastricht, Amsterdam, Nice, etc.) that over time have laid down how the EU is to be governed, although Eurosceptics accused them of forcing the pace towards some kind of superstate. In the event, the Treaty had to be put on hold when French and Dutch voters – for a range of reasons that had as much to do with a distrust of their political elites as the content of the document itself – voted against it in ratification referendums held in the spring of 2005.

KEY POINT

Like the EU Constitution that could not be ratified, the Lisbon Treaty that replaces it is seen by some as merely a necessary tidying up exercise to allow the EU to cope with twenty-seven (and possibly more) members and by others as a major step (for good or ill) along the road to some kind of federal superstate. A balanced assessment suggests that the irritation of its proponents is understandable but so, too, are the suspicions of its opponents.

The Treaty was not, however, abandoned. Instead it was reworked as a 'Reform Treaty' that amended the EU's existing treaties – something which made it look very different but actually kept a good deal of the substance of the proposed Constitution. The Treaty still gets rid of the 'three-pillar' structure set up by the Maastricht Treaty in 1992, although there are still special procedures for foreign, defence and security policy. It also reduces the number of ways in which EU law can be made, tries to streamline the institutions (by, for instance, reducing the number of European Commissioners), and creates, if not a full-blown EU minister of foreign affairs, then a 'High Representative of the Union for Foreign Affairs and Security Policy' chosen by the member states who will sit in both the Commission and the Council of Ministers. The Lisbon Treaty still augments the role of the EP by extending the 'co-decision' procedure (renamed the 'ordinary legislative' procedure) to around 95 per cent of all legislation, as well as attempting to improve decision-making in the Council of Ministers by extending QMV to more policies and changing its rules slightly. The Lisbon Treaty introduces a new system for voting by members where legislation passes if fifteen out of twenty-seven member states agree and those agreeing represent 65 per cent of the EU's population. Member states who are outvoted, however, have the option of applying an 'emergency brake' and trying to persuade the European Council that their vital national interests must be protected.

Under the Lisbon Treaty, as under the proposed constitution, the EU will have a full-time 'President of the European Council' chosen (by QMV) by the European Council to oversee the agenda and work of the European Council and hence the general approach and priorities of the EU, thereby providing more continuity than the current 'rotating presidency' held by each member state for six months. The EU is also granted a 'legal personality', allowing it to negotiate international treaties and agreements on behalf of its members; before it could really only do this on trade. And, as under the proposed constitution, the writ of the ECJ will be extended to justice and home affairs issues (including immigration and asylum) where previously it did not run, although two countries (the UK and Denmark) can claim 'opt-outs' on this score. Whether, however, the UK could, as it claimed, opt out of the Treaty's formal incorporation of a 'Charter of Fundamental Rights', including the right to life and liberty, and the right to take industrial action, is debateable. So, too, is the extent to which national parliaments, as under the proposed constitution, really will be able to get the commission to think again about a policy to which at least a third of them object. Similar doubts apply to the fact that a petition signed by 1 million European citizens from a significant number of member states can invite (not, note, oblige) the Commission to submit proposals to the Council and the EP.

Finally, those sceptical about European integration were presumably pleased that the Lisbon Treaty copied the constitution by providing, for the first time, an explicit 'exit option' for any member state that decides to leave. Anyone opposed to a European superstate was also pleased to see that the Lisbon Treaty abandoned the idea of making the hitherto *de facto* anthem (from Beethoven's Ninth Symphony) and flag (blue with twelve gold stars) official. On the other hand, they were clearly very worried indeed about the so-called 'ratchet-clause', simplifying the process of treaty revision in the future. This opens up the possibility that potentially fundamental changes, while still having to be made unanimously (unless all member states decide that henceforth they can be made by majority voting), can in the future be made without the fanfare (and therefore the visibility) of an intergovernmental conference (IGC).

The end of the nation state?

Given what we have learned about both minority nationalism and the EU, it is easy to present a picture of Europe's historical nation states menaced, on the one hand, by sub-national pressures that may one day lead to the creation of new nation states and, on the other, by European integration. Indeed, as we have already noted, there is a sense in which the two threats to state integrity and sovereignty are complementary. National minorities take control of cultural and educational affairs and service delivery, while the EU handles (among other matters) monetary policy, agriculture, trade and the environment, supposedly leaving little for the state to do. But this is too simplistic.

For one thing, by no means the majority of European states find themselves under pressure from national minorities, and are unlikely to institute changes that undermine their status as relatively homogeneous unitary states. Scandinavia is an obvious example, notwithstanding the autonomy granted by Nordic countries to Greenland and the Faroe Islands (Denmark), the Swedish-speaking Åaland Islands (Finland) and the Sami (Laplanders).

KEY POINT

By no means all European states face a threat to their territorial integrity from minority nationalism, although where it exists that threat is serious. However, all the states involved in European integration have incrementally compromised their sovereignty, even though they continue to command the primary loyalty of their (majority) populations and could, in theory, reassert their authority by leaving the EU.

Moreover, the collapse of communism has brought back into the European fold a handful of countries that, at first glance, are both unitary and linguistically homogeneous and unlikely to want to compromise a sovereignty that was so long suppressed by Soviet domination. Any list would include on it Poland and the Czech Republic, as well as the much smaller Slovenia.

That said, however, the new members of the EU also include countries, such as Slovakia and Hungary and the Baltic states, that contain minorities who (like Northern Ireland's nationalist community, although less violently) could feel more loyalty to neighbouring states. Whether, though, they will allow those minorities more autonomy is another matter – and will partly depend on the behaviour of those neighbouring states. Some are careful not to push things too far, relying on common EU citizenship to make things easier over time, although the fact that some countries involved look unlikely to join in the foreseeable future renders this strategy problematic (see Scott, 2006): Romania, for example, cannot apply this soothing logic to the Romanian minority in Moldova; but other states, like Hungary, have provoked concerns by granting special privileges to 'Hungarians' living in surrounding countries (Csergo and Goldgeier, 2004: 27–9).

Those concerns may put off those countries from ever following the UK, Spain and Belgium down the (quasi-) federal or devolutionary route, pushing them instead towards France's example and to cling to the constitutional ideal of being 'one and indivisible' in spite of the historic claims of certain regions for more autonomy. But they need to be careful. For one thing, as we have seen, France is not quite as inflexible as it presents itself. For another, France can get away with more because it is a country with clout. New EU members, such as Romania and Bulgaria (with Turkish minorities), might well need to make more effort under the watchful eye of fellow member states. On the other hand, pressure on such matters can prove counterproductive: Greek Cypriots clearly felt 'bounced' by the EU and the UN into accepting a federal solution to end the partition of their island and bring the Turkish-occupied north into Europe with them, and promptly voted 'no' to the plan in a referendum in April 2004 (see Box 2.11).

We should also remember that, while the EU boasts – if not formally, then informally – many of the outward symbols we traditionally associate with a state like a flag and a passport, it still lacks a good deal of the substance. The EU's parliament is not sovereign, executive authority is blurred and it fails to command the primary loyalty of those it likes to call citizens. On the other hand, anyone supporting European integration can point, on the evidence of this chapter, to the fact that many member states, too, fail to inspire loyalty or affection among all those living within their borders. And, as we shall see in Chapters 3 and 4, few European states can boast a genuinely independent or powerful parliament – or, for that matter, an executive whose competence is clear, unencumbered and unchallenged.

Yet even if there is no clear 'pincer movement' against Europe's historical nation states, they are no longer quite what they were. Only some of them are under threat from below; but all of them have ceded the final say in some areas of policy and law to the EU. Indeed, such is the reach of the EU into the economics, policy-making (see Chapter 3) and particularly the legal life of its member states, that it cannot be said merely to present a threat from above. Instead, it is embedded within the nation state. Whether, however, this represents an end to sovereignty is a moot point. Practically, European states that join the EU no longer have complete control or freedom of action: they have swapped full sovereignty for the greater security provided by an institution whose original purpose, after all, was to render states interdependent so they would not and could not make war on each other ever again (see Debate 2.1). On the other hand, there is nothing – beyond the enormous costs that would presumably be involved – to stop a state that has forgotten (or no longer believes in the necessity of) that basic bargain from leaving and reasserting whatever control and freedom it feels it has lost.

But while in many European countries the nation state as an institution is under threat, if not siege, it continues to exercise considerable cultural sway over many, perhaps even the majority, of Europeans. As we have seen in Chapter 1, people still see themselves as Czech or German or Dutch or Swedish or even (though in increasingly lesser numbers) Spanish or British or Belgian. This sense of identity is reinforced daily, not just by politics but, perhaps more powerfully by the 'banal nationalism' (Billig, 1995) of linguistic and spatial familiarity and popular culture, be it sport or prime-time television (see Chapter 7). The challenge for Europe is to reconcile its population's persistent attachment to

BOX 2.11

Cyprus – where the EU and minority nationalism meet

The internationally recognized Republic of Cyprus joined the EU in 2004 but, following the failure to win consent among Greek Cypriots for a re-unified federal state, the whole of the island of Cyprus did not. The area controlled by the self-styled Turkish Republic of Northern Cyprus (TRNC) – which has existed in various forms since Turkey invaded, ostensibly to protect the Turkish population of the island against Greek nationalists in 1974 – is still excluded. The population of the TRNC wants to rejoin the Republic but with a level of autonomy and continued (military) links with Turkey (which has spent much of the last three decades encouraging migration of mainland Turks to Cyprus) that is unacceptable to the Greek majority. Despite the occasional confidence-building measure from the leaders of both communities, the situation remains deadlocked and a thin strip of no-man's land – the demilitarized zone – still stretches across the island from east to west. Notwithstanding the commitments it made when it became a candidate for EU membership, Turkey refuses to open up its ports and airports to the Republic of Cyprus until the EU (which now grants aid to the TRNC) allows direct flights from its member states into the Turkish north. Meanwhile, the Republic of Cyprus threatens vetoes left, right and centre should any quarter be given. This stand-off nearly derailed negotiations on Turkish membership, parts of which have been frozen until progress on the issue is made. It was hoped that EU membership for Cyprus and, eventually perhaps, Turkey would help solve one of Europe's most persistent and dangerous minority nationalist problems. Right now it doesn't look that way.

DEBATE 2.1

Is EU membership a good idea?

YES

- Countries' businesses gain unrivalled and unlimited access to a market of nearly half a billion well-off consumers. Joining the 'eurozone' reduces costs even more.
- Poorer member states gain from the money redistributed from their richer counterparts via 'structural funds' aimed at developing backward regions. Richer ones benefit in the short term by being able to locate production in poorer counterparts where costs are lower. In the long term, redistribution produces more consumers with more money.
- Citizens gain the theoretically unhindered and legally-enforceable right to travel, live, work, set up businesses, and (to a limited extent) access social security in twenty-six other countries. As consumers, they benefit from competition legislation.
- Common standards – for example, on the environment – help promote the collective good and prevent 'free-riding.' They can also be used to spread best-practice.
- Many modern challenges – the environment, terrorism, immigration, organized crime and trafficking – make a nonsense of borders and are better tackled in unison.
- For many states, being represented in foreign policy and trade negotiations by a large and powerful player gives them more influence than they would otherwise have.
- The EU helps lock in democracy, links economies and promotes cultural and diplomatic understanding and interchange – a recipe for peace as well as prosperity.

NO

- The economic future is global not regional, with India and China rather than Europe being the markets of the future. The EU is inherently protectionist, giving aid to the developing world instead of opening up trade. It also subsidises inefficient businesses – particularly in agriculture – and backward, sometimes corrupt countries.
- Some citizens – affluent and mobile cosmopolitans – benefit more than others from all these freedoms, but all have to put up with legal obligations imposed by institutions that they have not elected and therefore cannot hold directly accountable.
- Common standards put up costs for business and prevent it competing globally. The EU is biased towards a consensus model that stymies liberal economic reform.
- Countries could still co-operate on transborder issues and form coalitions in international fora without surrendering their sovereignty on vital issues like immigration, currency, and foreign and defence policy. Why should larger, more powerful nations have their freedom of manoeuvre limited by minnows?
- To credit the EU with fifty years of peace and prosperity is to confuse correlation with causation: those who have stayed outside it, like Norway and Switzerland, have also avoided war and grown rich – in fact, even richer.

nation states with its movement toward a 'multilevel governance' that, institutionally anyway, can override and undermine those states. Failure to do so risks delegitimizing democratic politics as a whole: people will feel (and indeed be) governed by an institution over which they seem to have little or no observable control. Success might help pave the way for the co-existence of national and European identity that some experts on nationalism argue is by no means impossible (see Smith, 1992).

Learning Resources for Chapter 2

Further Reading

On the nation state and minority nationalism, the first port of call would be Keating (2001), *Nations Against the State*, and Guibernau (1999), *Nations without States* or, if you want something very short, Keating's chapter in the collection edited by Heywood *et al.* (2006), *Developments in European Politics*. The more up-to-date collection edited by McGarry and Keating (2006), *European Integration and the Nationalities Question*, is also very useful. See also Panayi (2000), *An Ethnic History of Europe since 1945*. O'Leary's essay in the collection edited by Paul *et al.* (2003), *The Nation State in Question*, and Schmitter's chapter in the book edited by Gustavsson and Lewin (1996), *The Future of the Nation State*, provide typically stimulating essays on some of the issues raised here. Work on the EU is voluminous to say the least. A justifiably popular introductory text is McCormick (2008), *Understanding the European Union*, and good ways into more complex and contemporary debates are Cowles and Dinan (2004), *Developments in the European Union 2*, and the 'state-of-the-art' collection edited by Jorgensen *et al.* (2007), *The SAGE Handbook of European Union Politics*. Bache and George (2006), *Politics in the European Union*, is comprehensive yet accessible. An excellent advanced, but very approachably presented, guide is Hix (2005), *The Political System of the European Union*, while there is plenty of contemporary and historical food for thought in the collection edited by Meunier and McNamara (2007), *Making History*, and in Bartolini (2007), *Restructuring Europe*; Schmidt (2006), *Democracy in Europe*; and the collection edited by Thomson *et al.* (2006), *The European Union Decides*. Anyone seriously interested in the EU should also check out the *Journal of Common Market Studies* (JCMS) and the *Journal of European Public Policy*. Other journals, of course, carry articles on the EU: a recent example of a stimulating contribution in a less specialist outlet is Mark Aspinwall's article on 'Government Preferences on European Integration', *British Journal of Political Science*, 37(1), pp. 89–114.

On the web

www.ethnologue.com – minority languages and cultures in Europe

www.expatica.com – twists and turns of Belgian politics

www.lehendakaritza.ejgv.euskadi.net – Basque Country

www.gencat.net – Catalunya

cain.ulst.ac.uk – Northern Ireland

www.moi.gov.cy and **www.trncinfo.com** – both sides of the Cyprus question

europa.eu – official overview of EU

www.euractiv.com – in-depth EU (and European) news, discussion and debate

www.epc.eu and www.cer.org.uk – EU think tanks

www.brugesgroup.com and **www.openeurope.org.uk** – Eurosceptic perspectives

www.europeanmovement.org and **www.fedtrust.co.uk** – Europhile perspectives

news.bbc.co.uk/1/hi/world/europe/6928737.stm#foreign – compares the EU Constitution and its Lisbon Treaty

Discussion questions

1 What are the historical roots of minority nationalism, and why do you think it has become more important in recent years?

2 Why have states like Belgium, Spain and the UK become (or made moves toward becoming) federal countries? Do you think these moves are a rational solution – and one that will last – to the problems they face? Or are these problems (and, indeed, the solutions) actually very different from each other?

3 In your opinion, can there be any justification for Europe's minorities to employ violence in order to make their case and impose their solutions?

4 There are lots of criticisms of the EU. Yet in less than fifty years it has gone from a group of six to a group of twenty-seven countries. Presumably, then, it has some attractions for the countries that have joined. What do you think explains its growth?

5 Why are some EU institutions thought of as *supranational* and some as *intergovernmental*? Do you think this is a useful or a false distinction? Is the tension between them creative or destructive?

6 What role have law and decision-making rules played in increasing European integration? Do you think they have eroded, or even ended, the sovereignty of EU member states?

7 How different is the EU's Lisbon Treaty from the supposedly rejected constitution and should countries have had a referendum on it? One MEP who argued that it was substantively different noted that the DNA of mice and humans is 90 per cent the same, but the remaining 10 per cent is rather important: did he have a point?

8 Has the European nation state had its day?

Chapter 3

From government to governance – running the state, making policy and policing the constitution

Passing power downwards – decentralization	72
'More control over less' – central government reform	77
Policy-making – sectors and styles	84
The booming third branch of government – the judicialization of politics	90

In Chapter 2, we looked at challenges to the supposed integrity and the impermeability of the traditional European nation state. We discovered that the latter was under pressure from both within and without. Not every country was affected by minority nationalism, but all had conceded important powers to the EU, not least in the economic and legal domains. Those worried by such developments can perhaps derive some comfort, however, from the fact that, notwithstanding such concessions, each country still retains its unique constitution. This formal legal framework sets out the rules of the game for politicians, citizens and the institutions by which they govern and are governed. As well as defining the rights (and sometimes the duties) of the citizen, the fundamental feature of most constitutions is a so-called 'separation of powers' between the legislature, the executive and the judiciary (see Box 3.1).

This chapter focuses primarily on the bureaucratic side and the policy-making of the second of the 'three branches', the executive. This is the body that traditionally 'runs the country' or 'governs', albeit under the supposed direction of democratically elected politicians who form the government of the day and who are themselves meant to be under the watchful eye of parliament (see Chapter 4). But this chapter also considers the increasing importance of the third branch – the judiciary and the courts. It has two main themes. The first is that, once again, we see some commonalities, but also the persistence of national differences.

The second main theme is that governing in Europe, inasmuch as it was ever easy, is not as easy – or as easy to describe – as it used to be. Like that of the nation state, the scope and even the size of the executive is everywhere questioned. Authority, even where it is accepted, is more diffuse or spread out. What we used to talk of simply as government, it seems, is giving way to what is now termed *governance* (see Peters and Pierre, 2000). The former conjures up an image of institutions run by or on behalf of the state delivering, in more or less top-down fashion, those public goods which citizens (and the groups we examine in Chapter 8) are presumed to need. The latter implies a more complex process by which executive institutions – public and private, central and local – combine more or less smoothly to deal with the demands of increasingly less deferential individuals and interests. In short, '[the] top-down use of authority which characterises government has given way to persuasion, incentivisation and other forms of mobilisation characteristic of networks' (Page and Wright, 2006: 4). It is this development, when combined with the growing impact of the EU, that has led

BOX 3.1

Separation of powers

The political philosopher Charles de Secondat, Baron de la Brède et de Montesquieu (1689–1755), known to us simply as Montesquieu, published his *On the Spirit of Laws* in 1748. In it, he famously argued that the 'checks and balances' required to safeguard a country against tyranny were best embodied in the 'separation of powers' between the following 'three branches of government'. These were a legislature to pass laws and agree taxation, an executive to administer those laws and take decisions where appropriate and a judiciary to broker disputes. In his time, Montesquieu believed that this division of labour was best exemplified by England. Since then it has become better entrenched – albeit with a rather more active executive than Montesquieu may have envisaged – in the US. It also helps structure politics in Continental Europe, and is an important part of an ideal that emerged in German constitutional theory but spread throughout the continent – namely, the *Rechtsstaat*, a state whose acts must conform with laws enshrining fundamental rights.

political scientists to talk of the spread throughout Europe of the multilevel governance we defined in the Introduction – namely, the dispersal of power, a multiplication of sites of authority and policy competence, and a mixture of co-operation and contestation between tiers of government that would formerly have been considered separate and hierarchically ordered.

This chapter begins by looking at how and why power has allegedly passed downward toward lower levels or tiers of government – a process often labelled 'decentralization' or, more specifically, 'devolution' (see Chapter 2) or 'regionalization'. It then returns to the topmost level – to the so-called core executive. It explores whether (and if so why) the core executive has shrunk, yet also possibly gained in strength, via measures to improve co-ordination between a formerly more fragmented bureaucratic machine. Have recent developments such as the establishment of arm's-length 'agencies' (running things on behalf of government but not run by government) helped to 'hollow out' the state (Rhodes, 1997) to a degree that undermines one of the key branches of government? Or have they simply allowed it 'more control over less'? The chapter then goes on to show how the authority of the executive (and possibly parliament) is now constrained by the activism of the judiciary to such an extent that we should perhaps see the latter, too, as a part of the multilevel governance emerging across the continent.

The **core executive** is a label given by political scientists to the heart of government. It comprises both the political part of the executive – normally Cabinet and Prime Minister – and its bureaucratic support, as well as key civil servants from the most important departments, ministries and intelligence chiefs. The core executive normally operates out of the national capital.

Passing power downwards – decentralization

In Chapter 2, we referred to the classical distinction between unitary and federal states (see Elazar, 1997) and noted that it was breaking down as some former unitary states moved toward federalism. This move between classical categories, however, has been made only by the handful of countries we discussed in Chapter 2 – namely, Belgium, Spain, the UK and (possibly) Italy. Apart from Germany, Austria and Switzerland, all the others remain unitary states: no CEE state chose to become or stay in a federation. Yet that binary distinction between unitary and federal has always been as much analytical as real. In 'unitary' Scandinavia (especially Denmark) local government has long collected (relative to other

KEY POINT

A variety of pressures – practical, financial and ideological – have ensured that it is not only in federal countries that powers are devolved from central to regional and/or local government. The EU has also played a part, although its influence – like the downward transfer of powers itself – is not quite as great as some assume.

non-federal states) a large proportion of state revenues (see Table 3.1). It has also been quite a big spender and runner of services, all of which has allowed room for regional variation. And even outside Scandinavia, local authorities in Europe are responsible for a raft of things that in some countries would be the preserve of central government (or private companies). These include public housing, public utilities, welfare and health. Consequently, even if they do not collect much of their country's revenue (see Table 3.1), they account for quite a high proportion of its spending. In Spain, in 1979, for instance, central government accounted for 90 per cent of public spending and town councils 10 per cent. By 2000, the figures were 59 per cent and 14 per cent, respectively, with the increasingly powerful autonomous communities (see Chapter 2) accounting for 27 per cent and destined to account for even more with the transfer to them of responsibility for health services (Colomer, 2002: 196–7).

Spain, as we saw in Chapter 2, is not a 'normal' federal country, but even the supposedly more conventionally federal Switzerland and Germany are by no means replicas of US-style federalism (see Box 3.2 and Church, 2004). German *Länder* (regional states) have less power and autonomy than their American counterparts (see Box 3.3). They do, though, have considerable influence on national politics via the *Bundesrat* (the upper house of parliament) and on political outputs more generally because (along with local government and insurance funds) they control two thirds of Germany's budget and employ over half of all the country's public servants. In Switzerland, the competence of the federal (i.e. central) authority has been growing. The Swiss states (called cantons) are still the prime source of identity and the ultimate authority when it comes to giving more power to the centre. But they are too fragmented to deliver all services and functions efficiently or effectively.

But if those countries moving toward federalism (full-blown or otherwise) are in the minority, they are by no means alone in pursuing decentralization. A variety of political, economic and institutional pressures have pushed – or are likely to push – all but the smallest European states in the same direction. From at least the 1970s onwards, central government finances in many unitary states were coming under pressure as the postwar boom began to tail off. This prompted the idea that they were suffering from 'overload' – too much responsibility

BOX 3.2

Alpine exceptionalism – the Swiss confederation

Each of the twenty-six cantons that make up the *Confoederatio Helvetica* (CH), or Switzerland, is linguistically homogeneous. They comprise German speakers (who make up 65 per cent of the population) or French speakers (18 per cent) or Italian speakers (10 per cent). Each tends, as well, to be dominated by either Protestants (who make up 40 per cent of the population) or Catholics (who make up 45 per cent), though by no means all German-speaking cantons are Protestant, nor all French-speaking cantons Catholic. Little surprise, then, that the state forged from this religious and linguistic patchwork is federal rather than unitary. Survey evidence suggests that, in contrast to Germans, who do not feel much emotional attachment to their *Länder* (regional states), the Swiss root both their cultural and political identity in their canton rather than in the nation. Why else, one could argue, would they tolerate a federal government that has places all but reserved for a handful of the biggest parties, pretty much irrespective of results, with senior politicians almost automatically getting a turn to be president? The federal government may control more areas of day-to-day life than some suppose. But its growth is limited by the constitutional requirement that any new powers must be agreed by the cantons, as well as a referendum of all citizens, Switzerland being one of the world's biggest fans of *direct democracy* (Chapter 6). Cantons largely determine their own taxes. They have a big say in federal legislation, too. Not only do they have an 'upper house' of parliament all to themselves, but this *Council of States* knows that its veto cannot be overridden in the lower house, no matter how many MPs are ranged against it.

BOX 3.3

Germany's *Länder* – not quite as autonomous as they look

Unlike most of Switzerland's cantons, Germany's sixteen *Länder* are largely artificial creations, designed not so much to reflect traditional regional identities as to disperse power efficiently in a country that the WWII allies needed to neuter. Under the 1949 Basic Law (Germany's constitution), every *Land* government is accountable to a separate parliament, is elected in different ways, and operates according to its own constitution. The split with regard to responsibilities is broadly as follows:

	State (*Land*)	Federal (*Bund*)
Exclusive responsibility	Broadcasting Transport Police and judiciary Education (incl. curriculum)	Defence Foreign and trade policy National budget
Shared responsibility	Environmental policy, business and labour market regulation	

However, the federal government also has the ultimate say on anything judged to require uniformity throughout the country. The federal government also delegates a good deal of the implementation and administration of the policy areas in which it has competence. Interestingly, the *Länder* can deal direct with the European Commission on issues for which they have competence and, following arguments over ratifying the EU's Maastricht Treaty, they have a constitutionally guaranteed right to a say on any transfer of sovereignty that may affect them. They are also allowed to make their own agreements with foreign states – but only with the consent of the federal government.

In short, there is a good deal more functional overlap and interdependence in the so-called 'co-operative federalism' that distinguishes Germany (and Switzerland) from the 'dual' federalism that operates in the US – and, therefore, still plenty of room for tension. An example is the *Finanzausgleich* – the constitutionally backed obligation on the most wealthy *Länder* to subsidize their poorer counterparts (especially those in the former East Germany). Disputes, ultimately, must be adjudicated by the Constitutional Court (see Table 3.4) but reforms passed in 2006 aim to reduce conflict by granting the *Länder* more autonomy in some areas in return for reducing their ability to block federal legislation in the powerful second chamber of Germany's bicameral parliament, the *Bundesrat* (see Chapter 4).

for too many aspects and activities (see King, 1975). Policy makers wanted to offload some of this overload (and some of the blame for cutbacks to services) onto lower tiers of government. But they were nevertheless aware that efficient and effective service delivery and economic planning were just too big a job for the lowest level of local administration (normally called 'the commune' or district in Europe) – a level that is notoriously fragmented (Italy and France, for example, have over 8,000 and 36,000 communes, respectively). They were also coming to terms with the fact that development aid from the EU was increasingly targeted at the level of the region rather than the state (see Keating and Hooghe, 1996).

This combination of ideological change and institutional pressure (domestic and to some extent European) drove a rationalization of central and local government. It also led to the setting up or strengthening of so-called 'meso-level' or regional

Table 3.1 Levels of government – three examples

UK	France	Poland
Government	*gouvernement*	*rząd*
(Unelected) regional offices (England); executives (Scotland and NI); assembly government (Wales)	*région*	*województwo*
County council or 'unitary authority'	*département*	*powiat*
City, town, borough, district council	*commune, municipalité*	*gmina*

Note: Multilevel governance implies all levels communicating with each other simultaneously rather than a 'nested' chain of command or hierarchical division of labour.

government that sits between the local and the central state (see Table 3.1). And in many (though not all) countries this level has, accordingly, progressed from being appointed to being elected (see Keating, 2000). This incremental trend toward 'functional decentralization' (the parcelling out of tasks and competences previously assumed by central government) first affected western Europe, including some of its administratively most centralized states. France, for instance, began by setting up appointed regional authorities to co-ordinate economic investment and planning in the 1970s, and the twenty-two in mainland France became elected bodies in 1986 as part of a general process of *déconcentration* (decentralization) pursued by governments of both left and right (see Box 3.6). Likewise, Italy, which had a similar so-called 'fused' system where provinces were overseen by prefects who reported directly to Rome, moved to a system of twenty popularly elected councils representing its historic regions. Greece still has prefects but they are elected at the regional level. The situation in the Netherlands is rather more complicated (see Andeweg and Irwin, 2005). The country maintains its system of twelve provinces, with elected governments and legislatures, dealing mainly with transport and environmental matters. These are much smaller than most European regions, hence a not altogether convincing recent attempt to group them into four 'Eurosized' *landsdelen* or 'country-parts' which some argued were set up primarily to adjust to the fact that, from the late 1980s onwards, the EU's 'structural funds' would no longer simply compensate member states for their own regional spending but supposedly go straight to the regions themselves.

These moves toward regionalization would appear on the face of it, indeed, to provide some of the most concrete evidence of Europeanization we have. In CEE, too, many states (except for the very small ones) proceeded to carve themselves up into sometimes quite artificial regions (Poland has sixteen, the Czech Republic eight) in order to qualify for the €200 billion plus of EU funding that goes to deprived regions within countries (see Chapter 1) – just as Greece, for instance, did in the 1980s and 1990s (see Sotiropoulos, 2004: 417). But recent studies have cast doubt upon this seemingly plausible narrative, emphasizing the relative importance of domestic pressure, the doggedness of domestic political and administrative actors, and the considerable diversity of outcomes (Hughes *et al.*, 2004). Regionalization may have been seriously undertaken in Poland, for instance, but in many other accession states it went no further than 'surface compliance' and in some 'remained formal, dysfunctional and mostly symbolic' (Sturm and Dieringer, 2005: 289, 290). Studies also show that the EU's concern about adequate financial control led the Commission to change its tune after 2000 and recommend that accession states manage their regional development programmes and policy centrally (Keating, 2006). In both Western and Central and Eastern Europe, it would also appear that central governments are using the advantages afforded to them by their greater presence and involvement in decision-making in Brussels to maintain a gate-keeping role between the EU and regions – the clear exceptions being Belgium and Germany (though not similarly federal Austria, see Falkner, 2000a) where regions/states have been adamant about their right to direct contact (see the various country studies in Wessels *et al.*, 2003).

We should also be cautious not to overstate the case for 'regionalization', irrespective of whether it is or is not driven by Europeanization. For one thing, as Table 3.2 makes clear, money does not follow structure in any simplistic way. Central governments

Table 3.2 The central/regional/local split of taxation, 1995 and 2005

	Local (%)			Regional (%)			Central (%)		
	1995	2005	Rank	1995	2005	Rank	1995	2005	Rank
UK	3.6	4.7	20	0	0	–	93.5	94.4	2
Czech Rep.	12.1	15.0	7	0	0	–	76.7	72.0	5
Netherlands	3.2	4.1	22	0	0	–	54.4	60.2	11
Sweden	29.3	31.7	2	0	0	–	60.2	56.6	13
Italy	7.8	15.8	6	0	0	–	59.9	52.6	21
Poland	12.5	12.1	9	0	0	–	57.4	48.2	22
France	10.6	10.9	12	0	0	–	41.4	40.5	24
Spain	8.7	8.5	15	4.7	22.1	2	49.8	36.4	25
Germany	6.4	7.4	17	21.2	21.2	3	27.8	28.5	27

Note: The remainder of taxes are taken by social security funds; rank is out of EU-27 – the lower the number, the more important that form of taxation is in the country concerned.

Source: Data from Eurostat, *Taxation Trends in the EU, 2007*.

in many countries – even those such as the UK or Spain that have supposedly devolved power to regions – continue to keep a tight hold on sources of revenue and, where possible, spending. National politicians are aware of the impact on the macro-economy (and perhaps their electoral chances) if they cede control of revenue-raising to sub-national government. Moreover, we need to be careful about treating the regions they are keen to keep an eye on as cohesive entities 'when the reality is that they are composed of diverse groups with multiple interests' (Keating, 2006: 151). Likewise, it is tempting (and not altogether incorrect) to see the EU's funding and efforts to diffuse best practice creating a network of increasingly assertive regions. But we should acknowledge that those regions which are keen and effective players at the EU level (such as the German *Länder*) are able to play that role not simply because of the EU but because they had already asserted themselves and gained recognition domestically (Keating, 2006: 152).

In any case, as Table 3.2 also hints at, regionalization is not the whole story when it comes to decentralization. Beneath the level of the region there have also been significant developments in local government, whose service delivery role still dwarfs that of regions. Most notable in this respect is the extension – on the grounds of improving both management and accountability – of personalized political control (see Box 3.4). 'Regionalization' also masks the potential for conflict between local and regional authorities: in Italy, for instance, regions took over some of the supervision of local authorities from centrally appointed prefects. This, and the failure of the regions to devolve some of their powers to the local level, has caused considerable tension. Indeed, some larger European towns and cities (especially in Italy) have even tried to bypass the regions by forming a more direct relationship with central government. And rarely are these conflicts merely institutional in the sense of an objective, if contested, search for the most rational and/or democratic way of running the country. Most reorganizations of local (and regional governments) will have a political tinge (if not a political motive) to them: the central governments that pursue them are made up of party politicians who may well be hoping to disadvantage their opponents or even do away with them altogether – as was the case when the UK's Conservative government abolished London-wide government in the 1980s, only for it to be reinstated when Labour took over in 1997.

We should note, however, that this kind of local–regional (and central) conflict is not endemic in Europe. True, in countries with more adversarial styles of politics (such as Spain, the UK, France and

Italy) parties in opposition at the national level use their occupation of local or regional office to 'grandstand' against the government. But in countries with more consensual political styles (e.g. Germany, the Netherlands and the Nordic countries) co-operation tends to win out over conflict. In Sweden, for example, decentralization is taken for granted and runs relatively smoothly, albeit not utterly without tensions. Each of its twenty-four counties has an elected council, but also a governor appointed from the centre. He or she leads an administrative board, but one made up of members chosen by the county council. The administrative board fulfils a planning role alongside not only the county councils but also the municipal authorities. The municipalities look after day-to-day service delivery according to goals set for them by government agencies. But they also raise a relatively large amount of their own revenue (see Table 3.2) and have a fair amount of discretion to decide how exactly they spend their centrally determined bloc grants (see Pierre, 1995: 153). Meanwhile in Germany, the fact that the *Länder* and the federal government, irrespective of party differences, effectively have to work together via the *Bundesrat* (the upper house of parliament) in order to avoid gridlock (see Chapter 4) also means that when conflict does flare up it eventually gives way to co-operation. This does not always happen in Spain (see Chapter 2), where the autonomous communities play only a minor role in Spain's upper house, the *Senado.*

'More control over less' – central government reform

Although many of its functions (and at least some of its funding) have been devolved downwards to regional and local authorities, the central state in Europe has by no means withered away. Many analysts, however, suggest that it has been 'hollowed out' (Rhodes, 1997). According to them power has passed upwards (to the EU), outwards (via the privatization we deal with in Chapter 9) and downwards (to arm's-length agencies, for example). At the same time as devolving responsibilities (if not always control), central governments across Europe have, to a greater or lesser degree, been changing how they do the things that are left (Box 3.4).

KEY POINT

There is considerable variation in the extent to which Europe's central governments have embraced the ideas associated with new public management (NPM), although most have been concerned to improve political co-ordination of, and control over, the bureaucracy. Convergence toward one model, however, is not on the cards and – as is the case with regionalization – seems unlikely to be driven any further as a result of states adjusting to deal with the EU.

Influenced in part by **new public management** (NPM) ideas, many have sought to separate policy-making and setting (the advisory and supervisory function) from policy implementation (the administrative function). But they have also taken steps to offset the potential fragmentation involved in this effort. This has been done by maintaining and, indeed, improving political control of the non-elected part of the core-executive.

For Europe's top civil servants, the NPM may well be a double-edged sword. Ostensibly, it provides a choice between a career in policy advice or more hands-on management, thereby ending any confusion between the two roles. But it also poses a risk: if, for example, politicians seek to expand the range of advice they receive, they will no longer rely so much (or at least so exclusively) on their top civil servants, and the latter may not appreciate the advantages of becoming '"network managers" rather than the wielders of public authority' (Page and Wright, 2006: 4) – especially if they face competition for such posts from executives with valuable private sector experience. The same goes for Europe's politicians. NPM offers the chance to reduce their day-to-day operational responsibility (and, indeed,

New public management is as much an ethos as a doctrine. It rests on the notion that the public sector can learn a lot from the private sector in terms of its competitive focus on efficiency, value for money and responsiveness to clients or customers. Indeed, it should actually be re-structured to resemble a market wherein, ideally, the purchasers of a service are split from its providers, with managers given more autonomy but also clearer targets.

BOX 3.4

The trend towards direct election in European local government

In June 2004, Ken Livingstone was elected for the second time as Mayor of London, the first directly elected mayoralty in the UK. London has since been joined by a handful of other towns and cities. Moreover, other local councils have moved away from the traditional system of an appointed chief executive overseen by committees of elected councillors toward a system of a council leader with a cabinet (see Wilson and Game, 2006).

But the UK has a long way to go to catch up with Italy. There, as in France and Germany, there is a stronger tradition of an individual (elected or not) exercising administrative powers on behalf of the state. Since 1993, any of Italy's eight thousand *comuni* (local councils) with a population of more than 15,000 can hold direct elections for their mayor. Some local authorities have also been able to take advantage of a new property tax, the rate of which they can determine, to enhance their autonomy.

On the other hand, both the UK (which, in the jargon, is traditionally a *monist* country, emphasizing collegial, elected and local supervision of council activities) and Italy (a Napoleonic or *dualist* country where elected bodies traditionally worked alongside an individual executive answerable to the state) are part of a European trend (see Borraz and John, 2004). The rest of Germany has been catching up fast with the southern *Länder*, which have a strong tradition of directly elected executive mayors. Meanwhile, the countries of Scandinavia, as in Britain, have been experimenting with more powerful council leaders and cabinets, and even directly elected mayors. In the Netherlands, mayors were traditionally appointed by the government, but this is no longer obligatory – a move which may pave the way for direct election.

The aim has been to increase the responsiveness of services to local demands, and hopefully to offset declining voter turnout. Doubtless, direct election will enhance the prestige (and perhaps the accountability) of mayors and council leaders, especially in the biggest cities, vis-à-vis regional and national government. However, the extent to which greater powers for the locality have accompanied this enhanced prestige is less easy to gauge.

accountability) and therefore free up time for a more political role. However, NPM poses risks, both for politicians and for democratic legitimacy and control. At least in theory, politicians will be blamed for policy failures over which they have less direct control. On the other hand, if a politician can reasonably claim NPM-style separation between their function and implementation, they may escape accountability, whether 'formally' enforced by electors, parliament, the head of state or the judiciary or more informally policed by the media and the interest groups we deal with in Chapters 7 and 8 (see Helms, 2006). It is already rare for policy failure to prompt individual ministerial resignation in contemporary Europe, even though there is some evidence that such resignations do actually boost government popularity (Dewan and Dowding, 2005). In the August heatwave that hit France in 2003, over 10,000 people, mainly elderly, died of heat-related illnesses, prompting the resignation of the Surgeon General but not that of the Health Minister, who denied responsibility and stayed on in his job until a cabinet 'reshuffle' in 2004. If NPM makes such denials even more plausible, it may be more efficient (and some would say more realistic) but it might not be good for democracy.

In fact, the extent to which NPM ideas are seen as common sense in a particular country is, research suggests, heavily dependent on cultural and institutional traditions (see Pollitt *et al.*, 2007; and also Wright and Hayward, 2000): NMP is not irresistibly inevitable and is almost always adapted rather than adopted wholesale. For instance, in Germany public service is more about administering according to legal procedure than managing service delivery, while the power of the *Länder* in the *Bundesrat* (see

BOX 3.5

France: plus ça change – perhaps not

France is routinely portrayed (and sometimes ridiculed) as one of the most inveterately centralized, 'statist' (and, indeed, elitist) states in Europe, or perhaps the world. This portrayal always needed some qualifications. Centralization, for example, was traditionally mitigated by the fact that so many of France's national politicians held (and continue to hold) elected positions (for example, as mayors) at the local level, guaranteeing that state policy took sub-national needs into account. But the portrait is also increasingly inaccurate. True, its civil servants or its politicians have not rushed to embrace what they see as the neo-liberal tenets of NPM. But there has been a concerted attempt by governments of both right and left, beginning in the early to mid-1980s, to transfer powers from Paris (and its agents, the *préfets* or prefects) to local and regional government, which now controls almost half of government expenditure. These lower tiers of government have responded positively to being given extra responsibilities, and governments have seen fit to add to them over the years. Nor have civil servants at the centre, as well as at local level, resisted reform completely (see Clark, 1998 and Rouban, 1995). Generally, reform has tended to accelerate when both president and prime minister are from the same side of the political spectrum: just as federalism slows what little enthusiasm there has been for NPM in Germany, *cohabitation* tends to do the same in France (see Pollitt and Bouckaert, 2000: 49).

Chapter 4) has always meant that rapid change is difficult to achieve politically. Not surprisingly, then, Germany has not proved particularly fertile soil for those hoping to sow the seeds of the NPM (see Pollitt and Bouckaert, 2000: 91–2). On the other hand, the British civil service values pragmatism, bargaining and flexibility; nor is it either compartmentalized or governed by a separate civil service law. This, and the relative absence of constitutional and legal constraints on a majority government, means that NPM could be imposed relatively effectively from the late 1980s onwards (see Pollitt and Bouckaert, 2000: 47). A Scandinavian country like Sweden, which combines a respect for legalism with an enthusiasm for decentralization and autonomy (see below) seems to lie midway between the two – not as resistant to the idea of management as Germany but not quite so gung-ho as the UK (see Christensen and Lægreid, 2002). Interestingly, there appears to have been little attempt by outside bodies (such as the IMF or the Organisation for Economic Co-operation and Development, OECD) or the EU to make the adoption of NPM (as it did with privatization) a condition of assistance to the new democracies of East Central Europe (Goetz, 2001).

National history, tradition and culture, then, play a big role in governance. Indeed, it can sometimes seem that the only structural feature that European executives share is the tendency (particularly when it comes to the civil service and particularly at the highest levels) for them still to be staffed almost exclusively by white, largely middle-class and usually highly-educated, middle-aged men! While there may be a common thrust, and even common pressures (fiscal, political and otherwise), each country adapts to them in ways that – unlike, say, their parties and party systems (see Chapter 5) – do not always fit obvious patterns. For example, we cannot simply fall back (as the media often does) on easily assumed differences between the practices and responses of 'northern' and 'southern' Europe: differences do exist, but only some of them (the 'Mediterranean' tendency towards large-scale political appointments to civil service jobs and the 'over-production' of formalistic regulations) can be said to be systematic (see Sotiropoulos, 2004). And the national stereotypes that inform not only journalistic but also academic analysis are only sometimes useful (see Box 3.5). Comparative research on public administration rightly lays great stress on the strength and explanatory power of national traditions. But we should not allow this to trap us into automatic acceptance of outworn stereotypes that caricature countries rather than capture a more complex and dynamic reality.

The fact that comparison in this area is difficult might explain (and to some extent be caused by) the relative paucity of truly cross-national research in public administration (though see Peters, 2001, Weller *et al.*, 1997; and especially Pollitt and Bouckaert, 2000 for honourable exceptions), even though there are several useful collections of single-country descriptions (see Bekke and van de Meer, 2000; Bevir, Rhodes and Weller, 2003; Page and Wright, 2006; Peters and Wright, 2000; Pierre, 1995; Verheijen, 1999). Many of these begin by estimating the number of 'civil servants' employed by each state. But even a cursory glance makes it clear that using these to compare the size of central states or core executives is highly problematic, because what counts as a civil servant varies so much between countries. What does emerge, however, is the fact that since the 1980s civil service numbers across Europe seem to have stopped expanding. This is especially the case if we accept the assertion that employees transferred, say, to regional governments or to bodies that used to be part of the central state but now exist at arm's length from it (in agencies) are no longer, strictly speaking, civil servants.

The state that regards itself as the pioneer of separating policy-making and policy implementation is the UK. Since the late 1980s the British government has been steadily 'hiving off' operations and delivery to what are known as 'agencies'. There are now around one hundred employing around three-quarters of what would traditionally have been called civil servants. Perhaps the most visible example is the 'Benefits Agency' which is responsible for social security payments and employs tens of thousands of people all over the country. Each agency is a more or less (see Gains, 2003) autonomous unit responsible for a particular function or service. It is headed by a chief executive reporting to a minister who, advised by senior civil servants, determines the agency's resources and goals.

Both fans and critics of 'agencification' in Britain point (either in sorrow or sceptically) to the fact that the model has not always been enthusiastically adopted elsewhere in Europe, with the exception perhaps of Denmark and more recently the Netherlands (see Pollitt *et al.*, 2007), as well as the EU itself (Williams, 2005). Yet they miss an important point. In fact, the 'hiving off' of policy implementation has long been taken for granted in many other countries, especially in Scandinavia, even if few of them expressed much explicit enthusiasm for the NPM ideas that held sway in Britain (see Box 3.6). In Germany and the Netherlands, for instance, the delivery (and to some extent, via their collection of insurance premiums, the funding) of much of the welfare state has traditionally been left to so-called 'parastatal' or 'parapublic' bodies. The Federal Employment Service (*Bundesanstalt für Arbeit*) in Germany, for instance, runs most of the country's job centres, while most healthcare is provided via insurance premiums collected by its *krankenkassen* – bodies organized either by sector or by geography and with the involvement of unions and employers. In the Netherlands, many of the institutions that originated in the days when the country was divided

BOX 3.6

Neither new nor neo-liberal – government agencies in Sweden

The hiving off of government business from ministries to agencies is often associated with Thatcherite Britain in the 1980s. In fact, social democratic Sweden was the pioneer of the notion that the formulation of policy should be institutionally separated from its implementation. Indeed, the separation is formalized in its constitution, which charges government departments (overseen by cabinet ministers) with policy formulation while implementation rests with around eighty legally autonomous agencies (*ämbetsverk*). This means ministers cannot be held accountable for bureaucratic mistakes, but it also means that, potentially, they have much less control than some of their counterparts in other countries (for example, the UK) over what is done in the name of the government by agencies (see Ziller, 2001). In fact, ministers are able to exert influence via informal contacts between civil servants and, more formally, via the *Riksdag* (the Swedish parliament), which can vote to reorganize agencies and which determines their budgets. Interestingly, these have shrunk in recent years as agencies' service delivery roles have passed to local government. The response of agencies has been to turn themselves into supervisors rather than providers of local services (see Pierre, 1995).

along the lines of its religious subcultures continue to deliver services (often organized regionally), albeit in a much more secular age.

Spain, it must be said, has less of an 'agency' tradition, and has been too preoccupied with territorial decentralization to develop one along NPM lines. Nor has there been much enthusiasm in France for agencies. On the other hand, they have always played a part in Italy – some would say too big a part: their proliferation as means of providing patronage opportunities for politicians and bureaucrats alike has done nothing to ameliorate the unimpressive reputation of its public servants (see Box 3.7).

Hiving off the job of implementation has its potential downsides. The most obvious is that the creation of more structures (and arm's length structures at that) will make it harder for the government of the day to co-ordinate, let alone control, policy and delivery (see Wright and Hayward, 2000) just as the latter may be becoming all the more important to voters who are no longer so tribal or hung up on ideology (see Chapter 6). This task is already rendered difficult in some states owing to a tendency toward compartmentalization on the part of ministries and departments (see Table 3.3) – a tendency that is only partly mitigated by the existence of finance ministries that oversee spending (and therefore all departments) and, in some countries, the appointment of a 'minister-without-portfolio' tasked with achieving what in the UK (a prime example of the trend) is called 'joined-up government'. Partly in response, to these problems, potential and actual, Europe's politicians have recently looked for ways to help them at least steer their state machinery, even if – because of the fragmentation inherent in functional and territorial decentralization – they can no longer control it. It is this that explains what those who cling to the ideal of a neutral civil service believe is a damaging trend toward the politicization of bureaucracy. This trend (see Peters and Pierre, 2004) encompasses two things. First, there is an increased willingness on the part of senior civil servants to acknowledge that they need to be politically sensitive networkers rather than dry-as-a-bone administrators (see Pierre, 1995: 207 and also Aberbach *et al.*, 1981 and Rhodes and Weller, 2001). This may explain why, despite it being increasingly possible to do so, not that many top civil servants are parachuted in from the private sector. Second, this notwithstanding, politicians seem ever keener to appoint to senior positions people they can trust.

BOX 3.7

Living up to the stereotype – the civil service in Italy

Lazy, offhand and wedded to interminable bureaucratic procedure which will be set aside only if you know him personally or pay him if you do not: such is the stereotype of the Southern European civil servant. Unfortunately, it is a stereotype that many familiar with the byzantine world of the Italian civil service would argue holds true (see Lewanski, 2000). Historically, many civil servants saw their posts not so much as a passport to progression or a vocation but, rather, as a slowly rising means of subsistence that could be supplemented either by kickbacks or by holding down another job outside of the notoriously short opening hours. The administrative culture is highly legalistic, which ensures that there are myriad opportunities for those involved to charge a private premium for anyone wanting to move things along. Of course, all this applies most to 'street-level' bureaucrats. But the senior levels of Italy's civil service also come in for criticism (see Cassese, 1999) for excessive legalism, reform-resistant culture (though see Lewanski, 1999) and a tendency towards little empires ruled over by men who are there because of their staying-power and social networks rather than their talent. Traditionally, none of this mattered too much because – in a manner that in some ways paralleled the situation in Communist East Central Europe before 1989 – the grip of Italy's political parties on society was so strong that politicians could effectively by-pass the civil service in order to get things done. Since the collapse of the old party system in the early 1990s, however (see Chapter 5), this is no longer the case, strengthening the case for reform.

Table 3.3 Joined-up government – compartmentalized civil services

The compartmentalized rule	The interdepartmental exceptions
NL: Highly autonomous departments with own specialized recruitment; consequent lack of joined-up government has given rise to reforms, among them the ABD (*algemene bestuursdienst*) designed to improve horizontal mobility among senior civil servants.	**UK:** Emphasis on centrally recruited generalists; good horizontal mobility; cross-ministerial committees.
Germany: Very specialized departments with own career patterns.	**France:** generalist administrators with good networks often based on highly sought after membership of a *grand corps* (functionally oriented groups of high-flyers), shared educational background in one of the *grandes écoles*, and movement between departments and ministerial staff, and in and out of politics.
Sweden: As in most Scandinavian countries, the civil service is highly sectoral.	
Spain: Departments and ministries colonized by particular and specialized functional structures, called *cuerpos,* which seem to have survived an attempt by centre-left governments in the 1980s to loosen their grip.	
Italy: Notoriously fragmented; low mobility.	
Poland and **Czech Republic:** Little central recruitment or horizontal mobility.	

Sources: Bekke and van der Meer (2000), Page and Wright (1999), Verheijen (1999).

No European country has anything like the 'spoils system' that sees incoming administrations in the US make wholesale and overtly partisan changes at the top of the civil service. But Greece and (to a slightly lesser extent) Spain come some way towards it (see Sotiropoulos, 2004: 410). Newly elected governments in 2004 (one right-wing, one left-wing) made fairly sweeping changes at the top of the civil service and even in corporations where the state still has some involvement. And there are other states which are more accepting of party involvement than some. In Austria and Belgium, for example, it has long been a convention that political parties were granted a number of positions according to their relative strength to which they would appoint their members. At the other end of the spectrum lie countries such as the UK and Sweden, where there is a strong cultural norm toward neutrality. Here, top civil servants are expected to switch seamlessly from outgoing to incoming governments of a different stripe. Indeed, it is by no means easy (especially in the UK) for a minister to replace staff whose attitudes he or she does not find conducive with those to whom he or she is better disposed. It is, however, increasingly accepted (as it is in the Netherlands) that ministers will supplement existing staff with a handful (and no more) of people who are acknowledged to be political appointments but join the civil service as temporary 'special advisors'. Often, they provide political or media management advice that would be considered beyond the pale for permanent civil servants.

Other countries lie along this spectrum. In the Netherlands and Germany, openly political appointments to senior civil service posts, especially by new governments, are increasingly common: notwithstanding its reputation for legal formalism, the German civil service saw significant changes at the top when the CDU–CSU joined the SPD in government after the 2005 election and took the Chancellorship. In France, ministers, in addition, to the departments they run, where they may, and often do, reshuffle the top posts, are also allowed what is called a *cabinet* – a group of, at the very least, ten high-fliers, some of whom will be plucked from departments and some of whom will come from outside the civil service altogether, to help them supervise and drive their ministries, as well as to keep an eye on the work of their ministerial colleagues. This practice of appointing advisory *cabinets* was copied in Poland, but not altogether successfully (see Zubek, 2006: 104). France's powerful president (see Chapter 4) also has a *cabinet,* in addition to his own general secretariat of civil servants who co-ordinate the work of the government. It is not surprising, perhaps, that many French ministers (who do not have to be – and while they serve cannot be – parliamentarians) have previous experience as civil servants, often working in a *cabinet*, before they become politicians and part of the elected government.

The governments of CEE also face the challenge of establishing political control over a bureaucracy that tends toward legal formalism without returning to (or failing to escape from) the profound party politicization of the civil service that characterized the communist era. They are not helped by the continuing antagonism between the centre-right and what, outside the Czech Republic, is a centre-left that more often than not rose from the ashes of the Communist Party itself. This antagonism tends to see new governments try to bring in their own more trusted servants which, in turn, militates against the development of the neutral civil service that observers in, say, Scandinavia and the UK, assume (wrongly) is (or should be) the norm everywhere. On the other hand, we should beware of too negative a portrayal: extensive interviews with hundreds of ministers from CEE suggest that by far the majority of them were not only happy with the work of their civil servants but saw them essentially as (neutral) administrators (Blondel *et al.*, 2007: 147–8). Europeanization might have played some part in this since accession arguably represented a countervailing force to what might have become clientelism or cronyism: 'Brussels' needed a professional set of administrators that it could deal with during negotiations and which could implement change, a demand which dovetailed with the recommendations of external bodies like the OECD. The result of these contrasting pressure has sometimes been, as in Poland, a gap between what is formally the case – the apparent erosion of politicians' ability to appoint their favourites to the civil service – and the informal reality on the ground; namely, 'tampering with the regulatory framework' so that 'far-reaching politicization' continues (Zubek: 2006: 116; see also Meyer-Sahling, 2004 and O'Dwyer, 2006).

Once again, then, cultural and institutional differences seem set to persist. Although we can identify a European tendency toward trying to tighten political control over a state machine that is now more 'loosely coupled', there is no such thing as conformity. But what of one potentially crucial force for such conformity – namely, the need to improve the 'fit' between national and European administrative structures (see Cowles *et al.*, 2001)? It is certainly common to hear suggestions (from both federalists and anti-federalists alike) that the differences between east and west, and north and south, and between individual countries, will gradually grow smaller as their executive structures are somehow brought into line by the demands of dealing with the EU.

Clearly, there is evidence of Europeanization in this respect: for instance, the *grands corps* (high-ranking civil service organizations) in France have arguably lost some of their self-confidence and grip on the policy process in recent years as a result both of European integration and the way reformers have used it to bolster their case (see Cole and Drake, 2000: 29–30). More generally, member states have had to develop mechanisms for interministerial and departmental co-ordination, not an easy thing given the extent to which civil servants can make direct contact with their functional counterparts in other countries, often via the some 1,000–1,500 EU working groups and committees operating at any one time. The member states have done this, however, in strikingly different ways. Traditionally, centralized states such as the UK and France have tried (not altogether successfully) to maintain central co-ordination of the European involvement of ministries, often via ad hoc committees, while other states – Sweden is an example – prefer a more formalized co-ordination and decision-making process that takes place at cabinet level. Meanwhile, some traditionally more fragmented, less streamlined states find co-ordination on issues with a European dimension more of a trial (see Maurer *et al.*, 2003: 69 and the individual country chapters in Wessels *et al.*, 2003).

This divergent response to a common adaptational challenge is confirmed in a useful summary of the research on the issue in western Europe; Klaus Goetz (in Hix and Goetz 2000) observes that 'the gap between expected adaptive reactions and the often rather modest effects that empirical analyses uncover' is wide. Most studies, he notes, testify to 'the importance of national context and the capacity of national administrative traditions to modify, accommodate . . . and, perhaps, even neutralize European pressures'. The signs, Goetz goes on, are little different in the newer members of the EU from East Central Europe – and anyway the impact of Europeanization would be difficult to disentangle from the effects of the wider changes that postcommunist countries have undergone. More generally, as Page and Wouters (1995) observe, the survival of profound differences in structures and procedures in the bureaucracies of the component states of the US – a fully federal system – should make us very cautious about predicting that the EU will somehow make Europe's state bureaucracies look more like each other.

Policy-making – sectors and styles

As for structures, so for policy-making – what actually goes on in those structures and emerges out of them? As Wessels *et al.*, (2003: xv–xvi) conclude from their comparative study of all fifteen states that made up the EU until May 2004, although 'the head of government, governmental administrations and interest groups . . . have increased their role as strong and active multi-level players' compared to 'weak adaptors' like parliaments (see Chapter 4) and (interestingly) regional administrations, '[f]undamental patterns of national policy-making have not changed'.

A state's **policy style** can be defined as the interaction between a characteristic problem-solving approach covering each stage of the policy cycle – initiation and formulation, implementation, evaluation and review – and a characteristic relationship between those involved, including (though not exclusively) politicians, bureaucracy and those groups affected by and/or seeking to effect change (see Richardson *et al.*, 1982: 13).

KEY POINT

EU membership may have strengthened some actors and organizations relative to others, but it has not erased fundamental cultural and institutional differences in the way policy is made in individual states. These policy styles can be compared but they are only approximations because sectors within countries vary and because contingencies always play a part. So, too, does Europeanization, but its effects are not uniform.

This firm rejection of the idea of 'Europeanization-as-convergence' when it comes to policy-making raises the question of what those patterns are in the first place. Is it possible to talk about each European state having some kind of identifiable **policy style**? The answer seems to be probably, but not without considerable qualifications. The first of these is the extent to which policy-making in nearly all advanced societies is 'sectorized', with each area engendering its own, more or less permeable, **policy network**. These involve, at the very least, government and those interest groups trying to get it to do something that could benefit them or prevent it from doing something that they see as detrimental (see Chapter 8 for more detail on such groups). This means that there might be more in common between the making of, say, energy policy between two countries than there is between policy-making in, for instance, health and education within the same country, making generalizations misleading if not meaningless.

The second qualification to the idea of national policy styles is that the reality of policy-making may differ considerably not just from the 'ideal type' or simplified model analysts use to understand it (the same is true for policy networks, as we note in Chapter 8), but also from the 'standard operating

A **policy network** is a range of actors (including, for instance, organized groups, national and European civil servants, regulators, firms and academics) that interact, more or less systematically, in a given policy area. Tight knit networks are labelled 'policy communities'; more loosely coupled ones 'issue networks'.

procedures' or 'norms' that those involved might prefer to adhere to – or, alternatively, might need to appeal or resort to if a deal cannot be worked out (see Hayward, 1982). Three examples of this – historical principles acting as a fallback, if you like – spring immediately to mind. First, there is the tradition of the state overriding objections in the public interest in France. Second, there is the insistence on 'parliamentary sovereignty' (a majority of the House of Commons ultimately trumping any intransigence by, say, interest groups) in the UK. Third, there is the *Rechtsstaat* tradition in Germany, whereby anyone proposing a policy, even on a relatively unimportant topic, should be able to show it is consonant with the constitution.

The point, though, is that on a day-to-day basis these principles are not brought into play: most of the time consultations and negotiations lead to deals. We therefore need to be careful about using these normative traditions to characterize (or caricature) a country's policy style. This still happens, as one of the examples just given illustrates: we now have ample evidence that French policy makers are no longer elitist apostles of *dirigisme*, directing things from the top because they assume they have all the answers as well as the right to do so; instead, they work with (and are sometimes severely constrained by) interest groups and local and regional governments (see Guyomarch *et al.*, 2001). Yet it is still not uncommon to see the country labelled, indeed almost dismissed, as 'statist'. The potential, and possibly the propensity, that has always existed for such statism may still be there, but it is rarely drawn on lest it waste political capital which politicians and bureaucrats might need in future policy-making.

This brings us to the third qualification to the idea of national styles, one which opens up a classic debate in political (and all social) science – namely, the relationship between 'structure' (institutions, procedures, processes and norms) and 'agency' (individual and group action). The paradigmatic European example of agency triumphing over structure is the Conservative government under Margaret Thatcher that governed the UK from 1979 until 1990. Possibly some of those triumphs were as rhetorical as they were real, but they ruthlessly exposed the fact that the policy style widely associated with that country (and, indeed, that party) before it came to power in 1979 – pragmatic, consultative, compromising – was in some ways misleading, relying on what had been done before, not on what could be done if politicians were determined enough. Ironically, it also demonstrated that the notion of 'parliamentary sovereignty' alluded to above might indeed be important when comparing the UK with other countries where political circumstances, culture, processes and institutions made this kind of untrammelled power highly unlikely (see Table 3.4). Then again, parliamentary sovereignty can tell us little about how UK governments (in fact, all European governments) have fared when dealing with matters that demand policy but on which parliament plays only a bit part, such as economic policy – which is why, incidentally, one cannot really cover policy-making by drawing a few standard diagrams of 'how a bill is passed' in various countries' legislatures. Nor does the concept (or the diagrams) help us much when it comes to governments having to deal with crises that demand immediate administrative action rather than parliamentary process – whether these crises are real (such as the floods in central Europe in 1998 or the spike in petrol prices that occurred in September 2000) or one of the less tangible matters that temporarily achieves prominence in the media-primed 'issue attention cycle' (Downs, 1972, and see Chapter 7).

Even the strongest 'agents', then, may find themselves undone by structures not of their own making (like the oil or credit markets) or by sheer contingency (most obviously, the weather). Or, as we have suggested, they might sometimes find it convenient to recall an idealized version of their role in policy-making rather than act, as they do on most days, more prosaically. Or, as we have also said, different 'standard operating procedures' may apply in different policy sectors. Nevertheless, it may still be worth essaying some broad generalizations about individual countries' policy styles. These should take into account the institutional influences on them (i.e. the other actors governments must deal with) and the normative influences on them (i.e. their problem-solving approach), since, as a valuable recent study found (Héritier *et al.*, 2001), they help to explain how essentially similar policy goals often produce sharply differing outcomes. The generalizations are illustrated in Table 3.4, the aim being to provoke discussion and promote comparison rather than to present an all-encompassing account.

Table 3.4 Policy styles and their institutional and normative influences

	France	Germany	Italy	Netherlands	Spain	Sweden	UK
Limits to action:							
Federal states/devolved regions?	No	Yes	No (may change)	No	Some	No (but increasingly decentralized)	Some
Accessible/assertive constitutional court?	Can be	Yes	No	No	Not often	No	No
Relatively powerful parliament?	No	Yes	Potentially	No	No	Yes	No
Institutionalized interest group participation?	Some	A lot	Some	A lot	Little	A lot	Little
Powerful coalition partners?	Rarely	Always	Always	Always	Rarely	Rarely	Never
Coalition agreement that really counts?	No	Yes	No	Yes, very much so	No	Sometimes	No
Interest groups required for implementation?	Sometimes	Often	Sometimes	Often	Sometimes	Often	Sometimes
Fragmented departments?	Occasionally	Often	Often	Often	Often	Often	Sometimes
Procedure over flexibility?	No	Yes	Yes	No	Yes	Yes	No
Intervention over 'hands-off'?	Yes	Yes	Yes	No	Yes	Depends	No
Consensus over majority rule?	No	Yes	No	Yes	No	Yes	No
Overall policy style characterized by:	Consultation within limits, then action	Interconnection and incrementalism, risking immobilism	Disconnection and heavy-going	Consensus where possible, action if not	Consultation within limits, then action	Consultation without immobilism	Consultation within limits, then action

An all-encompassing account of policy-making in Europe would prove impossible anyway, given the very little we know as yet about policy-making styles in East Central Europe. In fact, these styles are probably still very much in the making, just as they have been in older 'new democracies' like Portugal, Greece and Spain (on which see Magone, 2008). An exhaustive account would be equally difficult owing to the caveats already discussed above. Any comparative schema or shorthand characterization will inevitably fail to explain exceptions to what, in any case, are tendencies rather than rules.

For instance, the incrementalism and 'interconnectedness' that the Germans label *politikverflechtung* does not rule out major reforms being pushed through, often in the face of considerable doubts and opposition. One only has to think of the decision during reunification to allow East Germans to swap their weak communist currency one-for-one with the powerful Deutsche Mark then used in West Germany or, more recently, the Schröder government's 1999 reform making it easier for 'foreigners' to claim citizenship. On the other hand, one could argue that both examples show the dangers of departing from the norm: currency union is included in a fascinating comparative study of European 'policy disasters' (see Gray and t'Hart, 1998), while the political arm-twisting required to get the citizenship law saw it rapidly struck down by the Federal Constitutional Court, obliging the production of an amended version.

In other words, just as policy styles that potentially brook no compromises need not preclude them, styles that emphasize consensus are equally capable of fostering innovative solutions. Indeed, because they eventually achieve 'buy-in' from all concerned, they may even be better at producing policy that works and lasts. The welfare reforms in the Netherlands and Sweden that we touch on in Chapter 9 are good examples. The latter country's policy system is famously consensual to the point of being cumbersome. Governments wanting to do something routinely appoint a state commission (*statsutredningar*) composed of experts, interest groups, agencies and representatives of (other) parties to examine their ideas and produce a report. At the same time, a wide variety of opinion is canvassed under the pre-legislative *remiss* consultation procedure. All these views feed into legislative proposals that are then intensively debated in parliamentary committees, often resulting in cross-party agreement. Yet for all this, Sweden is one of the few countries in western Europe that has 'grasped the nettle' on the pension reforms that many think Europe's ageing population make vital (see Chapters 1 and 8). France, with its more 'heroic' policy style has achieved some reform, but more is needed – and has, in 2007, already occasioned more of the protest that occurred when it was last tried in 1995.

Amid all this talk of national variations, what of Europeanization, as defined in the Introduction? Is policy-making right across the continent increasingly interconnected, with state and non-state actors 'downloading' the prescriptions of the EU and/or other European countries at the same time as seeking to 'upload' their own? Studies seem to suggest a good deal of variation, with two things standing out as important. The first is the extent to which involving or invoking EU institutions and initiatives presents opportunities to domestic actors to speed up or slow down change as they see fit (see Héritier *et al.*, 2001: 288). In other words, Europeanization occurs or does not occur in part because its occurence or non-occurence suits policy makers: it need not be an unstoppable force but can just as often prove a valuable resource.

The second thing determining the extent of Europeanization is whether the EU has policy competence in the policy area concerned (see Zeff and Pirro, 2001; and especially Wallace *et al.*, 2005). So, for instance, policy-making on agriculture and fisheries, or on the environment, does, of course, go on at the domestic level, but those involved (across all member states) exhibit a 'co-ordination reflex' which means they are attuned to and involved in (and therefore thinking of the consequences for) the policy process at the EU level. Perhaps, for instance, they participate in an EU *groupe d'experts* (preparatory committee) and therefore meet fairly frequently in Brussels with their sectoral counterparts from other countries – the kind of activity that, incidentally, makes it harder and harder for Foreign Ministries to maintain their gatekeeping and co-ordinating role over the interaction of supposedly 'domestic' departments. In other areas – including, say, health and education where governments have not ceded much to the EU – policy makers could well be learning from other countries, and they

COUNTRY PROFILE

FRANCE

Area: 545,600 km^2 (13.0% of EU-27)

Population: 63.0 million (12.8% of EU-27)

Religious heritage: Roman Catholic and Protestant

GDP (2006): €1,794 billion (15.5% of EU-27)

GDP *per capita* as percentage of EU-27 average (2006): 113

Female representation in parliament and cabinet (end 2007): 19% and 47%

Joined EU: founder member, 1957

Top 3 cities: Paris – capital city (2.2 million), Marseilles (0.8 million); Lyon (0.5 million).

History: Present-day France is composed of various regions centralized in the seventeenth century by a monarchy that was then overthrown in a revolution which began in 1789. In the following two decades, the country emerged (under dictator Napoleon Bonaparte) as an imperial power. After Napoleon's defeat, the monarchy was restored, only to be overthrown once again in 1848. Following two decades of dictatorship and the loss of a war with what became Germany, France finally settled, albeit fractiously, into democracy, although under this 'Third Republic' it rapidly began to lose its status as a world power.

During the Second World War the northern half of France was occupied by Germany, while the southern half ('Vichy') was ruled by a collaborationist regime under Marshal Pétain. After an initially unstable period (the so-called 'Fourth Republic') during which both its constitution and its colonial policy were called into question, France pulled itself together under President Charles de Gaulle. After De Gaulle bowed out at the end of the 1960s, the centre-right held on to power in what was (and still is) known as the 'Fifth Republic' until 1981, when François Mitterrand constructed the first fully centre-left government since the 1930s. Its radical economic programme soon came unstuck, however, forcing a policy U-turn. Until 2002, government alternated between multiparty blocs of the left (including a much weakened Communist Party and the Greens, as well as the more mainstream Socialists) and the right (made up of conservatives and liberals who, for the moment, continue to shun the well-supported far-right National Front). But this pattern was broken when, in 2007, the centre-right was returned for a second term, its leader Nicolas Sarkozy having managed to build, after years of fragmentation, an unusually large single party – the UMP. The left, however, remains fragmented, although the Socialists were not routed as completely as they had feared at the parliamentary elections that followed Sarkozy's winning of the presidential contest in the spring of 2007.

Economy and society: France is still one of Europe's most powerful economies, and a notable exporter, especially of agricultural goods. With a generous, insurance-based welfare state but plagued by relatively high unemployment, the French enjoy a standard of living on a par with that of their German neighbours – and one which is more evenly distributed in geographical terms. That said, Paris remains by far the richest city, although some of its suburbs are notoriously blighted by crime and poverty. Some 4.5 million people in France are Muslim (most of whom have their origins in France's former colonial possessions in North Africa). There is some regionalist sentiment in the west and south, but it is only problematic in the Mediterranean island of Corsica.

Governance: France's elections are fought, unlike anywhere else in Europe, under a two-ballot, majoritarian system rather than under PR: the only other country which shuns the latter is the UK. France is also Europe's main 'semi-presidential' system. Its president is directly elected every five years and then

WHAT'S IN AN ANTHEM?

Probably one of the most instantly recognisable anthems on the planet, *La Marseillaise* was made famous throughout Europe by the French Revolution and its defence against invading German and Austrian armies. So much so, indeed, that it became something of an anthem for radicals everywhere and may well have been one of the first ever 'samples', making an appearance in Tchaikovsky's famous *1812 Overture*. It is essentially a stirring (if slightly gory) call to arms against 'tyranny's bloody banner' and 'savage soldiers' from foreign lands who would 'cut the throats of your sons, your wives' but whose 'impure blood' will end up watering the fields of France.

appoints a prime minister and cabinet who are accountable to a notoriously weak parliament, although a recently convened commission has called for the strengthening of the latter. This means that the French sometimes experience divided government if parties other than those who support the president win the parliamentary elections. In that case, the president has little choice but to appoint political opponents as prime minister and to cabinet. This so-called *cohabitation* should, though, become less common now that parliamentary elections are somewhat more likely to follow hard on the heels of the presidential contest. France's Constitutional Court is an increasingly powerful player in the political process, and potentially important interest groups include (despite their small membership) the public sector trade unions and the farmers. Notwithstanding its reputation for being one of the continent's most 'statist' countries, France has pursued a policy of decentralization for more than two decades. Its national and its local politics are, in any case, intimately connected by virtue of many national politicians – again, unusually so in Europe – continuing to hold positions as local mayors or heads of regional government.

A KEY CONTEMPORARY CHALLENGE

ENDING THE FEATHER-BEDDING OF (UNIONIZED) PUBLIC SECTOR WORKERS

French governments in the last decade or so have a habit of folding in the face of street demonstrations and strikes by public sector unions. President Sarkozy, however, made no secret of the fact that he would regard his election in 2007 as a mandate to change France. Among his first targets were the 'special pensions' that allow some public sector workers to retire as early as fifty and France's large civil service. The perks, which cost an estimated €6 billion per annum would, announced the President, have to go, while one in three of all retiring civil servants (which in France means plenty of front-line workers not just administrators and managers) would not be replaced. The government also announced plans to slim down the court system and to begin another rethink of higher education. Sarkozy talked about negotiation and mutual agreement but also promised that he would see things through. Thus, in mid-November 2007, within only a few months of taking office, the new President was facing his first huge test on a number of fronts: an open ended train strike backed up by stoppages on the Paris Metro and by workers in the electricity and gas industries in which the government still holds a big stake; protests by students and teachers and by court workers and lawyers, and a day of action by civil servants. He was widely expected to back down, but the signs were that the public might be less sympathetic to the protesters and strikers than previously. The clash is not just fundamental to France's economy and state sector, but also to democracy itself: should direct action defeat an elected government?

Foreign policy: After 1945, France dedicated itself to locking its old enemy Germany into Europe via an integration process that it was determined to lead and exploit. It has also attempted (much like the UK) to hang on to its former glory: France may have lost most of its overseas possessions by the 1960s (including, most bitterly, Algeria), but it still has far-flung colonies in the Caribbean and the South Pacific, still has its own nuclear weapons, and is still one of the five permanent members of the UN security council. France fell out badly with the US over the Iraq war, for which it could see no sound justification. The election of President Sarkozy, however, along with a shared concern over the nuclear ambitions of Iran, has seen a significant rapprochement. Differences on climate change, however, remain. Also notable in recent years has been France's willingness to put its armed forces at the disposal (and, indeed, at the head) of EU peacekeeping missions in the Balkans, Africa and the Middle East.

Contemporary challenges

- Rebalancing political institutions, especially to give the legislature more say and to stop politicians simultaneously holding multiple offices
- Attacking persistent disadvantage and discrimination suffered by citizens of immigrant origin, even if, say, collecting statistics on ethnicity will mean offending against the republican ideal of equality
- Ending what some see as the feather-bedding of (unionized) public sector workers in order to reduce the state's deficit and borrowing and help dynamize the economy (see box above)
- Reforming the country's creaking higher education system; tackling youth unemployment.

Learning resources. For an overview, start with Knapp and Wright (2006), *Government and Politics of France*. More discussion is provided in Cole *et al.* (2008), *Developments in French Politics 4*, and the collection edited by Cole and Raymond (2006), *Redefining the French Republic*. Keep up to date with the news at http://www.expatica.com/actual/toc.asp?subchannel_id=25

might well have a special 'desk' that deals with European affairs, as well as a man or woman on the ground in Brussels (in the government's Permanent Representation if they are a civil servant or, if they work for an interest group, at its office in the city). But they are not looking over their shoulders at other countries or seeking to anticipate their actions in anything like the same way. It is because of this variation between policy areas that we need to be careful before we assume that Europeanization necessarily disrupts or undermines the traditional (if informal) hierarchy that means some ministries tend to be seen as more important than others.

The booming third branch of government – the judicialization of politics

Talk of 'disruption' and 'undermining' brings us rather neatly to the extent to which the executive's job in Europe is made more difficult these days by the role of what in the US is traditionally a powerful 'third branch of government': the judiciary. Theoretically, its role is not just to enforce criminal sanctions, but also to adjudicate disputes by applying the civil law to particular cases. These might be between private parties, or between individuals and the state, or perhaps between central and local government. In so doing, the judiciary is meant to provide another 'check and balance' by ensuring that government and the state operate under the rule of law and do not exceed their powers and/or violate fundamental liberties laid out in the constitution. To some observers, however, the courts have taken things too far: their interventions have become so profound and frequent that we are moving, they claim, toward 'juristocracy' (Hirschl, 2004).

KEY POINT

To talk of 'juristocracy' is going too far, but it is apparent that the judges do play a role – and perhaps an increasing one – in the politics of European democracies, even where judicial review is restricted. And the ECJ is undoubtedly both influential and a driver of Europeanization. The judicial branch of government seems more popular than the executive or legislative branches – but this isn't saying much.

All European states, with the exception of the UK, which prefers the flexibility of tradition and precedent, have written constitutions. At least in the eyes of the ordinary citizen, these constitutions – even though they are almost all the product of popular regime change and new-found independence – rarely attain the sanctified and sacred status enjoyed by the US constitution, and they have often been amended or even replaced by new, improved versions (see, for example, Wolczuk, 2007). They are nonetheless important, helping as they do to structure politics by laying down the powers and roles of the various institutions (president, government, parliament, regions, etc.) involved in running a country. Many political 'rules of the game' can be rewritten pretty easily by the players; constitutions less so. They may not be totally fixed objects around which the executive is obliged to work, but they are seriously heavy pieces of scenery – very difficult to shift, and best not bumped into too often.

The UK is not only unusual in that its constitution is 'unwritten' (though since some documents are vital to it, it might be more accurate to say uncodified). With the exception of Scotland, its legal system is based on what are called 'common law' principles, whereas the bulk of European countries (including Scotland) operates systems based on 'Roman' or 'code' law. In England and Wales, and also Ireland (and to some extent former dependencies like Malta and Cyprus), statutes passed through parliament are important (especially for criminal law), but so, too, are precedents set by judges' decisions in past cases. These establish principles – based on notions of equity and individual rights (for example, to free enjoyment of property) that are binding on lower courts

In other European countries, however, civil law is much more likely to be 'codified' – systematically written down so it can be applied to particular cases by judges. These judges therefore enjoy rather less discretion than their counterparts in the common law system and are often seen (and, indeed, recruited and trained) as highly specialized civil servants rather than lawyers who have served their time arguing before other judges before going on to become one themselves. Roman law systems are generally less adversarial (and more 'inquisitorial')

BOX 3.8

What, no constitutional court?

Just because they do not have a constitutional court does not make politicians in the UK, the Netherlands and Sweden immune from legal intervention – or, just as importantly, the fear of it. Although judicial review is only rarely resorted to in Sweden, the 'Council on Legislation', made up of senior judges, can be asked by the government or by a parliamentary committee to rule on government proposals. This usually takes place prior to the bill being brought before the *Riksdag*, which also appoints *ombudsmen*. These are officials to whom ordinary people can appeal if they feel due process has not been followed – an idea that has been copied in the Netherlands and the UK (as well as in other Scandinavian countries, Portugal and Austria). In the UK, Acts of Parliament cannot be overturned by judges, but the actions of the authorities can be challenged on the grounds that they are taken without due authority, or are irrational and unreasonable, or not in accordance with proper procedure. And, while it is true that no court can actually strike down a statute as unconstitutional, it has for some time been open to a judge either to rule illegal the executive action required to carry it out or to declare that parts of it are unlawful to the extent that they deprive an individual (or company) of their rights under EC law. Indeed, after the passing of the Human Rights Act of 1998, judges can now declare statutes incompatible with the European Convention on Human Rights (ECHR or CPHR) – something that has already forced the government into re-writing the rules on holding terrorist suspects. This also holds true in Sweden and in the Netherlands. The Dutch constitution may explicitly deny the courts any right to constitutional review, but this has not prevented them considering many matters that many would consider political, most famously euthanasia and (more mundanely) employment issues (see Andeweg and Irwin, 2005).

than common law systems. They also tend to have more of a division of labour between various specialist courts set up to deal with, for instance, criminal, financial or administrative law (although we should note that over the last two or three decades, the British legal system has also developed a network of more specialized administrative tribunals).

This is not to suggest that all Roman law systems are the same. For instance, Germanic countries (and now most CEE countries) place more stress on a logical progression from general principles – the *Rechtsstaat* idea we referred to when defining separation of powers – than do 'Napoleonic' countries (France, the Benelux countries, Italy, Portugal and Spain) even though they rely heavily on codified law. In Scandinavia, codes are slightly less rigid and detailed – and public servants see themselves as managers as much as mere implementers of the law – but process is important. Nor should we fail to note that many countries are hybrids – Poland and Greece, for instance, sit somewhere between the Germanic and the Napoleonic style, while Scotland even mixes in common law influences. Generally, though, the distinctions between Roman and common law systems have traditionally been more important than the differences within them.

Anyone with a nodding acquaintance with US politics will be familiar with the idea of a Supreme Court that provides the ultimate insurance against government, be it central or local, undermining the rights guaranteed to citizens by the constitution. Similar courts exist in many European countries. The obvious exceptions are Britain, the Nordic countries and the Netherlands, though this by no means guarantees that politicians are free from judicial constraints (see Box 3.8). Where such courts do exist, the main difference between Europe and America is that in the US, any judge in any court, can declare a law or government action or decision unconstitutional. This ruling can then be tested in other courts right up to and including the Supreme Court. In Europe, this kind of **judicial review** has traditionally been rejected on the grounds that ultimate power rests with the people and is therefore invested in a democratically elected parliament rather than in appointed judges.

Alongside this belief in the supremacy of statutes, however, runs an enthusiasm for constitutionally

Table 3.5 Europe's constitutional courts

Country/Name	Membership	Reputation	Role	Record
Germany: Federal Constitutional Court	16 members (half appointed by *Bundestag,* half by *Bundesrat,* both needing a two-thirds majority).	Highly regarded as 'above politics' or at least balanced.	Considers constitutionality before and after legislation has come into force. Pre-legislation ('abstract review'), applied for by federal or *Länder* governments, or one-third of MPs, and can therefore be a means by which oppositions try to overturn a parliamentary defeat. 'Concrete' (i.e. *post hoc*) review initiated by courts or, most commonly, by individuals claiming violation of rights by a public body. Adjudicates between federal government and *Länder,* and civil liberties/human rights.	1990 forces changes to East German electoral system; 1993 rejects challenge to Maastricht Treaty, but stresses limitations on EU's power; 1992 lowers state funding to political parties; 1993 makes publicly funded abortion harder; 1994 clears way for German military participation overseas; 1998 clears way for Germany to adopt the euro; 2001 grants equal legal treatment of 'gay marriages'; 2002 forces government to rethink liberalization of citizenship law; 2002 upholds military conscription; 2003 rejects legal ban on neo-Nazi parties; 2006 throws out law allowing the shooting down of hijacked civilian airliners.
France: Constitutional Council	9 members (3 each chosen by President, National Assembly and Senate), including many former politicians.	Highly partisan: appointees of right-wing governments tend to oppose left-wing successors and vice versa.	Can consider constitutionality only before legislation comes into force (i.e. abstract but not concrete review possible) on request of the President, presidents of the two chambers of parliament, or 60 MPs. Lower courts cannot refer cases to it. Covers wide range of issues, but rarely involved in human rights cases. Seen by many as almost a third chamber, given the propensity of opposition parties, having lost the votes in parliament, to refer virtually all important bills and budgets to it.	1982 insists on adequate compensation for nationalizations; 1982 strikes down an attempt to boost the number of women candidates in local elections; 1984 blocks Left's plans to regulate media ownership; 1986 interferes with Right's plans to deregulate media; 1993 limits Right's attempts to tighten immigration and asylum regime; 1998 overturns Socialist by-election win over National Front because of media bias; 1999 grants same-sex couples full legal rights.

Table 3.5 Europe's constitutional courts (continued)

Country/Name	Membership	Reputation	Role	Record
Italy: Constitutional Court	15 members (5 chosen by President, 5 by parliament and 5 by judges in higher courts).	Only moderately partisan, and normally reasonably balanced between partisans of the various parties.	Carries out pre-legislation abstract review (usually on the initiative of national or regional government) and concrete review (i.e. *post hoc* referrals from courts). Wide range of activity but particularly active as gatekeeper for requests for referendums.	1971 allows sale of and information on contraception; 1970s strikes down sexist adultery laws; 1970–4 upholds constitutionality of divorce liberalization; 1976 breaks up government monopoly of media.
Czech Rep.: Constitutional Court	15 members, appointed by President and parliament.	Seen to favour government's establishment of liberal capitalism, notwithstanding social costs; early clashes with centre-left.	Abstract and concrete review – the former initiated by the President, or government or parliament; the latter by courts or individuals.	1993 upholds retrospective punishment for crimes under Communist regime and right to restitution of property, but strikes down criminal prosecution for defaming political institutions; 1997 forces immigration authorities to allow appeals in person; 2000 strikes down rent controls.
Poland: Constitutional Tribunal	15 members, appointed solely by parliament.	Seen initially as subservient to parliament and government's liberalizing agenda, but beginning to be more assertive.	Before 1999, it could be overridden by two-thirds majority in parliament, but now its say is final. Very accessible – abstract review on the initiative of political institutions at the national and local level, judges and even on its own initiative. Concrete review via referrals from courts.	1989–94 strikes down some of Poland's 'shock therapy' economic reforms; stymies President's attempts to extend powers; upholds rights of former regime officials to pensions; upholds rights and privileges of the church; keeps abortion ban; 2007 strikes down 'lustration' law.
Spain: Constitutional Tribunal	12 members, 2 each appointed by the judiciary and the government and 8 by parliament.	Partisan appointments (especially under Socialist governments), but not sufficiently so as to undermine its legitimacy.	Abstract review on application by Prime Minister, president of parliament, 50 parliamentarians, regional governments, ombudsman. Concrete review via referral from court or requests by ombudsman or individuals. Can also rule on the text of international treaties.	1983 counteracts legislative move to slow down (for fear of antagonizing conservatives) granting of regional autonomy and declares that state law prevails over regional law; 1993 strikes down key provisions of the government's internal security reforms (minister resigns).

Judicial review is the process by which legislation, regulations and administrative acts of the state are examined by the judiciary in order to check, among other things, that they are in accordance with the constitution and other law, and that neither the executive nor the legislature is going beyond its powers, breaking its own procedural rules or acting unreasonably. Review can make use of a particular case (concrete review) or not ('abstract review', which may take place before the law comes into force).

backed rights, freedoms and principles which – logically, anyway – would seem to constrain and take priority over parliament. Many countries have resolved this potential contradiction by setting up special constitutional courts that are – supposedly, at least – 'above politics' (see Table 3.5). Countries that have set up such courts include Germany, France and Italy and, more recently, Spain, Poland and the Czech Republic (see Procházka, 2002 and Sadurski, 2005), all of which emerged from dictatorship wanting an extra bastion against any return to arbitrary rule. Italy and Germany were, of course, in a similar position in the 1940s, and the latter would in any case have needed some kind of umpire to settle disputes between federal and state authorities.

However, unlike the US Supreme Court, which sits at the apex of the ordinary court system and is, in effect, that system's final court of appeal, Europe's constitutional courts sit outside that system (the only exception being Ireland, where the High Court and Supreme Courts do the job of a constitutional court). It is possible in most countries that have a constitutional court for that court to hear cases referred to it by ordinary courts concerning laws that are already in force – a process known as 'concrete review'. But it will also spend much of its time (and, in the French case, all of its time), responding to requests by politicians (local or national) to decide on the constitutionality of laws that have already been passed by parliament but that are not yet in force. This process – because no particular case is involved – is known as 'abstract' review.

From sometimes small beginnings, these constitutional courts have expanded the role of the third branch of government. For the most part, the expansion was largely unforeseen and, because it crept up on politicians only gradually, went largely unnoticed. In France, for example, the Court was seen as a tool of or prop for the executive and few made much of its 1971 decision henceforth to take into account the wide-ranging preamble to the constitution. This decision, along with a constitutional amendment in 1974 that extended the right to refer matters to the court to any sixty members of either legislative chamber, paved the way for a massive (and creative) increase in its competence and importance. Now, it may well have taken on a self-sustaining momentum of its own (see Stone Sweet, 2000). The use by opposition politicians of abstract review to try to strike down legislation and policy that they are unable to vote down in parliament is increasing. In France, virtually every contentious bill (and budgetary measure) is re-fought in this way and, because it takes time for judges appointed by previous administrations to be replaced by those more favourable to the present government, such bills stand a 50:50 chance of being declared in some way unconstitutional. Governments and parliaments, in the face of possible defeat during what amounts to an extra final reading of bills, and knowing that changes to constitutions require big majorities (especially if the article covers basic rights), are already obeying what political scientists call 'the law of anticipated reactions'. They are watering down their legislation to improve its chances of either avoiding or passing judicial scrutiny – something that calls into question the idea of a separation of powers.

Also being called into question are the differences between Roman and common law systems – a development that provides considerable potential for, as well as evidence of, Europeanization. Concrete review – whereby courts (and sometimes individuals or ombudsmen) can ask their national constitutional court for a ruling which they can then apply to their particular case – is blurring the formerly hard and fast distinction between ordinary courts and constitutional courts which, as a result, are arguably becoming more like a US-style Supreme Court. And the increasing stress on the interpretation of constitutional principles (as opposed to merely applying a code) may not differ that much from the use of precedent and the notion of the supremacy of decisions of higher courts that are already associated with common law systems. At the same time, common law systems, by developing specialized administrative tribunals and increasingly taking into account codified EC law, are becoming more like Roman law systems.

Law, and its contribution to governance, is one area in which Europeanization is without doubt important (see Cichowski, 2007). True, there are big differences in the extent to which European countries transpose European law into domestic legislation, and in the frequency with which they are hauled up in front of the ECJ for lagging behind or non-observance (see Table 3.6). And national politicians will often go for the most flexible interpretation of EU rules. They will also try to square the Commission, which is responsible for policing them and referring cases to court: government provision of 'state aid' to ostensibly private firms (which we touch on in Chapter 9) is a good example. But, as the decline in state aid can be said to show, the fact is that, for the most part, compliance eventually occurs (see Zürn and Joerges, 2005), even if it is sometimes only partial and contingent on attention being drawn to non-compliance by powerful interested parties (see Conant, 2002). This is because, as we noted in Chapter 2, both national politicians and national courts have accepted the supremacy of European law and, where appropriate, acknowledged that it has direct effect on their countries without needing transposition. Indeed, the alleged enthusiasm of some national courts (especially lower courts) for the ECJ – combined with the willingness of businesses, individuals and pressure groups to bring actions based on European law (see Chapter 8) – has been a major factor in blunting any incipient resistance to its power on the part of national politicians. At least in those areas where their predecessors have granted competence to the EU, then, Europe's elected politicians and the states they run find their room for manoeuvre restricted by non-elected judges.

Table 3.6 Persistent offenders – new actions taken by the ECJ for the failure of a member state to fulfil its obligations

	Annual average from date of joining until 2006	2006
Italy	10	25
France	7	9
Spain	8	19
Germany	5	11
UK	5	4
Sweden	3	4
Netherlands	2	5
Czech Rep.	1	4
Poland	1	3

Note: Long-term average is likely to be lower than any recent year's numbers because there were fewer laws to infringe on earlier.

Source: Data from *ECJ Annual Report, 2006*.

While Europe's politicians do not like being 'named and shamed' via the ECJ, they do not always object to being bound by European-level law. ECJ decisions, like those of domestic courts, can sometimes provide political opportunities as well as constraints. A good example would be the series of decisions that helped build momentum for the Single European Act (SEA) (see Chapter 2), which accelerated progress on the single market (see Chapter 9) – something most of Europe's politicians (even reluctant Europeans such as the UK's Margaret Thatcher) were keen to see. Another would be the ECJ's ruling that pension ages for men and women should be the same – something that allowed European governments to raise the age of entitlement for women which will, in the long-term, save them money. States also exploit the power of the ECJ in disagreements they have with each other: ECJ rulings (backed up by the possibility of large fines) were said to be instrumental in getting France to drop what the UK claimed was an illegal ban on the import of British beef. In judicial matters as in many other aspects of European politics, then, the EU 'lives' inside as well as outside the state and can be an opportunity and not just a threat.

Some claim to see in both domestic and EU affairs, and the blurring of the boundaries between them, the beginnings of a slide down a slippery slope they call the 'judicialization' of public life and politics. At the bottom lies a homogenized European legal system that, they argue, takes no account of national traditions which, supposedly at least, are culturally appropriate and have done the job well enough for centuries. Parliamentary government, they claim, is giving way to 'rule by judges' who owe their positions partly to their professional colleagues, mostly to politicians and not to the supposedly sovereign people. It is all too easy to assume that constitutional and other courts are inevitably 'a good thing'; the record, however, is more mixed: the experience of Central and Eastern Europe, some argue, is a case in point (see Sadurski, 2005).

As we have seen, however, judicialization, inasmuch as it is occuring, is not uniform throughout the continent (see Guarnieri and Pederzoli, 2002). Nor, we should remind ourselves, does it necessarily go against the wishes or the interests of either politicians or people in general. A number of the issues the courts deal with, such as anti-discrimination and the right to life, are seen by the former as 'too hot to handle' and by the latter as best kept free of partisan party politics. The same may be true of disputes between central, local and regional government, which will undoubtedly become more frequent with the popularity of decentralization, devolution and even federalization (hybrid or otherwise). In dealing with them, the judicial branch of government is, in effect, doing everyone a favour. It is also contributing a great deal to the governance not only of each country, but, especially with regard to EC law and the ECHR, Europe as a whole. Even if one disagrees that judges might do a better job than politicians (see Debate 3.1), it does seem to be the case that people trust the legal system in general far more than they do their elected parliaments and governments – though, as Table 3.7 shows, this is not saying much. It is to these supposedly venerable but clearly much maligned institutions that we now turn.

Table 3.7 'Trust' in the legal system, government and parliament

	Net trust (%) in:		
	Legal system	**Government**	**Parliament**
Sweden	+29	+3	+29
Netherlands	+23	+1	-12
Spain	+4	-8	-11
EU-15 average	+2	-28	-18
Germany	+16	-39	-30
EU-25 average	-2	-32	-25
Italy	-19	-31	-26
UK	-1	-45	-30
France	-16	-46	-35
Czech Republic.	-2	-42	-58
2004 accession states av.	-24	-49	-55
Poland	-33	-64	-71

Source: Data from *Eurobarometer*, 66 (2006).

DEBATE 3.1

Would rule by judges be better than rule by politicians?

YES

- Judges in established liberal democracies are normally appointed on merit and are highly objective and intelligent professionals without an axe to grind.
- Judges make decisions based on rational argument and the evidence in front of them, not according to ideology or facts selected to support their prejudices. They respect well-established principles rather than appease or whip up emotive public opinion.
- While judges announce (and often justify) their decisions publicly, they take them away from the glare of publicity, meaning the media are less influential.
- Because they are not subject to election, judges have longer time horizons: they can do what is best in the long-term rather than what will get them into, or keep them in, power in the next three or four years.
- Not having to worry about what the majority wants, judges do a better job of protecting the rights and interests of minorities.
- The judiciary in established liberal democracies is free of corruption and well trusted.

NO

- Judges are often recruited from a social elite with a very narrow experience of the real world, unlike politicians who come from a variety of backgrounds and occupations.
- Emotions, symbols, and identity are important to people and their instincts and desires have to be respected. Society also changes faster than the law, which is inherently conservative.
- The idea that there are objective facts or evidence is a nonsense. Society is full of conflicting interests, ideas, and institutions: only if they are properly represented can they be peacefully reconciled and scarce resources efficiently allocated.
- When it comes to almost any decision, it is better to trust to the 'wisdom of crowds' rather than the judgement of a handful of people: 'millions of people can't be wrong' is not merely a phrase; it's a probability.
- The more the media scrutinize the decision process, the more open and fair it will be.
- Politicians who live with the knowledge that they will be held accountable every so often tend to act in the interests of the majority.
- The 'tyranny' of that majority can be avoided by, for instance, making it difficult to override fundamental rights by entrenching them in a constitution or by proportional representation.
- Politicians in democracies are rarely corrupt and a lack of trust is healthy scepticism.

Learning Resources for Chapter 3

Further reading

On regions, see Keating *et al.* (2005), *Culture, Institutions and Economic Development*. On local government, see the collection edited by Denters and Rose (2005), *Comparing Local Governance*, and the collection edited by Coulson and Campbell (2006), *Local Government in Central and Eastern Europe*. For a discussion of governance, see Peters and Pierre (2000), *Governance, Politics and the State*; their edited volume (2004), *The Politicization of the Civil Service in Comparative Perspective*, also provides plenty of insights into how politicians are trying ensure they steer the bureaucracy instead of vice versa. On the central state in Europe, see Page and Wright (2006), *From the Active to the Enabling State*, and Dimitrov *et al.* (2006), *Governing after Communism*. The collection edited by Pollitt *et al.* (2007), *The New Public Management in Europe*, is the must-read if you are interested in this phenomenon. So, too, is the OECD publication, *Modernising Government* (2005). On the extent to which Europe and the domestic have (and have not) become enmeshed both bureaucratically and in terms of policy, see Wessels *et al.* (2003) *Fifteen Into One?* On policy-making, try the collection edited by Moran *et al.* (2006), *The Oxford Handbook of Public Policy*, and Rose (2004), *Learning Lessons in Comparative Public Policy*. For policy making in the EU, the first port of call must be the incomparable collection edited by Wallace *et al.* (2005), *Policy-Making in the European Union*. See also Compston (2006), *King Trends and the Future of Public Policy*. On the interface between law and politics, especially in those countries operating constitutional courts, see Stone Sweet (2000), *Governing with Judges*, and Sadurski (2005), *Rights Before Courts*. On law and the EU, see Stone Sweet (2004), *The Judicial Construction of Europe*, and Tridimas (2008), *The European Court of Justice and the EU Constitutional Order*.

On the web

confinder.richmond.edu – constitutions in English

www.concourts.net – constitutional courts

www.nispa.sk – CEE public administration and civil service

www.oecd.org – reports on governments and governance throughout Europe

international.lga.gov.uk – local and regional governments in Europe

curia.europa.eu – ECJ

www.palgrave.com

Companion Website

Visit the Companion Website to 'click and go'

www.palgrave.com/politics/bale

Discussion questions

1. Why do some analysts think it makes more sense to talk about governance rather than government? And why talk about multilevel governance?
2. Why does decentralization seem to be the trend across Europe? Does the trend mean that traditional distinctions between unitary and federal countries are now a little outdated and/or overstated?
3. What are new public management ideas and why aren't they uniformly popular in Europe?
4. The neutrality of the civil service is valued in some European states but less so in others: can you think of any advantages of a more politicized bureaucracy?
5. How do you think that Europeanization has affected the state machinery of European countries?
6. Some talk about national policy styles. How can we explain them? Why and to what extent do they persist?
7. Why do you think most European states have written constitutions and judicial review? Is it possible – or advisable – to do without them?
8. Given the record of Europe's constitutional courts, would you say judicial interference in politics has been either extensive or dangerous?
9. Has 'rule by judges' been made more or less likely by European integration?

Chapter 4

Governments and parliaments – a long way from equality

The head of state	101
Prime minister, cabinet and parliamentary government	102
Permutations of parliamentary government in multiparty systems	105
Minimal (connected) winning coalitions	105
Minority governments	106
Oversized or surplus majority coalitions	109
Government duration and stability	110
Dividing the spoils – 'portfolio allocation'	110
Governing	111
Parliaments – one house or two?	115
Parliaments – hiring and firing	117
Parliaments and the production of law	118
Parliaments – scrutiny and oversight	122
Parliament and government – the European level	124
Parliament, power and parties	125

Chapter 3 looked at governance, but, in addition to looking at policy-making, it concentrated mainly on the changing architecture of the state and the non-elected people who help to run it, be they civil servants or judges. Now, we turn to governments – the representative part of the executive. The elected government in almost all European countries must enjoy 'the confidence of parliament', normally expressed in a vote when it takes office – a vote it has to win or, at the very least, not lose. Europe's parliamentary governments are led by a prime minister and a group of colleagues, which political scientists call a **cabinet**. The fact that cabinet members very often sit in, and in all cases are responsible to, parliament blurs the distinction between the executive and the legislature that constitute two parts of the classical three-part 'separation of powers' that we outlined in Chapter 3. This clear division of labour is considered sacrosanct by some Americans, yet its blurring in Europe does not seem to exercise many Europeans. Conversely, Americans see nothing strange in the head of state and the head of government being one and the same person; namely, the President. However, nearly all European countries, more or less successfully, keep the two functions separate.

This chapter begins by looking at the largely attenuated role of the head of state in European countries. It then focuses on governments and, in particular, prime ministers and cabinets. Who and what are they made up of? Do they always command a majority in parliament? How long do they last? How is it decided who controls which ministry? What do they spend their time doing? Next, the chapter turns to Europe's parliaments. Most European legislatures have two chambers: we look at whether it makes much difference. The chapter then moves on to the basic functions of legislatures – hiring and firing governments, making law, and scrutiny and oversight. It explores whether and why some of Europe's parliaments are weak and some are stronger. The chapter ends by asking why, despite the fact that some parliaments are relatively powerful, they are rarely a match for governments.

Cabinet, which may be known in particular countries by a different name (for instance, in France it is called the Council of Ministers) is the final democratic decision-making body in a state. In Europe, the cabinet is made up of party politicians who are, more often than not, chosen from the ranks of MPs and are collectively (as well as individually) responsible to parliament.

The head of state

All European countries have a head of state. In the continent's monarchies (Belgium, the Netherlands, Denmark, Norway, Sweden, Spain and the UK), the head of state will be the king or queen. In republics, it will be a president, either elected directly by the people (as in Austria, Bulgaria, Cyprus, Finland, France, Ireland, Lithuania, Poland, Portugal, Romania, Slovakia and Slovenia) or 'indirectly' by an electoral college (as in Germany, Italy, Greece, Estonia and the Czech Republic) which is normally the parliament. The title of 'president', however, does not mean the post holder is, like the US President, both head of state and head of government. In Europe the two roles are normally kept separate. The only clear exceptions to the rule are Cyprus, the only fully presidential system in the EU-27 (see Ker-Lindsay, 2006), and France (see Box 4.1), although a number of other countries (among them Romania) can perhaps claim to be, like the latter, 'semi-presidential' (see Goetz, 2006: 78–81; and Wolczuk, 2007: 240–1). By far the bulk, then, of Europe's presidents, like its monarchs, do not wield executive power but are instead supposed to be above day-to-day politics. As such, they are trusted not just to represent the state diplomatically but also neutrally to carry out vital constitutional tasks such as the official appointment of a prime minister as head of government, the opening of parliament and the signing of its bills into law.

KEY POINT

By far the majority of Europe's heads of state do not wield or even share executive power, even if they are directly elected. This does not, however, mean they have no role or influence.

It is therefore tempting to write off Europe's presidents and monarchs as playing a merely legitimating and/or symbolic role. They are a reminder to people (and, more importantly, to elected governments) that, underneath the cut and thrust of inevitably partisan politics, something more steady and solid endures. And, like the flag and certain unique traditions, they can be rallied round by all sides in times of trouble. But heads of state – particularly when elected – do constitute an alternative locus of potentially countervailing power that can constrain the actions of governments seeking to push their mandates a little too far or, for instance, promote their

BOX 4.1

Monsieur le Président – France's executive head of state

Under France's 'semi-presidential' system (see Elgie, 1999), the president has executive (and especially emergency) powers that go well beyond those given to other heads of state in Europe, other than in Cyprus – the EU's only fully presidential regime. Not only is he head of the armed forces and the negotiator of international agreements, he can also dissolve parliament for fresh elections without consultation and can call a referendum on policy put forward by parliament or the government. Very often, he is also in charge of domestic policy – but not always. As in most other European countries, the French president appoints a prime minister who must command the confidence of the lower house of parliament, *l'Assemblée Nationale.* The prime minister and cabinet ministers are then collectively and individually responsible to parliament, which is what differentiates semi-presidential from full-blown presidential systems. This means that French presidents can exercise anything like full executive power only when the prime minister and cabinet are drawn from his or her own party, or (as is often the case in France) an alliance of parties. Since the mid-1980s there have been several periods (1986–8, 1993–5, 1997–2002) where this has not been the case, obliging the president to 'cohabit' with a prime minister and cabinet drawn from a party or parties on the other side of the political fence. While the tension and conflict arising from cohabitation has not always been as bad as it might have been, the situation certainly obliges the popularly elected president to take more of a back seat – though less so in foreign and defence policy and diplomacy than in domestic policy. Now that French presidential elections have been re-timed to take place every five years, and in all likelihood just before parliamentary elections, it could be that *cohabitation* becomes much rarer.

friends inappropriately. Italy's President is a case in point. In the early 1990s, for instance, Francesco Cossiga made it clear that, like the public, he thought little of some of his fellow politicians who were at the time mired in the scandal that brought about major electoral and party system change (see Chapter 5). In 1994, his successor, Oscar Luigi Scalfaro, appointed a non-party 'technocratic' administration which lasted just over a year instead of dissolving parliament at the request of Silvio Berlusconi (whose first attempt at being prime minister ended after just a few months), having earlier prevented Berlusconi from appointing his choice of Minister of Justice. Carlo Azeglio Ciampi, who came into post in 1999, provoked the outrage of Berlusconi (prime minister once again) by exercising his right, in December 2003, to veto a bill passed by parliament which many claimed gave Berlusconi *carte blanche* for a media monopoly in Italy (see Chapter 7). He was, however, constitutionally barred from vetoing the bill a second time when a slightly amended version was passed in April 2004.

This countervailing power is supposed to be used sparingly and for the good of the country. It is no bad thing that even elected governments are made to think twice once in a while: the right enjoyed by some presidents, for example, to refer controversial legislation to some kind of Supreme Court (see Chapter 3) probably does no harm if it is used sparingly, as it is in, say, Ireland. Frequent intervention of this or any other kind, however, leaves those heads of state who indulge in it open to the accusation that they are simply trying to undermine or obstruct an elected government with whom they (or their party) have policy disagreements. This happened early on in significant postcommunist countries like Poland, Hungary and the Czech Republic but, although they still have their moments, the situation has resolved itself (formally and conventionally at least) in favour of the parliamentary government: in Poland, for example, the 1997 constitution still allowed the president a veto over legislation, but it excludes the budget and can be overridden by a three-fifths majority in parliament; on the other hand, it is clear that left-wing presidents are more willing to use that veto if they are faced with a government of the right and vice versa (Zubek, 2006: 87).

In some countries, however, there is still sometimes debilitating (or at least headline-grabbing) conflict between prime ministers and presidents whose powers arguably continue to entitle them to an influence beyond that enjoyed by most of their European counterparts. Before he decided not to contest the 2007 election, for example, the Slovenian president Janez Drnovšek (who was prime minister from 1992 to 2002) had a few run-ins on both domestic and foreign policy with the government (see Fink-Hafner, 2007). His Portuguese counterpart, Aníbal Cavaco Silva (another former prime minister who served for ten years between 1985 and 1995) has also irritated not just the government (which as in Slovenia was on the opposite side of the left-right fence to the president) but also parliamentarians more generally by criticizing their chronic absenteeism (see Magone, 2007). To some this sort of conflict supports the idea that Portugal and Slovenia continue to merit the label 'semi-presidential' along with, say, France, Romania, and Lithuania (see Magalhães, 2007). Others might argue that, as in Poland, parliamentary government has become the convention, with presidential assertiveness depending more on the character, experience and political position of the incumbent than his or her formal rights, even if the latter do appear to be more than ceremonial.

Prime minister, cabinet and parliamentary government

In all European states except France and Cyprus, the person formally charged with the running of the country is clearly the prime minister. He or she is normally the leader of (or at least one of the leading figures in) a political party that has sufficient numerical strength in parliament to form a govern-

KEY POINT

Executive power in Europe is wielded by governments which are accountable to and rely on the support of parliament. They are led by cabinets comprised of ministers from one or more parties, many of whom retain their parliamentary seats. In theory, they are co-ordinated, if not controlled, by a prime minister whose power – which some argue is on the rise – varies between countries but also according to circumstances.

ment, whether on its own or (more usually) in combination with other parties. As long as the government he or she leads retains the confidence of parliament, and subject of course to how his or her party fares in general elections (and the inter-party bargaining that goes on after them in most countries), a prime minister can serve multiple terms: unlike most presidents, they are not time-limited.

Broadly speaking, the power of a prime minister depends on two things. The first is the power of the executive in general: this is facilitated, for example, by a strong central state and limited judicial oversight of government actions (see Chapter 3), as well as a weak parliament (see below). The second is his or her power within that executive itself. Helms (2005: 14) provides a helpful checklist of factors that contribute to this:

> the right to decide upon appointments and dismissals of members of the cabinet as well as on the major political appointments below the cabinet level; the right to determine the number and terms of reference of ministerial departments; a superior position within the cabinet; . . . the unconditional right to dissolve parliament (through an official proclamation of the head of state) without the need to secure the cabinet's approval[; being] the leader of the (dominant) governing party . . . [and governing] in single-party governments [rather] than in coalitions.

Not surprisingly, perhaps, the UK prime minister (strong executive, plenty of powers within that executive, and leading a single party majority government) can claim to be one of Europe's most powerful (see Helms, 2005: 12–13). Meanwhile, his Italian counterpart (relatively weak executive, few advantages within the executive, and leading a large coalition with an often insecure majority) is one of the continent's weakest. Other countries combine strong executives with limited prime ministerial power within the executive (e.g. the Netherlands) or vice versa (e.g. Germany), or they find that their strength on some dimensions is at least partially limited by running a minority government (which we go on to talk about below), albeit one that normally involves a single party (as in Sweden and Spain).

Because of their ultimate dependence on the confidence of parliament, it may seem at first glance that European prime ministers enjoy less autonomy than, say, an executive who is also head of state, such as the President of the US. In fact, this is far from being the case. First and foremost, unlike the US President, they can normally count on winning (or at least not losing) votes in the legislature. This is not only important domestically but at a European and global level, too. If a prime minister signs an international agreement at summit meetings – the increased frequency of which is said by some observers to contribute to a rise in prime ministerial prominence – his co-signatories can generally regard ratification (where it is required) as a done deal.

Back at home, prime ministers may well have a great deal of say in the appointment of their cabinet – the group of people who are tasked both with running particular ministries and co-ordinating government policy as a whole (see Blondel and Müller-Rommel, 1997). Moreover, the fact that they typically chair cabinet meetings means that they can wield considerable influence on what cabinet does and does not discuss, as well as over the conclusions and action points emerging from those discussions. Ultimately, too, most of them have the power to hire and fire cabinet colleagues, the exceptions being the Dutch and French prime ministers. The latter, though he can force ministers to resign, can also have ministers all but forced on him if operating under a president from the same party.

In general, prime ministers also have power-bases in their party and may be so popular with the general public that ministers dare not risk deposing such a figure, even if they feel that his or her treatment of them verges on the dictatorial. In fact, interviews with hundreds of ministers across Europe suggest that most of them accept prime ministerial authority and even prefer a strong Prime Minister, as long as he or she is also willing to listen to and involve his or her cabinet (Blondel *et al.*, 2007: 202). Even if this weren't the case, ministers would be at a comparative disadvantage because it is the prime minister, by dint of his or her co-ordinating function, who knows – inasmuch as any one person can know – what is going on across the whole range of government activity. They, on the other hand, may well be reluctant to intervene in the business of fellow ministers (unless of course it directly affects their own portfolio) for fear of getting a taste of their own medicine at a later date. This does not necessarily allow the prime minister to interfere as much as he or she might like to in the business of the ministry. Indeed, in Germany, for instance, there are strict conventions precluding such interference, notwithstanding an equally powerful convention (also included in Germany's, constitution, the *Grundgesetz* or 'Basic Law') concerning the Chancellor's right to set the overall direction of government policy. But the prime minister's overview does allow him or her to play one minister (or set of ministers) off against another. His or her prominence in the media may also be a source of power, and is one more thing that leads some to argue that European countries are undergoing what they call 'presidentialization' (see Poguntke and Webb, 2004) or, at the very least, witnessing a strengthening (see Hennessy, 2005 on the UK case) of the position of the prime minister relative to his cabinet colleagues. This represents not so much presidentialization as a move towards what some comparativists would call a 'centralized-prime ministerial core executive' and away from the 'centralized-cabinet' model or (in cases where ministers have considerable independence from their colleagues) the 'decentralized-ministerial' model (see Goetz, 2006, for more detail on this schema).

Notwithstanding all this (and to a much greater extent than is the case with an executive president), a European prime minister must also engage in collective decision-making with his or her cabinet – even if this often takes place outside and prior to the cabinet formal meeting which is then used simply to formalize decisions. Ultimately, he or she cannot function (or, indeed, continue in office) without its collective consent to his or her being *primus inter pares* or 'first among equals'. Inasmuch as it exists in its own right, then, 'prime ministerial power' is constrained not just by contingencies of time and chance and personality, but the multiple and mutual dependencies between the prime minister and his or her cabinet.

This is not to say, of course, that the extent of this interdependence is the same in all European countries (see King, 1994). And it clearly varies according to political circumstances: for example, in Poland 'the strength of prime ministerial leadership has been chiefly determined by political and personal factors, such as party standing, the nature of parliamentary support, the presence of important leaders outside the cabinet, personal style and the popularity of government policies' rather than the Prime Minister's relatively strong formal powers over his cabinet ministers (Zubek, 2006: 96). For instance, a prime minister trying to hold together a potentially fissiparous coalition of different parties will probably be less powerful than a textbook account suggests. At the very least, he or she will need to rely not so much on constitutional-cum-administrative means of co-ordinating his or her cabinet as on party-to-party relationships and mechanisms that are supplementary to formal processes.

That said, formal (or at least conventional) powers, accumulated over time and varying between countries, cannot be discounted. The UK prime minister, presiding over a single-party government and armed with the traditional prerogatives of the Crown, is more powerful, for instance, than his or her Dutch counterpart. This is because the latter is hemmed in by both a closely worded coalition agreement with other parties and a tradition of ministerial equality. On the other hand, even the most powerful UK prime ministers of recent years have had to defer to their finance minister. Indeed, in most European countries – west and east (see Blondel *et al.*, 2007: 176) – the latter is especially powerful: his (and it is almost always his) resignation would give markets and voters cause for alarm, while inside government the frequent contact his ministry has with all other departments gives him not only control and co-ordination capacities that rival those of his 'boss' but also a similarly bird's eye view of the work of the government as a whole.

The relative lack of personal autonomy enjoyed by the prime minister of a European country, however, has its upsides. Compared to, say, a US President whose hold over the legislature might be tenuous or even non-existent, the prime minister and the cabinet of a European country can generally feel confident that their decisions will, where necessary, be translated into legislation. European governments are, above all, party and parliamentary governments. The political face of the executive more or less accurately reflects the balance of power between the parties elected into the legislature and will often (though not always) be a multiparty coalition. The ministers who make up the cabinet formed from

BOX 4.2

The Netherlands' non-parliamentary executive

In the majority of European countries, ministers are also parliamentarians, though in only a few (the UK and Ireland are good examples) do they, in effect, have to be. The Netherlands (like France, Romania, Slovakia, Slovenia, Sweden and Norway) is more unusual in the sense that, there, members of the *Tweede Kamer* are constitutionally obliged to give up their seats once they become ministers. Their place is taken by substitutes from their own party so as to maintain the balance of party power in parliament. They can still appear in parliament to answer questions – and do so much more frequently than their cabinet counterparts in the US, for example. Interestingly, though, this formally enhanced separation between executive and legislature seems to do little to increase the willingness of the latter to stand up to the former: the *Tweede Kamer* is not seen as one of Europe's more assertive legislatures.

that coalition might or might not be MPs (Box 4.2). But they are there first and foremost because they represent a political party whose presence in the government is required in order to secure an administration able to command – at least for the time being and on crucial pieces of legislation (such as budgetary matters) – what is routinely referred to as 'the confidence' of parliament. Although confidence is understood by most people in, say, the UK to necessitate a stable majority of the MPs in parliament, this is by no means always the case.

Permutations of parliamentary government in multiparty systems

Many European governments do indeed command such majorities, some even when they are made up of just one party, although this is unusual outside the UK, Malta and Greece (see Figure 4.1). But, as

Figure 4.1 Single-party majority government – Greece, 2007

KKE	SYRIZA	PASOK	ND[1]	LAOS
Communist	Left	Soc. Dem.	Conservative	Populist radical right
22	14	102	152[2]	10

Notes: 1. Shading indicates government.
2. Seats required for overall majority = 151.

Table 4.1 shows, a significant number qualify as minority governments, i.e. administrations made up of one or more parties which together control less than half (plus one) of the seats in parliament. Such a prospect would be anathema in some countries, inside as well as outside Europe. But in others it is a far from frightening prospect. To understand why, we need to look a little deeper into the process of government formation.

Minimal (connected) winning coalitions

Few political scientists, even when conducting thought experiments, think of democratic politicians as purely 'office-seekers', interested in power either for its own sake or because of the personal profile, wealth, comfort and travel opportunities it can bring them. However reluctant the fashionably cynical among us might be to acknowledge it, the fact is that most people prepared to represent a political party are also 'policy-seekers'. They want to see some real progress (however limited) made toward realizing their vision of the good society. Even if we forget all the other aspects that might be

KEY POINT

The majority of European governments are coalitions between two or more parties. Most command a majority in parliament – sometimes a much bigger one than they actually need. A surprising number, however, are minority administrations. Which type of government forms is partly a product of parliamentary arithmetic but also of institutionally influenced cultural norms.

Table 4.1 Which type of government occurs most often in which country, 1945–2007?

	Percentage of postwar administrations that were:			
	Single-party majority	**Minimal winning coalition**	**Minority government**	**Oversized coalition**
Europe, 1945–2003	13	33	28	26
	UK[2] 100[1]	Germany 70	Sweden 70	France 70
		Czech Republic 60		Italy 60
		Poland 60		Netherlands[3] 50
		Spain 60		
		Netherlands[3] 50		
Europe, end 2006	14	45	24	27

Notes: 1. Figures for countries rounded to the nearest 10 per cent.
2. Note that the UK had one very brief single-party minority government in the 1970s.
3. The Netherlands appears twice because it has had almost as many minimal winning as oversized coalitions.

Source: Calculated from Gallagher *et al.*, (2006) and Bale and van Biezen (2007).

involved (from the psychology of bargaining to the personal relationships between party leaders), this dual motivation is enough to ensure that government formation is very rarely simply a matter of putting together what political scientists call a minimal winning coalition. True, around one in three governments in postwar western Europe have been **minimal winning coalitions**, while only around one in ten have been single-party majorities. But most of these coalitions have also been what political scientists call **minimal connected winning coalitions** (see Figure 4.2 for an example).

> A **minimal winning coalition** is a government made up of parties that control as near to just over half the seats in parliament as they can manage in order to combine their need to win confidence votes with their desire to have to share ministerial portfolios between as few claimants as possible.

Given that in most countries such a coalition would be theoretically, and often practically, possible, how then do we account for the fact that so many parties in Europe hold office, either singly or together, as **minority governments**? In fact, the answer is quite simple: they do it because they can.

Minority governments

In some countries minority government is difficult, if not impossible. These are countries that operate

> **Minimal connected winning coalitions** are made up of parties with at least something in common ideologically, even if governing together means having more parliamentary seats than would be strictly necessary and/or could be formed by doing deals with less like-minded parties (Figure 4.2).

> A **minority government** is made up of a party or parties whose MPs do not constitute a majority in parliament but which, nevertheless, is able to win – or at least, not lose – the votes of confidence that are crucial to taking office and/or staying there.

what political scientists call 'positive parliamentarism'. This refers to the fact that their governments have to gain at least a plurality (and sometimes a majority) of MPs' votes before they are allowed to take office – something that is normally tested in what is called an 'investiture vote' on a potential government's policy programme and cabinet nominations. Examples include Germany, where minority government is made less likely still by a rule that insists that no government can be defeated on a vote of no confidence once it has been allowed to form unless the majority voting against it is ready to replace it immediately with another government. Other examples of countries insisting on investiture votes include Belgium, Ireland and Italy. So, too, do Poland and Spain which, like Germany, have a 'constructive' vote of confidence, where a successor government has to be ready to take over before one can be called. But Spain also reminds us that 'politics' can often trump 'institutions': after the 2004 general election, the social democratic PSOE managed, in spite of the rules and conventions, to construct a minority government!

Other European countries, however, are characterized as operating 'negative parliamentarism'. Governments do not need to undergo an investiture vote or, if they do (Sweden, where the prime minister rather than the government has to step up to the plate, is an example), they are not obliged to win the vote, merely not to lose it. In other words, they can survive as long as those voting against them do not win over half the MPs to their cause. Likewise, the government has to be defeated rather than actually win on motions of no confidence. This makes it much easier for minority governments to form and to stay in power once they have formed. It therefore comes as little surprise that a list of countries operating negative parliamentarianism includes (as well as Finland, Portugal and the UK), countries such as Sweden, Norway, and Denmark, where minority government has, since the 1970s, become the norm.

These countries are all the more likely to experience minority government because elections, historically anyway, have often produced what political scientists refer to as 'strong' parties. These may well be the largest party in the parliament. Moreover, they are 'pivotal' in the sense that any minimal connected winning coalition would have to include them, and would, if you filled all the seats in parliament in left–right order, have one of its MPs occupying the middle seat (and therefore known in the jargon as the 'median legislator'). Pivotal parties are always at an advantage, even if they are not large: for example, the liberal FDP in Germany managed to turn its position midway between the Social Democrats and the Christian Democrats into almost thirty-one years of government in the forty-nine years between 1949 and 1998. But when a pivotal party is also parliament's largest, it is often in a great position to run a minority government. This is particularly the case when, as in Scandinavia, parties on their immediate flank (say, ex-communist or green parties in the case of the social democrats, or a far-right or zealous market-liberal party in the case of the conservatives) would not dream of teaming up in government with parties on the other side of the left–right divide or bloc. Unless these smaller, less mainstream parties are willing to increase what political scientists refer to as their 'walkaway value' by, say, threatening to support the other side or precipitate a new election, they become, in effect, 'captive parties', whose support (or, at least, abstention) in confidence motions can be pretty much guaranteed (see Figure 4.3).

In any case, life as what political scientists refer to as a 'support party' rather than a coalition partner might suit all concerned. This is especially the case if it involves some kind of deal – an understanding (possibly written and public) that may fall short of a full-blown coalition agreement but provides some promises on policy and consultation. This 'contract

Figure 4.2 A minimal connected winning coalition – Hungary, 2006[2]

MSZP[1]	SZDSZ	MDF	KDNP	FIDESZ	Others
Soc. Dem.	Liberal	Christian Dem.	Christian Dem.	Conservative	Ind.
190	20	11	10	154	1

Notes: 1. Shading indicates government.
2. Seats required for overall majority = 194.

Figure 4.3 A minority government – Denmark, 2007[2]

EL	SF	SD	RV	V[1]	KF	DF	Others
Left	Left	Soc. Dem.	Soc.Lib	Conservative	Christian Dem.	Populist radical right	Various
4	23	45	9	46	18	25	9

Notes: 1. Shading indicates government.
2. Seats required for overall majority = 90.

parliamentarism' (see Bale and Bergman, 2006) allows the party or parties in government not just to limit the extent to which they have to share power, but also to affect a 'respectable' distance from the parties that are helping them get into or stay in office. Those other parties might benefit, too. First, if they are relatively small and/or inexperienced full-blown membership of a coalition might thrust too much responsibility onto them before they are ready to accept it. Appointing ministers who are not really up to the job and subsequently have to resign can be very damaging, as the parties that made up the Polish government between 2005 and 2007 discovered – so much so, indeed, that two of the three lost all their MPs at the subsequent election. Not entering the government, on the other hand, but simply providing support, might have allowed them to go into the next election combining a claim to be contributing to political stability with a claim not to be responsible for all those things the government did that voters disliked. That election, or future elections, might have delivered them more seats by which time they would not only be more experienced but also better able to drive a hard bargain with a potential coalition partner. These agreements have occurred in the Czech Republic, Sweden and in Lithuania, where in 2006 a minority coalition took office by securing the agreement of a significant 'opposition' party in return for promises on policy and posts in parliament (see Krupavicius, 2007).

There is another reason why minority governments are more common than we might first suppose, and more common in some countries than in others (see Strøm, 1990). It is that in some systems being 'in opposition' is not nearly so thankless a task as it is in others, notably the UK. As we go on to show, some parliaments – particularly those with strong committee systems – offer considerably more scope for politicians whose parties are not in the government to influence policy and legislation. Again, it is the Scandinavian countries that experience frequent minority government where this so-called 'policy influence differential' between government and opposition is smallest. Finally, it is probably also the case that once a country has experienced minority government on a number of occasions and has lived perfectly well to tell the tale, it is more likely to embrace the possibility in the future. This does not mean it will never experience majority government, just that it will not be the default setting. For example, the centre-right coalition that took office in Sweden in 2006 was the first majority administration in that country for twenty-five years.

In short, the tendency toward minority or majority government has to be seen as cultural, as well as mathematical. There are few institutional barriers to minority government in the Netherlands, for instance. Even though the government has to get parliament to approve the often very detailed policy agreement the coalition parties spend months negotiating, there is no formal investiture vote, for example. Yet minority government continues to be almost unthinkable to the Dutch – possibly a hangover from the historical need to form governments that were sufficiently broad-based to include representatives of both the Protestant and Catholic churches that traditionally were so important to people's identity. Hungary, likewise, just doesn't seem to 'do' minority government: unlike any other country in Central and Eastern Europe, all its governments in the postcommunist period have commanded majorities. Conversely, and rather uniquely in a PR system, Spain's two main political parties seem to be so wedded to the idea of single-party government that, if it also means minority government, then so be it. This almost certainly has something to do with not wanting to court accusations that they are 'selling out' the unity of Spain to the regional parties with which they would have to coalesce in order to form a majority administration.

Cultural 'hangovers' and cultural realities also help to explain a tendency in some countries toward the last type of parliamentary government, **oversized** or **surplus majority coalitions.**

Oversized or **surplus majority coalitions** are governments that contain more parties than are needed to command a majority in parliament, to the extent that if one (or possibly more than one) party were to leave the government, it might still control over half the seats in the legislature.

Oversized or surplus majority coalitions

The traditional home of oversized or surplus majority coalitions in Europe is Finland. Because of its delicate proximity to the old Soviet Union, the country got used to putting a premium on national unity, on consensus and on including the left so as not to anger its bigger neighbour. So entrenched was the mindset that, until 2000, legislation that in most countries would have required only a simple majority in parliament required two-thirds of MPs to vote for it. In Italy, too, there were institutional reasons for oversized coalitions. Until parliament stopped voting – at least, routinely – by secret ballot, governments needed a stockpile of extra votes because they could not trust enough of their highly factionalized MPs to toe the party line! The tradition of including more parties than a coalition really needs also built up over decades during which the main aim of most parties was to stand together in order to prevent the Communist Party sharing power. Nowadays, it is reinforced by an electoral system that encourages parties into 'pre-electoral' pacts with each other. These occur in many countries (see Golder, 2005): Norway in 2005 and Sweden in 2006 provide a left-wing and a right-wing example.

Figure 4.4 An oversized or surplus majority government – France, 2007[2]

PCF	Verts	PS	UMP[1]	UDF	Other
Left	Green	Soc. Dem.	Conservative	Liberal	Various
15	4	186	313	22	37

Notes: 1. Shading indicates government.
2. Seats required for overall majority = 289.

They do not necessarily result in an oversized coalition, but they might well do so: pacts are generally honoured and the winning combination of parties will form a government even if it is composed of more parties than, strictly speaking, are needed, as was the case in France in 2007 (see Figure 4.4).

None of this is to suggest, however, that such governments are impossible, or even unlikely, in other countries. In the ten former communist countries now in the EU, for instance, oversized majority governments are almost as common as minimal winning coalitions. Under certain circumstances surplus majorities can turn out to be the best, or even the only, option (see Volden and Carrubba, 2004). A case in point is Belgium. There, the contemporary need to ensure a balance of parties from both the Dutch- and French-speaking communities may make oversized coalitions increasingly necessary. But other classic 'institutional' reasons also come into play. The federalization of the country we explored in Chapter 2 requires two-thirds of MPs' votes because it entails changes to the constitution. This reminds us that a country's 'preferred solution' to government formation can change over time as institutions and cultures change. The Netherlands is a case in point. True, it still prefers majority governments, but as the differences have blurred between religious and ideological groups – differences that traditionally encouraged broad-based coalitions – the country has moved from preferring oversized to

Figure 4.5 A 'grand coalition' – Germany 2005[2]

Die Linke	Die Grune	SPD[1]	CDU-CSU	FDP
Left	Green	Soc. Dem.	Christian Dem.	Market liberal
54	51	222	226	61

Notes: 1. Shading indicates government.
2. Seats required for overall majority = 308.

minimal winning coalitions: prior to 1975, the latter made up only one fifth of postwar Dutch governments; after 1975, over two thirds (see Keman, 2002a: 230). But, ultimately, preferred or conventional options are trumped by a combination of mathematics and ideological incompatability. The German election of 2005, for example, like the Dutch and the Austrian contests of 2006, produced a 'grand coalition' between the SPD and the Christian Democratic CDU–CSU which neither party really wanted but was inevitable once it became clear that other combinations could not work (see Figure 4.5)

Government duration and stability

Much of the fear of minority government in countries with a more or less institutionalized preference for majorities results from the conviction that it is somehow less stable. In fact, this does turn out to be the case, but with important qualifications. A useful rule of thumb is that single-party majority governments last longest, generally one year more than minimal winning coalitions and, in both western and Central and Eastern Europe, twice as long as minority governments. Also important, however, is the ideological affinity or 'connectedness' of the various parties that go to make up a government. A government composed of those who are politically close will be more stable than one which is not. Nor, of course, should we forget the influence of institutional rules. For instance, the rules we have already mentioned on votes of no confidence are bound to make a difference. Governments will often last longer where these are hard to lose or (as in Germany, Spain and Poland with their 'constructive' confidence votes) hard to stage in the first place. On the other hand, political culture or system traditions are also important. In western Europe, for example, minority governments in Sweden and Norway last longer than minority governments in Italy or Belgium. In Eastern and Central Europe, governments in the Czech Republic and Hungary last longer than most of their western counterparts, but governments in Latvia, Lithuania, Romania and Poland are notoriously short-lived (Blondel *et al.*, 2007: 49). Also important is the existence or absence of comprehensive and more-or-less binding coalition agreements. In some countries (for example, the Netherlands) these work well. In others where they are uncommon (such as Italy) they might actually undermine stability by removing the flexibility that particular system seems to demand. The new democracies of East and Central Europe have, of course, had less time to develop traditions, but it is already apparent that some (like Hungary) tend toward stability whereas others (like Poland) do not (see Nikolenyi, 2004).

KEY POINT

Multiparty systems do not necessarily produce unstable, short-lived governments. In fact, their duration and stability varies considerably – and not just according to type of government (majority or minority). Some countries routinely suffer from instability; some rarely, if ever, do so.

Another qualification is that the 'durability' of European governments to some extent depends on the number of parties that actually make up (or potentially could make up) a coalition. A parliament with a large number of small parties presenting each other (and larger parties) with multiple options can mean that relatively minor shocks caused by policy or personality conflicts are enough to precipitate a collapse of the government. This is especially the case when such a collapse does not necessarily entail fresh elections. All this holds true for Italy, and explains in part why it has 'enjoyed' so many more governments than other European countries – a habit it has found hard to shake. On the other hand, Italy's impressive postwar economic performance suggests there is no easy relationship between apparent 'instability' and poor (or at least socio-economically unsuccessful) government!

Dividing the spoils – 'portfolio allocation'

Putting together a coalition, of course, entails coming to some agreement both on policies and on the division of ministerial rewards. 'Who gets what, when and how?' is one of the classic political questions, and no more so than when it comes to what

KEY POINT

Which party gets which ministry partly depends on their preferences. But the number of ministries each party in a coalition gets normally equates to the strength of parliamentary support it can contribute relative to its partners in government – although sometimes those parties that are absolutely necessary to the formation of that government are given a disproportionate share of portfolios.

political scientists call 'portfolio allocation' – deciding which party gets which ministries. Except in the case of single-party governments, which in Europe tend to be the exception rather than the rule, this happens in two stages. First, the parties haggle over which ministries and departments they will occupy in the coalition cabinet. Next, they decide who in the party will take up the portfolios they manage to get. Actually, of course, the two stages are not quite so separate: which ministries a party wants may well be conditioned in part by the need to accommodate particular politicians. Indeed, sometimes the size of the cabinet will be increased in order to make a deal easier, although over time, it should be said, the size of cabinets appears to be decreasing marginally – possibly in response to the decline of nationalized industries and enthusiasm for bigger ministries that can cut across ancient and unhelpful departmental divisions (see Chapter 4; see also Peters, 2007: 242).

In theory, there are basically two methods governing the first stage of portfolio allocation: according to *bargaining strength* or according to some kind of rule of *proportionality*. In the first instance, parties that are part of the coalition can use their importance to that coalition as leverage with which to gain the highest number of seats around the cabinet table as possible – even if this number is disproportionate to the number of MPs they bring to the government benches. The other way is simply to give each party in the coalition the number of cabinet places that best reflects the proportion of MPs with which it provides the coalition. For instance, a party which provides 30 per cent of the MPs on the government benches should be entitled to claim around a third of the cabinet positions.

In the real world, both these systems of allocation operate, but other factors come into play as well. In Central and Eastern Europe, for instance, it seems clear that other parties are biased against former communist parties, even though they now claim to have transformed themselves into social democratic parties (see Chapter 5). The latter often participate in coalitions nowadays, but often with fewer seats around the cabinet table than they might expect (see Druckman and Roberts, 2007). And, right across Europe, it is often the case that certain parties have certain favourite ministries. For example, a party representing agricultural interests might ask for, and almost always get, the agriculture portfolio. Likewise, social democrats tend to want health and social security, and greens the environment. This risks sclerosis, as the party in control has little incentive for fresh thinking. On the other hand, it does avoid damaging policy swings and can give the party a chance to make a difference. This is not something that seems to be that easy (as we go on to explore in much more detail in Chapter 9). Yet there does seem to be some link between which particular party in a coalition controls a particular ministry and the policy direction of that ministry. Political scientists Ian Budge and Hans Keman (1990) looked at labour and finance ministries and found, for instance, that they tended to pursue policies to avoid unemployment more strongly when they were controlled by social democrats rather than conservatives, who in turn were more interested in reducing the role of the state.

Governing

The formation of a government via the naming of a cabinet and the swearing-in of ministers to whom particular portfolios have been awarded is, of course, merely 'the end of the beginning'. Most politicians in Europe, even the most mainstream

KEY POINT

Being a cabinet minister involves balancing the goals of the party with the constraints imposed by other ministers, who may be from other parties, and the existing policies of one's department, as well as taking into account ongoing engagement with EU partners. It also involves both collective and individual responsibility.

COUNTRY PROFILE

United Kingdom (UK)

Area: 241,600 km² (5.8% of EU-27)	
Population: 60.4 million (13.3% of EU-27)	
Religious heritage: Mainly Protestant	
GDP (2006): €1,910 billion (16.5% of EU-27)	
GDP *per capita* as percentage of EU-27 average (2006): 119	
Female representation in parliament and cabinet (end 2007): 20% and 23%	
Joined EU: 1973	
Top 3 cities: London (capital) (7.5 million), Birmingham (1.0 million), Glasgow (0.6 million).	

History: The United Kingdom of Great Britain (England, Wales and Scotland) and Northern Ireland took some time to assume its present shape (Box 1). Wales was all but assimilated into England in the 1540s. But the union of the two with the kingdom of Scotland, long an ally of France, was not achieved until 1707. A seventeenth-century Civil War established the supremacy of parliament over the crown. By then, after centuries of religious dispute that began in the sixteenth century when the English king broke with the Roman Catholic church, Britain was a largely Protestant country.

Across the sea, however, the island of Ireland, which Britain had conquered but found hard to subdue, was predominantly Catholic. There was, however, a Protestant minority in the north – one deliberately transplanted there (mostly from Scotland) in order to strengthen colonial power. When, in the wake of the First World War, Ireland began to regain its independence, this minority rejected a place in what (in 1948) finally became the sovereign Irish Republic, remaining part of the UK. By the beginning of the twentieth century, Britain had become the world's greatest commercial and imperial power, using the wealth generated by its pioneering role in the Industrial Revolution to establish control of huge swathes of the Indian subcontinent and Africa.

This imperial expansion helped put the country on a collision course with Germany. Although the ensuing First World War resulted in a British (and French) victory, it proved a big drain on the country's resources, just as its other ally, the US, began to supersede it economically. The Second World War (1939–45), from which Britain also emerged victorious, confirmed this relative decline, as did its inexorable surrender of its overseas empire. On the domestic front, however, the aftermath of the war saw the building by a Labour government of a comprehensive welfare state. Since then, power has alternated between Labour, on the centre-left, and the Conservatives, on the centre-right, with the former, under Tony Blair, winning a landslide victory in 1997 after eighteen years out of office. Blair has finally handed over to his long term collaborator and rival, Gordon Brown, who faces a seemingly rejuvenated opposition and a less benign economic environment.

Economy and society: The UK economy underwent severe restructuring under the free market policies of Conservative Prime Minister Margaret Thatcher during the 1980s, and has undergone something of a renaissance in recent years. The service sector – particularly finance – is especially strong. As a result, the country's 60 million people – around 6.5 per cent of whom came (or their parents or grandparents came) as immigrants from the Caribbean and the Indian subcontinent – enjoy a *per capita* annual income of about 20 per cent above the EU average. The south-east of the country, especially around London, however, is notably better off than some of the more peripheral regions. Tackling that disparity plus per-

WHAT'S IN AN ANTHEM?

No one is quite sure where the tune of the turgidly monarchical *God Save the Queen* came from, although the words date from the eighteenth century. Indeed, the anthem was probably the first to be consciously adopted as such. The first verse conveys the hope that Her Majesty will be around as long as possible and that the deity will ensure she is 'victorious, happy and glorious'. The less-often sung second verse is slightly less unctuous: said deity, it hopes, will see not only to the scattering of enemies but will also 'confound their politics' and even 'frustrate their knavish tricks'. It is not just Scotland and Wales that prefer to use a different anthem at sporting events: the England cricket team has experimented with *Jerusalem* – a hymn to 'England's green and pleasant land.'

sistent inequality (and child poverty) is proving tricky.

Governance: The UK employs not a PR but a 'first-past-the-post' (FPP) electoral system to elect MPs to its Westminster parliament. This almost always results in single-party majority governments and makes things difficult for the third largest party, the Liberal Democrats. It does, however, afford representation to nationalist parties from Northern Ireland, Scotland and Wales. As a result of the Labour government's pursuit of decentralization and 'devolution', these components of the UK now have their own legislatures, elected under more proportional systems. The UK government pioneered the privatization of formerly state-owned utilities. And it still likes to think of itself as at the cutting edge of new approaches to governance, contracting out civil service work to public agencies and promoting public finance initiatives, which use private sector money to build facilities that are then leased back by the public sector.

Foreign policy: The UK proved sceptical about European integration until the late 1950s, when it realized its days as a world power were numbered and that its economy was stagnating. It finally joined what was then the EEC (now the EU) in 1973. It retains its reputation as 'an awkward partner', and has chosen, so far, not to adopt the euro. EU membership is not seen as contradicting either the country's continuation of its self-styled 'special relationship' with the US (with which it retains close defence, intelligence and trade links) nor its contacts with its former colonies via the British Commonwealth. The special relationship has come under fire following the invasion of Iraq, with politicians and commentators on both left and right calling for a healthier distance with Washington. But continued concerns over terrorism, Iran's nuclear ambitions and a newly resurgent Russia suggest links will remain close.

A KEY CONTEMPORARY CHALLENGE

DEVOLUTION AND PARLIAMENTARY VOTING

The UK's devolved parliaments and assemblies – especially in Scotland – have, under devolution, been granted power over areas that used to be the preserve of 'Westminster'. But MPs representing Scottish, Welsh and Northern Irish constituencies still attend the UK parliament and can vote on issues that affect England – issues that are sometimes controversial, such as health service reform and the financing of higher education. Some English MPs are also raising the question of why their constituents (each of whom gets around €7k of public spending compared with €8.5k in Scotland) are subsidizing health and education provision that is clearly much more generous than they themselves enjoy, with free prescriptions being an obvious case in point. There is a partisan divide on the issue because the Conservatives have almost no MPs outside England, whereas the Labour benches (and cabinet) are full of Welsh and Scottish MPs. An obvious solution – a separate English parliament – would clearly favour the Conservatives, but they are reluctant to pursue it since they believe, like Labour, that it could hasten the break-up of the UK that they regard it as their duty to protect. Instead, the Conservatives look to be moving to a demand for 'English votes on English laws' – effectively preventing MPs sitting for constituencies outside England from voting on legislation that affects only the latter. The problem is that this would not only prevent various ministers voting for their own legislation, it would also render meaningless the government majorities on which British parliamentary democracy has come to rely, thereby creating what Labour has taken to calling 'constitutional anarchy'.

Contemporary challenges

- Fighting Islamist terrorism without alienating Muslim citizens
- Reconciling a situation in which Scottish, Welsh and Northern Irish parliamentarians can vote on legislation that affects the English when – because of devolution – the opposite does not necessarily apply (see box above)
- Freeing local government to decide (and raise funds for) its own priorities whilst ensuring that access to services does not become 'a postcode lottery'
- Meeting climate change targets in the face of seemingly insatiable consumption
- Providing sufficient housing and infrastructure to cope with migration and population growth.

Learning resources. A good all-round starting point is McCormick (2007), *Contemporary Britain*. Good textbooks include Moran (2005), *Politics and Governance in the UK* and the frequently updated Budge *et al.* (2007), *The New British Politics*. The latest in the series *Developments in British Politics* is always worth reading. Keep up to date with the news at http://news.bbc.co.uk/1/hi/uk/default.stm.

centrists, see themselves as having a particular job to do, above and beyond merely keeping the state ticking over. Normally, this involves the translation of policy into practice. More precisely, it involves ministers overseeing the drafting of legislation and the progress of civil servants in implementing the policies that have made it through the government formation process – the policies that are included in the coalition agreements that are becoming an increasingly common phenomenon in Europe (see Müller and Strøm, 2000). This, as we suggested in Chapter 3, has become more difficult. Most European states are no longer simply 'top-down' affairs although, as we also saw in Chapter 3, steps have been taken to tighten the hold of politicians over non-elected parts of the 'core executive'.

Ministers also have to meet with and take on board (or, at least, absorb) the views of pressure groups, particularly those on whom they might rely to some degree for the implementation of policy (see Chapter 8). In addition to interest groups and parties, another source of policy (and possible trouble) is the EU. As we noted in Chapter 2, ministers in some departments could spend two or three days a month consulting with their counterparts in the other member states. In these consultations, they are assisted both by their home departments and by their country's Permanent Representative in Brussels. This 'ambassador to the EU', along with his or her twenty-six colleagues on the intergovernmental committee routinely referred to as COREPER, works to achieve compromises that will protect and promote the 'national interest' and, quite frankly, ease the burden of work for ministers. Not everything can be 'fixed' beforehand, however. A trip to Brussels can often, therefore, involve ministers trying to get something done or, alternatively, trying to stop something happening. This might be at the behest of other departments, whose civil servants meet in interdepartmental committees with those of the department concerned, or it might come from pressure groups or the cabinet, or even, in Denmark, parliament (see Box 4.7). Ministers therefore play a vital linkage role between the national and the 'supranational'. Indeed, they are the embodiment of the blurring of the boundaries between them that is so important a part of contemporary European politics.

In Europe's parliamentary systems, ministers, even when they are not themselves MPs, also play a vital linkage role between citizens and the state by being individually answerable and, in most cases, collectively responsible to parliament. Being individually answerable means that they can, at least theoretically, be held to account for the actions of their department. This is vital if there is ultimately to be democratic control of the state, although not all countries follow Poland, for example, and allow parliament to officially vote 'no confidence' in an individual minister, thereby forcing him or her to resign. Being 'collectively responsible' means that ministers are expected to support government policy or else resign. This cabinet collective responsibility is also important in democratic terms because parliaments express their confidence (or at least their lack of confidence!) in the government as a whole. The fiction that ministers are all pulling in the same direction has therefore to be maintained, in order to preserve the political accountability of the executive in a system where the buck stops not with one individual (as it does in presidential systems), but with government as a whole.

This supposedly constitutionally necessary convention does not, in fact, hold everywhere. Belgium's cabinet ministers, for instance, are under no such obligation (Keman, 2002a: 229) and, notes one expert (Sanford, 2002: 165), their Polish counterparts certainly *feel* under no such obligation! Nor, of course, even where the convention has developed, does it preclude genuine and sometimes bitter disagreement within cabinet. Studies of cabinets across western and eastern Europe suggest that many governments (though not all governments, Sweden being an obvious exception) employ networks of cabinet committees to pre-cook and filter out issues different departments can agree on so as not to disrupt cabinet itself – although this technique cannot always prevent cabinet from becoming a court of last resort between disputatious ministers rather than a collegial and collective decision-making enterprise. But those same studies also show that cabinets themselves are mostly still meaningful forums: their deliberations actually change policy (Blondel and Müller-Rommel, 1997, 2001). The extent to which cabinets actually control ministers and prevent them from 'going native' (becoming more interested in protecting their departments than the interests of the government as a whole), however, is another matter (see Andeweg, 2000).

It is also one that feeds into another thorny issue – the extent to which cabinets made up of politicians from different parties, as is the norm in many countries, can actually work together. In fact, co-ordination often takes place outside the cabinet room itself. In an increasing number of countries, the formation process produces a written agreement which is used to bind the coalition partners (and their ministers) into a common programme: the most detailed study we have comes from the Netherlands, and suggests it is quite an effective technique (see Thomson, 2001). In a few countries, the cabinet as a whole is encouraged to 'bond' by spending time with each other (whether they like it or not!) at 'working lunches' and the like – this is famously the case in Norway, for instance.

More often, co-ordination involves not just ministers but other party political actors. Sometimes this kind of co-ordination goes on in so-called coalition committees. The three-way coalition that took over in Bulgaria in 2005 and saw the country safely into the EU in 2007 established a 'coalition council' of the chairmen of the parties concerned which helped smooth over disagreements between them (Spirova, 2007). But more often than not, it occurs informally. This might involve bilateral contacts by ministers or their political appointees to the civil service. In the case of disputes that are harder to resolve, it could involve troubleshooting by the prime minister and deputy prime minister, who are very often from different parties. But it might also involve meetings between party leaders, especially when, as occurs surprisingly often in Europe, those leaders do not actually play a formal role in government or even parliament (see Gibson and Harmel, 1998). In Belgium, for example, party chairmen meet frequently (often weekly) with 'their' ministers (see Keman, 2002a: 228) and thus exercise a kind of 'outside' influence on Cabinet that would be considered intolerable in a country such as the UK, for example.

Excessive ministerial autonomy (or 'departmentalitis') and intra-coalition co-ordination are not, however, the only problems facing the political part of a state's executive branch. Limited time is clearly a major – if largely overlooked – constraint. And a government's capacity to do what it wants to do may be constrained by events beyond its control such as war, terrorism, recession and opposition from important interest groups such as trade unions or business representatives, often backed by the media. One would also expect, on both a strict interpretation of the separation of powers doctrine and the assumption that they owe their very existence in most European countries to parliament, that governments would be constrained by the second 'branch of government', the legislature. Interestingly, however, the influence of Europe's parliaments over their executives – their governments – is widely dismissed as illusory. According to common wisdom, they are (or have over time been reduced to) talking shops and rubber stamps, while the prime minister and the cabinet call the shots. Indeed, the supposed 'decline of parliament' is often a given in media discussion. Academic contributions, however, question, first, the existence of some kind of golden age of parliamentary power and independence which has now passed and, second, the extent to which any decline has actually taken place (see, for example, Elgie and Stapleton, 2006). A comparative approach, which reveals significant variation in both the structure and the operation of parliaments around Europe, suggests a similarly nuanced picture.

Parliaments – one house or two?

In many European countries, as in the US, the legislature is 'bicameral', with an 'upper house' that sits in addition to a 'lower house': out of the fifteen 'older' democracies that constituted the EU before the accessions of 2004 and 2007, nine had parliaments made up of two houses – an arrangement traditionally favoured in particular by larger, as well as federal states. However, out of the twenty-seven countries now in the EU the majority (fourteen) are 'unicameral' – an arrangement traditionally

KEY POINT

Around half of all Europe's parliaments have just one chamber; the other half have two, although rarely is this 'upper house' – normally chosen on a different basis to the 'lower house' – as powerful as the latter. Hopefully, however, they improve the representativeness of the legislature and the quality of its legislative output.

favoured by smaller and unitary states (a definition that fits most of the EU's new joiners). Unicameral parliaments have only one chamber, although some (such as Norway) have developed ways of dividing this into what amounts to two chambers in order to scrutinize legislation better. In bicameral systems, the lower house (as in the sole chamber in unicameral systems) is filled by MPs or 'deputies' who are directly elected by all adults entitled to vote. Upper houses, on the other hand, are not always directly elected (see Table 4.2). A couple have appointed members, including the British 'House of Lords'. Many are composed of democratically chosen representatives from local, regional or, in federal countries, state-governments.

With the exception of Switzerland (where the upper house, the Council of States, has a veto that the lower house, the National Council, cannot overturn), Germany, Italy (see Boxes 4.3 and 4.4) and Romania, there is no doubt that in Europe's bicameral systems it is the lower house that is the more powerful, and therefore the focus of public atten-

Table 4.2 The upper house – who decides who sits there?

	Basis of upper house
Czech Rep.	Directly elected
France	Electoral colleges of mainly local politicians, and overseas territories
Germany	Delegates from state governments (*Länder*)
Italy	95 per cent directly elected on a regional basis; 5 per cent life-time appointments
Netherlands	Elected by provincial councils
Poland	Directly elected on a regional basis.
Spain	85 per cent directly elected; 15 per cent indirectly elected by regional authorities
Sweden	Sweden is unicameral: it has no upper house.
UK	80 per cent appointed for life; 15 per cent hereditary; 5 per cent church

BOX 4.3

The Italian *Senato* – powerful or pointless?

With the exception of a handful of senators-for-life, the vast bulk of the Italian *Senato* is directly elected to an upper house that has equal standing with the lower house, the *Camera dei Deputati*. Italy, therefore, would appear to have one of the most powerful second chambers anywhere in the world. But, as in Spain, because elections to the two houses take place simultaneously, the party complexion of each is remarkably similar. Consequently, there is far less of the partisan friction witnessed in Germany (see Box 4.4). This does not, however, prevent disagreements between the two chambers on particular pieces of legislation, not least because local and national interest groups lobby both assiduously. Because both houses have equal power, some bills can be batted back and forth between them for so long that they perish when new parliamentary elections are held. Given this tendency to delay legislation, Italians can be forgiven for wondering quite what the point of bicameralism is in their country. On the other hand, Italy's new electoral system (see Chapter 6) means the *Senato* is now elected on more of a regional basis, which might mean it takes on a more specific representative function. It also means that it may well contain a different balance of forces than the *Camera*, which is now guaranteed to provide a majority to whichever pre-electoral coalition wins the election – at least at the outset of the government it goes on to form. Both these developments could see the Italian upper house emerge as more of a genuine countervailing force. In January, 2008, Prime Minister Romano Prodi, in fact, saw his government collapse when he lost a senate vote of confidence. Perhaps he would agree with the French revolutionary philosopher and statesman, Sieyès, who famously observed that an upper house that agreed with the lower house was superfluous, while one that dissented was mischievous.

tion. In short, where bicameralism prevails in Europe, it is normally what political scientists label 'weak' as (opposed to 'strong') bicameralism. In most countries with two chambers, the power of upper houses lies primarily in their ability to amend and/or delay, rather than actually to block, bills passed by the lower house. However, in some countries even this power is very limited. This might be because the lower house has the ability to bring things decisively to a head, as in France, where the Senate can be overruled. Or it may be because the power is little used since the party composition of the upper house is so similar to that of the lower house, as in Spain. Despite this relative weakness, however, there seems to be no movement to dispense with them altogether in favour of unicameral systems: even in the Czech Republic, where debate about the need for such a body and its composition was initially so heated that it almost failed to get off the ground, people seem reconciled to its existence, if not exactly enthusiastic.

However, upper houses are not powerless. The power of delay is not necessarily to be sniffed at. Moreover, on proposed constitutional changes supported by the lower house, many of Europe's upper houses possess a power of veto. This makes sense given that their raison d'être – especially in federal systems – is often to protect the rights and interests of sub-national government. And even where such a role is denied them, one can argue that upper houses still, potentially at least, have a valuable role to play. For instance, they provide a forum that, because it is less of a focus for media attention, is somewhat less charged and therefore somewhat more conducive to clear-headed consideration of issues. The UK House of Lords, for example, might be ridiculed as a bastion of entrenched conservatism, but its European Union Committee is acknowledged as performing a useful role in scrutinizing EU legislation that will impact the UK.

Parliaments – hiring and firing

Generally, however, when most Europeans think of parliament, they think of the directly elected lower house. This is the place that not only passes laws, but makes and breaks – and in between hopefully scrutinizes – governments. As we have seen, running European countries rests on a party or a coalition of parties being able to command a majority in confidence and supply votes in parliament. Ultimately, then, parliaments are theoretically the most powerful branch of government. When it comes to the crunch, it is they who retain the right to hire and fire the executive, thereby translating the results of elections into a government and forcing that government to account to those whom electors elect, and perhaps the electors themselves. But how powerful does this make them in practice?

KEY POINT

Europe's governments require the support of their legislatures and, as such, can normally be dismissed by them. This power – easier to exercise in some countries than in others – is rarely used in practice but is almost certainly a constraint.

Hiring is indeed crucial, as we have suggested when looking at government formation. But it normally pits one party or collection of parties against another rather than the legislature as a whole against the executive. Moreover, once the task is complete, the power is essentially 'used up' until next time. Similarly, the power granted by the right to fire the executive lies more in the threat to use it than its actual use. The fact that it is a 'nuclear option' probably explains why, although the right of dismissal exists, it is surprisingly rarely used and few European governments are actually brought down by votes of no confidence. This is partly, of course, because some of them choose to jump before they are formally pushed. Others are sufficiently adaptable to avoid the kind of policies that would offend the MPs that originally supported their formation. Still others, when this cannot be done, are sufficiently prescient to have arranged alternative sources of support.

In a handful of cases, institutional rules make votes of no confidence, once a government has formed, even more unlikely. In the Czech Republic, for instance, for a government to form takes only the votes of a majority of the MPs in the chamber at the time the vote is held. But to remove a government it takes a majority of all MPs (i.e. 101 out of 200) whether or not they are all present. In Germany, Spain and Poland, as we have seen, they go even

BOX 4.4

The upper house with the upper hand? The German *Bundesrat*

Germany's upper house, the *Bundesrat*, is made up of sixty-eight members belonging to delegations from the governments of each of the Federal Republic's sixteen states (*Länder*), with delegations varying in strength from three to six members depending on the size of the state. These representatives of the *Länder* have quite a large role in the passing of federal (i.e. national) legislation. The *Bundesrat* has veto power over legislation impacting on states – which until recently meant that over half of all legislation had to be voted on and approved there. And even when a bill does not fall into this category, it is open to the *Bundesrat* to reject it. This obliges the lower house, the *Bundestag*, to produce a 'yes' vote as big as the *Bundesrat's* 'no' vote in order to overrule it. The extent to which this makes things awkward for the government depends, more than anything, on whether the party controlling it also controls the upper house. As in the US, this depends on it being able to win those state elections that take place in between federal elections. If the opposition win these (and they very often do as the government bears the brunt of 'mid-term blues'), the party composition of one or more states' delegations changes, causing the government to lose its control of the *Bundesrat*. When this happens, 'divided government' prevails and the upper house comes into its own. Perhaps through negotiation in the *Vermittlungsausschuß* (the mediation committee formed by representatives from both houses), the *Bundesrat* often obliges the government in the lower house to modify those aspects of its legislative programme that opposition parties do not support. It is this need to take account of the views of opposition parties that makes Germany's parliament (and perhaps its politics in general) so consensual. According to critics, though, it also makes radical reform practically impossible (see Chapter 9). Frustration on both sides led to the setting up in 2003 of a bicameral commission to look into modernizing the federal structure – a move that eventually resulted in a deal that saw the *Länder* get the right to determine more at local level (particularly on education) in return for a reduction in the proportion of bills (from 60 to 35 per cent) that could be blocked by the *Bundesrat*.

further: a government can be defeated only by a 'constructive' vote of no confidence, which demands that the opposition already has an alternative government ready to take over immediately. In many countries, a government defeat in the house can – although it does not always – lead to new elections that can come as a merciful release after a period of political crisis or legislative gridlock. But in Norway, where elections can be held only every four years, this option is unavailable. This makes motions of no confidence motions a less attractive way of 'solving' a supposedly intractable parliamentary problem. The fact that a government defeat on a motion of confidence can lead to fresh elections in other countries points to the fact that parliament's right to defeat the executive is, in any case, normally balanced by the executive's right to dissolve (or request the head of state to dissolve) parliament – a right that exists in all European democracies outside Norway, Switzerland and Finland. If, as an MP, your party is not likely to do well in a snap election, you are unlikely, however dissatisfied you are with the government, to stage a vote of no confidence and thereby risk cutting off your nose to spite your face.

Parliaments – the production of law

Parliament's other most important function is the making (or at least the production) of law – the consideration and passing of legislation. There is provision in most countries for so-called 'private members bills'. But by far the bulk of the proposals (and certainly the bulk of proposals that stand an earthly chance of actually ending up on the statute book) will come from governments. International Parliamentary Union (IPU) data from the 1990s showed not only that six out of ten bills originated in government (a figure rising to nine out of ten in

KEY POINT

Governments set the agenda on legislation and get most of what they want through. The pace of that legislation, and the extent to which it is modifiable by parliaments varies considerably. Some parliaments – notably those in 'consensus' systems – are stronger than others; namely, those that operate in more 'majoritarian' cultures. The committee system is a key variable.

countries like the UK, the Netherlands and Sweden), but also that over eight of ten of those bills made it on to the statute book. Moreover, although recent research suggests there are big differences in how long it takes for legislation to go through each parliament (see Box 4.5), these differences are generally due to inefficiencies in parliamentary process rather than government control. Most governments, especially those which control the agenda of the house, get their legislation through – particularly if it refers to a policy settled on in their coalition agreement (De Winter, 2004). Consequently, it is all too easy to buy into the caricature of European legislatures as merely 'rubber stamps' or 'talking shops' – or, worse, 'sausage machines' into which the executive shoves its bills, cranks the handle, makes mincemeat out of the opposition, and smiles as its statutes pop out at the other end. Without going too far the other way, it is fair to suggest that such metaphors disguise a good deal of variation, but once again it is patterned variation.

Broadly, one can divide parliaments in western Europe into two groups that correspond to the distinction between 'majoritarian' and 'consensus' democracies made by Dutch political scientist, Arend Lijphart (1999). In the majoritarian group, one would include the UK, and probably Spain, along with Ireland, Greece and France. In these countries, the government pursues its agenda with little regard for the input of other parties, which are more often than not clearly regarded as the opposition. This opposition knows that government is almost guaranteed to get its way. And anyway, it is likely to be sympathetic to the theory that its winning of the election gives it a mandate to do so. Therefore, opposition parties can do little more than offer the kind of criticism that (a) will allow them to say 'I told you so' at the next election, at which, hopefully, the mandate will pass to them; and (b) hopefully undermine the government's popularity in the meantime. It is unlikely to be able to use the upper house to block the government's programme because in majoritarian systems the lower house enjoys clear superiority. Parliament as a whole is an 'arena' rather than a truly 'transformative' institution – and one that reacts to, and can do little or

BOX 4.5

How long does law-making take?

In a comparative study of almost 600 bills across seventeen parliaments in Europe, Becker and Saalfeld (2004) found that having more parties in a coalition did not slow legislation down, even if they were ideologically quite far apart. By the time a bill is introduced, the partners in a coalition will normally have made the necessary compromises and, particularly if they operate with a majority that gives them the right to control the agenda of the house, can get their legislation through, although considerable time (an average of nearly 80 hours out of 128 hours) is lost in many countries by delays between the various stages – and it is this that accounts for the differences that are superficially so apparent (Table 4.3)

Table 4.3 Hours to pass a bill through parliament

Country	Hours
Sweden	101
Germany	127
17-country average	128
UK	219
Spain	228
Netherlands	378
Italy	620

They found that 75 per cent of bills passed, and that just under ten per cent of bills fail at each stage (pre-committee, committee and post committee). Interestingly, only 5 per cent of the bills that reached the second chamber (where one existed) failed.

BOX 4.6

France's feeble parliament

Most observers agree that the *Assemblée Nationale* is one of Europe's weakest legislatures. Its members do themselves no favours by often staying away in order to attend to the affairs of local government, in which many continue to hold elected office and have their main power-base. The government controls parliament's agenda. It can insist on it taking a yes/no 'package vote' on a bill in its unamended state. It has nothing to fear from committees which are unwieldy and oversized. And it has at its disposal a host of procedural techniques to overcome any residual power of delay. Parliament, constitutionally, can legislate only in certain prescribed areas outside of which government can issue what amount to decrees. The censure motion necessary to oust any government determined to insist on treating a particular bill as a matter of confidence is difficult to employ. Moreover, parliament is constitutionally unable to pass a non-governmental bill or amendment that would involve lowering state revenues or increasing expenditure.

Fortunately, France's constitutional court (see Chapter 3) has now made decree laws subject to much greater constraint. In addition, regulations can be amended by the Assembly. Theoretically, it also gets to subject all bills to committee scrutiny before the plenary session and now even gets to meet all year round, not just the six months initially allotted to it. But the picture painted is, nonetheless, one of weakness. This may, however, be mitigated if President Sarkozy decides to act on the recommendations of a Committee set up to look at the modernization and re-balancing of France's governing institutions and headed by former Prime Minister Édouard Balladur. Delivered in October 2007, they included curtailing the right to legislate by decree, giving parliament, as well as the government, the right to determine its own agenda, and granting it some power to approve presidential nominations.

nothing to stop or even seriously slow up government initiatives (see Box 4.6).

The same can be said of parliaments in consensus democracies like Germany, the Netherlands (and Belgium), Sweden (and other Scandinavian countries) and Italy, but not without some qualification. While they are still essentially 'reactive' (at least when compared to the US Congress) parliaments in these countries tend to feature more constructive criticism and operate at least sometimes in 'cross-party' rather than always 'inter-party' mode (King, 1976). These tendencies are, or have become, culturally ingrained, though they may be institutionally supported. At the macro-level, consensus democracies tend towards highly proportional electoral systems and multi-party politics that make coalition inevitable; they also tend to accord interest groups an important consultative role (see Chapter 9). At the micro-level, parliament's agenda might, for instance, require the unanimous (or near-unanimous) consent of all parties (as in Scandinavia, and the Germanic and low countries, as well as Spain and Italy) rather than being decided by the government majority (as in the United Kingdom, Ireland, France, Greece and Portugal) – something frequently used as an indicator of the overall power of parliament (see Figure 4.6). No doubt ministers who operate in a 'Westminster' system, where their government has all sorts of procedures it can resort to in order to curtail debate, would be horrified to learn that in countries like the Netherlands and Sweden such manipulation is virtually impossible.

Figure 4.6 European parliaments – the strong and the weak

Stronger parliament *(Sets own agenda; strong committee system)* →	**Weaker parliament** *(Government sets agenda; weak committees)*
1 Germany	6 Czech Rep.
2 Sweden	7 UK
3 Italy	8 Spain
4 Poland	9 France
5 Netherlands	

While, as some analysts are right to warn us, the differences between consensual and majoritarian democracies can be over-stated (see Arter, 2006), they are nonetheless significant when it comes to parliaments. And they are visual as well as rule-based. Some countries even have seating systems designed to take some of the heat out of the more adversarial aspects of parliamentary politics. Sweden, for example, makes its MPs sit in regional blocs rather than according to party, and many parliaments in Europe avoid the adversarial layout of the British House of Commons (see Andeweg and Mijzink's chapter in Döring, 1995, for the layout of European legislatures). Perhaps most important, however, for both the facilitation of cross-party activity and the overall power of parliament is the existence of powerful legislative committees. These are especially prevalent in Scandinavian parliaments (see Box 4.7), in Germany and in some of the newer democracies in Central and Eastern Europe, especially Poland. In many countries in those regions, such committees get to make amendments to (and in some cases redraft) bills before they are debated on the floor of the house by all interested MPs in what is known as 'plenary session'. In majoritarian systems, committees usually get to go over the bill only once it has received at least one, and possibly two, readings in plenary, by which time party positions have already hardened up and legislation is more 'set in stone'. Contrary to the position in their consensual counterparts, committee membership in these systems might not even be distributed according to each party's share of seats. In more consensual systems, proportionality is taken as given and (especially where there are minority governments) increases the chances of committees taking an independent line. As a result – and because what they do actually matters – committees in consensual systems are often quite conflictual (see Damgaard and Mattson, 2004). A very valuable table covering the composition, autonomy and powers of committees in west European parliaments provided by Mattson and Strøm (2004: 100–1) makes it clear, however, that such conflict does not undermine their importance compared with their counterparts in more majoritarian parliaments.

The parliaments of CEE are harder to locate in such a schema. At first, a combination of volatile party systems, arguments between presidents and

BOX 4.7

Power outside the plenary – Danish parliamentary committees

Although other Scandinavian parliaments – and Germany and Poland – boast influential committees, and although some Italian committees traditionally had the right of final assent on some minor legislation, experts agree that the Danish *Folketing* possesses Europe's most powerful parliamentary committees. It has twenty-four standing (i.e. permanent) committees, each with seventeen members, with membership roughly proportional to the party distribution of seats in parliament. Most committees cover the work of one particular ministry. When a minister proposes a bill, he or she can expect a flood of written questions by committee members and could well be asked to appear in person, too. Delay is not advisable because any bill that does not make it through all its stages in the parliamentary session in which it is introduced will have to start all over again. The committees' report on the bill outlines the parties' positions and amendments that they hope to see adopted in the second reading. In many parliaments that would be it, but in Denmark an MP can demand that the bill go back to committee after the second reading for a supplementary report.

All *Folketing* committees are potentially powerful because, as in other Scandinavian countries, minority government is so common, meaning that the executive will rarely have a majority in committee. But the two most powerful are, without doubt, the Finance Committee, whose say on the budget is much greater than its counterparts in other legislatures, and the European Affairs Committee, which is able to dictate to the country's ministers the stand they must take on certain issues when voting in Brussels. Ministers are first answerable to the Committee, and only then to their colleagues for their EU-related actions. This loss of executive autonomy is seen as a price worth paying by governments keen to ensure that rows over 'Europe' do not break them apart or cause other parties to withdraw their support.

prime ministers, and weak bureaucratic support for the executive seemed to suggest that parliaments in the region had, if not the upper hand, then rather more power than in the more established democracies (see Kopecký, 2007). Certainly, the Polish *Sejm* (which, it must be said, has a proud history stretching back over centuries) could claim to be one of Europe's more independent legislatures: it has a powerful committee system (a generally accepted indicator of strength, as we see below) whose members can initiate legislation, up to half of which (a very high proportion in relative terms) passes (see Zubek, 2006: 89–90). Moreover, 'the government possesses weak agenda control and few formal means of defending its legislation against rival bills and amendments' (Goetz and Zubek, 2007). Yet it is hard to know how much of this parliamentary strength and executive weakness is institutional and how much derives from the difficulties Polish governments face because of the unusually large number of parties and 'party-hopping' by Polish MPs, all of which makes things difficult for governments. Governments in Lithuania, where the first two years of the parliament elected in 2004 saw over one third of MPs change their affiliations, are similarly afflicted. Across the region as a whole, however, decreasing turnover among, and increasing professionalization of, MPs and the declining number of parties in most of its parliaments, have made them easier to manage (Kopecký, 2007). Also important in strengthening governments' hands have been the fast-track procedures brought in to ensure that parliaments could get through the huge body of legislation needed to meet the requirements of accession to the EU (Kopecký, 2007). It will be interesting to see whether such procedures are used for other purposes now that the accession process is complete.

Parliaments – scrutiny and oversight

MPs, and therefore parliaments, can exercise the crucial role of scrutiny and oversight over the executive via parliamentary questions, written or oral. The use of this technique (once a hallmark of 'Westminster', majoritarian systems) is now ubiquitous and rising throughout Europe, not least because of the realization, particularly by opposition parties, that hard-hitting questions and possibly inadequate replies are eagerly picked up on by the media. The latter (as we shall see in Chapter 7) is always looking to focus on the controversial and the dramatic in order to hold consumers' interest in a subject that they fear might otherwise cause them to change channels. In many countries, questions can lead direct to a special debate on the reply. These so-called 'interpellation' debates serve to keep the spotlight on the government for even longer, even if, critics argue, they tend (like many of the goings-on in parliament) to generate more heat than light.

KEY POINT

Europe's highly partisan parliaments are neither programmed nor resourced to do as good a job as their US counterpart in keeping an eye on governments. The situation is probably even worse when it comes to policing the EU.

The main way, however, that Europe's parliaments perform scrutiny and oversight on the executive is via the committee system. Interestingly, in some countries where committees play a relatively weak role in legislation, they play a much bigger role in holding ministers to account for the work of their departments. For instance, the UK parliament's 'select committees' are more specialized, have long-term membership and can instigate and take evidence in their own enquiries. They therefore offer far more of a challenge to the executive than the much larger, ad hoc 'standing committees' that are charged with examining legislation. Conversely, committees in Sweden are less active in this respect than they are in law-making, where they frequently (and successfully) make changes to legislation. The committee system of the *Riksdag* also helps ensure that it ranks (alongside the Hungarian parliament) at the most powerful European legislature when it comes to 'the power of the purse' (Wehner, 2006) – financial scrutiny over the government's budget (see Figure 4.7).

It is unusual for Europe's legislators to carve out a powerful niche for themselves as committee specialists in the manner of their US counterparts. But being seen to do a good job in this area can boost the chances of promotion into the ranks of government,

Figure 4.7 The power of the purse – how much influence European parliaments have over government budgets

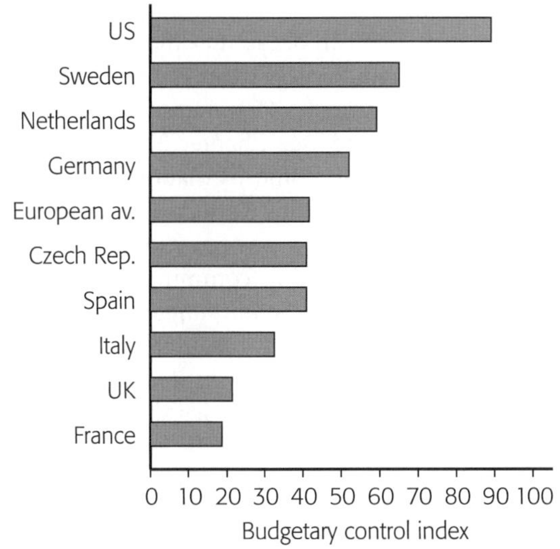

Source: Data from Wehner (2006: 781); Wehner's index (which includes nineteen European countries but not Poland) covers a range of parliamentary powers over the government budget.

although whether, as a government backbencher, 'a good job' means giving ministers a hard or an easy time is a moot point! Committee work also gives MPs a chance to bring to bear their own professional experience on questions of national importance: those with, say, a military or a medical background might be valuable on the Defence or Health Committee. But such work does more than merely pad out MPs' résumés. It can throw the spotlight on issues the executive would rather remain obscure.

Moreover, with the increasing impact of EU legislation on domestic affairs, committees can arguably go some way to closing the so-called **democratic deficit**. Germany's constitution, the Basic Law, for instance, obliges its government to inform the *Bundestag*'s EU Affairs Committee (attended by both MPs and MEPs) of impending European legislation before it becomes 'set in stone'. Indeed, national parliaments all over Europe – though more slowly in the weaker parliaments, perhaps (Dimitrakopoulos, 2001) – are waking up to the fact that, in order to have any influence at all on European legislation, they have to assert a right to examine and express their opinions on proposed EU law much sooner than governments would otherwise like them to (see Maurer and Wessels, 2001 and Raunio and Hix, 2000). Indeed, they can now invoke a protocol to the Amsterdam Treaty that obliges governments (though not, note, in urgent cases!) to give them a minimum of six weeks between notifying their national parliaments of a proposal and it coming to the Council of Ministers for a decision.

The EU's **democratic deficit** is the gap between the powers and competences assumed by the EU and the ability of European citizens to determine the make-up of those institutions and oversee the exercise of those powers and competences. It arises from the tendency of member states, via treaty or treaty-based legal decisions, to cede legislative and executive functions that would hitherto have been the preserve of elected parliaments and governments to unelected bodies (such as the Council of Ministers and the Commission) that the EP cannot effectively hold to account.

On the other hand, six weeks is hardly adequate, and, as a closer look at the German example shows (see Holzhacker, 2002), partisan considerations – protecting or damaging the government – are often only just below the surface in the work of European affairs committees. In any case, paying them too much attention can distract us from an arguably much more profound truth; namely, the fact that, because they continue to take the leading role in the relationship between states and the EU, governments (and, indeed, the executive) in general enjoy a profound institutional and informational advantage over their legislative 'colleagues' – an advantage they have always enjoyed with regard to diplomacy and foreign policy (see Putnam, 1988). To the extent that an increasingly important EU continues to rest, ultimately, on intergovernmental bargaining and to exclude national legislatures from that part of its governance which can be called 'supranational' (see Chapter 2), then Europe's parliaments look set to lose out even more to its governments (see Moravcsik, 2001). As a fascinating case study of the Austrian parliament shows (Falkner, 2000a), this includes even those parliaments that thought they had negotiated extra safeguards against marginalization prior to their country joining the EU. And it might even include parliaments in those countries that are not EU member states. A recent study of Switzerland, for instance, illustrates that when (as often happens) the country has to undertake legislative change so as to ensure that it remains roughly in line with what is going on within the EU itself, the executive wields more power than it would do on purely domestic legislation (see Sciarini *et al.*, 2004). Meanwhile, the legislatures of CEE found themselves sidelined in favour of the executives that the EU preferred to deal with during the accession process.

Parliament and government – the European level

It is perfectly possible to slot into our discussion of the functions and strengths of parliaments, and their relationships with governments, mention of the institution that, more than national legislatures, is supposed to help close the 'democratic deficit' – the European Parliament (EP). Indeed, recent academic work on the latter has argued strongly that the EP (and, in fact, the EU in general) be analysed, not as *sui generis* (constituting a unique class of its own), but using the same tools of analysis (coalition theory, disaggregating the various roles and functions of different parts of the system, etc.) that comparative politics uses to examine other political institutions (see Hix, 2004 and Hix *et al.*, 2007). This is not merely an analytical imperative, but a normative one, too: as we have suggested above, national parliaments find it hard to play much of a role in European law-making, while links with each other and with the EP through bodies such as COSAC (the Conference of Community and European Affairs Committees; see Corbett *et al.*, 2003: 282–5) seem unlikely to lend them that much leverage. This makes it all the more vital for democracy in Europe that we understand the workings of the EP, using what we already know about legislatures more generally to help us.

KEY POINT

The EP can be analysed as a legislature like any other: it has, for example, a party system that most Europeans, if they knew about it, would recognize. However, there is a disconnect between the ideological composition of the parliament and the political direction of the EU, which neither voters nor their elected representatives therefore seem to control.

For instance, one can argue that the EU has what amounts to a bicameral legislature along the lines of some federal parliaments. The increasing use of the co-decision procedure (see Chapter 2), for instance, gives equal power on some legislation to the two 'chambers', the EP and the Council of Ministers – particularly now that the two have to resolve their differences in a conciliation committee (not unlike the German parliament's *Vermittlungsausschuß* mentioned in Box 4.4) in order for legislation not to fail. On the other hand, at least until co-decision becomes the norm for every piece of EU legislation, one can argue that there remains a big difference in that, in the EU, the chamber representing the people (the EP) is weaker than the one representing the states or regions (the Council). And the dissimilarities do not, of course, end there. For instance, the Council of Ministers, despite its reputation as a 'bastion of intergovernmentalism' (see Chapter 2), often cooperates with the supposedly 'supranational' Commission (in its role as the 'executive' of the EU) on the rejection of amendments by the EP (see Tsebelis *et al.*, 2001); and, unlike any other legislative chamber in Europe, the Council gets to hold its debates in secret! The other big difference between the EU and its member states is that, in the EU, the 'executive' or 'government' (such as it is) is not formed by a majority in the legislature. Instead, it is divided between the Commission and the European Council, made up by the heads of government of the member states.

This means that there is a relatively (indeed, a very) indistinct relationship between the results of elections to the EP (see Chapter 6) and the political direction of the EU. Even if (as was the case immediately after centre-right parties did well in the EP elections of 2004) one side of the political spectrum, can occasionally claim what amounts to a 'majority' in the Commission, the Council of Ministers and the EP, it rarely lasts long. And it may not be that significant: national governments change, and there is no hard and fast relationship between commissioners' and ministers' party affiliations and the policy line they take. Moreover, while the EP can withhold its approval of the president and the Commission and can (and has on rare occasions, such as 1999) help to effect their removal, its role in 'hiring and firing' the executive is, again, rather less direct than its counterparts in the member states.

Another key difference between many national parliaments and the EP is that voting in the latter often proceeds along cross-party lines. Often this is because, in order to realize its potential legislative strength vis-à-vis the Council of Ministers, the EP needs to cobble together an absolute majority of all members, notwithstanding the fact that, as members of national parties, nearly all of them belong to increasingly consolidated European parliamentary groups (see Figure 4.8). This kind of majority is practically impossible unless the two biggest parties, the social democratic PES and the Christian Democrat/conservative EPP-ED, vote together (see Kreppel, 2000, 2002). Given they are often joined by the relatively large liberal grouping, the ALDE, this means that the EP is often dominated by a kind of 'grand coalition' that marginalizes the smaller, less centrist groups. The party line-up might, then, resemble that of, say, the Netherlands or Germany (see Chapter 5), but unlike those countries (and others) it shows little sign of moving from cosy centrism to more bipartisan competition between right and left (see Chapter 9). Of course, we should not forget that cross-party voting also goes on in some of Europe's more consensual parliaments, such as the Swedish *Riksdag*. There, it is largely the product of a law-making process in which parliamentary committees play an important role. Given that committees also play a similarly vital role in the life of the EP, this is one way in which it can be said to demonstrate significant similarities with national parliaments. Another is the attempt by the EP to improve its scrutiny and oversight of the Commission (see Corbett *et al.*, 2003: 241–68).

Figure 4.8 EP Party Groups, 2008 – from left to right

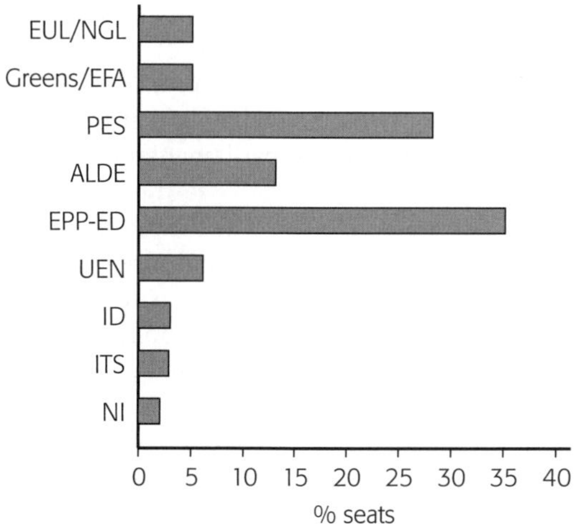

Notes:

EUL/NGL:	European United Left/Nordic Green Left (left parties)
Greens/EFA:	Greens
PES:	Party of European Socialists (social democrats)
ALDE:	Alliance of Liberals and Democrats for Europe (liberals)
EPP-ED:	European People's Party-European Democrats (Ch. Dem. and Conservatives)
ID:	Independents (includes United Kingdom Independence Party UKIP)
UEN:	Union for a Europe of Nations (Nationalist-Conservatives)
ITS:	Identity, Tradition, Sovereignty (populist radical right)
NI:	Non-attached members

Arguably, in fact, MEPs have more incentives than MPs to play the scrutineer and the overseer. Unlike at least some of their national counterparts (and even US Congressmen to some extent), they have no partisan interest in protecting the executive, which allows them more freedom to range across party lines in their criticisms. That said, we need to be very careful not to think that parties (or, technically, party groups) are not that important in the EP. If anything, they are becoming increasingly important. True, national parties, where issues are thought to be sufficiently important, can occasionally request (and normally rely on) their MEPs to vote differently to the EP group to which the party belongs (see Hix, 2002). But the extent to which MEPs now vote along party group lines (called 'cohesion' in the jargon) is higher than ever, and at nearly 90 per cent is much closer to European than to US levels. Meanwhile the bigger groups appear to be competing more often along predicable ideological lines (see Hix *et al.*, 2007; see also Faas, 2003).

Parliament, power and parties

Talk of cohesion and voting along party lines brings us back to the reasons why legislatures in Europe are generally relatively weak. While the patterned variation that emerges between consensual and majoritarian democracies can be summed up graphically (as in Figure 4.6), we should be careful not to think things are that simple. Because government in Europe is parliamentary and party government, there is no clear, US-style separation between the executive and the legislature. This means that the conflicts between the two branches are likely to pale into insignificance alongside conflicts between the government majority and the 'opposition'. Moreover, the power of parliament is as contingent on parliamentary arithmetic (and therefore electoral fortunes) as it is on constitutional conventions or internal organization. Even in consensual countries, an executive made up of a majority coalition or single-party majority will encounter fewer problems with the legislature than a minority government. In any case, schemas of strong and weak parliaments risk relying too much on comparisons of formal powers when, in fact, the strength or weakness of the institutions may lie elsewhere. A clue to where this 'elsewhere' might be comes in the observation made about the UK by French political scientist Maurice Duverger (see Duverger, 1954: 46): 'Parliament and Government,' he noted, 'are like two machines driven by the same motor – the party.'

KEY POINT

The majority of MPs (who are not, incidentally, descriptively very representative of most of the citizens who elected them) are committed to parties that support the government or, at least, do not wish to bring it down. Essentially, then, Europe's parliaments are relatively weak institutions because they contain strong parties.

How hard do most European governments have to work to command the votes of their MPs? In most countries, the answer – normally, anyway – is not terribly hard at all. Levels of party discipline are very high in most of Europe's parliaments. Parliaments in the newer democracies of Central and Eastern Europe initially experienced higher turnover of MPs and more party splits – something that, along with their role as constitutional founders and executives that initially suffered from divisions between presidents and prime ministers, made them appear rather stronger than they really were, constitutionally speaking (Kopecký, 2007). But, with the notable exception of Poland, turnover and defections – labelled 'party tourism' (see Millard, 2004: Chapter 6) – have in general dropped. Nowadays, all over Europe, most members in most parliaments stay loyal. They have more in common ideologically with their own party than with others and, even in CEE, they are becoming evermore professionalized, full-time politicians. As such, they are evermore dependent on the party to whom they owe their (re-)election, their salary, their staff (such as it is: US congressmen are far better resourced), their privileges, and their chance of executive office.

Europe's MPs, then, may have some vestigial loyalty to their home-base or perhaps the profession or pressure group with whom they were associated before they came into parliament. But, in general, it will weigh relatively lightly with them compared with, say, their counterparts in the US Congress. The same is even true for members of the EP, for whom domestic concerns, while still important, are giving way more and more to loyalty to what appear to be increasingly competitive party groups. Moreover, inasmuch as the links between national parliaments and the EP have increased over the years – and it is easy to overplay the extent to which even timetabled joint sessions of committees constitutes significant growth – any meaningful co-ordination in the future will probably need to take place at the intra-party as much as at the interparliamentary level (see Messmer, 2003).

All this means that the key to the executive dominance demonstrated in both the consensual and majoritarian democracies of Europe, is to be found inside parties – forums that, sadly, political scientists, although they can make educated guesses (see Heidar and Koole, 2000), are almost never allowed into. But it also means that the power of the executive can at least potentially vary over time according to the hold it has on its own 'backbenchers'. This might depend, say, on the selection processes of the parties that form the government, as well as on what those backbenchers think are its chances of re-election. Put bluntly, a government that (a) looks likely to suffer at the next election and (b) is made up of one or more parties that can do little to stop the reselection of recalcitrant MPs is probably going to have to pay attention to those MPs (and therefore parliament). One that is polling well, and maintains firm and centralized control over who gets to go

BOX 4.8

Europe's unrepresentative representatives?

As the political theorist Edmund Burke argued, parliamentarians are not delegates but representatives: their job is not simply to parrot the views of their parties, but to exercise their judgement in the best interests of their constituents and the country as a whole. Should they therefore be literally representative of its population? If 5 per cent of citizens, for instance, are of Arab descent, should 5 per cent of MPs also be Arabs? If 40 per cent are working-class, should parliament reflect the same proportion? And given that women make up at least half the population, then should not every other MP be female? Anyone answering 'yes' to all these questions is likely to be disappointed. Parliaments in Europe are notoriously unrepresentative of racial minorities. They are also becoming ever more middle-class: social democratic and other left-wing parties no longer see it as their mission to bring 'workers' into parliament, and the communist aspiration that parliaments should reflect ordinary people has long been abandoned by most parties in East and Central Europe, who now also largely field candidates drawn from the professions (see Millard, 2004: 156–83).

As for gender, there is huge variation across the continent, as Table 4.4 (correct as at November 2007) shows. It also shows that women lose out at cabinet level, too, although the fact that in some countries the proportion of women in cabinet exceeds that in parliament suggests there may be affirmative action being taken at this level.

Table 4.4 Women lose out?

	Percentage of women in:	
	Parliament	**Cabinet**
Sweden	47	41
Netherlands	37	25
Spain	36	47
Germany	32	40
EU	31	30[1]
Poland	26	25
UK	20	23
France	19	47
Italy	17	22
Czech Rep.	16	13

Note: 1. The EU has a parliament but no Cabinet: the figure given is for the European Commission.

Sources: Bale and van Biezen (2007), IPU.org and author's calculations.

There may be a link between PR (see Chapter 6) and greater representativeness, but it seems to depend on the precise system used and may be less important than the tendency of left-wing parties (an example would be the Spanish socialists elected to government in 2004) to promote women more heavily (see Threlfall, 2007). Yet any trend toward parliamentary gender equality is hardly impressive across the continent: apart from the odd earthquake election, turnover among MPs, at least outside the more volatile party systems of CEE, is not that great even if it is higher than in the US (see Matland and Studlar, 2004), so men have a built-in incumbency advantage that may well take time to overcome (see Schwindt-Bayer, 2005). Generally, women are best represented in those countries where they can expect to enjoy greater equality (in practice as well as in theory) in other areas of life. Rules to encourage 'parity' do not always work: they were introduced for the 2002 elections in France, but many parties simply paid the fines involved rather than change the habits of a lifetime (see Murray, 2007).

where on the party list next time around, is likely to have fewer problems.

We should, of course, avoid allowing the question of who is weaker and who is stronger, the government or parliament, to completely overshadow our thinking on these 'branches of government'. After all, although politics is about power, it is also about function. Parliaments hire and fire, produce laws, scrutinize the activities of the executive and its bureaucracy, but they also play a vital role in legitimizing (if not necessarily popularizing!) rule by a necessarily smaller set of people over a much larger group of us. Moreover, they perform a recruitment role by launching the political careers of that smaller set of people – though whether they do it very well (at least when it comes to being representative) is another matter (see Box 4.8). Even if parliaments are just 'talking shops', as some cynics allege, they would still be performing the function of a forum for interests (organized or otherwise), as well as expressing and channelling people's views to those whom they choose, more or less willingly, to contract out governance.

In fact, one of the main messages of this chapter is that anyone searching for evidence of the power of parliaments and governments in Europe probably needs to look behind closed doors. They will not find it by focusing on the kind of open confrontation that sometimes occurred between, say, kings and queens and their parliaments in times past or that still occurs between executive presidents and their legislatures outside Europe. Instead, they will find it, as Duverger implies, in institutions that, while they attract their fair share of criticism these days, nevertheless continue to play a crucial part in politics in Europe. It is to these institutions, the political parties, that we now turn.

Learning Resources for Chapter 4

Further reading

On the political executive, see Helms (2005), *Presidents, Prime Ministers and Chancellors*, and the collection edited by Poguntke and Webb (2004), *The Presidentialization of Politics*. For an overview of cabinet structures and norms, see the edited collecton by Blondel and Müller-Rommel (1997), *Cabinets in Western Europe*, and Blondel *et al.* (2007), *Governing New European Democracies*. The obvious starting-point on parliamentary, coalition governments is Müller and Strøm (2000), *Coalition Governments in Western Europe*. Also useful are the article by Strøm *et al.* (1994), 'Constraints on Cabinet Formation in Parliamentary Democracies', published in the *American Journal of Political Science*, and the chapter by De Winter in the collection edited by Luther and Müller-Rommel (2002), *Political Parties in the New Europe*. A good first port of call on parliaments and governments would be the contributions to the collection edited by Döring (1995), *Parliaments and Majority Rule in Western Europe*; the collection edited by Norton (1999), *Parliaments and Governments in Western Europe*; and the collection edited by Döring and Hallerberg (2004), *Patterns of Parliamentary Behaviour*. For an invaluable attempt to get at what goes on behind closed doors, see Heidar and Koole (2000), *Parliamentary Party Groups in European Democracies*. Also useful is the collection edited by Müller and Saalfield (1997), *Members of Parliament in Western Europe*. For CEE, see the chapter by Kopecký in the collection edited by White *et al.* (2007), *Developments in Central and East European Politics*. On the EP, an accessible yet sophisticated read – one that will also point to other useful sources – is provided by Hix *et al.* (2007), *Democratic Politics in the European Parliament*. On the distinctions between 'consensual' and 'majoritarian' democracies, see the incomparable Lijphart (1999), *Patterns of Democracy*. Millard (2004), *Elections, Parties and Representation in Post-Communist Europe*, not only provides, among other things, an account of the situation of women in that region's parliaments, but a good introduction to the issue of female representation more generally. The 'must-reads' on this topic, though, are Kittilson (2006) *Challenging Parties*, and Mateo Diaz (2005), *Representing Women?*

On the web

www.cia.gov – current PMs and cabinets

www.europarl.europa.eu – EP

www.rulers.org – heads of state and government

www.ipu.org – parliaments throughout Europe

www.riksdagen.se – Swedish parliament in English

www.idea.int/women/parl/toc.htm – women in parliament

www.palgrave.com
Companion Website
Visit the Companion Website to 'click and go'
www.palgrave.com/politics/bale

Discussion questions

1. Europe's presidents, and especially its kings and queens, are often seen as simply symbolic figureheads. Do you agree?
2. Some of Europe's prime ministers seem to be more powerful in relation to their cabinet colleagues than others. Why do you think that is?
3. Why would you expect most European governments to be 'minimal winning coalitions'? But why and how do some administrations govern without controlling a majority in parliament?
4. Why do you think some European governments last longer than others?
5. How is it decided which ministers get which jobs? What do ministers actually do, and how (well) do they all pull together as a cabinet?
6. Do the 'upper houses' of Europe's parliaments have much influence?
7. Some parliaments are more powerful than others: which are they, and how and why do they have more influence than their counterparts in other countries?
8. Has European integration undermined the power of national parliaments? And what about the EU's own parliament: what, in your opinion, most distinguishes it from its national counterparts?
9. Some of Europe's parliaments seem more representative of its citizens than others: do you think that they should all be striving to contain MPs who are more like those who elect them?
10. Most observers agree that, for all the variation between them, Europe's legislatures are not much of a check on its executives: why do you think that might be?

Chapter 5

Parties – how the past affects the present, and an uncertain future

What are parties, and what are they for?	131
Organization	132
Party systems and party families	135
The bases of party systems – social and institutional, luck and skill	150
Party system change?	153
Are parties in decline?	158
The Europeanization of parties and party systems?	162

In Chapter 4 we suggested that parties are the key to understanding how the executive in Europe dominates the legislature – how the government, in other words, controls parliament. In fact, parties are crucial to the government and politics of European countries more generally. Without them representative democracy could not function. And yet Europeans seem not to trust them very much (see Figure 5.1) In this chapter we explain what parties are, and how they came to be. We also look at the ways they organize, and at the way political scientists have tried, by looking at their ideas and their origins, to sort them into meaningful categories that they call 'party families', most of which are represented in almost every individual country's **party system**. We go on to look at these systems and at how political science tries to classify them, and ask whether, why, how and how much they are changing. Finally, we touch on debates on how parties should be funded and explore the popular notion that parties – unpopular with the public and struggling for members – are on the way out.

A country's **party system** is the more or less stable configuration of political parties which normally compete in national elections. It is normally characterized by how many parties there are, what they stand for and their relative strengths. Alternatively (see Mair, 1996) it can be characterized by the extent to which competition between parties is predictable or unpredictable, and post-election changes in government tend to be marginal or wholesale.

What are parties, and what are they for?

Although they have been around for some 200 years, **political parties** still sometimes seem easier to recognize than to pin down. We have made an attempt to come to a workable definition, but it is necessarily qualified. The qualification 'for the most part' is necessary because there are parties, for instance, that refuse either to contest elections at all or, if they do, make it clear that their eventual aim is not to work within the system but to dismantle it. Others exist only for their own (and hopefully others') amusement. 'More often than not' is also a necessary caveat because there may be no clear link between a party's ideas and certain interests and/or values. Its ideas might reflect the personal predilections of a charismatic leader. A party's ideas might also owe more to historical hangovers than current concerns.

Political parties are organizations that, for the most part, recruit candidates to contest elections in the hope that they can then participate in government, or at least push it in the direction of their own ideas – ideas that, more often than not, reflect the socio-economic interests and/or moral values of those who support them.

KEY POINT

Parties perform a range of crucial tasks in all European democracies: representing and packaging interests and values so that alternatives are simplified and meaningful; recruiting and supporting candidates; and forming governments with coherent programmes.

As far as functions go, a hypothetical job description for parties would include, at a minimum, the following:

- Representing socially or culturally significant interests at the same time as 'aggregating' (lumping together and packaging) their sometimes contradictory preferences
- Recruiting, selecting, socializing and providing material and ideological support to candidates and elected politicians who will do the representing, often at both national and sub-national level
- Structuring an otherwise bewildering array of choices available to voters at parliamentary and local elections, which, by their very presence, they render competitive
- Facilitating the formation of governments that produce relatively co-ordinated and coherent policy responses to perceived and real problems
- Effectively mediating between millions of citizens and a state that otherwise might act exclusively in the interest of those it employs and those whose economic clout could give them a disproportionate say in its direction.

Organization

As with ideas, so with organization (see Box 5.1). The structure of most parties, as well as being influenced by both electoral competition and the political philosophy the party claims to represent, is heavily constrained, if not wholly determined, by both their history and changes in their environment – an environment they can only do a little to help shape.

On a superficial level, accounts of modern party organization do not depart much from the common wisdom found in the media. This portrays parties as basically in the hands of leaders determined not to allow their more zealous supporters to scupper their electoral chances by remaining true to whatever cause the party was set up to promote or defend. In fact, however, when we look more closely, that portrait – and, therefore, the common wisdom – is far from describing the reality for many, if not most, parties. Repeated investigation by political scientists of what is sometimes called the 'law of curvilinear disparity' (the idea that leaders and voters are routinely less 'extreme' and more electorally-minded than activists) suggests that it is no more a law – or at least a universally applicable one – than is Michels' so called 'iron law of oligarchy' (see Box 5.2). Party supporters and members are just as interested in winning elections as leaders, while the latter care deeply about values and policy. Research also

Figure 5.1 (Lack of) trust in political parties

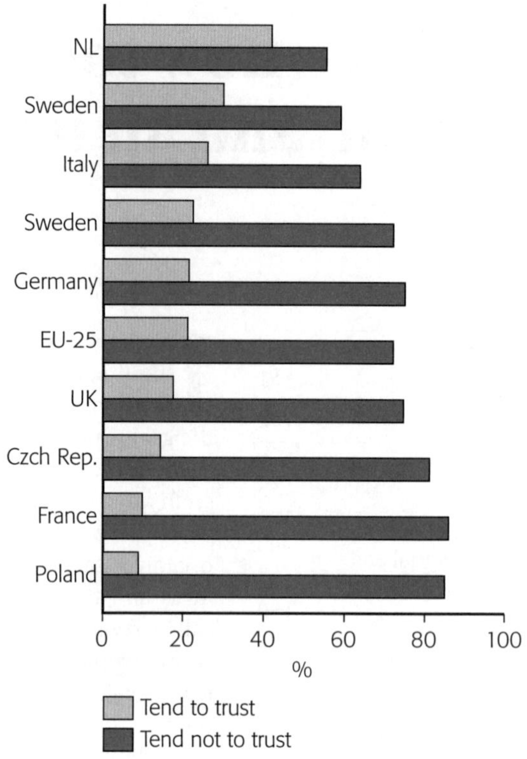

Source: *Eurobarometer*, 65 (2006).

KEY POINT

The way parties organize themselves varies over time and, to some extent, according to ideology.

BOX 5.1

The evolution of political party organization

Cadre parties (Duverger, 1954) were clearly controlled by an elite *caucus* (or small group) commonly consisting of parliamentarians and local notables, with the addition later on of a national organization to deal with members who were expected not so much to decide policy but simply to contribute funds and campaign at elections. Examples include **nineteenth-century Liberal and Conservative parties.**

Mass parties (Duverger, 1954) were founded by those who did not enjoy political power (at least to begin with) and tended to adopt a 'branch' structure in which members, as well as providing financial and campaign resources, could hope to contribute to policy. This meant that party leaders enjoyed rather less autonomy from the centre than their counterparts in the cadre parties. Examples include **early twentieth-century Socialist parties.**

Catch-all parties (Kirchheimer, 1966) seek to broaden their base beyond their traditional support and attract the 'floating voter' and interest group backing. Such parties downplay ideology in favour of pragmatism, and cede considerable autonomy and control to the leadership over the active membership. In the age of mass media, such parties could become **electoral professional parties** (Panebianco, 1988) – dominated by career politicians employing experts (see Webb and Kolodny, 2006) to track public opinion and market the party accordingly via resources derived not from membership subscriptions but from interest groups and the public purse. Examples include **mid- to late twentieth-century Social Democratic and Christian Democratic parties.**

Cartel parties (Katz and Mair, 1995) arguably become so reliant on public subsidies and so distant from their largely symbolic membership that they have become not so much brokers between society and the state as components of the latter. Organizationally, such parties shift or maintain the balance of power away from parts of the party that might be captured by activist members, such as the national, extra-parliamentary, organization (*the party in central office*) towards the parliamentary wing (*the party in public office*). The latter is controlled by the leadership, which communicates over the heads of activists with the rest of the largely passive membership (*the party on the ground*) and potential voters via direct mail and the mass media. Survival is their main goal and the existing 'winners' collude with each other over electoral and funding rules to exclude newcomers. Examples suggested include **most twenty-first-century mainstream parties**, although a number of political scientists reject the thesis, citing lack of hard empirical evidence: parties, they suggest, still maintain links with organised interests, seek members, and compete rather than collude (see Kitschelt, 2000; Detterbeck, 2005; and Allern, 2007).

Anti-system parties are a reaction to the collusive consensus which arguably results when established parties join a cosy, only superficially competitive, cartel. Examples suggested include **1980s Green Parties** and **1990s far-right parties.**

For a constructively critical discussion of all the models and their evolution, see Krouwel (2006).

suggests that present-day forms of party organization do not necessarily mean decreased democracy (see Allern and Pedersen, 2007).

There is a tendency for parties in European democracies to conform to 'common sense', essentially hierarchical, norms of organization that apply across a variety of social, government and commercial sectors. Whether or not this so-called 'isomorphism' (or fit) obeys the 'iron law' outlined in Box 5.2 is, however, a moot point. After all, the extent to which they conform to those norms varies considerably. For instance, the Italian party *Forza Italia* was founded in the early 1990s by continental media magnate and later Italian Prime Minister Silvio

Berlusconi (see Chapter 7). But it began very differently from traditional parties, being arguably little more than a hollow holding company and marketing organization for the ideas and interests of its charismatic leader (see Hopkin and Paolucci, 1999). Some would argue that the 'business firm model' represented by *Forza Italia* is, in fact, only the ultimate extension of a wider European (or possibly global) trend – an aspect of presidentialization (see Chapter 4) – whereby parties, even in parliamentary systems, play little more than a supporting role to the media stars (see Chapter 7) who are their leaders.

In fact, we are a long way off from that situation: even if one reduces parties to brands (Snyder and Ting, 2002), it is clear that the majority of them existed before and will survive the passing of the current 'face' of the brand. And they are often quick – though not always quick enough – to replace that face if he or she doesn't manage to attract customers. The idea that leaders will prove all-conquering also ignores the link we often observe between party ideologies and the way they go about organizing themselves. Left-wing parties, for instance, still tend to give members a greater say than their more conservative counterparts. But the paradigmatic example of this link is provided by Green parties. Despite modifying the 'flat' (i.e. non-hierarchical), ultra-participative values and structures that they brought with them from their beginnings in social movements (see Chapter 8), green parties still stress membership consultation, consensus, and limitations on leadership (Burchell, 2001). This is a big contrast, for instance, with far-right parties at the other end of the spectrum, which tend to afford their leaders a great deal of discretion and control. That said, in Europe's younger democracies there is less likely to be a match – even an inexact one – between ideology and organization. With the exception of communist parties and their successors, parties began with comparatively little infrastructure or grass-roots, and many have found it difficult or unnecessary to do anything about it (van Biezen, 2003).

Ideology, then, might be a guide to understanding the distribution of power within different parties, but it is by no means a complete explanation. This becomes obvious if one looks at how they go about selecting their candidates (see Rahat, 2007). For one thing, there are some states where the process is subject to legal obligations – Finland, for example, insists that all its parties give their members a vote. Another obvious institutional factor is the electoral system (see Chapter 6): in most European states, parties fight elections in multi-member constituencies or districts so need lists, chosen either at the national or the regional level; a few continue with the single-member constituencies associated with British- or US-style 'first-past-the-post' elections, so the choice needs to be much more local. Even then, however, there may well be intervention (or attempted intervention) from the national headquarters in order to prevent the adoption of an unsuitable candidate or parachute in a favourite of the leadership. In Germany, however, such intervention would be not just controversial – as it often is in the UK (and can be in Spain despite a tradition of central control) – but actually illegal. The law has also been enlisted to block or to allow gender quotas – an increasingly important institutional effect on the process (see Norris, 2006).

When it comes to candidate selection, size also matters – generally speaking, the larger the party, the

BOX 5.2

Michels' iron law of oligarchy

To an early theorist of party organization, Robert Michels, the adoption by mass, left-wing parties of elitist or cadre-style organization (and the concomitant watering down of their radicalism) was wholly predictable. According to his 'iron law of oligarchy', a combination of bureaucratic necessity, the inevitability of specialization, the trappings of office and the submissiveness of supporters would eventually ensure that power would pass from the membership to a leadership more interested in survival than social change (Michels, 1962). A later theorist like Angelo Panebianco might qualify the extent to which this necessarily implies a decline of ideological distinctiveness and question the existence of a truly cohesive leadership (Panebianco, 1988). But he, too, notes that party survival rather than the implementation of its founding philosophy becomes the name of the game.

more central control over the process – and it also seems different parts of Europe have different preferences on the subject. Nordic countries tend towards local autonomy whereas Southern European countries go for central control (Lundell, 2004). Finally, practices vary not just between countries and between parties in the same country, but over time and with political fortunes as well. For instance, very few countries or parties have followed the US and held 'primaries' where (virtually) anyone can turn up to select a party's candidates. Few, one suspects, would have predicted that it would be the world's oldest political party, the British Conservatives, which would at the turn of the twenty-first century choose to experiment with the idea. But then few would have predicted in the twentieth century that the party would suffer three consecutive landslide defeats between 1997 and 2005 – defeats that eventually brought about a 'modernizing' leadership keen to 'encourage' local branches to choose a more diverse range of candidates.

Party systems and party families

When it comes to parties, history matters, often far more so than the media's treatment of day-to-day political events would sometimes have us believe. It certainly influences what political scientists refer to as the party system. Most political scientists employ a dual approach to classifying party systems. Following the Italian political scientist Giovanni Sartori, who pioneered work in this area, they give equal weight to a consideration of the number of parties present in, say, parliament (referred to as the degree of 'fragmentation') and the ideological distance between them (referred to as the degree of 'polarization'). Both of these can be seen as dimensions that can be plotted against each other on a graph. Countries can then be located on the graph according to how they score on each dimension (see Figure 5.2). Doing this reveals similarities and differences between countries. Taking our core countries, we find only one – the UK – that has few parties and (relatively) little distance between significant parties on the left and the right – a situation we call 'moderate two party-ism'. There are rather more countries (Germany, Sweden, and probably the Czech Republic and Spain) where the distance between right- and left-wing parties might not be that great, but where there are more of them – a situation we know as 'moderate multipartyism'. The rest (Poland, France, Netherlands, Italy) are all illustrations of 'polarized multipartyism' – lots of parties and a big difference between the most left- and right-wing parties.

KEY POINT

Countries' party systems – and the parties themselves can usefully be categorised into 'ideal types' to facilitate comparison and contrast: systems vary in the extent to which they are fragmented and polarized, or open to innovation; parties vary according to ideology and organization.

More recently, one of Europe's top scholars of party politics, Peter Mair (2006a), has suggested that we employ a different method of classifying party systems on the grounds that nowadays so many party systems fall into the 'moderate multipartyism' category that it has become somewhat meaningless, and that any increase or decrease in the number of parties at the margins doesn't necessarily tell us much about the core or essence of a system. Mair suggests a more discriminating measure could be based on competition for government. The latter can be 'closed' or 'open'. Closed systems are those in which: (a) alternation in government tends to be wholesale (all the parties in office lose power after an election) rather than partial; (b) the combinations of parties that form governments are familiar rather than innovative (parties on the right govern together, as do parties on the left, for example); and (c) a narrow range of (mainstream) parties tends to govern. An example would be the UK. Open systems are more opaque, fluid, innovative, inclusive and rather less predictable. Outside the newer democracies of Europe, an example might be the Netherlands. This new means of classification would also have implications for how we measure change (see below) but, at the moment, it remains to be seen whether enough political scientists will pick it up to see it replace (or perhaps just supplement) the Sartori-style schema they have been familiar with for years.

These classifications are interesting because they provoke predictions and hypotheses that can be tested. One obvious hypothesis involves the relationship between party systems and the kind of party competition that occurs within them. For example, in a system with few parties and a narrow range of ideological difference (i.e. one that exhibits moderate multipartism or two-partyism), we might predict that parties will tend to campaign in the centre ground rather than emphasizing their left and right credentials. Party competition will, in other words, be 'centripetal' (tending toward the centre) rather than 'centrifugal' (tending toward the extreme). This is the case, for instance, in the UK. Under conditions of polarized multipartyism, we are likely to see more centrifugal competition as a number of the parties aim to occupy niches along the entire political spectrum.

These classifications of party systems, however, in some ways beg the question: How did countries' systems come to be the way they are? Many political scientists believe that party systems are rooted in social (or, increasingly, values-based) conflicts, which they call cleavages (see the definition given at the beginning of Chapter 1). Most of these were those already in place at the end of the nineteenth century and the beginning of the twentieth century, when democracy (or at least the vote for all adult males) was introduced. Indeed, one of the most famous theses in comparative politics holds that, as a result, they helped to structure – or even freeze – Europe's party system for decades to come (see Lipset and Rokkan, 1967). Some, of course, have developed since, while others have declined in salience or, as in CEE, had their development arrested, either temporarily or permanently (see Zielinski, 2002). The extent to which a cleavage was more or less important in a particular country helped to determine which parties (or, comparatively speaking, representatives of the various party families) were present, as well as which were stronger or weaker. So, too, did the extent to which existing parties were able to adapt in order to mobilize on that cleavage as well as the one that gave birth to them. Figure 5.3 shows the evolution of a hypothetical party system containing all the main cleavages and, therefore, all the party families we will go on to discuss. But clearly, not all countries will, in reality, have been affected by all cleavages and most will therefore contain representatives of only some rather than all the party families.

Figure 5.2 Party system classification, by fragmentation and polarization

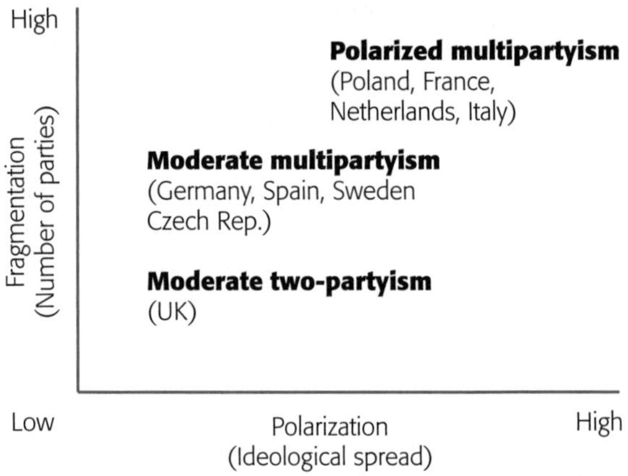

We can go through Figure 5.3 (which is, of course, a stylized diagram) from the top down. The different interests of landowners and those who were beginning to make money from industry or the professions had led, around the middle of the nineteenth century, to the foundation of, on the one hand, *conservative* parties and, on the other, *liberal* or *radical* parties. These parties stood on either side of the *land–industry* cleavage. The increased need and willingness among wage-earners to express their own interests gave rise, as the nineteenth century drew to a close, to *socialist* or *social democratic* parties, which then spawned *communist* parties that believed in a more revolutionary route to power. These mobilized one side of the *owner–worker* cleavage and reinforced the basic division between what we have come to call 'right' and 'left'. The rise of the city (especially in Scandinavia) saw the creation of *agrarian* parties dedicated to defending the interests of farmers (the *urban–rural* cleavage). Another conflict that influenced politics was the *church–state* cleavage that, in time, saw the creation of conservative *Christian democratic* parties opposed to the secularism, as well as the progressive social and economic policies, of the left in particular. Meanwhile, the *centre–periphery* cleavage encouraged, in some countries, the formation of *regionalist* parties which defended the autonomy of communities with separate identities (and possibly languages) against state centralization. More recently, agrarian

Figure 5.3 The evolution of Europe's party families, from the nineteenth to the twenty-first century

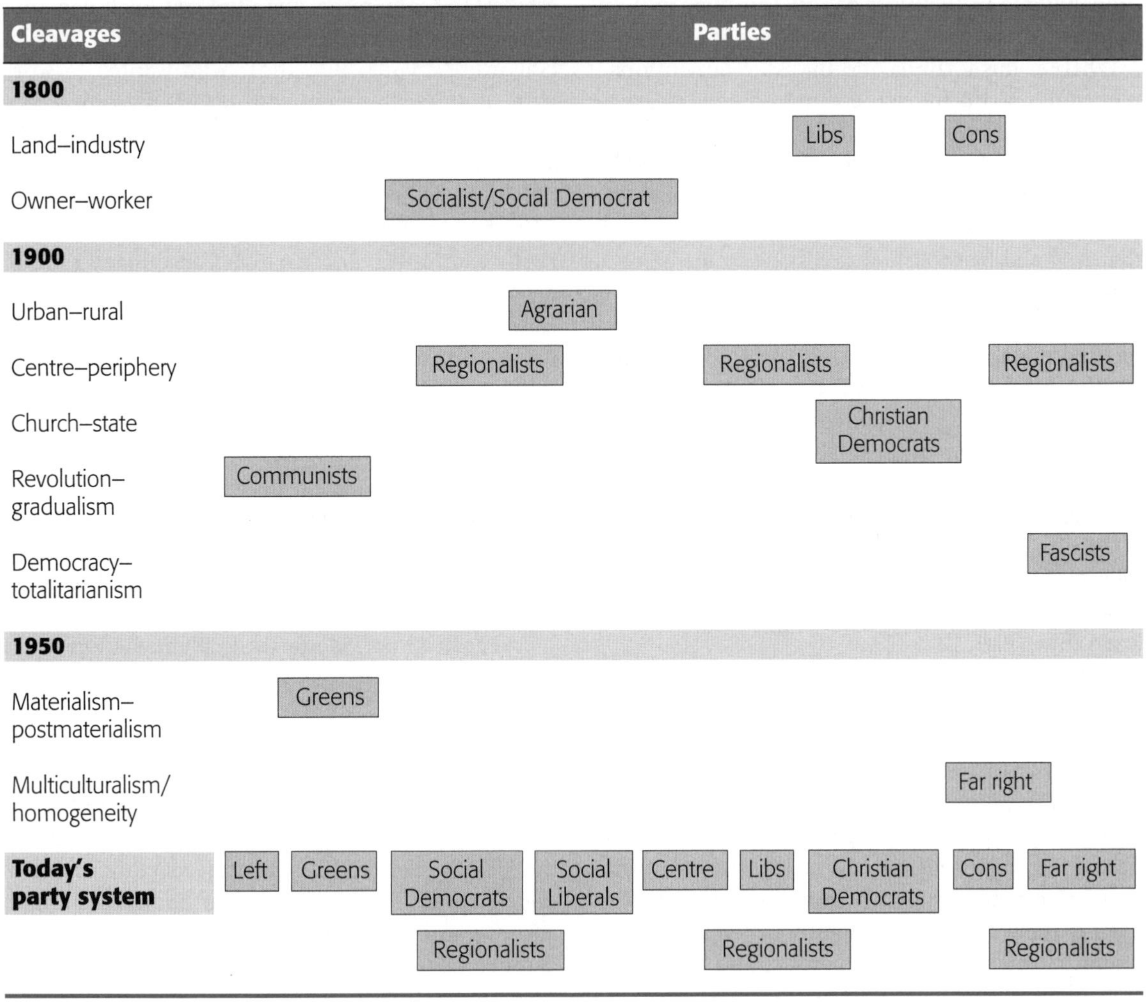

parties have become *centre* parties, and (with the end of the Cold War) some communist parties have become *left parties*. Even more recently, cleavages seem to have opened up around more values-based *post-materialism* (see Chapter 6 for a full definition). This focuses on matters such as the environment and multiculturalism, giving rise to *green* parties and possibly helping to give a new lease of life to *far-right* parties.

The relationship between cleavages (or, more precisely, the conflictual 'issue dimensions' they give rise to) and parties can, incidentally, be used to predict the number of parties in a system. This is done with a simple formula produced by influential Dutch political scientist Arendt Lijphart (whose distinction between 'majoritarian' and 'consensual' systems we have already referred to in Chapter 4). More often than not, there is a relationship between the number of issue dimensions and the number of parties. This can be expressed as $N = I + 1$; namely; the number of parties will equal the number of issue dimensions, plus one. So, for example, in the Netherlands, the issue conflicts are religious, socio-economic and post-materialist, which means (at least) four parties. Of course, this does not always hold exactly, and requires that one ignore very small parties that might well be influential at certain times or on certain issues – as the UK's and Spain's regional parties are, for instance. The number of parties might also change as issue dimensions become more or less important. Nevertheless, it is probably one of the more robust formulas in political science.

Whether this formula and the issue dimensions it relies upon – or, indeed, the notion that cleavages structure party systems – can be applied to Europe's newest democracies is open to argument. Many observers routinely assume, for instance, either that the transition from communism is still so recent that it would be foolish at this stage in the game to expect to find such deeply embedded conflicts or that, even if they are emerging, they will be very different from those that structure party competition in the established democracies. Recent research using large surveys of European voters, however, suggests that – due in no small part to the efforts of parties themselves to politicize them – 'the pattern of social cleavages and their political consequences is similar between the established and emerging democracies, with religion and the owner–worker cleavage dominating political conflict' (McAllister and White, 2007: 211–12).

If this turns out to be right, it could help explain why parties in many postcommunist European countries look not unlike their 'western' counterparts, and now of course associate formally with them in European party federations and parliamentary groups (see p. 163 below). Political scientists have long suggested that countries that had cleavages in common tended to contain similar parties, even if their names were slightly different. Political scientists interested in comparison and generalization often group these parties into 'party families' (see Mair and Mudde, 1998), on the basis that, while some national variation is inevitable, what each party stands for tends (historically, at least) to 'run in the family'. We now look at each party family in turn, not in order of foundation (as in Figure 5.3) but instead in broad order of contemporary political importance. We also provide examples of each, partly to show that, although generalizations are useful, membership of the family does not always involve direct lineage.

Socialist and social democratic parties

These parties first began to emerge in the last quarter of the nineteenth century as those on one side of the owner–worker cleavage began to agitate not merely for political rights, such as the vote, but also for an economy and a society run in the interests of the many rather than the few. Such demands were obviously anathema to conservatives. But liberals were divided into those who wanted to work with (and ideally retain control of) any progressive forces in politics and those who regarded socialism as a threat to private property and individual freedom. Many socialist parties allied with the increasingly powerful trade union movements. Partly as a result, and partly because many radicals departed to form communist parties following the Russian revolution (1917), it became clear that these parties aimed not to overthrow capitalism but to mitigate and even dynamize it. This they hoped to do by using the state: through the ownership (or at least the regulation) of key industries and utilities, the use of progressive taxation and redistributionary government spending, governments would co-operate with trade unions (and hopefully employers, too) to deliver full employment and social security, health and education for all (see Box 5.3).

The postwar period saw the implementation of key planks of the social democratic programme across western Europe. This was initially by social democrats themselves, but then also by parties of the centre-right who recognized that opposition presented electoral difficulties. During this period, social democrats had the support of at least a third (and in the UK, Sweden and Austria considerably more) of the electorate. When the postwar boom came to an abrupt end in the mid-1970s (see Chapter 1), social democratic parties with the misfortune to be in government – whether or not they or their policies were to blame (and with the exception of Austria and Sweden) – bore the brunt of public displeasure. Conversely, the social democratic success stories of the 1980s were in Spain, Portugal and Greece, where socialist parties turned out to be the main beneficiaries of the collapse of dictatorships (Merkel, 1992). The French *Parti Socialiste,* having won a historic victory in 1981, however, ran into far greater difficulties when, unlike its Mediterranean counterparts, it attempted to buck, rather than adapt to, the trend toward economic liberalism. Its radical programme of nationalizations and public spending quickly ran into trouble (not least with the financial markets) and it was forced to execute a U-turn toward austerity (see Ross *et al.*, 1987). This trauma, and ongoing defeats of sister parties in the UK and

Germany, led some commentators to predict 'the death of social democracy', its ideology outdated and its core support (the manual working class and trade unions) shrinking. A process of policy renewal and reaching out to middle-class voters, plus a series of electoral come backs in the late 1990s seemed to have put paid to such pessimism for a while. But the first elections of the twenty-first century have not been so positive (see Chapter 9).

In the postcommunist democracies of eastern Europe, the performance of, and prospects for, social democratic parties are better than some might have predicted – particularly when one considers that for the most part they began as the means by which Cold War communist parties attempted, almost overnight, to establish their newly moderate, democratic, credentials. In most countries in Central and Eastern Europe, social democratic parties have already made it into government on one or more occasions and either are, or are close to being, the largest single party.

While the likeness may not be exact, the newest members of the social democratic family, then, bear some resemblance to those in the west that have been around much longer. New or old, most social democrats, as we argue in Chapter 9, continue to believe in using the power of public initiative and the public purse to (at the very least) protect the less fortunate and, in the long term, reduce their numbers via strategies promoting equality of opportunity. All, however, realize that this power is constrained by what is deemed prudent by international

BOX 5.3

Modernization over Marxism – two social democratic parties

It is often said that the British Labour Party originated 'from the bowels of the trade union movement' rather than the philosophical beliefs of impractical ideologues. Its original purpose was to ensure that laws passed by parliament did not unfairly hinder unions in their role as protectors and promoters of the interests of ordinary working people. Once the bulk of those people became entitled to vote, it quickly became clear that Labour would become one of the UK's two main parties. Despite *Clause IV* of its constitution – committing it, in theory, to extending public ownership of the economy – Labour in practice came to be associated not so much with the more radical Marxist diagnosis and prescriptions that characterized continental social democratic parties but, rather, with redistribution via progressive taxation, the welfare state and the sort of 'nationalization' of key industries that made sense in the 1930s and 1940s but was seen by many as outdated by the 1950s. The very vagueness of Clause IV, and fear of the infighting that would greet any attempt to replace it, meant that it was only in the 1990s that the party finally equipped itself with what its leadership argued was a more relevant, realistic 'mission statement'.

All this is in marked contrast with other European social democratic parties. Despite close relationships with the trade unions (particularly in Scandinavia), these parties were not so financially or so organizationally dependent on them. Neither were they so uninterested in ideological direction and debate. In their early years, they were heavily influenced by the writings of Marx and his followers. Initially, indeed, the really significant difference between them and the more radical *Communists* (many of whom started out as social democrats) was their commitment to a peaceful and parliamentary road to socialism – even if the plan originally was to refuse (unlike the British Labour Party) to get involved in government until an electoral majority for their cause had been won. Ironically, it was their stress on social analysis – and frustration with ruling themselves out of government despite their relative electoral strength – that made these parties more open to change in order to adapt to new circumstances. One of the best examples is the German SPD, originally founded in 1875. At its famous *Bad Godesburg* congress in 1959, the party announced its abandonment of old-style, Marxist, socialism and its embrace of the 'social market economy', setting itself on a path toward both catch-all party status (see Box 5.1) and, quite soon afterwards, coalition government.

financial markets and reasonable, taxwise, by their electorates. To them, the state still has an economic as well as a welfare role, but it is as a regulator or framework-setter as opposed to an owner or driver. And while not immune to both differences of emphasis and internal division on the issue, all are basically in favour of an EU that aims to liberalize and increase trade – though not at the expense of social provision or labour standards, commitment to which is reinforced by continuing close links with the union movement. On issues of morality, conscience and sexuality, social democratic parties are firmly in the secular liberal tradition.

For all these reasons, and because in northern if not in southern Europe (see Astudillo, 2002) they continue to be closely linked to trade unions, Europe's social democrats might perhaps be more comparable than ever with the US Democrats. Those looking for a single 'European equivalent' of the Republican Party, however, will have a harder time. In their enthusiasm for a strong defence of the nation, no-nonsense policies on crime and punishment, and a low-tax, no-meddling government, the Republicans share much in common with Europe's conservative parties. But in their rhetorical commitment to 'compassionate conservatism' and their anti-permissive stance on family values and personal (and especially sexual) morality, they have strong affinities with Europe's Christian Democrats. These are the party families we go on to look at next.

Conservative parties

Europe's conservative parties were formed in order to co-ordinate the defence of the socio-economic privileges of the traditional, mainly landed, hierarchy against what were seen as the pretensions of the rising liberal middle class. Where liberals were supposedly motivated by theory, enthused by international free trade, obsessed with the individual and possessed of an off-putting earnestness, conservatives declared themselves to be more pragmatic, more patriotic, more paternalistic and yet also more fun! In the UK, for instance, they were backed by brewing and agricultural interests, as well as the dominant church. They were able to survive the granting of universal suffrage – first by poaching middle-class voters who were put off by liberalism's identification with sectarian, urban and (increasingly) radical politics and, second, by appealing to the nationalism, the traditionalism and the respectable aspirations of newly enfranchised working-class voters.

The second challenge for conservative parties was the advent of the welfare state. Although conservative parties were paternalistic, they argued that the less well-off were best protected by a thriving private sector and a mixture of self-help and charity. State intervention should be limited largely to policing law and order and providing for the defence of the realm. However, the obvious popularity of increased social provision and what, at the time, seemed the inevitability of public involvement in key sectors such as transport and energy, meant they concentrated their efforts for most of the postwar period on limiting rather than 'rolling back' state spending and activity. Following the economic difficulties encountered by European nations in the 1970s, when countries such as Germany and the UK were governed by the centre-left, the opportunity arose to pursue a more aggressive attack on the state (see Chapters 1 and 9). This was taken furthest in the UK, where the emphasis was on cutting state subsidies to industry, reducing the role of the trade unions and selling off state assets. Although welfare provision suffered, there were electoral constraints on how much could be cut.

This was in keeping with the fact that Europe's conservative parties have historically been careful not to allow their ideological instincts to sway them too far away from the centre of the political spectrum (Box 5.4). This might well be due to the fact that they are strongest in countries that display two characteristics. The first is the tendency among the country's voters, irrespective of the electoral system, to give power to one of two main parties (or blocs). A recent example would be Hungary, where over 80 per cent of the vote at the 2002 election went to the two main competitors, one of which, *Fidesz,* had rapidly transformed itself into the region's most successful Conservative party (see Kiss, 2002). The second is the weakness or absence of a traditionally more centrist *Christian Democracy* (see p. 142) in that country; instances include the UK, Malta, Spain, Greece and arguably, since the 1990s, Italy. Notable exceptions to the 'Conservative or Christian Democrats, but not both' rule, however, include Sweden and the Czech Republic.

BOX 5.4

Fighting in the centre-ground? – three conservative parties

The Spanish *Partido Popular* (PP) began life in 1976 as the *Alianza Popular* (AP), a home for high-ranking members of the Franco dictatorship who wished to pursue their conservative politics in the new, democratic Spain. Finally, in 1990, the centre-right, at the same time as reforming under the single banner, *Partido Popular* (PP), found a leader from a new generation of conservatives too young to be tainted by association with the authoritarian past. José María Aznar was able to exploit his image as a reliable, pragmatic, centrist – and, above all, clean – politician to his advantage. In 1996, PP assumed office as a minority government with the support of smaller regionalist parties. Centrist policies, and the support of young people for whom the Socialist opposition now meant monolithic, old-fashioned, corrupt politics, helped PP win itself an overall majority (in a PR system) in the general election of 2000. It seemed about to win again in 2004 when the Madrid train bombings carried out by Islamic terrorists blew everything off course and propelled a renewed Socialist Party (PSOE) into office. The booming (some would say dangerously so) economy, plus a raft of measures to counter discrimination on the grounds of gender and sexual orientation (see Chapters 1 and 8), as well as the PSOE's apparently more successful (because more flexible) stance towards demands for greater autonomy in the Basque Country and Catalunya (see Chapter 2), made things uncomfortable for PP, and its new leader Mariano Rajoy. Under pressure from, for example, the Catholic church, victims groups and Spanish nationalists, the party risked a return to the kind of (moral) conservatism that put it at odds with more moderate voters. Notwithstanding Spain's slowing economy and its desperate attempts to exploit immigration as an issue, PP lost the general election of March 2008.

For most of its life, the Conservative Party in the UK was a pragmatic operator, using its status as 'the natural party of government' and its unashamed nationalism to ensure that any concessions to social democracy (such as public ownership and the welfare state) were kept within limits. It was not until 1979, with the coming to power of Margaret Thatcher, that the Conservatives attempted – with some success – to roll back these concessions in pursuit of a more ideological free-market approach. Helped by the weakness of its Labour opponent, the party stayed in power for eighteen years, but the price of longevity proved high: by 1997 it was faction-ridden, sleazy, and had even managed to blow the reputation for economic competence that had allowed it to overcome suspicions about its supposed lack of social compassion. Its increasingly hostile attitude to the EU, and its traditionally tough line on immigration and law and order appealed to large numbers of voters, but nowhere near enough to win a general election against a rejuvenated Labour Party which appeared to combine economic efficiency with social concern. Seen as old, out of touch, and (ironically) too ideological, the party lost a second and third election before it finally turned to a leader, David Cameron, who committed his party to 'fighting on the centre ground' – for example, by balancing very specific and supposedly fully funded tax cuts with the need to maintain spending and improve public services.

Whether Cameron's strategy pays off, at least in the short-term, remains to be seen. He appeared, though, to have taken some heart from Sweden where, at a general election at the end of 2006, a centre-right (or *bourgeois*) alliance led by the Swedish conservatives, the *Moderata samlingspartiet* (the Moderates) was elected to office. Their leader, Fredrik Reinfeldt, had been something of a neo-liberal but, soon after taking on the job in 2003, he did everything he could to suggest the party would move to the centre: the country's generous welfare state and (in his view) overregulated labour market needed only adjustment not tearing apart; tax cuts, yes, but only for the lower paid. He even went so far as to ape Tony Blair by rebranding his party as *De Nya Moderaterna* – the New Moderates. Opponents suggested this was merely a marketing tactic and that once in office, his mask would slip to reveal him once again as a neo-liberal ideologue. Other observers pointed to the fact that, even if this were the case, the party would be severely constrained in what it could do by its more cautious and centrist coalition partners.

Christian democratic parties

These parties, especially those of Roman Catholic origin, were around in various forms by the beginning of the twentieth century (Box 5.5). But representatives of this centre-right party family really came into their own following the end of the Second World War (see Kselman and Buttigieg, 2003). While clearly opposed to the collectivist, class-based ethos of the left (and in particular the Communists), Christian democratic parties were markedly more positive about state and trade union involvement than some of their conservative counterparts (see Hanley, 1994 and van Kersbergen, 1995). Prizing social harmony above individualism and unfettered free markets, Christian democratic parties were instrumental in the development of 'corporatism' (see Chapter 8) in Austria, and to a lesser extent Germany, in the second half of the twentieth century. The stress was on 'capitalism with a conscience' and on a role for the state in facilitating long-term, mutually beneficial and institutionally supported relationships between business and unions. But the collective good wasn't everything, as it supposedly was to parties on the left: individuals mattered, too. Yet they had to be seen not as the autonomous, primarily self-interested actors beloved of economic liberals, but as socially embedded contributors and beneficiaries of an organic whole (an idea known as 'personalism'). The stress was also on support for the family – especially the traditional family that was seen as the embodiment and transmission belt for Christian moral values. But while compassion and help for the less fortunate was important, tolerance and compromise had their limits when it came to issues such as abortion and divorce.

Although strong feelings on those issues are most associated with Roman Catholicism, it is important to emphasize the fact that, outside traditional strongholds like Austria, Belgium and (until the early 1990s) Italy, some Christian democratic parties (for example, in Germany and the Netherlands) came to appeal to Protestants as well. In fact, in almost uniformly Protestant Scandinavia, they could do little else. Ecumenical appeals, however, cannot completely insulate the Christian Democrats from the decline in the number of western Europeans who are practising Christians (see Chapter 1). On the other hand, Christian Democrats outside Scandinavia (where they continue to concentrate their appeal to people of faith) have, since the Second World War pursued a 'catch-all' strategy (see Box 5.1). Their centrist, pragmatic policies consciously appeal to as wide an audience as possible even as they begin to adapt more 'neo-liberal' economic policies and, in so doing, start to look increasingly like secular conservative parties (see van Hecke and Gerard, 2004). Recent elections in Austria, the Netherlands and Germany show that it is a strategy that can work. The situation in the new postcommunist democracies is less hopeful, however. With the exception of Slovenia, Christian Democratic parties seem to be in decline. This is true even in places like the Czech Republic and Hungary where they had a foothold in the first place, while in (still very Catholic) Poland, the obvious potential for a successful 'family member' has yet to be realized.

Liberal parties

These parties were first set up to promote the interests of people who earned their living from commerce and the professions, and lived in the towns and cities that grew quickly in the Industrial Revolution of the nineteenth century (Box 5.6). Early on, they promoted the legal, property, political and religious rights of the individual in contrast to the arbitrary rule of a traditional, landed interest that was happy to see the state identify with a particular church. In the twentieth century, however, liberal parties seem to have gone one of two ways. The first, sometimes called 'neo-liberalism', prioritizes a commitment to the free market and opposition to state interference in the economy as well as in matters of morality – all of which distinguish it from centre-right parties belonging to the Christian democratic family. In very recent years, however, this brand of liberalism has been concerned not to appear too 'soft' (i.e. libertarian) on issues such as drugs and civil liberties issues, and has begun to incorporate a hard line on immigration into its platform. The second strand of liberalism, sometimes labelled 'social liberalism', has generally not abandoned its reputation for tolerance and the promotion of civil liberties. It is generally more sympathetic than the first strand toward government intervention in the economy and welfare policy, believing that it helps to ensure that people

BOX 5.5

Crossing classes and denominations – Christian Democratic parties

Germany's *Christlich-Demokratische Union* (CDU) traces its roots back to the predominantly Catholic Centre Party of the interwar years. Indeed, Christian Democracy in Germany still attracts disproportionate support from Catholics, especially in Bavaria, the stronghold of the CDU's sister-party, the *Christian Social Union* (CSU). But its appeal in the postwar period has been non-denominational and to a great extent non-religious in character. It became, in effect, one of Europe's archetypal 'catch-all' parties (see Box 5.1). Unlike its Bavarian sister-party, the CDU is not overtly nationalistic, nor morally or socially very conservative. Although in recent years it has been influenced – just like its similarly 'cross-confessional' Dutch counterpart, the *Christen Democratisch Appèl* (CDA) – by economic liberalism, it continues to see a place for government intervention, for consultation with trade unions and for a strong insurance-based welfare state (see Chapter 1). After dominating German politics in the 1980s and 1990s, the CDU then enjoyed rather less luck until it narrowly 'won' the 2005 general election under its new (and first) female leader Angela Merkel, who was, however, forced to form a 'grand coalition' with bitter rivals, the SPD. This constraint, plus the fact that comparisons between 'Angie' and 'Maggie' were always overdone, means anyone expecting Thatcher-style deregulation, state-shrinking and 'union-bashing' will be in for a very long wait!

Norway's *Kristelig Folkeparti* – the model for the Christian democratic parties of Scandinavia – might be a member of the same party family as the CDU, but is different in many ways that may even challenge the notion that there is such a thing as a pan-European party family. Far from being a catch-all party (see Box 5.1), it relies on a core support of Lutherans, many of whom feel very strongly (and conservatively) on social issues (particularly on their opposition to alcohol and to abortion) and/or their right to hang onto their particular Norwegian dialect *(Nynorsk).* The party, which was founded in 1933, is also geographically highly concentrated, and attracts nowhere near the catch-all cross-class vote of the CDU. For a while, its loyal support, plus the charismatic leadership of Kjell Magne Bondevik (who could claim the prime minister's post in centre-right governments even though his party was by no means the biggest in the coalition) managed to prevent it from dropping too far below 10 per cent. But, in 2005, it took less than 7 per cent – a share that may represent its core support.

can actually benefit from the freedoms they should enjoy.

The UK Liberal Democrats are a good example of this second strand, although the country's electoral system constitutes a big (if not necessarily insuperable) barrier to them gaining office – or regaining it, since they began life as one of Britain's two biggest parties (see Chapter 6). Elsewhere in Europe, however, liberal parties, whether on the neo-liberal right or in the more 'progressive' centre, have been involved in government far more frequently. Sometimes this has been as part of a so-called 'bourgeois bloc' against social democracy (as in Sweden). At other times, they have been 'third parties' able to join either a right- or a left-wing government (as in Germany) or a wider 'rainbow coalition' (as in Belgium and the Netherlands). In western Europe, they now poll on average around 10 per cent, though the range is large: from around half of the average in Scandinavia to two or three times the average in the Benelux countries, Switzerland and, recently, the UK. The liberal party family is similarly well represented in some of Europe's smaller, newer democracies such as Latvia, Lithuania and Slovenia. There is also a small liberal party that broke away from the Conservatives in the Czech Republic.

Green parties

In Europe, the Greens began to take shape in the 1970s and 1980s when 'new social movements' (which are defined in Chapter 8) campaigning

BOX 5.6

Two liberal parties; one country

The *Volkspartij voor Vrijheid en Democratie* (People's Party for Freedom and Democracy, VVD) may have been founded in 1948, but it benefited from a long list of liberal predecessors stretching back into the nineteenth century. During that time, politicians objecting both to the religious influences of Dutch conservatives and the statist inclinations of Dutch workers' parties were instrumental in progressive social reform and the expansion of civil and political rights. In the postwar period, the VVD grew to become the Netherlands' third largest political party and recently has commonly formed part of the government, usually in coalition with the Christian Democrats, but also with the Labour Party. Their focus was on tax reductions and on decentralization, and, in the 1990s under their leader Frits Bolkestein (later appointed EU commissioner for the internal market and tax reform), on the dangers of immigration and multiculturalism. This supposedly potent combination of liberal economics and populist calls for restriction and integration has not, however, helped the party at elections in recent years – and it has caused internal tensions between members prone to division over the issues. This turmoil, plus its loss of vote share at the election of 2006, not only stranded the party in opposition but led to what looked like a catastrophic split a year later (see van Kersbergen and Krouwel, 2008).

D66 (*Democraten 66*) is the Netherlands' other liberal party. It is much closer than VVD to the Labour Party on welfare and economic policy, and in recent years has stressed the need for investment in education and the environment. It has distinctive stances on constitutional reform (it believes in 'bottom-up' and direct democracy) and is very committed to the freedom of the individual above and beyond the market place. It traces its roots back to the *Freethinking Democratic League* founded at the beginning of the nineteenth century. But it really got going in the late 1960s as a reaction to the seeming impasse between liberals and social democrats – an impasse that was allowing the Christian Democrats to rule yet ignore the need to modernize the country. D 66's stress was on the need to bypass class and religious loyalties in favour of participatory democracy wherein all express their personal values – so much so that some see it shading into the 'postmaterialism' exemplified by the Greens. D 66 has tended to support governments of the left but, in 2003, entered a centre right-coalition – along with VVD! This did not prove an easy experience, especially when controversial support for conservative policies did not achieve the expected pay-off in terms of electoral reform, and internal splits began to occur. Finally, disagreement with VVD's hard-line Minister for Integration and Immigration caused D 66 to pull the plug on its coalition partners, although it performed abysmally at the ensuing election, taking just 2 per cent. Fortunately, the unusually low threshold employed by the Dutch electoral system (see Chapter 6) saved it from a parliamentary wipe-out – but for how long?

against the supposed unsustainability and exploitative nature of growth-oriented economic development sought parliamentary representation (Box 5.7). Their appeal was – and is – 'postmaterialist' (about quality of life rather than standard of living) or even anti-materialist. Although the environment (and particularly opposition to nuclear power) was the primary focus, it also encompassed anti-militarism and anti-discrimination, solidarity with the developing world, social equality and justice, and liberal tolerance of alternative life-styles. Greens also differentiated themselves from so-called conventional, 'grey' parties by their continued (if, over time, slightly diluted) commitment to participatory democracy and local autonomy – a commitment which typically saw them adopt much flatter organizational structures than other, generally hierarchically organized, parties.

Although not as successful as the far right, the Greens are clearly one of the 'success stories' of politics since the 1970s, having found what seems to be a secure footing in several major European coun-

BOX 5.7

The difficult art of compromise – two Green parties

The first Green Party to make it into government in western Europe was the Finnish *Vihreä Liitto*, whose 6.4 per cent of the vote in 1995 was enough to earn them a cabinet seat in a so-called 'rainbow coalition' stretching all the way from the Left Alliance to the Conservatives. This was only eight years after the formation of the party in 1988, though Greens had been elected as MPs in 1983 and 1987. The coalition was returned to power, with the Greens improving their vote to 7.3 per cent and retaining the Ministry of the Environment. During their time in government, the Greens scored notable successes in extending conservation land and introducing more sophisticated environmental taxes. They were unable, however, to prevent a majority of MPs (most other parties were split on the issue) voting to begin work on a fifth nuclear reactor. In May 2002, the party met and decided to leave the government in protest. They made a point of saying, however, that they would be willing to enter coalition negotiations following the next elections in 2003. This magnanimous offer was, not surprisingly, turned down by other parties. But the party's tactics did it no harm at the ballot box and the party increased its vote slightly. The upward trend was continued in 2007, when the party took 8.5 per cent – enough to take it once again into a coalition government, although interestingly one otherwise made up of only centre-right parties.

Ireland's Green Party is one of the newest entrants into government – and like its Finnish counterpart it has, rather controversially, chosen to do a deal with a predominantly centre-right administration (although in Ireland it has never been quite so easy as it is in most European countries to analyse politics using left–right categories). The Greens made their big breakthrough in parliament at the general election of 2002, and managed to match that performance in 2007. Two years previously, the party's National Convention had voted against forming a pre-electoral pact with the other broadly centre-left parties, but noises made before the election by its leader didn't seem to indicate going with the other side was likely either. But when the prime minister came calling, and after tough negotiations which netted them a few bankable policy wins and a couple of significant portfolios (Environment and Energy), the increasingly pragmatic Green leadership decided it was now or never – and just as importantly managed to convince their membership, who had to vote on the deal before it could go ahead. If the experience of other Green parties is a guide, the party won't find government easy – especially because it is part of a surplus majority or oversized coalition where its votes won't always be vital (see Chapter 4) – but it will probably acquit itself better than its opponents predict.

tries. And they have been in coalition government (see Rihoux and Rüdig, 2006) – not just in Germany, where the high-profile and popular Joschka Fischer became foreign minister, but also in Finland, Belgium, Slovakia and the Czech Republic, and in France and Italy, despite their electoral performance in the last two countries being poorer than it is in Sweden, Austria and Switzerland. The relatively poor performance in France and Italy is probably explained in part by their more majoritarian electoral systems (see Chapter 6). But it may also reflect the fact that Green parties have found it hard to progress in southern Europe generally: their strength in Spain, Portugal and Greece is negligible. It is not much better, interestingly, in Norway or Denmark. There, the lack of Green success may be due to the fact that the general level of environmental consciousness is so high that mainstream parties factored it in to their own platforms at a very early stage. In Denmark, however, there is a very small Red–Green party, as there is in the Netherlands.

As in southern Europe, the level of environmental consciousness in the post-communist democracies, where material necessities are still very much the issue for the vast majority of the population, is very low. Consequently, the Greens are virtually non-existent in electoral terms in Central and Eastern

Europe. Virtually, however, does not mean totally. Greens have been in government in Slovakia and now the Czech Republic has seen the fortunes of its Green Party improve considerably since it was joined, and then led in a much more pragmatic direction, by Martin Bursík, an ex-environment minister who, unusually for a Green politician, began life on the centre-right of politics. His more media-savvy leadership, and his background, helped the party not only to just over six per cent of the vote in the general election of 2006, but also to a place in the centre-right government that assumed office thereafter.

Far-right parties

Far-right parties were first founded as highly nationalist, conservative and militarist responses to the Communist revolution in Russia and the economic difficulties that followed the end of the First World War (Box 5.8). After that war, they seized power – sometimes after being elected to it – in several European nations including, most notoriously, Italy and Germany (see Chapter 1). The aggressively expansionist policies of those regimes, their blatant disregard for democracy and human rights, and their ultimately genocidal theories of racial superiority, were largely discredited following their defeat in the Second World War. But this did not mean that some of the tendencies they managed to mobilize disappeared completely.

While few far-right parties in the West actively celebrated their connection with the fascist past, some were still willing to play on similar themes in the postwar period. At first, they enjoyed little success. But more recently – as hostility to immigration has risen among Europeans (see Chapter 10) – this has changed. Along with its xenophobic (anti-foreigner) thrust, contemporary far-right rhetoric is characterized by populism – attacks on supposedly corrupt 'politics as usual' conducted by what is portrayed as a cosy cartel of mainstream politicians apparently more interested in their own survival than in the real needs or views of 'ordinary people' (see Albertazzi and McDonnell, 2007; Mudde, 2004; Taggart, 2000; and Zaslove, 2004). Often led by a charismatic leader who promises to clear up the mess at a stroke, many far-right parties began the 1980s and 1990s by offering potential voters a mix of strong support for a low-tax, low-interference, free-market economy, and conservative social values – all of which appealed most to middle-class ('petit bourgeois') voters. Recently, however, they have made big inroads into the working-class vote, focusing more on promises to cut immigration in order to cut crime and to ensure that the traditional welfare entitlements of the native-born are not compromised by allowing in foreigners with unrestricted access to them (an appeal known in the jargon as 'welfare chauvinism'). Meanwhile, their economic policies, such as they are, are, if anything, rather centrist (see de Lange, 2007).

It is these 'populist radical right parties' (see Mudde, 2007) that have gained ground recently in Italy, in Switzerland, Denmark, Norway and Austria (see Chapters 9 and 10). In Central and Eastern Europe, however, the issues of national minorities (see Chapter 1) and the Roma are more salient than immigration and multiculturalism (see Chapter 10). Consequently, the far-right in the region tends toward the older model of ultra-conservative nationalism (perhaps mixed with religion, as in the case of the *Liga Polskich Rodzin* or League of Polish Families that was wiped out in the election of 2007) and/or barely concealed or even open racism (for example, the Bulgarian *Ataka* or 'Attack' Party). Even an outfit which, compared to others in the region, could be seen as relatively 'modern' such as SPR-RSČ, the Czech Republican Party, which made it into parliament in the 1990s (see Kreidl and Vlachová, 2000), resembles its German namesake or the British BNP, both of which are at the extreme end of the far-right in western Europe. Everywhere, however, extremism – perceived or real – seems to present less of a barrier to office than before: in Slovakia, a government put together by the self-styled social democratic party, *Smer*, in the summer of 2006 included *Slovenská národná strana* (SNS), a party that seemed to specialize in demonizing the country's Hungarian, homosexual and Roma minorities.

Communist and Left parties

Communism provided an expression for those dissatisfied with the gradualism of social democracy and who believed that the replacement of capitalism by a collectivized, classless society could be achieved by rapid, revolutionary means (Box 5.9). In those countries that found themselves within the sphere of

BOX 5.8

Different, but all here to stay? Three far-right parties

Many people have heard of Jean-Marie Le Pen – one of Europe's most high-profile far-right leaders. A former soldier, active in extreme politics for decades and willing to flirt with Holocaust denial, he makes an ideal anti-hero for a media all too eager to associate the contemporary far right with the fascist past. There is no doubt that he deserves their attention, having taken his *Front National* (FN) from relative obscurity to what seems like a permanent place on the French political scene, where it can claim to enjoy around 10–15 per cent support nationwide – and much higher in certain regions in the East and the South of France. But there are limits to the FN's success. First and foremost, it tends to be more pronounced in presidential than parliamentary contests. In 2002, Le Pen's charisma, combined with a poor campaign by his Socialist opponent and a large number of surprisingly successful fringe candidates, helped him to not much less than 20 per cent of the vote for president, although France's electoral system, which severely handicaps smaller parties who might do better under PR (see Chapter 6), continues to stymie the FN's chances in the parliamentary elections. Moreover, some argue that the attention paid to Le Pen's favourite themes of immigration and law and order by Nicolas Sarkozy, leader of the centre-right *Union pour un Mouvement Populaire* (UMP) party and now President of the Republic, has diminished the Front's appeal (see Marthaler, 2008; see also Chapters 9 and 10). The party will also have to deal with the thorny question of who is to succeed its charismatic but ageing leader.

In other European countries, the far right is led by rather younger leaders who, unlike Le Pen, enjoy the advantage of operating under PR and have worked hard to render themselves more acceptable to potential allies on the centre-right, in the hope that they will one day share in (or at least influence) government. A good example is Pia Kjaersgaard, whose *Dansk Folkeparti* (DF) took 12 per cent of the vote in the Danish general election of 2001 (up from 7.4 per cent in 1998) and helped a centre-right minority government to take power by acting as a support party in parliament (see Chapter 4) – a role the party repeated after it upped its vote share to 13 per cent in 2005 and 14 per cent in 2007. This intermediate position gave DF considerable sway over immigration policy (see Chapter 10) without it suffering the fate suffered by another far-right party led by the best-known of the new breed of leaders, Jörg Haider. In 1999, his Austrian Freedom Party (FPÖ) could claim to be the continent's most successful party of its kind, winning 27 per cent of the vote at that year's general election, after which it became a full coalition partner with the Austrian Christian Democrats, the Austrian People's Party (the ÖVP). But being in power proved rather more difficult than carping from the sidelines and, at the end of its second consecutive term in office, the party eventually split in two, with Haider forming the Alliance for the Future of Austria (BZÖ) which only just squeaked back into parliament in 2006. The post-Haider FPÖ performed rather better: indeed, the parties' combined vote was higher than that achieved in 2002, the election prior to the split. In Austria, as elsewhere, the far right seems likely to be a feature of many European party systems for some time to come.

influence of the old Soviet Union, Communist parties were able to seize control in the fledgling democracies that briefly replaced the defeated dictatorships after the Second World War. The regimes they established resembled the Soviet Union's in that they were essentially party dictatorships that replaced the market with state planning, trading off political freedom and private property rights for near-universal (though low-level) economic and social security (see Chapter 1). In the West, however, the prospect of Communist parties winning power looked increasingly unlikely as the Cold War wore on. In Sweden and France, admittedly, the Communist Party supported social democratic administrations on more than one occasion. But in Italy, where the communists (the PCI) received

BOX 5.9

Making the best of a bad job? Four 'former' communist parties

The Swedish Left Party had its roots in the break-away from the Social Democrats by hopeful revolutionaries in 1917. The party remained loyal to the Soviet Union from the 1920s until the 1960s, when a newly independent stance led to a partial name change. The 'Communist' label was finally dropped in the 1990s since when it has spent time acting as a support party for minority social democratic (SAP) governments (see Chapter 4). This role, in the halfway house between government and opposition (see Bale and Bergman, 2006) resulted in some concrete achievements on the issues it has made its own – gender equality and resolute defence of the welfare state. However, it ate away at its support, which dropped from 12 per cent in 1998 to 8 per cent in 2002 and then just under 6 per cent in 2006. Now back in opposition, along with the Social Democrats, the party has the chance to rebuild its support, though some argue that it needs to decide between a 'new left' agenda built around issues like civil liberties, anti-discrimination, and environmentalism or the old-style 'class politics' of its leader Lars Ohly, who got into trouble for declaring himself a communist to a media that was all to happy to rake up old allegations about the party's past involvement with the Soviet bloc.

But 'keeping the faith' – choosing 'leftist-retreat' over 'pragmatic reform' (Hough, 2005) – need not necessarily mean electoral decline, at least in the short term. In the Czech Republic, the existence of the Social Democratic CSSD effectively closed off the latter option for the KSČM. Instead, it stuck to its traditional ideas about state ownership and opposed market reforms and membership of NATO and the EU. It also tapped into nationalist fears about the reclaiming of Czech lands by dispossessed foreigners (especially Germans) and antipathy to economic restructuring on the part of those who had lost their industrial jobs as a consequence. The party made the most of its relatively large, disciplined membership to maintain a healthy share of the vote, particularly among older people. In 2002, these strengths, along with widespread dissatisfaction with the social democrats, the collapse of a nationalist alternative on the far right, and an eye-catching campaign involving topless models, delivered the Communists 18.5 per cent of the vote. Things didn't go quite so well in 2006, however, and many observers predict that the party's 12.8 per cent is the beginning of a slow, demographically driven decline.

The one relic of the past the KSČM did ditch was the Soviet-style hammer and sickle on its logo (now a rather jaunty couple of cherries). Even this concession to modernity, however, proved too much for the Italian *Rifondazione Comunista,* which proudly retains the old symbol, and continues to attract sufficient support (5 per cent in 2001 and 5.8 per cent in 2006) to make itself a necessary but troublesome coalition partner for social democratic *Democratici di Sinistra* – essentially that part of the former Communist Party (PCI) which chose a more moderate path at the end of the Cold War. In fact, the Czechs and the Italians are not alone in their 'brand loyalty': it is shared by Europe's most successful left party, AKEL of Cyprus, which – for the moment at least – seems to have found the secret of combining ideological and policy modernisation with a nostalgic attachment to its traditional communist logo and subculture (see Dunphy and Bale, 2007). Its leader became Cypriot President in 2008.

significant electoral support, they were largely kept out of formal participation in government by an American-backed agreement on the part of other parties to form whatever coalitions were necessary to keep them out. This was in spite of their fairly flexible, forward-looking, democratic and less state-centric 'Eurocommunist' stance.

The end of the Cold War, however, has presented the radical left with a new opportunity. So, too, has the tendency of social democratic parties to back away, in word if not necessarily in deed (see Chapter 9), from state ownership, high taxation and generous social spending. In Sweden and Finland, for example, the former communists, now calling themselves *Left*

BOX 5.10

Insiders and outsiders – two successful regionalist parties

Europe's regionalist parties come in all ideological shapes and sizes. Among the most powerful is the *Convergència Democràtica de Catalunya* (CDC), the biggest partner in the Catalan nationalist union or CiU (see Chapter 2). Formed at the end of the Franco regime, it dominated politics in the province of Catalunya throughout the 1980s and 1990s, under its leader (and five-term head of the Catalan government, the *Generalitat*), Jordi Pujol. It also challenged the United Left (an alliance that, after all, covered the whole of Spain) for the position of third party behind PSOE and PP in the national parliament – a position it used to support the former and then the latter in government in 1993 and 1996, with ever-more autonomy for Catalunya as its price. It is able to do this partly because it is courted by the other parties but also because the size of the Catalonian population means it can win 3–5 per cent of the nationwide vote just by fighting there. The politics of the CiU have been described as slightly to the right of centre, but above all pragmatic.

In Belgium, the *Vlaams Belang* (formerly *Vlaams Blok, VB*) campaigns not only for a fully independent Dutch-speaking Flanders (see Chapter 2) but also for the barring and even the repatriation of immigrants. Founded in 1977 by radicals impatient with the gradualist nationalism of other Flemish parties, it has a solid base in the biggest Dutch-speaking city of Antwerp and took 12 per cent of the vote in the 2007 general election, despite (or perhaps because of) the decision of Belgium's other parties to treat it as an extremist 'pariah' with whom they would have no dealings. Although this 'cordon sanitaire' continues, they clearly have to pay attention to the support VB gathers on issues such as crime and immigration, while fear of increasing its support has undoubtedly led to further concessions to Flemish demands for more autonomy. Attempts to ban the party – at least indirectly – may not have proved as counterproductive as many predicted and may (along with the name change from *Blok* to *Belang*) even have accelerated a move away from the overt racism that alienated some potential voters (see Bale, 2007) – but neither, it seems, have they done it much harm.

parties, look to have a secure hold on some 5–15 per cent of the vote. They consciously provide a home for those dissatisfied with social democrats' defence of the welfare state and labour market protection. But they also stress so-called 'new politics' (or post-materialist) issues, such as anti-discrimination, aid to the developing world, environmental awareness, anti-militarism and, increasingly, anti-globalization, as well as opposition to what they claim is the neo-liberal agenda of the EU. These new politics values mean that many (western) former communist parties now have a lot in common with parties first set up in places such as Denmark and Norway in the 1960s to offer a radical alternative to both communism and social democracy.

Some left parties, however, have not adapted, neither have they fared so well. The French PCF, for example, is a shadow of its former self, and in Spain, the path toward modernization has been an uneven and slow one, perhaps because, for some time, the Communists were keener on using the IU (United Left) as a front organization they could control rather than a genuinely new formation. In Germany, the PDS – formerly the Communist Party that ran East Germany in the days of the Soviet bloc (see Chapter 1) – initially drew nearly all its strength from that part of the country and therefore seemed doomed to limited success. However, it then formed an electoral alliance with a breakaway party from the social democratic SPD, the Electoral Alternative for Labour and Social Justice (WASG), which won nearly 9 per cent in 2005 (more than double the PDS's previous tally). In June 2007, the two organizations merged to form *Die Linke.* (see Hough *et al.*, 2007). It may well be that the SPD's participation in a 'grand coalition' with the Christian Democrats (see p. 143) might well drive some 'progressive' voters its way.

In the former communist countries of eastern

Europe, Communist parties – as we note above – have generally transformed themselves into social democratic parties. As in Italy, however, where the PCI became the Left Democrats (DS), a minority of supporters who see this tendency as a sell-out have remained 'true to the faith', albeit with a now avowedly democratic stance. Support for these 'hardliner' parties is generally small. It has some similarities with the support base of the more traditionally inclined former Communist parties of the West, like the one which dominates the United Left or *Izquierda Unida* (IU) in Spain. But it contrasts with that of the Scandinavian Left parties, which appeal to younger, more middle-class, urban and educated voters, as well as to the trade unionists that both kinds of former Communist Party try to target.

Regional and ethnic parties

Some parties exist to promote the cause of those who argue (see Chapters 1–3) that their group and/or region merits autonomy or even complete independence from the state (Box 5.10). In some western European countries they play an important role in sub-national, and sometimes national, coalition governments. Most important are those in Belgium, where all parties in the families represented there are also regional, representing either Dutch-speaking Flanders or French-speaking Wallonia. Most numerous are those in Spain. The views of such parties on economic or social and moral issues vary considerably from left, through centrist to far right. Regionalist parties also exist in the postcommunist democracies, where they sometimes represent national minorities who identify with another country, perhaps one just across the border. In Romania and Slovakia, Hungarian minorities (and in Romania plenty of other minorities) are represented in parliament, and indeed in government, by their own parties; so, too, is the Turkish minority in Bulgaria. Indeed, one of the successes of the transition from communism in such countries is the extent to which such parties have been included in coalition politics for reasons of both political necessity and ethnic stability (see Millard, 2004: Chapter 9).

Agrarian and Centre parties

Some parties were originally set up to defend and promote the interests of farmers – often small-scale producers and peasants – especially in Scandinavia (Box 5.11). This is still part of their identity but, as the declining proportion of people employed in agriculture has eroded their core support, agrarian parties have repositioned (and often renamed) themselves as *Centre* parties, moving, as it were, 'from farmyard to city square' (see Arter, 2001). Currently the most successful example is the Finnish *Keskusta* (KESK) which took a quarter of the vote in the 2003 election. Centre parties target middle-class, often small-town, voters looking for a party that will moderate both the left and the right. Perhaps as a consequence, they cannot easily be pigeonholed ideologically. Private enterprise and traditional morality is important, but so, too, is generous welfare, agricultural support and in some cases environmental conservation. In postcommunist Europe – including Hungary where there was some early success – such parties barely exist, the one significant exception being Poland. There, agrarian parties reflect the suspicions of the still extensive (but often small-scale) agricultural sector that the larger, urban-based parties will sell out small producers to multinationals and the European Union.

The bases of party systems – social and institutional; luck and skill

Acknowledging that historical cleavages help structure present-day party systems need not blind us to the way parties may develop away from their original intentions and support. Neither does it mean downplaying the extent to which parties either enjoy or make their own luck. Often, a cleavage can be given political expression by a party founded on one side of another cleavage but sufficiently flexible to incorporate other concerns as well. From very early on, for instance, the British Labour Party managed to express the interests not just of the working-class (owner–worker cleavage) but also those of Wales (centre-periphery). But, by the same token, parties cannot rest assured that they have one or other side of a cleavage 'sewn up'. To take the same example, Labour 'inherited' Wales from the Liberal Party, but now faces a threat to its monopoly from *Plaid Cymru*, the Welsh Nationalists (as it does in Scotland

BOX 5.11

Two farmers' parties – 'ecohumanists' and populists

The Swedish *Centerpartiet* was founded in the second decade of the twentieth century as the Farmers' Federation, and functioned essentially as a parliamentary pressure group until the 1930s, after which it worked closely with the social democratic SAP. Co-operation continued until the late 1950s when the Federation, sensing it no longer had a future if it continued to appeal purely to its rural constituency and to cosy up too closely to the SAP, changed its name to the Centre Party and began to take a more independent stance. This strategy proved highly successful for a while: in 1956 it had polled under 10 per cent, but by the end of the 1960s, the *Centerpartiet* could claim to be the biggest non-socialist party in the country. In 1976, it took almost 25 per cent of the vote and its leader became the first non-social democrat prime minister in forty years. It was not, however, the best time to be in office (the world economy was in a mess) and the party arguably became distracted by its strong opposition to nuclear power. It was not in office again until 1991, but by then only as the smallest party (scoring only 8.5 per cent) in a four-way non-socialist coalition that lasted only three years. Following that unhappy period, it helped keep the minority SAP government in power between 1995 and 1998. At the 2002 election, fighting on what it calls an 'ecohumanist' platform, mixing social liberalism with environmentalism, it took just 6.2 per cent of the vote. In 2006, however, it threw in its lot with Sweden's centre-right parties and, not only raised its vote-share to 7.9 per cent but became part of the ensuing government.

Self-Defence (*Samoobrona*) started life as a Polish farmers' union in the early 1990s but – under the leadership of the charismatic populist Andrezj Lepper – soon turned itself into a political party and, in 2001, overtook the hundred-year-old Polish Peasants' Party (PSL) with 10 per cent of the vote. Where the PSL, as a member of several coalition governments, had headed toward the mainstream, *Samoobrona* put itself at the head of demonstrations and protests by Poland's large agricultural sector. But, by calling for greater government intervention in the economy, it also broadened out beyond its agricultural base to express the concerns of the many Poles for whom the transition to capitalism has not been easy – the 'transition losers' (see Szczerbiak, 2003). It combined this 'economic populism' with calls to get tough on crime and corruption and, unlike most of Europe's centre and agrarian parties (see Batory and Sitter, 2004), did not reconcile itself to the EU. After the 2005 election (which saw it marginally increase its support), Self-Defence swapped its role as the quintessential outsider for membership of the right-wing coalition government, but found the transition from sloganeering to sitting around the cabinet table a difficult one. The coalition fell apart and – true to form in Poland (see Chapter 4) – some of the party's MPs began to defect. At early elections, held in the autumn of 2007, *Samoobrona*'s vote collapsed from 11.4 per cent to just 1.5 per cent, a loss of 1.1 million votes!

from the Scottish National Party, the SNP). Similarly, some argue (see below) the conflict over the reach and power of the EU will become a new cleavage in many European countries, including the UK: now, there is a British party devoted to Euroscepticism (the United Kingdom Independence Party or UKIP). Yet it faces stiff competition on that score from the much older, much bigger, Conservative Party; whether it is wise for the latter to focus too much on the issue, especially at the expense of more traditional 'bread and butter' topics, is debateable (see Bale, 2006) but it will undoubtedly pick up more voters on the issue than UKIP – as long, that is, as the country's electoral system (see Chapter 6) continues to favour larger parties.

KEY POINT

A country's party system is influenced not only on historical and contemporary social and value conflicts, but also by institutions like the electoral system.

This brings us neatly to the fact that, as well as the skill shown or the luck enjoyed by particular parties, their relative strength (or even their very presence) – especially at a parliamentary level – is explained not just by social conflicts but also by man-made, constitutional arrangements. Academic observers who take an 'institutionalist' (as opposed to a sociological) approach argue that the political 'rules of the game' shape party systems just as much as cleavages, and neither rules nor systems should be seen as mere reflections of socio-economic 'reality'.

The most obvious institutional influence on party politics is the electoral system used in a particular country. These systems are examined in more detail in Chapter 6, so here we will limit ourselves to just a few key observations about their potential effects. Parties from some of the smaller or more extreme party families (such as the far right or the communists or the agrarians) could find it harder to win parliamentary seats in a country such as the UK. There, the electoral system does not award them seats according to the proportion of votes received, unlike a country such as Norway or Austria, where it does. On the other hand, a 'plurality' system with plenty of small constituencies, such as the UK's, might well make it easier for regionalist parties, whose share of the overall national vote might see them failing in a more purely proportional system to make it into parliament. But this effect, in turn, depends on the extent to which a proportional system has large or small constituencies or districts. The Netherlands' system treats the whole country as one district, offering little hope for regional parties. The Spanish system divides the country into regions, which makes it more likely that they will be represented at a national level.

Once again, however, it is important to stress that party systems are the product of both institutional arrangements *and* social forces – and that neither of these will necessarily prevent the emergence of a skilful or a lucky party or guarantee the survival of a short-sighted or unlucky one. Things are doubly complicated because parties are themselves involved in setting and changing the institutional framework in which they operate. All this is most obvious early in the life of the new democracies of postcommunist Europe. There, at a time when it was difficult to predict which social cleavages would become important or salient, those political parties which enjoyed initial success tinkered with thresholds and district magnitudes in order to ensure such success continued (see Bale and Kopecký, 1998). For some it did, but some have declined or even disappeared as they were rendered less relevant by more pressing social conflicts and outmanoeuvred by other 'political entrepreneurs' (see Millard, 2004). As the Spanish UCD, which disappeared almost overnight after seeing the country safely into the democratic era, could have told them, voters are not necessarily grateful once the job is done (see Hopkin, 1999).

And while postcommunist party systems still tend to be more fragmented, polarized and fluid (Lithuania is a good example) than those of their 'never-communist' counterparts, in some countries (notably the Czech Republic, Hungary and Slovenia) they are now presenting voters with a familiar set of options rather than a bewildering array of choices – at least when it comes to parties that have a chance of getting into or influencing governments (see Millard, 2004: Chapter 6). In many of Europe's new democracies (even those where party competition remains unsettled), a sizable social democratic party, sometimes flanked on its left by a smaller socialist or communist party, competes against a more or less fluid right, though there are still centrist (e.g. liberal) parties that may be willing to play a role in governments of either bloc. This pattern would, for instance, be readily recognizable to Scandinavian voters long used to this kind of basically *bipolar, two-bloc* competition. French (and, more recently, Italian and German) voters would recognise the pattern, too (see below).

Figure 5.4 illustrates the relative strength of the parties in the German party system mapping the actual parties' share of the vote in 2005 onto a graph of support for party families. Figure 5.5 performs a similar mapping exercise for the eight other 'core countries' considered in this book at the most recent available elections. There is always room for disagreement about which party belongs to which family, of course, but it emphasizes once again that, although not every party family is represented in every country, a good many of them are. This makes generalizations about European party systems more feasible and credible.

That said, there are of course 'exceptions that prove the rule'. Poland is often cited as such. Indeed,

Figure 5.4 The German party system after 2005

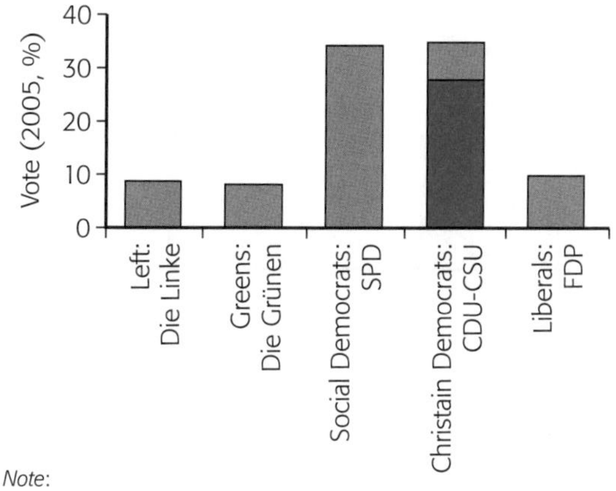

Note:
Left: Die Linke. (8.7%)
Greens: Die Grünen (8.1%)
Social Democrats SPD (34.2%)
Christian Democrats: CDU-CSU (27.8% + 7.4%)
Liberals: FDP (9.8%)

many analysts (see Millard, 2004) have questioned whether the country can be said to have a party 'system' at all in the sense that there was little evidence of a more or less stable pattern of interaction or number of parties (though see Jasiewicz, 2007). Yet for the first time, the election of 2005 saw the same parties that sat in parliament before the contest returned after it. On the other hand, there were massive swings in support, with the Social Democrats dropping from 41 to 11 per cent. And, because of the continuing importance of issues like religion, agriculture and unfinished business concerning the transition from communism, it is harder convincingly to collapse the various dimensions of politics into an encompassing, conventional left–right dimension, making it harder to line up parties along it or to pigeonhole them. For instance, Self-Defence, which took such a beating at the election of 2007 (see Box 5.11), saw itself as implacably opposed to the former-communists-turned-social-democrats but clearly believed in economic and social intervention by the state – populist, maybe, but right wing? There are two apparently conservative parties – one more into economic liberalization, one more nationalistic. Which is more right wing? Finally, the Peasants' or People's Party (PSL) has taken to (but is not alone in) calling itself Christian Democratic – does this mean we should unquestioningly label them as such even if they don't have much in common with their western 'counterparts' (see Bale and Szczerbiak, 2008)?

Party system change?

Interestingly, however, if the party systems of the continent's older and newer democracies are beginning to look more like each other, it may not simply be a matter of the former East 'catching-up' with the West – arguably a rather patronizing way of seeing things anyway. It could also be that politics in the latter is in flux – possibly, some would argue, because it is becoming detached from its historical roots. In other words, it could be that the Europeanization of party systems from west to east and north to south might be a two-way process. Voters and parties in the newer democracies might be taking time to discover where they stand. Meanwhile, in the older democracies both voters and parties are less and less likely to think, do or say things just because political custom and tradition dictates it.

This has led some political scientists to argue that, after years in which they were in effect 'frozen', party systems in western Europe since the 1970s are undergoing profound and accelerating change. The central features of this are an increase in fragmentation (the number of parties in the system), accompanied and in part explained by two things: **electoral volatility** and **dealignment**.

As we show in Chapter 6, the evidence that cleavage-driven voting has disappeared completely is weak: it might not necessarily be foolish, even now, to think we could predict a person's voting behaviour from his or her occupation or religion. However, we would, indeed, be less likely to make a correct prediction than we would have been thirty,

Electoral volatility occurs when voters switch their votes between parties from one election to another. **Dealignment** describes the way in which people's political preferences seem to be becoming less related to their location on one or other side of certain key cleavages than they used to be – preferences, in other words, seem to be increasingly individual and decreasingly collective, less fixed and more floating.

Figure 5.5 Eight contemporary European party systems

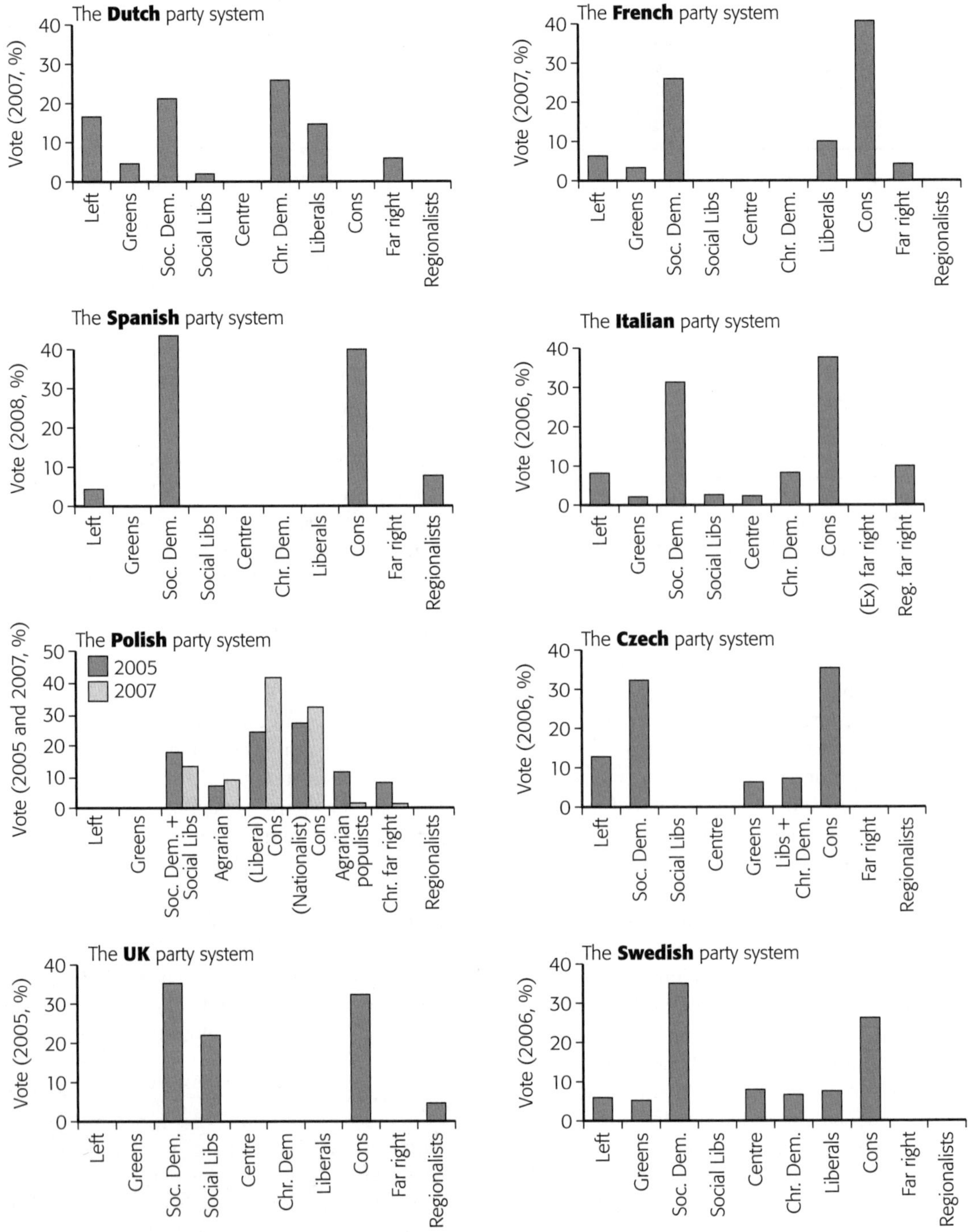

Note: See Figure 5.4 for the German party system after 2005.

Source: *Data from Parties and Elections in Europe*, 2007. www.parties-and-elections.de

KEY POINT

Party systems are changing: in the west there are more new parties and the fortunes of (and the alliances put together by) parties fluctuate more than they used to; further east, things will not necessarily 'settle down'. But change should be expected and is rarely wholesale: left and right score about the same as they ever did.

forty, or fifty years ago. It also seems, as we show in Chapter 6, that predicting how a person will vote based on how they voted last time is less easy than it was. In the 1990s, every west European country saw volatility rise compared to the 1980s – in many cases, to levels never reached before (see Chapter 6). The most comprehensive recent survey (Drummond, 2006) paints a picture of relative consolidation between 1945 and 1970 giving way to one clearly characterised by 'increasingly erratic party fortunes' thereafter – a trend evident not only in the new parties (where we might expect instability) but (more significantly) in the older, established parties. Scandinavia in particular, has not only experienced high volatility, but has seen the newcomers gain at the expense of the old-timers.

Volatility in postcommunist countries remains very high and looks likely to stay that way (see Millard, 2004: Chapter 5). Some analysts detect a certain amount of consolidation in Eastern and Central Europe as voters learn both where there interests are and which parties are likely to best serve them (see Dawisha and Deets, 2006 and Tavits, 2005). Others, though, maintain that the stabilization of political competition does not automatically occur after a few years of flux (see Mainwaring and Zoco, 2007) and note that the citizens of postcommunist states came to politics after, not before, the advent of mass education and media systems, meaning they might never take on the partisan loyalties associated with the earlier era (see Enyedi, 2006: 228). If the new century picks up where the old one left off – and judging by some recent elections, it might do – then change may become the rule and not the exception right across Europe.

What about *fragmentation*? Has all this switching of votes led to more parties? And are some of them new parties? Our answer – even if we exclude Italy, whose party system underwent an unusually complete transformation in the early 1990s once the corrupt Christian Democrats could no longer frighten voters with the spectre of communist takeover (see Newell, 2000) – has to be 'yes' – especially in Scandinavia (see Drummond, 2006). But it should be a qualified 'yes'. There is no doubt that in many west European countries there has been a rise in the number of parties capable of making it into parliament. The increase, however, is by no means large and, according to recent research (Tavits, 2006) would seem to depend (a) on how long the country has been democratic (older systems have fewer new entrants); (b) on an electoral system that is not stacked against small parties (see Chapter 6); and (c) on the extent to which parliament (as opposed to major interest groups brought together by the government – see Chapter 8) has much purchase on policy. In addition, there have indeed been many new parties, but also many (such as the pensioners' party, AOV, which suddenly made it into the Dutch parliament in 1994) that have proved to be what political scientists sometimes call 'flash parties', disappearing into obscurity as quickly as they appeared. Of course, the green, far-right and regionalist parties that first emerged in the 1970s have not only gate-crashed their way into the politics of many countries, but also look set, eventually, to become 'old' parties themselves.

Yet even the impact of these successful new parties can be overstated. This is because for the most part, and sometimes in spite of their own efforts to retain their 'anti-system' or 'anti-party' reputation, they often become identified with one side or other of the familiar left and right blocs. The far-right parties have ended up either joining (as in Italy) or effectively supporting (as in Denmark) coalitions led by more moderate conservatives. The greens may have argued that they were 'neither left nor right but out in front', but few voters buy this line and most green parties have gradually accepted their fate as part of the left – although recent developments in the Czech Republic, Finland and Ireland suggest this may be changing. Regionalist parties, it must be said, have always been harder to pigeonhole, but even this can be exaggerated. Few were surprised, for instance, when the Catalonian nationalists (CiU) supported the then minority government of the conservative *Partido Popular* (PP) in Spain between 1996 and 2000.

Table 5.1 Party family and bloc performance across sixteen European democracies since 1950

	1950s	1960s	1970s	1980s	1990s	2000–4
Left	7.9	8.4	9.1	8.0	5.3	4.3
Green	n/a	n/a	n/a	2.3	4.8	5.4
Soc. Dem.	33.6	32.1	31.8	30.7	29.9	28.8
Left bloc	**41.5**	**40.5**	**40.9**	**41.0**	**40.0**	**38.5**
Liberal	8.7	9.8	9.6	10.3	10.1	10.7
Centre	6.6	6.9	6.7	5.4	6.4	7.1
Ch. Dem.	22.9	23.4	22.1	21.5	17.6	16.9
Cons.	15.4	15.8	15.2	16.3	15	15.4
Far right	1.0	0.5	1.6	2.2	6.3	5.8
Right bloc	**54.6**	**56.4**	**55.2**	**55.7**	**55.4**	**55.9**

Note: n/a = Not applicable.

Source: Data from Gallagher *et al.* (2006: chapters 8 and 9).

In fact, if we look at the support for the two blocs, left and right, across Europe as a whole, it has remained remarkably consistent since the 1950s (see Table 5.1). If we include in the left bloc socialists (including former communists), greens and social democrats, it still commands around 40 per cent of the vote across Europe. The right, if we include not only conservatives, Christian democrats and the far right, but also liberals and agrarians, continues to poll around 55 per cent. Some have even suggested that, even if it is popularly believed that there is little policy difference between them (see Chapter 9) in many European countries, the two blocs or 'poles' are attracting smaller parties from both the centre and the flanks, thereby 'bipolarizing' political competition (see Bale, 2003; and Mair, 2001). On the other hand, one can make the argument that recent trends in both voting (see Chapter 6) and government formation (see Chapter 4), suggest that parties and voters may well be becoming more adventurous or 'promiscuous' (i.e. increasingly willing to give new parties a try) and thereby encouraging parties to be just as innovative when it comes to putting together coalitions – innovation that, in turn, may encourage voters to embrace novelty still further. It is noticeable that the years since the end of the Cold War have seen governments in many west European countries joined or supported by parties that previously might have been considered beyond the pale (see Table 5.2). Although, such innovation may (at least for the moment) go on within rather than between left and right blocs, these are exactly the kind of trends that may move some party systems from what Mair (see above) calls 'closed' to 'open'.

Should we, then, conclude that western European party systems are no longer 'frozen' but thawing fast? Rather than being 'caught up' by (unevenly) consolidating east European party systems, will they not instead meet them coming the other way? Quite possibly, yes. However, three points need to be made.

First, the apparently sharp increase in the pace of change in party systems should not blind us to long-term, albeit previously imperceptible, causes. These may well be sociological. The structural shifts in occupational, migration and family patterns discussed in Chapter 1 have almost certainly produced in every country a more heterogeneous and less tradition-bound electorate, for instance. But there will also be institutional causes. Mainstream centre-left and centre-right parties, for instance, might well have contributed to the partial 'de-coupling' of social class and voting (see Chapter 6) by their attempts to broaden their 'catch-all' appeal by stressing pragmatism and competence over ideology and particular interests (see Chapter 9).

Second, it is possible that, in focusing on what, some argue, is after all only fairly marginal change to party systems, we may in fact be peering down the wrong end of the telescope. Perhaps, given the huge changes to European societies over the fifty years since the end of the Second World War, it is the lack of any correspondingly huge change in the continent's party systems that needs explaining! And here again, the danger of putting things down to *either* sociology *or* institutions becomes obvious. The lack of change in party systems might indicate, for example, that political scientists have always tended to overstate the links between those systems and social realities. Perhaps parties – and especially old parties – have found it easier to adapt to (and maybe even help shape) those realities that they are sometimes given credit for. Or perhaps the constitutional and electoral arrangements they had a hand in designing have served to constrain the kinds of party system

Table 5.2 No longer beyond the pale – west European radical parties in or supporting governments after 1989

	Left parties	Green parties	Far-right parties
Austria			Government (1999–2006)
Belgium		Government (1999–2003)	
Cyprus	Government (2003–)		
Denmark	Support party (1993–2001)		Support party (2001–)
Finland	Government (1995–2003)	Government (1995–2002) Government (2007–)	
France	Support party (1989–1993) Government (1997–2002)	Government (1997–2002)	
Germany		Government (1998–2005)	
Greece	Government (1989–90)		
Ireland	Government (1994–7)	Government (2007–)	
Italy	Support party (1996–8) Government (1998–2001) Government (2006–8)	Government (1996–2001) Government (2006–8)	Government (1994–5) Government (2001–6)
NL			Government (2002)
Norway	Support party (1994) Government (2005–)		Support party (2001–5)
Spain	Support party (2004–)		
Sweden	Support party (1998–2006)	Support party (1998–2006)	Support party (1991–4)

change that a more sociological approach might have predicted.

Third, the fact that, arguably, such change does now seem to be gathering pace does not necessarily mean that Europe's party systems will for evermore be subject to such volatility, fragmentation and dealignment that we may as well abandon the search for patterns and predictions and kiss goodbye to the whole notion of party systems and even to parties themselves. If the twentieth century is anything to go by, change is a constant but often a gradual process, and by no means always in the same direction. Even so-called 'earthquake elections' (contests which see many of the old parties losing seats to new competitors appearing out of nowhere) rarely end up rendering the political landscape utterly unrecognizable – especially a couple of elections later. Party systems of the future will probably end up looking different from how they look today, but rarely completely so – just as how they look today strongly resembles how they looked three or four decades ago. Then, just as now, they will be the product of a subtle and reciprocal interaction of institutional arrangements and sociological realities, both of which will influence and be influenced by the behaviour of parties themselves.

Are parties in decline?

Whether party systems change profoundly or stay more or less the same, will many Europeans even care? Certainly few of them – particularly in bigger countries (see Weldon, 2006) and especially in East Central Europe but also in the west – join parties or stay very long if they do (see Figure 5.6). If ever there was a golden age for parties in the postwar period, it is over now. There are many other things that people with more leisure and money can now do with their time, and, for the politically inclined, there are many single-issue groups that seem to offer a more direct (and possibly more enjoyable) way to get what you want (see Chapter 8). Members are still useful to parties, in terms of finance or legitimacy or campaigning (see Scarrow, 1994) – and parties may be responding to the lack of supply by making themselves more democratic (Scarrow and Caul Kittilson, 2003). However, it would seem they are able to cope without too many people on the ground – especially if it means they will be free of the damaging impression that internal wrangling can cause in the media.

Figure 5.6 Party membership, c. 1980 and 2000

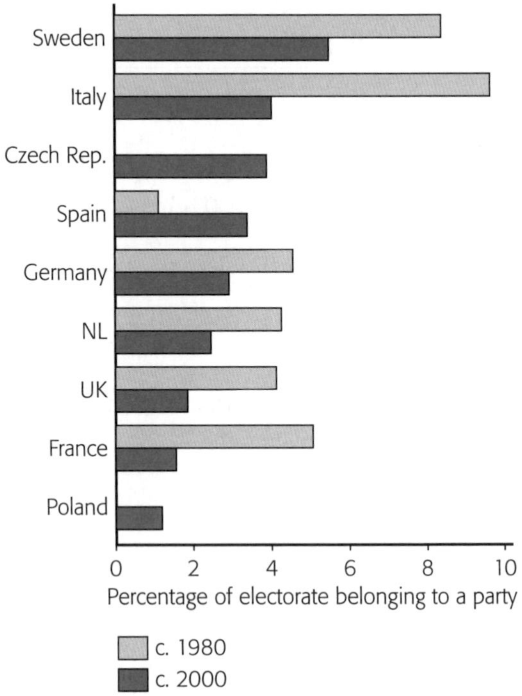

Sources: Data from Mair and van Biezen (2001).

KEY POINT

Parties may not be popular but there is no better alternative: partly because of this they are increasingly publicly funded and are likely to be with us for the foreseeable future.

To many media pundits, and quite a few political scientists, high levels of anti-party sentiment and electoral apathy across the developed world indicate something of a crisis – one which might mean the long-term, even terminal, decline of parties as genuinely representative institutions linking citizens to governments (see Dalton and Weldon, 2005 and Mair, 2006b). There might be some truth in these predictions of party 'failure', but we should not expect wholesale change – at least, not too quickly (see Debate 5.1). There is a great deal of inertia around and parties are adept at adapting. For instance, in the face of reduced (or never very significant) membership income and of donations that cannot always be be relied upon (or relied upon to be strictly legal!), parties in almost every country, especially in Central and Eastern Europe, seem to have persuaded the states they help to run that they are worth subsidizing (see Table 5.3 and Pinto-Duschinsky, 2002). This has fuelled allegations that they are indeed operating as cartels (see Box 5.1).

In fact, there are plenty of arguments which supporters of state funding can point to. Parties are the least worst option when it comes to ensuring competitive elections and contestable national governance. This is because they are at base information-economizing devices, providing distinctive but manageably-packaged alternatives (see Budge and McDonald, 2006) for voters who would otherwise be confronted with a chaotic choice of alternatives and agents whom they could neither conceivably hope to know nor trust. This is even the case in some of Europe's newer democracies where politicians swap party labels, and parties come and go, with aston-

Table 5.3 Party funding

	Parties obliged to disclose donations?	Limit per donor?	Ban on foreign donations?	Ban on corporate donations?	Tax privileges for parties?	Parties obliged to disclose spending?	Limit imposed on spending?	Direct public funding?	Public funding based on?	Free media access at election?	Media access based on?
Czech Rep.	Yes: all	No	Yes	Yes	Yes	Yes	No	Yes	Votes at current election + parliamentary seats held	Yes	Number of candidates
France	Yes: all	Yes: c. €5,000 per election cycle	Yes	Yes	No	Yes	Yes	Yes	Votes at current election + candidates	Yes	Parliamentary seats held
Germany	Yes: all	No	No (but limited to EU)	No	Yes	Yes	No	Yes	Votes at previous election	Yes	Mix of factors
Italy	Yes: above c. €6,000.	Yes: c. €10,000 per election cycle	No	No (unless they do work for government)	Yes	Yes	Yes	Yes	Votes at current election	Yes	Equal time
NL	Yes: corporate donations over c. €3,000	No	No	No	No	No	No	Yes	Parliamentary seats held	Yes	Parliamentary seats held (but also for new parties)
Poland	Yes	Yes: fifteen times minimum wage p.a.	Yes	Yes	No	Yes	Yes	Yes	Votes at current + previous election	Yes	Number of candidates
Spain	Yes: all	Yes: c. €60,000 p.a.	No	No (unless they do work for government)	Yes	Yes	Yes	Yes	Votes at current election	Yes	Votes at previous election
Sweden	No	No	No	No	No	Yes (but not public)	No	Yes	Votes at previous election + parliamentary seats held	Yes	Equal time
UK	Yes: above c. €7,000	No	Yes	No	No	Yes	Yes	Yes	Parliamentary seats held	Yes	Number of candidates

Source: Data from IDEA (2003) *Funding of Political Parties and Election Campaigns* (Stockholm: IDEA).

ishing speed (see Zielinski *et al.*, 2005). Parties – especially established ones – offer a reasonably predictable set of diagnostically based responses to both novel and perennial problems. They also offer – in extreme cases – some hope of bridging the gap between the majority and minorities who feel strongly enough to pursue armed struggle. They possess sufficient democratic credentials – often exemplified in their own internal practices – to spare citizens the worry that those whom they choose to govern will turn around and deprive them of that choice next time around. Finally, they make it easier for those who did not get the government they wanted: if your team did not finish top, then at least it was beaten by an outfit or outfits playing roughly the same game under the same rules, and who you might hope to beat in the future. Parties, in other words, are worth funding because they are, in a sense, public utilities – something we need but which, left to our own devices, we might be incapable of raising sufficient resources to obtain and supply (see van Biezen, 2004).

Supporters of the role of parties in a democracy also deny that other groups can fulfil a governing function because governing involves balancing various social claims for resources. By definition, pressure groups and protest movements – which may indeed be better at expressing the direct material or identity needs of their participants, but which also promote one interest or cause to the exclusion of most or all others – are unable to do this, at least with any degree of efficiency and legitimacy (see Chapter 8). The idea that neutral, non-political state managers will be able to help them do so is patently false, since (as we note in Chapter 8) state bureaucracies sometimes fall victim to 'producer-capture' by well-funded and well-organized interests – even when overseen by parties with different concerns and constituencies. How much more likely and worse would this be without those parties around at all?

This is not to say that Europe's parties are by any means perfect. They often talk as if they have a monopoly on good ideas, even though they know that they are heavily reliant on input from other players, including other parties – something which proportional systems that help facilitate coalition governments implicitly acknowledge. This, and other elements of their gamesmanship (and their salesmanship), can drive some citizens either to despair, or away, or both, as evidenced in recent British and EP elections, for example. But a great many others enjoy politics at least a little, even if only as a spectator sport. There is little evidence that those who stay at home would be any more actively involved by some other means of legitimately organizing the periodic, and at least semi-public, surrender of collective sovereignty to a handful of individuals. Parties might well be no more popular than (and just as stuck in the past as) other despised professions such as used-car salesman, but people will almost certainly continue to use them both for a very long time to come – something citizens themselves seem to recognize (Table 5.4).

Whether tomorrow's parties will look exactly like yesterday's, however, is another matter. So is the more normative question of whether government by organizations which survive for want of anything better, rather than because they are truly representative, can be said to constitute democracy. In order to cope with lower levels of partisanship and commitment,

Table 5.4 Feelings towards political parties – not close but necessary

	Feeling close to a political party (%)	Agreeing parties are necessary (%)	Identifying a party that represents their views (%)
Sweden	63	78	78
Spain	56	81	74
NL	55	85	n/a
Czech Rep.	53	73	78
France	51	n/a	59
Italy	48	n/a	n/a
UK	46	77	n/a
Germany	45	82	58
Poland	40	61	40
'Western' average	52	75	66
Postcommunist average	44	60	59

Note: n/a = not available.

Source: Data from Tóka (2006: 123, data covers 1996–2004).

DEBATE 5.1

Are political parties doomed to extinction?

YES

- Parties used to fulfil a social and a patronage function. Nowadays, there are more and better places to meet people and patronage tends to be seen as corrupt.
- They are losing members, especially active members: they are hollow shells.
- Fewer people identify with one party rather than another: football teams invoke more loyalty.
- The differences between them are less obvious now: its all managerialism, not passion and ideology.
- Fewer people are bothering to vote for them: if votes are like purchases, they are losing customers.
- According to opinion polls, they are some of the least trusted institutions in present-day society, and people don't believe parties care what they think and that they are only interested in power.
- Parties are closed, secretive institutions that call for discipline and dedication from their members. This puts them out of step with a wider trend toward transparency, autonomy and more instant gratification.
- They can't survive without state subsidies, which they don't deserve but still get, thereby increasing cynicism.
- People nowadays – especially the young – are more likely to get involved in pressure groups than parties.
- Developments in IT and telecoms will soon allow us all to vote on every issue in instant referendums, just like we do for television talent shows, rendering parliament (and therefore parties) redundant.
- The media does just as good a job of exposing government wrongdoing and thus ensuring accountability.
- The media is, anyway, what counts when it comes to appealing to voters: parties (at least, as they are traditionally organized) are relatively inefficient vehicles for tomorrow's aspirant politicians.
- Politics and governance is becoming more transnational or even supranational. Parties are irredeemably national institutions that will find it hard to adjust to this new era.

NO

- They have never had as many members as some like to think. And, in any case, the boundaries between membership and non-membership are now quite blurred.
- Loss of party identification is no bad thing: we shouldn't expect better educated, better-off people to maintain the old tribal loyalties.
- Turnout in elections can go up as well as down, and the media tends to pay more attention to low rather than high turnout. In any case, turnout varies a great deal between countries.
- It's hardly surprising that people don't think much of political parties and politicians given the way the media portrays them; when people do have direct contact with them they tend to feel more favourably. Anyway, you don't have to like someone or something to realise that they have a job to do: polls show that people still think that parties are necessary.
- State funding of parties varies considerably, but if we want representative democracy then we have to pay for it somehow. It's like any public good – left to the market it will be subject to undersupply.
- Pressure groups push only their point of view and their issue to the exclusion of all others – parties try to produce balanced programmes that will appeal to a wider audience. Pressure groups are rarely internally democratic and are often financed by special interests.
- Anyone who thinks that there is enough time in the day for all sorts of often very complicated issues to be debated and then voted on by people who are understandably not interested in everything is living in cloud-cuckoo land!
- The media doesn't actually do that much investigative reporting. It largely relies on parties to structure and inform coverage of political issues, and to blow the whistle on government.
- Even those entrepreneurs (be they individuals or cause groups) who make most use of the media find it necessary, if they want to get into government, to capture or create a party as well.

for instance, parties might well evolve into more 'open source', networked organizations with a much more shifting, less tightly-defined membership. Conversely (and rather more pessimistically), they might become even more like hollowed out brands – still useful to those with the resources and skills to exploit them but increasingly intangible.

The Europeanization of parties and party systems?

Primarily because they contest national elections, we tend to think of parties as national bodies. However, in many cases – in response to the trends identified in Chapter 2 – they are multilevel organizations, operating and constituting themselves in both subnational (see Deschouwer, 2006) and, as we now go on to discuss, transnational arenas. Sheer proximity aside, the EU provides not only opportunities to persuade and learn from other parties of like mind but also a whole new electoral battleground and set of issues (organizational and ideological) with which to contend (see Ladrech, 2002; and Mair, 2000). As a result, we have to consider the effect on parties and party systems of Europeanization – the potential we identified in the Introduction for European integration to impact on the constraints, incentives, resources and influences experienced by hitherto 'domestic' political actors.

KEY POINT

Parties are adapting to European integration but it has not undermined their primary 'domestic focus', although its indirect effects may pose problems as time goes on.

The impact on organization is immediately apparent. For instance, representatives of national parties elected to the EP need to work together, which they do by forming party groups in the EP (see Chapter 4). They may also be members of transnational federations outside the EP (see Table 5.5 and Johansson and Zervakis, 2002). Clearly, this transnational activity could lead to co-ordinated campaigning at EP elections – indeed, it has already done so in the case of the greens in 2004. The tendency for the various national leaders of the party families to caucus together before European summits might also both build on and facilitate transnational relationships that might have a policy impact at the European level, to the extent perhaps that centre-right leaders might, say, agree to co-ordinate a push for business deregulation.

But there is an awful lot of 'could' and 'might' about all this when, in practice, domestic politics and ideological differences between national parties belonging to the same federation often get in the way (see Lightfoot, 2005). Party politicians attend the European Council as heads of government and tend to push their national interests as much as their ideological positions. For example, centre-left leaders in Sweden, the UK and the Netherlands from 1997 onwards might have been interested in reforming the CAP but their counterparts in France and Germany did not stand shoulder to shoulder with them; and on liberalization of the European economy during the same period, the agenda was driven by an alliance between a centre-left prime minister in the UK and a centre-right prime minister in Spain. It is also doubtful in the near or medium term whether the increasing power of the EP will change the incentives parties have to keep their activities largely national. For one thing, organizational change not only disrupts vested intra-party interests (Panebianco, 1988), it also presents co-ordination problems at a time when many parties already have enough on their plates coping with sometimes increasingly decentralized systems (see Hopkin, 2003). For another, parties are not so rich that they can devote significant resources to relationships between national parties, transnational federations and EP party groups (EU funding for which cannot legally be filtered back to the national party). Notwithstanding all this, we should remember that parties are, above all, adaptive organizations, and it could be that in future they will adopt a kind of 'franchizing' model, whereby (like many fast-food chains) the component parts of the organization will be allowed a good deal of autonomy as long as they use and promote the basic brand (Carty, 2004). This less hierarchical structure might facilitate within parties the kind of multilevel governance they are having to adjust to both at home and in Europe.

On the other hand, political cycles in European countries show little sign as yet of synchronizing

Table 5.5 Transnational party federations

Party family	Federation	Website
Left	European Left Party[1]	http://www.european-left.org/
Greens	European Federation of Green Parties	http://www.europeangreens.org/
Soc. Democrat	Party of European Socialists	http://www.pes.org/
Liberal	European Liberal Democrats	http://www.eldr.org/
Cons/Christian Dem.	European People's Party	http://www.epp.org

Note: 1 = Formed in May 2004, includes Germany's *Die Linke*, the French PCF, the Italian *Rifondazione Comunista*, the Spanish *Izquierda Unida*). It was also supposed to include more 'unreconstructed' communist parties, such as the Czech KSČM (see Box 5.9). Their presence explains the reluctance of other Left parties (especially those from Scandinavia) to participate in the new party, although, ironically, the KSČM stormed out of the inaugural meeting in protest at criticisms of the Soviet era.

and are unlikely to, given different constitutional arrangements. This makes working together across national borders difficult. And, as we saw once again in 2004, the EP elections themselves are still fought largely on national issues under national systems and are not seen to impact that strongly on the policy direction of the EU (either by parties or by voters). They also tend to see incumbent parties suffer, irrespective of the party family they represent, making co-ordination between the levels (for example, between parties in national government and EP groups) difficult and, arguably, pointless. A party may have sent a lot of MEPs to Strasbourg at the last election but, if it is in opposition at home, its MPs could well be less enthusiastic than those MEPs are about European legislation, seeing it more as the product of a government they object to than the result of the hard work of their Euro-colleagues. Finally, there have been very major few changes in party practices to allow those colleagues a greater say in the running of national parties. The latter have adapted, recognizing that they need to operate in a multilevel environment, but the shift in resources and control has hardly been huge (for more detail, see Poguntke *et al.*, 2006).

None of this, however, should allow us to forget what should be apparent from almost every chapter in this book, namely that the structures and issues that form the environment in which parties have to operate (either as governments or in terms of electoral competition) are affected – often increasingly so – by European integration. A major development since the 1980s, for example, is the extent to which social democratic parties have reoriented themselves towards a more 'pro-European' position as they recognize, first, that co-ordinated continental action may make more sense than the pursuit of the same goals at a purely national level and, second, that the latter is no longer clearly demarcated from the transnational anyway (see Ladrech, 2000). Left parties have also had to come to terms with Europe, recognizing that unless they engage positively in transnational politics in general and with the EU in particular that their fears about the latter locking-in neo-liberalism (see Chapter 9) are more likely than ever to be realized (see Dunphy, 2004). Green parties, too, have learned to live with, if not completely overcome, their ambivalence. Indeed, more than that, a recent study suggests that 'Europeanization has accelerated both trends of professionalization of Green strategy and the mellowing of their ideological edge' (Bomberg, 2002: 45). In particular, success at EP elections has given the greens extra exposure, while perceived failure has helped speed up organizational reform (Bomberg, 2002, 34–5, 38). All of this indicates (Bomberg, 2002, 46) that 'Parties need not simply lie back and "let Europe happen to them": they can (and often do) actively engage and exploit European structures for their own party political gain.'

In keeping with this, we should reflect on other recent research which suggests that, despite the potential for 'Europe' to provoke internal tensions in some parties, most parties can, by and large, incorporate 'Europe' into existing and familiar modes of competition. Party (family) stances, and voter preferences, on European issues might well be consistent with, rather than cutting across, their left–right (and their postmaterialist–materialist) positions (see

Marks and Steenbergen, 2004). For instance, social democratic parties tend to favour a 'social Europe' that helps to correct market failures, while conservatives tend to favour a Europe that promotes the cause of economic liberalization and business deregulation – something that really worries left parties. Meanwhile, green parties appreciate the opportunities provided by the EU for environmental regulation, while far-right parties fear a loss of national sovereignty will undermine their ability to keep out immigrants and maintain a home-grown culture and welfare state.

Partly because of this and partly because of strategic and tactical imperatives, the pace, direction and extent of European integration is itself becoming an issue – if not always a central one, at least for mainstream parties – in national elections (see Gabel, 2000; and Grzymala-Busse and Innes, 2003). 'Europe' is now a potentially potent war cry – and some would argue even a new political cleavage (see Kriesi, 2007) not just in the UK and Scandinavia, where it has played a part in partisan competition for some time, but in elections all over the continent (see Szczerbiak and Taggart, 2008; see also de Vries, 2007). It is these contests that are the focus of Chapter 6.

Before moving on, however, it is worth pausing to ask whether, in all this talk of 'Europe' affecting (or not affecting) party organization and political competition, we might be ignoring more indirect effects – and more normative questions – that are just as, or perhaps even more, important. Research on these might be at an early stage, but it might well be the case that, as Peter Mair (2006a) suggests, any flow of policy competence to the European from the national level (inasmuch as the two remain separate) will (a) mean that, because so many previously available policy instruments (such as protecting certain sectors from competition) are no longer available, domestic political competition has to be carried out on an attenuated or at least altered agenda; and (b) weaken parties even further by making it obvious that the real power lies elsewhere (for instance, with unelected EU institutions and/or the interest groups that seek to influence them). This, combined with a lack of interest and respect for the EP that might spill over into views on national legislatures and elections, could lead to a crisis of representation (see also Bartolini, 2007) that cannot help but damage parties, except perhaps those that – in predictable populist fashion – jump on the bandwagon in order to exploit it.

Learning Resources for Chapter 5

Further reading

The standard text on political parties, Ware (1996), *Political Parties and Party Systems*, is excellent, though in need of updating. Fortunately, we now have Katz and Crotty (2006), *Handbook of Party Politics*, which is a great place to start. Mair and Mudde (1998), in the journal *Annual Review of Political Science*, is useful on party families. Good country overviews (and pointers to more detailed studies) are available in Broughton and Donovan (1999), *Changing Party Systems in Western Europe*, and Webb *et al.* (2002), *Political Parties in Advanced Industrial Democracies*. For the electoral performance of the main parties and party families in the postwar period, see Mair (2002), in *Comparative Democratic Politics*, edited by Hans Keman. The case for party system change is most easily grasped by reading Drummond (2006) in the journal *Political Studies*. Most of the key conceptual readings are helpfully collected in Wolinetz (1997), *Party Systems* and (1998), *Political Parties*. Anyone particularly interested in parties should consult the collections edited by Dalton and Wattenberg (2002), *Parties Without Partisans*; Gunther *et al.* (2002), *Political Parties*; Luther and Müller-Rommel (2002), *Political Parties in the New Europe*; and Mair *et al.* (2004), *Political Parties and Electoral Change*. For stimulating reads on decline, resilience and Europeanization, respectively, see Mair and van Biezen (2001), Yanai (1999) and Ladrech (2002), all in the journal *Party Politics*. Also recommended is the collection edited by Lawson and Merkl (2007), *When Political Parties Prosper*. For postcommunist states in particular, a brief yet typically lucid overview is provided by Enyedi (2006), in Katz and Crotty's *Handbook of Party Politics*, but see also Lewis (2006), in the journal *Democratization*; and Bakke and Sitter (2005), in the journal *Party Politics*. Best books on the region include the collections edited by Lewis and Mansfeldova (2007), *The European Union and Party Politics in Central and Eastern Europe*; and by Jungerstam-Mulders (2006), *Post-Communist EU Member States*; Millard (2004), *Elections, Parties, and Representation in Post-Communist Europe*; and the collection edited by Webb and White (2007), *Party Politics in New Democracies*.

On the web

www.wikipedia.org – type in 'politics' plus the name of the country for links to parties

www.europarl.eu.int/groups/default.htm – European party groups

www.idea.int – party funding plus more besides

www.parties-and-elections.de – links to parties' websites

www.palgrave.com

Companion Website

Visit the Companion Website to 'click and go'

www.palgrave.com/politics/bale

Discussion questions

1. What roles are political parties supposed to play in Europe's representative democracies? In your opinion, are there any conflicts and contradictions between those roles?
2. How has the way parties organize varied over time? Should we expect a party's ideology to relate to the way it organizes itself?
3. Why do you think some countries' party systems are more fragmented and/or more polarized than others'?
4. Do you think the 'party families' dreamed up by political scientists are useful guides to understanding European parties? What do you see as the pros and cons of categorizing parties in this way?
5. Why are there not representatives of each and every 'party family' in each and every European country? What is the relative importance of sociology, on the one hand, and institutions, on the other?
6. What are the symptoms and causes of party system change in Europe?
7. Are there any arguments and evidence that suggest to you that some observers might be overstating the degree of change in Europe's party systems?
8. Do you think that parties are dinosaurs on their way to extinction or are they destined to be around for some time still to come? If so, why?
9. Why is it easy to play down the impact of European integration on parties and party systems, and would be right to do so?

Chapter 6

Elections, voting and referendums – systems, turnout, preferences and unpredictability

Europe's myriad electoral systems	167
Turnout – decline and variation	175
Volatile voting	179
Preferences – what makes people vote the way they do?	180
EP elections	191
Direct democracy – useful tool or dangerous panacea?	192

The term 'democracy', like the term 'Europe', disguises a wealth of variation. Representative democracy, at a minimum, implies the chance for every adult to vote periodically (see Box 6.1) in order to help choose and hold accountable those who legislate and govern on their behalf. Democracy came to Europe in the late nineteenth and early twentieth centuries. But the process was far from complete even before it was set back for decades, first, by authoritarian dictatorships which began in the 1930s and, second, by the forty years of communist rule in East Central Europe which followed the Second World War. In France, Italy, Belgium and Greece, for instance, women won the vote only in the wake of that conflict, and in Switzerland they had to wait nearly another thirty years. On the other hand, in all European countries, the age at which people become entitled to vote (though not to stand as candidates) now matches the age at which they legally become adults, with some countries (such as the UK) either debating or even (as in Germany) experimenting with a reduction in the age.

This chapter begins by looking at different electoral systems and their effects, including their interaction with the party systems we described in Chapter 5. It then goes on to examine the decline in turnout that some believe is coming to afflict all liberal democracies. Is it happening, and if so, why? It also asks whether voters are becoming more footloose. Next, it tackles the thorny issue of electoral behaviour. Why do people vote the way they do? Have party identification, class, and religion given way to values as a source of preferences? Are elections, instead, being determined by more short-term considerations? Finally, the chapter looks at so-called 'direct democracy' – referendums and the like. Are they a viable substitute for the representative democracy that all European countries still seem to prefer?

Europe's myriad electoral systems

In all European democracies, the physical process of voting is still simple and similar. Notwithstanding some isolated (though interesting) developments in electronic voting (see Box 6.2), most voters still enact the same ritual. They enter a private space with a ballot paper, mark it in some way to record a preference and then deposit it in a ballot box for counting later. Only then do things get complicated. The number and percentage of votes each party gets has to be translated into a number and percentage of parliamentary seats. The match between votes and seats is rarely exact in any

BOX 6.1

The timing of elections

In most European countries, there is considerable flexibility with regard to when elections are held. Naturally, all have a maximum (generally four years, though five in France, Ireland and the UK), but only Norway (where elections can only be held every four years) has a minimum time between national contests. Sweden is also unusual in that it is committed to holding a general election every fourth September, irrespective of whether an early election has been held in between. Elsewhere, convention mostly has it that the government can decide when it wants to call an election providing that it is within the maximum permitted. Even in countries where this kind of 'cutting and running' is frowned upon and unusual, it is sometimes inevitable – as the Netherlands (in 2003) and Germany (in 2005) have both discovered in recent years.

BOX 6.2

'I-voting' in Estonia

The Estonian general election of March 2007 was the first in the world to allow voting over the Internet. On two days in the run-up to polling day, voters could use their chip-enabled national ID card to vote from the comfort of their home computer. If they changed their mind, they were able to annul that vote and vote physically, though very few did. By no means everyone took advantage of this opportunity: over one million people have ID cards but there were just over 30,000 'i-votes' out of a total of just over 550,000 votes cast – around 5.5 per cent – with younger people slightly more likely to vote this way than their older compatriots (see NEC Estonia, 2007). However, this was the launch of the process and, since there appear to have been no problems, many people who may have been reluctant to take the risk in 2007 may well do so next time. In July 2007, fellow Baltic state Lithuania announced that it would follow suit and hoped to have its own system up and running in time for its next election.

country, but in some it is more exact than in others. The crucial mechanism is the electoral system.

Europe's electoral systems can basically be split into two main groups: **plurality/majority**, on the one hand, and **proportional**, on the other. One can then split the first group into two – plurality and then majority – and the second group into three – list PR, mixed systems, and single transferable vote or STV (which is used by only two countries, Ireland and Malta). Each of the systems is explained in more detail below. Table 6.1, indicates which system each of our common core countries uses for its general elections. Research suggests that both the original decisions on which system should be adopted and the tinkering with those systems that follows are often (though not exclusively) the result of parties pursuing their own best interests (see Gallagher and Mitchell, 2005: 539–40). Experience suggests, however, that parties – perhaps fortunately – don't always get what they bargained for.

Plurality/majority systems use single-member constituencies or districts, with the candidate who gets a *majority* (more than half the votes cast) or a *plurality* (more votes than any other candidate) getting elected. **Proportional systems** – often known collectively as PR or proportional representation systems – make use of multimember constituencies or districts so that the seats a party gets in the legislature more accurately reflects its share of the vote.

Plurality and majority systems

Europe's simplest electoral systems are those that employ plurality and majority rules. These were also initially the most widely used systems, but they are now employed by so few countries that they may be

Table 6.1 Who uses which electoral system?

Plurality	(List) PR	Mixed
UK, France (majority required to win on first of what will otherwise be two ballots)	Czech Republic, Italy, Netherlands, Poland, Spain, and Sweden.	Germany

KEY POINT

Almost all European countries use PR, but some systems are more proportional than others. All systems are subject to manipulation, but each has its own more or less predictable effects and strengths and weaknesses. Electoral systems influence but do not determine party systems, so PR will support but not guarantee multiparty politics; likewise, a plurality system won't ensure two-party politics.

more familiar to Americans than most Europeans. A 'plurality system', often called 'first-past-the-post' (FPP), is one in which the candidate who gets the most votes is elected. It is the system employed in the UK, with the exception of elections in Northern Ireland and elections to the Welsh Assembly, and the Scottish and European Parliaments (for details see Mitchell, 2005). A 'majority system' is slightly different. It requires that the winning candidate get over half the votes, with the most common way of ensuring such an outcome being a second, 'run-off' election between the top two (or more) candidates. This method is employed in presidential but not parliamentary contests in Austria, Finland and Portugal.

France, like the UK, conducts its legislative elections in hundreds of single-member constituencies (also known by electoral systems experts as 'districts'). But there the similarities end. In France, there are two rounds of voting, the second held a week after the first. A candidate who wins over 50 per cent in the first ballot is elected but those who only win a plurality (i.e. the most votes of all those standing but not an overall majority) must contest a second ballot a week later against all of his or her opponents who won 12.5 per cent or more in the first ballot. In the second ballot, the winner is the candidate who wins the most votes (i.e. a plurality), although often (because many second-ballot contests turn into two-horse races) he or she will actually win a full-blown majority. France's president is also elected under a two-ballot majority system, with only the top two candidates going through to the second round. This system seems to encourage voters to 'vote with their hearts' first time around, spreading their votes around a diverse variety of candidates from extreme left to extreme right, and finally 'with their heads', eliminating the candidate furthest from their own stance (often at the request of the defeated candidate for whom they voted in round one).

Plurality systems can produce very disproportionate results, although the extent of the disproportionality can vary considerably from election to election. In France, for example, the centre-right UMP won 62 per cent of the seats with just 33.3 per cent of the vote in 2002; in 2006, however, while its vote share improved to 39.5 per cent, its haul of seats (while still disproportionate) dropped to 54 per cent. It all depends, in essence, on where a party wins its votes – a point well illustrated by the UK. On the one hand, a party doesn't want to spread its vote too thinly across the country. The Liberal Democrats may have won 22 per cent nationwide at the 2005 election but that netted them under 10 per cent of the seats in parliament because it was insufficiently concentrated to allow many Lib Dem candidates to win a plurality in individual constituencies. On the other hand, it doesn't do simply to pile up votes in so-called 'safe seats'. The Conservatives only lost out to Labour by 2.9 per cent of the national vote in 2005 but they were trounced in terms of seats by 55 per cent to 31 per cent because Labour's votes were more efficiently distributed in the hundred or so 'marginal constituencies' whose results, in practice, decide British general elections. This creates the real possibility (but one that has been realised only twice since 1945) that the party which wins most votes will nevertheless lose the election in the sense of not becoming the next government. Of course, this risk is by no means confined to plurality systems. Indeed, with the exception of Malta (which now has a rule declaring that whichever of its two largest parties wins the most votes must also win the most seats) and Italy (which has recently adopted a similar rule), it is a fairly common occurrence in more proportional systems where coalition government is the norm.

PR systems

In fact, by far the majority of European countries use electoral systems that attempt to ensure that the share of seats a party has in parliament more or less reflects the (nationwide) share of the vote it received at the election, accepting that this more often than not means multiparty politics and coalition government. However, there are many subtle variations in the systems used by each country, all of which affect just how accurately votes are converted into seats. Although the advocates of PR emphasize its 'fairness' when compared to FPP systems, most are aware that what are all too easily dismissed as dull, technical differences between proportional systems are actually crucially important in determining which parties are likely to do well, or at least better than their competitors.

That this is the case is not surprising, given PR's history. It did not replace FPP as the system used by most countries (beginning with Belgium in 1899 and Sweden in 1907) because it was universally acknowledged to be fairer or more rational. It actually started out – at least in part – as the means by which the various parties representing the privileged and the propertied hoped to survive the coming of universal suffrage, and thus the enfranchisement of the working class (see Boix, 1999). It was widely assumed that such parties would suffer if they stood in individual constituencies because their better-off voters would always be in the minority. The only way this could be avoided without a shift to PR was if constituency boundaries were drawn so as to make some of them middle-class strongholds and/or just one party could be pretty confident of mopping up the anti-socialist vote – both of which applied in the UK, which stuck to FPP. Since these first changes, parties of all stripes have continued to play a major role in determining the 'rules of the game' and, unsurprisingly, have done their best to ensure that they are helped (or at least not harmed) by the sophistication and the subtleties of those rules. However, their thinking on such things tends to be very short-term and their best-laid plans to protect and promote their own interests often prove futile and even counterproductive (see Andrews and Jackman, 2005). This might be no bad thing.

Before going on to look at some of the subtleties and sophistications of PR systems, we should first understand the basic differences between them. They can be conveniently divided (following Lijphart, 1999) into three:

- List PR systems
- Mixed systems
- STV systems.

List PR systems involve voters voting in multimember constituencies or districts for lists of candidates provided by political parties or alliances of political parties. When the votes are counted, each list is awarded seats in proportion to the votes cast for it. In the Netherlands, there is only one national constituency, which guarantees a proportional result overall. In other countries, however, regional variations could produce an overall result that is disproportionate. While some (like Spain and the Czech Republic) are prepared to live with such an outcome, others are not. A number of countries (mainly Scandinavian states, including Sweden) reserve a certain proportion of seats (normally 10–20 per cent) in order to correct any such imbalance – the so-called 'higher-tier' seats.

There is one more important difference between countries employing list PR. Some (e.g. Spain and now Italy) employ 'closed' lists, in the sense that the party (or parties if they are fighting as an electoral alliance) determines the rank order of the candidates on the list: those voting for the list can do nothing to change that order. Others (such as Finland, Estonia, Switzerland and Poland) employ 'open list PR', where the candidates who make it into parliament off the list are determined by the voters who rank order or actually simply vote for the names on the list. Still others employ hybrids, whereby voters can express a preference within a party's list. In some (e.g. Sweden and the Czech Republic, as well as Cyprus and Greece), their preference can and does make a difference (see Karvonen, 2004). Popular candidates can leapfrog into parliament over those placed higher on the list by their parties, although the proportion of MPs thus elected is often only around 5 per cent. In others (e.g. the Netherlands), the rank order provided by the party nearly always determines things. Clearly, 'closed list' PR makes it more difficult for candidates who make themselves unpopular with their parties and therefore end up with a low list position, and thus strengthens the disciplinary capacity of party managers.

Mixed systems give voters two votes. They use one to vote for a candidate in their local constituency or district. They use the other to vote for a list in a multimember constituency (often covering a particular region). The list is 'compensatory': it is used to ensure that, whatever the results of the constituency contests, the overall result of the election is more or less proportional. Its ability to do this, however, is to some extent dependent on how many seats in parliament are constituency seats and how many are party or list seats. In Germany, about half of all parliamentary seats are non-constituency seats, a number adequate to produce a pretty proportional result: this is why its system, still sometimes called AMS (alternative member system), is increasingly labelled MMP (mixed member proportional). In Lithuania, however, the number of party or list seats is insufficient to compensate fully for a disproportionate result in the constituencies and its system can therefore be labelled 'mixed-parallel'. Hungary's hybrid system is, broadly speaking, a variant of MMP, though its subtle contortions mean that, strictly speaking, it is 'a mixed-linked, majoritarian-proportional, two-vote system, with two-round majority-plurality and regional PR list elements and a compensatory national list' (Birch *et al.*, 2002: 60)!

In STV systems, voters in multimember constituencies or districts, are presented not with lists but with names of individual candidates (along with their party affiliations) which they are then invited to rank order. Candidates receiving a certain quota of first-preference votes are deemed elected, after which any of their votes over and above the quota are transferred (as if they were first preferences) in proportion to that candidate's voters' second choices. The same thing happens to the second-preference votes on the ballots of the weakest candidate. The transfer process continues until all the seats allocated to the constituency are filled by candidates reaching the quota (for a full description of this process, see Farrell, 2001: 126–39). It may sound complicated to the uninitiated, but Irish and Maltese voters seem to cope perfectly well. To many, STV has the considerable advantage of ensuring reasonable proportionality at the same time as maintaining a strong link between individual legislators and voters, who will often pay as much, if not more, attention to the candidate than to the party he or she represents (see Marsh, 2007).

PR's subtleties and sophistications

The subtleties and sophistications mentioned above are myriad, but only two or three of them are worth focusing on here. The first two are features that impact on the proportionality of PR systems; namely, 'thresholds' and 'district magnitude'. The third is the mathematical formula adopted to working out the allocation of seats. All three can negatively impact on the proportionality of PR systems (see Anckar, 1997).

A threshold is a percentage figure of the vote that a party (or electoral alliance) has to score before it is awarded a share of seats in parliament or, if a higher-tier exists, a share of those seats. Thresholds exist in almost every country that employs PR, normally because of a desire to limit fragmentation (i.e. a large number of parties in parliament) for fear that this would threaten stable government – and, of course, the position of existing parties. Thresholds vary between a low of 0.67 per cent in the Netherlands and a high of 5 per cent in the Czech Republic, Poland and Germany, where avoiding a return to the extreme multipartism of the interwar years was uppermost in the minds of those who designed its electoral system. Basically, the higher the threshold, the higher the hurdle and the harder it is for small parties to make it into parliament. Given this, it is not entirely surprising that thresholds have been tinkered with in many European countries by those parties with a vested interest in preventing competition. This was a lesson quickly learned by the parties that initially did well in elections in the postcommunist democracies (Bale and Kopecký, 1998). After the 'velvet divorce' that saw Czechoslovakia split into two countries, for example, both new republics raised thresholds, particularly for parties that formed alliances to fight elections, and in 1999 the Romanian parliament voted to increase its threshold from 3 to 5 per cent, with electoral alliances needing to obtain an additional 3 per cent of the vote for every party belonging to it. In fact, such manipulative measures are rarely fool-proof (Andrews and Jackman, 2005), as the smaller parties in Poland quickly discovered (see Box 6.3). But they are by no means confined to Europe's newer democracies: Belgium, for instance, upped its threshold to 5 per cent in time for the 2003 elections (see Hooghe *et al.*, 2006), although, as often seems to happen, the goal of reducing the number of parties does not seem to have been realised.

The number of MPs allocated to each constituency – known in the jargon as 'district magnitude' – can make a significant difference to the

BOX 6.3

The uncertain science of electoral engineering – Italy and Poland

In 1993, Italians voted in a referendum to abandon their country's relatively 'pure' form of list PR in favour of a mixed system, combining party lists and first-past-the-post contests in individual constituencies. This, they hoped, would bring political stability by making it harder for small parties to gain parliamentary representation. But a fantastically intricate rule (the *scorporo*) brought in to buy off the resistance of smaller parties to the change, plus the willingness of parties to form electoral alliances meant the number of parties in parliament has not decreased anywhere near as much as many people expected. As the 2006 election approached, however, the then prime minister, Silvio Berlusconi (see Chapter 8), attempted to stave off defeat by passing a new electoral law which returned the country back to list PR. However, the new system (see Massetti, 2006 for details) differs from its pre-1993 counterpart by establishing higher thresholds (10 per cent for a coalition; 4 per cent for a party not in a coalition; and a minimum of 2 per cent for each coalition party), the intention being to encourage broad left-wing and right-wing coalitions. More unusually, the new system also featured a winner's bonus: a coalition with the most votes but which wins under 340 seats in the 630 seat parliament is awarded that number of seats, thereby ensuring that one or other coalition will be able to govern. Berlusconi's gamble backfired: the election was incredibly close, with the left-wing coalition beating his right-wing alliance by 49.8 to 49.7 per cent (around 25,000 votes out of 38 million) and, with the winner's bonus, ousting the prime minister from office. Although no parties outside the two pre-electoral coalitions made it into parliament, the latter still contained nineteen parties – so much, perhaps, for consolidation.

This would come as no surprise to Poles. Poland undertook a number of changes to its electoral system in its first few years as a democracy, with larger parties insisting that a reduction in fragmentation – the number of parties in parliament – would be good for stability and good government (as well as, of course, reducing the competition). Many casual observers noted that these seemed to work: the number of parties in parliament reduced quite markedly. After the 1991 election, the *Sejm* contained eighteen parties (though, significantly, the Senate, elected by plurality, afforded representation to thirty-one). In 1993, with the introduction of thresholds of 5 per cent for single parties and 8 per cent for alliances, the number declined to just six. However, the extent to which this reduction was directly due to rule changes, rather than a more general 'learning curve' that saw Central and East European voters avoid wasting their votes on tiny parties with poor prospects (see Tavits and Annus, 2006), is debatable. In any case, smaller parties were able to offset some of the negative effects of the rule changes by creative strategies, such as forming alliances that, for instance, they were careful to call 'committees' and not 'coalitions', thereby avoiding the higher threshold (8 per cent) imposed on the latter. Their efforts did not however, prevent, over a third of votes being 'wasted' on parties that failed to make it into parliament.

proportionality of a PR system, especially where there is no second tier of seats to correct any disproportionality at the regional level. Basically, the lower the district magnitude (i.e. the lower the number of MPs allocated to each constituency), the lower the proportionality of the overall result. This arithmetical relationship results from the fact that, as some of us may remember from primary school, dividing a relatively small number by a relatively large number entails a greater likelihood of a remainder. Proportionality is therefore pretty easy to achieve in the Netherlands where (like Slovakia since 1998) the whole country is treated as one constituency with 150 MPs. But it is much less likely in Spain. There, in addition to having strong regional differences, the country is split into fifty-two constituencies with an average of seven MPs per constituency. At the general election of 2000, this allowed the centre-right *Partido Popular* (PP) to form a single-party majority because its 44 per cent

Table 6.2 PR electoral formulas and the parties they favour

Formula	Largest remainders	Modified Sainte-Lagüe	D'Hondt
Formula favours	Smaller parties		Larger parties
Countries using formula for constituency seat (first-tier) allocation	Italy	Sweden, Poland	Netherlands, Spain, Czech Rep.
Countries using formula for list seat (higher-tier) allocation	Germany	Sweden	

Sources: Adapted from Birch *et al.* (2002: 27, 86), and Gallagher *et al.* (2006: 352–3).

of the vote afforded it 52 per cent of the seats. The opposition PSOE could hardly complain, however, because it had taken advantage of the same sort of disproportionality in the 1980s and early 1990s. Almost invariably, such disproportionality favours larger over smaller parties: at the Czech elections of 2006, for instance, the Greens won over six per cent of the vote but only three per cent of the seats, whereas the Civic Democrats (whom they eventually joined in government) won 40 per cent of the seats with 35 per cent of the vote.

An electoral system can be made to work to the marginal advantage of larger parties according to the mathematical formula used to allocate seats to parties in PR systems. Table 6.2 deliberately eschews a detailed discussion of the mathematical merits of each formula (on which, see Farrell, 2001), but summarizes their effects. Some countries use one formula for allocating constituency seats and another for the compensatory higher tier of list seats. This combination can cancel out the bias toward larger or smaller parties. Others, which generally employ a formula that favours larger parties, do not have a higher tier and therefore the bias goes uncorrected: Spain is an obvious example. While these matters can seem awfully abstruse to some of us, they matter a lot to parties. For instance, in Poland, prior to the election of 2001, right-wing parliamentary parties, fearing (correctly) that the more unified social democrats were about to win a big victory, got together to change the electoral formula from d'Hondt in favour of St-Laguë, which is thought to favour smaller parties. It might well be that the change did enough to deny the social democrats an outright victory that year. Not surprisingly, the new government, led by the social democrats, changed back to d'Hondt in time for the 2005 election – although its move did little to save it from near meltdown in that contest.

Generally, we can say that the Netherlands (and Denmark) have the most proportional PR systems, with most others somewhere in the middle. The exceptions are Spain and Greece (and to some extent Portugal) where larger parties do better than, strictly speaking, they should. On the other hand, levels of disproportionality are still under half of that experienced by the UK and under a third of that experienced by France. This is what we would expect: political scientists have constructed what they call an index of disproportionality (the higher the figure, the less proportional the system); worldwide, plurality and majority systems score 12 to 15, while List PR and MMP systems score 4 and STV systems, at 5, only marginally more (see Farrell, 2001). Figure 6.1 illustrates the scores for our core countries.

Electoral systems and party systems

We noted in Chapter 5 that political scientists have constructed another kind of index to ensure that they don't overestimate the amount of party system change. The effective number of parliamentary parties (ENPP) combines a simple count of political parties in a system with a sense of their strength, ensuring that the presence of one or two very small parties won't lead us to record a big change. They have also used this to see whether the type of electoral system is associated with a country having more or less parties. Looking again on a worldwide scale and using the ENPP rather than simply the absolute number of parties in a system, there does, indeed, seem to be a relationship. Again, it is in the expected direction: plurality and majority systems tend to have two . Aor three significant parties, STV systems three, and List PR and MMP systems four or five (see Farrell, 2001). Figure 6.2 gives the figures for our core countries.

However, one of the biggest mistakes we can make is to confuse correlation (some kind of relationship between two factors) for causation (suggesting that one causes the other). Doing so would lead us to think that, because countries with proportional electoral systems tend to have multiparty systems, the latter must be the result of the former or that two-party systems are all down to FPP – views sometimes associated with Maurice Duverger, one of the 'founding fathers' of comparative politics. There are two problems with such reasoning. First, it does not quite fit contemporary and historical reality. For instance, the most solid two-party system in Europe is in Malta, but Malta uses STV. Historically, most of the countries that moved to PR just before or just after the First World War already had multiparty systems even under plurality rules – even if some of those parties did not get their fair share of parliamentary seats. And the move toward multiparty politics in, say, Austria and Ireland, occurred only recently despite decades of using PR systems. Italy's

Figure 6.1 The mismatch between votes and seats at the most recent election

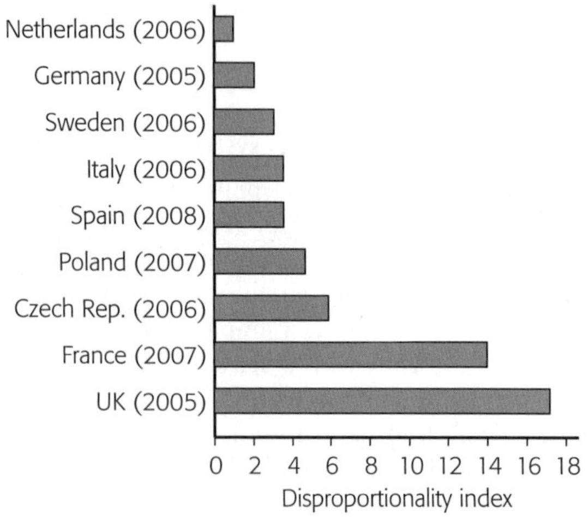

Note: The higher the score the greater the mismatch, zero being a perfect match.

Source: Data from Gallagher (2008)

Figure 6.2 The effective number of parliamentary parties at the most recent election

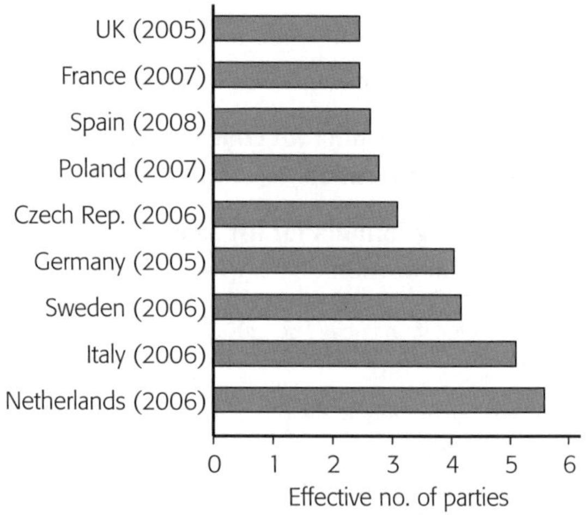

Source: Data from Gallagher (2008).

(as it turned out, temporary) move towards a less pure proportional system did not, as people hoped, cut down on the number of parties in parliament – something Poles could have told them (see Box 6.2). Secondly, as we have already suggested in Chapter 5, treating the electoral system as the prime cause of party systems would be to place too great a weight on institutional factors and too little weight on the social factors that also help to shape things.

Obviously the electoral system plays a role, but it is not necessarily a determining one. If plurality systems really did create two-party politics and PR multiparty politics, how would we explain either the virtual duopoly that exists in Malta, which operates STV, or the range of parties on offer to French voters under their plurality system? Giovanni Sartori (whose work on party systems we referred to in Chapter 5) has persuasively argued (Sartori, 1997) that a plurality system cannot in and of itself produce a two-party system. This is because the existence of the latter also depends on limited polarization and on the absence of geographically concentrated minorities that are unwilling to be represented by either of two big parties (and therefore elect MPs from regionalist parties instead). On the other hand, Sartori suggests, if two-party competition does take hold, a plurality system will exert 'a brakelike influence' and 'a freezing effect'. By the same token, moving to PR (or a more 'pure' form of

PR) will, of course, remove obstacles to new entrants. It may also encourage the splitting of old parties whose two wings previously had to put up with each other in order to avoid the electoral wilderness. But Sartori argues that this simply gives institutional expression to what was going on anyway – 'freedom to increase [the number of parties]', he writes, 'is no more the cause of increasing than freedom to eat is the cause of eating'. Given the extent of obesity in the developed world, however, one might be forgiven for wondering whether his argument holds water. Knowing you can walk out of the party taking some of your colleagues with you and/or start up a new party and still stand a chance at the next election surely might cause political actors to do something they otherwise might not even contemplate. Likewise, the consequent expansion of the alternatives on offer may well also encourage voters to vote in a way that would otherwise never have occurred to them. This goes beyond even the 'psychological effect' posited by Duverger (1954), who concentrated on the tendency of voters under FPP not to bother voting for smaller parties that (because of the 'mechanical effect' occasioned by their failure to win their fair share of seats) have no chance.

Academic disputes over the causal relationship (or lack of it) between electoral and party systems, however, pale in comparison to wider arguments about the relative merits of proportional and plurality systems. These are summarized in Box 6.4 and, given the perceived political effect of different systems, understandably generate considerable passion on either side. It is possible that we might be dealing here with what philosophers call 'an essentially contested question' – one involving so many underlying assumptions and motivations that it is unlikely ever to be satisfactorily answered.

Rather more practically, however, we can follow political scientist Michael Gallagher (see Gallagher and Mitchell, 2005: 571). He synthesizes a set of eight qualities that the ideal electoral system would deliver: (1) 'accuracy of representation of voters' preferences'; (2) 'socio-demographic representation in parliament'; (3) 'personal accountability of MPs to constituents'; (4) 'maximization of participation opportunities for voters'; (5) 'cohesive and disciplined parties'; (6) 'stable effective government'; (7) 'identifiability of government options'; (8) 'opportunity for voters to eject governments from office'. Different electoral systems score high or low on each of these desired qualities. Which one you prefer will depend on how you rank those qualities. In short, the choice of electoral system is like any other political choice: as well as depending a great deal on where you are starting from (since the past determines the present and the present constrains the future), there are always trade-offs involved, ensuring that there is no such thing as a perfect or one-size-fits-all solution.

Turnout – decline and variation

The fact that people bother to vote, even though the chances that an individual ballot paper will change the result are miniscule, has always preoccupied those who see politics as rational choice (see p. 00; see also Dowding, 2005). Recent elections throughout the democratic world, however, have given cause for concern among pundits and politicians because the number of voters appears to be dropping – in some cases, like a stone (see Table 6.3). Some political scientists like Mark Franklin (2002) argue, the decline, while not insignificant (just compare some recent elections against long-term averages), is not as large as is often thought. Franklin also suggests that we need to start taking the levels achieved in the 1950s as an unusual high point rather than as a norm from which we have now sadly departed. Nowadays, for better or worse, he argues, there may be fewer 'great causes' and profound disputes. And we need to remember that a handful of high-profile cases of low turnout (most notably perhaps the UK election of 2001) do not necessarily constitute a trend so much as point to the importance of contingency in explaining variation over time within one country – something that is also stressed in a recent exploration of turnout in

KEY POINT

Turnout seems to be declining but still varies – between people, between countries and regions, and between elections – in ways that we can predict.

BOX 6.4

PR or plurality – for and against

The case for plurality

Voters vote directly for governments and MPs: less horse-trading by parties forced to water down their election promises in order to become part of a winning coalition; better chance of calling to account or completely getting rid of governments and MPs, forcing the latter to take account of local feeling rather than simply toeing the party line.

Stronger, and very often single-party, governments: administrations can pursue mandated programmes instead of delaying or rendering them incoherent through compromise, allowing them to tackle problems properly rather than waste time on searching for a consensus; governments more stable and durable; not prone to being blackmailed into unpopular policies by small, fringe parties.

The case for PR

Fewer 'wasted votes' on the part of people who vote for parties or candidates that do not go on to get into parliament.

More representative parliaments: MPs come from right across the political spectrum in line with voter preferences, providing them with a real choice; more women and ethnic minority MPs because parties do not need to worry about the risk of putting up a female and/or an ethnic candidate in an FPP constituency when voters are assumed (rightly or wrongly) still to prefer white men.

More coalition governments: legislation and policy theoretically has the support of a majority of voters and not just a majority of MPs; the need to balance the interests of various parties necessitates and promotes consensus politics – and prevents an essentially unrepresentative executive inflicting its programme on the country even though a majority of voters did not vote for it; the increased likelihood of having to take account of ethnic parties promotes consensual solutions to ethnic conflicts.

Little or no opportunity for parties to tinker with electorate boundaries (redistricting) in the hope of giving themselves an advantage – something that occurs frequently in the US, and has occurred occasionally in the UK and Ireland.

Boosts electoral turnout and female representation – the proportion of people who actually go to the polls at a general election, as well as the number of women elected – tends to be measurably higher under PR, although the impact can be overstated in both cases.

CEE (Millard, 2004: 75–81; see also Kostadinova, 2003) and is, of course, obvious at particular elections, such as the presidential contest in France in 2007 which saw 84 per cent turn out compared with 72 per cent five years before.

Franklin's analyses suggest that a shorter than usual period between elections, for instance and, more significantly still, a highly predictable result, both tend to depress turnout. So, too, does a feeling on the part of the electorate that, first, the differences between the alternatives on offer and, second, the connection between who is in power and the policies pursued, is vague. These factors can sometimes work in opposite directions: for example, the German election of 2005 looked like it would be desperately close, which should have encouraged turnout, but in the end voters' scepticism about the actual effect that a change of government would have on policy seems to have trumped everything, producing the lowest turnout in Germany since the war.

Such a result points to the fact that talk of fluctuation and only marginal change in turnout might, however, be masking the beginning of a trend

Table 6.3 Turnout in selected European countries, 1945–2007 – long-term decline or trendless fluctuation?

	Italy	Netherlands	Sweden	Germany	Czech Rep.	UK	France	Spain	Poland
1950s	94	96	79	87	n/a	80	80	n/a	n/a
1960s	93	95	86	87	n/a	77	77	n/a	n/a
1970s	91	84	90	91	n/a	75	76	73	n/a
1980s	89	84	89	87	n/a	74	72	77	n/a
1990s	85	76	85	80	75	75	69	78	48
2000s	81	80	81	78	61	60	60	73	43
Mean, 1945+	89	87	86	85	68	74	74	74	46

Note: n/a means not applicable because state was not a democracy at the time. All calculations based on registered voters only (which tends to give a slightly higher figure than figures based on age-eligible population). Mean is the average at all elections from 1945 onwards. Italy has (barely enforced) compulsory voting.

Source: Data from IDEA (2007).

downwards. Political scientist Peter Mair (2006b) draws an analogy with climate change – one that anyone who has seen Al Gore's environmentalist film, *An Inconvenient Truth*, will readily appreciate. Of course, says Mair, there has been fluctuation before, just as previous decades have seen ups and downs in temperature and carbon dioxide. But, just as when we look at, say, temperature and notice that a disproportionate number of record highs seem to have occurred in the 1990s, so too have record lows in turnout (see Figure 6.3).

Just as interesting as the apparent decline in turnout are the variations in turnout between European countries (see Table 6.4). We know that the richer and/or more educated and/or more interested in politics a person is, the more likely he or she is to vote. And, in most countries, older people are more likely to vote than younger people, although one can debate whether this is inevitable due to a natural 'life-cycle effect' (see Goerres, 2007) or whether it is the product of a media environment hostile to politics that is affecting young people first but will eventually have consequences right the way through the age-range (see Wattenberg, 2007). Arguably, however, none of this demographic variation really matters as much as the fact that a voter is from, say, Sweden (where turnout is generally high – 82 per cent in 2006) or from Poland (where it is much lower – just under 41 per cent in 2001, although this rose to 54 per cent in 2007).

Figure 6.3 Record lows in turnout – when have they occurred?

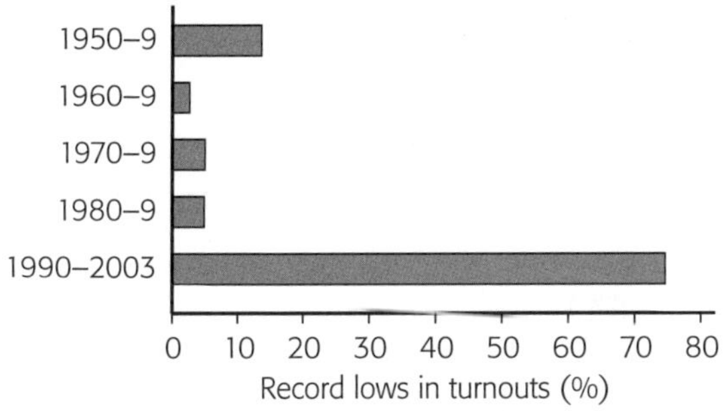

Source: Data (encompassing elections in sixteen postwar European democracies) from Mair (2006b).

There seem to be several reasons behind these geographical variations, as Franklin's work shows. Compulsory voting, postal voting and weekend voting, and proportionality itself, are significant, as is the extent to which one party or another is close to getting an overall majority. But by far the most important factor is 'electoral salience' (the extent to which elections are seen actually to impact on the complexion and conduct of government). Countries in which elections are seen to mean something boast turnouts up to 30 per cent greater than countries such as Switzerland, in which 'whoever you vote for the government still gets in'. Compulsory, postal and weekend voting seem to increase turnout by just over 5 per cent each, while every percentage point closer to perfect proportionality a country gets is

Table 6.4 The European turnout league table, 1961–99

85% +	80–84%	75–79%	70–74%	65–69%	50–60%
Malta, Belgium, Italy, Austria, Iceland, Luxembourg, Sweden, Denmark	Germany, Czech Rep., Greece, Netherlands, Norway	Portugal, Romania, Finland, UK, France	Spain, Bulgaria, Ireland	Estonia	Hungary, Switzerland, Poland, Lithuania

Source: Adapted from Franklin (2002).

apparently worth around half a per cent in additional turnout. Countries that present voters with the possibility of voting for or against a party that is close (but only close) to getting an overall majority seem to have turnouts around 5 per cent higher than those that do not. Smaller countries have higher turnouts, but the difference turns out to be minimal.

Clearly, then, things need not be set in stone, but turnout does seem to be something of a long-term cultural phenomenon, albeit one that might also be affected by institutional arrangements. Fluctuation will occur over time, but even a record turnout in some countries may never come close to matching what would be a record low in others. Variation occurs between countries but there are also obvious regional differences. Within 'western Europe', Scandinavians – perhaps because they continue to display a stronger all-round sense of civic literacy (see Milner, 2002) and see voting as a duty – are the champion voters. Meanwhile the postcommunist democracies of CEE seem unlikely to reach the comparatively low levels seen in non-Nordic European states, although there is variation within the region. As Figure 6.4 shows, Poland seems to suffer from persistent low turnout in parliamentary elections – a die that also seems to have been cast in the Baltic republics of Lithuania and Estonia (but not Latvia). However, Slovenia, Slovakia and Hungary (apart from a blip downward in 1998) seem to have relatively 'healthy' levels of turnout with around seven or even eight out of ten people voting. Meanwhile, the Czech Republic is a good illustration that what goes down can come up. There (as Figure 6.4 shows) turnout seemed to be trending downward after an initial burst of enthusiasm, and dropped alarmingly in 2002. Yet at the next election (which promised – and turned out – to be close), turnout ticked up again. Interestingly, turnout rose markedly (albeit from a very low base) in Poland in 2007 – an election widely portrayed as a close clash between two visions of the country, one outward looking and the other traditional and nationalistic. That voters were more interested than they had been two years earlier when the parties promoting those visions were at the time seen to be basically on the same side and supposedly on course to form a coalition supports

Figure 6.4 Turnout in two postcommunist democracies, 1990–2007

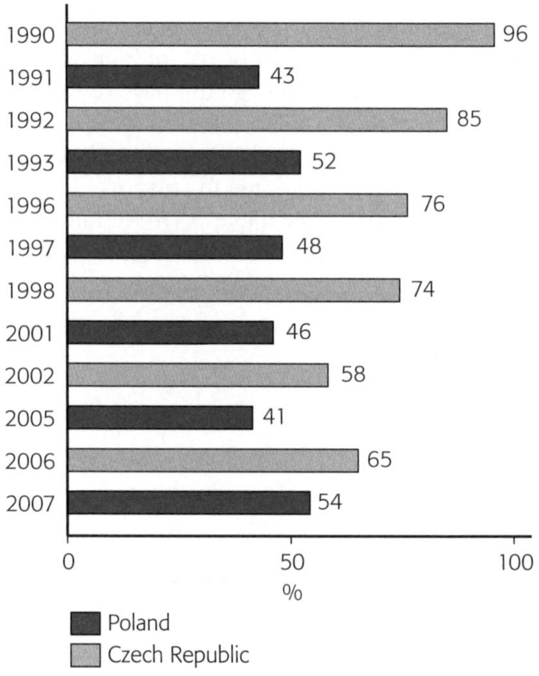

Note: 1990 and 1992 figures relate to Czechoslovak elections.

Source: Data from IDEA (2007).

the idea that citizens in postcommunist countries are just as 'rational' as those in other European democracies – when more is at stake they vote in greater numbers (Pacek *et al.*, 2007).

A recent 'meta-analysis' (a study of other studies) on turnout comes to some pretty clear conclusions on what makes for higher turnout (see Geys, 2006). Turnout is higher in countries with historically higher turnouts, in countries with smaller populations (presumably because there is an increased chance that a handful of votes can make a difference to the result), where (for the same reason) the result is forecast to be close, where parties spend more on campaigns, where PR is used, where voter registration is easy, and where a number of elections are run concurrently. The most robust finding, however, is something of a no-brainer: compulsory voting ensures higher turnout. To some, we should ignore this: the right not to vote is as important as the right to do so, and there are (as yet seemingly unfounded) fears that obliging people to turn out will lead to frivolous or protest voting. Others, however, are much more worried about low turnout. There comes a point, they claim, where so few people vote that the legitimacy of the polity is called into question. They also worry about the fact that rational politicians are bound to pander to those who do vote (the better off and the elderly) and ignore those that do not (the poorer, the less educated and the young). Indeed, so worried are they that they now advocate the extension of compulsory voting to all mature democracies (see, for example, Wattenberg, 2007).

Volatile voting

We touched on volatility (the extent to which people switch their vote from one election to another) when discussing party system change in Chapter 5. In fact, volatility may be even more of a phenomenon than the headline figures suggest, even though we should stress (as we did in Chapter 5) that much of it involves voters transferring their votes within rather than between left and right blocs. Peter Mair (2006b) once again draws an analogy with climate change, noting that 'the more recent the election, the less likely it is to yield a predictable outcome' (see Figure 6.5). The idea that we might be understating the extent of volatility is also supported if we compare figures based on aggregates calculated from election results and figures based on survey research that actually asks people how they voted. Research suggests that aggregate figures disguise, first, the extent of switching (between parties and between voting and non-voting) that goes on between one election and the next at the individual (or 'micro') level and, second, the extent to which such switching has risen (though not always in strictly linear fashion) from the late 1960s/early 1970s onwards. For instance, in 1960 only 7 per cent of those surveyed by the Swedish election study said that they had changed their vote from four years previously; in 1998 the figure was 31 per cent (see Dalton *et al.*, 2002) – an increase seemingly replicated in other European countries where the question was asked (see Table 6.5, which uses a year-on-year average which has the effect of 'smoothing out' highs and lows in particular years caused by exceptional circumstances).

This picture of flux fits with figures from the same surveys which seem to indicate that voters are increasingly leaving their decision about which way to vote until nearer polling day. To use the Swedish example again, only 18 per cent made up their

KEY POINT

Voters switch parties more, and make up their minds later, than they used to. Votes seem to switch within left and right blocs more than they switch between them.

Figure 6.5 Record-breaking volatility – when has it occurred?

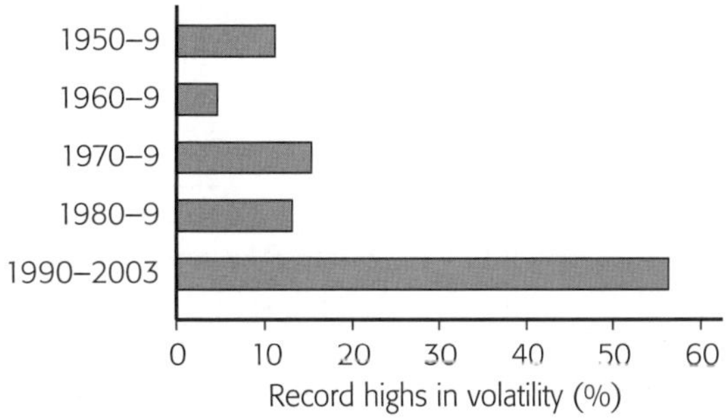

Source: Data (encompassing elections in sixteen postwar European democracies) from Mair (2006b).

Table 6.5 Switching votes and deciding later, 1970s-1990s

	Yearly increase in volatility	Period covered	Yearly increase in 'late deciders'	Period covered
Austria	0.60	1979–99	0.65	1979–99
Denmark	0.25	1971–98	0.03	1971–98
Germany	0.30	1961–98	0.30	1961–98
Netherlands	0.20	1971–98	0.95	1971–98
Norway	0.60	1969–93	0.90	1969–93
Sweden	0.50	1956–98	1.10	1956–98
UK	0.10	1964–97	0.45	1964–97

Source: Data from Dalton *et al.* (2002).

minds during the campaign in 1964; thirty-four years later, in 1998, the figure was 57 per cent. This might, of course, have been particularly high in the latter year because many social democrats defected (temporarily) to the Left Party in protest at the government's welfare squeeze (which may also explain the high level of volatility in that year). But, once again, compiling an average which 'smooths out' peaks and troughs in the data (see Table 6.5) suggests that there has been an increase over time – and not just in Sweden.

Preferences – what makes people vote the way they do?

Despite the increasing sophistication of the research tools employed by political scientists, explaining why people vote the way they do has always been much harder than we would like. The reason is that there are so many possible factors that go into such a decision that it is impossible to control for all of them – certainly at the individual level. This does not mean, however, that we cannot make educated guesses based on aggregate data – in other words, by using survey research to see if there is a correlation between certain characteristics (which become the 'independent variable', the thing doing the influencing) and voting for one party or another (the 'dependent variable', the thing being influenced). Decades of research in this area has traditionally accorded particular significance to three things: class and religion (both of which fitted quite neatly with Lipset and Rokkan's (1967) idea of 'cleavages' discussed in Chapter 5) and 'party identification' (the extent to which someone feels 'close to' a particular party). The problem is that the same research now suggests that the effect (or at least the predictive power) of all three has not necessarily disappeared, but has almost certainly declined. Indeed, so much so, some argue, that we would have just as good a chance of predicting which party someone is going to vote for if we were to flip a coin instead of bothering to ask them which party they identify with or about their social background and religious beliefs.

KEY POINT

Social class, religion and party identification are less important to voting than they were, but have not been simply or completely replaced by 'values voting' or by short-term considerations based on issues, the economy, and leadership. Voters are individuals but what seems important to them is in part determined by parties.

Party ID

The idea of party identification (often referred to simply as 'party ID') is often associated with the 'Michigan model' of voting (so-called because it was pioneered at the University of Michigan in the US). This model held that the majority of people were socialized into feeling closer to one party rather than another. Although this did not necessarily mean they would always vote for it – judgements about economic conditions or particular issues or candidates could play a part as well – normally they would. This 'homing instinct' made party identification a powerful predictor. Many political scientists in Europe question whether survey respondents are able to disentangle their current political preference from any long-term identification they might or might not have, but others argue the concept is useful outside the US (see Evans, 2004).

Many analysts remain unconvinced that there is a clear-cut answer to the question: Has there been a Europe-wide decline in party ID over time? (see Schmitt and Holmberg, 1995). Individual countries aside, by no means all cross-national studies suggest there has been any overall decline in party identification (van Deth and Janssen, 1994). On the other hand, some researchers are now convinced that the evidence both for decline of party ID and a declining relationship between party ID and party choice at elections is there (see Dalton, 2000), even if it does vary between countries and is sometimes pretty marginal (Thomassen, 2005). If they are right, this will of course leave political scientists with another challenge – not simply showing that people are less attached to parties than previously and that remaining attachments count for less, but explaining why that has happened.

Two possibilities spring to mind in this respect. One is to suggest that the decline in (and the decline in the predictive power of) party ID is linked to public dissatisfaction beginning in the 1970s with the relatively unimpressive performance of their countries' economies. This was transferred to the parties, which seemed to be incapable of doing much to make things better and which more recently have had their reputations badly damaged by scandals, financial and otherwise. The evidence for this is not particularly impressive, however. Those who are least partisan are not necessarily those who are most dissatisfied, and vice versa. The other explanation for a decline in party identification links it to the increased educational capacity of most electors and the greater access they have to information supplied by the media rather than by parties (see Chapter 7). Taken together, these mean that people have less need to rely on instinct and loyalty and, instead, can make the kind of consumerist, individual choice they are increasingly used to in other areas of life – an idea sometimes labelled **the modernization thesis**. This will almost certainly sound plausible to readers of this book, but there is a problem: comparative research suggests that the relationship between more education and less partisanship is non-existent in some countries (e.g. Netherlands and Germany) and declining over time in others (e.g. the UK and Sweden) as people (especially younger people) with little education also appear to be turning their backs on parties as much as those who have, say, been to university (see Thomassen, 2005: Chapter 5).

> The **modernization thesis** (see Dalton 2002) holds that economic progress, mass education and media penetration will create 'new citizens' who are more knowledgeable, confident and autonomous, and because they are 'cognitively mobilized' are more willing and able to make up their own minds about politics and try different ways of getting what they want. They will be less inclined to develop or rely on old loyalties, and more sceptical about what parties and elections can offer them. Many will be attracted by 'new politics', driven less by concerns over the distribution of economic gains than by issues like the environment and multiculturalism.

A second, simpler but perhaps more robust explanation is that party ID was associated with the very social characteristics that we go on to explore below; namely, class and religion. As their hold on people has waned so, too, has the tendency to feel closer to the parties most associated with such collective identities (like the social and the Christian democrats), while newer (and often smaller) parties have not made up for the decline by generating similar loyalties. This certainly seems to be the case in Germany, where partisanship has been gradually declining over at least thirty years (see Arzheimer, 2006) – a fact that may help explain why, at the election of 2005, the country's biggest parties the CDU/CSU and the SPD achieved their lowest combined share of the vote for fifty years. And, of course, any decline in party identification will feed on itself: there is less loyalty to pass down to the next generation of voters, ensuring that more and more young people never develop identifications (strong ones anyway) in the first place. This possibility calls to mind the postcommunist democracies. There, partisan identification was weak to start with and, in the opinion of some analysts, is by no means logically bound to develop at all (see Vlachová, 2001).

The 'end of class voting' and the rise of values?

As Chapter 1 suggested, class has not disappeared, either as a useful categorization or as an identity that means something to many, perhaps even most, people. So we should be careful before we rush to write its obituary as an influence on voting – something that many commentators have been accused of doing (see Franklin *et al.*, 1992). On the other hand, there is some truth in the suggestion that, for too long, researchers tended to let class overshadow other cleavages, such as religion, language and ethnicity, that are more cultural than economic, social or geographical (see Dogan, 2001). Perhaps we should ask first whether class is as important in some countries as it is in others, and then whether there is evidence that it has declined as an influence over time. On the first question, there is reasonably broad agreement that class voting (the extent to which, put at its most basic, the working class votes left and the middle class votes right) varies considerably across countries (see Table 6.6).

Table 6.6 The historical importance of class voting

Low	Relatively low	More significant	Relatively high
US, Postcommunist countries	France, Ireland, Italy, Netherlands, Portugal, Spain, Switzerland	Austria, Belgium, Germany	Denmark, Finland, Norway, Sweden, UK

Source: Data from Nieuwbeerta and De Graaf (1999).

The second question – the decline (or not) of the influence of class on voting – is rather more controversial. What is *not* at issue is that, however measured, the proportion of the population that can be categorized (or thinks of itself) as working class has shrunk by around one third in the postwar period (see Chapter 1) – this is sometimes labelled the 'composition effect.' What *is* at issue is the extent to which people vote in a certain way because they belong to (or at least can be labelled as) a certain class – the so-called 'correlation effect'. There are, of course, plenty of country studies that do support such an effect: for example, work on the French party system (see Evans, 2002) shows very convincingly that the left-wing parties have lost whatever claim they had to be the party of the working class. It also suggests that many blue-collar workers (as in Austria, too) now vote for the far right (see Chapter 9) – evidence of both 'dealignment' (see Chapter 5) and a certain degree of 'realignment' (i.e. groups of voters not so much losing their loyalty as taking it elsewhere).

All this certainly fits nicely with the tale told by most media commentators and one often repeated in academic texts. Actually, however, there is considerable debate about its truth. Some country-level and cross national studies would appear to contradict, or at least severely qualify, this conventional wisdom (see Brooks *et al.*, 2006 and Evans, 1999). On balance, recent research suggests that, while overall there has been a significant decline in class voting from the late 1960s and early 1970s (see Knutsen, 2006), it is more pronounced (and the trend more linear) in some countries than others (see for example Thomassen, 2005: Chapter 4; see also Achterberg, 2006). For instance, Ireland and the Netherlands do not appear to have experienced a decline; Austria, Belgium, France and Italy have experienced a decline, but not as pronounced as that in Britain, Germany and above all Scandinavia, especially Norway and Sweden. This variation, it is argued, puts paid to the modernization thesis, which would surely apply to all advanced industrial or postindustrial countries at pretty much the same time.

And even if we do accept the dealignment thesis, of course, we are still left with the task of explaining *why* class is now a less reliable predictor of vote. This is not an easy one, and explanations so far are more deductive (based on theoretical speculation which might or might not fit data from a process that is still unfolding over time) than inductive (emerging from a clear body of evidence). These (largely sociological) explanations are summarized in Box 6.5 (see Evans, 1999: 6–7).

It is, of course, possible to argue that class was, and is, a relatively vague way of categorizing voters and thereby explaining their political choices. Much better, perhaps, to employ more precise distinctions based not just on what they do for a living but also on which sector – service or manufacturing, private or public – they work in. Quantitative cross-national research by Norwegian political scientist Oddbjørn Knutsen (2005) does just this.

Knutsen finds that there is a relationship between the sector worked in and party support but that its strength varies considerably between countries, being strongest in a Scandinavian welfare state like Denmark, moderate in France, Italy and the UK, small in Germany and the Netherlands, and insignificant in a country with a comparatively underdeveloped welfare state like Ireland. Interestingly, the strongest relationship between sector and party choice is not just between those who work in the private sector and conservative parties (which tend to be in favour of a smaller state and lower taxation) but also between those in the private sector and populist radical right parties, which are not necessarily keen on shrinking the state (see Chapter 5). There is (perhaps more predictably given their vested interest in the election of a government committed to upholding the welfare state rather than trimming it to cut taxes) a relationship between being employed in the public sector and voting for parties on the left. However, there is considerable variation between countries when it comes to which parties benefit most from this relationship: in Britain and France, for example, it seems to be the social democrats (Labour and the *Parti Socialiste*), while in Germany and the Netherlands it seems to be green and/or left parties. Finally, the political impact working in the public or private sector tends to be greater if you work in services.

Both class and occupational or sectoral explanations were focused on western European countries. As such, they could be of limited use in helping us to understand the links between social structure and voting in CEE. One could argue that in post communist countries, such as Poland and the Czech Republic, class will in fact increase its influence on

Postmaterialism refers to the supposed trend in advanced countries, once the basic needs of the educated and reasonably well-off have been met, for such people to eschew political beliefs and behaviour based on the defence or promotion of material interest in favour of an interest in 'quality-of-life' issues, self-expression and ensuring the rights and well-being of minorities and/or the less fortunate (see Inglehart and Rabier, 1986).

BOX 6.5

Why people's class might no longer predict their vote

1. As services supersede industry, creating so-called 'postindustrial societies' (see Chapter 1), other cleavages (such as gender, nationality, ethnicity) could be superseding class which, after all, had its roots in industrialization.
2. As suggested by the modernization thesis, the growth of education and an emphasis on individual over collective identities has increased people's ability to think for themselves and make more rational, calculating and issue-based political decisions.
3. As most people now have met their basic material needs, some experts argue that they tend to think more in terms of values rather than interests: this **postmaterialism** cuts across class voting, encouraging, for example, many middle-class salary earners to vote for social liberal, new-left and green parties, while many workers gravitate toward the far-right.
4. As the manual working class has declined as a proportion of the population (something not even those who are sceptical about the decline of class voting dispute), mainstream social democratic parties have had to – or at least convinced themselves that they have had to – extend their appeal to the middle classes. This 'catch-all strategy' has met with some success, but the downside is (supposedly) a loss of some disillusioned working-class supporters.
5. European societies may not be becoming 'classless' in the sense that life-chances are no longer influenced by social background (see Chapter 1). But class has never been an objective category; it is a cleavage and an identity that is latent and dormant unless (explicitly) mobilized by political actors: if parties choose not to appeal to such antagonisms and to pick policies that polarize debate, then it is hardly surprising that they cease to drive people's voting behaviour.

voting, as 'marketization' since the early 1990s makes it clearer to people with which side of the left–right divide their material interests (perceived as much collectively as individually) lie (see Whitefield, 2002; see also Evans, 2006). Whether this is primarily because the electorate has taken its cue from politicians, or because politicians are reflecting the feelings of the electorate (in the jargon 'preference-accommodating' rather than 'preference-shaping') is very much a moot point – and one already mentioned when we discussed the concept of volatility (first touched on in Chapter 5) above. On the other hand, not all analysts agree that class, any more than party identification, will necessarily come to take its 'proper place' as a cue for voters in CEE countries such as Poland and the Czech Republic (see Zielinski, 2002). Instead, it can be argued that a voter's self-placement on a left–right scale – one that is often more rooted in historical understanding and moral values rather than socioeconomic issues – may continue to be a much better predictor of political preferences than, say, occupation (see Gijsberts and Nieuwbeerta, 2000, Mateju and Vlachová, 1998 and Szczerbiak, 2003).

Interestingly, a stress on the electoral importance of the values held by voters rather than their class position is by no means limited to those interested in East Central Europe. Not everyone agrees that older cleavages such as class and religion (see below) are paling into insignificance beside something we touched on in Chapter 5 in the context of green parties and go on to talk about in Chapter 8 namely, postmaterialism. Although the existence of such a trend is often taken for granted, and has even been used to help explain not just the rise of the greens but also that of the far right (see Ignazi, 2003: Chapter 12), there are those who are highly sceptical (see, for instance, Wilensky, 2002: 191–207). Yet many analysts argue that 'values voting' is at least as important as 'cleavage' or 'structural' voting (see Knutsen and Scarbrough, 1995), although they might, of course, be connected (see Kriesi, 1998).

Yet many of those who support the idea of 'values voting' (the tendency to cast one's vote according to a conception of 'the good life' held irrespective of one's occupation, religion, etc.) are by no means sure that it began in the 1970s. It may, they note, have been important (but unmeasured) in the 1950s and 1960s, helping to explain in part why party systems have not undergone the kind of change we might have expected given the huge changes in society in the postwar period (see Chapters 1 and 5). In other words, 'values', even if they weren't 'new politics' values have always informed people's voting decisions. Obvious candidates here would be where people placed themselves (or could be placed by their answers to certain survey questions) on a 'left–right' or an 'authoritarian–libertarian' dimension – a location which, interestingly, appears to have little to do with their social class (Thomassen, 2005: 260). Recent research (Thomassen, 2005) suggests, in fact, that, as with class, the impact of all these value orientations is not determined by an inevitable modernization process – one that would predict either the rise of new politics and the decline of more traditional orientations or the declining impact of all value orientations as voters become more and more individualized and therefore idiosyncratic. Rather their impact depends, once again, on the extent to which political actors effectively mobilize them: if parties choose (or manage) not to frame their disagreements in terms of a left–right or authoritarian–libertarian conflict, then voters are less likely to bring such value orientations to bear on their choice of party or candidate.

Religion – another death announced prematurely?

Just as some political scientists are beginning to challenge the common wisdom on the putative end of class voting in an era where individual values are supposedly coming to the fore, others are warning that, likewise, we write off religion (see Chapter 1) at our peril. Similarly, their criticisms do not involve an attempt to refute the obvious. Just as those who see a continuing link between class and voting do not try to argue, for instance, that there are just as many manual workers as ever there were, those who still see religion influencing votes do not contest the fact that fewer and fewer people go to church these days – a 'composition effect' which means religion is having less and less of an impact on voting. What they argue, however, is that a 'correlation effect' still exists; namely, that for those who are religious, religion remains a strong a predictor of their vote. Specifically, they maintain that (a) religion impacts most on the voting behaviour of those who attend regularly; and (b) even many non-attenders still consider themselves to be believers/members of churches and that this continues to have at least some influence on their vote. This influence may be direct, in that they vote for, say, a Christian democratic party. Or it may be indirect, in the sense that it encourages them to support a certain party because of the stances it takes on issues on which their opinions are in part shaped by their religious convictions.

So what about the evidence (see Broughton and Ten Napel, 2000, Norris and Inglehart, 2004; and Knutsen, 2004)? Certainly, there does seem to be evidence that, in some countries, differences between Christian denominations might matter less than differences between those who go to church and those who just think of themselves as members of one. In Germany, for instance, people are more likely to vote for the CDU/CSU if they are regular churchgoers, be they Protestant or Catholic. But things are complex. In a country such as France, for example, there is still a difference between denominations (Catholics still tend to vote for right-wing parties), though one reinforced by regular attendance (at least on the Catholic side) and, significantly, by higher social status – a warning to us of the risks of dismissing either class or religion simply because, investigated in isolation, they do not seem to make much of a difference. They also seem to be linked in Scotland (and to a lesser extent) England, where Catholicism is – very unusually – associated with centre-left rather than centre-right voting. In the Netherlands, active Protestants vote disproportionately for explicitly religious – Protestant – parties and practising Catholics are most likely to vote for the CDA. Interestingly, however, research lends little support to the suggestion that there might exist widespread indirectly religious voting for particular parties owing to their stances on 'moral issues' such as abortion or marriage and the family. Research also suggests that if right-wing parties have traditionally benefited more than the left from the impact of faith on voting, there is a flip side. People who consciously reject religion tend to vote for left-wing parties – either for social democrats or (especially if there is a parliamentary left or green alternative) for smaller parties on their flank.

So, religion remains a better predictor of voting than other social characteristics, including class, even if the extent to which religious belief predicts one's political stance might (according to Norris and Inglehart's massive cross-national study) gradually be weakening over time. But we should not let this lack of dealignment on the part of those who have faith obscure the possibly more important fact that (as we saw in Chapter 1) fewer and fewer people are going to church regularly (if at all) nowadays. Hence, the value of this relationship (especially to the right side of the political spectrum) would appear to be a wasting asset – much as the decline in trade union density we consider in Chapter 8 may well harm the left. Accordingly, mainstream centre-right parties all over Europe have been attempting to reduce any reliance they may have had on religious voters, just as their social democratic counterparts have been scrambling to ensure they can cope with the decline of the 'traditional working class.'

Secularization, in other words, might not make things easy (see Duncan, 2006, 2007), but it need not spell the death of parties whose appeal may have begun as religious – as long as that appeal is leavened or tempered by a show of concern with other issues. True, Christian Democrats have struggled in, say, France (where they were never strong), in Belgium (where the French speaking Christian Democrats re-labelled themselves as the 'Humanist Centre Democrats') and Italy (where voters deserted the party in droves for more secular right wing parties when the extent of the party's corruption became clear after the end of the Cold War). But in Germany, support for the Christian Democrats has remained fairly steady, notwithstanding unification with the former East Germany, where levels of religious belief (let alone church attendance) are very low. Meanwhile, in the Netherlands and Austria, Christian Democratic parties seemed to have turned things around in recent years. In Scandinavia, the recent performance of some Christian parties might suggest a niche (though no more than a niche) audience worth pitching for in these supposedly more postmaterialist times.

In CEE countries, many of which were (officially anyway) atheist under communism, religion is likely to be less of an influence on voters. There are, however, exceptions (see Whitefield, 2002), to this rule. A big one is Poland, where Roman Catholicism, and the extent to which it is actually practised rather than simply adhered to, continues not just to

COUNTRY PROFILE

Italy (Italia)

Area: 294,000 km^2 (7.0% of EU-27)

Population: 58.7million (12.0% of EU-27)

Religious heritage: Roman Catholic

GDP (2006): 1,477 billion (12.7% of EU-27)

GDP *per capita* as percentage of EU-27 average: 104

Female representation in parliament and cabinet (end 2007): 17% and 22%

Joined EU: founder member, 1957

Top 3 cities: Rome – capital city (2.7 million), Milan (1.3 million), Naples (1.0 million).

History: Italy was, for centuries, a collection of sometimes foreign-ruled city-states. In the nineteenth century, however, nationalists led by Garibaldi built on the achievements in the north by Cavour and, by 1861, had succeeded in unifying the country under a constitutional monarch. Italy held its first mass elections on the eve of the First World War, a conflict from which Italy emerged on the winning side.

From the 1920s onwards, Italy, like Germany, collapsed into authoritarian dictatorship (in its case under the fascist leader Benito Mussolini). Following its defeat in the Second World War, in which it allied itself with Germany, Italy became a republic. Its politics were dominated by the centre-right Christian Democratic party (DC), which benefited from an unwritten pact between most political parties to keep the powerful communist party (PCI) out of office at the national level. The DC's constant presence in every postwar administration until the early 1990s provided a kind of disguised stability for a system that saw forty-seven governments between 1947 and 1992. But it also relied on clientelistic corruption, as well as links with organized crime. With the collapse of Communism, Italians were finally able to express their discontent, and the early 1990s saw the end of the DC. The electorate divides between a left-wing bloc based around the former PCI, and a right-wing bloc composed of a former fascist party (the now conservative National Alliance), a xenophobic regionalist party (the Northern League) and the dominant partner, *Forza Italia,* led by media mogul Silvio Berlusconi. The Right narrowly lost the election of 2006 to the Left, led by former Prime Minister and President of the European Commission, Romano Prodi. In 2007, Italy's centre-left parties, including the former PCI, merged to create the *Partito Democratico* (Democratic Party). Its first outing at the snap election of 2008 was a baptism of fire.

Economy and society: Interestingly, Italy's superficially chaotic politics did little to harm its postwar economic revival, and the country retains its reputation for producing stylish, high-quality goods in demand all over the world. Its population, however, enjoys a *per capita* GDP only a handful of percentage points above the EU average. This is because there is a big gap between the rich industrialized and service-oriented north and the poorer, more agricultural south (or *Mezzogiorno*) that also includes the islands of Sicily and Sardinia. This has led to tensions, with people in the North feeling resentment at having, as they see it, to subsidize the South. Partly because there is a relatively low level of identification with the nation state, Italians have historically been very pro-EU. Traditionally, they have also been among the most tolerant toward migrants, although this has changed in recent years, as foreigners have been sucked into the North. More are likely to join them, since Italy, along with Spain, has one of Europe's most rapidly ageing populations. (see box on p. 187).

Governance: Italy is a parliamentary democracy elected, between 1994 and 2001, under a mixed system that failed

WHAT'S IN AN ANTHEM?

Il Canto degli Italiani was written and popularized in the middle of the nineteenth century during the ultimately successful campaign for a free and united Italy. But it did not become the country's anthem until the founding of the Italian Republic in 1946. The first verse (the only one that is really sung) dips a toe into classical imperial glory, with Italy wearing the helmet of Roman general Scipio and God having apparently made the goddess Victory 'Rome's slave'. Italy, goes the chorus that winds up the anthem, has called and 'we are ready to die'. And just to leave no one in any doubt that they are, the very last word is a resounding 'Yes!'

in its intention to reduce the number of parties. Very unusually, both houses of the legislature have practically equal power. Also, in recent times, Italian presidents, elected by parliament and supposedly with little more than ceremonial power, have shown themselves more willing than their counterparts in other European countries to criticize the government of the day. Italy's judiciary is also renowned for its willingness to investigate its politicians and their actions. Relations became even more strained during Silvio Berlusconi's second period of office, although he managed to stave off his legal pursuers. He also managed to effect a return to a much purer form of proportional representation just in time for the election of 2006. His hope that this would save his government turned out to be a false one, however. And there is talk of yet more reform on the way. These high-profile spats, should not, however, obscure other fundamental developments in the governance of Italy, not least the move toward granting its regions much greater autonomy, although this is as yet more true in theory than in practice.

A KEY CONTEMPORARY CHALLENGE

BRINGING IN MIGRANT LABOUR IN A CLIMATE OF FEAR

After a century of so of being an exporter of labour, Italy is now a net importer – people still move from the south to the north in search of better prospects but not enough of them to do the jobs that are either beneath or beyond Italians. Until recently, much of the debate surrounding immigration in Italy focused on North Africans, particularly if they were Muslims. Recently, however, a new group has become the focus for mass anxiety – the Romanians who, since their country joined the EU in January 2007, have been arriving in Italy in such numbers that many have had to be housed in makeshift camps. These, according to many Italians (many of whom equate Romanians with Roma or gypsies) have become breeding grounds for crime: Mayor of Rome, and leader of the new Democratic Party, Walter Veltroni, claimed that three-quarters of those arrested for rape, murder and robbery in the city were Romanian.

In November 2007, the Italian government responded to these anxieties in draconian manner that stands in marked contrast with Italy's reputation as an enthusiastic European. By decree, it gave permission to police and local authorities to expel all foreigners, including EU citizens, thought to pose a risk to public safety. To many, however, it was little more than a desperate move by politicians who know that they cannot, in the long term, restrict the free movement of labour that so many of Italy's employers and, ultimately, Italy's pensioners will have to rely on unless younger generations of Italians do something to raise the country's plummeting birth rate.

Foreign policy: Italy, like Germany, spent most of the latter half of the twentieth century atoning for its over-assertiveness before 1945. A staunch member of the EU and NATO, it has, however, often been accused of not living up to the commitments it often seems to observe more in word than in deed. In recent years, Italy has modified its knee-jerk enthusiasm for European integration and, with the UK and Spain, its right-wing government (in contrast to its population) was a strong supporter of the Iraq war. Following the change of government in 2006, relations with Washington have cooled slightly, with Italy seeking, at last, to punch its weight closer to home: the country was instrumental in putting together an EU peace-keeping mission after the Lebanon War of 2006.

Contemporary challenges

- Welfare reform, possibly aiming at shifting so much spending away from the growing army of pensioners and towards, for example, providing better unemployment coverage
- Bringing in, in a climate of fear and prejudice, sufficient migrant labour to fill vacancies and offset the shrinking population so that future pension commitments can be met (see box above)
- Making devolution (and even federalism) a reality without further worsening the disparity between the rich north and the poor south
- Disentangling the continuingly complex and close relationship between politicians on both sides and banks and other enterprises; rooting out organized crime from government and business.

Learning resources. There are a number of books that serve as useful primers to the colourful politics of recent years, while trying to give a journalistic/historical insight into Italian society more generally. The best of these include Ginsborg (2003), *Italy and Its Discontents*; Jones (2007), *The Dark Heart of Italy*; and Stille (2007), *The Sack of Rome*. For something more academic, try Newell and Bull (2005), *Italian Politics*; and `cotta and Verzichelli (2007), *Political Institutions in Italy*. Keep up with the news at http://www.ansa.it/site/notizie/awnplus/english/english.html

influence voting but (along with attitudes to the communist past) actually structures popular conceptions of what is and is not right- or left-wing (see Szczerbiak, 2003). Many parties on the right make a specific pitch for the country's most religious voters, combining a scathing attitude to the supposedly aggressive (but, in practice, very tame) secularism of the left with an assertive nationalism that means they have little in common with the larger, more moderate, Christian democratic parties of the west (Bale and Szczerbiak, 2008).

Few other countries in Europe, however, can come anywhere near matching the US in terms of religiosity and, therefore, the potential impact of religion on politics. However, once again, we should stress that (as with class) any such impact depends not just on the voters themselves – the 'demand side' of the equation, if you like – but also on the supply side, namely the parties that compete for their votes (and to some extent the interest groups they listen to). If parties choose, or feel obliged, to mobilize on the church–state cleavage (see Chapter 5), then what are otherwise dormant religious attitudes among voters can begin to seem more relevant when choosing between parties. For instance, having won the election of 2000, the PASOK socialist government in Greece decided to remove religious affiliation from some state-held identity data, thereby provoking a huge row with the powerful Orthodox Church. Its campaign to stymie the move was publicly backed by the opposition conservative party, which moved ahead in the polls and won a convincing victory at the next election. The fight with the church was by no means the only reason that saw voters turn away from PASOK, but it might well think twice before picking one again. Its counterpart in Spain, however, seemed to many to be determined to do just that after unexpectedly winning the 2004 election. Prime Minster Zapatero's PSOE government quickly began passing all sorts of liberal legislation, provoking the Catholic church to urge its most devoted adherents onto the streets to protest and also call on the conservative opposition, the PP, to join it. Aside from the fact that the socialists clearly believed in what they were doing, the calculation might have been that identifying PP with values that fewer and fewer Spaniards now seem to share would allow PSOE to paint its main opponent, once again, as the party of the past.

Other social characteristics – ethnicity and gender

The fact that, as we noted above, Catholics in England tend to vote Labour, can be explained by the fact that Catholicism was the religion of (poorer) Irish immigrants. But this begs questions about whether the relationship in question is actually to do with religion or with ethnicity. The same goes for the fact that Britain's black and minority ethnic (BME) population continues to vote overwhelmingly for Labour. Is it because some of them are non-Christian (a problematic explanation because Afro-Caribbeans, for example, are relatively observant Christians)? Or is it because they are non-white and therefore suffer disproportionately from discrimination, are more likely to be in lower-paid occupations, and less likely to favour a party (the Conservatives) that (rightly or wrongly) has been perceived as tougher on immigration. The UK, however, would seem to be unusual: as in the US, there is one party (Labour in Britain, the Democrats in the US) that picks up the majority of the 'multicultural' vote. This does not seem to be the case elsewhere. However, there is very little research published (at least in English) on the voting patterns and political participation of ethnic (and particularly immigrant) minorities in Europe, especially outside of the UK (see Dancygier and Saunders, 2006; Garbaye, 2005; Saggar, 2000) – although we do, of course, know much more about the more obvious link between minority nationalism (which relies in part on ethnic if not racial identity) and the success of regionalist parties (De Winter *et al.*, 2006).

This gap in our knowledge is serious, especially given the growing presence of such minorities all over Europe and the distinct possibility that a backlash against immigration is helping to create a new ethnic cleavage (see Chapter 10 and Dogan, 2001). Until it is remedied, however, we are fortunate enough to have most of what we do know ably summarized by Anthony Messina (2007: Chapter 7). First, although immigrants who hold citizenship participate more than those who do not, they still tend to vote in lower numbers than the native born, although the longer someone is resident the more they vote. This is partly because it takes time to build up an interest (material and otherwise) in political outcomes in the new country, especially when one retains an interest in these matters in one's country of origin. It is also because some immigrant groups (particularly those who do not do well or who feel especially discriminated against) are clearly prone to alienation and apathy. Second, where immigrants do vote, however, there is a clear tendency across Europe for them to support parties of the left: this is as obvious in, say, Germany (where parties on the left receive between two thirds and three quarters of the votes of naturalized Turks) and the Netherlands, as it is in the UK. And this appears to occur irrespective of class: parties on the left, even though they have in recent years moved to change the perception that they are 'soft' on immigration (see Bale *et al.*, 2008), are seen to be more immigrant-friendly; their interest in promoting equality and support for a welfare state also seems to resonate with migrant voters. Third, there are significant differences between participation rates not just between different immigrant groups in the same country but between the same immigrant group in different countries – differences that we lack the research to explain.

The relationship between gender and voting is also relatively under-researched especially at cross-national, comparative level. This is not because of small sample sizes (women, after all, constitute the majority of the adult population) but possibly because in most countries there appeared to be little difference between the voting behaviour of men and women – although in the UK, for instance, it is well-known that the Conservatives would have lost almost every general election in the postwar period had only men been entitled to vote. Inglehart and Norris (2000), however, suggest that things may be changing throughout the advanced industrial world and, therefore, in Europe. Women used to be more conservative than men, at least insofar as surveys were able to determine their position on a left–right scale; however, outside of postcommunist democracies, they appear to have moved to the left of men. Whether this development is as significant as they suggest, and whether gender differences in ideological self-placement has (or will) influence voting, remains open to debate (see Brooks *et al.*, 2006: 110). We have some interesting country studies (e.g. Campbell, 2004 and Johns and Shephard, 2007). What we need is more comparative work.

Issue-voting, retrospective judgements and leadership

If long-term factors like class and religion seem to matter less, if values haven't taken their place as determinants of party choice, and if voters are more footloose, then perhaps we should look for an increased impact on voting of more short-term factors. Perhaps contemporary, 'cognitively mobilized' voters, knowing their own preferences on a range of concerns, now vote for those parties whose policies most closely match those preferences: has 'issue voting' increased? Or perhaps, just as rationally, they now place more emphasis on whether the parties (or party) in power have (or has) delivered on promises made, especially, say, on the economy. It would appear that these 'retrospective judgements' have more impact on voting in some countries rather than others, with the rank order – the UK, Sweden, Spain, Germany, France, Italy and finally the Netherlands – appearing to vary according to the extent to which parties (or predictable coalitions) can reasonably be blamed (or given credit for) economic policy (see Duch and Stevenson, 2006). But is economic voting more important than it used to be? And what about the leaders that, especially in the contemporary media (see Chapter 7), now loom so large in political life? Are voters – not altogether irrationally – more swayed than they were by personality? If we wrap all these questions up together, is it the case that European voters have grown out of their tribal instincts, care more now about competence and delivery than ideology, about **valence** rather than **position issues**? Do they then believe that one of the best ways of getting what they want is to elect individuals rather than worry overly much about parties, whose claims to **issue ownership**

Position issues are those on which people tend to take sides (e.g. more or less tax and spending), whereas **valence issues** are those on which most people want basically the same thing (e.g. sustainable economic growth or safer streets) and, as a result, judge politicians according to their competence in achieving more or less rather than either/or. **Issue ownership** refers to the fact that certain parties are seen by the majority to have consistently better policies and/or to care more about certain issues than their opponents; this leads parties during elections to try and ensure that 'their' issues dominate the news agenda (see Chapter 7).

seem meaningless given the fact that (a) virtually all of them believe in more or less liberal capitalism; and (b) globalization means their policy options are severely narrowed?

Leaving aside objections, or at least qualifications, to the idea that parties are all the same and globalization means they cannot make a difference anyway, which are dealt with in Chapter 9, the answer (for the moment at least) would seem to be no. There is little evidence to suggest that issues, retrospective judgement and leaders drive voters' decisions more than they used to. A recent cross-national study looking at six European democracies since the 1960s (Thomassen, 2005) found that

- Although there was evidence voters preferred parties that 'owned' the issues they thought were important (or 'salient' – see Chapter 7), there was no increase in 'issue voting' over time. In fact, issues have always played a role in voters' choices but that part hasn't grown.
- Although voters tend to punish the parties they perceive as responsible for their own and the country's economic difficulties, they don't do so now any more than they have always done
- The importance of leadership evaluations to voting differs between countries – leaders (of large parties) are more important in countries in which they are seen to be serious prime ministerial contenders (as in the UK). But it doesn't differ significantly over time.

Of course, it might be that we are just at the beginning of a era in which these short term factors come to trump 'cleavage' or 'values' voting. After all, it seems to make so much sense. As we saw in Chapter 5, Europe's parties (especially mainstream parties) can no longer rely on large numbers of members either to reflect back the views of the electorate to them or to spread their message to the electorate and keep some of it loyal. Acting increasingly on the basis of opinion polls and focus groups, and having to rely more and more on a media they cannot control (see Chapter 7), parties stress their 'catch-all' centrist pragmatism and emphasize their leaders and their stances on valence issues – the things that every government is expected to deliver – rather than on the issues they traditionally (and generally still) 'own'. For instance, parties of the mainstream left and right will make more of their ability competently to run a stable and growing economy than they will of their intentions – albeit ones they still profess and even act on (see Chapter 9) – to, say, decrease taxation (the centre-right) or defend the welfare state (the centre-left). Europe's voters, taking their cues from the parties, begin to vote on the basis of the content and the credibility of the more specific offers being made to them by the salesmen (or women) concerned – in other words, they vote ever more instrumentally than ideologically. The parties pick up on this consumerist response and adapt their appeals accordingly. And so on and so on.

But just because this is intuitively plausible – and has even taken on the guise of common wisdom in some quarters – doesn't mean that it's right, at least as far as the available evidence goes. Voters are driven by a mix of class, religion, values and shorter-term factors. And, as the evidence from postcommunist countries suggests, they also learn over time, taking previous results into consideration during any current election (see Dawisha and Deets, 2006). The importance of each factor varies between elections, but we are a long way yet from explaining – let alone predicting – how and why. Moreover, individual psychology, political interest and knowledge, and intellectual capacity also play a part. Different people, for instance, will use different 'heuristics' (short-cuts) to make their decision on which party to vote for – or, indeed, whether to bother voting at all (see Baldassarri and Schadee, 2006). And a psychological predisposition to traditionalism and security, and acceptance of inequality, is associated with support for the right of the political spectrum, whereas openness to new experiences and a preference for equality is associated with support for the left – at least in western Europe. In the east, individuals with a strong psychological need for security favoured the left (which under Communism had provided it), whereas those who were most open to new experiences tended towards the right of the political spectrum, presumably because it was associated with capitalist risk-taking, all of which suggests an interaction between individual character traits and collective history (see Thorisdottir *et al.*, 2007). The fact that political scientists are beginning to acknowledge this kind of complexity doesn't make their task any easier, but it at least brings us closer to the real world.

EP elections

Elections to the EP take place every five years. Notwithstanding the increasing power of the EP in the EU's law-making system, turnout at the elections (which, note, are fought as simultaneous national contests not as one pan-European election) has dropped across the continent in recent years (see Table 6.7). True, a modest recovery in some countries can be hidden by the average figure, which now includes very low turnout countries in CEE. And, over the years, the average has also dropped with the inclusion of other less 'Europhile' countries, the position of the elections in national election cycles, the reduction in compulsory voting – and, of course, the trend toward turnout decline discussed above (see also Franklin, 2001a, 2001b). But the turnout difference between national and European elections is marked.

Political scientists are divided on the extent to which voters currently (or could potentially) fit EU issues into their existing left–right and materialist–postmaterialist orientations (see Gabel and Anderson, 2002; and Marks and Steenbergen, 2004). There is considerably more agreement on the point that EP elections are still what political scientists call 'second-order' contests (though see Blondel *et al.*, 1998). Like local and regional elections, they are often used by voters to send a message (often one of dissatisfaction conveyed by voting for small and/or opposition parties) to the national government of the day (see van der Eijk and Franklin, 1996). This means that EP elections seem unlikely, at least for now, to contribute much to the creation of a European identity among the citizens of the member states. Whether, though, this is because those citizens are irretrievably nationally focused or whether they are encouraged to be so by parties who are neither ready nor willing to supranationalize their appeals or their focus, is a moot point (see van der Eijk and Franklin, 1996: 364–5). As we noted at the end of Chapter 5, many political scientists argue that it may only be a matter of time before 'Europe' becomes a key political cleavage – something that will depend not only on how voters are affected by EU policies but also on whether and how parties choose to mobilize on the European issue and thus provide 'cues' for those voters (Hooghe, 2007).

The current 'second-order' status of EP elections can give rise to co-ordination problems. Because EP elections are largely national contests and because of

KEY POINT:

The EP has become more powerful but voters – even if their preferences on European integration may dovetail with their views on other issues – still accord it relatively little importance. EP elections can be (and are) used, though, as a useful test of opinion and tactics in domestic politics.

Table 6.7 Turnout in EP elections, 1979–2004

	1979	1984	1987	1989	1994	1995	1999	2004	Prev. gen. election
Czech Rep.	–	–	–	–	–	–	–	28.30	58.0 (2002)
Poland	–	–	–	–	–	–	–	28.32	46.3 (2001)
Sweden	–	–	–	–	–	41.6	38.8	37.80	80.1 (2002)
UK	32.2	32.6	–	36.2	36.4	–	24.0	38.83	59.4 (2001)
Netherlands	57.8	50.6	–	47.2	35.6	–	30.0	39.30	79.9 (2003)
France	60.7	56.7	–	48.7	52.7	–	46.8	42.76	60.7 (2002)
Germany	65.7	56.8	–	62.3	60.0	–	45.2	43.00	79.1 (2002)
Spain	–	–	68.9	54.6	59.1	–	63.0	45.10	77.2 (2004)
Italy	84.9	83.4	–	81.5	74.8	–	70.8	73.10	81.3 (2001)
EU average	63.0	61.0	–	58.5	56.8	–	49.8	45.70	–

Source: Data from www.elections.eu.int

the tendency (particularly pronounced when national elections are a long way off) to punish incumbents, there are always likely to be 'mismatches' between member state governments (and maybe the commissioners they nominate) and the EP. These mismatches, given a legislative process relying on 'co-decision' between the EP and the Council of Ministers (representing national governments), could make European law-making more conflictual, especially if the EP begins – as it seems to be doing (see Hix *et al.*, 2003) – to vote more on left–right (or at least party-bloc) lines. Whether this will mean that at least some national governments will be faced with more European legislation of which they do not approve, however, is another moot point. Hypothetically, a centre-right government which loses out in the Council of Ministers under QMV (see Chapter 2) might be able to rely on centre-right MEPs of whatever nationality to make the kinds of changes it desires at a later stage of the legislative process – changes which, if the EP carries on expanding the range of legislation over which it has some control, could have big (budgetary) implications.

Irrespective of these unintended consequences of EP elections, the latter play an important part in the domestic politics of member states (see Gabel, 2000). Both parties and voters use them (and their results) as signals and portents, which may then affect their subsequent behaviour. A party may finally realize, for instance, that it has to dump its underperforming leader, while a protest vote allows voters to register their dislike of the direction in which a particular party is travelling and/or provides an opportunity for catharsis, after which they return to the fold by the next general election. Or the effect of that vote is perhaps to allow a new entrant onto the political scene who then stays around for good. For instance, EP elections – fought as they are under PR even in countries that ordinarily use majoritarian systems – gave the far-right *Front National* and the Greens an early boost. Similarly, EP elections have finally given voters in Europe's other majoritarian system, the UK, the chance to make a vote for a small party count. Conceivably this may make them more willing to vote for smaller parties in other elections – a logic that also applies, incidentally, to the use of PR for elections to the Scottish Parliament and the Welsh Assembly, and could well spill over into increasing support to change the system at national level. These possibilities, however, probably pale into insignificance alongside the more immediate fact that European integration more generally (rather than the EP in particular) is increasingly part of domestic political disputes, either on its own or because hostility to it is becoming a now familiar favourite for populist politicians all over the continent (see Szczerbiak and Taggart, 2008).

Direct democracy – useful tool or dangerous panacea?

Representative democracy is not the only form of democracy in Europe: all of the continent's states, apart from Germany, also have experience of **direct democracy** at the national level – most famously in Switzerland (see Box 6.6). The referendums used in the latter take various particular forms (see Table 6.8). But the issue is worth studying for anyone interested in European politics. For one thing, direct democracy has played and could well continue to play a role in European integration (see Hobolt, 2006), notwithstanding the fact that referendums (in France and the Netherlands) famously scuppered the EU's Constitutional Treaty in the Spring of 2005 (see Chapter 2). Just as importantly, direct democracy is also put forward as an alternative, or a cure, for the supposedly moribund state of party-driven politics in Europe. Direct democracy would also seem to be particularly attractive to younger

> **Representative democracy** is the election of parties and candidates to parliament where they then form governments and pass legislation on the people's behalf. By **direct democracy**, we mean the holding of referendums in order to decide policy and/or constitutional changes.

KEY POINT

Many European countries use referendums, but their purposes and powers vary considerably. Direct democracy comes with risks but can be a useful adjunct to representative politics.

BOX 6.6

The home of direct democracy

The Swiss confederation is famous for a century or more of referendums. Nationally, it takes just 50,000 of the country's 7.3 million citizens who so object to a law or policy that they want to see it struck down to sign a petition to force a binding referendum. To win, they need to muster 'a double majority': Switzerland is made up of *cantons* (mini-states that enjoy a great deal of independence from the federal government at the centre); in order to pass at the national level, a referendum proposal has to win not only a majority of all those voting but also has to pass in a majority of cantons. Switzerland is also one of the few places in Europe to allow its citizens the right of initiative. As in California, they can propose a new law and, if passed, it becomes binding on parliament. Getting a vote on a proposal, however, is more demanding than getting one that seeks to strike something down; 100,000 citizens must sign and, more often than not, their proposal will be rejected. Frequently, though, the campaign (perhaps even before it has achieved all the signatures needed) will prompt the government into a counterproposal. Indeed, research suggests that the Swiss political class have become increasingly adept at doing deals in order to head off, or at least control, the effects of referendums (Papadopoulos, 2001). Whether this means that, ultimately, no one can beat politics-behind-closed-doors, or that those who conduct such politics are nonetheless more responsive to those outside the room, is a moot point.

people (see Donovan and Karp, 2006).

Supporters of direct democracy, like its opponents, put forward a whole host of arguments (see Debate 6.1). At the more fundamentalist or populist end of the spectrum lie claims that referendums have the potential to save democracy from parties that are portrayed as distant from the people and a distortion of, or even as parasites on, democracy. In the middle are claims, first, that referendums encourage participation and informed voting on crucial issues that would otherwise be subsumed in the packages of policies on offer at elections and, second, that parliaments make better laws if they know they risk being overturned. At the minimalist or pragmatic end of the spectrum lies the argument that they provide, first, a useful safeguard, particularly on constitutional issues that affect the political 'rules of the game' (be they domestic or European or the interaction between the two) and, second, that they prevent particular issues paralyzing the system.

This pragmatic argument for direct democracy certainly seems to reflect reality. In western Europe, the most widely used type is the ad hoc referendum and most referendums (of whatever type) have been used in order to decide questions that are considered too difficult (perhaps because they involve moral judgements on such things as abortion or divorce) or too crucial (normally because they touch on the constitution or on matters of sovereignty, particularly with regard to the EU, see Chapter 2) for parliament to decide for itself. This has been the case especially when an issue looks like splitting parties and/or when governments are hoping to insulate themselves from negative electoral effects it might have on them. The UK government's surprise announcement in 2004 that it would hold a referendum on the EU's Constitutional Treaty is typical: in light of the Treaty's rejection by Dutch and French voters, no referendum was held, but the promise of one was enough to get Labour safely through the 2005 general election.

Referendums on social or economic policy are not uncommon in the twenty-four US states which have citizen-initiated referendums. But (outside Switzerland) they are very unusual in Europe. Votes on moral issues – despite media interest in them – are also quite uncommon, especially outside Italy and Ireland. Three European countries have resorted to referendums on the divisive – and possibly post-materialist – issue of nuclear power (Austria, 1978, Sweden, 1980 and Italy, 1987). All rejected it (the Italians voting to ban their country's activity in projects outside of Italy). Spain's socialist government in the 1980s used a referendum to legitimize its decision to remain in NATO, and Hungary held a referendum in 1997 before joining it – unlike Poland and the Czech Republic, neither of whom felt in necessary to hold one before doing the same thing. Referendums have also been held in Southern and East Central European states during their transition to democracy, not least as a way of gaining legiti-

Table 6.8 Types of referendums and where they can be used

Called by	'Law-controlling'	'Law-promoting'
Constitutional requirement	*Mandatory* (law in this area – normally constitutional) requires a referendum before coming into force) **Austria, Denmark, Estonia, Ireland, Latvia, Lithuania, Romania, Slovakia, Spain, Switzerland**	
Elected representatives	*Abrogative* (overturns laws already in force). **Italy, Switzerland**	*Ad hoc/optional* (called on a particular issue and may or may not be declared binding) **Austria, Belgium, Denmark, Finland, France, Greece, Hungary, Norway, Portugal, Slovenia, Sweden, UK**
	Rejective (overturns – normally constitutional – laws passed but not yet in force) **Austria, Bulgaria, Czech Rep., Denmark, Estonia, Greece, Ireland, Italy, Lithuania, Poland, Romania, Slovakia, Slovenia, Spain, Sweden, Switzerland**	
Citizens	*Abrogative* **Italy, Switzerland**	*Popular initiative* (draft law proposed by citizens which becomes binding if passed) **Hungary, Latvia, Lithuania, Poland, Romania, Slovenia, Switzerland**
	Rejective **Switzerland**	

Source: Adapted from Setälä (1999); entries for postcommunist states from Auer and Bützer (2001).

macy for new constitutions.

Indeed, constitutional referendums are the biggest single group, closely followed now by EU referendums, not least because so many CEE states held referendums for both purposes (see Szczerbiak and Taggart, 2004). Some (the Baltic states and Slovenia) used referendums to declare themselves independent; significantly this was an option denied to the Czech and Slovak people by their politicians, who feared their plans for a 'velvet divorce' might be vetoed. With the odd exception, referendums on new constitutions have resulted in 'yes' votes. This stands in marked contrast to referendums on constitutional amendments that have sought to extend the power of one branch of government, normally the executive, or somehow seem to advantage the ruling party and do not have cross-party support (as was the case in Ireland in 1959 and 1968 when the *Fianna Fáil* party tried unsuccessfully to introduce FPP). The exception to the rule is provided by France, where Charles de Gaulle persuaded the people to back the creation of a directly elected president in 1962. But even this is only a partial exception: when de Gaulle tried to limit the powers of the Senate in 1969, his plans were rejected in a referendum and he resigned.

Most states limit such votes to those proposed by the legislature or the executive, though interestingly there are some grounds to think that they propose them more often in states where the judiciary may

DEBATE 6.1

Should we have more referendums?

YES

- Direct democracy bypasses an unpopular and disconnected political class which is either too ideologically blinkered or too 'politically correct' to deliver common-sense solutions in accordance with the views of ordinary people.
- Referendums can encourage lively debate and informed decisions on an issue which may not only cut across party lines but are also too important to be decided at general elections when voters have to take into account a whole host of topics.
- Direct democracy can help decide questions that would otherwise cause ongoing division and distract the country from other important matters.
- Referendums ensure that constitutional issues that will effect the political 'rules of the game' are not decided by those who play – and, indeed, only temporarily play – it.
- Governments and parliaments that know any legislation they produce may be overturned by a referendum will tend to ensure that such legislation is in accord with the will of the people. And – in the case of citizens' initiatives – allowing the people to recommend or even compel politicians to act on certain issues means they can never drift too far out of touch or close their eyes to a vital matter of public concern.
- Improving technology will allow us to vote instantly – think of TV's *Big Brother*.

NO

- Boiling down a complex issue into a straightforward question that everyone can understand will encourage dangerous oversimplification; it also rips particular issues out of context. People may end up voting for something that, for instance, will impact negatively on other programmes that they value or for policy that, given wider constraints, can be neither implemented nor afforded.
- Turning issues into either/or questions provides a field day for populists and a dumbed-down media – forces that will encourage voters to make irrational and prejudiced decisions when they might be better off leaving things to politicians who, when all is said and done, have been elected to do just that job and have more time and resources to do it properly.
- Low turnout is a problem: getting less than, say, half of the electorate to vote will throw the legitimacy of a referendum result into question and can even mean the result is not binding; this can encourage campaigners for the status quo to call for mass abstention – not what we need in a democracy.
- Even a 'respectable' turnout will be unrepresentative, given that older, better-off and better-educated people are more likely to vote.
- Referendums don't always bring closure – what is to stop the losing side calling for another vote on the same question at a later date?

be called on to oblige them to do so (as has happened in Ireland on three occasions in the postwar period; see Qvortrup, 2002: 105–7). However, two states – Switzerland and Italy – allow citizens themselves to call a vote on a particular question, requiring only that they gather sufficient signatures to show that such a vote would be worthwhile holding. The relative ease with which this can be done, however, is balanced in both countries by safeguards designed to reduce the risk to minority rights by requiring that any vote be passed by a 'double majority'. In Switzerland, this involves the cantons (see Box 6.5).

In Italy (where referendums can only repeal an existing law and where 500,000 signatures or five regional councils' support must be obtained first) they require at least 50 per cent of the country to actually turn up and vote, and the repeal option has to gain majority support among those who do. After a golden period in the early 1990s, when voters used referendums practically to oblige politicians to overhaul the electoral system, Italian referendums have failed to attract sufficient people to turn out and vote, rendering them – in the eyes of critics, anyway – an expensive waste of time. The same has happened in Lithuania, which holds the record for the most referendums in CEE, and in Poland, where the referendum turnout is even lower than at elections: in 1996 just 32 per cent turned out to vote on privatization, in 1997 only 43 per cent bothered on the constitution. However, turnout on EU accession improved to 59 per cent, higher than in other 'candidate countries', although generally turnouts in the referendums they held before joining could have been predicted by their levels of turnout in other contests (see Szczerbiak and Taggart, 2004). Even countries where referendums are used sparingly can have trouble with turnout, The Portuguese government abandoned plans to liberalize abortion laws when the restrictionist case 'won' a referendum on the issue with a 1 per cent majority in 1998 but on a turnout of only 32 per cent despite weeks of high-intensity media coverage. When the same subject was put to a vote in February 2007, turnout (at almost 40 per cent) fell short of the 50 per cent required, although this time the government made it clear that it would regard the 59 per cent vote for liberalization as a mandate to legislate.

This falling-off of interest is not, of course, the only argument against direct democracy. Another is that, owing to the correlation between political participation and both affluence and education, those voting in referendums will be particularly unrepresentative of the electorate as a whole. Some critics also hold that they they risk the basest instincts and blinkered prejudice of the majority being whipped up by populist politicians who want to override the law and the rights of ethnic and other minorities – just as they were used by fascist regimes in the 1930s. Others believe that they discourage compromise, oversimplify complex matters and can produce contradictory laws and policies which are popular only because their wider context is not considered.

However, outside of Switzerland (where there is some evidence to suggest that poorer, less-educated voters are disproportionately less likely to vote in referendums) opponents of direct democracy have, as Yet produced no evidence to show that this is the case in other European countries or, if it is the case, that this underrepresentation is any worse than it is in parliamentary elections. The same goes for the suggestion that voters in referendums are ill-informed. Again, this is unproven and, even if it were, the situation would probably be just as bad in parliamentary elections where some voters' knowledge of party and candidate positions (and names) is woefully poor. Advocates of referendums can point to evidence from Denmark and Switzerland that they actually help improve citizen understanding of the issues under consideration. This could affect not just the result of the referendum, but opinion on the wider issue of which it might be just one facet. For instance, those who know more about the EU tend to be more supportive of it: holding relatively frequent referendums on EU matters could then affect levels of support for the EU more generally, even perhaps if the referendum in question is 'lost'. That they are sometimes (though rarely) lost reflects a problem to which EU referendums are particularly (but not exclusively) prone; namely, that they become party political popularity contests rather than a carefully considered answer to a specific question – something which is even more likely if the governments that order them are obliged neither to obey the result nor to hold them in the first place (see Hug, 2002; see also Qvortrup, 2002: 76)

This raises another common criticism of referendums; namely, that governments more often than not pull the strings, holding them only if and when they think they can win. However, the accusation is not borne out by the record, which suggests that over three-quarters of referendums held in Europe between 1945 and 1997 were not within their control. It also shows that just over a third did not turn out to be supportive of the government's stance on the issue in hand (see Qvortrup, 2002). Neither is there any evidence that national-level referendums in Europe have oppressed minorities. This is the case even in Switzerland, where some local referendums have produced some 'near-misses' for supporters of xenophobic measures: in September 2000, two-thirds of those voting rejected an initiative limiting immigration, for instance The Swiss also overwhelmingly supported the decriminalization of homosexuality in 1992. Often, indeed, voters turn out to be surprisingly liberal. Referendums on moral issues are very rare outside Italy (where divorce was controversially permitted in 1974) and Ireland (which has had long debates on both divorce and abortion). But voters in these two Catholic countries have on several occasions surprised commentators by voting for the more liberal option – though in Ireland, it took a second referendum on both issues (abortion in 1992 and divorce in 1995) before this result was achieved.

Yet referendums very rarely resolve an issue if it reflects deep-seated divisions within a society. For instance, in 1950 a majority of Belgians voted for the restoration of the monarchy, but only because of such strong support for the idea from the Flemish community; riots ensued (mainly involving French speakers from Wallonia) which forced the king to abdicate in order for the monarchy to survive. More recently, the British government's ability to garner referendum backing for the Northern Ireland peace process in 1998 may well have helped prevent things slipping back into chaos, but it took longer to bring a lasting settlement appreciably closer. Meanwhile, the recent history of referendums in the Republic of Ireland, shows that those on the losing side of the argument (whether they be citizens or the government) do not necessarily give up; instead they go for another referendum. This happened on abortion in the 1990s and, more recently, the ratification of the EU's Treaty of Nice.

Demands for direct democracy are often a function of disenchantment with and distrust of 'politics as usual' and, as such, we might expect them to increase. But, going on the evidence, referendums are not a 'silver bullet' that can revivify ailing democracies. Indeed, evidence suggests that they are just as (or more) likely to mobilize those who are already sufficiently interested to participate as they are to encourage those who are turned off politics to join in (see Donovan and Karp, 2006: 683–4). On the other hand, fifty years of experience suggest that they no longer need be tarred by association with the rigged 'plebiscites' of Fascist and Communist dictatorships. Instead the evidence suggests that, used sparingly, referendums can help democracy function more efficiently and, in some cases, provide a valuable reminder to politicians that getting elected every four or five years does not give them licence to ignore voters' views, particularly on issues of fundamental concern.

There is, however, one caveat, relating to a common criticism of direct democracy. The argument that money can buy, or that 'special interests' can manipulate, referendums can in part be dismissed by noting that it applies with equal force to parliamentary elections. Indeed, one could argue that it is much easier for a wealthy interest group to 'buy' a small group of legislators than it is for them to 'purchase' the votes of millions of citizens. We also know that the overwhelming imbalance of financial resources in favour of the 'yes' campaigns in recent EU accession referendums was nowhere near reflected in the results, with substantial minorities voting 'no' in many countries. Those contests, like the one that resulted in the Swedes rejecting a switch to the euro, showed that 'it is possible to run an amateurish but populist and effective campaign against a much more glossy but off-putting one' (see Szczerbiak and Taggart, 2004: 767).

But the argument that the media might sometimes play a part in swinging the result one way or another could have some force, notwithstanding the fact that referendum results (as they did when voters in Sweden and Denmark rejected the euro) have often gone against the media consensus. As we go on to suggest in Chapter 7, fears of media influence on voting (if not on politics more generally) are often overplayed, yet they are not totally groundless, particularly when it comes to very close results. In most proportional systems, such marginal 'distortions' will be spread across the parties. But in referendums, just as in two-horse races in FPP systems, media influence on just a few thousand voters can – just occasionally – mean the difference between winning and losing (see Siune *et al.*, 1994). On the other hand, analysis of the EU accession referendums (see Szczerbiak and Taggart, 2004) strongly suggests that voters – who also, of course, have their own opinions and knowledge-base – are not influenced simply by the media per se but also by the cues they receive in (and not exclusively in) the media by parties and politicians, as well as by other, sometimes more credible actors, up to and including formally non-partisan presidents and even popes! In short, and once again, while it may be fashionable in these somewhat populist times to insist on separating voters from politicians, the preferences and actions of each have an impact on those of the other. This is also the case when we come to examine the relationship between politics and the media, the subject of Chapter 7.

Learning Resources for Chapter 6

Further reading

For amazingly accessible yet erudite and informative coverage of the electoral systems debate in Europe and elsewhere, see the collection edited by Gallagher and Mitchell (2005), *The Politics of Electoral Systems*. Anyone really interested in voting and elections should also check out the journal *Electoral Studies*. For the more academic arguments about the relationship between electoral and party systems and political behaviour, see Norris (2004b), *Electoral Engineering*, and see Sartori (1997), *Comparative Constitutional Engineering*. Franklin (2004), *Voter Turnout and the Dynamics of Electoral Competition in Established Democracies Since 1945*, discusses turnout and plenty more of interest besides. Electoral behaviour in (western) Europe, and particularly the decline (or not) of class voting, is discussed in the collections edited by Evans (1999), *The End of Class Politics?*, and by Thomassen (2005), *The European Voter*. A useful introduction to political science's attempts to understand voting behaviour is Evans (2003), *Voters and Voting* (Sage). A stimulating discussion of some of the issues raised here is the chapter by Pennings in the collection edited by Keman (2002b) *Comparative Democratic Politics*. On referendums, the first port of call should be Le Duc (2003), *The Politics of Direct Democracy*; but see also Kaufman and Waters (2004), *Direct Democracy in Europe*. Also useful are two books by Qvortrup (2005), *A Comparative Study of Referendums*, and (2007), *The Politics of Participation*.

On the web

www.aceproject.org – all things electoral

www.sussex.ac.uk/sei/1-4-2.html – election reports online

www.parties-and-elections.de and wikipedia.org – election results

www.unc.edu/~asreynol/ballots.html – examples of ballot papers

www.idea.int/vt – global survey of turnout

www.iri-europe.org – referendums

www.palgrave.com
Companion Website
Visit the Companion Website to 'click and go'
www.palgrave.com/politics/bale

Discussion questions

1. There is more than one type of proportional representation or PR electoral system used in Europe and they all have their strengths and weaknesses. Which do you prefer, and why?
2. What sort of rules can affect, and even undermine, the proportionality of PR systems? Can you give some examples of where these things have had an impact?
3. A handful of European countries employ 'plurality' or 'majority' systems: what do you see as the pros and cons of such systems?
4. Many people assume that a particular electoral system automatically leads to a particular party system: are they right to do so?
5. What causes variations in turnout at elections, and how seriously should we take concerns about turnout dropping right across Europe?
6. Voters seem to be less loyal to parties than they once were: how would you go about explaining this?
7. Do you think class and/or religion make much difference to the way people vote any more?
8. If you were asked to sum up the differences between today's European voters and those of thirty or forty years ago, what would you say?
9. Do people vote differently in EP elections?
10. Referendums are distrusted, even disdained, by their critics: do you think they have some justification for their dislike of direct democracy?

Chapter 7
The media – player and recorder

Variations in usage and style	201
Structure and regulation	204
State and public service broadcasting	208
The connection between media systems and political systems	210
The changing coverage of politics	212
Bias and its effects	220
Pressure groups and populists	226
The impact of ICT – cyber-optimism or cyber-scepticism?	227
The media and 'Europe'	230
'Overseas' news	233

In a representative democracy made up of millions of people, politicians need to communicate with those whose votes they rely on and whose welfare should be their main concern. To do so, they rely on the media – so much so, in fact, that some analysts talk about the 'mediatization' of politics (see Schulz, 2004). Inasmuch as politics and the media operate as separate institutions – and the media is best seen as an institution since it persists over time with norms and rules that impact systematically on those who work in and deal with it (see Schudson, 2002 and Cook, 1998) – the membrane that separates them is highly permeable. The media in Europe does not simply observe political activity but also helps to drive, structure and police it. It is a source (and, on many matters, for most citizens practically the only source) of information and interpretation. It thereby produces and reflects what (admittedly rather loosely) we call 'public opinion'. It also acts as a 'watchdog', not necessarily doing good or behaving admirably but exposing and preventing abuses, keeping politicians on their toes for the rest of us who are too poor or too busy to do so ourselves (see Schudson, 2005). It provides what those who conceive of it as a kind of 'fourth estate' see as a pseudo-constitutional check and balance – particularly in countries where, for instance, parliament (and therefore political opposition between elections) is weak. This is not just theoretical: extensive cross-national empirical research strongly suggests a positive association between good governance and human development, on the one hand, and media freedom and accessibility, on the other (see Norris, 2004a).

Partly because it is recognized that the market might fail to perform these valuable functions, the state in most European countries continues to own, or at least subsidize, public broadcasting. Rather less obviously (via lower rates of sales tax or postal/telecommunication rates), it also subsidizes the press (see Murschetz, 1998). State 'interference', however, does not stop there: the state – at both national and local level – regulates the media in myriad ways, from the granting of broadcast licences to the imposition of obligations towards political impartiality. In some countries, it goes even further, with the government of the day exerting a degree of control over output, or even indulging in plain old censorship (see Newton and Artingstall, 1994) that in others would be regarded as illegitimate and even dangerous.

Given the state's concern to maintain a degree of control of the media – and we should never forget that in most countries broadcasting in particular was originally monopolized by states lest this frighteningly powerful new technology fall into the 'wrong' hands – it is hardly surprising that the Europeanization of media regimes has been slow. This does not mean that there are no similarities in the political role and impact of the media in individual countries. Indeed, it could be that the media – especially television – varies less across Europe than do many of the other institutions (governance, parliaments, parties, etc.) we have examined in previous chapters. There is of course some patterned variation, and this chapter begins by providing some general and country-specific material on media use which suggests significant regional differences. It then goes on to look at the structure of the media and the regulatory and ownership environment in which it operates across Europe, with a particular focus on the implications for government control and for the coverage of politics. It then looks at possible connections between states' media systems and their political systems. Next, it explores how that coverage has changed in recent years, particularly with regard to the media's increased focus on personality-driven and 'presidential' coverage even in parliamentary systems and its move toward a less deferential style. It then deals with the difficult question of the media's effect on politics: is it overblown, can we measure it, and is it more about agenda-setting than directly influencing either voters or those for whom they vote? It goes on to explore the contribution of the media to the visibility and success of pressure groups and populist politicians. It moves on to examine the impact of new information and communication technology (ICT) on European politics and the contribution of the media, old and new, to European identity and integration. It ends with a brief look at the way the media in Europe covers foreign (including other European) countries.

Variations in usage and style

Broadly speaking, the further south and east you go in Europe, the less people read (or at least buy) newspapers: if you take a thousand Swedish adults over 400 of them will buy a paper, a figure that drops to around 300 in the UK, Netherlands and Germany, 200 in the Czech Republic and France, and only 100 in Poland, Italy and Spain (see Gulyás, 2004 and McQuail, 2001). This is probably because mass education and democracies with entrenched freedom of the press came later to Mediterranean countries and Eastern and Central Europe. Certainly, as Hallin and Mancini (2004: 64) show, there is (with the exception of France) a striking correlation between a country's newspaper circulation today and its adult literacy rate at the end of the nineteenth century – an example, if ever there was one, of the 'dead hand of history'. Conversely, the further south you go, the more television people watch, the big exception to the rule being the UK. There adults watch well over three and a half hours a day, which puts them just ahead of people in Spain, Italy, Poland and the Czech Republic, who are in turn just ahead of the Germans and the French; it is only when one gets to the Dutch and the Scandinavians that the figure drops to around two-and-a-half hours (Gulyás, 2004; and McQuail, 2001).

KEY POINT

Television is far and away the most important medium. Newspaper-reading is more important in Northern than in Southern and Central and Eastern Europe, but is on the decline everywhere, especially among young people.

These regional variations also apply to media styles: for instance, the Scandinavian media, despite its mass reach, takes its mission to inform and educate more seriously than most and, especially when it comes to local newspapers, is financially supported by the state for so doing (De Bens and Østbye, 1998: 14). This does not mean, however, that Nordic necessarily means high-minded. True, the UK tabloid press is even more heavily focused on entertainment than its equivalents elsewhere in Europe. But Sweden has its *Aftonbladet* just as Germany, where the 'tabloidization' of news has arguably proceeded at a slower pace than in, say, the UK (Esser, 1999), has its *Bild.* Elsewhere, tabloids quickly took hold in Poland, Hungary and the Czech Republic following the fall of communism (Gulyás, 2004: 84–5). Interestingly, it is newspapers in Southern Europe that are, by and large, relatively serious affairs bought by relatively few people, with most going to weekly magazines (the *prensa del corazón* most famously exemplified perhaps by *¡Hola!* in Spain) for the celebrity gossip that the

BOX 7.1

Going, going, gone? Age and the decline in newspaper reading in Europe

American Political Scientist Martin Wattenberg, who is concerned about declining electoral turnout among young people (see Chapter 6), suggests that decreasing exposure to media that carries political coverage may well have something to do with it. He notes that newspaper consumption is indeed going down generally, but shows that it is dropping further and faster among young people – with the possible exception of Italy, where older people have traditionally not been big readers (but interestingly where relatively more young people turn out to vote). For those of our core countries on which he has data (see Wattenberg, 2007), we can compare the situation now with twenty years ago (Table 7.1).

Table 7.1 Percentage of people regularly reading a newspaper

	18–29 year olds (c. 1983)	18–29 year olds (2003)	Change (c. 1983–2003)	Over-65s (c. 1983)	Over-65s (2003)	Change (c. 1983–2003)
UK	76	43	−33	83	65	−18
Netherlands	82	39	−43	90	75	−15
Sweden	90	37	−53	96	80	−16
Italy	47	30	−17	32	32	0
Germany	72	28	−44	86	74	−12
France	34	21	−13	69	51	−18

The big question is: will younger people pick up the newspaper habit as they get older? Wattenberg – and others (see Lauf, 2001) – suspect not.

British (and the Germans and the Swedes) get every day.

These variations, however, should not be allowed to disguise one very obvious trend throughout Europe, and indeed the US (see Meyer, 2004); namely, the decline in circulation (see Papathanassopoulos, 2001: 111) and, very probably, daily newspaper reading. Irrespective of income and gender (which still matter in some countries, with the better-off and men reading more than the poor and women) and education (which interestingly is no longer a good predictor of readership anywhere), fewer people than ever are reading newspapers; the problem is particularly acute among young adults (see Box 7.1) – a fact that may have a negative impact over time in overall interest in and understanding of politics. What we do not yet know is whether the rise of the so-called free-sheet – newspapers that can be picked up at no cost at, for example, railway stations and which often contain re-worked content from the same day's paid-for papers – might arrest, or at least slow, the decline. And those who scoff that, even if they were to do so, it would make no difference because they contain so little political content need to be careful because they vary considerably. Viennese commuters, for example, can indeed pick up *Heute*, whose 'lite' political coverage is on a par with what Londoners expect from, say, *Metro* or Parisians from *20 Minutes*; but, if they were to plump instead for *Österreich*, they would be getting more politics for free than, say, British tabloid readers pay for when they read the *Mirror* or the *Sun*.

If we look at news in particular, similar patterns prevail. Firstly, the north of Europe seems to have more appetite for news than the south and the east, where relatively low use of newspapers is not, it would appear, made up for by watching television and listening to the radio (see Figure 7.1). Second, young Europeans use traditional sources for news much less frequently than average. If we take the EU population as a whole, we find that in 2006 some 66 per cent watched TV news daily, 40 per cent listened to news on the radio daily, and 35 per cent got news from newspapers everyday; the percentages for those aged 15–24 were just 42, 28, and 20, respectively. Before thinking that this is a recipe for apathy and depoliticization, however, we should note that there appears to be no consistent relationship between an appetite for news and, say, the electoral turnout we discussed in Chapter 6. Italy, for instance, ranks low on news hunger but is a highly politicized society where lots of people vote in elections. Its low ranking should also give us pause for thought before swallowing whole the idea that the country's ex-prime minister, Silvio Berlusconi, was somehow able to control politics because he controlled the media (see Box 7.12).

One aspect of the media in Europe that is seemingly universal is 'news values' – the criteria that determine whether editors include or reject a story (see Brighton and Foy, 2007 and Palmer, 2002). All over the continent, stories have much more chance of seeing the light if they are visual, emotive, conflictual, intense, unambiguous, of majority relevance, unpredictable and apparently capable of some kind of 'commonsense' solution. Nevertheless, one can detect subtle national variations in journalistic methods and ethics (see Weaver, 1998), notions of objectivity (see Donsbach and Klett, 1993) and, more generally, style. A fascinating comparative study (Donsbach and Patterson, 2004) of journalists in Germany, Italy, Sweden and the US, reveals all sorts of significant differences. German journalists, for example, are quite happy to provide both reportage and commentary on events, whereas, at the other extreme, US journalists tended to do either one or the other, not both. The Italians, like the Germans, were much less concerned with what their counterparts in other countries would think of as objectivity; Swedish journalists were much more likely than their counterparts in the UK and Italy to seek out their own information rather than more passively relying on the cues of parties, interest groups and government. When it comes to broadcast news styles, there are also variations. Programmes in Italy, Spain, and France, for instance, tend to carry more domestic news, longer items with fewer contributors and more studio-based content,

Figure 7.1 Appetite for news in Europe, 2006

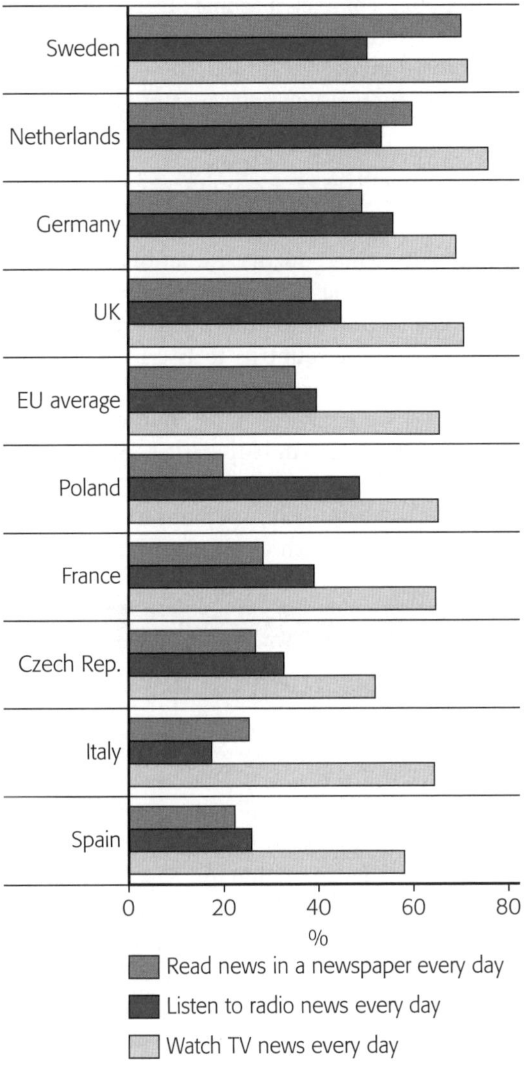

Source: *Eurobarometer*, 65 (Spring 2006).

whereas more 'Germanic' (as opposed to 'Romantic') news cultures, such as the UK and the Netherlands, go for short, sober, location-based reports (see Heinderyckx, 1993).

Interestingly, there is little hard evidence that increasing commercial competition in broadcasting has led to the 'dumbing down' of news provision, either when it comes to the privately owned channels themselves or to public broadcasters (though see Gunther and Mughan, 2000). Some detect 'divergence' – public broadcasting stays or gets even more 'serious') – while others observe 'convergence' – news on public channels becomes less 'serious' but commercial stations raise their game away from mere 'infotainment' in order to compete (see Pfetsch, 1996, for a fascinating case study).

Structure and regulation

The extent to which media is national or more regionally based varies considerably in Europe, particularly when it comes to the press. We would be hard pushed in some countries to assert the existence of a national newspaper market. The latter might exist in the UK, with the main division between downmarket 'tabloids' and upmarket 'broadsheets'. But regional titles continue to play a big, indeed bigger, part elsewhere. This is perhaps to be expected in a federal republic such as Germany, where many of the titles routinely cited in overseas press reviews (such as the *Frankfurter Allgemeine Zeitung* and the *Süddeutsche Zeitung*) are regional newspapers, albeit nationally distributed. Nor is it surprising in 'asymmetrically federal' Spain (see Chapter 2), where the combined circulation of the four top-selling national dailies is only a quarter of that of the regional press (Sanders with Canel, 2004: 199). Yet the same is true of supposedly centralized France where daily titles that are well known abroad (*Le Monde, Le Figaro* and *Libération*) sell predominantly in Paris; elsewhere regional papers rule the roost, to the extent that 'three out of four French citizens never read a daily national paper' (Kuhn, 2004: 26). The regional daily, *Ouest France,* for instance, has a higher circulation (700,000) than any of its 'national' competitors (De Bens and Østbye, 1998: 9).

While regional titles do cover national news, there is clearly less room for it, meaning that citizens in

BOX 7.2

The agenda-setting Cinderella – radio and politics

Writing on Spain, Sanders (with Canel, 2004: 200–1) observes that radio is both 'a key source of political news' and 'the most unconstrained medium for the discussion of politics'; it is also, she notes, an important agenda-setter, whose journalists are trusted more than their counterparts in TV and in the newspapers (an assumption confirmed in Figure 7.3). Generally, however, there is little mention of radio in work on the media and politics in Europe, even though many governments in Europe, especially in the UK, Germany and Scandinavia, continue to protect both local and national public radio (see Lang, 2004), and even though audience figures are actually quite high, while the medium's possibilities are still as endless as they ever were (see Hendy, 2000). This is partly because much of radio's output is music rather than speech, but also because surveys suggest the majority of people rely on TV for news (see Figure 7.1). Yet most of those listening to music hear news bulletins on-the-hour-every-hour, and talk radio, (particularly the 'flagship' programmes made by public broadcasters that feature news and interviews with major political figures), often plays an important role in setting the day's news agenda. Appearing on those programmes is also a means by which those figures signal their positions and intentions to each other, as well as the audience. Since the advent of television, governments have paid rather less attention to radio. However, in a 24/7 news culture that continually seeks new angles in order to refresh and move a story on – and where there is considerable cross-ownership of radio, TV and print media – a radio story is more than capable of causing politicians headaches. In addition, radio, more than television perhaps (see McNair *et al.*, 2002), can be a genuine public-access medium allowing people to break through into what they – rather than the media or the politicians – want to talk about (see Ross, 2004). The phone-in 'talkback' show is nowhere near as developed or significant a format in Europe as it is in the US, but politicians ignore the medium at their peril, even if research suggests that their appearances on it are unlikely to improve their image much.

KEY POINT

The media is subject to country-specific regulation and restrictions on ownership, but these are being undermined by EU law and a tendency toward commercial concentration and co-operation.

those countries where they predominate might be, first, more likely to think that what goes on in regional and local politics counts for something and, second, even more likely to turn to television for national-level political information. This serves to reinforce television's dominant role as most people's main source of political information, and hence the tendency of government and politicians to focus on broadcast (for which read television – see Box 7.2) rather than print media. The latter still has a place, though – both as a forum for elite-level, in-depth debate and, paradoxically, as creator of and conduit for populist opinion and political pressure. Unfortunately, the range of opinion and the direction of that pressure is not as diverse as it might be: the newspaper market in all European countries, with the partial exception of Scandinavia, has seen a fall in the number of titles, as well as increasing concentration of ownership of those that survive; the huge entry costs into the market also make it very difficult for newcomers to make it (De Bens and Østbye, 1998: 11). For many, a worrying aspect of the capital required to run a media outlet is the tendency in some countries for them to be owned by companies with outside, non-media interests which may (directly or indirectly) bias the editorial line. France is just one example (see Box 7.3)

Owning newspapers is now a rich man's sport and rich men are not generally noted for their left-wing views. This does not, of course, mean that all Europe's newspapers are conservative or neo-liberal

BOX 7.3

Defending whose interests? Ownership and the French press

In 2004, the centre-right supporting daily, *Le Figaro*, was bought by Serge Dassault, ex-boss (and still honorary chairman) of the Dassault group which, among other activities, produces military equipment, including the famous Mirage and Rafael jets. By 2005, he was reported as telling his senior editors that 'you have to take a lot of care with the news. Some of it does more harm than good', while later reports hinted at suppression of articles on the company's products and associates. *Le Figaro*, however, is not the only paper to have connections with the defence industry. In early 2005, Lagardère, which has interests in aviation as well as media, and supposedly began its media investment as a platform to oppose suggestions that it be nationalized, took a stake in the more liberal *Le Monde*. But it's not only defence companies who are involved in the media in France: so, too, are utility and public works companies like Bouygues, Suez-Lyonnaise, and Vivendi; they depend on government contracts and are naturally concerned about government regulation. And, of course, these companies' interests are by no means limited to France: Lagardère and Vivendi own publishing and broadcast assets in a range of European countries.

Whether ownership by these companies makes a difference to how particular outlets cover politics is predictably hard to prove, but there are frequent suggestions, for example, that French president Nicolas Sarkozy has received preferential treatment because of his open friendships with Martin Bouygues, Serge Dassault and Arnaud Lagardère. And during the 2007 presidential campaign, his other opponent, centrist François Bayrou, claimed Canal Plus (owned by Vivendi) had cancelled a TV debate between himself and the socialist candidate under pressure from M. Sarkozy. The first post-election 'scandal' came in August 2007 after *Paris-Match* (owned, via Hachette Filipacchi Media, by Lagardère) was accused by the (Belgian-owned) French weekly news magazine *L'Express* (which published rather convincing 'before and after photos') of having touched up a photo of the president, bare to the waist while canoeing with his son during an overseas trip, in order to remove his *poignées d'amour* (love-handles).

Sources: Harcourt (2005), Lloyd (2005).

BOX 7.4

Poland and political interference

Although not generally as bumpy as it has been in the Czech Republic and Hungary, the relationship between politicians and the media in Poland has never been plain sailing and still gives rise to controversies. In July 2001, the popular Justice Minister Lech Kaczynski was sacked after being accused of fraud in a documentary shown by the country's public service broadcaster, Telewizja Polska (TVP), whose boss at the time was close to the left-wing president, Aleksander Kwaśniewski. Kaczynski's claims that the programme was politically motivated were backed by some TVP journalists. The public, too, seemed to take his side: the government from which he was fired went down to a catastrophic election defeat at the 2001 general election, while the nationalist conservative party he (and his twin brother Jarosław) set up in disgust, Law and Justice (*Prawo i Sprawiedliwość* or PiS), came from nowhere to win 9.5 per cent of the vote – a share it then went on to treble at the next election in 2005.

Lech then became President and Jarosław Prime Minister until the coalition they put together fell apart, forcing a snap election in 2007. Before then, however, the brothers were able to use their party's control of the Board, which chooses the Head of TVP, to appoint one of Lech's right-hand-men, Andrzej Urbanski. Supposedly a temporary appointment, Urbanski remained in charge in the run-up to and during the election campaign, much to the chagrin of some journalists at the station who – along with political opponents – accused him of trying to bias output in favour of Law and Justice. They may have had a point: the electoral monitoring mission sent by the OSCE (see Chapter 11) noted 'a lack of qualitative balance by public television', although according to the twins they were nobbled by the tone of TVP's advertising campaign to boost turnout. Following the election, moves were afoot to remove Urbanski, although the President was believed to be keen to keep him in order to offset Law and Justice's loss of influence after it was ejected from office. Any attempt by the clear winner of the election, the Civic Platform party, to change the way the appointment is made in the future will be difficult because political control of the Radio and TV Board is provided for by the Constitution.

in persuasion. The logic of the market dictates that there is money to be made from papers that cater to the tastes of the millions of potential readers with a rather different outlook on life, and it is possible to argue that a decline in the number of titles will actually result in a decrease in 'political parallelism' (outlets being closely linked to one 'side' or other), which may in turn reinforce the 'catch-all' tendencies of parties we discussed in Chapter 5 (see Hallin and Mancini, 2004: 267ff.). But it does mean that those newspapers are unlikely to put themselves at the head of campaigns for, say, root and branch redistribution of wealth or a tax on international financial transactions.

Television may be dominant in Europe, but it has undergone considerable changes in recent years as technological progress (not least the arrival of digital and satellite) and free-market ideas have combined to turn what was once the fiefdom of a few (often state-run) terrestrial providers into a fragmented multi-channel world of round-the-clock choice. This poses major challenges for democracies and for the politicians and governments trying to run them. Deregulation of the broadcasting environment has, if anything, multiplied the tasks and the complexity of those charged with its oversight, albeit increasingly at arm's-length through 'independent' bodies that in a number of European countries (Germany and the Netherlands, for instance) contain representatives from supposedly important social interests.

Governments have to reconcile the demand for free speech with the fact that the market can potentially lead to monopolistic (and perhaps foreign-owned) media empires narrowing rather than widening the range of opinions on offer. This requires them to pass media laws that are often controversial, either because they are said to be overly restrictive or too lax – or sometimes because they attract accusations of political interference (see Box 7.4). But, once these laws are passed, this simply means an unending series of decisions to be taken on, say, awarding licences and on preventing or allowing takeovers. These decisions, rightly or wrongly, often draw flak from those who believe that they are influenced by the promise of political favours. Successive Spanish governments of both left and right have been attacked, and even successfully challenged in both domestic and European Courts, by opponents for allowing sales to go through in contravention of rules on concentration (see Sanders with Canel, 2004: 201).

In most west European countries, some foreign ownership of newspaper titles occurs. In Spain, for instance, the campaigning daily *El Mundo* is Italian-owned, while in the UK US-based News International owns a number of British titles. But it is actually still quite uncommon (see De Bens and Østbye, 1998: 12). In postcommunist countries, however, it is by no means so unusual, not least because overseas interests were often able to buy into print media markets – local as well as national (see Lang, 2004: 166–7) – relatively cheaply; they also had more money to do so than domestic concerns. This was certainly the case in Hungary, where foreign-owned daily newspapers account for almost 90 per cent of circulation (see Gulyás 2003, 2004). Foreign ownership, however, is less of a concern to most governments than cross-ownership (where one firm has, say, newspaper and television holdings) and overconcentration (where a few firms own most of the outlets). But they might be fighting a losing battle as technological advances and free-speech arguments, plus the logic of the market – and, in particular, the single European market (SEM) – begin to overwhelm them. Europe's increasingly corporate (as opposed to individually or family-owned) media groups are co-operating with each other more and more, which arguably promotes efficiency (if not genuine competition) and possibly reduces political partisanship. It does, however risk reducing diversity, not least because the need to deliver shareholder value drives out relatively expensive home-grown production in favour of imported (which means American) content (see Harcourt, 2005: 117–57).

True, states still have their own rules – dictating, for instance, the number of titles and channels in which a single firm is allowed to have a stake based on proportions of shares owned and/or audience share. Some even give this responsibility to lower tiers of government: public broadcasting in Germany may be controlled by a supposedly socially representative Federal Broadcasting Council, but most media regulation is done at the *Land* level. Yet as Harcourt (2005) points out, EU member states have had to accept the principle, laid down by the ECJ (see Chapter 2), that broadcasting is not a cultural matter, and therefore under national control, but a tradeable service and therefore subject to European competition law. The ECJ also prevented states from blocking broadcasts from abroad into its domestic market, and, as Harcourt shows, has been a lever for liberalization. It has obliged governments in the Netherlands, Greece and Belgium to abandon legislative attempts to restrict competition. It has also limited the privileges of state-owned or subsidized public service broadcasting, even though the continued role of the latter received a vote of confidence and a measure of protection in an important protocol to the Amsterdam Treaty of 1997 (see Box 7.5).

Meanwhile, the Commission, in its role as regulator of the internal market, has had to get involved in the policing (and – especially in Germany and also in Spain – the prevention) of mergers and takeovers of media firms, many of which now have holdings in a number of European countries. Some governments have objected to such interference. But, interestingly, some have been grateful to Brussels, even if only privately: they find it very difficult to take on media empires for fear of alienating a potentially powerful political opponent (see Harcourt, 2003: 196) – a good example of a hard task being contracted out to the EU. On the other hand, there is, of course, a tension – as there always is – between allowing a degree of concentration in order to create European businesses which can compete effectively with large overseas conglomerates (one of the main drivers of the single market project, after all) and preventing monopoly at home. It is also increasingly difficult in such a fast-moving environment to use audience share (which changes all the time) or share ownership (which can be hidden by complex inter-business networks) as measures of market dominance (Trappel and Meier, 1998: 204).

That said, the EU is clearly a force, not just in terms of legal and competition decisions but also in terms

BOX 7.5

The EU as protector of public service broadcasting

Governments and public service broadcasters were concerned that commercial concerns should not use EU competition law to try to undermine them completely on the grounds, say, that such broadcasting was an example of illegal state aids. They therefore inserted a protocol into the EU's Treaty of Amsterdam. This notes that 'the system of public broadcasting in the Member States is directly related to the democratic, social and cultural needs of each society and to the need to preserve media pluralism'. It goes on to note that nothing in the Treaty should be allowed to infringe on 'the competence of Member States to provide for the funding of public service broadcasting', although, it also observes, only 'insofar . . . as such funding does not affect trading conditions and competition in the Community to an extent which would be contrary to the common interest'. The tension between cultural and economic logic, therefore, has not entirely disappeared (see Harrison and Woods, 2001) and, if the recent past is anything to go by, the latter logic is likely to win out in the end: as Alison Harcourt shows, the EU – especially through the ECJ, which is even less sensitive to concerns about media pluralism and the public interest than the Commission, and under pressure from powerful commercial enterprises – has 'ridden roughshod over political choices made at the domestic level, regardless of national claims of subsidiarity (Harcourt, 2005: 4). One battleground still being fought over, for example, is the use of licence fee income by state broadcasters to fund their digital and especially their extensive web services: is this an unfair subsidy, as commercial opponents and some in the Commission allege, or a logical extension of public service provision in the twenty-first century?

of setting the agenda for, and promoting the convergence of, national regimes (see Harcourt, 2005, for details). If one is looking for evidence of Europeanization, then media regulation (although not, as we shall see, output) is a very good example. Recent media legislation in the member states (including those who joined in 2004), and even in Switzerland, shows significant signs of having been influenced by and redrawn to take account of the EU's 1989 and 1997 *Television Without Frontiers* Directives which (notwithstanding general moves toward liberalization) attempt to limit advertising and boost European content (see Wheeler, 2004). The latter aim does not go down well with the US, but the EU (especially under French pressure) has tried to hold the pass on the issue at international trade forums like the General Agreement on Tariffs and Trade (GATT) and the World Trade Organization (WTO). Whether, as US companies buy into European media firms and satellite transmissions really do create television without borders, resistance in the end is futile, remains to be seen. States can still exert control and, for example, protect the public from what they see as damaging material, but they have to act smart in order to do so (see Box 7.6)

State and public service broadcasting

In 1980, television in every European country, apart from Britain, Luxembourg and Italy, was public television, but by 2000 every country had allowed commercial competition (Semetko *et al.*, 2000: 123). But while public broadcasters might be under pressure, they have not disappeared. Outside Luxembourg, there is no European country without a state-funded or (if advertising revenue is permitted) at least a state-subsidized public broadcaster existing alongside commercial stations. True, the daily audience share of public broadcasters in post-communist countries such as the Czech Republic

KEY POINT

Television in Europe has changed considerably since the 1980s towards a more commercial and multi-channel environment, but public broadcasting is still important – and, in some countries, still not entirely free from government interference.

BOX 7.6

It's not what you do, it's the way that you do it – protecting public decency

Many people across Europe are concerned about pornography and the increased access to it provided by cable and satellite television, often beamed in from other countries in an attempt to evade censorship. In 2002, the French broadcast regulator, the Conseil Supérior de l'Audiovisuel (CSA), drew up plans to do something about the situation, after research and a campaign by teachers and the press revealed the sheer extent and range of what young people could see (and apparently were watching). But the attempt foundered, not so much because the Head of the CSA was spectacularly (and it turned out falsely) accused of sleaze in the media (see Fletcher, 2006) but because it was seen to be too difficult to frame legislation in such a way as to get round European competition and media law. Interestingly, there seems to have been no attempt to follow the UK, which managed to do just that by a bit of lateral thinking. The British government made the sale of smartcards, decoders and subscriptions for channels like Red Hot Television, xxxTV, Channel Bizarre, and Satisfaction Club, a criminal offence – and therefore outside the jurisdiction of the EU, which has no influence on that branch of the law.

Source: Fletcher (2006).

and Hungary is low (around 30 per cent and 15 per cent, respectively), and some commentators question whether they can ever really emulate their western counterparts. The latter were not faced with the same legacy of distrust of state television as a provider of propaganda; they also had years to establish themselves (in terms of ethos and audience) before facing commercial competition (see Jakubowicz, 2004 and EUMAP, 2005). In western Europe (including Norway, Sweden and the UK, where they are advert-free and rely largely on the licence fee), relatively embedded public broadcasters are not without their own troubles. But they can still boast considerable audience share (around 50 per cent or above), as well as the support of politicians who may be groping around for a new media policy paradigm but have not (yet) abandoned the public service model completely (see van Cuilenburg and McQuail, 2003; also Thompson, 2006).

European governments' support for public broadcasting – symbolized both by funding and by the common insistence that cable or digital services must include public channels in their subscriber packages – is driven by genuine concern to preserve national culture and a well-informed civil society, as well as by a suspicion that, without a mix of public and private, the technologically-driven expansion of choice will lead not to diversity but to dumbing down. But it also stems from the belief – strengthened by fears of commercial concentration – that democratically elected politicians, and those who vote for them, should have access to at least one source of information and opinion that is insulated from the interests of this or that entrepreneur or enterprise, as well as bound by codes (some of them statutory) promoting political impartiality or, at least, 'balance'.

Most (if not all) politicians in Europe are now used to the fact that state ownership (or rather funding) no longer provides them with direct access to quiescent cronies dedicated to serving the needs of the government of the day. But it has taken rather a long time (as well as public and legal pressure) to get some political players to recognize the fact. This is not only the case in new democracies (see Box 7.7), where state control, even if it was never as absolute or uniform as we might think (see Sparks, 2000: 37–40), was considerable. It is also true in countries that emerged from dictatorship over quarter of a century ago, such as Greece (see Box 7.8) and Spain (see Papatheodorou and Machin, 2003). Each incoming administration in Madrid gets to appoint a new Director General of public broadcaster TVE, whose news broadcasts are widely criticized for favouring the government of the day – not only by the public but even by journalists who work there. French broadcast journalists have also complained about the way in which their bosses seem to indulge in anticipatory self-censorship. During the suburban riots that shook France in November 2005, broadcasters around the world eagerly transmitted vivid images (and even a nightly tally) of burning cars; their French counterparts,

BOX 7.7

People power and Czech public broadcasting

In January 2001, the Czech capital Prague witnessed the biggest street protests since gatherings in Wenceslas Square brought down the country's Communist regime during the so-called 'velvet revolution' of 1989. People were demonstrating on behalf of journalists working for Czech television who were occupying their workplace, and broadcasting alternative news programmes, in protest against the appointment of a Director-General whom they believed was in the pocket of the country's two main political parties, which at the time were co-operating in running the country. Initially, the government took a hard line: the television centre was placed under virtual siege, forcing supporters of those inside to hoist food parcels (and, at one stage, chemical toilets) up through the windows to grateful staff. After a month, however, it became clear that many of the two parties' own MPs agreed with the protestors. The government promptly caved in under the pressure, and rushed a new media law through which allowed parliament to appoint a new, independent Director-General while the man they had just appointed resigned 'on health grounds'. In early February, journalists agreed to remove the logo 'Strike' from the corner of the screens and signed (on live TV, of course) an agreement with a new interim Director-General, who fired the old station manager and news director. Another triumph for Czech 'people power', but hardly a ringing endorsement of postcommunist media policy.

however, were much more cagey about showing such graphic pictures (and keeping a tally), apparently because they believed their duty not to inflame the situation further (and possibly boost support for the far right) came before their duty to show what was going on. We should be careful before condemning their attitude as pompous and spineless, however: many media outlets (print and broadcast) in Europe and elsewhere took a similarly 'responsible' stance when it came to publishing (or rather not publishing) the 'Danish cartoons' of the Prophet Muhammed that caused such a furore at the end of 2005 and beginning of 2006 (see Ryan, 2008).

Most other states in Europe (with the partial exception of France) try to avoid these problems by eschewing this 'politics-over-broadcasting systems' mode of governance. Instead, they operate the kind of 'formally autonomous systems' which exist in, say, the UK and Sweden, or the 'politics-in-broadcasting systems' (where governing bodies include representatives of political parties and interest groups) that still characterize Germany and the Netherlands (see Brants and Siune, 1998: 129). In the latter, this mode of media governance has led, following the introduction of commercial television in the late 1980s, to a system of three public service channels (one serving up supposedly family fare, one sports and entertainment and the third more 'cultural' and informative material). On each channel, time is allocated (partly in accordance with their membership numbers) to eight not-for-profit associations of social and religious groups which make programmes reflecting their interests and points of view – a system that promotes considerable diversity (see van der Wurff, 2004). In Italy, the 'politics-in-broadcasting' mode was taken to its logical extent by giving control of each state channel to one of the main political parties. Recently, however, elite agreement on this *lottizzazione* system has broken down, with accusations from the left that the right-wing government of media magnate Silvio Berlusconi was not playing fair (see Box 7.11).

The connection between media systems and political systems

What we observe, then, is considerable variation in the way media works and is regulated and consumed. But our task should also be to look for patterns in and essay an explanation of that variation – ideally, one that connects the political systems of states and the media systems they help structure but which in turn help shape them. Until recently, academics had avoided such a daunting comparative

BOX 7.8

Greece – the battle against government control

In most European countries, surveys suggest that citizens trust television, be it public or commercial, to deliver them relatively unbiased political news and information. But Greece seems to be different: an opinion poll in 2000 revealed that not only did half of those questioned mistrust the political output of state TV, three-quarters of them regarded it as a mouthpiece for the government. This is not so surprising when one remembers that broadcasting in Greece began in earnest under a military dictatorship and that, although the democratic constitution of 1975 guaranteed a free press, it left broadcasting 'under the immediate control of the state'. This monopoly saw the government intervene again and again in both management and output on the grounds that, to quote long-time socialist prime minister Andreas Papandreou, 'impartiality and pluralism on state media were incompatible because this distorts government policy'. This monopoly lasted another decade and was brought to an end only when a corruption scandal involving the Papandreou government emboldened the mayors of Greece's biggest cities (all members of the main opposition party) to establish not only independent radio stations but also TV channels. Government attempts to use the courts to stop them were – significantly – stymied by the intervention of the ECJ, which, after a referral from the Greek courts, made it clear that the attempt to maintain a monopoly was 'ostensibly illegal'. The consequence was an almost overnight and relatively anarchic deregulation, and a media environment that is still heavily politicized and where government has on several occasions undermined the ESR – the supposedly independent regulatory body. Meanwhile, the directors of the state broadcaster, ERT, still report to the Minster of Press and Mass Media.

Sources: Chondroleou (2004) and Harcourt (2003: 185).

enterprise. In 2004, however, Daniel Hallin and Paolo Mancini published what must rank as one of the most important books in the field of media in politics. In it, they argue that it is possible and useful to categorize Europe's media systems and link them to types of political systems that rest on the distinctions familiar to comparative politics. Three distinctions are particularly important to their schema. The first is the distinction between polarized and moderate systems, as suggested by Sartori for party systems (see Chapter 5). The second is the distinction between majoritarian and consensual systems developed by Arend Lijphart, which we mentioned when dealing with governments and parliaments in Chapter 4. The third is a distinction, which we go on to explore in more detail in Chapter 8 but which we touched on in Chapter 1 when talking about different types of welfare states. This is the distinction between more 'corporate' systems (where governments tend to take a hands-on role, working alongside powerful economic interest groups, and where the welfare state is comprehensive, if not necessarily delivered by the public sector) and more liberal 'pluralist' systems (where the government tends to take less of a role and interest groups tend to be more fragmented and competitive, and where the welfare state is not quite so comprehensive).

KEY POINT

Research into how variations in countries' media systems may be connected to their differences in their political systems is at an early – but fruitful – stage.

Hallin and Mancini argue that it is feasible and fruitful to think of European countries as members of one of three 'media systems': (i) the *Mediterranean* or *Polarized Pluralist model* (e.g. France, Greece, Italy, Portugal; and Spain) (ii) the *North European* or *Democratic Corporatist model* (Benelux, Scandinavia, Germany, Austria and Switzerland); and (iii) the *North Atlantic* or *Liberal model* (UK and Ireland), which also includes the US and Canada. Each of these is associated with – and influenced (though not absolutely determined) by – different types of political systems. In each media system there will be, among other things, a characteristic level of circulation, a characteristic degree of linkage between the media and parties and/or interest groups, a tendency toward advocacy or 'objectivity' among journalists, a characteristic regulatory regime, and a different role for the state. Naturally, they expand on these system characteristics, and the links between them and political factors, in a book which relies on sophisticated historical reasoning and lots of empirical evidence, but they can be summed up as follows:

- **Polarized pluralist model.** State and parties involved in many aspects of life, including the media, and adherence to widely differing ideologies is strong, both among the general public and journalists, meaning that there is relatively little sense of an objective common good or, for journalists, professional norms which trump ideology. Politically active minority consumes heavily-slanted, comment-heavy output of predominantly serious newspapers, while less-interested majority sticks more to television.
- **Democratic corporatist model.** Extensive state intervention in the market – including the media market – to facilitate (and subsidize) the representation and reconciliation of different interests and viewpoints, as well as transparency and local autonomy, for the common good. The value placed on the latter ensures that while journalists may advocate for one side or other, they do so within a framework of shared professional norms. Serious news is produced for and consumed by a mass as well as an elite audience.
- **Liberal model.** State not so involved, especially when it comes to the print media. Journalists (with a strong rhetorical commitment to objectivity and independence) are less concerned with representing interest groups and/or ideologies than with playing a watchdog role on behalf of citizen-consumers. Many still read papers but rely more on television for news.

Of course, there are all sorts of criticisms to be made and debates to be had about Hallin and Mancini's schema. For one thing, one can argue that it captures traditions very well but that these traditions (while still important) are being by-passed as media systems – no longer as insulated as they once were – converge (in part because of technology) on more globalized, homogenized, or at least hybrid practices (see Nord, 2006; and Petersson *et al.*, 2006 on Swedish election coverage, for example). For another, one can argue that the systems of Ireland and the UK, where there is, first, still a very strong assertion of the importance and subsidy of public broadcasting and, second, a highly partisan print media, simply don't belong in the same category as the overwhelmingly private broadcasting and non-partisan system of the US. In addition, their speculation that the media systems of East Central Europe will fit into the democratic corporatist model seems highly questionable. The polarization and partisanship that characterized the region's media in the early 1990s might have been dampened by commercial concerns, but has by no means withered away, while public service broadcasting is finding it difficult to compete against commercial stations with little interest (but considerable bias) in politics; the arbitrary interpretation of media of law and the lack of an institutionalized professional ethos among journalists also stand out (see Gross, 2004). All of this is surely more reminiscent of the Mediterranean or polarized pluralist model than any of the others. Yet most of these are issues which Hallin and Mancini themselves wrestle with and invite further discussion on. This, after all, is how comparative study progresses: models are proposed, criticized, qualified and adjusted, the better to resemble (and to explain) reality.

The changing coverage of politics

Fragmentation

Just as Europe's politicians – or, at least, most of them – can no longer guarantee that state broadcasters will do their bidding, they can no longer rely on the fact that by speaking on two or three television channels they will get their message across to the majority of citizens. Admittedly, some futurologists oversell the pace of fragmentation: 'the true "break-up" of the "mass audience" is, as McQuail (1998: 125), points out, not yet upon us. As in the

KEY POINT

Media coverage of politics is more fragmented across a bigger range of outlets, possibly more personalized, and certainly less respectful towards politicians. Whether, though, this has led to increasing cynicism on the part of voters, or a serious loss of agenda-control by parties (especially at elections), is debatable.

rest of the developed world, most Europeans still rely on three or four channels for the vast bulk of their viewing (see Curran, 2002: 190). This will continue to be the case while a stubborn but large minority refuses to pay directly for its television services and for the technology that makes digital services possible. It is also true that whereas over 20 per cent of households in western European countries presently have digital TV, the figure in some eastern European countries (though not all: in Poland the figure is similar) is lower. But the cost is coming down fast. It is also becoming a matter of a one-off payment rather than a long-term subscription, and could soon be unavoidable as analogue services are switched off.

The advent of on-demand services and 'narrowcasting' – the arrival of specialist channels providing an exclusive diet of, say, sport or music or wildlife or celebrity or life-style programmes – means that many people will be able to do what they have always wanted; namely, tune out politics and current affairs altogether. Political junkies, however, will increasingly have to search for what they crave (and perhaps pay for it via a subscription to a specialist channel) rather than being spoonfed for free. Given that the linkage between the public and parties has come to rely so much on mass rather than face-to-face communication, this development threatens to erode what is already a rather tenuous link even further. One can argue already that a market-driven media is unlikely to provide the kind of 'public sphere' or forum that is supposedly necessary for informed, democratic and hopefully rational politics and decision-making (see Habermas, 1989). Whether any such space can be meaningfully said to exist when so many can contract out of it altogether is, anyway, questionable. In fact, contracting out is a feature of the non-digital environment, too, given the increased provision in recent years of regional and minority-language stations – something digitization will only make easier. It may be no accident, for example, that the difficulty countries such as Belgium and Spain – and possibly now the UK – have in holding themselves together has been accelerated by the opening up of 'sub-spheres' that allow minorities to cut themselves off from the rest of the state.

From 'party logic' to 'media logic'

Many European media outlets are cutting down on – or at least changing – their coverage of politics and current affairs not just in between elections but also during them. For commercial newspapers and broadcasters, this is largely on the grounds that elections and politics more generally do not deliver audiences and, therefore, advertising revenue. But even public service broadcasters are seen to be backing away from what used to be thought of as a responsibility to inform and educate voters, irrespective of whether the low turnout at elections they use as justification for their shrinking coverage could conceivably also be a function of that shrinking (Semetko *et al.*, 2000: 127–8).

In some cases, we are talking about a simple reduction in coverage, but this can be overdone. Rooney (cited in Hallin and Mancini, 2004: 280), for example, found that whereas two UK tabloids, the *Sun* and the *Mirror*, devoted 33 and 23 per cent of news content to public affairs in 1968, this had dropped in both cases to 8 per cent by 1992. Winston (cited in Hallin and Mancini, 2004: 281) found that politics as a proportion of news items on the main BBC news shrank from over 20 per cent in 1975 to under ten per cent, with crime stories reversing the trend. Cross-national research by Brants (cited in Hallin and Mancini, 2004), however, suggests that not even commercial television can be said to have marginalized politics as much as is often suggested.

What does seem to be clearer, however, is that programmers and editors are less and less willing to allow politics and politicians to operate in some kind of 'reserved area' in which normal news values are suspended at crucial times (such as elections) in order to give people what they supposedly need as citizens rather than what they apparently want as consumers. Kuhn (2004: 35) notes, for example, that in the 2002 French presidential election, not only the commercial brand leader TF1, but also the main

BOX 7.9

Ads and debates

European political parties spend much less on political advertising than their US counterparts. But that is partly because they are less well-resourced and partly because many countries prohibit paid spots (see Table 7.2), although (as in Norway, where the right were keen to open things up but lost power to a left-wing government that halted the plan) there are party political differences on the issue. They do, however, allow parties a limited number of party election broadcasts (PEBs) funded by the tax-payer (see Chapter 6). Research (see Kaid and Holtz-Bacha, 2006) reveals that advertising does have an effect – although it may not always be in the direction the candidate or party intends! Interestingly, it also reveals that, unlike their US counterparts, Europe's parties produce overwhelmingly positive rather than negative advertising; this is possibly because many of them know they have to work with other parties in coalitions.

Table 7.2 What the media provide at elections

	Paid election ads?	Free time on public TV	Leaders' debates?
Czech Rep.	Yes	Yes	Yes
France	No	Yes	Yes
Germany	Yes	Yes	Yes
Italy	Yes	No (but on private TV)	Yes
Netherlands	Yes	Yes	Yes
Poland	Yes	Yes	Usually
Spain	No	Yes	Usually
Sweden	Yes	Yes	Yes
UK	No	Yes	No
US	Yes	No	Yes

public service broadcaster, France 2, 'devoted significantly less time to election news and debates than in the previous presidential contest' and that 'frequently the election was not the lead story on television news'.

But this is not simply a question of a decrease in the time allotted to politics, but also the way in which it – and hard news in general – is treated. It now has to interest and entertain as well as inform – an imperative that used to be stronger in 'liberal systems' (see Donsbach, 1995) but has now spread to others. As one very prescient study of Italian election-time broadcasting put it, coverage has moved from 'party logic', where political institutions' right to set the agenda and occupy a prominent place in the schedules went unquestioned, towards 'media logic', where neither can be taken for granted (see Mazzoleni, 1987). There has for some time been a 'struggle for the agenda' between the media and politicians (see, for example, Asp, 1983, on its manifestation in Sweden in the 1970s). But, increasingly, normal news values – presumed topicality, obvious visuality, surprise and drama, easy intelligibility, personalization and negativity – are now applied to political stories. This means politics either falls out of favour or it becomes more entertaining – either by being more gimmicky or gladiatorial or, more subtly, by associating itself with the media's celebrity and lifestyle focus.

Gimmicks there are aplenty; but it is hard to identify a trend. Perhaps fortunately, few European politicians followed a spate of Italian politicians who, in the early 1990s, appeared naked or semi-naked in order to court publicity and earn a reputation for liking a bit of good, clean fun (see Roncarolo, 2004: 113). As for gladiatorial contests, more and more parliamentary democracies seem to be going in for televised candidate debates (see Boxes 7.9 and 7.10). The UK, however, has never staged one, and even those that have during one election have not at the next, largely because the incumbent resists taking part. This happened in Spain in 2004, where, despite polls showing that 75 per cent of the public wanted a debate, the man who expected to win the election, PP's Mariano Rajoy, refused to 'get into the ring' with the man who actually won it, Jose Luis Rodriguez Zapatero, around whom PSOE conducted a notably 'presidential' campaign. In most countries, however, the weaker performer has no choice but to go head to head (see Box 7.10).

BOX 7.10

Mars or Venus? Head-to-head debates in France and Germany

In 2002, some forty-two years after they began in the US, German TV held its first head-to-head debates – watched by almost half of the voters – between the 'Chancellor Candidates' of the two leading parties. The reporting of them may have been predictably dominated by boxing metaphors, but academic research suggests that they made a difference: exposure to them seems to have increased turnout and believing one candidate to have won the debate increased the chances of voting for him – effects that were magnified among voters without strong party identification (see Faas and Maier, 2004). The 2005 election represented another first in that one of the televised contenders was a woman. Angela Merkel was widely judged to have been bested by the media-savvy incumbent, Gerhard Schröder, during the single head-to-head debate to which she agreed. After it, her party's ratings began to slide badly, although not enough to prevent her becoming Chancellor after the election.

A couple of years later, another male–female pairing took place in France, as the favourite Nicolas Sarkozy took on the less-fancied (but, as the media typically never tired of mentioning, supposedly highly fanciable) Ségolène Royal. As in other countries, the instantaneous judgements provided by pundits, pollsters and party PR flaks were probably as important as the debates themselves – which was why, for instance, the Royal camp was incensed by the release of what it saw as a dubious post-debate poll that saw Sarkozy as the clear winnner despite the fact that the balance of opinion among 'commentators' and 'analysts' called the two-and-a-half hour marathon, watched by 23.1 million people, a score-draw. Whether Royal's decision – after the confrontation was billed as 'Action Man vs Mrs Nice' – to put in a highly combative performance was a wise one, however, was debatable: a display that might have been seen as simply robust had it been given by a man was condescendingly dismissed as hysterical by opponents.

How much longer British leaders will be able to refuse debates without it counting against them, however, is another matter. Such behaviour, after all, runs counter to the trend that many political scientists claim to have identified toward the 'presidentialization' of not just campaigning (Mughan, 2000) but also European politics more generally (see Poguntke and Webb, 2004). Moreover, in the face of the common wisdom (see Chapter 9) concerning the ideological convergence of mainstream left and right (summed up nicely during the 2002 presidential election in France by *L'Express* publishing a despairing article entitled *A la recherche du clivage perdu*: 'In search of the lost cleavage'), parties feel they must seek new ways to demonstrate that they are different. Given that politics, some claim, is no longer about big ideas but about competent and credible management, it makes sense for parties to try to embody their claim to such qualities by increasing the focus on their leaders. Ironically, however, as leaders become more important to party campaigns, it is not only competence and credibility that count: all-round personality could become more important, creating a premium on candidates who can project personal warmth and charm irrespective of worthiness. Perhaps, as some seriously suggest they should (see Coleman, 2003), both those who do politics and those who cover it are learning from TV shows such as *Big Brother*. The obvious risk – one that is theoretically greater in countries (such as the UK) where ministers are normally elected representatives and not prime ministerial (or presidential) appointees from outside of parliament – is that voters end up with politicians who come over well on television but can't do the very serious job they are elected to do.

What certainly seems to be embedding itself in political coverage, irrespective of gimmickry and gladiatorialism, is what Kuhn (2004: 34) calls 'the mediatization of intimacy' – the deliberate courting by politicians of appearances by themselves and often their wives (less commonly their husbands) in supposedly non-political formats. These – the chat-show or the magazine portrait are the archetypes –

purport to concentrate on the 'real' man or woman behind the public persona in the knowledge that in so doing they are (a) likely to reach voters who might otherwise be turning off and tuning out of politics; and (b) avoid hard questions by experienced and knowledgeable specialist journalists. There is of course a flipside to all this. Since politicians have allowed the cameras into their lives in order to film friendly stories about just how like the rest of us they are, they are finding it increasingly difficult to prevent the media from exposing sides of them that might not go down so well. In many European countries there are strong privacy laws: France, where stories about the state of the main presidential contenders' relationships with their spouse/partner were suppressed during the election of 2007, is a good example. But even that suppression was far from complete, suggesting that protection of privacy is gradually being eroded as politicians who decide to live by the sword are deemed liable to die by it, too (see Stanyer and Wring, 2004). And even if domestic law or journalistic custom is still strong enough to prevent the emergence into the public domain of matters that many would regard as essentially private, the availability of many foreign newspaper titles on the internet and the advent of cross-border satellite broadcasting mean that it is almost impossible to keep things from anybody interested enough to find out.

We need, however, to bear two or three points in mind. First, it is still possible for politicians, particularly if they live fairly conventional lives and are determined not to become celebrities, not to be treated as such – and perhaps to benefit from such distance (see van Zoonen, 2006). Second, even if their private lives are paraded all over the papers, voters may well (as they famously did in the US with Bill Clinton) separate the politician from the person. For instance, in 2006 and 2007 the leaders of the Czech Republic's two biggest parties (both of whom have now served as prime minister) had to endure titillating press-coverage of their personal lives, but it made little dent in either's support.

Third, we should be wary of thinking that packaging politics and politicians is a recent phenomenon in Europe. Kuhn (2004: 31) reminds us that, before he won the 1981 French presidential election, François Mitterrand underwent an 'image make-over'. So, too, did his British counterpart Margaret Thatcher before becoming Prime Minister in 1979, and she famously eschewed inquisitions by trained interrogators from the ranks of political journalism in favour of rather more cosy chats with sympathetic radio DJs. Even in the 1974 French election, Kuhn reminds us, 'the youthful Valéry Giscard d'Estaing presented himself as a man of the people by being photographed in a football strip and playing the accordion (though not both simultaneously)'. Holtz-Bacha (2004: 48–9) reminds us that a 1960s TV-ad for former Chancellor Willy Brandt sought to portray him as a man of the people by showing him driving himself to work through West Berlin, where he was mayor. Indeed, 'personalization' seems to have been part of election campaigning and coverage in Germany as far back as 1949 and, rather than there being an overall trend towards an increase, it tends to vary from election to election, often depending on the charisma of the candidates involved (Wilke and Reinemann, 2001: 301–2). We should also note that, in the UK, a *Times* newspaper editorial was already lamenting in 1970 the fact that people were being asked 'to vote not for a Member of Parliament, but for a Party; not for a Party but for its Leader; and not for its Leader but for a pre-packaged television presentation of what Market Research suggests the Leader should be'.

This is not to say that there is nothing new under the sun: simply that some developments we see as recent have being going on rather longer than we think. In any case, there are some changes in the media's coverage of politics that do stand out as genuinely novel – if not always welcome – developments. For instance, media providers throughout Europe are, especially during elections, crowding out their already limited discussion of policy issues and party programmes with a focus on speculation on who is winning (poll reporting and the 'horse race' aspect). Analysing Germany between 1980 and 1994, for instance, Brettschneider (1997) recorded a big increase (from 65 to 168) in the number of polls reported in the German media in the twelve weeks before federal elections. Broadcasters also seem to be 'dumbing-down' their coverage by forcing politicians into ever shrinking soundbites (see Schulz *et al.*, 2005: 74–5), at the same time, it must be said, as politicians themselves are moving away at election time from old-style party political broadcasts (a

5–10 minute lecturette from a talking head) to 2-minute spots that resemble the US-style adverts that many European countries now allow them to pay for in addition to publicly funded air-time.

It is also argued across Europe that the media is allowing prediction, punditry (including journalists interviewing other journalists) and 'the ranters, columnists with little knowledge but strong opinions' (Riddell, 2006: 77) to crowd out the space and time devoted to the 'straight reporting' of political events, especially if those events are routine, complex and parliamentary (see Negrine, 1998). Research has even noted a trend towards the media reporting not simply on politics but also on how it (the media) reports on politics (Esser *et al.*, 2001). We need to be careful, however. The media in European countries might be spending less time on reporting parliament (and/or reporting only those parts of it that are dramatic and conflictual, such as question times), but they are still fairly reliant on familiar political institutions to provide a steady stream of the raw material for much of what still passes for news (policy conflicts, calls for legislation, airing of issues, and the like). What in the UK is called the 'silly season' – that period where news organizations struggle for stories as parliamentarians go on their long summer break – is testament to the ongoing (if uncomfortable) mutual dependency between politics and the media, between journalists and their sources (see Ericson *et al.*, 1989).

'Disdaining the news', or at least the parties

In the face of this ongoing dependency, there is a tendency by journalists in many European countries to assert their autonomy from politicians in the face of increasingly intense efforts on the part of the latter to control the news agenda and the way they are presented within it. Political parties all over the continent have professionalized their media relations (see Farrell and Webb, 2002) or at the very least adapted their practice (rarely as 'amateurish' as is often rather patronizingly suggested) to changing media technologies (see Negrine and Lilleker, 2002). At election time this has seen them seeking, first, to bully journalists into their version of what is and is not important and fair and, second, to spoonfeed them with neatly pre-packaged stories based on stage-managed 'pseudo-events' from the so-called 'campaign trail'. Notwithstanding a putative move towards stressing 'valence issues' such as economic competence over more ideological 'position' issues, parties still aim, broadly speaking, to keep the focus of the campaign on the issues they 'own' or are associated with – for instance, health and welfare for social democrats or smaller government for conservative parties (see Chapters 5 and 6).

To maintain control and cope with media change, parties (and governments) in Europe are engaging in what one critic calls 'institutionalized political impression management' (Louw, 2005: 26) – the agenda setting and celebrity-handling that we now routinely associate with so-called 'spin doctors'. Although there are some exceptions, notably in the postcommunist democracies in Europe, where politics is still party-centred rather than candidate-centred, these almost iconic figures are rarely roving consultants-for-hire or 'parajournalists' (see Schudson, 2003: 3) in the American mould (see Plasser and Plasser, 2002). Instead, they are partisans with considerable experience in the media who are either explicitly employed or simply relied on to get the party's message across (see Esser *et al.* and Fan, 2000, for a comparative study of the UK and Germany).

As a response, European journalists have taken, like their American colleagues, to 'disdaining the news' (Levy, 1981). They were already just as (if not more) prone to a much-criticized tendency to use 'strategic or game frames in political reporting, which focus on the strategies of political elites and their success or failure in playing the political game, at the expense of the policy concerns that motivate ordinary citizens' (Hallin and Mancini, 2004: 141). But they began to go even further, undermining the efforts of politicians by pointing out to viewers the spinning and the strategic intent behind their statements and pseudo-events, and by revealing the tensions beneath the shows of unity and the fluster and flap beneath the calm and collected exterior (see de Vreese, 2001: 170);

Journalists have also become less deferential and even aggressive, moving from the 'watchdog journalism' of earlier decades to the so-called 'attack-dog journalism' that seems to assume that all politicians are in it for themselves and out to put one over on the people (see Barnett, 2002). These developments have not, however, proceeded at the same pace throughout the continent. The populist 'disdaining',

COUNTRY PROFILE

Spain (España)

Area: 499,500 km^2 (11.9% of EU-27)

Population: 43.7 million (8.9% of EU-27)

Religious heritage: Roman Catholic

GDP (2006): €981 billion (8.5% of EU-27)

GDP *per capita* as percentage of EU average: 102

Female representation in parliament and cabinet (end 2007): 36% and 47%

Joined EU: 1986

Top 3 cities: Madrid – capital city (3.13 million), Barcelona (1.6 million), Valencia (0.8 million).

History: Modern Spain was created in 1479 by dynastic intermarriage. After defeating and expelling the last remnants of the Arab kingdom of Andalusia in the south in the name of Catholicism, its monarchs led the Counter-Reformation against Protestantism in Europe. Further intermarriage joined them to the Habsburg dynasty. As a result, Spanish monarchs ruled not just Spain, but also Austria and what was to become Belgium and the Netherlands, as well as parts of modern-day Italy, France and Germany. Meanwhile, the discovery of America gave Spain an empire (Florida, Mexico, part of the Caribbean and Latin America) and, of course, gold and silver.

By the eighteenth century, however, imperial decay had set in. Spain became a backwater, ruled by a conservative aristocracy determined to preserve its own privileges, as well as Madrid's control of industrially and commercially more advanced regions such as the Basque Country and Catalunya. The nineteenth century saw Spain consumed by a series of wars between liberals and monarchists who were supported by the still-powerful church. This conflict witnessed the brief flowering of a federal republic before the return of the monarchy and a level of repression which radicalized both peasants and the growing urban working class into anarchism and communism. Following a short-lived dictatorship in the 1920s, free elections ushered in a republic and then a left-wing government that threatened not just the privileges of the church and the propertied, but the very existence of the nation state. A military *coup* in 1936 led to three years of civil war (see box below) that also served as a proxy conflict between Fascist Germany and Italy and Communist Russia.

The victor in the civil war, Francisco Franco, established an authoritarian dictatorship, backed by the Catholic church, that lasted from 1939 till his death in 1975 (see box p. 219). The early years saw thousands of opponents put to death, diplomatic isolation (notwithstanding Spain's neutrality during the Second World War), and the country's economic and social development all but arrested. In later years, Franco bought his country a place in the 'West' by allowing US air bases on Spanish soil. He also allowed millions of Spaniards to work abroad in northern Europe and eventually millions of tourists to make the trip south. This assisted economic development but also helped open up the country to foreign influences and the possibility of change. Following Franco's death, his anointed successor, King Juan Carlos, combined with reformists within the regime to restore democracy. After a failed army *coup*, the Socialist Party (PSOE) assumed office and held on to it from 1982 to 1996, until it was finally overhauled by the centre-right Popular Party (PP). The latter won a bigger majority in 2000 and was forecast to win again in 2004 until, just days before the election, Islamic terrorists exploded bombs in Madrid, and the Socialists snatched a narrow victory. They defended it successfully in 2008

Economy and society: Spain's inhabitants have seen their standard of living increase markedly since the end of the Franco era as the economy has become

WHAT'S IN AN ANTHEM?

The answer, in the case of *La Marcha Real*, has been absolutely nothing as far as the words go – at least, since the death of Franco, under whom the lyrics were (predictably enough) about Spain triumphing, the 'hymn of the faith' and 'Glory to the Fatherland'. With the coming of democracy, clerico-fascism was no longer in fashion and coming up with something that might prove acceptable to the Basques and the Catalans was always going to be difficult. But decades of having to stand mutely at international sporting events while the other side belted out a song finally took their toll. The hunt is now on for a new set of lyrics that everyone can feel comfortable with.

integrated into Europe and boosted by EU funding. Agriculture and fishing (Spain has easily the largest fleet in Europe) has become less important as the economy has diversified, particularly in the more industrial and commercial north. Annual per capita income essentially matches the EU average. Other big changes since the advent of democracy include a steep decline in the influence of the church, vast improvements in health, welfare and education, and in the position of women, who now have one of world's lowest birthrates. Perhaps the most visible change of the last few years, however, has been brought about by the influx of immigrants, both from sub-Saharan Africa and from Spain's former colonies in Latin America – an influx that is testimony to the construction led economic boom that the country has enjoyed in recent years but which is also due, critics claim, to the tendency of successive Spanish governments to grant amnesties to hundreds of thousands of formerly illegal immigrants.

Governance: Spain is now a solid parliamentary democracy, with both houses of parliament elected by a PR system that favours the two largest parties and parties from the country's regions. Under the 1978 constitution these 'autonomous communities' have been granted so much power that the country now resembles a federal state. This has not been enough, however, to end calls for independence from some regions, especially in the Basque country (where the terrorist movement ETA operates) and Catalunya, which in late 2007 saw students demonstrate against the arrest of Catalan separatists for publicly burning photographs of the king.

A KEY CONTEMPORARY CHALLENGE

COPING WITH THE LEGACY OF A CIVIL WAR

The Socialist government that won the post-Madrid bombing election of 2004 proceeded with a series of measures calculated to enrage the centre-right and the Church. These included the legalisation of same-sex marriage, moves toward negotiations with Basque separatists, devolution of even more power to Catalunya and other regions, and the passing of the *ley de la memoria histórica* (law on historical memory), which recognizes and rehabilitates the victims of the Franco regime – the regime in which the Popular Party has its origins. Moreover, like the governments of many former dictatorships, the administration has begun to press ahead with the removal of statues, street names etc. that commemorate the former regime. Controversially, churches that do not remove plaques and other fixtures that do the same risk losing state funding. The government even hinted at alterations to Franco's gigantic mausoleum in the *Valle de los Caídos* (Valley of the Fallen) which was built by forced labour. Some – probably unfairly, given the process was started years before and the Socialist foreign minister attended the ceremony – accused the church of counter-attacking when almost simultaneously the Vatican beatified nearly 500 Roman Catholic victims of the Republican forces that ran democratic Spain before they were defeated by Franco.

Spain's so-called *pacto de olvido* (pact of forgetting) may, then, by encouraging everyone to put the past behind them and move on, have facilitated its swift and peaceful transition to democracy. But it also bottled up rather than erased painful memories – memories which clearly still inform the cleavage between left and right even seven decades after the Civil War.

Foreign policy: Spain, initially concentrated on 're-joining' western Europe, via NATO (1982) and the EU (1986). Since then, it has tried to persuade its fellow member states to take Europe's relations with North Africa more seriously and, before it pulled its troops out after the Madrid bombings, angered many of them with its pro-American stance over Iraq.

Contemporary challenges

- Reconciling population decline with a generous pension system
- Managing separatist feeling and consequent terrorism
- Coping with the legacy of a civil war that for years was never really talked about (see box above)
- Controlling but not preventing immigration
- Cooling an economy at risk of overheating without tipping over into recession
- Living with reduced EU funding as consequence of Eastern enlargements, 2004–7.

Learning resources. For a good all-round textbook, see Magone (2008), *Contemporary Spanish Politics*. Gunther *et al.* (2004), *Democracy in Modern Spain* also repays reading. Anyone wanting a broader take on this fascinating country should head straight for Hooper (2006), *The New Spaniards* and Tremlett (2007), *Ghosts of Spain*. Keep up to date on the news at http://www.expatica.com/actual/toc.asp?subchannel_id=81

'attack-dog' stance was first evident in the US and it is therefore no surprise that it spread first to the UK. Other media cultures have been slower to adopt it – at least wholesale. A recent study of election coverage in (admittedly quality) newspapers in Germany from 1949 onwards did find that journalists tended to do more of their own interpreting rather than simply reporting what politicians said and did – a trend also identified in the Netherlands (see de Vreese, 2001: 172). But its authors could find 'no overall trend toward negativism' (Wilke and Reinemann, 2001: 291; see also Schulz *et al.*, 2005: 75). Nor, apparently, are German journalists as interested in their British colleagues in 'exposing' the black arts of the spin doctors, possibly because they are less subject to direct pressure from them, which might in turn be because German parties (whose chancellor candidates are not always the undisputed leaders of their parties) have neither centralized their media operations to quite the same extent nor spent so much money on them (see Esser *et al.*, 2000). It could be, of course, that academic studies are simply lagging behind a reality that British commentators (see Lloyd, 2004) were the first to pick up on.

France, too, according to Kuhn (2004: 38) provides something of a contrast: 'there remains a strong journalistic culture of deference to politicians at the apex of the state apparatus'. Others have noticed the same thing: according to one UK journalist sent out to cover the 2002 presidential election in France, watching a key TV interview with the incumbent, Jacques Chirac (who, he claimed, would have been hounded out of politics years ago by the British press), 'was like watching an old man being gummed by a toothless spaniel' (Jeffries, 2002). Disdain there may be; as Yet however, it is still largely confined, at least in France, to satirical TV programmes and magazines. In both Poland and the Czech Republic, too, public broadcasters have had to combat accusations that they are too respectful to the governments, even if those governments did not necessarily share that view and (particularly in the mid-1990s) made fairly blatant attempts to interfere. But politicians had a notably less easy ride on the main commercial stations and some of their 'disrespect' began to rub off on their public service counterparts (see the contributions by Goban-Klas and Kettle to O'Neil, 1997).

Some commentators, especially in the US where it has gone furthest, think that this style of journalism is contributing to falling trust and rising cynicism among voters. Others rebut this argument, claiming that watching the news has a positive effect on political knowledge, participation and trust (see Norris, 2000) or that, if disdainful strategy-obsessed coverage does provoke a degree of cynicism, then the latter might well be temporary and appears to have no significant impact on participation (de Vreese, 2005). It might, also depend on which side you're watching: Aarts and Semetko (2003) found that, in the Netherlands, the effects were positive for those who got their news from public service broadcasters but negative for those who watched the news on commercial television. If more and more people switch from one to the other, perhaps we will indeed witness the 'spiral of cynicism' and apathy that some critics are worried about.

Yet for all this talk of a struggle for control between politicians and journalists, they are still playing what is essentially a collusive, albeit edgy, game with each other – one that in many ways excludes the very public both sets of players claim to represent. This is most obvious at elections. These events, as demonstrated by the frequent disjuncture between what opinion polls show are the issues that most matter to voters and the subjects actually covered in the media during the campaign, are still largely 'about what politicians talk about rather than what the public want them to talk about' (Brookes *et al.*, 2004; see also Brandenburg, 2002). Polling data is used by the media not to help set the agenda but largely as a supposedly real-time measure of how each party is doing, with the results used both to predict outcomes and to challenge politicians about their 'performance' so far. If, say critics, those same polls suggest alienation and/or apathy (findings which are, somewhat ironically, then used by both media and politicians as a stick with which to beat one another) why would we be surprised?

Bias and its effects

Most politicians at election time, however, are less worried about supposedly media-fuelled cynicism than they are about whether they are getting a fair deal on TV and in the press compared with their

KEY POINT

The ability of the media to influence both voters and politicians, even indirectly, is easier to assume than to prove, not least because there are so many other influences at work.

opponents. So aware are they of the importance of media coverage, that they are acutely sensitive to, and often complain about, bias. It would be easy, but not entirely correct to dismiss these complaints as predictable paranoia. This is especially the case when they come from smaller parties. These parties, sometimes on the extreme of the political spectrum, claim – with some justification – that they are squeezed out of mass coverage by their larger and possibly more mainstream competitors: the Liberal Democrats in the UK, the *Front National* in France, *Izquierda Unida* in Spain and the Czech Communists, for instance, routinely make this point. Mainstream parties, of course, will reply that coverage should be based on support and the likelihood of getting into government, not on some abstract idea of giving all voices an equal say. This might make sense between elections, but less so, perhaps, during election campaigns that should presumably be about everyone getting the chance to put their point across. Nevertheless, in many countries free election broadcasts are allocated according to party support: in Spain, for example, parties are allocated between 10 and 45 minutes in total, though they can divide this up between however many individual spots they like (see Sanders with Canel, 2004: 197). Interestingly, however, the media in general does devote more news time to so-called minor parties at election time, which conceivably could have the effect of boosting their vote by improving their visibility.

But smaller and/or extreme parties are not the only ones complaining. Larger, mainstream parties are also acutely concerned. We have already seen that public broadcasters in those states that have not created an arm's-length relationship between government and broadcasters are accused of bias (normally, in their case, in favour of the government of the day). But so, too, are privately owned media outlets – particularly those whose owners are said to exert undue influence on coverage, either directly or via the anticipated reactions of their journalists or even politicians themselves. For instance, French commercial broadcaster *TF1* allegedly promoted (though it has to be said unsuccessfully) the candidature of Edouard Balladur in the run up to the presidential election of 1995. It was said to have done so because the head of the company that controls it, Bouygues, had close links with other politicians in his camp (see Kuhn, 2004: 29). Accusations of bias and improper influence have been levelled at Rupert Murdoch in the UK (see Curran and Leys, 2000) and, before his empire went bust, Leo Kirch in Germany, both in relation to editorial interference and for allegedly using their large share of media markets to 'bully' politicians afraid of their influence on voters into granting them policy concessions and regulatory exemptions. And then, of course, there is Europe's one-man media-minefield, Silvio Berlusconi (see Box 7.11).

But is the influence of these 'moguls' – and the media in general – on voters really as great as it seems? Even assuming that biases exist, do they really matter? Certainly, at first glance, it is logical to think that since (as we suggested in Chapter 6) people are becoming less attached to particular parties and more volatile in their voting behaviour, their political choices at election time might be more and more open to influence through and by the media. But being convinced, for instance, that 'campaigns make a difference' is one thing (see Farrell and Schmitt-Beck, 2002); being able actually to prove 'media effects' on political behaviour is another. One noted expert on politics and the media (Mughan, 2000: 76), for instance, warns us that 'It must be remembered that a great deal of myth and hyperbole suffuses discussion of the political role of television. In truth, much remains shrouded in mystery' – so much so, in fact, that he quotes another authority to the effect that: 'The state of research on media effects is one of the most notable embarrassments of modern social science . . . [T]he scholarly literature has been much better at refuting, qualifying, and circumscribing the thesis of media impact than supporting it.'

In short, while the common wisdom nowadays is that 'elections are won on television' or 'people vote the way they do because they believe what they read in the papers', we are a long way from knowing whether this is indeed the case. The fact that such sentiments are common wisdom – among political

BOX 7.11

Silvio Berlusconi – *il cavaliere*

Acres of newsprint and thousands of hours of air time throughout Europe have been devoted to Silvio Berlusconi. This is not just because of his allegedly dubious business dealings. Nor is it simply because of his infamous 'gaffes' (comparing a German MEP to a concentration camp commandant, claiming that 'the war on terrorism' was a clash between Christian civilisation and the rest, and suggesting that he might introduce the photogenic Danish Prime Minister to his wife on the grounds that he was better-looking than the man with whom she was rumoured to be involved). It is also because of the conflict of interest inherent in his dual role as Prime Minister of Italy and owner of multiple media interests both in that country and abroad (see Ginsborg, 2004). Given the history of government interference and politicization of the public broadcasting system (RAI) in Italy, and the fact that Berlusconi dominates the commercial TV sector, becoming prime minister gave him potential control of 90 per cent of Italian television, in addition to the fact that he also has indirect control over a number of print media and advertising outlets. He stands accused by opponents of using his position in government to protect and promote his business interests (including opening up the possibilities for cross ownership), of politically interfering (even more than they did!) in RAI's affairs by fixing its board, securing the silencing of critical journalists and the appointment of toadies, measurably reducing the airtime devoted to opposition politicians on both RAI and his own channels, and of using the latter to drive the supposed 'dumbing down' of political and other coverage. All this, plus the way Berlusconi was able to use his media power to leverage his overnight entry into politics in 1993, challenges comforting but perhaps outdated beliefs in a separation of powers between those who do politics and those who supposedly watch over them on our behalf.

Sceptics could point out that, for all Berlusconi's media power, his coalition still lost the general election of 2006. An obvious retort, however, would be that the big bias towards Berlusconi during the campaign saw his opponents' lead dwindle to virtually nothing (see Chapter 7) by polling day, and that things might have been even closer had the communications regulator, Agcom, not prevented a plan by one of Mr Berlusconi's channels to replace a feature film with a two-and-a-half hour show with the Prime Minister as the only guest. Whether, though, the man they call 'the cavalier' can keep going is another matter. Now in his seventies, the surgical procedures he undergoes are no longer purely cosmetic – Berlusconi had a pacemaker fitted in 2007. Perhaps this explains why, in the summer of that year, he was accused of trying to manoeuvre a successor into place behind the backs of the other party leaders in his centre-right electoral coalition. True to form, however, he picked not a political hack but a flamboyant, flame-haired and female entrepreneur – and former TV presenter and Miss Italy finalist – Michela Vittoria Brambilla, known as *La Rossa*.

elites as well as the rest of us – might help drive the continuing mediatization of politics throughout Europe. But the evidence is very thin – especially for some kind of 'direct' effect like the conversion of what would have been, for example, a Socialist vote to a Conservative one. Against this scepticism, it must be said that the absence of proof for such effects might be down to the inability of political scientists to find convincing ways of measuring them and isolating them from all the other impacts on vote choice. There are so many factors and influences that intervene between us receiving a message from the media and our making political decisions, many of which could well be far more powerful and persuasive than anything we have read or seen (see Newton, 2006 and Box 7.12). Moreover, media messages often cancel each other out (see de Vreese and Boomgaarden, 2006a). This has not, however, stopped academics trying to explore media influence – for both the print and for the broadcast media.

Few newspapers in Europe nowadays can be dismissed as no more than mouthpieces for particular

BOX 7.12

Other influences

One obvious, but easily overlooked, example of non-media influence is talking to family and close friends. German political scientist Rüdiger Schmitt-Beck is by no means a sceptic when it comes to the possibility of media and campaign influence: his comparative study of the UK, Germany, Spain and the US (Schmitt-Beck, 2004) suggests that knowing the extent to which voters were exposed to the media added to our ability to predict their vote, especially in the more volatile Spain and the US. However, the very same research showed him that – outside Germany – 'the informal political exchange between voters in their everyday life world has a higher capacity to influence their votes than the mass media.' Interestingly, but perhaps not surprisingly to people who are married, 'spousal relationships stand out as particularly conducive to interpersonal influence'. In a nutshell, then, it might be more fruitful for researchers to worry less about what people are reading or listening or watching as they eat their breakfast and pay more attention to who they are eating it with.

parties. Although many have faced closure (the Italian Communist daily, *Unità,* is often on the brink), a few party organs (normally on the far left) still exist (such as the French Communist *l'Humanité*), but they sell very few copies. This is not to suggest, however, that European newspapers do not have their biases, even if those in the UK tend to be very much more strident about their partisan loyalties than most of their continental equivalents. But just because they are not diehard supporters of one party, and almost never 'announce for' one candidate or party in the way that British papers are expected to, does not mean that that in France and Germany, for example, both regional and national newspapers do not lean fairly obviously to the left or to the right. And because the bias is obvious, it is to some extent self-selected: a right-wing reader chooses a right-wing paper rather than the paper making her right-wing. It is also discounted, not least because trust in newspapers is not high (see Figure 7.3).

Figure 7.2 TV as the main source of news

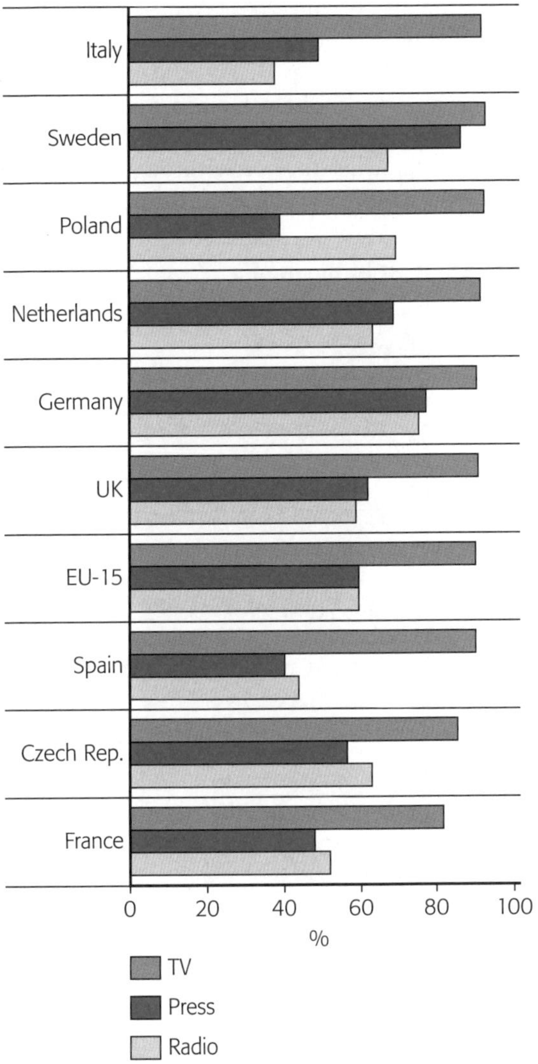

Note: Figures represent those reporting they use the media in question for news every day or several times a week, and are for 2001 because later surveys question respondents only about use of media for EU news.

Sources: Data from *Standard Eurobarometer* (56, 2001) and *Candidate Country Eurobarometer* (2001).

This scepticism notwithstanding, there is some recent research from the UK which suggests, first, that newspapers may influence our outlook on the economy which might then feed through to voting (see Gavin and Sanders, 2003) and, secondly, that newspaper bias might have more electoral effect than we were previously able to detect, though only sufficient to make a difference in very close contests (see Newton and Brynin, 2001). Yet even one of the researchers who argues for this possibility, Ken Newton, also emphasizes that it is severely limited by the considerable distrust many people display towards newspapers (see Figure 7.3) and by the fact that they filter what they read through their own upbringing, experience, values, and social contacts.

Figure 7.3 Trust in the media

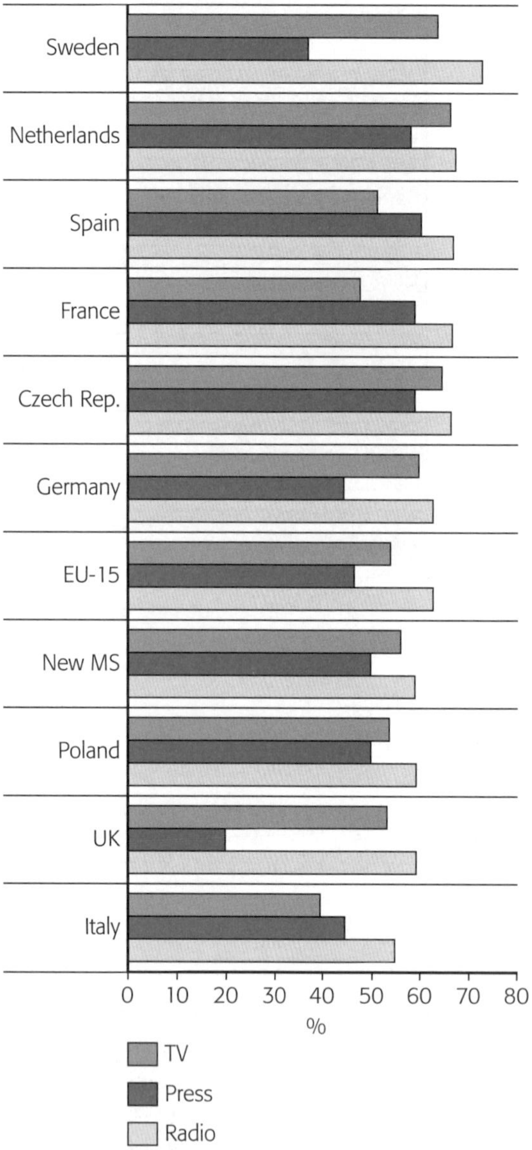

Source: Data from *Standard Eurobarometer* (61, 2004).

In short, 'people do not so much believe what they read in the newspapers, but read what they believe' (Newton, 2006: 217).

The same can be said to the way people filter television. Yet TV is nonetheless seen as more of a problem by many of those worried about the impact of bias: it is clearly the major source of news for most Europeans (see Figure 7.2) and, except where partisanship in one branch of the media is a particular 'problem' (e.g. newspapers in the UK; television in Italy), generally more trusted than the press (see Figure 7.3). With regard to television, there is some limited research evidence of what are called 'indirect effects'. Most of the time, TV seems to reinforce partisanship (in short, the viewer has her prejudices confirmed whatever she watches), although some would argue for a stronger, short-term effect on the politically undecided and inattentive (for a summary of this more qualified position, see Curran, 2002: 133). Given the fact, (as we saw in Chapter 6) that more and more people could be said to fit into these categories, this short-term effect on elections could become more and more important. Against this, however, we have to weigh the fact that if 'those who are least interested, involved and knowledgeable about politics are the most susceptible to media influence' they are also the least likely to be watching and reading anything remotely political (Newton, 2006: 225).

It is also possible to argue, though not without qualification (e.g. Semetko, 2000: 362–3), that the media already has considerable 'agenda-setting power'. This power derives from **priming** voters' sense of what is and is not important to think about when casting their votes (see Box 7.13) – all the more important if 'issue voting' (see Chapter 6) as well as personality preferences are indeed becoming more crucial to results (see Kleinnijenhuis *et al.*, 2001). More particularly, some claim that TV

> Media **priming** occurs when emphasis on a particular issue makes it more salient, makes it seem, in other words, more important to us than perhaps it might be otherwise, opening up the possibility that we can be persuaded to change our political decisions and judgements according to what the media is or isn't talking about. Priming is an 'indirect effect' – the media doesn't so much tell people what to think as tell them what to think about.

BOX 7.13

Priming '*l'insécurité*' in the French presidential election

Liberals the world over reeled in shock at the results of the first round of the French presidential election when the leader of the far-right Front National, Jean-Marie Le Pen, emerged in second place ahead of the Socialist Prime Minister, Lionel Jospin, and earned himself a run-off election against the eventual winner, Jacques Chirac. But perhaps the result was more of a surprise than it should have been. After all, the media, in effect, decided that the central issue of the campaign would be *l'insécurité* (law and order) – an issue that the right (both mainstream and extreme) had made its own in the previous year and one on which the left was widely seen to be vulnerable. This does not mean, suggests one expert on both French politics and the media, that there was a conspiracy, expressly designed to favour one side over the other. As Kuhn (2004: 30) notes, a regular diet of crime may have helped make the latter an important criterion on which voters evaluated the candidates, but it did so largely because it conformed to conventional news values, suited TV's claims to be in touch with 'the people' and tapped into (as well as perhaps feeding) what opinion polls suggested were genuine concerns. The winner of the next contest in 2007, Nicolas Sarkozy, certainly did all he could do emphasize insecurity and his hard-line reputation on crime, famously promising during a 2005 visit to a run-down housing estate to hose the *racaille* (variously translated as 'scum' or 'riff-raff') from the streets.

debates (and, importantly, media reporting of who won and who lost) can help shift votes if held sufficiently close to election day so that their effect does not wear off (see Denemark, 2002; also Gunther *et al.*, 2000). Interestingly, given the developing common wisdom surrounding the importance of 'presidentialization' in campaign coverage, the very latest work into 'leader effects' in elections (mainly in Europe) finds that, generally, individual leaders are not nearly so important to voters as the media thinks (King, 2002; see also Brettschneider *et al.*, 2006; Schulz *et al.*, 2005). Not surprisingly, perhaps, there is some indication that the influence leaders have on voters could vary with how high-profile those leaders are (see Schoen, 2007) or between parties, with very left-wing parties and voters discounting leadership, for example, whereas their more right wing opponents make a virtue of it (see Costa Lobo, 2006).

What about the agenda-setting power of the media when it comes to politicians themselves? Again, there is more common wisdom that there is hard evidence. According to many liberals in the UK, for instance, politicians are increasingly driven by the press into populist stances that they otherwise might eschew, particularly on immigration (see Chapter 10). And such effects, if they exist, might not be limited to the British tabloids. Writing on France, Raymond Kuhn (2004: 29) notes that *Le Monde* in particular has acquired the reputation of exerting independent, but also unaccountable, power through its capacity to support or undermine particular politicians and policy options'.

The problem for political scientists, of course, is that, however well connected or persuasive they are, they are unlikely to tempt politicians into admitting that this or that policy was pursued (or such and such a minister was dismissed) because of a press or television campaign (see Kepplinger, 2007). But because it is difficult to measure or prove media influence, does that mean it is unimportant? Given the current state of our empirical knowledge, it would be more 'scientific' to say that the capacity of the media to help determine politicians' beliefs, behaviours and agendas is minimal; but would that be true? A degree of agenda setting would seem plausible: as Walgrave and Van Aelst (2006) observe, politicians are avid consumers of the media; they use it to signal to each other and to the public, and they are – whatever the research shows – convinced that the media plays a big role in determining public opinion. Perhaps, as they suggest, the first task is to assume that the media's influence on political actors varies and to think about when it is more, and when it is less, likely to count.

Researchers from a Marxist and/or cultural studies perspective would also suggest that the effect of the media simply cannot be traced over a short period, like an election. For them, the political power of the media has much more to do with the general legitimation of governments sitting atop (and doing very little about) pervasive structural inequalities. We might, the argument goes, struggle against some of these if our attention were not so distracted and our aspirations so limited by the 'non-political' product served up to us nightly by a corporate oligopolists, as well as by the public broadcasters increasingly forced to compete with them on their terms (see Curran, 2002). We might also profitably turn to examine the political effects of supposedly non-political programmes: research suggests, for example, that regular viewing of cop-shows increases concern about crime and that such concern influences opinions about politicians (see Holbrook and Hill, 2005); it has also shown (this time using the environmental issue) that people draw on a blend of fictional and non-fictional television in the construction of their views (Delli Carpini and Williams, 1994).

These warnings are important. For one thing, some argue (though not uncontroversially) that television militates against active involvement in society, political and otherwise (see Putnam, 2000; see also Hooghe, 2002). For another, it is hardly the stuff of crude conspiracy theory to suggest that the media, particularly the privately owned media, is unlikely to produce shows of any genre (current affairs or soaps) that routinely question and undermine the idea that liberal capitalism is the inevitable and best system, especially with advertisers breathing down their necks – evidence for which is plentiful in the US (see Campbell, 2004: 62–3) even if the topic is under-researched in Europe. Even if the media avoid systematically (though perhaps unconsciously) excluding those who question the consensus completely, it may well be **framing** them negatively. It is not hard for journalists, if they want to, to present people as extreme (far-right or far-left organizations), disruptive (unions in industrial disputes or environmentalists taking direct action) or possibly violent (animal rights and anti-globalization protest groups).

Framing is an 'indirect effect' of the media, which decides on the way stories are packaged so as to highlight (often subconsciously) who should take credit and blame, or who are the good guys and who we should trust less or take less seriously.

On the other hand, none of this is going to make much difference if those watching the broadcast know from their own experience that things are not as they seem, or if they share the concern of those who are demonized. An obvious example of this is when rioters are shown smashing property or strikers disrupting daily life; if they are expressing a cause for which there is sympathy, then they will be supported by many of those watching at home, whether the media or politicians like it or not – something to which numerous French presidents and prime ministers, who have been forced to back down in the face of street demonstrations, can attest (see Chapter 8).

Pressure groups and populists

This might explain why, if all this partial exclusion and negative framing is going on, it does not seem to have marginalized all the groups just mentioned. Indeed, as we shall see in Chapter 8, a number of them seem to be flourishing – something that is often put down (not least by their corporate opponents and by governments) to their skill in exploiting, of all things, the media! Rather than being a target for the media or running the risk of being ignored or sidelined by it, many pressure groups are an ideal source of stories. As a result, they can claim to play an important part in the agenda-setting 'issue–attention cycle' (see Downs, 1972) that politicians and governments might try to manipulate but – given the disdaining attitudes and the acceleration of news delivery – are possibly less and less able to control.

KEY POINT

Changes in the way politics is covered arguably advantage media-savvy pressure groups and populist politicians at the expense of more conventional actors.

On a practical level, the groups' now-professionalized media staff do a lot of the investigative work news organizations cannot themselves afford to do, and go on to reproduce it in effective, easily digested formats that the organizations can rapidly turn into finished product. Their sometimes conflictual and often highly visual modes of engagement – mass protests, daring stunts, and so on – dovetail well with conventional news values, especially those of television. They also provide journalists with an alternative to more conventional news sources, such as governments, parties and corporations, to whom the public and journalists alike seem to afford less and less trust and respect. This is particularly the case where groups appear to be taking 'the public's' side against those other institutions in situations where the latter seem intent on ignoring popular feeling: hence the media 'sexiness' of protests against genetically modified (GM) crops. Groups are also finding that the Internet helps them mobilize and aggregate otherwise passive and fragmented audiences whose feelings and/or purchasing power (see Bennie, 1998) can then be used to outflank companies and, indeed, states (see Rodgers, 2003: Chapters 4 and 5).

All this brings some comfort to those on the progressive end of the political spectrum, seeming as it does to bear out Habermas's reformulation of the public sphere as a much more contested, congested and potentially transnational space in which civil society can use the media to transmit concerns to the political core and which thus acts as a countervailing power (see Curran, 2002: 135–6). But this also has what some would see as darker side. Supposedly liberal and progressive 'media-savvy' cause groups are undeniably attractive to a media keen to put itself onside with the public against a 'political class' that increasingly has to justify inclusion in coverage on news values alone. But so, too, are charismatic populists from the other end of the political spectrum. Prepared to say what 'everyone' is thinking in terms that anyone can understand, and launching attacks on 'the establishment' that 'no-one' likes or trusts in a style that resonates with almost universally-held news values, men like Jörg Heider in Austria, Jean-Marie Le Pen in France and the late Pim Fortuyn in Holland are (or were) a news editor's dream. Recent research certainly seems to suggest that the media were an important resource – and one skilfully used – for the radical right wing populist parties we discuss in Chapters 5, 9 and 10 (see Art, 2007 and Mazzoleni *et al.*, 2003; see also Jagers and Walgrave, 2007).

Little wonder that, in a public sphere increasingly dominated by media logic, their more mainstream opponents, constrained by the compromises inherent in responsible politics but condemned for 'spin' if they try to compete, are finding life harder and harder. It is not only their fault. If the populism we discussed in Chapter 5 is, indeed, the spirit of the age (see Mudde, 2004) – a *Zeitgeist* that fashionably sees politics as a problem rather than a solution – then what some see as the media's 'culture of the contempt' (see Lloyd, 2004) should perhaps shoulder some of the blame as well. As one respected foreign correspondent from Germany (Krönig, 2006) notes, 'politics is more often than not undramatic, complex, not easy to understand and therefore . . . difficult and boring to report'; worse still, its results take a long time in coming. If the typical response on the part of journalists, who still feel obliged to cover some (if less) politics but despair of making it sufficiently attention-grabbing, is 'permanent linguistic overkill' (billing every critical report as 'damning', devastating' or 'scathing', all internal disagreements as 'dramatic splits', all warnings 'stark' and all developments 'alarming') then it is hardly surprising, say some critics, that so many sensible people are turned off the whole business.

The impact of ICT – cyber-optimism or cyber-scepticism?

It is not just trends in the conventional, 'mass' media that play into the hands of populists and promotional groups. By speeding up communication (including communication with the mass media), information and communication technology (ICT) has significantly cut the cost of starting from

KEY POINT

The Internet may really change and open up politics, but it has yet to realize that potential – and, because of inequalities of access and its capacity to insulate users, it may not be an unalloyed benefit if it does. At the moment, mobile telephones and consumer databases are having just as big an impact.

scratch. It also has the advantage of appealing to some who might otherwise by-pass politics, particularly the young who are especially attracted by what Castells (2007: 248) calls 'mass self-communication' – a form that is 'self generated in content, self-directed in emission, and self-selected in reception by many that communicate with many'. Theoretically anyway, this new form allows non-conventional political actors rapidly to network their way to prominence, and perhaps success (see Van de Donk *et al.*, 2003). It is also encouraging more conventional political actors across Europe – such as parties (see Gibson, Nixon and Ward, 2003; Gibson, Römmele and Ward, 2003; Pedersen and Saglie, 2005) and trade unions (see Ward and Lusoli, 2003) – to try and pull off the same trick, even if they are still at the stage of using the new technology simply to speed up and spruce up what they do already.

But academic research on all this is still in its infancy (see Bentivegna, 2006; Chadwick, 2006; and Gibson and Römmele, 2005) and the extent to which the web has blown (or will blow) 'politics-as-usual' out of the water can be overdone according to 'cyber-sceptics' (see Zittel, 2004). According to this point of view, there is a great deal of potentially unfounded speculation concerning the impact of new technology on how people use the media and how the media will interact with politics. Anyone, then, who assumes that the potential proliferation of spaces for political expression and genuinely two-way exchange offered by information technology (IT) will be realized might be fooling themselves, especially when one considers, first, the uses (largely passive and commercial/'leisure' oriented) to which the web is currently put by most citizens and, second, the extent to which politicians current use of the same medium 'has more to do with adaptive self-preservation' and self-presentation than a desire to move beyond conventional ideas about representation (Coleman, 2005). And while it might well lead to what some would consider a welcome expansion of ideological diversity, the extent to which that expansion will be meaningful (in the sense of altering policy outcomes, for instance) is equally open to doubt, notwithstanding some suggestions that, for example, 'e-petitions' on its 'Downing Street' website (see UK Government Petitions, 2007) might have given the UK government pause for thought on the subject of, say, road pricing.

This is not to say that things will not change significantly. Generally, it seems clear that the web is becoming an evermore more interactive (and less male) medium. In 2007 an authoritative British report, for instance, confirmed the huge boom in internet shopping, but also noted that social networking sites like Bebo, MySpace, and Facebook were, along with YouTube, all in the UK's top ten sites by time spent (Ofcom, 2007). More specifically, research from the US suggests that, in fact, a steadily increasing number of people do use the web to get political information, although they prefer single-issue sites rather than those provided by party politicians (Howard, 2005). Nor should we assume that styles of political communication that are now relatively peripheral will never catch on in ways that profoundly alter, say, the relationship between electors and elected, and between leaders and led. Blogging by (strangely enough) journalists, politicians, party activists – self-confessed political anoraks – is one potentially fruitful example (see Coleman, 2005 and Ferguson and Howell, 2004). But of course blogs can also have much less benign effects: the destructive November 2005 riots in France were in part fuelled by bloggers (some of them later arrested) on sites like skyblog.com (now skyrock.com/blog/) who were accused of urging other young people to burn cars and attack the police. Meanwhile, the press reported, future candidate for the French Presidency, Nicolas Sarkozy, was at the very same time buying ads on Google so that his compatriots searching for info on the riots would readily find a petition to support him in his hardline stance.

But at the moment it is, to coin a cliché, too soon to tell whether the web will transform politics and/or the coverage of politics. Future works may well describe a politics and a media that are unrecognizable and even unimaginable from those described here. Yet inertia is a powerful force, and Europeans are just as likely as anyone else to adapt to novelty rather than adopt it wholesale, using the Internet to complement rather than replace existing information sources (see Nguyen and Western, 2006; see also Dutta-Bergman, 2004). There will also be considerable cultural (albeit institutionally-influenced) differences in uptake and use (see Box 7.13)

BOX 7.14

Legislators 2.0?

Thomas Zittel (2004) carried out an interesting project to compare legislators' use of the web in the US, Germany and Sweden. US congressmen were much quicker to set up personal websites than their counterparts in the *Bundestag* and *Riksdag*, but few of the sites were very impressive, used not so much to enhance two-way communication but as a place for press releases, a bit of biography and some basic contact details. The Swedes, like the Germans, were not just limited by resource constraints (whereas US representatives employ about eighteen staffers, German MPs get three staffers and Swedish members barely one each); they also had concerns about individualized communication undermining the importance of the party–voter relationship. On the other hand, the Europeans were less concerned about discussion fora than the Americans, who were much more concerned about their inability to moderate or control disruptive or embarrassing contributions due to the strong tradition of free speech.

To some, the fact that the impact of the Internet on politics is perhaps oversold might not be such a bad thing. To them, the **digital divide** seems likely to perpetuate existing political inequalities and participation rates. Interestingly, however, one thing that Figure 7.4 indicates is that access to the Intenet seems to vary as much, if not more, across European nations as it does across social classes, although if we were to include growth figures it would quickly become apparent that the nations that logged in later (including France, which held on to its telephone-based information system, Minitel, for some time) are catching up.

To talk of a **digital divide** is to remind ourselves that access (and willingness to use) to the internet is not equal (see Norris, 2001). It varies between countries and (see, for example, Korupp and Szydlik, 2005) between people within countries – men, the better off, and the young, for instance, are more likely to make use of the Internet. Variations between countries are largely determined by their wealth, the extent of democratic freedom and the extent to which they are plugged into the global political economy. But they also depend on government policies: privatization and telecommunications deregulation and competition tend to boost the introduction, take up and usage of the Internet (see Guillén and Suárez, 2005).

Figure 7.4 also shows figures for mobile phone penetration, which in some countries is running at more than one phone per person – a figure that may come as no surprise to some of us. The inclusion of these statistics is not just for good measure; it is perhaps the case that if we are looking at the Internet for the impact of ICT on politics, we may be looking in the wrong place. It could be that mobile telephony will have a far bigger impact.

Figure 7.4 Penetration of ICT in the EU and US

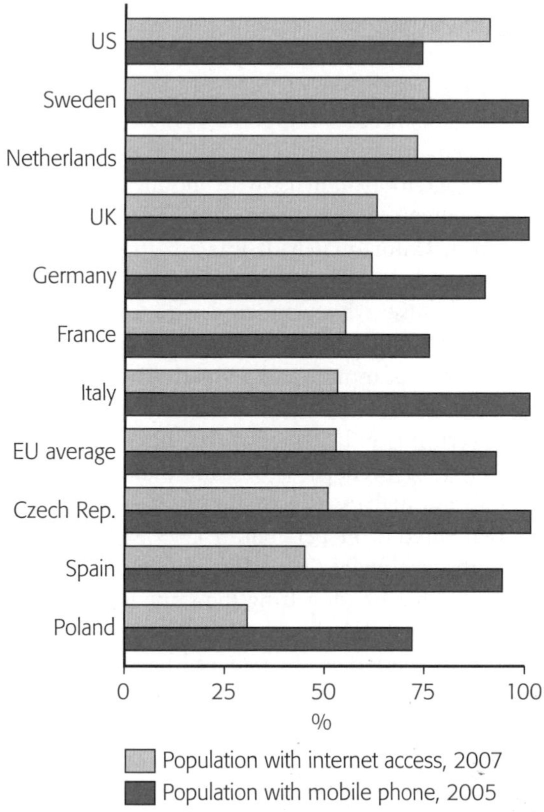

Note: US mobile penetration is a media estimate.

Sources: Data from Internet World Stats (2007) and European Commission (2007).

The political impact of the mobile phone is becoming apparent in the activity of some of the protest groups we look at in Chapter 8. Both fuel protesters and environmental activists – and, indeed, those who have helped kick off violence at recent EU and G8 summits, as well as rioting in the French suburbs – use mobiles to organize and to send pictures which undermine attempts at government censorship or spin. So, too, did hundreds of thousands of Spaniards who came onto the streets to protest the then government's attempt to blame ETA for the Madrid bombings of 2004 and who could well have changed the result of the subsequent general election as a result. At the other extreme, those Islamists who committed the atrocities used mobiles to detonate their explosives and Islamist use of the Internet to recruit and organize is also a cause for concern (see Ryan, 2007). European parties have already made huge advances in campaigning not via the Internet, but via call centres. Now, they are beginning to use text messaging on election day in order to get their known supporters out to vote. In some cases, governments have woken up to the potential, too. Predictably, perhaps, it was the Italian government run by Silvio Berlusconi which sent a text message to all Italians with mobiles reminding them to vote in the European elections of 12 and 13 June 2004. Unfortunately, it was a course of action that landed him in hot water with political opponents and those who wondered who had paid the estimated €3 million cost: if it was the government, was it a waste of money and a breach of privacy; if it was *Forza Italia,* why did the message go through the government? Leaving aside these questions, however, it is perhaps significant that turnout in Italy (always high) was actually up in 2004 (73 per cent compared to 71 per cent in 1999), when across many other countries the decline was steep.

On the other hand, getting the same text message as millions of other people is unlikely to impress many of us these days. It may well be the case that personalization is the way ahead for the media as it is for other goods and services: futurologists, for instance, have predicted generic news sources will be replaced by 'The Daily Me' which electronically delivers us only the kind of news we are interested in from multiple sources. Leaving aside the potential downsides for democracy of people being able to insulate themselves from inconvenient truths and the potential withering of collective concerns (Sunstein, 2007; see also Howard, 2005), parties operating in such an environment will have to work harder to produced customized appeals. One way they are already doing this is via the most under-studied (because it seems so boring) yet most heavily exploited uses of ICT – direct mail based on sophisticated consumer intelligence (garnered from shop loyalty cards, magazine subscriptions, official censuses, and credit records, for example) that allows marketers to predict preferences and target people accordingly (Gertner, 2004). The 2005 general election in the UK saw both main parties pour resources into such efforts, with the Conservatives using the same 'Voter Vault' software that supposedly won the Republicans the US presidency. Although it did that particular party little good in the end, the same technology – or something very like it – will undoubtedly continue to be used in the UK and elsewhere in Europe.

The media and 'Europe'

A certain amount of scepticism is warranted when it comes to considering the extent to which the media has affected politics in Europe by helping to construct a 'European' identity (see Chapter 1) or promote a greater understanding of either other countries or the EU among its citizens. It is difficult to see its impact in these areas as much more than minimal, not least because there is as yet no genuinely pan-European media presence on the Continent. There is, as we have seen, a degree of Europeanization at the level of regulation and ownership. And there are clearly a handful of countries that have so much in common with their neighbours, not least linguistically, that they are happy to, say, watch their television and even read their news – even if the flow tends to be one- rather than two-way (see Collins and Butler, 2004 on Ireland, for instance). The Internet, too, theoretically makes a

KEY POINT

The media may be Europeanizing when it comes to regulation and ownership, but not when it comes to content. Coverage of the EU varies according to country and issue, but is generally very low.

nonsense of borders, although the extent to which most people actually view non-entertainment content from other countries, particularly those with which they have nothing in common linguistically, is more limited than 'the world's informationized networking elite' who look forward to everyone sharing their own 'cosmopolitan globalism' might have us believe (see Louw, 2005: 133–8).

There is, then, as yet, no genuinely European media market at the level of product. This is in spite of it being over a decade since the EU's 1991 *Television Without Frontiers* Directive came into effect (preventing member states from placing restrictions on the transmission of broadcasting from other member states) and despite the growth of cable and satellite television, to which getting on for a half of households in the Union now subscribe. Ultimately, European media integration faces a huge hurdle; namely, the cultural and language barriers that do so much to make the continent the diverse place it is (see Richardson and Meinhof, 1999). Attempts to create genuinely 'Euro-TV' have so far proved difficult: the audience share of pan-European channels 'rarely passes the 1 per cent mark' (Chalaby, 2002: 189). In 2003, for instance, 'pan-European satellite services offered 188 chat channels, 80 teleshopping channels, 36 music channels, 35 religious stations, 13 fashion stations, and seven (continuous broadcast) "adult film" channels' (Harcourt, 2005: 121). Programming like this, which like sport, has obvious cross-cultural appeal, has achieved limited success. But even this – like the 'reality TV' concepts that turn into quite different shows when they are exported into foreign markets – has required skilful (and expensive) 'localization' or tailoring to different national audiences who, on balance, prefer domestically oriented (even if foreign-inspired) programming (see Chalaby, 2002).

This preference, moreover, is supported by governments and parliaments who routinely insist on broadcasters showing a prescribed quota of domestically produced material as a condition of their licences. This insistence (mirrored by the EU Directives that insist on quotas for European programmes, apparently in order to stave off American hegemony) characterizes not just western but also central and eastern Europe. There, an acute awareness of the importance of the media in 'nation-building' (maintaining a sense of identity and community) has, in combination with the still widespread belief among elites that the media should reflect the views of the government, often trumped enthusiasm for market liberalization (see Sparks, 1997: 112–14).

All of this means that, with the possible exception of a few transnational 'top people in the Brussels micro-polity' of the EU and their interlocutors in government and business circles in Europe's capitals, there is no such thing yet as a 'European public sphere'. Apart from the *Financial Times* and a handful of upmarket satellite news broadcasters, there is little or no media space in which 'European citizenship' (see Meehan, 1993) can fully develop, certainly not without major inequalities in access and information (see Schlesinger, 1993; and Schlesinger and Kevin, 2000).

On the other hand, these kinds of analyses might be unduly pessimistic. For one thing, the conception of a 'European public sphere' that they employ is arguably too ambitious. To pass their test, such a sphere would need to be truly supranational rather than (less ambitiously) simply multidimensional, encompassing multilevel linkages in mediated political coverage between the national and the European. In fact, with the exception of the UK (where the focus remains heavily internalized) these multilevel communication linkages are becoming more common. It is possible, for instance, to point to a handful of EU stories that gain Europe-wide coverage that differs systematically from the coverage of the same story in, say, the US media (see Van de Steeg, 2006). And while political stories covered by the 'continental' media are still predominantly national, they can also involve national figures commenting or 'making claims' about other European countries or the EU – especially where these 'European' actors can reasonably be expected to have an impact on policy (for instance, monetary policy and currency matters, rather than, say, pensions). As a result, the most thoroughgoing (and ongoing) comparative investigation argues that (with the exception of the UK) 'we can speak of a Europeanized public sphere to the extent that a substantial – and over time increasing – part of public contestation neither stays confined to its own national political space . . . , nor extends beyond Europe without referring to it' (Koopmans, 2004).

This qualification notwithstanding, it remains true that a media beginning to Europeanize at the level of ownership and regulation seems unable to do much to Europeanize its product and, by implication, those who consume it. But can it at least improve their knowledge and their goodwill concerning the European Union itself? With the possible exception of attitudes towards EU enlargement where media coverage may have made a difference (see de Vreese and Boomgaarden, 2006b), the answer seems to be 'no' – for several reasons. One former EU Commissioner, the UK's Chris Patten, probably put his finger on one of the key, but possibly intractable, problems at a conference held in London in February 2002 to discuss the British media's ignorance and negative treatment of European affairs: 'So much of what the EU does is, frankly, boring and technocratic. It does not lend itself to simple or attractive reporting.' Although there is evidence to suggest that European elections, for instance, do spark at least a modicum of interest in and information gathering on the EU by ordinary people, the effect very soon wears off – and it seems to be decreasing (along with turnout!) with each election (see Lord, 2004: 60–1). But the media also share some of the burden of responsibility: people cannot be expected to take much of an interest if the media simply takes that lack of interest as a given and reacts accordingly – sometimes in spite of the fact it complains in the same breath that 'Brussels' is controlling more and more aspects of Europeans' lives. According to *The Economist* (3 November 2007), in 2005 UK's famously Eurosceptical daily newspapers had a total of six staff correspondents based in the Belgian capital; now there are only three.

This should come as no surprise, however, given what research has revealed about media coverage – research summarized as part of Christopher Lord's admirable (and surely timely) 'democratic audit' of the EU (see Lord, 2004: 62–4; see also Kevin, 2003). First, media coverage is 'sporadic' and 'events-based', often concentrating (unsurprisingly) on personalized conflict and bad news. It also varies across countries with regard to the amount of time and space devoted to EU matters, though there is no simple connection between lots of attention and enthusiasm in that member state for the EU. Second, while we should be careful not to forget that different media outlets in the same country will place their own meanings on the same piece of EU news (see, for example, the study of Italian portrayals of the launch of the euro in Triandafyllidou, 2003), the EU is nonetheless presented largely through national frames and filters. In other words, the focus is often on what 'it' (an external actor) is doing for or to 'us'. Not only is each nation therefore supplied with a different take on the same issue, but each is presented with a different notion of what the EU is about. For instance, if one compares German and British media coverage, the latter tends to present the EU as all of a piece whereas the former more often breaks it down into its component institutions. When the UK media does that, however, supranational institutions (the ones 'we cannot control' like the Commission) are four times more likely to be mentioned than the (arguably more powerful) intergovernmental ones. Lastly, the coverage of EP elections differs between countries, but only to the extent that some countries' media provide their publics with the most basic coverage while others fail to do even that. In the Netherlands in 1999, for instance, the EP elections 'took up only 1 per cent of total [TV] news coverage during the campaign', compared to the 27 per cent devoted to the general election campaign the year before – probably because those responsible for producing the news saw the EP elections (rightly or wrongly) as a 'non-issue' that meant nothing to voters (de Vreese, 2001: 168–9).

Interestingly, however, if one compares the EP election years of 1999 and 2004, there does (outside of France, Italy, Austria and Portugal) seem to have been a significant increase in television coverage of EU news right across Europe, although perhaps unsurprisingly, given they were experiencing their first ever EP elections, the media in the new member states (at least outside the Czech Republic) was generally much more interested (see de Vreese *et al.*, 2006). The same research, however, noted that the visibility of the EU was greater in public service broadcasting than on commercial stations, and in 'quality' as opposed to 'tabloid' newspapers. Perhaps surprisingly, the tone of coverage, when it was evaluative, was largely negative – particularly in the older member states. But, for the most part, coverage everywhere could be described as neutral. Of course, this increased visibility did nothing to boost turnout at the elections – another illustration, some might argue, of weak media effects.

Outside of elections, as a summary of recent research (Machill *et al.*, 2006) puts it, 'EU topics account for an extremely small proportion of reporting' while 'the players at EU level also only feature in minor roles' even in EU stories, while coverage of fellow member states is skewed towards the most economically powerful. On the other hand, it does suggest that there are significant differences between countries, with media in Germany, Denmark and the Netherlands paying most attention to 'Europe'. The other Scandinavian countries come next, followed by France, Spain and Austria, with Italy, Ireland and (perhaps surprisingly) Belgium giving the topic relatively little space. The UK is in the last group, although discussion there, when it occurs, can be very intense and heated. Other research (Koopmans and Erbe, 2004) suggests – very plausibly – that the amount of attention paid in the media to 'Europe' varies according to the extent to which the EU has policy competence in the matter being discussed: on agriculture, for instance, Europe will be brought up; on taxation or health, it won't.

Hardly surprising, then, that the public throughout Europe confess in *Eurobarometer* surveys that they are not very knowledgeable about the EU. The average self-assessment hovers between 4 or 5 on a scale of 1–10, with men, the better educated and 'opinion formers' claiming to know more than most. Generally, however, people feel that media coverage of the EU is sufficient and, indeed, objective, although, interestingly, more people in the UK than elsewhere seem to think that coverage there is too negative, which suggests that the rabid Euroscepticism of some British newspapers does not go unnoticed even if its effects are possibly exaggerated (see de Vreese, 2007). This low level of knowledge does not help support for the EU, which (as Table 7.3 suggests) seems to be correlated with thinking it is a good thing (though which way round the correlation runs is not clear). Clearly, this lack of support does little to boost participation in EP elections, and, therefore, neither can those elections boost interest in the EU. We should, though, qualify this gloomy picture by remembering that the issue of European integration might be becoming part of party political debate (see Chapter 5) and has recently featured in several European elections –

Table 7.3 Support for EU membership and self-perceived knowledge about the EU

My country's membership is . . .	Knowledge low (1–3) (%)	Knowledge average (4–7) (%)	Knowledge high (8–10) (%)
A good thing	37	55	64
Neither good nor bad	37	28	16
A bad thing	14	15	19
Don't know	12	3	1

Source: Data from *Eurobarometer* (60, 2003).

something that is reflected in campaign coverage (see Semetko *et al.*, 2000: 130–1). Whether this will be enough to stop what seems to be a vicious, rather than a virtuous, circle from turning, however, is a moot point. The low level and poor quality of coverage of EU issues could well have major implications for any attempt to offset the relatively low level of European identification in some countries (see Chapter 1). But it also has more serious, less normative but more nitty-gritty implications. While the 'general public' of European countries is looking elsewhere, organized groups who, by definition, do not necessarily have 'the general interest' at heart are busy making their presence and their pressure felt. It is to these groups that we turn in Chapter 8.

'Overseas' news

Before leaving the media, however, it is worth pausing to think about one of its most important roles, but one we have only briefly touched on so far. This is its capacity to improve citizens' (and, indeed,

KEY POINT

Although there are some differences between countries, the European media as a whole is not very different from, say, its US counterpart in providing only a very limited window on a world that is supposedly more interconnected and interdependent than ever.

politicians') understanding of Europe and the world (see Chapter 11). Given not just European integration but also challenges like migration, global poverty, terrorism and climate change, it is reasonable to argue that the boundaries of the domestic and the international are increasingly blurred nowadays: as one commentator (Franks, 2006: 100) puts it, 'More than ever before, we can only make sense of what is happening in our own back yard if we are properly informed about what is happening far away.' As a result, the extent to which, and the manner in which, the European media covers other countries (both inside and outside Europe) is a vital question. The answers may not appear particularly encouraging.

While it almost certainly remains the case that, irrespective of exposure to media, Europeans remain more aware of things going on beyond their countries' borders than Americans, their media is no less prone to the hierarchy of coverage that applies elsewhere (see Rössler, 2006: 275). This hierarchy, because it is shot through with historical variation, ensures that for the most part the foreign news watched by one country's viewers will not bear much resemblance to that watched by another's, even on the same night. First, come the 'news centres' that gain consistent coverage (the country itself plus, in most cases, the US). Second, come the 'news neighbours' that appear reasonably often (important – but not necessarily geographically or linguistically proximate – countries). Then come the 'topical news neighbours' that are covered because they are important to ongoing stories (Iraq and Afghanistan are the most obvious examples, especially for those countries who have troops there). And finally, a long way back, comes the 'news periphery' made up of countries that feature occasionally, perhaps because of some kind of disaster, and then disappear (for example, the countries afflicted by the Indian Ocean earthquake and resultant tsunamis of Boxing Day 2004).

Neither is the media in Europe much less prone than its US counterpart to 'domesticate' foreign news by pointing out not just the relevance of a story for domestic affairs but the similarities with events at home and, of course, the actual or possible involvement of nationals. Interestingly, however, there may be slight variations in the time devoted to foreign stories by television news in different countries: Rössler (2006) reports on his own research that showed Spanish and Italian TV news programmes even more likely to stick to events at home than their US counterparts (73 per cent and 67 per cent compared to 64 per cent), while in France, Denmark and Norway over half of their time was devoted to domestic news. Only in Germany, Switzerland and Austria did foreign news seem to have the edge, and they were also more likely to bring in the periphery than simply concentrate, like the Spanish and the Italians, on the US. Interestingly, European countries' television news was far more likely than its US counterpart to include other nations' political leaders. There were some commonly featured stories, but not enough for researchers to spot any trend toward convergence of coverage – in other words, as Rössler (2006) puts it, we may all be part of one world but each nation is getting different pictures.

Whether this is depressing depends, in part, on one's point of view. Those who routinely complain about globalization could take some comfort from this continued heterogeneity. Those who believe we should be all be focusing on common problems, or who believe that it is possible to identify objectively what does and doesn't matter, might be disappointed. On the other hand, an encouraging finding from Rössler's research (as well as more recent research on British coverage of overseas countries by Dover and Barnett (2004) which shows trendless fluctuation in time devoted year-on-year) is that it seems to be driven by events rather than – as some pessimists claim – by an editorial desire to cut down on foreign news. Where things have gone downhill, however, at least in the UK, is in non-news factual programming which took up 40 per cent less time in 2003 than in 1989–90, with the drop even more precipitate for programmes about developing countries. Worse still, if one believes that knowing something about the outside world is useful, was the fact that the remaining output increasingly involved 'genres that reveal little about the realities of life for non-British people living outside [the] country: travel programmes; series following British adventurers, documentaries about "Brits abroad" and reality game-shows in "exotic" locations' (Dover and Barnett, 2004).

Even this may be too encouraging a picture. One former BBC producer, now an academic, focuses on the combination of cost-cutting and technology that can satisfy the demand for instant pictures in advance of coherent journalism to run alongside them – all of which means a future of for foreign coverage as 'a series of disassociated disasters' fronted by globe-trotting 'dish-monkeys' who, tethered to their satellite phones in order to service 24-hour rolling news, are unable to gain or communicate any real understanding of context (Franks, 2006: 94). This is not a recipe for the informed (if not necessarily active or engaged) citizenry that an increasingly interconnected world might demand. We ought to remember, however, that the insulating effects of any decrease in the quantity or quality of media coverage of foreign countries could, in theory, be offset by the massive increase in foreign travel enjoyed by Europeans as the result of increasing wealth and ever-cheaper flights, especially within Europe itself. On the other hand, it is interesting to note that the British, who have taken particular advantage of these trends and are regular (and, at least in economic terms, welcome) visitors to cities all over the continent, remain as firmly Eurosceptic as ever.

Learning Resources for Chapter 7

Further reading

The literature on politics and the media is massive. A conveniently concise start is the chapter by Dahlgren (2000) in the collection edited by Axford and Huggins, *New Media and Politics*, or Chapter 5 of Curran (2002), *Media and Power*. A broad range of material is conveniently collected in the volume edited by Negrine and Stanyer (2006), *The Political Communication Reader*, while McNair (2007), *An Introduction to Political Communication*, is also a good first port of call. Anyone wanting a full-length comparative study should consult Hallin and Mancini (2004), *Comparing Media Systems*. Also useful are the collection edited by Esser and Pfetsch (2004), *Comparing Political Communication*, and by Gunther and Mughan (2000), *Democracy and the Media*. On Europe and the media, see Kevin (2003), *Europe in the Media*. A piece that should stimulate argument and thought is the article by Newton (2006), in the *European Journal of Political Research*. So, too, should Norris (2000), *A Virtuous Circle*. Anyone interested in political advertising should read the collection edited by Kaid and Holz-Bacha (2006), *The Sage Handbook of Political Advertising*. Books on the Internet include the controversial Sunstein (2007), *Republic.com 2.0*. Then, check out the article by Bentivegna (2006) 'Rethinking Politics in the World of ICTs', in *European Journal of Communication* and the book by Chadwick (2006), *Internet Politics*.

On the web

www.europeunie.com – news from all 27 EU countries

www.iht.com/global.html – English language editions of European newspapers

www.thesun.co.uk, www.bild.t-online.de and **www.aftonbladet.se** – tabloids

www.ketupa.net and **www.pressreference.com** – media facts and history

www.eumap.org/topics/media/television_europe – comparative info. on TV in Europe

drseansdiary.blogspot.com – quirky academic take on Czech politics

iaindale.blogspot.com and **www.order-order.com** – UK political blogs

www.bbc.co.uk/blogs/thereporters/markmardell – BBC Europe correspondent's blog

www.depts.washington.edu/bennett/internet.html – Political Communication Resources

Discussion questions

1 There are some very obvious regional variations in media use in Europe: how would you sum them up?

2 How do governments in Europe attempt to regulate the media, and how has European integration impacted on those attempts?

3 What is public service broadcasting? Despite its problems, do you think it still has a future in Europe?

4 What do people mean when they suggest that political coverage now conforms to media rather than party logic – and what are the implications for politicians?

5 Do you have any sympathy with the view that the media are actually undermining democracy by the way they report it?

6 Are European politicians right to pay so much attention to, and get so worked up about, bias in and the influence of the media?

7 Why might trends in media coverage benefit pressure groups and populists rather than more mainstream, conventional political actors?

8 Do you think new information and communications technology (ICT) will have a fundamental impact on politics in Europe?

9 How well do the European media cover 'Europe' and foreign news?

Chapter 8

Participation and pressure politics – civil society, organized interests and social movements

Participation – the expanding but not necessarily alternative repertoire	240
Pressure groups – different types, different opportunities	245
Pluralism, corporatism and policy networks	247
Rebels with a cause? NGOs and (new) social movements	255
'Venue shopping' and the Europeanization of pressure politics	263

The idea at the heart of representative democracy in Europe (see Chapter 6) is that citizens play a role in their own governance via the election of parliaments (and possibly presidents). It is also generally accepted that, like it or not, parties play a mediating role, helping to structure choices and aggregate interests, be they economic or cultural or religious (see Chapter 5). At the very least, according to the Austrian economist and political analyst Joseph Schumpeter – a man who thought too much citizen participation would be unworkable – parties provide competing teams of managers that we can choose between at the ballot box. But it would be a very 'thin' conception of democracy indeed that supposed citizens would – or, indeed, should – limit their participation to joining parties and voting or, indeed, between elections be content simply to leave the politicians and the bureaucrats to get on with it. After all, the policies initiated and implemented between those elections will rarely suit everyone and may even be seen as unfair by some people. As individuals, people are rarely so powerful that they can hope to influence policy on their own, and they also recognize that voting and political parties are not the only way to exercise that influence or simply to get involved. They are therefore likely to engage in other forms of political participation. And they might well band together in order to secure the introduction, prevention, continuation or abolition of whatever measures they feel are important to them – a tendency that, ever since de Tocqueville (a famous nineteenth-century French analyst of politics and society) wrote his comparative work on America, has been celebrated as one of the indicators and bastions of a healthy democracy.

Forms of political participation other than voting or joining a political party can be relatively low cost and episodic – signing a petition is a good (and, as we shall see, increasingly common) example. But they also include the collaborative or 'associative' activity that creates **pressure groups** which,

Pressure groups are more or less organized collections of people who aim, if they feel their interests or their ideals are at stake, to influence (but not to get elected to) government. This influence may be pursued directly, through access to politicians or bureaucrats, and/or indirectly – for instance, through the media or perhaps the legal system. Groups can be highly institutionalized or very informal. They can be permanent (and possibly well funded) fixtures in the political landscape, involved in a wide range of policy debates, or organizations that come and go according to whether their particular issue preoccupies (or can be made to preoccupy) people.

no less than parties, mediate between the state and the individual, expressing the demands and preferences of citizens and helping government to formulate, and sometimes even to deliver, the policies that meet them. Such activity and such groups constitute what is now routinely referred to as 'civil society' (see Box 8.1) – something that, it is claimed, not only minimizes the risk of an over-mighty and unresponsive state, but also helps create (at the same time as it draws on) the '**social capital**' that some see as essential for a genuinely participatory democracy and a healthy economy (see van Deth *et al.*, 2006; Hooghe and Stolle, 2003; Putnam *et al.*, 2000). It is this kind of collective participation and action, and the political response to it, which this chapter explores.

In the words of its most prominent promoter (Putnam 2000: 19):

> Whereas physical capital refers to physical objects and human capital refers to the properties of individuals, **social capital** refers to connections among individuals – social networks and the norms of reciprocity and trustworthiness that arise from them.

The chapter begins by looking at forms of political participation other than voting or joining political parties. It goes on to focus on pressure groups, the ways they have been classified and variations in the way they work and in their relative success. It then moves on to look at two classic categories in which

BOX 8.1

What is civil society, is it a good thing, and how much does each country have?

Civil society is a term more often bandied about than defined. The best short definition is probably by the political theorist David Held (1987: 281), who sees it consisting of 'areas of social life – the domestic world, the economic sphere, cultural activities and political interaction – which are organized by private or voluntary arrangements between individuals and groups outside the direct control of the state'. A good longer definition is the one used by the London School of Economics' Centre for Civil Society. According to the CCS (2004), civil society is:

> *the arena of uncoerced collective action around shared interests, purposes and values. In theory, its institutional forms are distinct from those of the state, family and market, though in practice, the boundaries between state, civil society, family and market are often complex, blurred and negotiated. Civil society commonly embraces a diversity of spaces, actors and institutional forms, varying in their degree of formality, autonomy and power. Civil societies are often populated by organizations such as registered charities, development non-governmental organizations, community groups, women's organizations, faith-based organizations, professional associations, trades unions, self-help groups, social movements, business associations, coalitions and advocacy groups.*

The common wisdom is that not only is all this is a terribly good thing in itself, but also that being involved in such activity breeds social trust and confidence in political institutions. Recent research across twelve European countries, however, provides little or no support for this claim (see Zmerli *et al.*, 2007). And although some research reveals even apparently non-political groups have 'a remarkably high level of . . . contacts' with local politicians, parties, and bureaucrats (Lelieveldt and Caiani, 2007), it also finds that the vast majority of groups focus on leisure pursuits, with ostensibly 'political' groups in a small minority that contains more passive than active members (Maloney and Roßteutscher, 2007a). Wider survey research also reveals that people are much more involved in groups of any kind in the established democracies of Northern and Central Europe than they are in the South and, especially, the newer democracies of Eastern Europe (see Figure 8.1).

Figure 8.1 Variations in associative activity in selected European countries

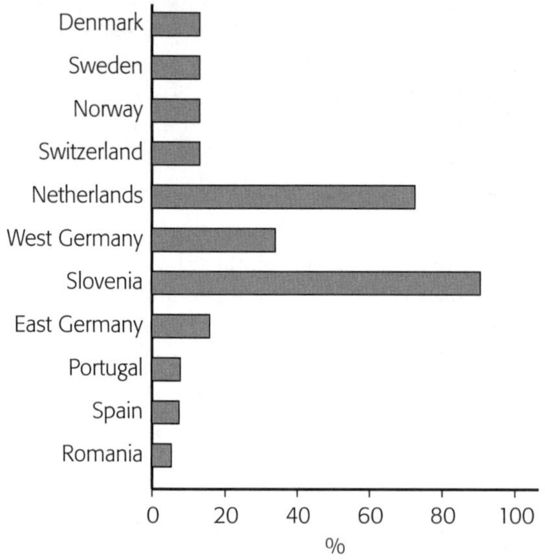

Note: Figures represent percentage of respondents claiming membership in at least one association.

Source: Data from Morales and Geurts (2006: 138).

European states have been placed in relation to the role of organized interests – pluralism and corporatism – to see to what extent these 'ideal types' (used by social scientists to simplify analysis) tell us anything useful about the real world. It focuses in particular on two key real-world examples: first, a group that is often said to be very close to government and successful all over Europe – the agricultural lobby – and, next, one that many casual observers believe, we argue mistakenly, has been frozen out – the trade unions. It then looks, conversely, at business and notes that, although powerful, it does not always 'win'.

Both of these groups can be defined as 'interest groups' in the sense that they have something material to offer their members. To some theorists, this explains their success despite being outnumbered, if you like, by the general public. We question this idea by pointing to big national variations in the willingness of different nations to join groups and by looking at one of the most significant developments in Europe over the last three decades – the mobilization of so-called *new social movements* (NSM) (Box 8.2). These groups offer people the chance to support a cause and, in so doing, express themselves and their values. We should not, though, be too naive. Many such groups have turned into 'protest businesses'. Others are testament to the fact that the comfortable distinction between civil society (supposedly good) and direct action (widely regarded as questionable) is not necessarily hard and fast. Finally, we look at the extent to which all the groups previously examined are operating at the European, transnational level.

Participation – the expanding but not necessarily alternative repertoire

In Europe's liberal democracies there are many more ways of being involved in politics than simply voting. People might, for example, confine themselves to casting a ballot every four or five years or signing a petition on the street or the Internet. They might take the next step by demonstrating against a law or a proposal that they don't agree with, realizing perhaps that they might end up breaking the law, or at least confronting those charged with upholding it, as a result. Or they might go so far as to join a political party or a group concerned with a particular issue or set of issues and end up being the kind of person who seeks the votes, the signatures and the attendance of others. In the most extreme circumstances, the group they join may even be clandestine, like an animal rights group prepared to countenance illegal and even violent action to stop what it regards as unwarranted cruelty. The opportunities, in other words, range from very 'low cost' to 'high-intensity' activities that suck up an individual's time and possibly his or her money too. And

KEY POINT

There are plenty of other (normally complementary rather than alternative) ways of participating in politics beyond parties and voting. But those that have increased most in recent years tend to be more ad hoc and require little ongoing commitment, while the likelihood of engaging in them varies considerably according to where in Europe people live and their demographic and socio-economic profile.

BOX 8.2

New social movements

The label *new social movement* (NSM) is applied to pressure groups, many of which began to emerge in the 1960s, expressing a radical critique of mainstream societies, cultures and institutions for ignoring people and issues that did not fit conveniently or inexpensively into 'politics-as-usual'. Characteristic concerns include equality for women and for racial, ethnic and sexual minorities, the environment and animal rights, international peace and, more recently, globalization. Many observers see such concerns as typical of 'postmaterialism' and/or 'identity politics', wherein solidarity with a cause not directly associated with one's self-interest combines with a need for self-expression and self-realization to mean that 'the personal is political'. NSMs are also distinguished (at least, initially) by their commitment to more general anti-authoritarian and pro-egalitarian values. This commitment also underpins the way they (supposedly but not, in fact, in all cases) work: informal and fairly pluralistic networks, non-hierarchical structures and (what used to be thought of anyway as) non-conventional forms of protest, often involving (normally) non-violent direct action, such as marches, demos, sit-ins and boycotts.

some of the more 'unconventional' types cross (or at least come close to crossing) the line between what is within and what is outside the law: the entire 'repertoire', however – even those which involve violence – can claim to count as political participation (see Dalton, 2002: 61).

Participation – especially when it is peaceful and legal – is generally seen as a good thing, although there is a long-running argument among political scientists about whether, like all good things, you can have too much of it. For example, in what is now regarded as one of the 'classics' of comparative politics, Almond and Verba (1963) promoted the 'civic culture' they claimed to have identified in the UK as the best compromise between 'subject cultures', where the government was accorded possibly too much respect and autonomy, and 'participant cultures', where citizens were so active and demanding that they made it difficult for representative politicians to get on with their job. This argument, however, seems to have faded as observers have become increasingly worried about a supposed decline in political participation in Europe, as well as other advanced liberal democracies – worries we have already touched on in Chapter 6 when we discussed turnout at elections.

Survey evidence (see Table 8.1) clearly suggests, however, that 'petitions, boycotts, and other forms of elite-challenging activities are no longer unconventional, but have become more or normal actions
for a substantial part of the citizenry of post-industrial nations' and that '[a]lthough passive and elite-directed forms of public participation, such as voting and church attendance, have stagnated or declined . . . these newer forms of public participation have become increasingly widespread' (Inglehart and Catterberg, 2002: 302). In other words, if one looks at new forms of political action, the oft-voiced fears that Europe (and other advanced nations) have over the last two or three decades been experiencing worrying levels of 'civic disengagement' are unfounded. For the former communist countries, the data covers a rather shorter period, but suggests a different pattern (see Figure 8.2). There seems to have been a 'post-honeymoon' dip in 'elite-challenging action' as the inflated expectations surrounding the transition to capitalist democracy were punctured by a more grim reality (see Bernhagen and Marsh, 2007 and Inglehart and Catterberg, 2002). However, generally speaking, this dip either did not take place at all or was much less significant in Central Europe, especially where people-power played a part in bringing down the former regime (for instance, in the Czech Republic and Poland) than it was in those states that were part of the former Soviet Union and where transition was elite-dominated (for instance Latvia, Lithuania and Estonia).

The other, normative concern about participation is that it is socially skewed, thereby disadvantaging the already disadvantaged. Essentially, participation in all its forms tends to be positively associated with socio-economic status and education, although clearly it is also driven by party and union

Table 8.1 The rise of 'elite challenging' participation in Europe, 1974–2000

	Percentage who:	1974	1981	1990	2000	Net shift
(West) Germany	signed petition	31	47	57	47	+16
	demonstrated	9	15	21	22	+13
	boycotted goods	5	8	10	10	+5
Italy	signed petition	17	42	48	55	+38
	demonstrated	19	27	36	35	+16
	boycotted goods	2	6	11	10	+2
Netherlands	signed petition	22	35	51	61	+39
	demonstrated	7	13	25	32	+25
	boycotted goods	6	7	9	22	+16
UK	signed petition	23	63	75	81	+58
	demonstrated	6	10	14	13	+7
	boycotted goods	6	7	14	17	+11

Source: Data from Inglehart and Catterberg (2002: 305).

membership, by an interest in politics, by individual psychology (see Bekkers, 2005) and by family traditions. Classing yourself as left-wing also counts for a lot – although interestingly, being right-wing, which in western Europe tends to make you less likely to participate in 'elite-challenging' or 'uninstitutionalized' activity, is positively correlated with such activity in Central and Eastern Europe. On the other hand, being environmentally aware in that region seems to make no difference but it is associated with such activity in the west (see Bernhagen and Marsh, 2007: 61, 64). Age makes a difference in the west as well, with middle-aged people (often with more secure jobs and an interest in the system because they have children in education and parents receiving healthcare and welfare/insurance benefits) more inclined to participate. So, too, does length (and indeed security) of residency, which means that it generally takes time, for instance, for immigrants to participate as much as the native population, although this might be offset by their very strong interest in securing policy that benefits or does not discriminate against their compatriots. Many of the factors that predispose an individual to involve themselves in these kinds of activity are, incidentally, the same as those that make them more likely to join a group of any kind, be it purely social, sporting or cultural, or political, although group membership is even more skewed towards men (see Armingeon, 2007, Badescu and Neller, 2007, Zmerli *et al.*, 2007).

The rise of political activities like petition signing, consumer boycotts, and demonstrations potentially increases the range of people who will get involved in politics. The fact that they are more sporadic, take up less time and are less hierarchical might make these new forms of participation more attractive to, say, young people and women. Fascinating new research by Stolle and Hooghe (2005) suggests that the latter is indeed the case, although the closing of the gender gap is more significant than the closing of the age gap: it seems that increasing numbers of people are carrying the protest 'habit' of their youth into middle age (see van Aelst and Walgrave, 2001), while it may be the case that younger people are finding newer, more technological ways of protesting (see also Hick and McNutt, 2002) like 'netstrikes' and 'jamming' (see also van de Donk *et al.*, 2003).

But the same research also shows that, while these forms of participation are no more likely than 'old-style' political activities to attract and favour people who are comparatively well-educated, well-to-do, and politically interested and driven, they are nevertheless still engaged in disproportionately by those groups. To take just one example of the 'emerging

Figure 8.2 Patterns of protest in 'western' and postcommunist Europe, 1999–2002

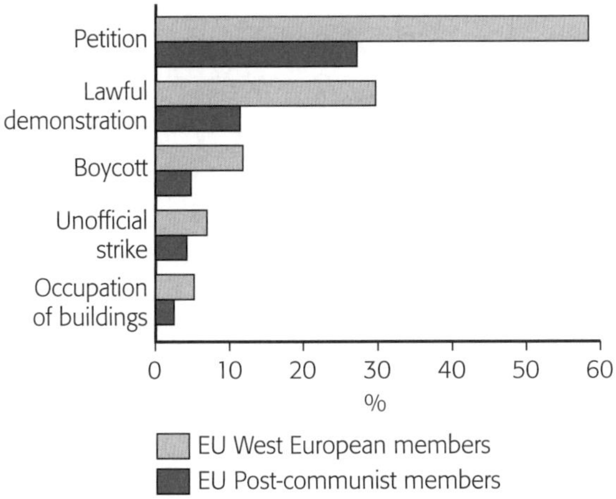

Sources: Data from Furusawa (2006: 213), based on World Values Survey.

action repertoires', the consumer boycott, the most highly educated are three-and-a-half times more likely to engage in such action than the least educated. In other words, the people who are more likely to vote, join parties and pressure groups, and contact MPs and officials (see Aars and Strømsnes, 2007), are also more likely to sign petitions, attend demos, and support consumer boycotts and 'buycotts' – the purchase of goods which, for example, promote 'fair trade' (see Stolle *et al.*, 2005). 'Elite-challenging' participation, then, is not so much an alternative but a complement to 'conventional' participation (see Norris, 2002): the same researchers, indeed, found that only 1 per cent of Europeans surveyed had engaged only in the former and not in the latter.

On the other hand, just as with voting (see Chapter 6), these individual-level drivers of activity could ultimately be less important than the region of Europe (Figure 8.2) or the particular country a person comes from (Figure 8.3). The latter might also have an effect on what people engaged in campaigning on what is ostensibly the same issue actually think they are doing (see Box 8.3)

There are, however, some caveats to this largely rosy picture of continued participation. Should we, for example, equate the relatively brief and episodic participation required by signing petitions, going on demos and boycotting certain goods with the more high-intensity participation required by, say, active (not simply passive) engagement in a political party or pressure group? It seems absolutely

BOX 8.3

The F-15 anti-war demo, 2003

15 February 2003 saw what was the largest transnational protest event the world has ever seen. Millions of Europeans – among others – marched in opposition to the upcoming US-led invasion of Iraq. Luckily for those interested in comparative politics, a team of academics was there distributing surveys in order to find out who they were and what they thought they were doing. It turns out that there was a fairly even mix of men and women, but that most were young to middle-aged, disproportionately highly-educated (in most countries researched, over half had been to university). They were also much more interested in politics than most people and overwhelmingly left-wing (60 per cent putting themselves on the left and over 20 per cent on the far left), with a large minority working in the caring professions. Seven out of ten were active members of a group or association. So far, so postmaterialist, some would say. Interestingly, however, there were significant variations when it came to what protesters from each country actually wanted – beyond, of course, preventing war. There was consensus on the war being really about oil, while nearly half the protesters in every country believed the Americans were conducting some kind of crusade against Islam. But when it came, for example, to believing that war was always wrong, protesters in the UK (and the US) were much less likely to agree that this was the case than their counterparts in Spain, Italy, the Netherlands, Sweden, Belgium and Germany – and were much more focused on getting a diplomatic solution to the conflict as opposed to simply stopping any invasion. Even transnational protest, then, seems to be shaped by national concerns and traditions.

Source: Verhulst and Walgrave (2007).

right to argue that 'elite-challenging' activity, even if it is relatively 'non-institutionalized', should be seen as just as important to civil society and to building social capital as, for example, membership of voluntary associations (see Welzel *et al.*, 2005). Yet it is difficult to escape the feeling that there is an important difference in the character and quality, if not the quantity, of participation involved (see Bale *et al.*, 2006). Moreover, if we cut the same figures a different way, do we get a less optimistic impression? If, instead of looking (as we do in Figure 8.3) at the proportion of people claiming to have engaged in at least one act, we compare, on the one hand, those who did nothing at all plus those who only did one thing (most probably signing a petition) with, on the other hand, those who engaged in two or three or all of the four activities, the picture of participation isn't quite as rosy (see Figure 8.4).

Against this more pessimistic picture, however, we should note that relatively low-intensity protest activity is not the only participatory indicator on the up. So, too, at least in some countries (as Table 8.2 illustrates), is membership – including membership by young people under the age of 25 – in 'sociotropic' associations (as opposed to religious or 'utilitarian' associations like political parties, trade unions or professional organizations), such as community, charity, environmental, international or cultural groups (see Welzel *et al.*, 2005: 127–8; see also Norris, 2002). We should also note, in all fairness, that research on the less institutionalized protest activity referred to above (petitions, boycotts, demos, etc.) suggests that the level of such activity is strongly correlated with open, accountable and efficient government – indeed, more strongly than is the case with the membership of groups which those interested in social capital tend to concentrate on (Welzel *et al.*, 2005).

Figure 8.3 Percentage of people who engaged in at least one 'protest activity'

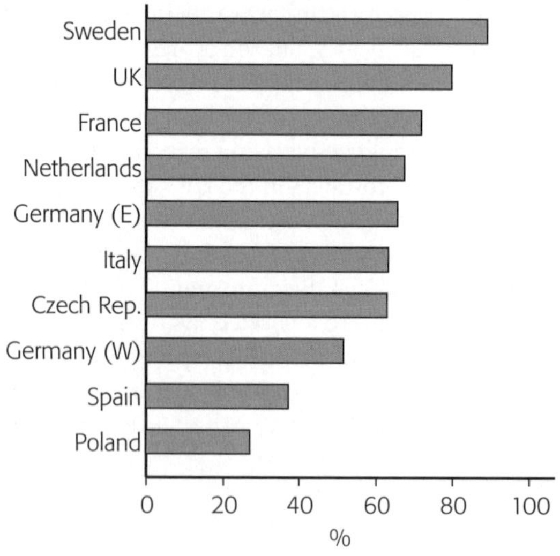

Note: Bars shows percentage who engaged in at least one of the four 'protest activities' in the 1999 World Values Survey (signing a petition, joining a boycott, attending a lawful demonstration, or joining an unofficial strike).

Source: Data from Bernhagen and Marsh (2007).

Figure 8.4 The gap between less and more active 'protesters'

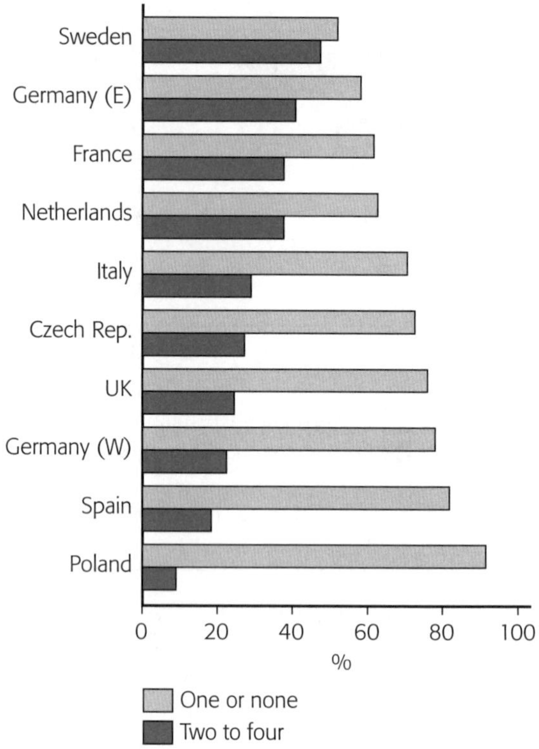

Note: The first bar shows the percentage of those who engaged in only one or none of the four 'protest activities' in the 1999 World Values Survey survey (signing a petition, joining a boycott, attending a lawful demonstration, or joining an unofficial strike). The second bar shows those who engaged in at least two of the four activities.

Source: Data from Bernhagen and Marsh (2007).

Table 8.2 Group and party membership in selected European countries, 1981–2000

	Belonging to/volunteering in a group				Belonging to a political party			
	1981	1990	2000	Trend	1981	1990	2000	Trend
Sweden	62	73	81	+19	15	10	11	−4
(West) Germany	41	39	24	−17	8	7	3	−5
Netherlands	46	64	81	+35	9	11	9	0
France	25	24	20	−5	3	3	2	−1
Italy	18	19	28	+10	6	6	4	−2
Spain	26	13	17	−9	4	1	2	−2

Note: 'Group' includes all voluntary associative activity except church and religious groups and parties.

Source: Data from Dekker and van den Broek (2005).

Pressure groups – different types, different opportunities

Any organized attempt politically to promote a particular course of action or way of life which falls short of founding a party to contest elections can be labelled a 'pressure group'. But such groups take on many forms in twenty-first-century Europe. Some will clearly be based on self-interest on the part of those involved, most of whom will be tied to the group through their occupation: these are sometimes labelled 'sectional' or even simply 'interest' groups since their core function is the protecting the interests of a section of society. Others may well be less self-regarding (at least in theory), and are known as 'cause' or 'promotional groups', though recently they may choose to call themselves NGOs (see Box 8.3).

Analysts have for some time found it useful to distinguish between what British political scientist Wyn Grant labelled 'insider' and 'outsider' groups. The former had cosy, private and possibly more influential relationships with those in power, while the latter were excluded and therefore obliged to take a different, more public route that involved trying to shame rather than inveigle the government into action. More often than not, sectional interest groups were seen as insiders, providing the state with the information and the implementation infrastructure that otherwise it might have lacked in exchange for a degree of influence on policy. Cause groups, on the other hand, were seen as outsiders.

KEY POINT

Pressure groups may be in the business of defending a tangible (often economic or 'sectional') interest, or they may promote a cause or ideal. There are now no hard and fast distinctions between the tactics both types use, their choice (and to some extent their success) being based on the political environment (or 'opportunity structure') they have to work in.

These distinctions, which were never hard and fast (see Box 8.4), might, however, be proving increasingly redundant. Governments have tried, in the spirit of 'the new public management' (NPM) to insulate themselves from the 'producer capture' (control of policy by insider groups) that too cosy a relationship with a pressure group may engender. And, as the structure of the economy has changed and economic growth weakened, they have also been less and less keen to provide the kind of pay-offs that some of those groups might traditionally have expected. Conversely, the success of increasingly professional outsider groups at getting their issues onto the agenda has forced governments to take them more seriously and suggested to insider groups that they may have something to learn, particularly when it comes to using the media (see Chapter 7).

Nowadays, then, instead of particular strategies being associated with particular groups, they are best seen as a range of options which any group may exploit as it sees fit – bearing in mind, of course, that there may be a trade-off between, for example, a group embarrassing the government and how keen the government is to keep it in the loop. Often, the decision of which path to pursue will be determined by circumstances or by what is sometimes referred to as the **political opportunity structure** prevailing not just in each state but also, given the importance of the EU for some policy domains, Europe as a whole.

The idea of a **political opportunity structure** originates from research into social movements (see McAdam *et al.*, 1996). The strategies and the success of groups, while obviously dependent on contingency and on factors such as effective leadership or resources, also depend on more consistent institutional and even cultural factors: Is there a supranational authority above the nation state?; Who are the 'veto-players'?; Is the party system fragmented and polarized, or restricted to just a few relatively centrist parties?; Are the media centralized and are they independent?; Do people regard all or only some forms of direct action as acceptable in a democratic, civilized society?

A good illustration of the point is provided by the extent to which (and the ways in which) pressure groups in different countries bother with parliament. In CEE, where communist states would have nothing to do with anything remotely resembling a pressure group and where even now governments remain ambivalent and unsure about such groups' legitimacy and rationale, the regions' fledgling interest groups are more likely to lobby parliament than lobby government direct (see Pérez-Solórzano Borragán, 2006). The studies of western European countries gathered together by Philip Norton (1999) suggest that for most of them, however, government is the main focus. However, they also suggest that the more chance the parliament has to modify and even make policy, the more effort groups put in to influencing it. Accordingly, the Italian parliament is seen not just as a channel to get to where the real power lies, but a target in itself. Generally, pressure groups focused on committees, not only because they regarded this as the best way of getting their views on record – a particular attraction for 'outsider' groups – but also because this was where small, but perhaps significant, changes could be made. The country studies also suggested a significant difference in the relationships between groups and parliamentarians. In Germany and the Netherlands, the relationship is both formalized and in some ways incestuous: many MPs started off in pressure groups and maintain strong links with them, although, interestingly, this is now declining with the rise of the 'career politician'. Such a decline will make those countries rather more like the UK, where the relationship between pressure groups and parliamentarians has always been rather more indirect.

BOX 8.4

The church – sectional or cause group, insider or outsider?

One of the most successful pressure groups in many European countries – even if it is not thought of as such – is the church. Given the precipitate decline in the number of devotees, the traditional religions have managed to retain many of their privileges and to maintain a possibly disproportionate influence on national life. Churches in Scandinavia and Germany for instance, still collect revenues, albeit on a voluntary basis, through the tax system. In Scandinavia, they have been instrumental in dissuading governments from liberalizing laws on alcohol consumption and opening hours. Meanwhile, in other countries, including Ireland and especially Poland, they have managed not only to protect vast financial assets but also to exert a brake-like effect on political responses to social change – most obviously when it comes to education and, in particular, the abortion law. But this influence might not last forever: in 2005, Spain became only the second country in Europe (after the Netherlands) to put same-sex marriage on exactly the same legal basis as conventional marriage; a determined centre-left government – boosted by opinion poll findings that it was reflecting majority opinion – drove through the measure notwithstanding the Roman Catholic Church (which apparently claims the loyalty of some 80 per cent of Spaniards) organizing counter-demonstrations and encouraging legal challenges.

This parliamentary manoeuvring serves to emphasize that the relationship between pressure groups and political parties is not a zero-sum game. In other words, rather than being self contained, alternative ways of doing politics, they continue to need and to use each other. This is a very important point – particularly in the context of the common wisdom surrounding the so-called 'cartel party', referred to in Chapter 5, that political parties have somehow lost their links to interest groups and are somehow less embedded in civil society. Contemporary studies of these links – the most obvious are between social democratic parties and trade unions, business groups and parties on the centre right (including liberals, Christian Democrats and conservatives), and environmental groups and the Greens – are few and far between. However, by far the most comprehensive recent case study of one European country – Norway – suggests that these links are still strong, even if they take different, less instutionalized forms (see Allern, 2007). In short, representative politics and pressure group politics are part of the same game: the latter is not replacing the former.

Pluralism, corporatism, and policy networks

Underpinning the political opportunity structure in each state are national traditions – not immovable, but nonetheless influential – concerning the extent to which groups, particularly groups representing employers and employees, are expected (and expect) to play a role in governance alongside the state. Some European states can be said to have a tradition of pluralism, while others are traditionally corporatist. In pluralist countries, the government might, of course, take advice from and occasionally rely on groups, especially for implementation of its policies; generally, however, groups are supposedly kept at arm's length, granted access to make their case but given no special favours. Countries with a corporatist tradition, on the other hand, are those in which so-called 'peak organizations (such as the national federations of trade unions and employers) have an institutionalized role in the planning and the implementation of certain key state policies, notably on the economy and social policy. Traditionally, meeting with each other and with the government in so-called 'tripartite' bodies, groups make (and, crucially, stick to) trade-offs which are supposedly in the best interests of the whole country: a typical example would be unions agreeing to wage restraint in return for employers' efforts to maintain employment, with both trusting the government to do its best to maintain a stable and benign economic environment.

However, as is often the case in political analysis, these are ideal types. Even supposedly corporatist European states have been wary of the degree of compulsion, monopoly, and (some would argue) economic sclerosis that full-blown corporatism might potentially entail; they can at best be labelled 'neo-corporatist'. In these countries there is, in certain sectors, a degree of 'concertation' between government and groups that other countries (and certainly neo-liberal right-wingers) might frown on. Indeed, as we suggest later, such concertation, far from disappearing, has made something of a come-back in recent years, even if (as we shall see) commitment to it (particularly in some former communist countries) is more rhetorical than real. But, even where it is meaningful, such concertation comes nowhere near undermining or replacing democratic government, as some critics of corporatism allege. Some of the countries in which this kind of sectorally specific 'liberal corporatism' and 'tripartism' is especially strong also have strong parliaments: Germany is one, Sweden another (see

KEY POINT

Some countries institutionalize the relationship between powerful interest groups, especially business and labour – a system labelled corporatism. Others see more advantage in a more arm's length and ad hoc relationship with groups, all of which have to compete with each other for access and attention – a system labelled pluralism. Most policy areas attract what are known as policy networks of interested groups – networks that are more or less insulated from outside interference. Insulation and influence, however, is not necessarily permanent, as the case of agriculture suggests. Nor is the power of business relative to, say, the trade unions necessarily a done deal.

BOX 8.5

Sweden – the coexistence of corporatism and parliamentary democracy

The trade unions, via two federations – the massive LO (*Landsorganisationen*) and the smaller, more white-collar, TCO (*Tjänstemännens Centralorganisation*) – have an institutionalized place at all levels of Swedish governance. They have places on the boards of many of the agencies that play such an important part in the running of the country (see Chapter 3). The employers, via the SAF (*Svenska Arbetsgivareföreningen*) used to enjoy the same rights, but have recently argued that such bodies should be left to politicians alone. Despite this, and despite their criticisms of labour law and national wage bargaining, however, they continue to work with the unions and the government to maintain an 'active labour market policy', aimed less at creating employment and more at maintaining and improving 'employability' by facilitating training and mobility (geographical and between benefits and work). This helps to ensure that the economy, which is heavily export-oriented, retains its flexibility and capacity for low-inflationary growth despite the relatively high wages, taxes and benefits that are associated with what is sometimes called the 'Swedish model' (see Chapter 9). Yet none of this means there is no place for parliament. Indeed, the *Riksdag* is acknowledged to be one of Europe's most powerful legislatures (see Chapter 4). In fact, there is no 'zero-sum game' between corporatist-style concertation and parliamentary democracy. The *Riksdag*'s *remiss* system illustrates this nicely: each piece of proposed legislation is sent out to pressure groups (and to the wider public, if they wish) for comment before being formally introduced as a bill before the country's MPs.

Box 8.5). In any case, by no means all pressure groups or sectors are involved in, or benefit from, what tend to be framework agreements between what are routinely called in Europe (and in EU jargon) 'the social partners' (i.e. unions and employers or their 'peak – sometimes called 'umbrella' – associations'). Equally, as we shall see, there is no European state (and whatever its zealous advocates in the US might maintain, probably no state in the world) where pluralism is so pure that it does not systematically advantage some groups over others.

The way in which a group tries to exert influence depends on the political opportunity structure of the state or states in which it operates, but in all cases its success is likely to be based on its ability and willingness to:

- Recruit all, or at least a very high proportion, of those people who have a stake in a particular issue
- Bring to bear significant economic resources and/or connections
- Provide the state with something it needs but cannot or is unwilling to provide for itself in sufficient measure to allow it complete autonomy: financial/human capital; information/expertise/knowledge
- Seriously put at risk the popularity either of the parties in government, or those that hope to be when that government is brought down.

To the extent that a group meets these criteria, and also to the extent that it is pressing a case to which there is little or only diffuse (rather than organized) opposition, it will tend to have a cosier relationship with those charged with the executive. Political scientists, as we saw in Chapter 3, label the cosiest of these institutionalized relationships (or policy networks) 'policy communities', while at the other end of the spectrum are what they call 'issue networks'. Once again, of course, we have moved into the realm of the ideal type. In real-world Europe things are rather more messy and, indeed, changing over time, as we can see when we look, for example, at agricultural policy.

Farming – a real-world example of power under pressure

The archetypal policy community in many European states is often said to be agriculture. As we saw in Chapter 1, farming contributes less and less to European economies relative to other sectors. Yet it continues to attract vast subsidies from all

European states, the bulk of which are now disbursed through the EU's CAP – a mechanism which, critics argue, allows the cost of subsidizing the sector to be hidden from voters at the domestic level. That might be true, but there are good reasons to suppose that even if it were not the case, agriculture would be relatively insulated from interference. For one thing, while European consumers do pay more for food than they need to, food nevertheless takes up a steadily declining proportion of family expenditure as increases in real wages have, over decades, outstripped increases in prices. Traditional notions about the rejuvenating simplicity, beauty and tradition of rural ways of life also continue to occupy an important place in our conceptions of what it means to be, say, French, or Danish, or Polish.

Taken together, this means that there is little opposition to what, if it were applied to industry, for example, might be seen as 'featherbedding' (making life so easy for producers, often via subsidies or protective measures, that they have no incentive to remain competitive). This makes for what political scientists refer to as an 'asymmetry of interests'. You have, on the one hand, a group of individual or family consumers who are not particularly bothered by subsidies just as long as food is reasonably cheap and plentiful. On the other, you have a highly organized group of farmers for whom the continuation of subsidies is a matter of the utmost importance, as well as politicians and bureaucrats who rely on them for their expert knowledge and their help in policy implementation. Given this asymmetry, the power of farming groups in every state – and, just as importantly, at the EU level, where they operate effectively under the umbrella of the the Committee of Agricultural Organizations (COPA) – to extract money from governments with almost no questions asked by taxpayers is hardly surprising. Neither, of course, is it unique to Europe (see Smith, 1993).

Yet the politics of agriculture also suggest that not even the tightest policy community can insulate itself entirely or forever. First, this is because one sector invariably impinges on others. Second, once we dig a little deeper, we find that even the most well-organized pressure group contains within it a number of potentially conflicting interests. An illustration of the first point is the way in which the rather cosy relationship between farmers and governments has been disrupted in recent years by a number of food-scares (over BSE or 'mad cow disease') and dioxin contamination, for instance) whose trans-European implications are testimony to the extent of integration and interdependence. In such cases, the fear that practices in one sector, agriculture, might have negatively impacted on another (namely, health) meant that the policy community lost control over policy to the extent that political (though, interestingly, not agricultural) heads rolled. Common wisdom suggests that it sacrificed some long-term trust and legitimacy by being less than open about the issues involved. This can be overdone, however. In fact, levels of trust in food and farming in individual European countries seem to be related more to levels of general political and personal trust than to whether or not a country has experienced food-scares or not. For example, the Italians, who have little experience of food-scares, are not very trusting compared with the British or even the Germans, who have had more than their fair share but appear to have been reassured somewhat by government reforms (see Poppe and Kjærnes, 2003).

Second, we need to realize that even the so-called 'agricultural lobby' is made up of many potentially conflicting parts. 'Feisty French farmers' are a common media stereotype across Europe, and especially in the UK, where their theatrical forms of protest – blocking roads, dumping manure, and so on – are guaranteed a place in the news. Interestingly, such antics are by no means an indicator that agriculture is an outsider group in a country that is still one of the largest exporters of food in the world. Indeed, they are testament to a political culture in which direct action has long been an acceptable (and effective) way of getting what you want and to the willingness – perhaps increasing willingness – of even well-connected pressure groups to pursue tactics that belie their categorization as 'insiders'. Yet insiders is very much what they are. FNSEA (the French Farmers' Federation) for example, sends representatives to sit on state commissions responsible for setting both policies and prices, on ministerial advisory councils and on regional economic development bodies. Its former leaders have even held prominent political posts, particularly in administrations formed by the centre-right, which is particularly strong in the rural districts that some would say get a disproportionate number of seats in the National Assembly. In 1986, for instance, former FNSEA leader, François Guillaume was made agriculture minister in the Chirac government.

To some French farmers, however, 'insider' status has compromised their representatives, encouraging them into even more radical action: José Bové, who grabbed world headlines (and plenty of support) for an attack on a McDonald's franchise to protest at the plight of small farms in an increasingly globalized market, is one example. Similar protests about the agri-business domination of the National Farmers' Union (NFU) are occasionally heard in the UK, especially when times are tough (as they were, for example, in the foot and mouth outbreak in 2001). In Italy, the split is institutionalized: large- and small-scale farmers have traditionally organized in different groups, with the former's group, *Confagricoltura,* traditionally being less powerful than the latter's, *Coldiretti,* which historically controlled the parapublic body, *Federconsorzi,* responsible (with the Agriculture Ministry) for overseeing the sector.

There is (still) power in a union

Interestingly, Italy's farmers, whether large- or small-scale, are not as powerful as their counterparts in France (or Britain, via the NFU, or Germany, via the *Deutscher Bauernverband*), which would seem to indicate that 'unity (especially when combined with the ability to recruit a majority of the potential members of a group) is strength'. The old adage certainly seems to hold good for one of the potentially most important pressure groups in any European country; namely, the trade unions.

Although set up, at least in theory, to defend the interests of ordinary people, the vast majority of whom earn salaries and wages, unions are not universally popular. A pan-European survey (*Eurobarometer* 66, 2006) revealed that in the EU-25, they were trusted by some 38 per cent of respondents – more than double the figure (17 per cent) for political parties admittedly, and a few percentage points above government (30 per cent) and parliament (33 per cent), but still a few points behind the press (44 per cent), and way below, say, the police (64 per cent) and the army (69 per cent).

Unions have also suffered significant declines in membership over the last three decades (see Visser, 2006) – a decline most obvious and rapid in the former communist countries, where unions that had recruited around nine out of ten workers could count only two or three out of ten within a decade of the end of the Cold War. Indeed, the proportion of the total workforce that are union members (known as 'trade union density' in the jargon) now is lower than in 1970 in almost every European country, with the picture becoming worse for the unions in each successive decade – and younger people are these days considerably less likely to join a union. The exceptions to the general decline over time were Finland, Sweden, Denmark and Belgium, where, significantly, the unions managed to secure themselves a big role in the delivery of unemployment insurance and where, crucially, unions have managed to maintain wage bargaining processes at the national or at least the sectoral or industry level, rather than at the level of the firm, which theoretically allows employers (to use a slightly pejorative term) to divide and rule (see Table 8.3). In all countries, however, union membership has held up much better in the public than in the (more internationally competitive) private sector (Visser, 2006): in the UK, the ratio is 59:17, in France 15:5, Germany, 56:22, Spain, 32:15, and the Netherlands, 39:22; in Sweden, the gap (at 93:77) is much smaller, but still significant. The union movement therefore has a considerable vested interest in the survival of a welfare state (see Chapter 9).

On the other hand, there is a great deal of variation, with some countries (mainly in Scandinavia) displaying density rates around five times those in the US (12 per cent on latest figures), while others (notably in CEE, as well as in France) dipping below even that figure. The patterned nature of that variation is very clear (Table 8.4). Although, as Table 8.3 suggests, density isn't destiny as far as workers being covered by collective bargaining agreements is concerned, it is on balance the case that countries where trade unions are fragmented by ideological and/or historical divisions, and where they fail to recruit to their full potential, take less account of the interests of labour, as opposed to those of business. In countries where the unions are concentrated (or at least willing to subordinate themselves to one 'peak' federation) and where they have high membership density (i.e. they recruit a large proportion of the workers available for recruitment) labour can expect

Table 8.3 Which wage deals are done where?

	National level	Sector/industry level	Firm/company level	Workers covered by collective agreements (%)
Czech Rep.		•	•••	21–30
France		•	•••	91–100
Germany		•••	•	61–70
Italy		•••	••	61–70
Netherlands	•	•••	•	81–90
Poland		•	•••	41–50
Spain	••	••	••	81–90
Sweden		•••	•	91–100
UK			•••	31–40

Notes: ••• main level; •• important; • some bargaining done at this level.

Source: Adapted from Avdagic and Crouch (2006: 209).

to have its views taken into account. Often, indeed, it will be institutionally involved in neo-corporatist economic and social management.

Once again, geography is not as good an indicator as history. True, Scandinavian unions (dense and concentrated) are powerful, but there is no typically 'Southern European' case. For instance, Italian unions might be fragmented but, even discounting for the large number of retired employees they continue to represent, they have far more members than unions in, say, France or Spain, where the importance of employee-elected works councils entering into binding deals with firms means that there is little incentive for workers thus represented (and bound) to join a union. And, just as they were in the run-up to qualification for the single currency in the 1990s, Italian unions can be persuaded (at least, by centre-left governments) to dampen their demands for the supposedly 'greater good' of the country – something that is supposed to happen only in more corporatist countries.

Elsewhere in southern Europe, Cyprus and Malta have density levels approaching those of Scandinavia, and Greece 'beats' Germany, the UK and the Netherlands, where density levels match those of Portugal. Density varies considerably in CEE, too: Slovenia and Slovakia (at around 40 per cent) are comparable with Ireland, while Hungary has only half as many unionized employees, and Lithuania, Latvia and Poland (see Box 8.6) even fewer. In the Czech Republic, workers disaffected with the communist regime infiltrated rather than (as in Poland) opposed the official trade unions, thereby enabling them, once democracy arrived, to benefit from their assets and organization (see Waller and Myant, 1994): this may explain why their density is on a par with that of the UK. Yet clearly, unions are not perceived as worthwhile by most postcommunist workers, particularly younger people and those who work in the private sector. They were tainted by association with the 'official trade unions' of the Communist era and possibly suffered from what some see as a more general retreat into private life once 'people power' brought that era to an end (see Greskovits, 1998). Moreover, they faced these difficulties at a time (the early 1990s) when the region's economic difficulties, along with the widely-perceived need to cede power to markets to facilitate a transition to capitalism, virtually guaranteed that the unions would not effectively protect or promote their members' short-term interests. Whether the difference in attitudes towards, and membership and powers of, trade unions in western and East Central Europe can be explained by some kind of uniform 'legacy effect' (see Crowley, 2004) is, however, debateable given the differences between countries (such as the Czech Republic and Poland) in the latter region (see Avdagic, 2005).

We should be careful, however, not to equate low union density and high fragmentation with powerlessness on the part of workers. Just like their (rather

Table 8.4 Unions in Europe

	Concentrated structure (%)	Loose structure (%)	Highly fragmented structure (%)
High membership density	Sweden (78)		
Medium membership density	Czech Rep. (27) Germany (23)	UK (29) Netherlands (22)	Italy (34)
Low membership density		Poland (15)	France (8) Spain (16)

Source: Data from Visser (2006).

more numerous but equally divided) Italian counterparts, France's trade unions have on several occasions since the mid-1980s (most famously in 1995), employed direct action (strategic strikes and demonstrations) to derail plans by centre-right governments to make what they argued were much-needed labour market and pension reforms. And notwithstanding this kind of action (and the widespread belief that it is the only way to make France's supposedly aloof and elitist state listen), French unions are by no means absent from the dense undergrowth of advisory councils attached to all levels of the country's government. Some even accuse them of being powerful enough to be responsible, like their counterparts in other continental European countries like Spain and Germany, for the difficulties experienced by young people in getting a job, or at least a permanent contract, from employers who find it practically impossible to fire or lay-off older workers who are protected either by unions directly or by the labour market regulations to which they have obliged governments to adhere.

Conversely, we should remember that much of the power of the dense and concentrated (in the jargon 'encompassing') trade union movements is perhaps more contingent than we think. True, their power is to some extent institutionalized through government consultation and (as in Sweden and Germany) membership of agencies and para-public bodies that help make and deliver welfare and labour market policies (see Chapter 3). But it also relies on their close relationship with social democratic parties. If the latter either lose office or, in office, are pushed by economic difficulties into taking 'tough decisions', then their trade unions allies might not appear quite so strong after all – especially if they simultaneously face rising unemployment. True, British trade unions were never able to embed corporatism in the same way as some of their continental and Scandinavian counterparts; but their swift marginalization in the 1980s, after two decades or more of influence ('beer and sandwiches at Number Ten', etc.) is a case in point.

Looking outside the UK, however, it seems clear that corporatism – or at least government-facilitated 'concertation' between employer organizations and trade unions – has not gone away. If anything it has made a comeback recently – sometimes in the most unlikely places (supposedly liberal and pluralist Ireland being the most obvious example). Partly, this has been a response to exceptional circumstances. In the Netherlands, whose so-called 'polder model' (named after co-operative efforts needed to create and maintain land reclaimed from the sea) in some ways pioneered this new style of corporatism, co-operation between government, workers and employers came about in the 1980s in order to deal with fast-rising unemployment. In the 1990s, elsewhere in Europe, co-operation originated in the economic stability (and in some cases belt-tightening) that was required to ensure qualification for the single currency (see Chapters 1 and 9). Moreover, this new kind of corporatism is not necessarily (as, in fact, it is in Ireland) at a highly institutionalized national or 'macro' level. Instead, it seems to be occurring at a more flexible, loosely-coupled, sectoral or 'meso' level, with success depending rather more than

BOX 8.6

Poland's trade union movement – defeat from the jaws of victory

Poland's overthrow of Communist dictatorship was a triumph for the independent trade union, Solidarity (*Solidarność*), to whom some 60 per cent of Polish workers had belonged in the early 1980s and whose leader, Lech Wałesa, went on to be elected President of the newly created democratic republic. But any euphoria was short-lived. In contrast to its willingness to stand up to the old regime, Solidarity – legal, once again – became an avid political sponsor of governments whose 'shock therapy' liberalization of the economy disadvantaged (at least, in the short term) many ordinary people. As a consequence, it never recovered its prestige – or, indeed, its membership. Taking into account the membership of Solidarity's rival, the OPZZ, which has close affiliations with the social democrats, and a few much smaller unions, only 15 per cent at most of eligible Poles are union members; only in France is membership lower. As for those who do join, they tend to be older, poorer and much less likely to be employed in the go-ahead sectors of the economy that attract foreign capital, and whose owners seem determined to keep unions out. Such low density and fragmentation explains why most observers (not altogether fairly, see Iankova, 2002) see Poland's 'Tripartite Commission on Socio-economic Issues' not as an indicator of incipient corporatism, but as a toothless 'talking shop' whose union delegates cannot possibly hope to deliver the co-operation of the Polish workforce – even if government and business organizations were of a mind to seek it. Perhaps it is not surprising, then, that a Eurobarometer survey in 2006, suggested that only 27 per cent of Poles trusted trade unions.

used to be the case on there being a social democratic presence in the government (see Baccaro, 2003, Blom Hansen, 2001, Compston, 1998; and Molina and Rhodes, 2002).

This kind of 'post-corporatist concertation' (O'Donnell, 2001), then, is more than a matter of cultural tradition: it is an instrumental and slightly more (party) political affair (see Hamann and Kelly, 2007). Rather than creating obstacles to the growth that hopefully gets parties re-elected, government-enabled pacts between 'the social partners' have the potential to ensure that wage inflation does not undermine it. Getting unions on board also makes it easier for economies to promote active labour market strategies that enhance a country's human capital and workers' flexibility – both key factors in competitiveness and productivity. Unions are also the key in many countries to governments pushing through pension reforms (see Anderson, 2001 and Baccaro, 2002) although, again, this is more likely to happen under centre-left governments (with whom the unions are more willing to work) than centre-right governments (whom they trust even less). Agreement between the social partners also helps to 'proof' policies against attempts to undo them by governments that might be composed of their opponents.

That said, as the examples of Sweden and especially Italy (see Vatta, 2001) suggest, the support of the social partners, particularly the employers, is far more contingent than in the so-called 'golden age' of corporatism in the first three decades after the Second World War. We should also sound a note of caution about CEE. There, early moves towards setting up corporatist-style consultation between government, business and workers – the Polish 'Tripartite Commission on Socio-economic Issues' is a good example – produced (with the possible exceptions of Hungary and especially the Czech Republic; see Avdagic, 2005; Greskovits, 1998: 155–76; and Myant *et al.*, 2000) what have been labelled little more than time-wasting talking-shops (see Ost, 2000; see also Mailand and Due, 2004). Certainly, there seems to be little sign that any of the region's states will be emulating their western counterparts by experimenting with 'concertation' (see Bruszt, 2002: 135), although this could change when they, too, need to ensure economic stability in order to qualify for the euro. Even in western Europe, there is some doubt whether the attempt to blend supposedly 'neo-liberal' and 'corporatist' approaches to governing the economy really will allow some countries 'to continue having their cake and eating it too' (Boucher and Collins, 2003; see also Teague and

Donaghey, 2003). But the fact that it is taking place at all strengthens the argument against the idea (discussed at greater length in Chapter 9) that Europe will and must eventually move in an 'Anglo-Saxon' or American direction. On the other hand, some would argue that the relative weakness of trade unions in CEE – especially now that so many of the countries of the region are in the EU – might encourage more labour flexibility through, as it were, the 'backdoor' (see Crowley, 2004).

Taking care of business

The power of farmers or unions in Europe, then, cannot be directly 'read off' from the quality or the extent or the coherence of its organization. And the same goes for the power of business. Take, for instance, the Spanish Employers' Association, the CEOE (*Confederación Española de Organizaciones Empresoriales*). The federation represents an impressive nine out of ten Spanish employers across a range of sectors. Yet in the democratic era, and facing an ostensibly fragmented union movement with few members, it has been unable to stave off labour market regulation which, while light compared to more corporatist countries, looks heavy compared to the regime in, say, Poland. There, in common with most CEE countries, civil society, at least as measured by associative activity, can hardly be described as burgeoning (see Howard, 2003). This is partly because many of those who might have taken an active leadership role were attracted instead by parliamentary politics. It is also because those who took over the old state enterprises stuck with the personal and clientelistic *nomenklatura* (communist bureaucratic elite) networks they already knew. The fact that many new businesses were run by self-employed people or were very small also militated against associative activity (see Padgett, 2000). So, too (and this applies to pressure groups in general), did the desire of postcommunist governments of all stripes to avoid the creation of groups that could exercise countervailing power at a time when they were already concerned about their states' capacities to implement transitional reforms – concerns that probably led international organizations and, indeed, the EU, to do little or nothing to prod them into filling this 'institutional void' (see Bruszt, 2002). Over time, however, business associations are showing signs of institutionalizing and potentially becoming more influential, though often (and perhaps unfortunately) more through reputational and informal contacts than as-of-right formal processes (McMenamin, 2002). In the meantime, it must be said that Polish employers, relatively unencumbered as they are by government regulation, hardly seem to have been handicapped by the absence of powerful organized pressure groups fighting on their behalf.

Conversely, the vast majority of France's employers, accounting for some 800,000 firms, are represented by MEDEF (*Mouvement des Entreprises de France*), which, especially under the leadership of the combative Ernest-Antoine Seillière between 1997 and 2005, has called for economic liberalization. It has not been entirely unsuccessful, but its influence has, first, been greater under conservative governments and, second, has not proved sufficient to budge them when they dig in their heels. For instance, France's centre-left government, elected in 1997, controversially introduced a maximum 35-hour week in order to 'share out jobs'. MEDEF managed to bring 30,000 businessmen out onto the streets to protest, albeit in vain, in 1999, but pressure on centre-right politicians seems to have done the trick (see Chapter 9). Yet the 'failure' of successive French governments – at least, before President Sarkozy – to make it easier for bosses to hire and fire and to grasp the nettle on pensions and health costs belies MEDEF's claims to have put *l'entrepreneur au cœur de la société française* (the entrepreneur at the heart of French society). Similarly in Italy, the employers' organization, *Confindustria,* after a period of drift in the 1960s and 1970s (when individual firms such as Fiat exercised far more influence over policy than *Confindustria* ever could) has emerged as a dynamic advocate for liberal reforms. Indeed, much was made of its partisan support for Silvio Berlusconi's *Forza Italia* party at the general election of 2001, particularly by Berlusconi himself. Yet the resulting centre-right government failed to deliver the pension reforms, tax cuts and labour market deregulation that the pressure group had demanded.

To some on the right of the political spectrum, the failure of business in some European countries to get government to deliver on its neo-liberal agenda is illustrative of the vestigial but nonetheless damaging influence of quasi-corporatist or statist arrangements. On the other hand, the fact that 'capital' in European countries cannot always get what it wants can be seen in positive terms. Perhaps it reflects the vitality and value of pluralism in the face of criticisms from so-called 'neo-pluralists' (see Lindblom, 1977) that business is inevitably at a huge advantage, given the structural dependence of politicians on it to provide the economic growth that is normally vital to their re-election (see also Bernhagen, 2007 and Przeworski and Wallerstein, 1988). Of course, the fact that so many groups (unions being only the most obvious example) have a vested interest in a status quo that some regard as ultimately self-defeating can also be taken to illustrate the tendency of pluralism towards 'hyperpluralism' or 'overload' – a situation in which the sheer weight of groups forces governments to take on more than they can handle and makes them unable to tackle serious problems (King 1975; see also Olson, 1982). This is precisely the interpretation that lent momentum to the 'new public management' (NPM) discussed in Chapter 3.

Rebels with a cause? NGOs and (new) social movements

Away from these arguments, however, there was traditionally a consensus that the prominence of business and unions, however qualified, proved that 'sectional' pressure groups which defend and promote the collective material interests of their members were likely to exert more influence in society than those that tried to do the same for so-called 'diffuse interests' (such as those of consumers) or for causes (such as 'the environment', 'peace' or 'developing countries'). This consensus was based on a theoretically persuasive explanation from what is labelled the *rational choice* school of political science (Box 8.7).

Sectional groups, the argument goes, tend to possess more of what government wants (in terms of resources, information and implementation). And, because they are more likely actually to pick up potential recruits in whichever sector they represent, they make it difficult for governments to appeal 'over their heads'. They recruit so well by offering what political scientists, following economists, call 'selective incentives' – largely material rewards that benefit only that group. Cause and even consumer groups, face a 'collective action problem' in that they have no significant selective incentives to offer a set of potential recruits. Even if material benefits exist, as they might for consumers if, say, price-fixing by a cartel of companies could be brought to a halt, recipients of those benefits are so numerous that any gain would be thinly spread and would be tiny compared to the gains of those doing the fixing – this is the 'asymmetry of interests' we referred to when discussing farmers. Additionally, if peace, an end to world poverty and sustainability are achieved through the efforts of a cause group, then everybody (aside, perhaps, from arms manufacturers and producers of pollutants!) will benefit. The fact that they can't be excluded from those benefits makes it rational for people to 'free-ride' on the efforts of a few activists.

That, of course, is the theory, but the reality – at least, in many European countries – is rather different. Domestic consumers, it has to be said, are still hard to organize, and pressure on prices and cartels tends to come from those businesses disadvantaged by them, rather than from the small consumer associations that do exist in Europe. The pressure also comes (as we shall see below) from the EU. However, the theory does little or nothing to explain why it is that the willingness to join groups – be they pressure groups or any of the other

KEY POINT

While 'rational choice' explanations would lead one to expect people not to participate in groups that give them nothing tangible that they could not otherwise get, this is clearly not the case. Social movements that see often relatively privileged people mobilizing on behalf of entities that cannot protect or promote themselves have been a persistent, and even growing, feature of European politics – although there are considerable regional variations in the willingness to get involved. We should not, however, draw too big a distinction between such movements, and more conventional political actors, nor between the strategies and tactics both employ, especially as movement organizations are often highly professional operations.

BOX 8.7

Rational choice

Rational choice is the name given to the idea, borrowed by political science from economics, that political phenomena can be explained by remembering that all actions are purposive, goal-oriented and 'utility-maximizing' within given constraints (see Elster, 1986 and Hargreaves Heap *et al.*, 1992). This allows the construction of formal models – often using 'game theory' – that enhance the study of politics' claim to be a science rather than a humanities subject, such as history. This has its downsides: in the wrong hands, it is capable of rendering the interesting uninteresting and the intelligible unintelligible; more profoundly, it relies on unrealistic assumptions about human behaviour and motivations, and can often be stronger theoretically than it is empirically (see Green and Shapiro, 1994). But it also has its upsides: in the right hands, it can cut through the detail to provide generalizations; in addition, proving why its hypotheses do not hold (or at least modifying them so that they accord with more realistic assumptions) can be an enormous boost to creative thinking and empirical research (see Dunleavy, 1991 and Friedman, 1996). Work on coalitions (i.e. why are there so many minority governments when a slim majority is surely the most rational option?) is one example (see Chapter 4). Work on those who join and do not join groups is another: Jordan and Maloney (2006), for instance, show that non-joiners are not simply 'free-riders' as rational choice analysis would suggest; instead they are very doubtful about the efficacy of groups (and, for that matter, personal sacrifices); nor do they have the kinds of skills and resources that would lead others to ask them to join or that would make joining (or even knowing about the organizations in question) easy for them.

myriad social and cultural groups that make up civil society – is so different across Europe. As we noted when talking about civil society at the beginning of the chapter, study after study has found that people in Scandinavian countries (and the Netherlands, possibly because of the tradition of church-based activity) are much more willing to join (and join several) groups than are Southern Europeans, particularly those in Greece, Portugal, Spain, Italy (as a whole) and France, where activity is often more family- and friendship-based. Countries such as the UK, Germany, Belgium and Ireland sit somewhere in the middle. Eastern Europeans (see Howard, 2003) are very much in with their Southern counterparts. In other words, while individual characteristics (gender, age, income, education, political interest, etc.) make a difference, it is often easier to make a prediction about how likely someone is to be a joiner by knowing which country or region they are from than by their personal characteristics. Associative activity would seem to be related, then, to the length of time the country in which you live has been a democracy and perhaps even to the extent to which the dictatorship that formerly ruled allowed non-party or state groups to exist.

These regional differences are not the only reason to cast doubt on the rational choice approach. Notwithstanding the variation just mentioned, one of the major developments in Europe in the second half of the twentieth century was the growth of groups associated with what were (and still are) sometimes labelled 'new social movements' (NSMs) (see Kriesi *et al.*, 1995). They are postmaterialist (see Chapters 5 and 6) in that they often focus on issues that, arguably, people struggling to make ends meet do not normally spend much time worrying about, especially if they lack the education that helps prompt or facilitate such thoughts in the first place. The spread of education and the comparative wealth that seem to have freed up so many Europeans (at least in the more prosperous west and north of the continent) to think about such issues have also given them the capacity to voice their concerns and to put their money where their mouths are. They also seem to have fuelled a concern with self-identity and the (emotive) expression of that identity not just in consumption but also in politics (see Goodwin *et al.*,

2001). Simultaneously, the postwar growth of the electronic mass media (see Chapter 7) provided a platform for the increasingly well-funded cause groups and non-governmental organizations (NGOs) to promote their ideals and exert pressure on both business and government.

That is not to say that the task of social movements is an easy one. They have, after all, to balance a number of sometimes competing or even contradictory means and ends: as one observer (Rochon, cited in della Porta and Diani, 2005: 179) notes 'the ideal movement strategy is one that is convincing with respect to political authorities, legitimate with respect to potential supporters, rewarding with respect to those already active in the movement, and novel in the eyes of the mass media. These are not entirely compatible demands.' Indeed, the mainstream media can be particularly hard to please: as we noted in Chapter 7, it craves and rewards the providers of novel and innovative action but, at the same time, is conventionally censorious about anything too 'radical' or 'extreme'.

That said, social movements have clearly been helped by, and might have done something to drive, something we have already discussed; namely, the increased willingness, especially in western Europe, to take political action that was previously seen as unconventional, if not illegitimate. However, we need to be careful about drawing too strong a distinction between both the tactics and the concerns of materialists and postmaterialists. When it comes to the tactics, groups of both types often use similar techniques (see Box 8.8). When it comes to concerns, solidarity with (for example) the oppressed and exploited peoples of the developing world can be accompanied by anxiety and anger about the supposed impact of globalization on the domestic front. This fusion, after all, is partly what the global justice movement is all about, bringing together a diverse coalition or network of groups under the banner of opposition to what it insists is neoliberal globalization – an agenda apparently pursued by transnational corporations, international organizations (the IMF, the World Bank being the chief culprits) and supposedly spinelessly compliant governments (see della Porta and Diani, 2005; see also Diani and McAdam, 2003).

When dealing with social movements, we also need – once again – to stress (see della Porta and Diani, 2005: 210–18) that many, even most of them, inhabit the same universe and often overlap with more conventional interest groups (most often trade unions) and political actors (almost inevitably left-wing political parties). The need to transcend this 'normalization' of mass action may go some way to explaining what in recent years seems to have been a ratcheting up of those protests and groups that

BOX 8.8

Different aims, similar tactics – direct action, old and new, in Germany

German 'postmaterialist' anti-nuclear activists pioneered direct action tactics in the 1970s, so there was little that was new about the social movement-style protests that attempted to block the passage of a train carrying nuclear waste from France to a storage site in Gorleben in north-western Germany in November 2001. Thousands of police officers, with dogs and helicopters and hundreds of metres of barbed wire, kept 1,000 protesters from disrupting unloading. Earlier, they had been forced to remove protesters who had chained themselves to railtracks. The shipment and the unloading went ahead, notwithstanding the government's commitment, long-term, to phase out nuclear power.

Just over a year before, in September 2000, Germany (as France, Italy, Spain and the UK) was hit by blockades mounted by lorry drivers, farmers and taxi drivers protesting against what they saw as unreasonably high petrol prices. Even though there were protests across Europe, they were not 'European' in the sense of being co-ordinated or targeted against the EU – in fact, their targets (and, in the end, the solutions they accepted) were domestic (see Imig, 2002: 917–18). In Berlin, more than 7,000 truck drivers brought the city centre to a standstill. This form of direct action had more effect, with the government (like other governments in Europe) announcing tax concessions to fuel users, notwithstanding its commitment to hiking eco-taxes.

COUNTRY PROFILE

Poland (Polska)

History: Poland was for centuries one of Europe's most disputed territories, its borders shifting time and time again as it fell victim to German and Russian imperial ambitions. For a time in the seventeenth century, it was one of the continent's largest states. Yet between the end of the eighteenth century and the end of the First World War, Poland officially ceased to exist. It regained its independence in 1918 but democracy, always fragile and fractured by inordinately large numbers of parties, collapsed in 1926 when war-hero Marshal Pilsudski began a dictatorship that endured until 1935. Within four years, Poland had once again ceased to exist, initially carved up between Nazi Germany and Soviet Russia, and then occupied solely by the former after it invaded the latter in 1941, two years into the Second World War.

During the war, Poland lost around 6 million nationals or about one fifth of its population, with half the victims Jews who perished in the Holocaust. Most, of course, were killed by the Germans. But the Russians, too, were brutal, massacring and secretly burying tens of thousands of Poland's military and civil elite at Katyn and other sites. And by failing to come to the aid of the Warsaw uprising in 1944, the Russians effectively allowed the Germans to kill hundreds of thousands of the city's population.

In the elections that followed the end of the war, the Russian-backed Communists took power and immediately began the process of dismantling democracy (see p. 259). Winning the hearts and minds of the people, however, proved far harder: both anti-Russian feeling and the Roman Catholic church remained strong. In 1978, Polish cardinal Karol Wojtyła was chosen as Pope Jean Paul II. His visit to Poland a year later, combined with industrial unrest in the country's important shipbuilding industry, saw the birth of the *Solidarność* (Solidarity) trade union, led by Lech Wałesa. Faced with the threat of a Russian invasion, the Communist authorities banned the union and imposed martial law in 1981. When, however, it became apparent some eight years later that the threat from the east no longer existed, the authorities began the round table process that led to the end of the Communist regime and the election of Wałesa as president. Since then, Poland has been governed by coalitions led either by a fragmented centre-right or by the former communists now standing as social democrats, although the former bloc seems to have concentrated itself into two large parties (one more liberal and one more nationalist than the other) while the latter has still to recover from a catastrophic election defeat in 2005.

Area: 304,500 km^2 (7.3% of EU-27)

Population: 38.2 million (7.7% of EU-27)

Religious heritage: Roman Catholic

GDP (2006): €271 billion (2.3% of EU-27)

GDP *per capita* as percentage of EU-27 average: 53

Female representation in parliament and cabinet (end 2007): 26% and 25%

Joined EU: 2004

Top 3 cities: Warsaw – capital city (1.7 million), Łódź (0.8 million), Kraków (0.8 million).

Economy and society: Initially touted as a shining example of 'shock therapy' (deregulation, currency reform and price liberalization), Poland's economy has recently given cause for concern: growth is back, but unemployment and state finances remain chronic problems. Poland's population has a GDP *per capita* that is only around half the EU average. Although the importance of heavy industries such as coal and steel is declining as services begin to grow, the number of Poles working in what is a fragmented and inefficient agricultural sector is unusually high: whether it will drop with EU membership and any improved economic growth that follows will be interesting to watch. The Poles also stand out on account of the

WHAT'S IN AN ANTHEM?

Mazurek Dąbrowskiego, which was penned at the end of the eighteenth century, was officially adapted as the country's anthem in the late 1920s. Perhaps predictably, given that it was written as a call to resist one of the numerous foreign occupations that Poles have had to endure over the years, it begins with the stirring first line 'Poland has not yet perished'. 'Sword in hand', it claims, we will seize back what the foreign foe has taken and save our country, taking (possibly a little naively in hindsight) Napoleon Bonaparte as an inspiration. Fortunately, perhaps, especially in view of recent diplomatic spats, the verses that mention resisting Germans and Russians with sabres and scythes are not part of the official version.

strength of their religious faith: Roman Catholic churches are well attended and remain an important influence on education, the media, and social mores and policy.

Governance: After flirting with the idea of a powerful president, Poland came down on the side of parliamentary democracy in its 1997 constitution, although even now the president (like the Senate in the country's bicameral legislature) has a veto over legislation. The veto can be overridden if the lower house (the *Sejm*) can muster a three-fifths majority – not always simple given that the country's proportional electoral system helps an unusually large number of personalized and antagonistic parties into parliament. The ability to build and sustain coalitions is therefore a key competence of the head of government, the prime minister, who is formally appointed by the president with the approval of the *Sejm*. There is a constitutional court, but only recently, with its striking down of the government's lustration (or vetting law) in May 2007, can it be said to have made a major intervention in Polish politics. As for pressure groups, neither the trade unions (including the once-popular *Solidarność*), nor business associations are particularly powerful. Government in the country's sixteen regions (*województwo*), however, is becoming more significant.

Foreign policy: The Poles have succeeded in achieving their two main priorities – protecting themselves from Russia and locking themselves into the European economy – by joining NATO (in 1999) and the EU (in 2004). Cordial relations with Germany were accorded a particularly high priority by both countries but (hopefully temporarily) came under severe strain while a strongly nationalist government held power between 2005 and 2007. That government also presided over a further deterioration of relations with Russia – a situation that any new government is going to find difficult to improve, even presuming it wants to. Relations with the US, however, are generally very good: nearly 9 million Americans have Polish ancestry and many Poles remain grateful for the role the US played in defeating Communism in Eastern Europe; the country contributed forces to US-led missions in Afghanistan and Iraq. The new government elected in 2007 may rethink these commitments, but it is unlikely to withdraw its offer to site intercept weapons as part of the US's proposed missile defence system.

A KEY CONTEMPORARY CHALLENGE
COMING TO TERMS WITH COMMUNIST COLLABORATION

The 'Law and Justice' party that governed Poland between 2005 and 2007 promised voters that it would dedicate itself to root out not just contemporary corruption but also those who had collaborated with the former communist regime. The watchword would be 'lustration' – shining a light into the dark corners of the past and ensuring that anybody with a less than spotless record, or at least the honesty to finally come clean, would be denied employment by the state. Under a new law, the Institute for National Remembrance would vet declarations that an estimated 700,000 Poles (civil servants, teachers, politicians, managers and board members of publicly listed companies, and journalists) would be obliged – on pain of being barred from their job for up to ten years – to file.

The new era, however, began awkwardly when it was revealed right at the start of 2007 that the man just about to take up the post as Archbishop of Warsaw had, despite his initial denials, collaborated with the Communist secret police. Things then went from bad to worse in May of the same year when the Polish Constitutional Tribunal struck down the new law, provoking accusations from the government that its members were ideologically motivated. Before the government could put together a more measured response, however, it fell apart and eventually lost a snap election called in the autumn. The new administration will have to balance its desire to get on with the future against accusations that, by not pursuing lustration (or indeed corruption), with quite as much vigour, it is sheltering people with something to hide.

Contemporary challenges

- Mending fences with European partners, especially Germany, in the wake of an idiosyncratic and nationalistic government that fell in late 2007
- Continuing rationalization of the economy, moving out of low-value heavy industry and agriculture
- Tackling the region's most persistent unemployment problem and reversing the 'brain-drain' of young Poles to western Europe
- Coming to terms with communist collaboration in the past without paralyzing the country in the future (see box above)
- Refusing to be bullied by Russia without causing a complete breakdown in relations or being seen as a US government stooge.

Learning resources Start with Lukowski and Zawadzki (2006), *A Concise History of Poland*. Then go on to Sanford (2002), *Democratic Government in Poland*, Szczerbiak (2002), *Poles Together?* and (2009), *Poland within the EU*. Keep up with the news at http://www.masterpage.com.pl/outlook/.

attract young people in particular. Certainly, some kind of rioting seems to have become par for the course at meetings of the G8 industrialized countries and, since 2001 when it met in Gothenburg, Sweden, the EU's European Council. On the other hand, it is easy to forget that European protest activity has often sparked violence in the past: the scenes in Gothenburg and in Genoa were as nothing, for instance, to the demonstrations in Paris in 1968. It is also easy to dismiss violence as ultimately counterproductive: a recent study of Germany (see Rucht, 2003) suggests it has to be seen, along with other unconventional 'social movement' tactics, as helping to provoke change and an increased sensitivity among conventional politicians towards the concerns of the less conventional. In other words, we might not like it but (in central and eastern Europe as well as in western Europe) it may be wrong to draw too hard and fast a distinction between civil society and what has been termed 'uncivil society': they are part of a continuum (see Kopecký and Mudde, 2002). On the other hand, it would be wrong to suggest that violence predominates in the 'anti-globalization' movement, which is not only extremely diverse but something that social and political scientists are only just beginning to get to grips with (see Poitras, 2003).

Just as it would be wrong to tar all 'internationalist' activism with the same brush, it would be wrong to fall too easily into the idea that it is detached from 'real' problems at home which might benefit from all the energy 'wasted' on its rather diffuse targets. Sidney Tarrow, one of the world's foremost experts on 'contentious politics' makes a very persuasive case in his recent work that 'transnational' activists often embody (as well as help forge) the link between the local and the global: the most effective – those, in other words, who get things done as well as protest – are '"rooted cosmopolitans" – people who grow up in and remain closely linked to domestic networks and opportunities' (Tarrow, 2005: xiii). He also reminds us that we need to be careful not to categorize all protest activity, especially among 'young people' as 'a reflex against globalization' that, given both the vague nature of the latter and the absence of a genuinely transnational government, is unlikely to achieve much: a great deal of protest activity is still targeted, just as it was in the 1950s, 1960s and the decades that followed, against an institution that continues to count; namely, the state.

Despite its darker side, then, all this might give heart to those who believe that democracy is ultimately about 'the people' triumphing, or at least controlling 'the interests'. But digging a little deeper suggests that this view might be a little naive. This is because it fails to come to terms with the fact that groups like Greenpeace, Friends of the Earth, the Worldwide Fund for Nature or even Amnesty International, which are active in virtually every European country, and even some of the larger domestic cause groups, have so institutionalized their operations that they are not by any stretch of the imagination 'bottom-up' or even democratic organizations. Rather, they are professional movement organizations (McCarthy and Zald, 1977) or even 'protest businesses' (see Jordan and Maloney, 1997) or 'transnational social movement organizations' (TSMOs) (see della Porta and Diani, 2005: 146–7). Even groups that do not qualify as such now tend to join European or, very often in fact, worldwide federations in order to boost their presence – and, hopefully, their clout. For example (see Table 8.5), Birdlife International, a worldwide partnership of groups dedicated to the promotion and protection of birds and their habitats, provides a home for small groups that are little more than promoters of an interest in birds and birdwatching (such as the Swedish society), as well as groups which are quasi-commercial concerns (such as the Royal Society for the Protection of Birds (RSPB) in the UK). Even accounting for population differences, the latter has fifteen times as many members, as well as a much bigger profile and a larger role in actually managing projects in lieu of government – an 'insider' role, incidentally, which, critics suggest, prevents it from taking an effective (or, at least, publicly aggressive) stand against detrimental environmental practices

Much of the activity of traditionally 'outsider' transnational protest businesses such as Greenpeace is capital-intensive (as opposed to labour-intensive) and media-intensive. So, while membership is important for providing them with legitimacy, it is most important for providing them with the finance to carry on their occasionally stunningly successful campaigns (see Bennie, 1998). Most people who do join them do so for short periods and without

Table 8.5 Bird protection societies

Country	Society	Members	Staff
Czech Rep.	*Česká spolecnost ornitologická* (ČSO)	2,100	7
France	*Ligue Pour La Protection des Oiseaux (LPO)*	35,000	127
Germany	*Naturschutzbund Deutschland (NABU)*	405,000	90
Italy	*Lego Italiana Protezione Uccelli (LIPU)*	42,000	95
Netherlands	*Vogelbescherming Nederland (VBN)*	125,000	153
Poland	*Ogólnopolskie Towarzystwo Ochrony Ptaków (OTOP)*	2,000	12
Spain	*Sociedad Española de Ornitologfa (SEO)*	8,000	50
Sweden	*Sveriges Ornitologiska Förening (SOF)*	11,000	24
UK	*Royal Society for the Protection of Birds (RSPB)*	1,049,000	1,440

Source: Data from Birdlife International (2007).

expecting or desiring to participate actively beyond perhaps signing a petition, possibly joining a march and – most importantly to the group concerned – giving the account details or credit card number that constitutes their donation to the cause. Some of this activity is counted by some political scientists as 'participation', but whether all such activities, simply because they go beyond turning up to vote every so often, really deserve to be included under the umbrella term of 'collective', let alone 'unconventional', action is a moot point. It is easy to overstate popular involvement in groups and other forms of pressure politics. When it comes to politics (and, indeed, the non-political group activity that some political scientists believe may facilitate involvement in politics; see Bowler *et al.*, 2003), 'low-intensity participation' is certainly the keynote for most Europeans at the beginning of the twenty-first century.

The fact that groups campaigning for supposedly postmaterialist causes, such as human rights and the environment, do not necessarily have more spontaneous or 'flatter' structures than traditional sectional or interest groups does not, of course, mean that they play exactly the same role. Some of the functions of a campaigning environmental group outlined by a director of such a group (Box 8.9) would presumably not sit well with an 'insider' interest intent on maintaining the convenient insulation of its 'policy community'. 'Outsider' groups, of course, have to weigh up whether some of these functions are worth trading off in return for being kept in the loop by government. Conversely, they have to consider whether incorporation may also mean neutralization. It would appear, however, that just as more

BOX 8.9

Functions of a campaigning group

Broker: carrying information between parties and actors

Demonstrator: demonstrating new responses and solutions

Educator: education of specialists, concerned parties and the public

Ferret: digging for information and conducting investigations

Innovator: developing new responses, solutions and policies

Orchestrator: engineering and manipulating events

Scout: scanning for future problems

Watchdog: monitoring legal processes and agreements

Whistle blower: alerting the public, the government and other groups.

Source: Burke, cited in Rawcliffe (1998: 20–1).

traditional, sectional interest groups simultaneously (and not just as a fall-back option) pursue 'indirect strategies', such as media campaigns, as well as 'insider access'. By the same token, so-called 'outsiders' ('cause groups' and the like) pursue more traditional forms of direct contact with the government, the bureaucracy and with legislators at the same time as acting in the media and on the streets – not just because the latter strategy can pay off in terms of influence but because, even if it didn't, they have to compete with other groups for members and public attention and must therefore do everything they can to show they are active (Binderkrantz, 2005; see also Gamson, 2004).

Media presence is, of course, one of the keys to social movement influence, much of which rests on its ability to put new problems and possible solutions on the agenda of public policy makers. This is not, however, the only way that influence occurs or can be measured (see della Porta and Diani, 2005). Even if it is hard, using another traditional measure, to say this or that piece of legislation would not have been passed (or, indeed, properly implemented) without them, we can trace their involvement across a range of government responses that once were novel but are now fairly standard. These include referendums, the setting up of expert commissions, arm's length regulatory and consultative bodies (that

DEBATE 8.1

Are pressure groups good for democracy?

YES

- Despite the criticisms, as long as groups operate in a competitive and transparent environment and governments are strong, savvy (and rich) enough to stand up to them, then they perform valuable functions; members who want them to be more democratic are free to leave or to agitate for better representation; people who don't join groups only have themselves to blame if those who do get what they want.
- Without pressure groups, citizens would, between one election and another, have to rely on politicians and possibly the media to hold the government to account: this would be particularly problematic where parliament and the press are relatively weak.
- Government can neither know nor do everything: groups provide expert, on-the-ground information to policy makers and often ensure effective implementation of the policy they make. The work of groups does not therefore reduce efficiency, it increases it. The interchange of personnel adds to the knowledge and capacity of groups and politicians.
- Participating in groups teaches people about the importance of working together, encourages them to think about and come to workable solutions, and promotes the trust and the networks that hold society together. The alternative would be a 'mass society' of individuals incapable of pursuing the collective good and at risk from a consequently more powerful state.

NO

- Groups only think of their own interests or ideals, which they pursue to the exclusion of the collective good, and often sell easy, quick-fix solutions when real life is more complicated.
- Some groups are more powerful than others: policy should depend on what works or what is right, not on who can mobilize the most money or members.
- Pressure groups and lobbyists may make sophisticated use of the media, but much of their contact with politicians and decision makers is inherently 'off-the-record'. This lack of transparency damages the political process and its reputation.
- The growth of groups has created a multi-million dollar, euro, and pound industry that is essentially parasitic on democracy, wasting resources that would be better ploughed into more productive economic and social activity.
- The world of pressure groups and representative politics is now so closely intertwined that it contributes to the formation of a hermetically sealed 'political class'.
- Pressure groups – even those that sell themselves as the defenders of the environment or the oppressed and disadvantaged – are not themselves very democratic or very socially representative organizations. Those who join them can become even more zealous and unwilling to listen to alternatives.

might well employ former representatives of social movements), and participative fora (citizens' juries, etc.). Social movements could also be involved in information exchange and other activities conducted under the auspices of the EU (see Lahusen, 2004), although some radicals write off such developments as nothing more than window-dressing and/or capture.

'Venue shopping' and the Europeanization of pressure politics

Traditionally, the activity of pressure groups in Europe went on at or below the level of the state. With the increasing importance of the EU, however, the activity of some groups has taken on an additional 'European' dimension. Business interests, for instance, have had to adjust to the fact that the regulatory environment in which they operate – one which may well have a fairly direct impact on their 'bottom line', their investment decisions and their ability or willingness to compete in certain markets – is, depending on the sector, increasingly subject to European rather than simply domestic rules (see Majone, 1996; Young and Wallace, 2000).

Take competition policy, and mergers and acquisitions (M&As). This issue is attracting ever-more attention from a European Commission determined to make a reality of the single or internal market. This clearly poses a threat to both firms and sectors that previously relied upon domestic rules to help maintain what some would argue are restrictive practices and/or cosy cartels – notorious examples would include the airline industry and (often highly subsidized) national carriers, or the automotive industry and its ability to restrict the sales of its products to franchised dealers. Since the Single European Act (SEA), the Commission has made efforts to liberalize such sectors. Trying to limit the damage, the big players in both sectors sought to lobby national governments, but also found it necessary to take their case direct to the Commission. The effect may have been to slow down the reforms, at the very least buying time either to work out an exit strategy or how to compete in the new environment. But liberalization, since it is part of the logic of the EU's single market and is backed up by European law (see Chapter 2), cannot be held off forever.

KEY POINT

The EU provides a forum for groups representing both sectional interests and social movements. The former are better resourced, and have been quicker on the uptake when it comes to lobbying, at the transnational level. But the European policy process is not necessarily rigged in their favour. Again, however, there are considerable national (or, at least, regional) variations in the extent to which groups are willing and able to operate at this level.

In any case, other groups that stand to benefit from entering the market or from the lowering of costs – and, indeed, governments who see liberalization as the key to faster growth through a more dynamic economy – will be lobbying in its favour. They might also, as a result of a better 'fit' between their domestic traditions and the EU's way of working, be better lobbyists. The inability in recent years, for instance, of state-owned companies and their government sponsors to prevent an EU-assisted attack on what were, in many mainland European countries, their virtual monopolies, might well be a case in point. Schmidt (1999: 164) notes more generally, the UK's 'larger, more fluid, more fragmented, horizontally integrated policy networks' do better at promoting domestic interests 'in the multi-polar, competitive decision-making structure of the EU' than, for example, what she calls 'France's smaller, tighter, more cohesive, vertical, state dominated networks' or Italy's traditionally 'under-the-table' mode of business influence. Realizing this perhaps, French governments, far from being concerned at being outflanked abroad by groups it can more easily control at home, have, since the beginning of the 1990s, been encouraging France's domestic interest groups to get active and involved at the European level (Szukala, 2003: 230).

Liberalization, however, is not inevitable across all sectors once responsibility for their regulation no longer resides solely with the state and takes on a supranational element. We shall discuss this further in Chapter 9. But, for the moment, one has only to think of the continuing support for agriculture as testimony to the capacity of some groups to maintain their grip even after the national state has lost (or voluntarily surrendered) its own. This is not surprising. Pluralism is no more 'pure' at the European than at the domestic level. Just as national governments are vulnerable to pressure because they rely on groups to provide them with information and help with implementation, so too are European institutions – perhaps even more so. Most obviously, the Commission – for all the talk of 'armies of Brussels bureaucrats' – has very few staff relative to its very large and very varied responsibilities. Even at the policy initiation stage, Directorate Generals (DGs) rely heavily on pressure groups to give them a sense of both what is needed and what is feasible. Given the limited time and resources available, the 'one-stop shops' provided by so-called 'Euro-groups' – groups often composed of the various national federations in a particular sector – are an attractive option. Bringing them on board, or at least getting them on-side, boosts the chances of an initiative being taken seriously and, if adopted, actually being implemented.

Implementation and enforcement is something which the Commission has great difficulty in ensuring, given its reliance on the member states. The fuss made (and law suits begun) by businesses and pressure groups (and individuals) whose interests or ideals are adversely affected by non-compliance on the part of member states (see Falkner *et al.*, 2004) are a good example of and a vital part of what have been called the 'horizontal enforcement' mechanisms (Neyer and Wolf, 2003) of the EU – an entity that ultimately depends not simply on rules but on the political willingness of states to follow them. Consulting with groups also provides a way – if not an entirely convincing one – round the so-called 'democratic deficit'. Even if the Commission cannot claim that its policies are subject to the will of the populace, the fact that some of the most well-informed and potentially vocal sections of it have been involved in the process provides them with at least some legitimacy.

So, whether pressure groups are campaigning to stimulate or to stave off change, the EU is now an important part of the political opportunity structure in which they operate. This explains why over a thousand lobby groups have offices in Brussels. In some ways, 'Europe' has obvious potential advantages over the state level for pressure groups. For a start, it affords the possibility of obliging (or at least giving an excuse to) domestic governments to make changes that might otherwise be difficult, either for electoral reasons or because there are plenty of institutions (corporatist structures, strong parliaments, active courts, etc.) that might combine to block reforms. The transnational firms that were active in lobbying the Commission to come up with the SEA (see Chapter 2) were certainly aware that it would be one way of getting governments and states that were reluctant (or, at least, claimed they were reluctant) to deregulate and privatize eventually to do just that once it came into effect in the early 1990s.

Likewise, for some interest groups, in marked contrast to cause groups, success depends in part on their ability to insulate their sector from the cut and thrust of mediatized and party politics. The EU theoretically provides a relatively benign environment where agendas can be set and deals cut in even more privacy than they are used to domestically. Depending on your point of view, what some have termed the 'network' governance of the EU (see Eising and Kohler-Koch, 1999) – multilevel and transnational 'problem-solving' between interested parties – either brings with it a much-needed maturity and flexibility to policy-making or effectively depoliticizes it, putting it even further beyond the reach of democratic control. The chemical and pharmaceutical industries are often cited as examples of sectors that are prepared to swap the supposed limitations imposed by banding together as a 'Euro-group' (the European Chemical Industry Council, or *cefic*, and the European Federation of Pharmaceutical Industries and Associations, or EFPIA, respectively) in return for a fairly cosy relationship with the European institutions whose decisions could impact on their business. Whether this means, of course, that they, or any other interest group with similarly good access, actually get what they want – a charge frequently made not just by anti-globalization protesters but also by cause groups with objections to specific policies – is another matter.

In any case, some would say, cause groups can hardly complain about the 'business-friendly' nature or 'corporate domination' of EU policy-making because many of them, too, have found 'Europe' conducive to pursuing their goals (see Ruzza, 2004). For one thing, getting changes made to EU rules and standards sometimes allows them to 'outflank' governments (and otherwise more powerful rival groups) at the domestic level (see Fairbrass and Jordan, 2001). For another, the EU provides them with considerable subsidies. For instance, it provides environmental groups with information via the European Environmental Agency (EEA) – information that can be used in campaigns, and the legitimacy of which is hard for opponents to question and for which otherwise campaigners would have to pay themselves. The Commission also makes a point of consulting such groups at all stages of the policy-making process as a counterweight to commercial interests. And they, too, can provide it with information (for example, on implementation failures by member states) and nudge it into action. Certainly, the Commission is already aware that environmental policy is one of the few areas where there is majority public support (even in supposedly 'Eurosceptic' countries) for a greater EU role. Moreover, some member states (e.g. in Scandinavia) are concerned lest those that have lower environmental standards (in southern and Central and Eastern Europe), for example, exploit them 'unfairly' to attract more foreign direct investment (FDI). Hence, there has been a perceptible increase since the 1990s in environmental legislation and action plans on matters such as air and water quality, and waste. Again, though, no one should come away with the impression that means, motive and opportunity necessarily add up to overwhelming influence for pressure groups, at least when it comes to environmental policy (see Jordan, 2001): their efforts, after all, are balanced by those on the opposite side (see Box 8.10)

'Europe' also provides pressure groups with other opportunities to influence policy. Given the 'judicialization' of politics referred to in Chapter 3 and the potential power of the ECJ as well as the Court of Human Rights, it is hardly surprising that even supposedly 'counter-cultural' movements, such as those set up to promote gay and lesbian rights, have pursued a legal route to getting what they want. It is important, however, to realize that recourse to the courts often occurs alongside (rather than going on instead of) the strategies more commonly associated with NSM pressure groups, such as media campaigns or some kind of direct action – or, of course, more discrete lobbying. There is no necessary 'zero-sum' game between the various strategies on offer (see Hilson, 2002). Similarly, many of the large firms that are represented by sectoral interest groups and associations are increasingly willing to lobby simultaneously on their own behalf at both domestic and European levels (see Coen, 1998). Indeed, they are encouraged to do so by the Commission if not all the EU institutions (see Table 8.6). Meanwhile (as Table 8.5 suggests) national associations are often members

BOX 8.10

REACH and the Services Directive

December 2006 saw the EU finally pass two pieces of legislation that were so disputed by those for and against that they took literally years to get onto the statute book. REACH (the Registration, Evaluation, Authorisation and Restriction of Chemicals) was fought tooth and nail by a sustained lobby and media campaign by industry bodies and individual firms, which insisted health and safety concerns were exaggerated and the new regime would render them uncompetitive. On the other hand, the eventual compromise they agreed to left some environmental campaigners furious that the EU had watered down what they believed were essential safeguards. The so-called 'Services Directive', which aimed to make the single market a reality for the non-manufacturing sector that (as we saw in Chapter 1) is increasingly the most important sector in contemporary Europe, also roused passions. Thousands of (mainly trade union) demonstrators came out onto the streets in 2005 to protest against what they saw as a neo-liberal threat to their jobs. After various amendments were made, particularly on areas (mainly in the public sector) that could be excluded from the requirement to open up competition, the unions – still quite influential, especially when it comes to centre-left and left-wing parties in the European Parliament (see Chapter 2 and 4) – calmed down and the legislation was passed. Some business representatives, and economists, claimed victory, but some believed that the directive had been essentially neutered, ending up as a codification of existing law rather than a genuinely liberal development.

Table 8.6 Who they like to see most – EU institutions and corporate lobbying

Commission	Council of Ministers	Parliament
(1) Individual large firms	(1) National associations	(1) European associations
(2) European associations	(2) European associations	(2) National associations
(3) National associations	(3) Individual large firms	(3) Individual large firms

Source: Adapted from Bouwen (2002: 383).

of European associations (the so-called 'Eurogroups' referred to above), but this does not stop them lobbying EU institutions directly.

More generally, one would be mistaken to think that pressure groups, whether they represent causes or interests, have to choose between the domestic or the European stage. Many of them pursue their aims at both levels simultaneously. And being well or poorly connected at the level of the state does not mean they tend, in turn, to ignore or stress the EU level (see Beyers, 2002). In short, in an era of multilevel governance, pressure groups and their individual or corporate members – especially if they are well resourced – are happy to be 'promiscuous'. As Richardson (2001) points out, with the possible exception of Germany, 'the EC/EU as a polity presents an American-style plethora of opportunity structures for interest groups, which respond accordingly by "venue shopping"' (see Richardson, 2001: 105–6). In other words, they will work both domestically and transnationally, and tolerate a fair amount of duplication on the grounds that, on balance, it is better to risk wasting one's time and money (especially when it constitutes a tiny fraction of an annual turnover that may run into millions of euros) than miss a potential opportunity.

By the same token, it is clear from some very impressive recent research (Beyers, 2004) that, as at the 'domestic' level, pressure groups operating at the European level do not (at least nowadays) need to choose between 'voice' and 'access', between more public 'outsider' strategies and more private 'insider' routes to influence – a finding that holds good not just for 'interest' groups like business sector associations and trade unions, but also for more 'diffuse' and 'cause' groups, such as consumer groups and environmental and other NGOs. That said, the same research does suggest that groups tend to vary their strategies according to which EU institution they are trying to influence: interest groups getting access to the relatively technocratic DGs of the European Commission tend to tone down public pressure. Interestingly, though, it also suggests that groups representing causes and diffuse (as opposed to sectional) interests do not find that their very public activities put off Commission officials from dealing with them. Given this, and given the Commission and the rest of the EU is concerned to counter accusations of a lack of transparency and a democratic deficit, there is no reason to expect that the process by which pressure groups seek influence will become as depoliticized as some who are sceptical or worried about European integration's impact on democracy suggest.

Groups are also, of course, involved in lobbying the most obviously politicized of all the EU institutions – namely, the EP – not least because it has gained more legislative power and can therefore help or hurt them more than ever before (see Earnshaw and Judge, 2002 for a useful summary of this activity and an interesting case study involving tobacco). It certainly appears that groups will try the more political, lobbying route first before they resort to (more expensive!) litigation at, say, the 'non-political' European Court of Justice (see Bouwen and McCown, 2007). But even when it comes to the influence process that characterizes the supposedly 'de-politicized' and technocratic realm of the Commission, recent research reveals, first, that 'the policy networks [involved] reflect a basic cleavage between a progrowth and a prosustainability coalition' and, second, that 'the granting of access by public officials is not predominantly a matter of functional resources' like expertise and information.

These things are not unimportant but access is also based on 'the perceived capability of interests to mobilize public support or to deal with issues on which the public may be easily mobilized', all of which means that policy networks 'are not reducible to functional information exchange processes' but remain 'channels through which principled political debates are triggered and public concerns are represented' (Beyers and Kerremans, 2004: 1147).

Given the activity of business interest groups at the European as well as at the state level, it may be hard to understand why some critics, especially in the UK, accuse the EU of introducing what former British Prime Minister Margaret Thatcher termed 'socialism by the back door'. What they really object to, however, is what they see as the institutionalization of corporatism in the EU system, symbolized by the so-called 'Social Chapter' of the Maastricht Treaty. Under the procedure it lays out, it is possible for legislation affecting the labour market – for example, the equal treatment of part-time workers or rules governing maximum working hours – to be agreed on by the so-called 'social partners' and then be simply rubber-stamped by the EU's normal legislative bodies, the Council and the EP. To (mainly British) critics of limitations on business, this is 'Europe' handing back unwarranted power to the trade unions just as they have been finally 'conquered' at home.

Many politicians in countries without a strong tradition of social partnership might have some sympathy. Governments in CEE, for instance, will be hoping that accession to the EU does not provide the region's fragmented unions (or, indeed, its similarly poorly organized, if not utterly uninfluential, business groups) an opportunity to make up for their domestic weakness, although there is some evidence that interest groups are beginning to take advantage of their enhanced ability to network with and learn from their 'western' counterparts (see Pérez-Solórzano Borragán, 2006). Some observers, however, would point out that because the EU's policy-making process is so dependent on interest groups, such an attitude is naive: as a member state, better to risk having groups that can constrain you at the domestic level if it means they are also capable of exerting some influence on the country's behalf in Brussels (see Bruszt, 2002). In any case, there are politicians, even right-wing politicians, from more long-standing member states where 'concertation' between the government and economic interest groups is par for the course, and who therefore have few qualms about, at least, a limited reproduction of the process at the European level. In fact, social partner agreements are not that common, nor are they exactly rushed into. Indeed, the ETUC (the trade union federation), and particularly UNICE and CEEP (the private and public sector employers) are often persuaded to take such a route only in order to stave off what might be even less welcome legislation made in the normal way (see Falkner, 2000b). UNICE in particular should not be caricatured as a corporatist soft-touch, even if it is willing to engage with the other social partners on concepts like 'flexicurity' (combining, in Scandinavian style, liberal and active labour market policies with top-drawer social security). Renamed *BusinessEurope* in 2007, its president, after all, is Ernest-Antoine Seillière, who was, as we have already mentioned, a doughty campaigner for liberalization when he was head of the French employers' association.

That said, institutions such as the Social Chapter, and the embedded respect for trade unions it seems to symbolize, help in part to explain why the latter have reconciled themselves to Europe (see Visser, 1998) – even in the UK, where Euroscepticism was and is unusually strong (Strange, 2002). In short, the EU has provided trade unions with a way of putting the brakes on, and even reversing labour market deregulation and 'anti-trade union legislation' at the domestic level.

When it comes to social movements, however, the evidence for Europeanization is, so far, quite limited, although this could be a case of academic research catching up with the reality on the ground (see della Porta and Caiani, 2007). At the moment, it seems as if the existence of European federations to which national groups belong (environmental groups are a good example) can give a misleading impression of the extent to which they actually co-operate and/or work at the European level (see Rootes, 2004). This is partly a matter of resources. Even the larger environmental organizations, for instance, are nowhere near as well staffed as some of their corporate counterparts: for instance, Birdlife International has only three permanent staff in Brussels and fewer than ten at its European headquarters in the Netherlands.

Campaigning organizations out of the mainstream, who may object, even violently, to some of what is done in their name (and in the name of the EU), are even less able to afford to 'venue shop'.

But this is also about focus. For instance, notwithstanding the increased competence of the Union in environmental policy, one of the most recent studies of environmental protest in western Europe stresses 'the extent to which both issues and forms of protests reflected the distinctive concerns and idiosyncratic dynamics of politics within each of the several states' it looked at (Rootes, 2004: 255). Other researchers have also found that most attention and direct action is directed at the domestic level, even when the target might (directly or indirectly) be the EU. And while the headlines surrounding violence at EU summits might suggest a Europeanization of contentious politics, the day-to-day reality for many of groups is less transnational (see Balme *et al.*, 2002 and Imig and Tarrow, 1999, 2001), while many of the protests against the EU are carried out not by NSMs but by occupational interest groups, especially farmers and fishermen (see Imig, 2002), whose livelihoods are, of course, directly affected by its policies. As hinted at above, however, the reality on the ground might be running in advance of the academic research – indeed, some of the latter is beginning to suggest that things are changing and social movements are beginning to act more frequently at a European level and against European targets (see della Porta and Caiani, 2007). Nevertheless, it will undoubtedly take time before most Europeans – if they ever do – stop thinking of home not just as where the heart is but also where power lies. The most pressing problem, many of them argue, is not so much Europeanization but that it no longer makes much difference which set of politicians, left or right, holds that power. This, and the common wisdom that surrounds it, is the focus of the Chapter 9.

Learning Resources for Chapter 8

Further reading

On political participation in Europe, see the collection edited by van Deth *et al.*, (2007), *Citizenship and Involvement in European Democracies*, and on associative activity in Europe, see the collection edited by Maloney and Roßteutscher (2007a), *Social Capital and Associations in European Democracies*. Anyone interested in social movements should begin with della Porta and Diani (2005), *Social Movements*, and Snow *et al.*, (2004), *The Blackwell Companion to Social Movements*. They should then move on to the superb collection edited by della Porta and Tarrow (2005), *Transnational Protest and Global Activism*. Imig and Tarrow (2001), *Contentious Europeans*, and Rootes (2007), *Environmental Protest in Western Europe*, are also very useful, while Tilly (2004), *Social Movements, 1768–2004*, provides plenty of historical (and contemporary) food for thought. On pressure group activity at the European (as well as the domestic) level, see the authoritative and recently updated Greenwood (2007), *Interest Representation in the European Union*, and an invaluable special issue on EU Lobbying of the *Journal of European Public Policy*, 14 (3), 2007, a publication that often has useful articles on this topic. On the apparent revival of corporatism, see the excellent collection edited by Berger and Compston (2002), *Policy Concertation and Social Partnership in Western Europe*. On civil society in Eastern Europe, see Howard (2003), *The Weakness of Civil Society in Post-Communist Europe*. See also the special issue on interest politics in CEE of the journal *Perspectives on European Politics and Society*, 7 (2), 2006.

On the web

www.etuc.org – trade unions in Europe

www.eurochambres.be and **www.businesseurope.eu** – European business groups

ec.europa.eu/civil_society – pressure groups and civil society in Europe

www.sociosite.net/topics/activism.php – social movements

www.palgrave.com

Companion Website

Visit the Companion Website to 'click and go'

www.palgrave.com/politics/bale

Discussion questions

1 Do you think a country needs a healthy civil society and, if so, why? How and why does the level of popular participation in non-party political activity vary across Europe?

2 What role do you think cultural and institutional factors play in how a pressure group goes about trying to gain influence?

3 How can we explain the power of the agricultural lobby in European countries? Do you think it will last?

4 Have trade unions all over Europe lost their influence?

5 Does the power of business in European countries depend simply on its importance to the economy?

6 Do you have any sympathy with, or are you actually involved in, the activities of new social movements? If so, why? If not, why not?

7 Do you think that big NGOs with their roots in new social movements remain true to their ethos, or have they become part of the mainstream and even the establishment?

8 Why has lobbying at the EU level become an integral part of most interest groups' strategies, and why might groups from some countries be more successful at it than others?

9 Do you think Europeanization poses a threat or an opportunity to groups whose aims do not dovetail neatly with liberal capitalism?

Chapter 9

Politics over markets – enduring differences between left and right

Has politics ever really mattered?	272
Drifting to the right? The centre-left in Europe	274
Party positions on the welfare state – words and deeds	275
Privatization	283
Flexible labour markets?	288
The EU – deadweight or driving force?	289
The end of the welfare and regulatory state? Separating the facts from the hype	293
Why it still makes sense to be different	295
No easy explanations – the rise of the far right	299

There are several easy assumptions about the current state of European politics and the European economy that, put together, constitute some sort of common wisdom. Perhaps the most prevalent is that 'left' and 'right' are becoming meaningless concepts as governments and parties from both sides of a political divide that used to be organized around more or less state intervention, spending and taxation are obliged to follow the same policies in order to cope with globalization and (less often mentioned in the media) Europeanization. Centre-left parties, the argument goes, may talk about a 'third way' between old-fashioned **social democracy** and **neo-liberalism**, but this is supposedly little more than a fig-leaf to cover their retreat from the former and their embrace of the latter, even in those states (France and Germany are often cited) where the tradition of government intervention is strong. All mainstream politicians nowadays, the common wisdom continues, know that 'Anglo-Saxon' or 'American-style' capitalism (with its labour market flexibility, private ownership and a limited, low-spending role for the state) is the way of the future, anything else being seen as recipe for continued low growth, high unemployment, uncompetitiveness and international decline. Most of the EU's newest members will, it predicts, reinforce this trend. Accordingly, the EU, once it overcomes its vestigial support for economic interference, will – via the discipline imposed by its new single currency – help ensure the triumph of more or less global neo-liberalism and the collapse of any serious social (or even Christian) democratic alternative to the essentially laissez-faire policies that conservative and market liberal parties have always argued for. Purveyors of the common wisdom also suggest that the absence of such an alternative is leading either to political apathy, reflected in ever-decreasing electoral turnout (see Chapter 6), or to the rise of populist politics which, especially on the xenophobic far right, sucks in the supposed 'losers' of globalization.

Social democracy – the ideology associated with the centre-left – advocates the promotion of equality and well-being via universal welfare provision that ensures the cross-class support necessary for its continuation. It also involves state intervention in the economy to ensure the stability and growth that supposedly creates jobs, helps pay for welfare, and shifts power from the market to politicians who, in theory, are more accountable to ordinary people.

Neo-liberalism advocates 'shrinking' the state by lowering taxation and privatizing its assets, opening up the economy to free trade, de-regulating the labour market, keeping inflation low and rewarding and encouraging individual responsibility and achievement – in other words, the kind of things that conservative and market liberal parties (see Chapter 5) have long stood for.

The problem with this common wisdom is that research suggests that it is probably misleading and possibly just plain wrong. Europe is not becoming inevitably and ever more like the US. Its traditions of social welfare and state intervention remain strong. They have never, however, precluded political differences between right and left, and, notwithstanding polling evidence that shows voters claiming they can no longer distinguish them, those differences remain relevant today, even if their specifics have inevitably changed over time. The supposed triumph of neo-liberal globalization is in reality severely constrained by (a) the fact that the left of the political spectrum does not want it to triumph and many on the right are either ambivalent about such a triumph or worried about the electoral consequences of being seen to pursue it too vigorously; (b) the fact that the welfare and regulatory state is path dependent and cannot simply be rolled back at will; and (c) the fact that the political-cum-institutional arrangements of many countries would make change difficult even if (a) and (b) did not apply.

This chapter, then, looks at whether 'politics matters', first, in the sense of being an activity that counteracts, mitigates and channels (global) market outcomes and, second, in the sense of those effects being dependent on which side of the political spectrum controls the government. It suggests that, even if we acknowledge and engage with the complexity of the challenges European states face, right and left are still meaningful concepts, especially if we don't insist on defining them in absolute, unchanging terms.

The chapter begins by tackling one of the most exhaustively researched questions begged by the idea that European politics has moved 'beyond left and right': Has politics ever really mattered that much, or have 'left' and 'right' never been much more than interchangeable management teams? It then goes on to explore the extent to which 'politics matters' in key areas such as welfare spending and taxation, privatization, and labour market policy. Each of these areas also allows us to look at the collapse or persistence of national regimes that seem to stand out against the supposedly uniform trend toward liberal capitalism. And it allows us to comment on the extent to which postcommunist countries really have gone all the way from full-blown communism to capitalism 'red in tooth and claw'. The chapter continues by examining how European integration both hinders and hastens what the common wisdom would like to claim is a necessary drive toward liberalization, deregulation and 'sound' policies. It goes on to suggest that, once we separate the facts from the hype about the triumph of liberal capitalism and the decline of left and right, differences between ideologies (and, just as importantly, nations) persist. The chapter ends by challenging the idea often put forward by media pundits that the supposed collapse of a political alternative to neo-liberalism in Europe has helped cause the rise of the far right.

Has politics ever really mattered?

Representative democracy in Europe assumes, and even relies on, political parties standing for a set of ideas-based policies rather than simply competing for the spoils of office. We should expect, then, that who governs (and, therefore, politics as a whole) matters. In other words, there should be some observable link between a particular party or set of parties being put into power and public policy. In fact, the impact of parties is harder to measure than might be imagined: even the smallest 'ship of state' resembles a supertanker rather than a speed boat – a small touch on the tiller or turn of the wheel takes a long time to register as a change of course, by which time the party or parties in question may be out of office. Nevertheless, political scientists have made some effort to make such measurements – and in a variety of ways. Few of them, however, are without problems.

One way of trying to find out whether parties make a difference is to see to what extent parties' manifesto promises (the promises that they make in writing at election time) are translated into the formally announced programme of the governments they form or help to form. But this means of mea-

KEY POINT

Historically, at least in the latter half of the twentieth century, there does seem to be a relationship between which parties were in office and government policy.

surement is only talking about the translation of one form of words into another, not the translation of words into action. For this, we have to look at studies examining the extent to which governments actually redeem the pledges made in their programmes. Unfortunately, these studies are surprisingly rare, and tend to be confined to countries such as the UK and Greece, which are unusual in Europe in that they normally have one-party majority governments (see Chapter 4). The fact that they seem to show (see Kalogeropoulou, 1989 and Rallings, 1987) that over two thirds of promises are kept – quite a high figure, given the contingencies of office – does seem to support the case for parties making a difference. But most European democracies are run by multi-party majority coalitions or either multi-party or single-party minority governments, making it much harder for a single party to see its ideas translated into deeds. This assumption is confirmed by one of the first comparative studies in this area involving the Netherlands and the UK (see Thomson, 2001), although the study, by showing that governing parties did most of what they said they would, also gives us some grounds for optimism that parties (and, by extension, politics) do make a difference.

Other studies aim to answer the question by looking at public spending – mainly on the grounds that left-wing parties (historically supportive of the welfare state and improved access to education) would be expected to spend more than right-wing parties (which historically have tended to worry more about, say, defence, and also where the money is going to come from). Again, taking these studies as a whole (see Alvarez *et al.*, 1991; Blais *et al.*, 1996; Hicks, 1999; Imbeau *et al.*, 2001; Schmidt, 1996, 2002) the verdict would seem to be a cautious 'yes', though it is important to note that some scholars would argue that 'politics hasn't mattered – much' (Caul and Gray, 2000: 234). Taking cross-national studies first, states that have experienced left-wing government for a considerable time (in Scandinavia and Austria) seem to have a bigger public sector than those for which the opposite is the case (Ireland, Switzerland and Germany). There also seems to be a link over time between left-wing government and more spending on education and welfare, though not health. Within-country studies (which can, of course, be added together to produce a cross-national conclusion) also seem to show a relationship between left-wing governments and higher spending and conservative governments and lower spending, although the effect is confined to majority as opposed to minority governments and is influenced by the size and strength of the opposition (as well as the existence of a strong trade union movement). On economic policy, there also appears to be a historical tendency for governments of the right to prefer lower inflation at the cost of higher unemployment, and governments of the left to prefer the opposite. Income inequality also seems to be affected – going up when there are right-wing parties in government and down when their counterparts on the left are in charge.

Historically, then, there does seem to be at least some truth in the argument that 'politics matters' or 'makes a difference'. Parties and governments of the left and right do different things and have different priorities – even if, as we shall see, many assume that the differences have narrowed (see Huber and Stephens, 2001). Indeed, politics might even make more difference than studies involving large-scale averages suggest. Such indicators cannot possibly hope to capture the myriad policy acts by an individual government that even the casual observer of politics would say were unimaginable under a government run by another party or set of parties. We can all cite examples from countries we know well. Would a Conservative government in the UK have announced a national minimum wage as its Labour counterpart did in 1997? Would the Popular Party in Spain have withdrawn Spanish troops from Iraq had it, rather than PSOE, been elected in the wake of the Madrid bombings in 2004? And would it have gone on to legislate for same sex marriage in 2005? In the unlikely event that the former communist social democratic party had been re-elected in Poland that same year, would it have attempted, like the Law and Justice led administration headed by the Kaczynski twins, to once again re-open the files in order to discover and sanction people who collaborated with the Communist regime? Now that government is out of office, will its successor, the Civic Platform party, pursue those collaborators with the same vigour or will it concentrate more on mending fences with Poland's neighbours (see Chapter 11)? These, however, are individual acts. They do not necessarily constitute long-term trends.

Drifting to the right? The centre-left in Europe

One such trend – or supposed trend – has become something of a commonplace these days. It is that Europe's centre-left parties have moved away from a traditionally social democratic emphasis on government intervention, welfare spending and prioritizing full employment. The charge does not come solely from crowing conservatives. But neither is it simply the catch-call of left-wingers torn between despair and trying to capitalize on the ensuing discontent of social democratic traditionalists (see Callaghan, 2000; and Callinicos, 2001). In fact, the abandonment of old-style socialism has been reflected in the rhetoric of some of social democracy's most prominent leaders, particularly in the UK and in Germany. In the mid-1990s, while seeking (successfully) to win office from centre-right parties which had been in power for over fifteen years, both Tony Blair and Gerhard Schröder insisted they were pragmatic centrists. Their so-called 'Third Way' or *Neue Mitte* sought not to expand or to 'shrink' the state, but to reconstruct it in order better to equip ordinary people to cope and compete in an increasingly global economy (see Green-Pedersen *et al.*, 2001).

KEY POINT

Social democratic parties have updated, but have not necessarily abandoned, their traditional goals and even the traditional means of achieving them. They are, however, being more honest with themselves and with electors about what they want to (and are able to) achieve.

To devotees of the Third Way, globalization, voter resistance to tax rises and inflation, and market antipathy to profligate spending, were – rightly or wrongly – to be treated as givens. The state, whatever the evidence to the contrary (see Weiss, 1998), was no longer so powerful. The majority had a stake in the health rather than in the hounding of capitalism. Governments of the left therefore had to work with, not against, the grain of what was a 'post-ideological' age – an era where (see Green, 2007) 'valence politics' (the question of who can best deliver progress toward broadly accepted goals) had replaced 'position politics' (the clash of opposing worldviews). They had to admit that they had no monopoly on good policies, and that some of what their opponents stood for made sense: unions were important but they could not be allowed to run the show; welfare benefits should provide 'a hand-up not a handout'; sometimes the market did know better than the state, the consumer better than the civil servant. Dogma, they claimed, had to take a back seat: 'What counts is what works.'

But was all this really such a quantum leap from the past? Common wisdom relies on the assumption of some kind of postwar 'golden era' during which ideologically committed social democratic parties in Europe were conquering capitalism, building welfare states and economies safe from the depredations of international markets. But the reality was rather more prosaic. The European centre-left spent most of the twentieth century trying not just to tame and humanize capitalism, but also to make it work better, all the time operating within constraints imposed by both moderate voters and powerful international markets (see Pierson, 2001 and Sassoon, 1997). Recent developments are part of an ongoing story. Of course, one can compare contemporary and 'classic' social democracy 'now' and 'then', and find the latter wanting (see Thomson, 2000). Yet such comparisons not only risk caricaturing both periods but also downplaying the fact that social democracy has always been a particularly plastic ideology which varies over space as well as time (see Stammers, 2001).

This plasticity has, it would seem, allowed social democrats in Europe to internalize the 'common sense' surrounding the advisability of, say, low inflation, balanced budgets and (to a much lesser extent) the new public management (or NPM) (see Chapter 3). Moreover, they know that pursuing such policies earns them valuable credibility with finance markets. No doubt, some are also privately relieved that, when their political opponents carry out painful reforms, they could be doing social democracy a favour by doing what it would find difficult to do itself in the face of opposition from its own supporters. But none of this learning and adapting necessarily means that Europe's social democrats threw the baby out with the bathwater (see Green-Pedersen *et al.*, 2001 and Martell, 2001). Part of the

BOX 9.1

Manifesto tracking

One of the longest continuous research projects in political science is the collection and coding of the manifestos of (western) Europe's political parties. One of the latest pieces of analysis from the project (Volkens, 2004; see also Volkens and Klingemann, 2002) explores the extent to which parties of the mainstream right and left have converged over time. Its findings are clear: in the 1940s–1960s, most centre-left parties moved to the left; but it also finds that they were followed in the same direction by almost all their centre-right opponents. From the 1970s onwards, the move was in the opposite direction: the centre-right moved right, and the centre-left, needing to keep in touch with the electorate, followed. Volkens' study cautions us, however, against exaggerating the extent of these shifts. Contrary to other scholars who use similar data (see Caul and Gray, 2000), Volkens also argues strongly against the idea of convergence: parties continued to maintain, at least, a semantic distance from each other. Interestingly, she also concludes that the 'policy shift to new Third Way issues . . . is no recent development, but started as early as the 1950s'. Other analysts of the manifesto project data, including those, such as Caul and Gray, who do see more convergence, also make the point that it has been going on for four or five decades, rather than being a knee-jerk response to resurgent neo-liberalism.

claim of key leaders like Schröder and Blair, after all, was that means can be de-coupled from ends, that values such as fairness and equality of opportunity (if not outcome) are best realized in up-to-date ways (Blair and Schröder, 1999). Utilitarianism and pragmatism has always been a strong streak in European social democracy: if the old ways of achieving the greatest good for the greatest number 'cannot be successfully implemented in the socio-economic and cultural environment of advanced capitalism' then they 'ought no longer be pursued' and, instead, be swapped for something that might work better (Kitschelt, 1994: 7).

Neither should we forget that the sheer size and inertia of polities and economies has meant – and will mean – that the differences between right- and left-wing governments (if not parties) tend to be ones of degree rather than kind. It will also mean – especially given that a measure initiated by one government might end up coming into effect under a successor from the other side of the political spectrum – that partisan differences in policy outputs might be difficult to pick up, making it difficult for us to see if they are still relevant. Nevertheless, it is important to make the effort to do so. In politics, discourse and rhetoric are undoubtedly important and arguably revealing (see Schmidt, 2001). But much of it – including the manifestos that political scientists have spent so much time studying (see Box 9.1) – is designed to reassure and reposition, rather than provide a blueprint for action. It might be fashionable to say there is no longer much difference between left and right, but it might not be true, or at least not wholly so. This can be illustrated by looking at parties records on what has long been a key battleground in European politics – the welfare state.

Party positions on the welfare state – words and deeds

The extent and form of the welfare state has traditionally been a matter of ideological and partisan contention between left (basically pro) and right (either anti or, at least, anti overly generous welfare provision). It is often suggested, however, that this is no longer the case, that there is a 'new politics of welfare' marked by retrenchment and austerity (see

KEY POINT

When it comes to welfare spending, redistribution and taxation, there has been no big roll-back of the state. Moreover, left-wing and right-wing governments still seem to behave in a manner consistent with their ideologies. The differences might have narrowed in the 1990s but, if they have, this is due to the centre-right, as well as the centre-left, moderating its policies.

Pierson, 1996) in the midst of which the left in particular has given up its values and its fight to maintain, let alone extend, welfare. Is this really the case?

One way of answering that question is, of course, to look at every European country and check out the debate in each one. However, this would be a highly intensive exercise and, because they vary so much on so many different dimensions, coming to a convincing conclusion either way might be difficult. One more practical way of trying to find out whether the left has collapsed in the face of neoliberalism – or, for that matter, whether the right is too comfortable or too scared to fight for it – is to restrict the analysis to a group of countries that are not only broadly similar, and therefore more comparable, but also well known as strong welfare states. If the left has moved away from its commitment there, the argument runs, then it will almost certainly have done the same in countries where that commitment is less strong.

A recent and very relevant attempt to pursue this more focused strategy used party manifestos to explore the changing positions of political parties on the welfare state in four Nordic (or Scandinavian) countries – Denmark, Finland, Norway and Sweden – between 1970 and 2003 (Nygård, 2006). Each has seen (in the light of shared concerns about competitiveness, spending and employment) retrenchment and reform – sometimes carried out by the left and sometimes the right. But all continue with a level and a style of welfare that continues to ensure that the region stands out as a beacon (at least for those of a left-wing persuasion) of equality and universal provision. The findings of the study make for interesting reading, not least because, once again, they question and qualify the common wisdom. First, although there was more interest in market-based solutions to social problems expressed as time went on, there was no overall decline in partisan support for welfare state expansion; if anything, support increased towards the end of the period. True, there were calls for cutbacks, but these tended to be made during economic recessions. Second, the clear trend was for parties on the left to continue to be staunch promoters of the welfare state, even though they had at times to recognize that reform and retrenchment might be necessary, whereas parties on the right were more likely to be the ones calling for limits and more market-based solutions, although this instinct was often muted (possibly by electoral concerns, possibly because of genuine attachment to the Nordic model). In the words of the author of the study, 'the left-right axis still plays a significant role' and 'parties still matter' (Nygård, 2006: 376–7).

Focused studies like this are useful, especially where they can be cross-checked and fleshed out by other similarly focused research. For instance, there is work which suggests that Scandinavian social democratic parties not only undertake welfare reforms because they are under pressure – and because the public trust them more to do the job (see Ross, 2000) – but also because they are well aware that the welfare state is a political asset that must be maintained and, therefore, kept up-to-date (see Klitgaard, 2007). On the other hand, focused studies have their limitations. They don't tell us about all the countries we are interested in and – especially if they analyse manifesto promises rather than government actions – they may tell us more about rhetoric than reality. This is why it makes sense to complement them with cross-national studies, often of a more quantitative type.

Two such studies – contributions to a branch of political science known as 'comparative political economy' – have been carried out by Allan and Scruggs (2004) and Korpi and Palme (2003). Both make a strong case for the continued importance of class-based political differences when it comes to welfare. Looking at the value of benefits paid to those who do not or cannot work, they find, admittedly, that – if only on this crucial dimension – the welfare state is not as generous as it once was, although they do not put the retrenchment of the 1990s down to 'globalization'. Yet they also have no doubt that politics still matters: right-wing governments, especially when the economy is in poor shape, are more willing to make cuts in benefit entitlements and levels – things which really do make a difference to rates of both relative and absolute poverty (Scruggs and Allan, 2006b; see also Brady, 2003). Support for the idea that parties and politics matter also comes from economists: a study of eighteen countries between 1981 and 1999 found a very clear effect – 'left-wing governments reacted to shocks not with cutbacks [as did right-wing administrations, even if few could match the stringency of Margaret Thatcher's in the UK], but with a rise in welfare-state generosity in order to cushion the effects of structural changes' (Amable *et al.*, 2006: 437). This finding, especially as it applies to right-wing parties, suggests that if (as we go on to discuss) the latter have reconciled themselves to the welfare state, then that reconciliation is either merely rhetorical or else comparatively recent.

The direction of these findings is reinforced by studies which look not just at the welfare state but at what, for those on the left anyway, was traditionally one of its key rationales; namely, its ability to redistribute income not just between different age groups or between, for example, the well and the unwell, but also between the better and the less well-off. In short, if parties and politics matter, we would expect to see a relationship between the redistributionary effect of welfare states and who governs. In countries where the centre-left has been in power more, we should see more redistribution between rich and poor compared with those where the centre-right is strong. Bradley *et al.*, (2003) explore this question and set up a particularly hard test by comparing (Scandinavian) social democratic states not just with Anglo-Saxon or liberal welfare states (such as the UK and the US) but also with states like Germany and the Netherlands where Christian Democrats, who are traditionally less hostile to generous welfare provision than their conservative and market liberal counterparts, dominate the centre right. Their findings (see Bradley *et al.*, 2003: 225–6) are unequivocal:

> leftist government very strongly drives the redistributive process directly by shaping the distributive contours of taxes and transfers and indirectly by increasing the proportion of GDP devoted to taxes and transfers. By contrast, if we add the direct and indirect effects of Christian democratic government, the net result is actually negative though not strongly so . . . [If] Christian democratic welfare states have slightly more egalitarian effects than liberal welfare states, our analysis shows that this is the case because they spend more and they have stronger unions or longer periods of left government, and not because of Christian democratic governance.

Inevitably, given the room for argument over how to measure it, there are quantitative studies which are more sceptical about the impact of 'partisan politics' on the welfare state. For instance, Kittel and Obinger (2003) clearly reject the suggestion that there has been some kind of 'race to the bottom' wherein governments have made swingeing cuts to welfare entitlements and provision in order to cope with globalization. But they note that the 1990s was a fairly difficult time for many governments when it came to social spending and argue that, during the last couple of decades, parties have made less of a difference on that score than they did in the past – certainly when compared with more structural drivers like ageing populations and unemployment. Indeed, which party or parties were in power mattered less than how many of them were in power, since larger coalitions made compromises on welfare reform difficult.

If Kittel and Obinger are right, and differences in welfare spending from the 1990s onwards were not influenced by parties quite as much as they were before, then this would, indeed, fit with the idea that the centre-left has recently begun to re-think welfare, at least at the margins. But their findings – especially their insistence that reforms might have meant retrenchment but never 'roll-back' – could also accord with criticisms coming from neo-liberals that the right in Europe is no longer (and perhaps never was) as convinced as it should have been that, to quote former American President Ronald Reagan, 'Government is not a solution to our problem, government *is* the problem'.

In fact, there is research which suggests that Europe's mainstream (centre) right parties (like the conservative *Moderaterna* in Sweden) have toned down any enthusiasm for liberalizing reforms – and not simply in order (successfully in the Moderates' case) to get re-elected but because they genuinely believe it makes more sense to patch up the welfare state rather than put it to the sword (see Lindbom, 2006). Certainly, anyone observing the Danish election in February 2005 would have found it difficult to pin the neo-liberal label on the incumbent and soon-to-be re-elected conservative prime minister, Anders Fogh Rasmussen. Seeking to close down any space between his own party and the Social Democrats, Rasmussen boasted of his plans for increased social spending and promised that any welfare reforms would be passed with the agreement of the opposition after consensual negotiations – a promise he went on to honour after the election (see

BOX 9.2

East is east? Left and right in the Czech Republic

It has become commonplace – and probably sensible – for most analysts of CEE party politics to warn readers unfamiliar with the region that definitions of left and right derived from Western Europe do not necessarily apply. And there are plenty of examples of former communist parties that repackaged themselves as social democrats after the fall of the Berlin Wall appearing, for instance, to espouse the cause of socio-economic and cultural modernisation (often via European integration) more loudly than some of their right-wing opponents, even if that meant painful – and electorally costly – reforms.

Arguably, however, the differences between right and left in postcommunist Europe will, in the long term, come to resemble those elsewhere. In some countries, the similarities have long been apparent. One such is the Czech Republic, whose president, Václav Klaus, during his time as prime minister in the 1990s, was already being called a Thatcherite.

It should have come as no surprise, then, that the coalition government dominated by Klaus' own party, the conservative ODS, announced in April 2007 a package that combined cuts in income and corporation taxes with reductions in entitlements to benefits, increases in VAT (sales tax) on many staple consumer goods and a hike in healthcare charges.

By the same token, the promise to fight the package (notwithstanding the fact that it was partly justified on the grounds of helping the Czech Republic to prepare join the eurozone) on the part of the opposition Social Democrats and the smaller Communist Party was also very much in line with what anyone familiar with left-right politics in 'the West' would have predicted. So, too, was the trade union-led demonstration by 30,000 people against the government's plans held in Wenceslas Square – scene of the protests that helped bring down Communism – in June 2007.

Bille, 2007). At the snap election he then called in the autumn of 2007, he again stressed his commitment to maintaining, while modernizing, the welfare state.

Of course, the suspicion among some ideologues that the right in Europe is reneging on, or at least rowing back from, neo-liberalism can be countered by a few recent examples of conservative governments clearly trying (as in Greece after 2004) to reduce their allegedly 'bloated' welfare states, not least because membership of the single currency supposedly obliges them to do so (see Box 9.2; also Box 9.9). One could also point out that the centre-right in Europe was never wholly committed to neo-liberalism in the first place – particularly not the continent's Christian Democrats who traditionally have been more welfare-friendly than their conservative and (market) liberal counterparts (see Chapter 5). In Austria, for example, the Christian Democratic ÖVP did, once in office after the 1999 elections, try to make good on its promise of *weniger Staat, mehr privat* (less state, more private), but the leadership of its German counterpart, the CDU-CSU, encountered more internal opposition to its policy of *mehr Markt, weniger Staat* (more market, less state) – a policy that also frightened voters so much that the party ended up having to govern with the Social Democrats after the 2005 election (Haupt, 2007).

However, if the Swedish example does apply more generally – and some would argue, for instance, that the British Conservative Party under David Cameron has shown the same tendency towards a move to the centre ground – it also slightly qualifies our argument that partisan differences are still strong, albeit not from the direction of the common wisdom, which tends to concentrate on the left rather than the right 'selling out'. That said, we should be cautious about assuming that the centre-right in Europe really has reconciled itself to 'tax and spend'. For one thing, research suggests that the enthusiasm for cutting, or at least stemming, welfare spending among parties on this side of the spectrum tends to vary according to trade union strength. Given the differences on this last score between, for instance, the UK and Sweden (see Chapter 8), we might expect the Conservatives and the Moderates to take a very different stance, notwithstanding media stories about David Cameron learning all he could from the Moderates' modernizing leader (and now Swedish Prime Minister) Fredrik Reinfeldt.

Returning again to the left, if there is a 'new macroeconomic consensus: fiscal stabilization = reduction in government debt burden = lower interest rates = more investment = increased economic growth = lower unemployment and stable inflation' (Teague and Donaghey, 2003: 110), this does not necessarily mean that, when they can, Europe's social democrats have given up spending. In Spain, for instance, PSOE may have been accused of selling out to market liberalism throughout the 1980s, but public expenditure, especially on health and education, climbed relentlessly as the party, in power for the first time in over forty years, attempted to make up for decades of neglect under a right-wing dictatorship (see Astudillo, 2002: 16–19; and Boix, 1998). More recently, the UK Labour government, supposedly keener than most to surrender social democracy to the market and the middle classes, presided from the late 1990s onwards over unprecedented rises in spending, particularly on youth unemployment, family support, education and (above all) on health, where by 2007–8 spending (in real terms, note) was double that of 1997. Moreover, it did not pay for this largesse simply via economic growth and a decline in unemployment (which have always been social democrats' favourite sources). It also did it through tax rises – primarily via an early hit on the excess profits of privatized utilities and pension funds, and then via carefully disguised raids on personal income that have hit the middle classes hardest.

Little surprise, then, that, at the same time as left-wing critics in Spain, the UK and elsewhere have been hounding social democrats for not doing enough, the centre-right in Europe continues to accuse them of doing both far too much and the same old thing. According to conservatives, centre-left politicians remain addicted to spendthrift policies that promote inefficiencies, stifle initiative and swallow up resources that would be better employed in the private sector. Yet when these criticisms hit home and the right is re-elected, it finds it difficult to throw things into reverse, possibly increasing voters' cynicism and their inability – much, if not all, of the time (see Box 9.3) – to see the differences between the parties that, objectively speaking, do still seem to be there.

In fact, both politicians and voters are to blame, if 'blame' is the right word. Historical evidence suggests that levels of taxation and public spending, while not utterly impervious to government action, are very 'sticky', making it difficult even for supposedly right-wing (let alone supposedly left-wing) administrations to do much 'dismantling of the welfare state' (see Green-Pedersen, 1999). This is partly because programmes create powerful constituencies with large numbers of votes. It is also because a great deal of public spending (and therefore taxation) is devoted to items which have been seen by most west Europeans – for good or ill – as rights rather than privileges. These include (above all) pensions, education, health care and social security in the event of illness, accident, or unemployment. Many people also expect the state to supplement wages that no one can realistically live on, although there is more ambivalence throughout western Europe about helping the supposedly 'undeserving poor' who could do more to help themselves (see Wilensky, 2002: Chapter 10).

There is little to suggest that Central and Eastern Europeans (many of whom were, after all, brought up to believe that state provision of these things was automatic) view things very differently. Certainly, their political representatives seem to reflect those preferences, notwithstanding some initially radical rhetoric, reinforced by the recommendations of international bodies such as the IMF and the World Bank (see Ferge, 2001), about moving toward a more 'residual' or 'Anglo-Saxon' welfare state. Take healthcare, for instance. Reforms in most postcommunist states 'have not been noteworthy for their emphasis on market competition or privatization' but were instead 'geared to securing universal access to health-care funded out of compulsory public or state-owned insurance schemes' and payroll taxes (Deacon, 2000: 155; see also Wagener, 2002).

In many of the areas just mentioned, in fact, there is an almost inbuilt pressure for spending increases right across Europe. Countries' government

BOX 9.3

A clear choice – the French elections of 2007

It has become something of a truism that voters these days aren't offered a clear alternative. But no-one who had to choose between Nicolas Sarkozy or Ségolène Royal at the French presidential elections in the spring of 2007 could have argued they couldn't tell the difference. Royal's 'Compact with France' was, to some, a real blast from the socialist past, although, in part, one foisted on her by her less centrist party. It proposed, among other measures, raising pensions, disability and housing benefits, and the minimum wage. The programme – costed at anything between €35 to €50 billion – also guaranteed jobs or training for young people, and promised to abolish a government scheme that made it easier for small businesses to hire and fire workers. Sarkozy, on the other hand, made no bones about his admiration for the world's more flexible economies: he promised to cut red-tape and taxes, especially for higher income earners, and get around the country's 35-hour week by making overtime easier and more profitable. All this, in order to liberate France's entrepreneurial spirit.

The obvious difference between the candidates probably helped produce a high turnout (85 per cent) and saw a comfortable 53–47 win for Sarkozy, who thereby claimed a mandate to change France (forgetting perhaps that his party and its predecessor had held the presidency for the previous twelve years). Once in power, he made immediate moves to make good his tax promises and looked like he was prepared to take on the trade unions over pension reform. However, he was noticeably more vague about cutting spending and few would bet on him giving up his penchant for promoting (and subsidizing) French industrial champions, especially after he insisted, in mid-2007, that an explicit reference to the EU's commitment to 'free and undistorted competition' should be excised from any new Treaty, and clashed with Neelie Kroes, the EU's competition commissioner, on protectionism. He also made interesting moves to appoint a cabinet drawn from across the political spectrum, although the Finance Minister he chose – Christine Lagarde, the first woman ever to hold such a post in a G-8 country – is generally thought of as an economic liberal who, like Sarkozy, is an admirer of the US.

Figure 9.1 Average annual growth in public spending on health, 1997–2002

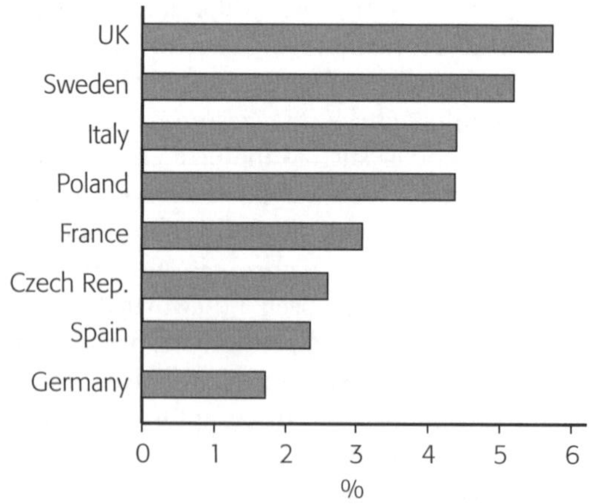

Note: No equivalent data for the Netherlands.

Source: Data from OECD Health Data, 2003 and 2004.

spending on education, for instance, varies between 4 and 8 per cent of GDP, with an average of around 5 per cent; but it is generally recognized that in order not to get left behind economically, a country's 'human capital' has to be constantly improved. Sweden and the UK, for instance, upped the numbers going into higher education between 1991 and 2001 by 85 per cent and 64 per cent, respectively. In health (see Figure 9.1), improvements in medical technology mean that people expect to be treated for conditions that previously would have been ignored and that might have served (as Charles Dickens' Mr Scrooge once put it) to 'decrease the surplus population'. As regards social security, there are several reasons why the state is more likely to spend in the future rather than save. These include the end of the concept of a 'family wage' (i.e. one big enough to support a non-working wife bringing up children) brought about by the entry of women into the labour force (see Chapter 1), the inability (or unwillingness) of governments to ensure full employment and the low wages paid to many in the (largely non-unionized) service sector economy – all situations that the state often ends up subsidizing through income support.

The other 'big-ticket item' – in some countries, the biggest ticket item – is old age pensions. We noted in Chapter 1 that Europe's ageing population was one of the biggest challenges facing its politicians. But, outside the UK (where governments of both right and left have made use of the highly majoritarian system to force through pension reform with little consultation) many have ducked it, or at least had to take things very slowly (see Schludi, 2005). Here is one issue on which there does seem to be a consensus among political elites, be they on the right or the left. Unfortunately, however, the consensus often seems to unite those that are in government rather than in opposition.

An obvious exception to this rule has been Sweden, where a commission involving stakeholders and five political parties in the 1990s managed to produce a package which essentially supplemented the state earnings-related scheme with private provision and went some way to means-testing the basic pension. Something similar was agreed in Denmark in 2006. Elsewhere, however, the situation has, sadly, been very different. In office, most governments in Europe have at least attempted to tackle the problem by a combination of the following: by reining back entitlements, most obviously by indexing to inflation rather than average wages; by raising the retirement age; by de-privileging public sector employees on particularly generous schemes (a real problem in France and Italy); and by encouraging or mandating private provision. In opposition, however, many parties have opportunistically supported (or, at least, declined to criticize) protests even when, had they been in government, they might well have been taking the same action. This is important because recent research suggests that governments can escape punishment for welfare rentrenchment as long as it is (a) done incrementally and combines reforms affecting only a small segment of the population and/or provision that is widely perceived as inefficient (see Levy, 1999); and (b) is not made much of by opposition parties (and the media) at election time (Armingeon and Giger, 2006).

In many European countries, the lack of explicit (as opposed to tacit) consensus, especially when combined with popular protest, makes it difficult, and even impossible, for those supposedly in power to act decisively. Of course, this is not always the case. Austria's right-wing government faced mass protests and strikes over its planned pension reforms in the summer of 2003, but promised to soldier on – partly perhaps because the country has no recent history of such events bringing down governments. Elsewhere, however, things are different. The right-wing Italian government of Silvio Berlusconi, for instance, almost forfeited office in the summer of 2004 when – in the face of mass public protests reminiscent of those that had brought it down in the mid-1990s – it just managed to pass relatively minor changes to a pension system that swallows up a large proportion of GDP and current spending by the state. Similarly, until President Sarkozy declared, quite reasonably, that he had a mandate to tackle the problem after his election in 2007, the French government pursued only piecemeal reform, and that almost by stealth, lest it spark off a repeat of the 1995 demonstrations that effectively brought down the only other government willing to face the situation (and the trade unions) head-on. This is a serious problem because both countries operate what are effectively 'pay-as-you-go' systems, where pensions – be they state earnings-related schemes or occupational schemes – are paid by contributions from those currently working: since the size of that group is going to shrink relative to pensioners (see Chapter 1), those countries will face an increasing (and perhaps politically intolerable) tax burden unless something is done.

It is clear from these examples that the capacity or willingness of parties and governments to make these 'hard choices' (Pierson, 2001) does not necessarily vary according to whether they can be described as 'left' and 'right'. This is just as true in Central and Eastern Europe, where governments have taken the opportunity offered by majority acceptance that there needed to be at least some reform to put in place multi-tiered (Swedish-style) pension systems that many of their western counterparts are struggling to implement (see Keune, 2006; Wagener, 2002: 162–8;). In Hungary, for instance, it was the ex-communist Socialist Party which, in the

BOX 9.4

Finally, an honest politician? Who's to blame in Hungary?

In September 2006, Hungary was thrown into turmoil when a radio station played a recording of a speech – made behind closed doors – by Prime Minister, Ferenc Gyurcsany, to his Socialist Party MPs a month or so after his government was re-elected in the spring (for a transcript, see BBC, 2006). In it he admitted, at times in very strong language, that they had spent most of the previous term lying to the electorate about the dire state of the country, afraid to take vital but painful reform measures lest they were thrown out of office. Now, he pleaded with them, they had to get real, tell the truth and implement the programme they'd been preparing in private.

Violent demonstrations against the government erupted in Budapest, spurred on by condemnation from the centre-right opposition, which made the most of the situation in the local elections that followed. The incident seemed to confirm people's worst suspicions of politicians as cheats. But was Mr Gyurcsany really such a villain? Both main parties had promised way more than they could possibly deliver at the general election a few months previously. Nor was it entirely surprising that *Magyar Szocialista Párt* (the Socialist party) had been cagey about pushing through painful measures in the run up to the election, even though it believed they were necessary: in previous spells in office it had done the right thing by the country only to find itself voted out by a population convinced it could have its cake and eat it, too. Indeed, from the first free elections of the early 1990s right up until the election of 2006, no Hungarian government had been able to win itself two consecutive terms. That doesn't necessarily excuse the Prime Minister, but it does once again raise the possibility that we get the politicians we deserve.

mid-1990s, radically reformed the country's pension system, introducing mandatory second-tier private provision (see Deacon, 2000).

Again, this does not necessarily mean that 'right' and 'left' have no meaning. But because Europe's voters seem to want to have it all (for instance, low taxes and early retirement on generous pensions) they have helped create a new division that does, indeed, threaten to go 'beyond left and right'. This is the division between parties and politicians who, however reluctantly, force voters to face up to the impossibility of 'having it all' and those who are prepared to pretend for the sake of office that 'hard choices' can be avoided (see Box 9.4). Unless voters change, it may be facile (even if very fashionable) to put all the blame for 'the state we're in' on politicians. After all, they are simply trying to make the 'least worst' trade-offs they can between what Europeans want and what they need (see Kitschelt, 2000: 160–6). What Europe's politicians are not doing, however, is taxing much less (see Table 9.1) or (see Table 9.2) spending much less either.

Of course, one can argue that overall tax take is not what is important. What really matters politically is where (or rather who) it is coming from. Perhaps supposedly spineless social democrats are sneakily shifting the overall tax burden away from

Table 9.1 Total tax revenue as a percentage of GDP, 1973–2004

	1973	1981	1986	1995	2004
Sweden	38.8	47.4	49.3	48.5	50.4
France	34.0	40.9	43.4	44.0	43.4
Italy	24.4	31.6	35.9	41.2	41.1
Netherlands	39.8	43.0	43.4	41.9	37.5
Czech Rep.	n/a	n/a	n/a	40.1	38.4
UK	31.4	36.7	38.2	34.8	36.0
Germany	33.0	34.2	34.0	38.2	34.7
Spain	18.0	24.3	29.6	32.8	34.8
Poland	n/a	n/a	n/a	39.6	34.4
EU-15	31.0	36.5	39.2	40.1	39.7
US	26.9	27.5	25.9	27.6	25.5

Note: Years chosen coincide with EU enlargement

Source: Data from *OECD Revenue Statistics*.

the forces they were traditionally supposed to be trying to control and onto those who they claimed to be protecting, in other words from capital to labour? In fact, there is little evidence for this: although in most European countries revenues from taxing labour have increased from 1970 onwards (from just over 15 per cent of GDP then to around 20 per cent now), mainly in order to pay for welfare expansion, revenue from taxing capital remains pretty much the same (between 5 and 7 per cent of GDP) as it was nearly forty years ago (see Genschel, 2004). That said, it is true that corporate tax rates (as opposed to revenues) have fallen in Europe (and all over the world) in the last two decades, and research strongly suggests, as globalization theorists argue (see Box 9.5), that these falls were down to governments keen to ensure that their countries were seen by companies as good places in which to do business – a concern shared just as much by left-wing as right-wing governments (Ganghof, 2006). On the other hand, the same research shows that when it comes to top rates of income tax, which are more obvious to electors and which apply to individual actors who are not always as internationally mobile as is sometimes reported, left-wing parties consistently preferred higher and more progressive taxes than their right wing counterparts.

Privatization

Of course, progressive taxation and support for (as opposed to scepticism towards) the welfare state were not the only touchstones for the centre left: there are other indicators we can use to answer the question as to whether politics makes a difference. State involvement in, or even public ownership of, certain key sectors of the economy, for example, was seen by many to be the *sine qua non* of socialism and, therefore, parties on the left. Of course, the extent of state involvement varied not just according to government ideology but also national tradition and each country's 'style of capitalism' (see Chapter 1) – a style often bolstered by its legal

KEY POINT

Left and right can at times do things that look very similar but that does not mean that they are the same and that it makes no difference which side is in power. The selling-off of state-owned enterprises is another case in point. Left wing governments have privatized less because (like right-wing governments) they were ideologically committed to the policy but more because they needed the money.

Table 9.2 Government expenditure as a percentage of GDP, 1961–2006

	1961–73	1974–85	1986–90	1991–95	1996–2006
Sweden	n/a	57.5	57.9	63.8	58.8
France	36.7	n/a	51.4	54.0	53.0
Czech Rep.	n/a	n/a	n/a	61.0	43.7
Italy	32.3	43.9	52.2	55.6	48.7
Germany	n/a	46.6	45.0	48.6	47.5
EU-15	n/a	45.5	47.5	50.0	47.5
Netherlands	37.1	53.2	54.9	54.3	46.3
Poland	n/a	n/a	n/a	49.8	44.3
UK	35.7	49.2	42.5	44.9	41.9
Spain	n/a	31.0	41.0	45.4	39.6
USA	30.5	34.1	35.8	36.2	33.8

Notes: 1. Data for Czech Republic and Poland is 1992–5.
2. n/a Not available.

Source: Data for 1961–95 (and US) from European Commission, DG Economic and Financial Affairs, *European Economy, Statistical Annexe* (Spring 2004). Data for 1996–2006 from Eurostat.

BOX 9.5

Does globalization render politics powerless and pointless?

Political Scientist Philipp Genschel (2004) observes that 'there are basically three stories about the globalization–welfare state nexus'.

Globalization theorists assert that globalization opens up economies to the international market and forces them to be more competitive. In order to ensure that their nation can compete, and in order to be able both to attract investment and to borrow money on international markets, governments lose their autonomy and power: they are, in effect, obliged to reduce the tax burden and spend sensibly, meaning that costly welfare programmes have to be cut or, at least, cut back.

Gobalization sceptics claim there is precious little evidence of any relationship between increasing international interdependence and welfare strain. In fact, the welfare state has not shrunk, there remain big differences in welfare spending and delivery between countries that have supposedly been subjected to the same all-consuming pressures and, in many countries, governments are still playing a very active role. Globalization may indeed be going on, but that shouldn't scare governments and voters into thinking politics is powerless or pointless.

Revisionists argue that globalization is real enough, but that it is not the main threat to welfare states. That comes from structural problems caused by, for example, demographic trends and cumbersome and self-defeating government intervention. The ironic – but good – thing about the crisis rhetoric surrounding the impact of globalization on the welfare state is that it encourages governments and voters to think that something must be done to tackle the underlying structural problems that are the real issue.

system: historically, state involvement has tended to be higher in France and in other continental European countries (e.g. Germany) where codified civil law is more important than common law (see Chapter 4 for more on this distinction; see also Bortolotti and Siniscalco, 2004: 49–50). In addition, the capacity to change things (i.e. to 'roll back the state') varies across countries: it might (as in Portugal, France and Germany) necessitate constitutional change or involve getting agreement among institutions (second chambers, powerful regional governments, presidents, the public through referendums) that in some countries (Italy, Germany, France, and Switzerland, for example) are powerful 'veto players' but in others (the UK, for instance) either don't exist or don't matter. However, there are good reasons to think that more right-wing political parties would favour reducing state involvement and therefore be keen on privatization (the transfer of state assets into private hands most commonly achieved by selling shares in those assets with the proceeds going to the government). Parties of the right believe, after all, in the market as the most efficient way of providing for people's needs and wants, and they were in part created to defend the sanctity of private property. It is also possible that, by creating a 'share-owning democracy' or 'popular capitalism' via selling off state-owned enterprises (SOEs) to the general public, they might boost support for their values in the electorate.

In the postcommunist countries of course, as we suggested in Chapter 1, privatization was a crucial part of the move away from the party-state past: outside Romania and Bulgaria (though they are now 'catching-up') most governments (even those run by communist successor parties) showed themselves to be reasonably keen 'systemic' privatizers (see Box 9.6). In the West, public ownership was clearly far less important than it was in the Soviet bloc, but the decision on whether to reduce or maintain it was theoretically no less political: the left should, on the face of it, have tried to block privatization and the right should have been associated with promoting it. Given, then, that privatization, after being pioneered in the 1980s by the UK's Conservative government, supposedly took off all over Europe, we would seem to have a *prima facie* case not so much for convergence between right and left but at least for the ideological dilution of the latter. So what is the evidence? Is there a clear correlation between a country being run by right-wing governments and it 'selling off the family silver' (see Boix, 1998) – a correlation that would suggest that partisan differences are still meaningful? Or is privatization a game that all governments play irrespective of which parties are in power, indicating that rhetorical differences between left and right matter very little in practice?

Sophisticated statistical analysis by Zohlnhöfer and Obinger (2006) suggests that in the countries that made up the EU before the 2004 and 2007 enlargements, privatization receipts between 1990 and 2000 were – perhaps unsurprisingly – largest in those countries where the state sector (and economic regulation more generally) had initially been most significant. Institutions also mattered: receipts were lower where there were more 'veto players'; namely, in countries with an important upper house of parliament and in federal countries. Interestingly, however, neither trade union density nor constitutional constraints appeared to exert much of a restraining effect. In addition, the findings suggested that budget deficits – especially at a time when the pressure to get them down in order to qualify for the single currency was intense – were an important driver of privatization (Clifton *et al.*, 2006 and Parker, 1998).

On the question of whether privatization was more associated with right-wing than with left-wing governments, however, the results were less clear – at least for the EU countries. In the OECD as a whole, there was a statistically significant relationship between the ideological complexion of governments and the amount of privatization business countries did. In the EU, it was only towards the end of the period – specifically once the decision had been made that every member state that wanted to adopt the euro had brought its deficit sufficiently under control to allow it to do so – that the association between centre-right government and privatization receipts was unambiguous. This led the researchers to conclude in a manner that supports the idea that left and right – and, indeed, politics and political institutions in general – still matter. Social democratic parties, they note, 'are indeed ready to sell off SOE[s] when under intense fiscal strain, but . . . they – in contrast to bourgeois [i.e. centre-right] parties – do not regard this policy as an effective instrument to enhance economic growth and thus abstain from using it in the absence of fiscal problems'. In short, selling off state assets 'was not caused by a fundamental change of the ideological positions concerning privatization on the part of left parties'. And both the extent to which it was done and the extent to which it could be done did, indeed, depend not just on economic pressures but also on countries' arrangements – no one should expect a country like Germany, for instance, whose federal system means power (and, indeed, ownership) is shared between the centre and the regions, and between the executive and the legislature, to be the world's biggest privatizer.

Given the obstacles – ideological and institutional – it is not surprising, then, that privatization has not proceeded quite as rapidly as some would like and has often taken place in stages rather than as a 'big bang'. On the other hand, it has happened. For instance, the nominally socialist government of France in the late 1990s introduced the 35-hour-week, spent millions on public schemes to reduce unemployment, upped welfare benefits, and was distinctly lukewarm about the 'Third Way' touted by its British and German counterparts (Clift, 2001, 2002). But, as it worked hard to qualify for the euro, it chose (rather than, say, raising taxes on the middle classes) to preside over what was the biggest sell-off of state assets in the country's history. Even though many of them were only part-sales (the state continued to hold majority stakes in *France Télécom* and *Air France*, for instance, and still owned a quarter of well-known car-maker, *Renault*), the Jospin government raised over €30 billion between 1997 and 2002. The left-wing government in Italy, at the same time, also sold off state assets in a desperate, and ultimately successful (if not entirely convincing), attempt to bring down its budget deficit in order to squeak into the single currency.

Those who are sceptical about the continued difference between left and right also point out that, even if the economy forced social democrats into something they would not otherwise have done, they have done nothing to reverse the trend once those pressures have come off. Others would see this criticism as unfair and unrealistic. Compensating shareholders would cost a fortune.

BOX 9.6

Privatization as politics

Privatization can be motivated by politics rather than pure economic theory. These political motives are often mixed, but can be analytically separated as follows.

Systemic privatization hopes to alter a country's socio-economic and political environment fundamentally by reducing the state's role (and people's expectations of the state's role) in it. The privatization programmes of CEE and, to a lesser extent, those of Southern Europe before it, could be labelled 'systemic'. So, too, could those pursued towards the end of the 1980s and the early 1990s by the Thatcher and Major governments of the UK; they also aimed at the reduction of the power of organized labour, which is often at its strongest in the public sector.

Tactical privatization, by contrast, is mainly about achieving the short-term, often electoral, goals of parties, politicians and the interest groups that support them. The adoption of privatization by centre-right politicians in France during the late 1980s was driven by a desire to distinguish themselves from their Socialist opponents, as well as the need to reward key supporters. The revenue thus gained, however, allowed the government to finance measures to combat unemployment (and, ironically, to keep afloat other state-owned holdings) that otherwise it would have had trouble affording.

Pragmatic privatization is even more ad hoc and often crisis-driven: governments simply need the money to offset debt or public spending and are prepared to override even their own reservations in order to get it, especially because selling off SOEs can be politically easier than raising taxes or restraining public sector pay. The privatization that went on in European countries in the late 1990s was one way of ensuring that countries such as Italy qualified for entry into the single currency – a process that required them to bring their budget deficits, their debt and their current spending into line with agreed norms. Privatizations carried out by centre-left governments in France and Germany also qualify as pragmatic.

Source: Based on discussion in Feigenbaum *et al.* (1998).

And international financial markets would take a dim view of any government going against neo-liberal orthodoxy, even if there is evidence that organizations such as the World Bank, IMF and the OECD are beginning to question some of that orthodoxy's component parts (see Deacon, 2005). Attempting, therefore, to turn back the clock would be insane. Neither, it has to be said, is there any evidence that private business provides any worse a service than the state for consumers, and therefore voters, some of whom (though often fewer than is imagined and certainly fewer than in the US) now hold shares.

In other words, one does not need to posit some sort of damascene conversion to gung-ho neoliberalism on the part of the mainstream left in Europe to understand privatization (and the unwillingness to reverse it) was driven by instrumental rather than ideological motives (see Box 9.6) – not least the desire to join the euro. Indeed, there was another EU motive, too. This was the need to respond to demands (expressed through the European Commission, but coming from corporations in countries that had already privatized such sectors) that states open up their telecoms and energy markets to competition. Such demands were designed to kick-start the so-called 'Lisbon process' by which European leaders – left and right – rather ambitiously promised at a summit in Portugal in March 2001 to make the EU economy the world's most competitive and dynamic economy by 2010 (see Wincott, 2003).

In fact, privatization is rarely so thoroughgoing as media headlines might suggest or true believers might want. We noted in Chapter 1 that, even in the keenest postcommunist states, sales are still by no means always complete and often proceed in stages.

The same is true for countries in western Europe. For instance, Norway seemed to stand out among Scandinavian countries as a keen privatizer, raising approximately €1.5 billion from the sale of shares in its fantastically wealthy *Statoil* company and almost €500 million from a massively oversubscribed sale of shares in *Den Norske Bank* in 2001. But, even after the latter sale, the state continued to own 47 per cent of the shares and, in the case of the former, still controlled a full 80 per cent. The centre-right government that took over from the Labour government that sold those assets did not, in fact, go much further because both right- and left-wing politicians are sensitive to voter opposition to the foreign takeover of domestic firms – something a continuing controlling share on the part of the state can prevent.

This kind of 'economic nationalism' is still important in other European countries, notably France. But in other countries, too, governments supposedly keen to privatize surreptitiously left the state in *de facto* control by awarding it a 'golden share' that allowed it to intervene, for example, to block a takeover bid. Indeed, the technique originated in the 'home' of privatization, the UK, in the 1980s. Recently, however, the British government, and governments in Germany, Italy, the Netherlands and Spain, have been taken to task over the practice by the European Commission. In May 2003, the ECJ ruled that both the UK and Spain, which had owned 'golden shares' in numerous companies that had supposedly been set free by privatization, would have to give them up. The only justification for such shares will henceforth be confined to enterprises involving national security considerations – a definition which, judging by experience, will probably be stretched to the limit.

We should also note that there has been a considerable slowdown in privatization since the peak of the process in the late 1990s, both in the number of sales taking place and in terms of value. This is due, in part, to the economic slowdown that struck large parts of the world's economy (i.e. Asia and the US, as well as Europe) and sent share markets downwards. Sensible governments postponed asset sales in the hope that they would find a better price in the future. The slowdown in privatization in Europe is also due to the rather prosaic fact that much of what can easily be sold has, in many countries, already been offloaded. To coin a phrase, many of the 'cash cows' have gone and only the 'lame ducks' remain.

European governments are also having to face the fact that some sectors might simply be too risky (strategically or financially) to privatize – at least, to privatize fully. True, this does not mean a complete halt to private sector involvement in previously state-run areas. For instance, the UK Labour government elected in 1997 initially disappointed those observers who hoped it would carry on where its pro-privatization Conservative predecessor had left off: the not-very-successful part-privatization of the air-traffic control system was about as far as it went. However, it has also angered left-wing critics with its enthusiasm for 'public–private' financing (PFI, the Private Finance Initiative), whereby the private sector builds roads, transport systems, prisons and (increasingly) hospitals which are then leased back to the state. Yet even under that government, one can argue that things have gone backwards. In 2001, for example, the UK government had to re-establish state ownership (albeit via a not-for-profit company) of the railway track operations that a Conservative government had privatized in the early 1990s. Interestingly, nobody suggested that this *de facto* 're-nationalization' was a sign that 'New' Labour was returning to its socialist roots. It might not be any more accurate, then, to see its plans to involve the private sector in public projects as proof that it has sold its soul to neo-liberalism.

By the same token, it is easy to pick up on headlines that seem to suggest that, 'at last', privatization is embedding itself in countries that have a tradition of what neo-liberals would see as 'state meddling' in the business sector. Thus, much is made of Germany's grand coalition's apparent desire to float *Deutsche Bahn*, which is now not just a railway but also a highly profitable logistics and freight business. But the culture of state involvement is very strong in many countries, especially in France, despite the liberal hopes that the EU will undermine it in the long term (see Cole, 1999 and Cole and Drake, 2000). Nicolas Sarkozy might have won the French presidency in 2007 by promising to liberalise the economy (see Box 9.3), but only a few years before, as Finance Minister, he famously prevented the Swiss pharmaceuticals giant *Novartis* from gatecrashing a merger between *Aventis* and *Sanofi*, two French firms that together could create a French 'national champion' to compete on the global stage. Sarkozy also bailed out *Alstom* (the trains, turbines and ship maker) by converting an €800 million loan it had been granted into a government shareholding worth just over 30 per cent.

In fact, what in EU jargon is called 'state aid' is not confined to France, even though, on balance, it has declined in the last decade. A recent European survey (Curzon Price, 2004) notes that it is 'gradually being brought under control, but most governments find it difficult to relinquish this instrument of policy'. It also notes that the European Commission 'still has problems enforcing discipline on member states' and that any decline could still be put at risk in an economic downturn – not just in France (and Germany), but also in other big 'offenders' such as Spain and Italy.

Flexible labour markets?

One of the other key shifts in economic and social policy since the 1970s has been a de-emphasis of 'demand-side' solutions to unemployment towards 'supply-side' measures and 'smart' welfare states that help people into, rather than holding them back from, employment. The former attempted to use Keynesian government spending to smooth out the business cycle and offset recessions (see Chapter 1). Supply-side solutions, however, concentrate on removing rigidities in the labour market. These rigidities include 'excessive' worker protection or bureaucratic benefits systems that put people off taking up offers of work. Supply-side measures also focus on providing education and skills training better to equip firms and people to adjust to economic change. Generally, it is governments of the right that are most associated with a desire to move towards more 'flexible labour markets'. For example, despite the general strike staged by Italian unions against such policies in April 2002, Silvio Berlusconi's centre-right administration could claim a mandate for trying to untangle the mass of laws and regulations that some would argue protect the rights of those with a job at the cost of those trying to get one. It was also a centre-right government in France that tried to do something about the country's high rate of unemployment among the under-25s (one in five of whom are jobless) by introducing the CPE (*le contrat de première embauche* or first employment contract). This was designed to make it easier for companies to hire (because they knew they could also more easily fire) workers, albeit one that was strangled at birth by street demonstrations and sit-ins by the very young people it was apparently supposed to help.

There is no doubt, however, that some social democratic parties, though not all of them, have been part of this shift, or that much has been made (by both critics and fans) of their going with the flow instead of trying to stem the tide. Much to the chagrin of its union backers, for instance, the UK's Labour government made it clear on assuming office in 1997 that, like its Conservative predecessor, it would not allow the EU to re-regulate the country's comparatively unregulated labour market. Meanwhile, the SPD–Green government in Germany tinkered with that country's heavily bureaucratic and heavily taxed labour market. Its *Agenda 2010* package, announced in the spring of 2003, was designed to make it more tempting for small and medium-sized enterprises (SMEs) to take on workers and to ease rules on collective bargaining. These changes (plus following the UK down the road of making it harder for unemployed people repeatedly to refuse offers of work) seem, along with wage restraint and an economic upturn, to have begun to make a dent in the country's high unemployment rate.

The adoption of supply-side measures, however, should not be taken as proof that differences between right and left have disappeared. The evidence suggests that the social democratic version of supply-side policies – which some see as the essence of the 'Third Way' (see Green-Pedersen *et al.*, 2001) – can be quite different to the version preferred by the right. Unlike the centre-left, the centre-right has tended not to balance deregulation with more spending on human capital (see Boix, 1998). Social democrats in countries such as the Netherlands

KEY POINT

The embrace by social democrats of the idea of flexible labour markets as a sensible supply-side response to unemployment and the need for a competitive economy is not necessarily a new departure in a right-wing direction

might not grab the headlines like their counterparts in the UK or Germany, but they have long demonstrated there is nothing inherently 'right-wing' about a shift to supply-side policies (see Hemerijck and Visser, 2001). If there were, then we would have to re-write the record on what is widely acknowledged to be Europe's (not to say the world's) most persistently 'social democratic country' (Box 9.7).

In any case, even if we look at (say) Labour, in the UK, which has gone further than many of its left counterparts in embracing de-regulation, we see a government that extended trade union recognition, a government that for the first time ever brought in a minimum wage and a government that is regularly attacked by employers' organizations for introducing too much worker protection. We also see a government that signed up to the EU's 'Social Chapter' – a measure that allows some EU labour law (examples so far include maximum working hours and rights for part-time workers) to be made by union–employer agreement (see Chapter 8). On the other hand, as if determined to make itself difficult to pigeonhole, the Labour government, since signing, has done its best to limit 'European interference' in labour market matters, claiming that light-touch' regulation is one of the keys to the UK's relatively low unemployment. It has also attempted to 'upload' its ideas into EU discourse by encouraging other countries to follow its liberalizing lead. The relatively residual nature (see Chapter 1) of the British welfare state, however, means that fellow EU members with more generous systems look likely to look more favourably at the 'flexicurity' – the use of a comprehensive welfare state combined with liberal labour laws to promote a responsive economy – pioneered by Denmark and the Netherlands (European Commission, 2007). The spread of these kinds of ideas lends weight to the more general argument that, when looking at the state in Europe, the picture is not one of either 'decline' or 'path dependent inertia' – instead the state is 'evolving . . . shifting in its purposes and modes of intervention'; if the future lies in liberal markets, it is also with those states that remain strong and large enough to facilitate adjustment (Levy, 2006: 21–2, 27).

BOX 9.7

Supply-side social democracy in Sweden

Social democratic Sweden's relative economic success has long been underpinned by supply-side policies and, in particular, an 'active labour market policy' through which the state provided a safety net, social services and skills development that would allow people and firms to adjust swiftly to changes in the international markets. This also had the considerable economic advantage of maximizing women's employability. In recent years, Sweden has looked less immune than previously to recession, and social democratic led governments have had little compunction in slowing the growth of welfare spending, not least on pensions. They have also, like Labour in the UK, granted independence to the central bank to set interest rates. Indeed, they have gone further than their UK counterparts by cutting income tax and privatizing the Swedish postal service in order to allow it to compete more efficiently in Europe. The so-called 'people's home' might not be quite what it used to be, but few accuse Sweden, or the party that has run it for so long (the SAP), of a comprehensive betrayal of the ideals of social democracy. None of this, of course, is any guarantee of continued support for the SAP. Indeed, its failure, notwithstanding the above, to make more of a dent in unemployment, combined with the centre-right parties decision to publish a joint manifesto which made clear they were not intending to undermine the welfare state, turned the general election of 2006 into that rare thing – a defeat for the Swedish social democrats.

The EU – deadweight or driving force?

We have already observed that the EU has played a role in privatization and the debate over flexible labour markets. In fact, it is a key factor in any discussion of the triumph (or otherwise) of liberal capitalism and the constraints on governments, especially of the centre-left. Not only does it provide a framework of binding legislation and decision

KEY POINT

The EU is dedicated to opening up Europe to competition and encouraging governments into making structural changes, but this is not necessarily inimical to the interests of ordinary people, nor is it a passive surrender to markets.

rules within which both economic and political activity in European countries must take place, it provides an arena in which politicians and the representatives of interest groups articulate their views and attempt to move that framework in their desired direction. It also – and this should never be forgotten amid all the talk of globalization – helps constitute what for all European countries has become by far their biggest market (see Chapter 1).

Like social democracy, the EU seems to get it in the neck from both sides. On the one hand, neo-liberals characterize it as pathetic, self-delusionary refuge from the bracing winds of globalization. Seeing the EU's commitment to enforcing fair competition (Box 9.8) as a mere sideshow, they also see it as a bastion of 'continental corporatism' (see Chapter 8), whose support for labour and environmental standards and excessive product regulation risks clogging up still further the arteries of an already ailing European economy. On the other hand, their opponents see the EU as a potentially anti-democratic (and anti-social democratic) attempt to embed or institutionalize neo-liberalism that has taken on its own momentum – a momentum that the largely domestic focus of Europe's centre-left is likely to prevent it doing much about, even assuming it wanted to (see McGowan, 2001). To these radical critics, the EU is the creation of politicians who are convinced that there is no alternative, yet sceptical about their own ability (or the ability of their counterparts in other countries) to persuade their voters of the case. The key to this project is the single market, and the single currency. These will apparently encourage capital, among other things, to relocate to where labour is cheapest, regulation is lightest and taxes are lowest and, in so doing, force governments to 'shrink' the state in order to ensure that their country remains an attractive place in which to do business.

More explicitly, the run-up to joining the euro was supposed to oblige Europe's overspending governments to tighten their belts by forcing them to meet 'convergence criteria' (set levels of debt, deficit and inflation) in order to qualify. And, when the single currency was adopted, it meant governments surrendering control of interest rates to the European Central Bank (ECB) (see Chapter 2), thus depriving them of an important tool of economic policy and control. At the same time, their new-found inability to devalue their currencies in order to adjust to balance of payments problems was designed to force them into structural measures (such as squeezing real wages and taxes, and introducing supply-side measures) to regain international competitiveness. Moreover, in order to ensure that all countries in the 'Eurozone' (the name given to the collection of states that have adopted the euro) play the game and preserve the credibility of the new currency, they have to sign up to the Stability and Growth Pact (SGP), policed by the Commission (see Box 9.9; Heipertz and Verdun, 2003 and Howarth, 2004). This is supposed to stop them building up debts and deficits by, for example, countercyclical spending to offset a Eurozone ('one-size-fits-all') interest rate that might be set so high that it risks choking off their economic growth.

We should be careful not to portray all these obligations as externally imposed by the EU on unwilling victims in the member states. Clearly, there were many conservative interests in many of them who were keen that their politicians swallow the medicine, and many politicians willing to use European Monetary Union (EMU) – as they use EU compliance more generally – to help them do what they wanted to do anyway (see Dyson and Featherstone, 1999 and Radaelli, 1997). But we should also be careful before assuming that the need to qualify for the single currency in the first place did, in fact, force European countries into swingeing cutbacks: as Rhodes (2002: 44) puts it:

> [i]n reality, 'getting in shape for EMU' did nothing to prevent even the most debt-ridden and poorly managed European economies from reducing their deficits and debts while also boosting spending on social and employment policy. Higher taxes, privatization and lower interest payments, facilitated by falling interest rates on smaller national debts, all allowed welfare states to keep on growing.

BOX 9.8

EU competition and de-regulation – good for business or good for people?

The European Commission is committed to opening up competition in sectors where, traditionally, firms have hidden behind national barriers in order to keep competitors out and prices up. Very often it will give a sector a chance to dismantle those barriers itself. But, if necessary, it will legislate them away or, if rules already exist, even raid firms to uncover evidence of anti-competitive practices – cartels and the like. Two obvious examples in recent years are the energy sector and telecoms: 2006 saw raids conducted on energy companies across several European countries and the threat of new legislation to break up existing monopolies; 2007 saw the EU legislating price caps on the roaming charges that meant excessively expensive international calls, after the mobile operators in question dragged their feet on a voluntary agreement.

So, is this neo-liberalism in action or unwarranted interference in the affairs of legitimate businesses? If it is the former, it is difficult to see how it harms the people that opponents of the free-market claim to be trying to protect, most of whom presumably benefit from cheaper gas and electricity and mobile charges. On the other hand, will competition – and therefore consumers – be damaged in the long term if (as many predict will occur in Europe's energy market) smaller, less efficient and state concerns are eventually swallowed up by a few big players who will then be in a stronger position than ever to exploit their strength? Just as importantly, given that few of these big players are genuinely pan-European, will some countries benefit more than others as they expand? Does this explain why, in the spring of 2007, the governments of Italy and Spain were accused of encouraging an Italian firm, *Enel*, to increase its stake in Spain's largest electricity producer, *Endesa*, in order to block a takeover bid by German firm *E.on*? Or was *Enel's* interest inevitable once it was effectively prevented from taking over the French firm *Suez* when the French government changed the law to reduce the state's stake in *Gaz de France* (GDF) in order to allow it (and not *Enel*) to merge with *Suez*? Economic nationalism can complicate things considerably.

And what of left and right in all this? Clearly, the willingness and ability of the Commission to take action is an example of politics winning out over the market. But it is also operating on an essentially pro-market agenda. Research – and the response of governments in these cases – suggests that the reaction of politicians to such action varies less according to their party affiliation and more according to their nationality, mainly because (as we saw in Chapter 1) countries differ markedly when it comes to how liberal or co-ordinated their economies traditionally are. Less a clash of ideas, perhaps, than a 'clash of capitalisms' (Callaghan and Höpner, 2005).

Now that the euro is in use, it would appear that the will of politicians has proved far stronger than the rules they (or, rather, their predecessors) designed in order to constrain themselves. So far, anyway, European governments have responded to the limitations of the interest rate regime simply by breaching the SGP – and so far earned nothing more than a scolding for so doing (Box 9.9). Neither, with the partial exception of Germany after 2002, is there much sign of governments trying to exert significant downward pressure on real wages. In fact, real wages continue to grow throughout Europe and are one reason why, for instance, the EU's huge agricultural budget, which adds considerably to the price Europeans pay for food, is still more of an issue for Eurosceptics than it is for ordinary consumers.

Of course, these are still early days, and two important parts of the supposedly neo-liberal single market jigsaw are yet to fall into place. One is ensuring that the service sector is as much of a single market as manufacturing (see Box 9.10). The other is the idea of 'tax harmonization' – the bringing into line of all member states' tax rates and policies – which is argued for on two grounds. First,

BOX 9.9

Big stick or big joke? The EU's SGP

Under the terms of the Stability and Growth Pact, Eurozone countries are not supposed to run budget deficits of more than 3 per cent of GDP. If they do, they are eventually liable to fines payable to the European Commission. However, it is not the Commission but the other member states, acting through the Council of Ministers, that decide on punishment. So far, they have proved reluctant to allow the Commission to do anything other than issue warnings and reprimands. One of these, issued in 2001, was enough to make Portugal cut spending in order to keep below the ceiling in 2002. Since then, however, the failure to take action against Germany and France, the most persistent offender, has rendered the Pact something of a laughing stock – so much so that, in 2004, six of the twelve eurozone countries (France, Germany, Greece, Italy, the Netherlands and a rather bitter Portugal!) looked set to breach the rules. The Commission responded by taking the Council of Finance Ministers to the ECJ for failure to act. In July 2004, the ECJ found in favour of the Commission, although this 'moral victory' became something of a pyrrhic victory when it was rendered partially redundant by a review of the Pact in the spring of 2005 that made it easier for countries to claim temporary exemptions from the 3 per cent rule.

This victory for large member states that seems to have emboldened one of them, France, to wonder out loud whether, in fact, there should be more political control over what some now see as the last bastion of orthodoxy – the ECB. Nevertheless, to dismiss the pact too lightly would be a big mistake: the fact that the eurozone's supposedly sovereign nations have agreed to permanent surveillance (and potential sanctioning) of their governments' spending and borrowing by a supranational institution represents a major development in the political economy of Europe and European integration (see Jones and Verdun, 2004).

from a neo-liberal point of view, national differences in tax regimes and rates represent inefficient and trade-distorting barriers to genuine competition. Second, there are those who believe there must be European control of tax and fiscal policy in order to offset the ECB's control of interest rates and monetary policy – something that some neo-liberals might support if they could believe (which, interestingly, few can) that rates would, as a result, be lower rather than higher. There are few signs, however, that either Europe's politicians or their electorates are listening to such arguments. Opinion polls show next to no support for tax harmonization. Consequently rates of VAT, of corporation tax and excise duty continue to vary (though, especially in the case of the first two, less so once necessary statistical adjustments are made to the standard or headline rates always quoted in the media). And whether these variations really make much of a difference to business decisions, or whether they really are used by governments as means of enticing firms to set up or stay in their countries, is very difficult to judge (see Radaelli, 2004).

But if the EU has 'failed' to get compliance and harmonization on tax and spending, does it matter? Perhaps not, if it means that there ends up being a balance between what Scharpf (1998) neatly characterizes as 'negative integration' (the EU attempting to prevent governments from doing things such as protecting industries or running deficits) and 'positive integration' (EU regulations, social policies and subsidies). By the same token, the apparent preservation of welfare and labour relations systems at the national level means that the absence of such institutions at the EU level might not actually matter as much as some – particularly those who insist such a capacity has to be developed as a counterweight to the EU's liberal agenda – think it does (see Rhodes, 2002). Moreover, we should not understate the level of aid to backward regions, let alone to farmers. Structural funding to these regions between 2000 and 2006 totals €183 billion (Molle, 2001), much of which is devoted to 'supply-side measures' such as retraining and not simply job-creating infrastructure projects. Neither should we forget the fact that by enlargement, the EU, irrespective of whether its institutions increase their power over national governments, has expanded both the opportunities and the options available to businesses in Europe –

BOX 9.10

Vive le plombier polonais! The EU's Services Directive

The service sector, as we saw in Chapter 1, now constitutes around two thirds of Europe's economy. The European Commission's desire to open it up to the same kind of cross-border competition that manufacturing has had to get used to was thus wholly understandable. But so, too, was the anxiety of trade unions. They worried about companies based in other European countries, companies that would only have to meet the standards imposed in those countries rather than the one they were operating in, forcing down pay and conditions – or simply taking the jobs to countries where they were already lower. There were also concerns that workers in the service sector would be undercut by migrants from the new member states – concerns that crystallised around *le plombier polonais* (Polish plumber) who EU commissioner Frits Bolkestein, in charge of the Services Directive, said he'd like to hire to help out at his second home in France!

Some on the left took the trade unions' side and, as we saw in Chapter 8, the Directive was diluted so as to exclude certain key publicly provided services. Others, however, made the point that inefficient and overly expensive services – whether public or private – were of no great benefit to the ordinary people social democrats were supposed to represent. And, they argued, denying the chance of earning better salaries and working in better conditions to hundreds of thousands of poor people in CEE was hardly progressive either. Interestingly, many supposedly Eurosceptic politicians of a conservative persuasion didn't seem too exercised about this particular piece of Brussels 'interference' in domestic affairs and, indeed, complained when the Directive was watered down. National sovereignty, it seems, doesn't always trump ideology.

both of which they can use to their advantage. In 2004, for instance, German-owned industrial concerns, *DaimlerChrysler*, *Siemens* and *Bosch*, were able to force longer working hours in factories in Germany and France partly by threatening to relocate plants to the Czech Republic and Hungary, where wages are lower.

How much longer that wage differential will last, however, is debatable. Clearly, it will not close in the next decade, but it is unlikely to last for ever. For one thing, the economies of the new member states are growing much faster than their western counterparts – and the continuation of such growth is not only likely but also clearly in the interests of the EU and all its member states (see Gros, 2002). For another, the gradual institutionalization of welfare states in the postcommunist countries (see below) is likely, in the long term, to lead to higher-wage economies. Neither is it something that the EU, as an institution, seems to want to do anything (or to be capable of doing anything) about. For one thing, the EU's competence over 'social policy' (see Hantrais, 2007) has, at the behest of the member states, been limited so as not to impact too directly on what most people would consider to be core areas of welfare, such as social security and healthcare provision. And, although the ECJ, for instance, has forced changes at the margins on, for example, on the retirement age and the eligibility of EU citizens for benefits in other member states, the latter continue to remain 'highly reluctant to shed their national welfare-state obligations in favour of pan-European solutions' Hermerijck *et al.*, 2006: 276). As a consequence, the EU can neither enforce 'European' models of welfare (see Chapter 1) on the region nor, as seems on balance more likely, prevent its governments adopting them, albeit in hybrid fashion (see Keune, 2006; Kovács, 2002, and Wagener, 2002).

The end of the welfare and regulatory state? Separating the facts from the hype

Comparative scholar Martin Rhodes provides a concise, no-nonsense but authoritative attempt to separate the European facts from the globalized

KEY POINT

The welfare state is not dead, nor is it in imminent danger. There is no race to the bottom on workers' terms and conditions driven by supposedly footloose firms.

hype about the triumph of neo-liberalism and the market over politics generally and the state in particular (see Ohmae, 1996 for an example). He notes the following (Rhodes, 2002: 41–2):

- European welfare states remain large, expensive and highly redistributive and their systems of labour market protection both generous and extensive.'
- '[T]here is no necessary correlation between welfare-state size/redistribution and the competitiveness of a country's companies in export markets' – something that markets are well aware of.
- '[A]nalyses of transnational investments patterns provide no support for the argument that multinationals are exploiting the differences in labour-market standards and regulatory institutions' between European countries (i.e. engaging in what is called 'social dumping').
- Broadly speaking, richer European countries are preserving levels of social spending while poorer ones tend to increase it in order to catch up. Meanwhile, 'permanent contracts remain dominant (and highly regulated by collective agreements and statute), and although there has been a spread of new contract forms (short-term, part-time work) in Europe, countries with high levels of social protection have also extended that protection to these "new" forms of work'.
- Because companies base their location decisions on myriad factors and governments find it hard to estimate the gains from tax competition with other countries, little such competition (and, therefore, downward pressure on revenues) has taken place.

Rhodes is not alone (see, for example, van Kersbergen, 2000), and his general conclusions are backed up not just by the findings of large quantitative projects (see Stephens *et al.*, 1999), but by country studies and cross-national studies of particular policy areas. Studies of both types point not just to the lack of any relationship between economic internationalization and welfare provision but also to the continued persistence of welfare states and national differences (see Swank, 2005: 187 and 184), most of which continue to correspond to Esping-Anderson's (1990) regime types outlined in Chapter 1. Three recent examples should suffice.

In the first example, Virpi Timonen outlines some of the changes made to the welfare states of Finland and Sweden – changes which include more private delivery of publicly funded services and a trend towards means-tested pensions – but nevertheless concludes that, because they continue to cover almost everyone and are therefore supported by almost everyone, they have not changed fundamentally, even when confronted with globalization and recession (Timonen, 2003).

The second example is Central and Eastern Europe. True, there is considerable debate between those (e.g. Ferge, 2001) who see the regions' governments, pressured by the need to persuade the World Bank and the IMF that they have really changed, heading down the Anglo-Saxon route and those (e.g. Deacon, 2000) who see a more 'European model' beginning to bed down. But, on balance, a mixture of institutional inertia, electoral constraints, and reasonably intelligent picking and mixing on the part of politicians (see Kovács, 2002 and Wagener, 2002) means that the region's welfare states, while not generous or particularly 'smart', are far from non-existent, even if they are difficult to pigeonhole as belonging to one or other of the welfare regime types we identified in Chapter 1 (see Keune, 2006). One analyst (Kovács, 2002: 198–9) captures the situation quite neatly:

> The 'communist welfare state' is being transformed but its relatively tightly knit safety net (including traditional protecting ropes) has not disappeared. At the same time, transformation is not excessive, the institutional experiments do not go much beyond their counterparts in Western Europe.

In our third concrete example, researchers focused on maternity benefits and child care programmes across Europe (and North America) and found, first, continued support (despite some limited convergence) for the idea of different countries belonging to different welfare regimes; second, that 'reports of the welfare state's demise do not hold true in these areas'; and, third, that while cultures and past patterns and choices influence current provision, 'the specific decisions that governments make' were just as vital (see Henderson and White, 2004). A similar conclusion is reached, incidentally, by a study (Mahler, 2004) which supports the idea that domestic politics plays a bigger role than globalization in determining the level of income inequality and redistribution in advanced countries. In other words, because politics still matters (and matters as much, if not, more than markets) Europe's welfare states – still largely protected from EU 'interference' – remain distinctive and, though not unchanged, relatively intact.

Why it still makes sense to be different

Just as Europe's welfare states are still welfare states, its social democrats can still claim, with some justification, to be social democrats, though not perhaps without qualifications. The biggest of these is that they have largely abandoned their goal of a more equal society – a goal that survived (at least as rhetoric) even long after most social democrats had embraced (more or less grudgingly) a role for the market as well as the state. This does not necessarily mean they are happy to let the poor get poorer – certainly in absolute terms – although both the persistence and the continued redistributionary effects of welfare mean that there is (reassuringly perhaps) little danger of that happening (Scruggs and Allan, 2006b and Kenworthy and Pontusson, 2005). But it does mean that they are less concerned than previously about the gap between rich and poor which, as we saw in Chapter 1, has got wider all over Europe (largely as a result of the rich being allowed to get richer). Instead, they seem more willing to admit that their primary concern has always been with *horizontal redistribution* (between old and young, sick and healthy, employed and unemployed) rather than *vertical redistribution* (between rich and poor) (see Bonoli, 2004).

> **KEY POINT**
>
> **It makes political and economic sense for parties to continue to differentiate themselves from their main opponents. This is especially the case in PR systems, but differences are still evident in countries operating FPP.**

Europe's social democrats have also admitted the difficulty of maintaining full employment via demand management and shifted their focus onto maximizing employment via the 'active labour market policies' successfully pursued in, for example, the Netherlands, even if this means a level of obligations to retrain and seek work that some see as draconian. They have also gone beyond the idea that 'more is (necessarily) better' when it comes to state involvement and public spending, and admitted the private sector into areas that previously might have been thought to be public sector preserves. Such an agenda might not be what some radical critics want; but it may be sensible (even superior) in the light of increasing evidence that, in the real world, individuals slip in and out of need over their lifetimes far more than we previously imagined – and far more than media-sexy terms like 'underclass' or 'middle-England' (and their European equivalents) imply (see Goodin *et al.*, 1999). But simply because social democracy is not what it was (what political ideology or institution or policy regime is?) need not mean that it is no longer social democracy. The latter has never been interested in being a prophet crying in the wilderness. Indeed, it has left that role to Europe's 'left parties', many of whom, incidentally, are in the forefront of opposition to the supposedly 'neo-liberal' side of the EU (see Dunphy, 2004).

In fact, these left parties are far from impotent or unimportant, not least because most European countries operate proportional representation systems (which interesting new research – see Iversen and Soskice, 2006 – suggests are themselves associated with more left-leaning government and redistribution). PR makes it all the more unlikely that social democrats will ever take what their critics call 'betrayal' too far: if they did, then many of the votes of the disillusioned and the disadvantaged might accrue to more radical alternatives which stand every chance of gaining seats at their expense, which would in time probably swing the centre-left back to the left in order to win them back. This

COUNTRY PROFILE

The Netherlands (Nederland)

Area: 33,900 km^2 (0.8% of EU-27)

Population: 16.3 million (3.3% of EU-27)

Religious heritage: Roman Catholic and Protestant

GDP (2006): €534 billion (4.6% of EU-27)

GDP *per capita* as percentage of EU-27 average: 132

Female representation in parliament and cabinet (end 2007): 37% and 25%

Joined EU: founder member, 1957

Top 3 cities: Amsterdam – capital city (0.7 million), Rotterdam (0.6 million), The Hague (0.5 million).

History: After breaking free from Habsburg and Spanish rule by the mid-seventeenth century and French rule by the beginning of the nineteenth, the Netherlands assumed its present status as a constitutional monarchy in 1848. Even though much of its Roman Catholic-dominated south became part of Belgium in 1839, the Netherlands remained a religiously divided society, with profound cultural differences not just between Catholics and Protestants but also between different branches of the latter. These differences were both maintained and contained by the *verzuiling* ('pillar') system: social groups marked off from each other by their denomination or ideological affiliation led largely separate existences, with their own welfare services, unions, business groups, political parties and media. From 1958 to 1973, all coalition governments were dominated by the centrist Christian Democrats. By the 1970s, however, the declining importance of religion and the consequent crumbling of the pillar system, allowed more governing flexibility. After a period of 'grand coalitions' with the Christian Democrats, the social democratic Labour Party finally got together with the economically liberal VVD and the more centrist D66 party to form what became known as 'the purple coalition'.

The Christian Democrats finally made it back into office in 2002, but not without the help of the far-right *Lijst Pim Fortuyn* (LPF) – a collection of political novices put together by a media-savvy maverick who was assassinated by an animal rights activist just before the election. After it, the LPF – and, consequently the government – fell apart. At the election of 2003 something like 'normal service' was resumed, but the Labour Party's recovery proved insufficient to oust the Christian Democrats, who formed a second centre-right coalition with VVD and D66. Labour again performed poorly at the next election but made it back into government as part of a 'grand coalition'. Since then, there have been big upheavals on the right of the political spectrum, with the founding of two new parties by high-profile, populist former members of the VVD.

Economy and society: The Dutch economy is one of the strongest in Europe, resulting in a *per capita* GDP for its 16 million citizens that is around a third better than the EU average. Rotterdam, half of whose population are said to be immigrants or from immigrant families, is the continent's biggest port, but the country as a whole is strong in road transportation, petrochemicals, consumer electronics and banking. It also has a highly efficient agricultural sector. This export-oriented economy may be vulnerable to downturns in big markets such as Germany, but it has helped the Dutch build one of the world's most developed welfare states; indeed, the supposedly successful combination of the two became known as the 'Dutch miracle'. Recently, however, more attention has been paid to its downsides, not least the extent to which sickness benefit and part-time work masks unemployment. And, while the Netherlands' (or at least its cities') famously tolerant attitude to drugs and alternative life-styles continues, its embrace of multiculturalism appears to

WHAT'S IN AN ANTHEM?

Popular from the end of the sixteenth century, *Het Wilhelmus* is the oldest song in the world to be used as a national anthem, although it was only sanctioned as such in 1932. At fifteen verses (the first letters of which combine acrostically to spell the name of its hero, William of Orange) it is also one of the longest, although (not uncommonly) only the first verse (sometimes along with the sixth) is usually sung. Written (unusually) in the first person, it's an account of a 'free and fearless' prince's struggle – more in sorrow than in anger and along with God and his fellow countrymen – for the 'Fatherland' against the 'tyranny' that is Spanish rule.

be under strain especially after episodes of religiously motivated violence. This may make life more difficult for the country's substantial Muslim population.

Governance: The Netherlands is a parliamentary democracy, elected under a PR system with a generously low threshold that facilitates a large number and spread of parties in the more powerful, popularly elected *Tweede Kamer* (Second Chamber). The less powerful First Chamber is chosen by the councils of the country's twelve provinces. Majority coalitions are very much the norm, even if two or three months of hard bargaining elapses between election night and the government being sworn in by the Queen. Notwithstanding this preference for majorities, the policy process is typically consensual – indeed, some say getting anything done takes too long (the so-called 'Dutch disease').

Foreign policy: The Second World War put paid to the Netherlands' century-old policy of trade-boosting neutrality, as well as to its empire in South America and the Dutch East Indies (most of which is now Indonesia). It was a founding member of NATO, and worked hard to maintain a good relationship with the US, as well as the UK, despite the fact that the latter was initially cagey about joining the EEC, which the Netherlands helped found in 1957. This traditionally 'Atlanticist' outlook came under strain in the 1980s, following huge public protests against the siting of US nuclear missiles in the country. Some observers also argue that the Netherlands, one of the biggest net financial contributors to the EU, is also cooling in its enthusiasm for further European integration (Box 2). This would seem to be borne out in recent European Parliament elections and, most spectacularly, in Dutch voters' rejection in the unprecedented 2005 referendum of the proposed European Constitutional Treaty.

A KEY CONTEMPORARY CHALLENGE

SHORING UP SUPPORT FOR EUROPEAN INTEGRATION IN A POPULIST CLIMATE.

In June 2005, Dutch voters resoundingly followed their French counterparts and rejected the proposed EU Constitutional Treaty – and by a massive 62–38 margin. Some feared that the proposed new voting arrangements might make it more difficult for the Netherlands to protect and promote its interests. They also resented paying more per head than any other member state into the EU budget, especially when the euro had apparently stoked price rises. Present, too, was the fear that EU integration might at some point allow other countries to interfere with the Dutch way of life, whether it be the tolerance reflected in the decriminalisation of prostitution and drugs or the solid, Christian bourgeois values of its more conservative inhabitants. Populist politicians also linked the treaty with the putative end of national controls on immigration and asylum.

The defeat also reflected a wider disconnect between citizens and not just the EU but also their own mainstream politicians, whose official agreement that the treaty was a good thing simply reinforced the suspicion – fuelled by populist politicians – that 'the elites' were trying to hoodwink 'the people'. That said, the overwhelming majority of the 'no' campaigners and voters made it clear that they objected not to the European train itself but to where it might be heading and the speed at which it seemed to be heading there. And interestingly, as in France, the government's decision not to hold a referendum on the Lisbon Treaty that replaced the Constitution in 2007 did not bring about mass protests.

Contemporary challenges

- Defending the Dutch tradition of toleration in an era of mass immigration and concerns about Islam
- Responding to the widespread distrust of and distaste towards mainstream, conventional politics and politicians
- Shoring up, in an increasingly populist climate, citizens' support for the elite consensus surrounding further European integration (see box above)
- Dealing with organized crime in big cities and glaring failures in the penal system
- Acting to do something serious about global warming which, given that half of the country lies below sea level, is a real threat.

Learning resources

An excellent overview is provided by Andeweg and Irwin (2005), *Governance and Politics of the Netherlands*. For incisive treatments of the dilemmas posed by immigrant integration, try Baruma (2007), *Murder in Amsterdam* and Sniderman and Hagendoorn (2007), *When Ways of Life Collide*. Keep up to date with the news at http://www.radionetherlands.nl/thenetherlands/

happened at the 1998 election in Sweden, when the Social Democratic SAP lost significant support to the Left Party and was henceforth distinctly more cagey about rationalizing the welfare state. Likewise, the existence of the Greens (and more liberal or libertarian variants of the left) relies on social democrats failing – at least, in the eyes of their critics – to defend core values (in this case, civil liberties and the interests of developing countries). But the presence of alternative parties on the social democrats' left flank also ensures that, looking over their shoulders, they do not completely forget such things.

Of course, the 'anchoring' effect of Green and Left potential depends in part on the extent to which this potential is likely to cause serious damage to the capacity of the social democrats to get into and dominate government. In some countries – Germany and Sweden are the most obvious examples – the social democrats have been able, in effect, to 'contract out' at least part of the conscience vote to smaller parties to their left, banking on the fact that the latter will probably join them in a progressive bloc that should prove capable of amassing more parliamentary seats than the bloc on the other side. The Swedish SAP, for about ten years after the mid-1990s, could count not only on the Greens, but also on the Left Party, notwithstanding its concern not to cede it too many of its voters. The German SPD, however, was stuck with the Greens alone, since it refused to work with the former communist (and largely East German) PDS or its successor (the more all-German party) the Left (see Hough *et al.*, 2007). Indeed, concern about losing too much support to the latter (as well as dissent in its own ranks over negotiations with the centre-right Christian Democrats) meant that, although Chancellor Schröder managed to steer his '*Agenda 2010*' welfare reform package through the notoriously cumbersome German system (see Chapter 4), he was forced into an early election and, eventually, early retirement (see Saalfeld, 2006).

In other countries, the centre-left has to be even more careful about not allowing too much space to open up on its left flank. France is the best example, though Italy and the Netherlands, to cite just two more examples, also have party and electoral systems that consistently deliver up small, radical parties to whom unwary 'centrists' can lose votes if they stray too far. The French socialist's candidate for the presidency in 2002, Prime Minister Lionel Jospin, for example, is widely thought to have blown his chances by taking too centrist a stance, leading some on the left either to abstain or vote for no-hopers who wore their radical hearts on their sleeves. But perhaps he was in a no-win situation: when the party's candidate at the next election, Ségolène Royale, presented a more left-wing programme (see Box 9.3), it looked outmoded and jarred slightly with her own image as something of a 'Blairite' modernizer.

But France, which operates a variant of FPP (see Chapter 6), suggests that keeping a respectable (if not respectful) distance from the other side of the political spectrum is not merely an artefact of the electoral system. So, too, does the UK, where, as we have already suggested, facile clichés about a move to the right under Blair and Brown obscure more than they illuminate. Indeed, defenders of Labour's continued centre-left credentials cannot only point to the huge rises in health and education spending already mentioned. They can also argue that, by focusing on (and delivering) economic growth and employment, and concentrating government help on working families, the UK government has pursued a 'classic postwar' social democratic strategy – even if, by 'talking right and acting left', it has done it by stealth. In any case, the radical rhetoric that characterized Labour before the party began its 'modernization' in the mid-1980s was always rather unconvincing given what (with the exception of 1945–8) was its very modest style of socialism in government.

European social democracy, then, has always been accommodating and has always operated in diverse institutional, cultural and competitive settings. These have, of course, increased as the end of communism in Central and Eastern Europe has produced a new bunch of parties that have adopted – some would say simply pasted on – the 'social democratic' label. This is problematic because, as we suggested in Chapter 5, the differences between left and right do not as yet (and might never exactly) replicate traditional western distinctions (see Sitter, 2003). The latter are rooted in the extent of state involvement in the economy and welfare provision. Distinctions in some postcommunist democracies have more to do with attitudes to the communist past, moral and family values and, indeed, to European integration, with 'social democrats' in Central and Eastern Europe being generally more favourable to the EU than their slightly more 'sceptic' right-wing opponents. These different bases for distinguishing the two sides are particularly the case in Poland, although the left and right in the Czech Republic (see Box 9.1) and Hungary could possibly claim to be more like their western counterparts (see Millard, 2004). They, too, hope to make moderate use of the power of the state to enhance citizens' quality of life and to maximize their equality of opportunity and their access to decent and hopefully helpful support whenever markets fail. But they, too, have stopped trying to pretend that they have either the will or the means to prevent those markets failing in the first place.

So, the supposed collapse in the distinction between right and left, and the concomitant weakening of the welfare state, is, to say the least, an idea in need of severe qualification. It is also one that offers us little purchase on one of the defining features of party politics since the 1990s and perhaps longer. This is the 'bipolarization' of politics we referred to in Chapter 5 – the fact that many of Europe's party systems appear to be structured by competition between blocs of parties, cleaving to either the left or the right, even if (as in Germany in 2005 or the Netherlands in 2006) the electoral arithmetic (and the unwillingness of one of the mainstream players to govern either as a minority or alongside more radical alternatives) can still effectively oblige the formation of a 'grand coalition' across the blocs. The left bloc generally contains left parties, greens, social democrats and some progressive or social liberals. Its counterpart on the right includes Christian democrats, conservatives and market liberals. It also includes, increasingly, the far right (see Bale, 2003) – a force whose rise is also blamed by some on the presumed decline of difference between right and left and reforms to the state that apparently make it incapable of protecting people from the predations of globalization.

No easy explanations – the rise of the far right

It is common wisdom that a combination of political convergence and economic dislocation has led inexorably to the rise of apathy and more extreme

KEY POINT

If voters are nonetheless finding it increasingly difficult to tell the mainstream parties apart, this is not an adequate explanation for the rise of more extreme parties on the right.

alternatives. We have already suggested in Chapter 6, that apathy and 'disconnect' can be overdone, at least when measured by turnout at general elections. Declines in the latter have not yet gone on long enough, neither are they uniform enough, to constitute a definite trend. Likewise, the rise of protest politics on the left, and the tendency for what appear to be increasingly large numbers of young people to become alienated from conventional politics and attracted to postmaterialist alternatives (see Chapter 8) might or might not turn into something more permanent than, say, the hippie and street-fighting movements of the late 1960s and early 1970s. Rather more concrete, though still a little hyped, is the rise of the far right (see Chapter 5) – something which pundits and politicians themselves often put down to what they claim is 'the lack of clear alternatives' presented by the political mainstream.

This explanation for the impressive performance of far-right parties since the 1990s has some merit. Class-based appeals, overt or even covert, have declined, and media-oriented, leader-focused campaigns might not have encouraged the far right to claim all the parties are the same (they have always done that) but they might have perhaps made that claim easier to believe. Also, one of the keys to their electoral fortunes in recent years has been the success those parties have enjoyed in recruiting young, poorly educated working-class men (although we should note that support for the far right is by no means confined to them). These are the sort of people who in previous generations would have been expected to vote for left-wing or centre-left parties. Perhaps it is the case that those parties (or, at least, the economies they 'run') are no longer providing these people with the standard of living or, more particularly, the job security that they were brought up to expect. Equally, by emphasizing equality of opportunity (often based on educational ability) and by tolerating more inequality of outcome than previously, the centre-left may have helped the 'winners' in society to pull away more obviously from the 'losers'. Perhaps social democratic parties, along with a shrinking trade union movement, are also failing to supply these 'losers' with the class-conscious comradeship that their fathers (or at least their grandfathers) might have enjoyed.

Ultimately, however, the 'decline of difference'/'victims of globalization' explanation is just too pat. Things are more complicated than that (see Norris, 2005). Indeed, as an explanation it is deeply flawed and inadequate. It is flawed because it relies on what we have seen is a partial reading of social democracy's past and present orientation, and an overly pessimistic impression of economic change and welfare decline. It also relies on a model of voting (i.e. class-based) that, as we noted in Chapter 6, many analysts are sceptical about. We should therefore be careful about blaming the centre left for supposedly letting down and losing what 'should' be 'their' voters. It is inadequate because it does not explain why, when large numbers of voters claim to have trouble telling the difference between the parties, only some of them plump for the far right. Neither does it explain why the far right is much more successful in some countries than others. This variation appears, incidentally, to have little to do with how, or how well, those countries have adjusted to economic change. The far right has done particularly well in top-performing, low-unemployment, welfare states such as Austria, Denmark Norway, and the Netherlands, and hopelessly in countries whose economies are either in much worse shape (e.g. Germany) or have much bigger differences between rich and poor (e.g. Spain and the UK). Moreover, and rather depressingly for the social democratic parties, the loss of office many of them experienced in the late 1990s – early 2000s – losses that could be blamed on the far right helping the centre right back into power (Bale, 2003) – occurred even though nearly all of them that lost office did so after presiding over economies that were performing pretty well.

In other words, things just are not as conveniently simple as the 'decline of difference'/'victims of globalization' explanation makes out. Moreover, those who buy into it also make the mistake of assuming that support for the far right is simply a protest vote – something the other parties could do something about if they were somehow more responsive and less convergent. Yet research shows that far-right voters are far less likely to be protest voters than is widely assumed. They vote for extremist parties because they are convinced by their populist arguments – arguments that perhaps include, but go way beyond, the hardly novel suggestion that the 'old parties' are 'all the same' (see Mény and Surel, 2002). Those arguments also have less to do with left–right competition on the socio-economic dimension, where centre left and centre right are supposed to have converged, than they have with 'values', where the evidence of convergence between the largely liberal left and the more conservative right is even thinner. In particular, people voting for the far right are worried about an issue that has come to dominate populist discourse – the growing presence of immigrant minorities in what they consider to be 'their' countries. It is to this issue that we now turn.

Learning Resources for Chapter 9

Further reading

For stimulating reads on the survival of the welfare state and the continuing power of politics, see Geoffrey Garrett's article in the journal *International Organization*, 52(4) 1998; Francis Castles (2004), *The Future of the Welfare State*; and the collection edited by Peter Taylor-Gooby (2004), *New Risks, New Welfare*. The review essay by Peter Starke in the journal *Social Policy and Administration*, 40 (1), 2006 is also helpful and his book (2007), *Radical Welfare State Retrenchment*, will almost certainly repay reading. Useful literature reviews on twenty-first century social democracy are provided by Kees van Kersbergen in the journal *Acta Politica*, 38 (2003), and Martin Powell's chapter in the collection he co-edited with Giuliano Bonoli (Bonoli and Powell, 2004), *Social Democratic Party Politics in Contemporary Europe*. An accessible, subtle and refreshingly balanced attempt to link developments in the European and international economy with the words and deeds of centre-left governments is provided by Peter Hall's chapter in the volume edited by Oliver Schmidtke (2002), *The Third Way Transformation of Social Democracy* – a volume that also contains useful contributions on the UK, Italy and France. Further debate on the politico-economic challenges for social democracy can also be found in the collection edited by Andrew Glyn (2001), *Social Democracy in Neoliberal Times*. Anyone interested in a long-term comparative political economy and its links to politics should also dip into Wilensky (2002), *Rich Democracies*. On the potentially restrictive (or at least restructuring) effect on social policy of belonging to the eurozone, see the collection edited by Martin and Ross (2004), *Euros and Europeans*. As for the far right, see Chapter 10.

On the web

www.tni.org – left wing takes on neo-liberalism

www.stockholm-network.org – neo-liberal enthusiasts

Discussion questions

1. How might we tell whether having a left- or right-wing government makes any difference to a country? Going on the evidence, does it make a difference?
2. Why did some on the centre-left of politics in Europe think social democratic and labour parties needed to 'modernize' and follow a 'Third Way'?
3. Privatization may still be fashionable – in some parts of Europe, at least. But is it quite as thorough-going as many assume?
4. Are so-called 'supply-side' economic policies necessarily right-wing?
5. Figures suggest that the era of 'tax and spend' in Europe is not really over: why do you think this might be?
6. In your opinion, is the EU locking in neo-liberalism in Europe or is it, instead, something of an obstacle to free-market, 'Anglo-Saxon' capitalism?
7. Does a move toward the centre-right make electoral sense for Europe's social democratic parties? Even if it does, is it possible that the move is more one of positioning than policies, rhetoric rather than reality?
8. It is not uncommon to hear the rise of far-right parties in Europe being blamed in part on the decline in difference between mainstream parties of the centre-right and the centre-left, as well as on the apparent failure of the latter to do much for the 'losers' of globalization. What do you think of this argument?

Chapter 10

Not wanted but needed – migrants and minorities

Migration into Europe – then and now	304
Europe's immigrants – grim realities and perceptions	307
Asylum-seeking	310
Encore le plombier polonais! Intra-EU migration since enlargement	314
The new stereotype – migrants and minorities as terrorists	315
Political responses – populism, priming and 'catch-22s'	315
Integrating and protecting migrants and minorities	323
Policy responses – towards 'Fortress Europe'?	326
The Roma – Europe's oldest ethnic minority	330

We observed in Chapters 2 and 3 how European states were devolving power, sometimes to the extent that traditional distinctions between unitary and federal states seem less and less useful. We also observed that these moves were often, at least in part, a response to claims for autonomy or even independence made by minorities who feel they constitute a nation or even a race apart. But those who feel that they are somehow trapped in the wrong body politic are not, however, the only minorities in Europe. The population of most, if not all, European countries is now made up not just of the descendents of those who lived there centuries ago, but also of those who have arrived much more recently – and, indeed, are still arriving. Whether these minorities are distinctive through **race** or only **ethnicity**, their presence, and the fact that they are being joined by more immigrants every day – at a rate of over two million per year from various sources – is the source of considerable anxiety and friction in many European countries. Migrants and minorities – no matter if they have been here for decades or even centuries – do not always find Europe as welcoming as they might have hoped. Indeed, they routinely encounter misunderstanding, mistrust, and sometimes outright hostility, from the ethnic majorities whose states they share and of which they might even become citizens.

This presents governments of all political stripes in Europe with a dilemma. Their majority populations, it seems clear, are anxious about, not to say hostile towards, any increase in immigration. On the other hand, experts are telling politicians that short-term labour shortages, combined with the ageing of majority populations whose fertility rates are way below replacement levels (see Chapter 1), make immigration more and more

> Although frequently (and, often, very reasonably) used interchangeably, the terms 'race' and 'ethnicity' do have different origins and connotations. **Race** is essentially about visually obvious physical characteristics that mark out some individuals from others, even if advances in genetics have put paid to the notion – at least at the level of science, if not popular culture – that such differences were somehow immutable and/or more than skin-deep. **Ethnicity** is to do with belonging to a social group that is tied by shared background, culture and language (and perhaps race, as well) and that may see itself (and be seen as) distinctive from the wider society. Inasmuch as it is ever really possible, one can perhaps escape or mask one's ethnicity, should one choose to do so. Persuading others, particularly if they are prejudiced, to ignore one's race might well be more difficult.

necessary, although few claim it is some kind of magic bullet. Indeed, even if it were, there is no guarantee that the consequent relief of politicians would be shared by their voters or by the media – witness the horrified reaction in some quarters to projections released in autumn 2007 suggesting that (due in part to immigration) the UK's population might well buck the European trend and actually rise by ten million in the next few decades. Some politicians, of course, will choose to side with 'the people' against the experts – one of the essences of populism (see Taggart, 2000). Others argue that democratic leadership sometimes entails leading (or even standing out against) public opinion instead of following and even inflaming it. Most politicians simply try to hold the ring, hoping that, as in times past (see Lucassen, 2006), the incomers currently seen as presenting such a threat will gradually be accepted.

This chapter begins with an account of patterns of migration into Europe, explaining why so many people have chosen, and been able, to make the place their home in the past, and why so many are joining them. It then looks at who Europe's newest arrivals are, what they do and where they live, before going on to examine some of the less-than-edifying public, political and media responses to their coming, focusing on anxieties about their impact on jobs and welfare, about asylum seekers, about immigration from the new member states of the EU to their richer counterparts in the west, and about Islamist terrorism. Next, the chapter looks at the ways in which European countries have begun, via the EU, to cooperate on immigration. It asks whether this is just one more surrender of sovereignty or yet another way to help preserve it, along with the distinctive immigration regimes that reflect (but are not wholly determined by) their past choices. The chapter ends by exploring the situation of the Roma minority that has been around in Europe for nearly a thousand years, but is still at the bottom of the heap.

Migration into Europe – then and now

Most of Europe's minorities have always lived there – or, at least, their ancestors have. But Europe is also home to millions of people who came, or whose ancestors came, from other places. Immigration is nothing new in Europe. It has been going on for centuries: the state system whose development we traced in Chapter 1 created national borders, they were rarely impermeable. European countries might not have encouraged immigration as much as 'settler' societies such as the US. But they often relaxed their restrictions when the labour market was tight and (perhaps more reluctantly) when claims were made upon them by citizens of their former colonies – Arabs from French North Africa, Afro-Caribbeans from the British Commonwealth or Surinamese from the Dutch East Indies (see Box 10.1).

KEY POINT

Europe is a continent forged by immigration and will continue to be so whether people like it or not: it attracts, and almost certainly needs, people to offset labour shortages and demographic problems.

Sometimes the flow of people into Europe has been a gradual, barely contested process, with intermarriage making a scientific nonsense of the idea of racial purity and bouts of emigration from Europe to the Americas and Australasia balancing out the numbers coming in. At other times, immigration has been more high-profile. Periodically, it has become the kind of influx that – especially when accompanied by media hysteria – causes widespread anxieties about 'overcrowding', about competition for jobs, housing, welfare and sexual partners and about cultural practices (such as forced marriage, honour killing and female circumcision) that many Europeans regard as alien, even barbaric. Migration, like European integration and especially eastern enlargement, has the capacity to both undermine and reinforce people's notions of where they come from, who they are and where they are going (see Spohn and Triandafyllidou, 2002).

For centuries, then, people have moved in and out of Europe without attracting much attention or doing much to alter, at least visibly, the ethnic balance. But there have also been several waves of immigration, often into particular countries, that have skewed the distribution of the continent's minorities, sometimes temporarily, sometimes permanently. For instance, by the late nineteenth-

BOX 10.1

Out of Africa, but not necessarily everywhere else – European decolonization

France, after almost eight years of fighting, left the Americans to try and sort out Vietnam after 1954. After another eight years of fighting, it left Algeria in 1962, having long disposed of its colonies further south in Africa. It continues, however, to hang on to territorial possessions in the Caribbean, Indian Ocean and in Polynesia – the so called DOM-TOMs. The DOMs (*Départements d'Outre-Mer*) – Guadaloupe, Martinique, French Guyana and Réunion – are fully integrated into France politically. The TOMs (*Territoires d'Outre-Mer*) are still effectively colonies: they are Wallis and Fortuna, French Polynesia (including Tahiti) and the nickel-rich island of New Caledonia, where in recent years an independence movement has forced France into granting it more autonomy.

The UK got out of the Indian subcontinent and Burma (Myanmar) reasonably peacefully, and out of Palestine, as it was then called, rather more violently just after the Second World War. During the 1950s, the British fought limited armed conflicts (but eventually saw the installation of friendly governments) in places such as Malaya, Cyprus, Kenya and southern Arabia. In the 1960s, it not only got out of Africa – rather too hurriedly, some say, given the instability its sudden departures engendered – but also withdrew from a major defence presence in South East Asia. On the other hand, it fought a war to re-take the Falkland Islands that Argentina decided to occupy in 1982. Fifteen years later, in 1997, the UK handed Hong Kong back to China.

The Netherlands withdrew from Dutch East India in 1949, when it became Indonesia. It granted independence to Surinam, next to French Guyana in the northern part of South America, in 1975.

Belgium was forced out of the Congo in 1960 by nationalist movements, with the chaos surrounding the withdrawal doing much to convince British policy makers that they, too, must accelerate their own withdrawal from Africa.

Portugal pulled out of the African countries of Mozambique and Angola in 1975 when, partly as a result of the strains imposed by trying to hang on to them, there was a peaceful (and eventually democratic) overthrow of the authoritarian regime that had ruled Portugal since the 1930s. It handed over Macau to China in 1999.

Italy and **Germany** both had limited colonial empires, based mainly in Africa, which they were forced to surrender after the Second World War ended in 1945.

Spain lost the last of its South American and Caribbean imperial possessions in the nineteenth century, but continues to hold on to its African outposts of Ceuta and Melilla in what is otherwise Morocco.

century, Jews had lived in Europe for centuries, although they had often encountered both acute and chronic discrimination. But then the Jewish populations of several countries were swollen by others fleeing nineteenth-century 'pogroms' (organized massacres and expulsions that today we might call 'ethnic cleansing' or even genocide) in the Russian empire. East Central Europe and Germany were the obvious places to escape to. Tragically, however, they were also those most afflicted by the Nazi Holocaust of the 1940s (see Chapter 1), once again reducing, in the most terrible way imaginable, the previous expansion.

After the Second World War, waves of immigration were experienced, first, by nations that were victorious and/or possessed colonies in Africa and the Caribbean: the 1950s and 1960s saw West Indians coming to the UK and Moroccans, Algerians

BOX 10.2

Immigration types and terms – legal, illegal, primary, family reunion, asylum, refugees, non-refoulement, residency, citizenship and amnesties

Immigration can be *legal* (i.e. people enter countries according to the rules set down by states for accepting them) or *illegal* (i.e. people enter illicitly without permission). Legal immigration can be split into a number of categories. *Primary immigration* occurs when an individual (perhaps with his or her immediate family) moves to another country, having got its permission to do so, for economic reasons – in other words, to work. *Family reunion* occurs when individuals move to another country (again, with permission) in order to join their relations who are already there, often, but not always, as a result of primary immigration. It is also possible for people to move legally to another country because they have a well-founded fear of persecution (commonly, though not necessarily, by the state) in their own country – this is known as seeking or claiming *asylum.* If the claim is accepted, the claimant will be granted *refugee* status under the 1951 UN convention. It is often the case with such applications, of course, that the person arrives prior to his or her claim being accepted and, in fact, it may turn out to be rejected (possibly because he or she is, in fact, an economic migrant trying to avoid the need for prior permission to enter the labour market). This leaves the individual with the choice of returning home (and he or she may be obliged to do so by the receiving country) or evading the authorities and becoming an *illegal immigrant.* In reality, the application process and any attendant appeal may take time, and the decision of the authorities might be to deny someone refugee status but still allow him or her to stay on other (humanitarian) grounds and/or because deportation would go against *non-refoulement* – a principle of international law which prevents states from returning people to a country where they would be likely to come to harm. In the long term, this might allow the individual concerned to apply for *residency* (the permanent right to remain) or even *citizenship* (the adoption of the receiving country's nationality). This is also a possibility when, as happens in many southern European countries, *amnesties* are granted to illegal immigrants who are offered the chance to 'regularize' their status in return for making themselves known to the authorities (and therefore paying tax and insurance contributions).

and Tunisians coming to France. In both countries, they came because labour shortages created demand for (often unskilled) workers at wages that seemed princely compared to what they could earn at home. The same was true, especially from the early 1960s on, in (West) Germany. There, *Gastarbeiter* (guest-workers), often Turkish, poured in to do the relatively low-paid jobs that (in the days of full employment we described in Chapter 1) Germans turned their noses up at but which needed doing if the country's 'economic miracle' was to be sustained. The UK, Germany and France also took in large numbers of Spanish, Portuguese and Italians. They were either leaving dictatorships (in the case of the first two) or (in the case of all three) the poverty of their native lands. Greeks and Greek Cypriots came for similar reasons, though in smaller numbers. The only countries relatively unaffected by these waves of essentially 'primary' migration (see Box 10.2) were in Scandinavia and the Soviet bloc. In the case of the former, this was because they were too hard to get to and had no historic, colonial links. In the case of the latter, it was because, quite simply, nobody wanted to go there.

Before the end of the Cold War in 1990, then, Europe's minorities came largely because it made economic sense for those directly concerned. It still does, given the numbers of foreign-born workers in the labour force of most European countries (see Table 10.1). It did not always benefit the underdeveloped countries from which immigrants came: they lost skilled, or at least potentially skilled, labour – and they still do, especially in the health sector. On the other hand, the remittances they sent back home were useful in economies starved of cash and, in the case of poorer European countries, of the durables

Table 10.1 Where they are – foreign population as a percentage of total population, 2005

	Foreign-born in population (%)	Foreign-born in labour force (%)
Czech Rep.	5.1	2.0
France	8.1	11.2
Germany	12.9	14.9
Italy	2.5	8.1
Netherlands	10.6	11.6
Poland	1.6	n/a
Spain	5.3	13.3
Sweden	12.4	13.1
UK	9.7	10.1

Note: Data for Germany is 2003; for Poland, 2003; and for Italy, and Spain, 2001.

Sources: Data from OECD, *International Migration Outlook* (2007).

that were increasingly taken for granted in the richer north.

Since then, however, the situation has become considerably more complicated. A more unsettled geopolitical environment has increased the numbers of people in Africa and the Middle East desperate to flee persecution and civil war, some of whom attempt officially to claim asylum (see Box 10.2). Meanwhile, the economic situation has gone from bad to worse. The insistence on the part of developed countries (often via the multinational agencies that they dominate, such as the IMF and the World Bank) that developing nations pursue what some see as a counterproductive conversion from subsistence to cash economies that will help them to honour overseas loans has made it very difficult for ordinary people. This is particularly the case when, at the same time, critics say, the EU's highly subsidized, highly protected, agricultural sector is allowed to dump its products in their markets without having to face free and fair competition from their producers (see Castles, 2004). Even where people can manage to feed their families, they have little hope that they can attain a standard of living that comes close to what, with the advent of global brand advertizing and media, they see being enjoyed – apparently by all – in the prosperous parts of the world. Little wonder, then, say some critics of the developed countries, that more and more people than ever before will do what ever it takes to make a new life for themselves and their families.

All this means that European countries with a history of immigration are finally having to come to terms with the fact that those who have come are unlikely ever to want to go 'home'. It also means that those countries with no history of immigration – often countries, in fact, that supplied immigrants to those that did – are having to adjust to the fact that they, too, are now destinations rather than points of departure (see Box 10.3).

Europe's immigrants – grim realities and perceptions

Given the role of civil and international conflict in pushing people into migration, we should be forgiven if we often concentrate more on where immigrants come from than who they are. But the latter matters, too. Sociological research suggests that they tend to cluster at either ends of the educational spectrum. Some are university graduates filling skills shortages in particular sectors, but Europe also needs unskilled workers willing to do menial jobs, especially in the expanding service sector. Research – and common sense – also suggests that immigrants are rarely the poorest of the poor. Most not only come from countries where there is already some economic development, but have had to amass funds to get themselves, legally or otherwise, to Europe in the first place: in Kurdistan, it costs about twice as much (€6,000) to buy illegal entry into Europe as it does to build an average family home. Many media stories about the plight of asylum-seekers ('bogus' or otherwise) feature women and children, either to elicit our sympathy or to provoke

KEY POINT

Most migrants come to Europe because they are poor, discriminated against or in danger. While the majority contribute positively, they are also over-represented in all sorts of negative statistics. The stereotypes are rarely positive – scrounger, job-stealer, criminal, terrorist – and many people buy into them, just as many people vastly over-estimate how many immigrants there are.

BOX 10.3

Spain – from sender to receiver

Spain used to export labour northwards and import tourists southwards. It still does the latter, although more and more of those coming from northern Europe never go home: some 300,000 UK citizens now live there, for example – a useful reminder that immigration is offset, at least in part, by citizens who leave to live elsewhere. The mass emigration of Spaniards, however, was coming to an end even before their country joined the EU in 1986. Nowadays, Spain imports not only tourists from the north, but also immigrants from the south, particularly from sub-Saharan Africa, many of whom work in 'polyculture' – the mass cultivation of fruit and salad crops under plastic in Southern Spain. For a few years, the favoured route was across the Straits of Gibraltar from northern Morocco, until, that was, Spain spent millions on surveillance equipment for the most vulnerable parts of its southern coast and on reinforcing the huge fences around its African outposts in Ceuta and Melilla. Since then, the Canary Islands, just off the Atlantic coast of Africa, have taken over as the main destination for immigrants: getting from there to the Spanish mainland, after all, requires no passport since the islands are fully a part of Spain and, in 2006, some 31,000 Africans landed on the islands (with another 6,000 tragically drowning in the attempt). The other big source of immigrants, this time by air straight to Madrid, is from (Spanish-speaking) South America, with people coming in as tourists (often visa-free) and going straight to the building sites of Spain's booming construction industry.

Like next-door-neighbour Portugal, Spain is still relatively homogeneous, with a foreign population of only 5 per cent, half of whom are in any case affluent – and often retired – northern Europeans (see Casado-Díaz, 2006). Notwithstanding some pretty ugly incidents of racist chanting by Spanish fans at football matches (Spain v. England in November 2004 being one shameful example) and some evidence that both anti-Latin American and anti-African sentiment is on the rise, surveys generally suggest that its population is also less prone to anti-immigrant sentiments than that of many other European countries (see Table 10.6). Spain (like Italy) has also tolerated a degree of illegal immigration, which it has regularized through periodic amnesties that have offered hundreds of thousands of people who had managed to evade the authorities to stay permanently. The most recent amnesty, in 2005 which regularized the status of over 600,000 people, infuriated other European governments, especially when they were then asked to help out in the Canary Islands: in their view the boatloads of Africans arriving in 2006 were a natural consequence of the previous year's decision. They were doubly frustrated because Spain (along with Italy and now, of course, the tiny islands of Malta and Cyprus as well) is supposed to play a big part in policing what is the EU's vulnerable southern border. Meanwhile, Spain has done its own deals with, among others, Senegal, Mauritania, and Morocco, which – along with television ads paid for by Spain – are reported to have resulted in a big drop in illegal immigrants.

our outrage. Far more commonly, in fact, Europe's immigrants are single men in their twenties and thirties, chosen by the families who help to get that money together because they are seen to have the best chance of making it to, and in, the promised land. If they do, they can then send for family members or at least send back the remittances that a recent study has shown 'significantly reduce the level, depth, and severity of poverty in the developing world' (Adams and Page, 2005: 1645).

Although some use kinship connections and aim for a particular destination, many have only the vaguest idea of where they might end up. Neither do they necessarily want to come forever – indeed, some experts think that stricter immigration regimes actually trap people into not leaving what might otherwise have been a temporary home. Given the restrictive climate, people quite justifiably fear not getting back in again should the planned return home not work out. On the other hand, if

Figure 10.1 The jobs gap between natives and immigrants in Europe, 2005

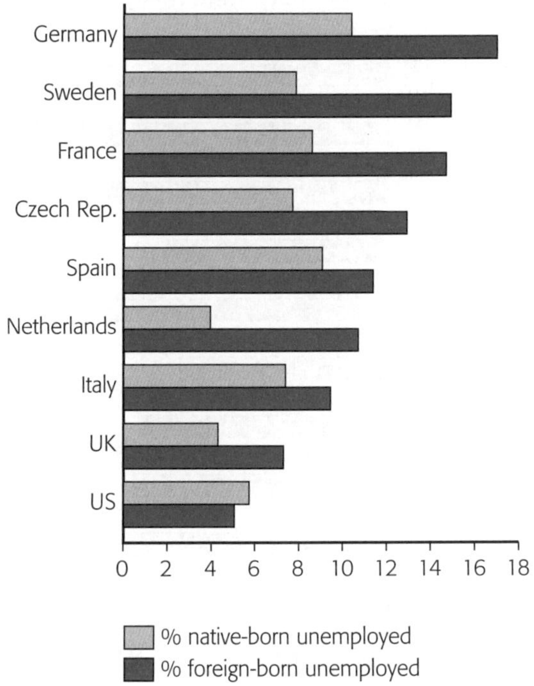

Note: No data are available for Poland.

Source: OECD, *International Migration Outlook* (2007). Note that these are official statistics: given the fact that immigrants may be more likely to work in the 'black economy', the real gap may be narrower.

they do stay, it is often because they find it easy (legally or illegally) to get work. This is one of the reasons why the UK is a relatively popular European destination (and why, by the same token, immigrants there make a positive contribution to GDP and state revenue). Once they do find work, and as long as they regularize their status, many immigrants send for their relations and, in some cases, pick up a spouse from overseas. In Europe, just as in the US, family reunion is (and this is something worth emphasizing) by far the biggest source of legal migration – and not necessarily one that contributes skilled or even able-bodied immigrants.

Many immigrants in Europe do badly paid work, just as they do in the US. Unlike the US, however, European countries have high unemployment and more generous welfare systems. Although, because they are younger, they tend to be economically more active than the population as a whole (see Table 10.1), immigrants there are generally more likely to be unemployed than non-immigrants of working age (see Figure 10.1), with some ethnic groups suffering even more than others. In Belgium, for instance, the highest unemployment rates amongst all groups are those for Turkish and Moroccan nationals (45 per cent for males, 56 per cent for females) compared to the unemployment rates for Belgian nationals of 10 per cent (Fundamental Rights Agency, 2007: 45). This feeds into a negative stereotype of the immigrant as a drain or even a parasite on the welfare system. At the same time, and somewhat paradoxically, immigrants are also accused of 'stealing jobs' because in many countries – especially those that have enjoyed reasonable employment growth in recent years – there has been a big (and probably very visible) increase in the number of jobs done by foreign-born workers (see Table 10.2).

The perception and the reality also feed into another powerful stereotype – that of immigrants (and those of immigrant origin) as criminals. Unsurprisingly, the children of immigrants often grow up poor. They also under-perform at school and in the labour market. In Germany in 2005, of German people aged 20–26, 41 per cent were students, 43 per cent were employed and 16 per cent were economically inactive; the figures for Turks of

Table 10.2 Growth in employment, 1995–2005, foreign-born compared with total population

	Employment growth, 1995–2005 (%)	
	Foreign-born	**Total population**
Italy	2038	13
Spain	979	58
Sweden	129	5
NL	73	18
UK	52	8
Germany	16	–1
France	9	10

Source: Data from OECD, *International Migration Outlook* (2007).

the same age were 24, 37 and 38 per cent, respectively (see *Migration News*, 14(1), 2007). This can become a vicious circle of deprivation, into which crime – particularly street crime – often enters. For instance, in Rotterdam, in the Netherlands, it has been calculated that nearly eight out of ten who are jailed for such offences are from ethnic minorities. Of course, not everybody in Europe swallows the stereotype whole, but there is enough reality (or perceived reality) in it to mean that plenty of people do buy into it (see Figure 10.2).

These perceptions are very difficult to shift, especially because they have some basis in reality. But the same goes for those that do not. As Figure 10.3 shows, Europeans (like Americans) massively overestimate the numbers of foreign-born people resident in their countries, especially in France and the UK.

Asylum-seeking

Although over 1 million people per year still enter the EU legally, the barriers to primary (i.e. economic) immigration were first raised in Europe during the recessions of the 1970s and 1980s. These troubled economic times marked the end of the postwar boom and, partly as a result of the sometimes counterproductive policies pursued to improve matters, saw unemployment return to levels not seen since the 1930s (see Chapter 1). Neither the barriers nor the recessions did much to reduce the push factors for people in developing or conflict-ridden countries: anything was better than where they were, and would-be immigrants were simply driven into increasingly desperate and unlawful measures to get around restrictions. Currently, illegal immigration into the EU is put at about half a million people per year, with many paying thousands of dollars to 'people-smugglers' or traffickers to help them make it, if not to the European mainland, then to some of its remote islands, often with tragic results. Bodies being washed up on the beaches of Spain and Sicily hardly

Figure 10.2 Do immigrants make things better or worse?

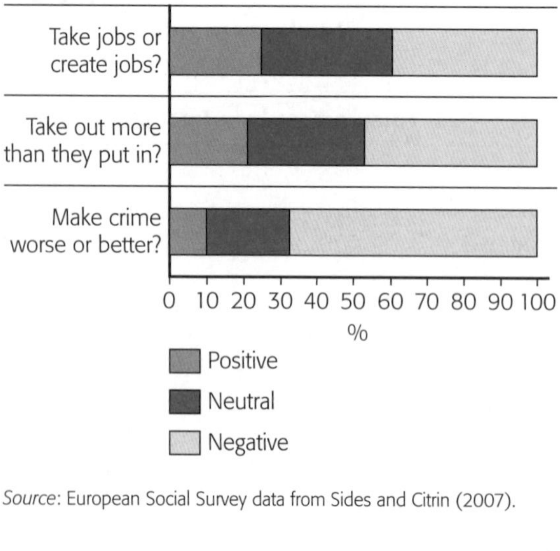

Source: European Social Survey data from Sides and Citrin (2007).

Figure 10.3 Perception is reality? The gap between how many 'foreigners' people think there are and how many there really are

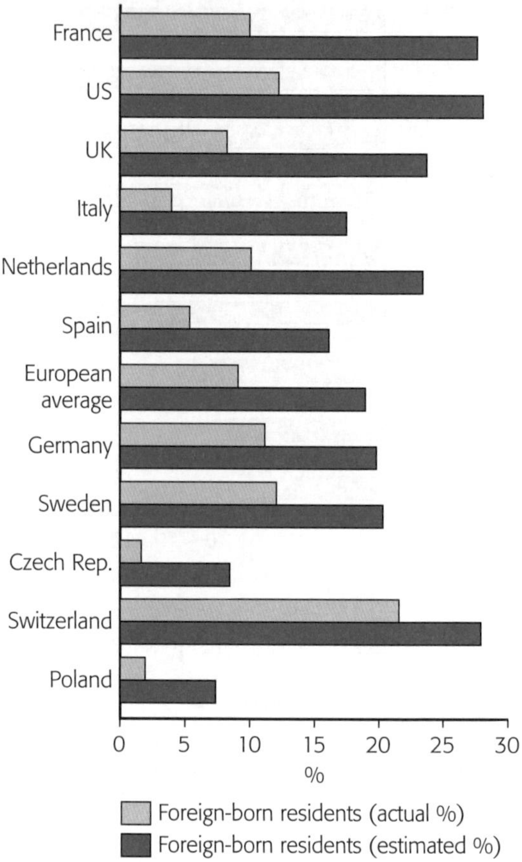

Source: 2002–3 OECD and European Social Survey data from Sides and Citrin (2007).

merit a mention in the news nowadays, so common are they.

This estimate of half a million per year for illegal immigrants covers those who, on arrival, simply disappear, having no contact with the authorities, often melting into the communities already established by their (legal) forerunners, although some of them, of course, make the headlines by being discovered or dying either *en route* or while working illegally. Large numbers of immigrants, however, make it to Europe every year and then claim asylum. Some will be economic migrants pure and simple, and therefore 'bogus'. Research suggests that the wealth of a country – but, interestingly, not the generosity of its welfare system – does impact on the number of asylum applications it receives (see Neumayer, 2004). But – like Jews from Germany in the 1930s, who also had difficulty persuading authorities in liberal democracies that they were genuinely in need of a place of safety – many will be fleeing for their lives. This is because the number of asylum applications, as well as being related to poverty and discrimination, is in part a function of civil conflict, state failure and human rights violations (see Table 10.3; see also Neumayer, 2005). For instance, the 192,000 asylum applications to EU countries in 2006 is only 30 per cent of the 670,000 received in 1992, at the height of the war that followed the break up of Yugoslavia (see Chapter 1). A more secure situation and/or fewer human rights abuses in Iraq or Afghanistan or the Kurdish regions of Turkey or Sri Lanka or Somalia or Sudan or the Democratic Republic of Congo or the former Soviet Union and Yugoslavia would also do much to reduce numbers of people desperate to get away from those countries and seeking to come to Europe. On the other hand, their choice of country is rarely random: asylum seekers often make for countries in which there are already communities from their homeland; a common language and colonial connections also count for something (see Neumayer, 2004). Obvious examples include people moving from the Congo to Belgium, Algeria (France), Somalia (UK and the Netherlands) and Russia (Poland). Sweden, by being particularly welcoming to Iraqis fleeing the chaos prompted by the US-led invasion, has experienced something of a snowball effect: in 2005, it got just over 2,000 applications, in 2006 over 9,000 – just under half of all the Iraqis applying in the EU; around 70,000 Iraqis now live in Sweden.

KEY POINT

Asylum is driven by need, if not always by the imminent threat of persecution that refugee status demands. Some countries seem to get more than their fair share of people seeking that status, although this is disputable if their size is taken into account. Asylum claims have dropped markedly in recent years.

Table 10.3 Top five countries of origin for asylum seekers in the EU-27, 2006

Country of origin	Total	Percentage of total applications
Iraq	19,215	10
Russia	12,760	7
Serbia and Montenegro	12,705	7
Afghanistan	7,430	4
Turkey	7,220	4

Source: Eurostat, *Asylum Applications in the European Union*, Issue 110/2007.

It is also worth pointing out, of course, that European countries' contribution to the problem of displaced persons is nothing like as generous as some claim. This is especially the case when judged against that of countries that are geographically much nearer crisis zones and inevitably receive many more refugees, both in absolute terms and relative to their capacity to cope – at least, as measured in terms of their existing population and their wealth, even if some countries (notably the Netherlands and Germany) could fairly claim to be under pressure when it comes to space (see Table 10.4).

Understandably, of course, most Europeans either do not compare their situation with other countries at all or compare it with other European countries. If we do the latter, we can see that certain countries are affected more than others, although the situation varies according to whether the comparison is done on absolute or relative terms. In absolute terms, it is

Table 10.4 Country capacity and contributions, 2001–5[1]

	Refugees per 1000 inhabitants	World ranking	Refugees to US$1 GDP *per capita*	World ranking	Refugees per 1,000 km^2	World ranking
Armenia[2]	80.0	1	236.3	17	8147.3	1
Sweden	12.1	10	2.9	65	245.9	28
Germany	10.7	13	26.7	40	2483.1	5
Netherlands	8.4	21	3.9	63	3909.2	2
Switzerland[2]	7.1	23	1.0	82	1256.1	10
DR Congo[2]	4.6	32	231.4	1	114.0	47
UK	4.6	33	7.7	56	1125.6	11
France	2.2	48	4.0	82	245.5	29
US[2]	1.5	59	11.5	50	48.4	66
Italy	0.2	93	0.5	95	45.0	67
Spain	0.1	99	0.3	107	12.1	92
Czech Rep.	0.1	100	0.1	113	17.8	88
Poland	0.1	113	0.4	98	7.6	101

Notes: 1. World ranking out of 154.
2. Armenia, DR Congo, US and Switzerland are added for comparison with core countries.

Source: *UNHCR Statistical Yearbook* (2005).

clear that at the top of the list of countries most affected by asylum-seeking are Germany and the UK (see Figure 10.4)

In relative terms, or at least in terms of annual applications per head of population, the rankings are very different, with very small countries like Malta and Cyprus, and a relatively small non-member state, Switzerland, appearing to be most affected, while the comparative generosity of Sweden becomes more apparent (see Figure 10.5). On these grounds, the UK, where the press hysteria surrounding asylum seekers has perhaps been greatest, has little to complain about.

But it doesn't work like that, largely because it is absolute numbers, their geographical concentration and the peak years that seem to count most – both for ordinary people and (perhaps significantly) for the media they consume. In 2002, for instance, the UK received (counting dependents) over 100,000 asylum applicants – far more than other European countries, including Germany, and more than any other country in the industrialized world. In fact, 2002 saw a 12 per cent increase on the previous year, while across the North Sea in the Netherlands and in Denmark, which both tightened their regimes, asylum applications dropped by 57 per cent and 48 per cent, respectively. London alone played host to over 200,000 asylum seekers and refugees. Meanwhile, the annual cost of processing and supporting asylum seekers in the UK in 2002 was said to be running at almost €2.5 billion – much of it going not simply on welfare benefits, but also to landlords and lawyers and the like catering especially for such people. Just over 40 per cent of those applying for asylum were granted permission to stay on one ground or another. The others simply helped to clog up the system, contributing to massive delays in processing genuine cases. Moreover, as all European states find, it has been one thing to turn down an application and another actually to return the person concerned to their country of origin (real or imagined). As politicians and the press never tire of pointing out, many remain regardless of a decision going against them, either because they simply escape the supervision of the authorities or because nowhere else will agree to take them back.

Figure 10.4 Total asylum applications, 1998–2006

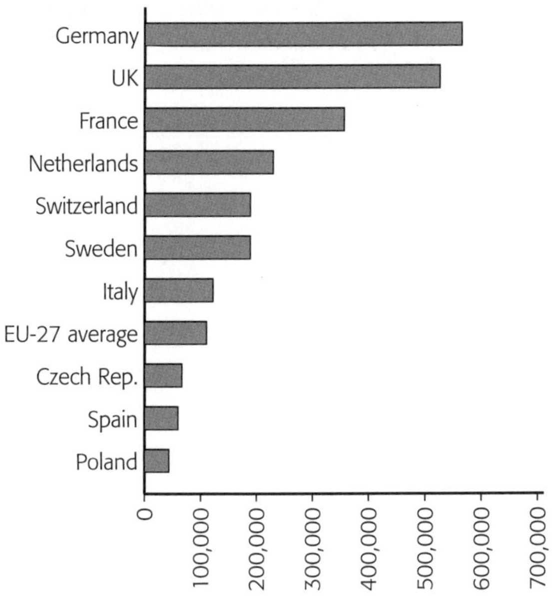

Source: Eurostat, *Asylum applications in the European Union* – Issue number 110/2007.

Figure 10.5 Annual asylum applications, per 1,000 inhabitants, 2003–6

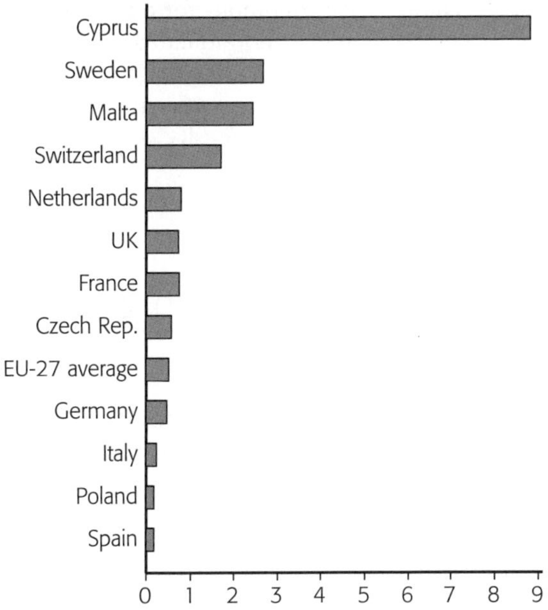

Source: Eurostat, *Asylum Applications in the European Union*, Issue number 110/2007.

'The numbers game' played in the media involves claim and counterclaims that are very hard to cut-through, not least because there is no one authoritative source of statistics for each country, let alone for Europe as a whole. But it is important, because many Europeans have very little direct contact with migrants and rely for their sense of what is going on (and for many of them what is going wrong) on the media. Indeed, there is research that suggests that politicians (who may themselves be influenced by newspaper and TV coverage, of course) take account of this: there appears to be a correlation between media coverage and governments taking action to toughen their stances on immigration and integration (see Givens and Luedtke, 2005). Certainly, the media, which made much of the numbers going up, has said relatively little about the fact that from 2002 onwards they appear to be going down all over Europe (Figure 10.6), even if the UK (with 27,800 applications in 2006) still gets the most and Sweden, along with Greece, currently seems to be bucking the trend. The fall may be due to the efforts made by most governments to

Figure 10.6 Rise and fall in asylum applications in the EU-27, 1998–2006

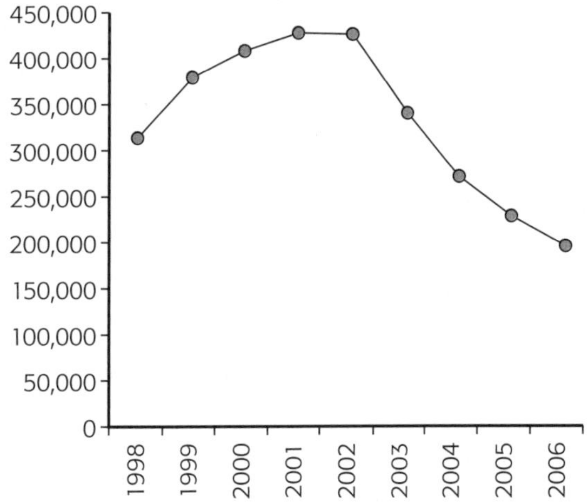

Source: Eurostat, *Asylum Applications in the European Union*, Issue 110/2007.

strengthen their border controls – often, as we shall see, via co-ordinated action with other receiving states – and to make conditions for asylum seekers (and other immigrants) more onerous. But it may well be the case that the civil conflicts which help drive asylum applications (or at least those made in Europe) have reduced in intensity or extent – at least temporarily.

Encore le plombier polonais! Intra-EU migration since enlargement

As asylum appears (rightly or wrongly) to be coming under some kind of control, however, new sources of anxiety have arisen. One of them is the huge increase in legal labour migration prompted by the enlargement of the EU to include much poorer countries from CEE (for background, see Górny and Ruspini, 2004). Once again, some countries are more affected than others. The UK, Ireland and Sweden decided from the outset that, unlike the rest of the EU-15, they would not introduce restrictions on workers from the postcommunist new member states (the so-called 'A-8'). This meant that anyone from the latter who was not willing to declare themselves self-employed, accept a limited seasonal work permit, or work illegally had only three choices if they wanted to earn a western wage. Indeed, given that the power of the trade unions in Sweden seems to have prevented employers from paying immigrants lower wages than their Swedish counterparts, making them less attractive to hire, the choice for many who wished to work in the West effectively came down to the British Isles, although the number of mainly seasonal work permits on offer from Germany still made it a popular destination (see Table 10.5). Consequently, the projections made of the numbers who would come to the UK and Ireland were hopelessly inaccurate.

KEY POINT

The distribution of those moving from the post-communist East to the richer West is also uneven but, interestingly, does not appear to be associated with increased hostility on the part of people in the countries most affected.

Table 10.5 Where the Polish went

Destination	Number of permits/ registrations issued to Polish citizens, 2004–5	Percentage of total
Germany	321,800	51.6
UK	129,400	20.8
Ireland	64,700	10.4
Italy	33,500	5.4
Netherlands	26,500	4.3
Austria	18,100	2.9
Spain	11,600	1.9
France	9,700	1.6
Belgium	3,400	0.5
Sweden	2,800	0.4
Denmark	1,200	0.2
Other EU-15	400	0.1

Source: Data from 'Move to Britain?', *Guardian*, 9 September 2006.

Initial government estimates on how many new EU citizens from CEE would come looking for work in the UK ranged around the 15,000 mark. In the event, official statistics from the UK released in August 2007 confirmed that between May 2004 and June 2007 some 683,000 people from the A-8 registered to work in the UK, seven out of ten of whom were from Poland and eight out of ten of whom were aged 34 and under, which perhaps explains why there have been so few claims on the benefits system (see BBC, 2007). Many of these will, of course, have gone home again, but the numbers of those returning might have been more than made up for by those who do not register or who declare themselves self-employed. The backlash against this 'flood' – as the tabloid newspapers who led the charge insisted on calling it – led the UK government, notwithstanding a very positive EU report on the economic impact of A-8 migrants (see European Commission, 2006), to join other member states in imposing restrictions on workers from Bulgaria and Romania (the so-called A-2) when those countries joined the EU in 2007. This was just as some member states which had originally imposed restrictions on the A-8 countries in 2004 – Finland, Greece, Italy, the Netherlands, Portugal and Spain – lifted them, while others (Belgium, Denmark, France and Luxembourg) were at least easing them. Only Germany and Austria seem destined to hold out until 2011, and even they have very large seasonal schemes that allow them to employ large numbers of Central and Eastern Europeans to do the jobs their own workers (notwithstanding continuing high unemployment in Germany) will not do, especially in agriculture. The latter sector, which – especially if involves manual picking – finds it hard to recruit right the way across western Europe, the work being backbreaking and the pay low, is a major source of jobs for migrants, many of whom are unfortunately prone to exploitation by 'gangmasters' who hire them out to flower, fruit, vegetable growers with no questions asked.

The new stereotype – migrants and minorities as terrorists

The other contemporary source of anxiety, along with labour migration from 'the new Europe', is Islamist terrorism, especially since the September 11 2001 attacks on New York and Washington have been followed by the March 2004 attack in Madrid, the July 2005 bombings in London, the attack on Glasgow airport in June 2007, as well as by numerous plots foiled by police, especially in Germany – the country where the 9-11 attacks were, at least in part, planned. This has contributed to what some analysts refer to as the ongoing 'securitization' of European (and, indeed, global) debates and policy on migration and minorities (see Guild and van Selm, 2005, Huysmans, 2006 and Karyotis, 2007), as well as adding yet another to a long list of negative stereotypes with which immigrants have to contend. On the other hand, Islamophobia in Europe has very deep roots and the spread and visibility of the Islamic population was already the subject of debate in the late 1990s in a number of countries, irrespective of the fact that Muslims – the vast majority of whom reject radical violence (see Klausen, 2005) – were not then automatically linked with it (see Box 10.4).

KEY POINT

There was Islamophobia in Europe before there was Islamist terrorism, but the latter has almost certainly made things worse.

Political responses – populism, priming and 'catch-22s'

The numbers, concentration and visibility of migrants and minorities in Europe, along with the negative stereotypes (welfare parasite, job-stealer, criminal, terrorist) mean that they are a hot-button political issue in contemporary Europe. As Figure 10.7 shows, attitudes towards them vary between countries (they seem generally less positive in the EU's new member states) as well as according to sex, education, occupational status and (very significantly) ideological self-placement. These attitudes are not as overwhelmingly hostile as some assume, nor are they necessarily getting worse – especially, interestingly enough, in those countries (the UK, Sweden and Ireland) which have seen big influxes from the new member states in recent years. Nevertheless, there is no doubt that large numbers of Europeans, among elites as well as the so-called masses (see Lahav, 2004: 105–6), are very worried by the situation. These worries, rather than varying much with the numbers of immigrants or levels of unemployment, spring from deeply held preferences for cultural unity and national sovereignty and identity, albeit preferences that are offset by friendships and length of education (see Sides and Citrin, 2007). Predictably, Europe's populist politicians have not

KEY POINT

In a climate of anxiety, pumped up by the media, populist radical right parties have thrived – but only in some countries, suggesting that it is the skills of the parties concerned, and the reactions of other parties, that matter more than 'objective circumstances'.

been slow to pick up on – or even to help drive – these concerns. But the mainstream has had to respond to them, and to some extent has also had a hand in driving them, too.

In the 1990s, parties of the far right, or 'populist radical right parties' (see Mudde, 2007), scored some

BOX 10.4

Islamophobia

It is the extent rather than the existence of European Islamophobia (fear or hatred of Muslims) that is novel. The threat posed by Muslim militancy has long been a familiar tune sung by Europe's populist politicians, particularly in Denmark and Italy. Both countries have a tradition of orchestrated campaigns against the building of mosques – campaigns that have now spread to many European countries (see the special issue on 'Mosque Conflicts in Europe' of the *Journal of Ethnic and Migration Studies*, 31(6) 2005), including Germany where, in the summer of 2007, there were huge protests against a new mosque in Cologne, home to 120,000 Muslims. But, since 9-11, fears that the latter present a clear and present danger have ballooned. Take the Netherlands, where something approaching a moral panic has been going on since 2002. In that year, media reports (backed up by undercover recordings) suggested some of the religious leaders of the country's 800,000 Muslims (who make up 5 per cent of the population) routinely railed against 'the West' and 'western values' such as gender equality and tolerance of homosexuality. In 2004, people's worst fears were confirmed when outspoken film-maker Theo van Gogh was killed by an Islamist fanatic after his film about the oppression of Muslim women was shown on Dutch TV – a crime which forced one of his collaborators, high-profile MP and apostate, Ayaan Hirsi Ali, into constant police protection (see Buruma, 2007, and Sniderman and Hagendoorn, 2007). Since then there has been talk of banning the wearing of the *burqa* (which covers the whole body) as a security risk, even though apparently only a few hundred women among the Netherlands' one million Muslims wear it.

Figure 10.7 Proportion of people disagreeing that 'immigrants contribute a lot' to their country

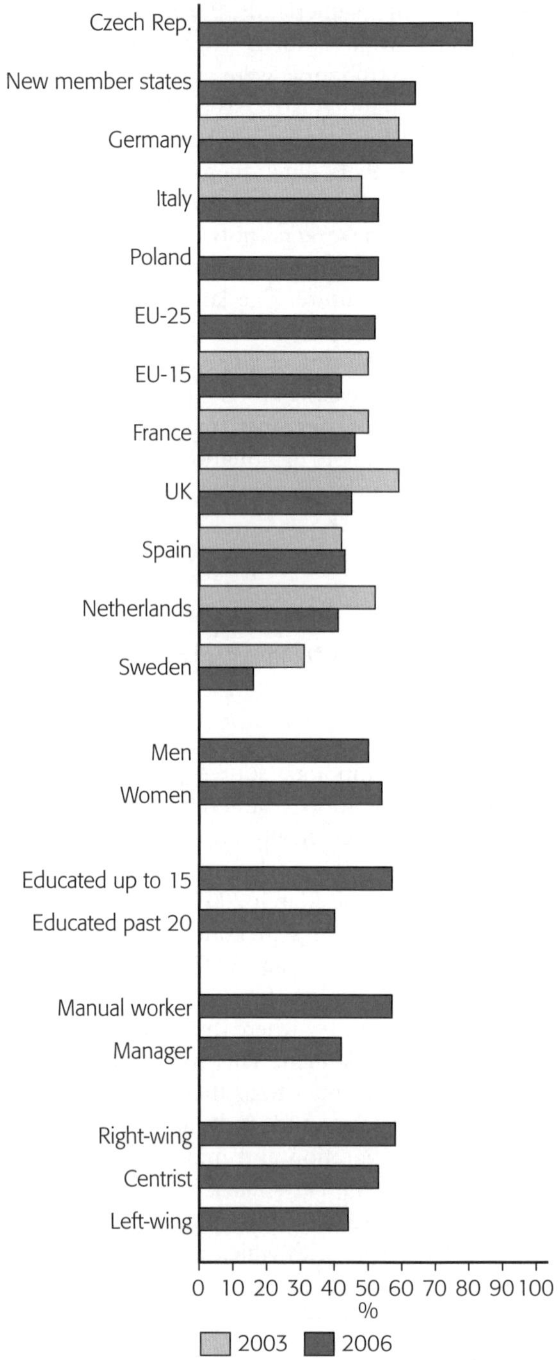

Note: Some might argue that this is a poorly-worded question – Central and East Europeans might be answering the way they do because their country has few immigrants at the moment.

Source: *Eurobarometer*, 66 (2007) and 60.1 (2004).

Table 10.6 'Successful' populist radical right parties in Europe – electoral performance and parliamentary/government status[1]

Election:	Turn of the century	New century	Latest	Parliamentary/Government status	
	% (date)	% (date)	% (date)	Previously	Currently
Austria (FPÖ)	26.9 (1999)	10.2 (2002)	11 (2006)	Coalition partner	Opposition
BZO*	n/a	n/a	4.1 (2006)	n/a	Opposition
Belgium (VB)	9.9 (1999)	11.6 (2003)	12.0 (2007)	Opposition	Opposition
Bulgaria (Ataka)	n/a	n/a	8.2 (2005)	Opposition	Opposition
Denmark (DF)	12.0 (2001)	13.3 (2005)	13.8 (2007)	Support party	Support party
France (FN)	14.9 (1997)	11.3 (2002)	4.3 (2007)	No seats	No seats
Italy[2] (AN)	15.7 (1996)	12.0 (2001)	12.3 (2006)	Coalition partner	Opposition
(LN)	10.1 (1996)	3.9 (2001)	4.6 (2006)	Coalition partner	Opposition
Netherlands (LPF)[3]	17.0 (2002)	5.7 (2003)	n/a	Coalition partner	No seats
(PVV)	n/a	n/a	5.9 (2006)	n/a	Opposition
Norway (FrP)	15.3 (1997)	14.7 (2001)	22.1 (2005)	Support party	Opposition
Poland (LPR)	7.9 (2001)	8.0 (2005)	1.3 (2007)	Coalition partner	No seats
Slovakia (SNS)	9.1 (1998)	3.3 (2002)	11.7 (2006)	Coalition partner	Coalition partner
Switzerland (SVP)	22.5 (1999)	26.6 (2003)	29.0 (2007)	Coalition partner	Coalition partner

Notes: 1. Party names are given in full in the List of Abbreviations and Acronyms, p. xiii.
2. The inclusion of AN in 1996 would be uncontroversial, but by 2001 its leadership (if not all its followers) had moved to a more 'respectable', conservative position; in contrast, the LN's inclusion in 1996, when its main appeal was regionalist and it had not yet moved so clearly into xenophobic territory, is disputable.
3. Not all observers would classify Pim Fortuyn as a *right-wing* populist, but his party is included.

notable successes, especially in western Europe (see Table 10.6). To many people, these successes are clearly related to xenophobia: in other words, the more hostile to foreigners a country is, the more likely it is to see the far right do well. This is an easy assumption to make. And it goes well beyond media pundits in Europe: research suggests that the presence of a significant far-right party in a country is enough to discourage would-be asylum seekers from the developing world from trying their luck there, presumably because it suggests they will encounter more hostility there than elsewhere (see Neumayer, 2004). However, back in Europe, perceptions of immigration being a problem or there being too many foreigners in a country – a perception that might or might not relate to the actual number of foreigners there (see Lahav, 2004: 120) – is, in fact, by no means a guarantee that the far right will do well.

Take Greece: attitudes to immigrants there are among the most hostile in Europe according to most surveys (see, for instance, Sides and Citrin, 2007: 484). Yet there is little evidence of a far-right breakthrough: the only party that one could label a far-right party, the populist Orthodox Rally (LAOS) took only 3.8 per cent of the vote at the 2007 election (though this was up on its score of 2.2 per cent in 2004). Real numbers of foreigners rather than simply exaggerated perceptions or genuine hostility, is also no guarantee of success. For every Switzerland (see Box 10.5) there are many more countries with high foreign populations (and much more difficult economic and social conditions for that matter) that go for years without the far right making an impact. This suggests that only part of its success can be put down to its nativist (and populist) stance – to its assertion that the nation belongs to those who are born there and is at risk from both outsiders and their ideas, as well as from mainstream politicians and other elites who will sell 'the people' down the river.

BOX 10.5

Too many black sheep? Switzerland's immigration debate

Switzerland is famous for its wealth (some of it stored in the famously secret bank accounts that allegedly still hold Nazi gold) and for its direct democracy (see Chapter 6). June 2005 also saw a referendum on a challenge to governmental and parliamentary approval of Switzerland joining the Schengen area, meaning that those travelling to and from member countries do not have to show passports, while their governments share information relating to cross-border crime, as well as migration and asylum (see Box 10.10). Turnout among the country's 4.8 million registered voters was 56 per cent and the decision to join was upheld by 55 per cent to 45 per cent. The vote also meant that Switzerland would be allowed automatically to turn back asylum claimants travelling from EU countries. Later on in the year, in September, the Swiss also approved the extension (in 2011) to the ten newest member states of the EU of the right to work freely in Switzerland – a freedom enjoyed by citizens of the pre-accession EU-15 from 2007 onwards.

Notwithstanding its being part of the government, the populist radical right party, the SVP (see Skenderovic, 2007) campaigned for a 'no' vote, building on existing anxieties about immigration in a country that probably gets more than its fair share of asylum seekers (see Table 10.4) and in which non-nationals make up a quarter of its workforce, along with an estimated 100,000 illegals. During the first referendum the SVP joined the 'Association for a Neutral and Independent Switzerland' in a campaign that included the erection of a large-scale Trojan horse in order to reinforce the message that the country would be flooded by foreigners. This was a fairly mild stunt considering how hysterical the debate can get in Switzerland. In December 2002, for instance, Swiss media revealed the plans of one town (Meilen near Zurich) which had a holding centre for asylum seekers to ban them from places such as schools and sports grounds, to prevent them from congregating in public places, and to forbid them from using the municipal swimming pool unless accompanied by a local resident or local official. According to media reports, this *apartheid*-style regime was based on a map showing no-go areas, indicated on the key by four black men with a line through them.

It should perhaps have come as no surprise, then, when in 2007 the SVP launched an eye-grabbing election poster showing three cartoon white sheep standing on the Swiss flag with one of the sheep raising its rear legs to administer a swift kick to the butt of a fourth, black, sheep effectively shoving it off the map. The poster went hand-in-hand with its campaign to force a referendum on the deportation of serious criminals and to put forward a parliamentary bill (which has little chance of passing but sends a clear signal to supporters) allowing the deportation of the entire family of any non-national under 18 convicted for a criminal offence. The SVP increased its vote to 29 per cent and remains Switzerland's biggest party.

Clearly, electoral systems have some impact on success or failure – it is difficult to imagine a populist radical right party making it into the UK parliament, for instance, while proportional representation systems clearly offer more of a chance for such parties to make an initial breakthrough; they might even offer some insurance against a complete wipe-out later if things go wrong later on – something that often happens when (as in Austria, for example) the stirring and simplistic promises of opposition can't be delivered in government. Yet give or take some of the differences in electoral thresholds and formulas covered in Chapter 6, the PR systems in use in most countries do not vary sufficiently to explain why some have successful populist radical right parties and some do not (see Carter, 2005). All of which brings us back to something that might perhaps have been more obvious in the first place had political scientists not been so keen to find more structural explanations that focused, to use the jargon, on the 'demand side' rather than the 'supply side' of politics. Put simply, a good deal of the success or failure of populist radical right parties must be down to how well organized and led they are. Obviously, being able to tap into a well of anxiety about immigrants and social breakdown helps, as does a receptive media (see Art, 2007), but only flexible and competent outfits with savvy leaders can take advantage of the opportunities with which they are presented (see Mudde, 2007; and Norris, 2005; see also van der Brug *et al.*, 2000; and Lubbers *et al.*, 2002).

There is also another important but often forgotten point to make about far-right success. This is that, in terms of getting into government, it has harmed the centre-left more than the centre-right. The latter obviously has to be careful not to go too far down the anti-immigrant line lest it alienate its business constituency, which is often in favour of anything that fills labour shortages (especially at a knock-down price), and (in the case of Christian democratic parties) a Catholic charity sector known for its good work among newcomers in difficulties. But unlike its counterpart on the left, the mainstream right has fewer dues to pay to progressive values such as liberalism and tolerance, and less compunction about getting together in government with more extreme parties on platforms that emphasize their need – and their willingness – to 'do something' about a 'crisis' they themselves have done more than a little to talk up in preceding years (see Bale, 2003, 2008; see also Arzheimer and Carter, 2006; and Meguid, 2005). Both mainstream and more populist right-wing politicians, in other words, have, along with the media, helped to 'prime' immigration (and its supposed accomplices – crime, welfare abuse and terrorism) as an issue, helping to boost its salience among voters (see Chapter 8). The common wisdom that it is in those countries that maintain what is pejoratively labelled by pundits a 'conspiracy of silence' on the issue that the far right do best is inaccurate: take Scandinavia, where immigration has been talked about quite openly and quite vituperatively for years in Norway and especially Denmark, but not in Sweden (see Box 10.6).

Interestingly, with the exception of those representing *Ataka* in Bulgaria and the PRM in Romania, not even Europe's populist politicians now justify their hard (some would say hostile) line on immigrants on the explicit grounds of racial difference or superiority. Instead, they talk of 'a clash of cultures', of ways of life that cannot be reconciled when immigrant minorities refuse to 'assimilate' and adopt the dress, customs and ideologies of their host country (see Eatwell, 2000: 411). They also talk about the links between immigration and rising crime and chronic abuse of the welfare state – both issues that the right has traditionally owned. The left is vulnerable on these issues because it is seen as soft, as 'out of touch' with how things really are for ordinary people.

Certainly, many social democrats rightly fear a loss of working-class support to the far right on this issue, notwithstanding the easily forgotten fact that an individual's views on immigration and minorities are in part structured by an individual's left–right orientation (see Lahav, 2004: 127–35). Theoretically, the left faces a 'catch-22'. If it adopts a more hardline attitude in order to appear responsive to public concerns, and therefore lower support for more extreme parties, it risks rendering legitimate (rather than squeezing out) the very xenophobia its strategy is designed to contain – xenophobia that might then boost support for those parties it is trying to defeat. In reality, though, the centre-left in Europe has chosen to join rather than beat those who argue for a tougher line on immigration control and integration. Especially in countries where the populist radical right has scored big successes (such as Denmark, Norway, the Netherlands and Austria), social democratic parties have moved to close down the gap by assenting to, or even promoting, a harder line on migration and multiculturalism. But even where the right has gained less traction, the UK being the most obvious example, they have done the same, suggesting perhaps that the move is not simply a reaction to other parties but – and some would say this was democracy in action – a response to the very real concerns of the electorate they seek to represent (see Bale *et al.*, 2008).

One question raised, of course, by the response (and possible contribution) of mainstream parties to the success of the populist right is how much influence the latter have had on public policy. Certainly, as we note below, there appears to have been a turn away from the official promotion of

COUNTRY PROFILE

The Czech Republic (Česko)

Area: 77,300 km^2 (1.8% of EU-27)	
Population: 10.3 million (2.1% of EU-27)	
Religious heritage: Roman Catholic (with Protestant minority)	
GDP (2006): €114 billion (1.0% of EU-27)	
GDP *per capita* as percentage of EU-27 average: 79	
Female representation in parliament and cabinet (end 2007): 16% and 13%	
Joined EU: 2004	
Top 3 cities: Prague – capital city (1.2 million), Brno (0.4 million), Ostrava (0.3 million).	

History: The present-day Czech Republic began life in January 1993, after seventy-five years as part of a federal state known as Czechoslovakia. The latter was created when the Austro-Hungarian Empire was broken up following the First World War. During the nineteenth century the rise of nationalism in 'the Czech lands' of Bohemia and Moravia made the provinces a thorn in the side of the Germanic Habsburg dynasty. Slovak nationalism also developed in parallel opposition to Hungarian rule in what was eventually to become the Slovak Republic. The exceptions were the German-speaking areas of the Czech lands, later known as the Sudetenland. Claims of discrimination against its inhabitants gave Hitler's Germany an excuse to annex part of what, by the mid-1930s, was one of Europe's most prosperous democracies. When Germany then grabbed the entire country in 1939, Slovakia, already chafing against membership of the rump federal state, declared itself independent. Following Hitler's defeat in 1945, a reunified Czechoslovakia seized the opportunity to expel 2.5 million ethnic Germans, thousands of whom died on forced marches or in reprisals by Czech paramilitaries. Elections in 1946 brought the Communist Party to power with a degree of mass support unusual in Eastern Europe but, by 1948, it had effectively put an end to democracy. Over the next four decades, the country developed into a repressive regime, punctuated by an attempt at liberalization (known as 'the Prague Spring'), which was crushed by Soviet-led military intervention in August 1968. However, the Soviet-backed regime ultimately found itself unable to resist massive demonstrations (labelled 'people power') which, as elsewhere in Europe, hastened the collapse of the Communist governments in 1989.

After a bloodless handover of power to democratic reformers, dubbed the 'velvet revolution', came the 'velvet divorce' with Slovakia in late 1992. This happened against the wishes of founding president (and former dissident) Václav Havel, whose petition signed by a million Czechoslovak citizens for a referendum was ignored by parliamentary politicians on both sides. Since then, the Czech Republic has been ruled by coalitions led initially by the centre-right Civic Democrats and then, following corruption scandals in the late 1990s, by the centre-left Social Democrats. The latter, though, have found it hard to find a majority, not least because they cannot work closely with a largely unreformed Communist Party that is still capable of garnering up to a fifth of the vote. This has sometimes resulted, critics maintain, in an unhealthily cosy relationship with the centre-right: before the 2002 election, for instance, something of a disguised 'grand coalition' ran the country. In 2006, the Civic Democrats squeaked back into power, but only after a highly protracted attempt to put together a coalition – an episode that led to more calls (especially among supporters of the two biggest parties) for a less proportional system that would supposedly make elections more decisive.

WHAT'S IN AN ANTHEM?

Kde domov můj? may well be the only national anthem in the world to have emerged (in the mid-nineteenth century) from a musical comedy, as well as one of the few to end with a question mark. It originally had two verses but the second was replaced by a Slovak verse when the two nations were forced together after the First World War. This was then removed after the 'velvet divorce' of the early 1990s, leaving the anthem with just the one verse, thereby rendering it one of the world's shortest. The lyrics conjure up a rural idyll – waters murmur, pinewoods rustle, spring shines in the orchard and all's well with the world in the beautiful Czech land that the singer calls home.

Economy and society: The country's 10 million people have one of the highest standards of living in CEE although clearly still some way below the EU average. This relatively high standing is due not just to tourism but to industry – Czech car-makers and defence manufacturers have, like banking and property, proved attractive to foreign investors for whom the country's proximity to the huge German market is an obvious plus. A reasonably comprehensive welfare state and fairly moderate economic policies have helped ease the strains of transition on a population that sees itself as largely homogeneous and is generally opposed to sharp growth in social inequalities.

Governance: The Czech Republic is a parliamentary democracy whose government is led by a prime minister appointed, at the suggestion of the speaker of the parliament, by the president. The latter – a largely ceremonial head of state – is elected every five years by both chambers of the bicameral parliament. The more powerful lower house, the Chamber of Deputies, is elected by PR. Members of the upper house, the Senate, however, are elected in single-member constituencies under a two-round majoritarian electoral system. Electoral reform seems to be favoured (in their own interests) by the largest parties but will be resisted by their smaller counterparts.

Foreign policy: The Czechs have devoted themselves to returning to the heart of Europe by achieving membership of NATO, which they joined in 1999, and the EU, of which they became part in May 2004. Other objectives include establishing a reputation for reliability and stability in order to attract foreign investment. Relations with Germany are accorded a high priority in spite of (or perhaps because of) continuing sensitivities on both sides over the expulsion of the Sudeten Germans and the German occupation. Relations with Russia, which in the days of the former Soviet Union kept a tight hold over the Czechs, have, however, come under strain as the result of the latter's willingness to host the radar systems for the US's proposed missile defence system.

KEY CONTEMPORARY CHALLENGE

REFORMING THE EDUCATION SYSTEM

The autumn of 2007 saw the resignation of the (Green) Education Minister from the Czech Republic's centre-right government after less than a year in the post. Party political machinations were partly to blame: she was one of a handful of Green ministers in a centre-right government which does not seem altogether comfortable with their presence, while Green supporters are continually wary of being betrayed. But there were also substantive policy concerns that go to the heart of problem that the Czech Republic has to deal with if, in the long term, it is to carry on catching up fast with its Western neighbours. Her resignation came as it looked as if her department's poor organization would see the country miss out on millions of euros' worth of EU funding for much needed higher education reform and expansion. But problems also abound in primary and secondary education, where teaching and learning is, according to many observers, far too traditional and technically specialist for the needs of the twenty-first century 'knowledge economy'. The difficulty is persuading staff to change their ways – not only do many of them still believe in what they regard as tried and trusted methods, they are also de-motivated by what, relative to other professionals, are the low salaries paid to teachers. Even more problematically for the government, they are also well represented by trade unions who appear to be willing and able to bring their members out on strike unless they are better rewarded for implementing change.

Contemporary challenges

- Seriously attempting to combat discrimination against Roma minority
- Overcoming the inability of what is still an overly politicized (and, some say, corrupt) public administration to manage and draw down EU funding efficiently
- Reforming the education system in the face of resentment and resistance of those who work in it (see box above)
- Tackling a deficit that makes adoption of the euro difficult and a pension system that will struggle as the working population shrinks.

Learning resources Try Hanley (2006), *The New Right in the New Europe*, which deals with Czech politics since 1989. Another useful read is Fawn (2000), *The Czech Republic*. Keep up to date with the news at http://www.radio.cz/en/ and http://www.drseansdiary.blogspot.com

BOX 10.6

Sweden – still immune?

Sweden is often held up as unusual in that populist radical right parties have – with one temporary exception (called New Democracy) in the early 1990s – fared miserably at the polls; this is in spite of the fact that polls suggest some public concern about immigration, even if it is not as high as in other European countries (see Figure 10.7). It is also in spite of a worrying degree of organized racist violence. The poor performance of the far right stands in marked contrast with Sweden's Nordic neighbours, Denmark and Norway, where such parties perform well. At the 2002 election, however, the populist mantle was taken on, a little surprisingly, by the Liberal Party, which focused on welfare dependency among newcomers, arguing that those unable to find work should, after a short period, be repatriated and that those who stayed should be helped to integrate by language and citizenship classes. It seemed to work as an electoral strategy: in a matter of months, the Liberals went from being a party in danger of slipping below Sweden's 4 per cent threshold to 13.4 per cent, trebling its score at the previous election. Some predicted that the genie had escaped from the bottle for a second time: we would, they argued, now see the erosion of the cross-party consensus which seems to have succeeded – contrary to so much common wisdom elsewhere in Europe concerning the dangers of a 'conspiracy of silence' – in damping down the vote for the far right. They were wrong. Sweden remains exceptionally open to asylum and immigration, especially in comparison to its neighbour just across the Oresund bridge, Denmark (see Green-Pedersen and Odmalm, 2008). The Liberals said very little about the matter in the 2006 general election, concerned as they were to maintain the unity of the pre-electoral alliance with other (essentially pro-immigration) centre-right parties that for once overhauled the Social Democrats. Whether the fact that the far-right *Sverigedemokraterna* doubled its vote to just under 3 per cent represented an ominous sign for the future remains to be seen – one of the reasons for the relative failure of the radical right in Sweden, after all, is that for many voters the party is still associated with boots not suits.

multiculturalism (although explicit encouragement of the latter was never as great as is sometimes suggested) and more emphasis on integration, if not full assimilation. And most European countries have made efforts to tighten up their immigration control, even if one can argue that they did this from the early 1970s onwards – before the far-right was a political force – and that they are nonetheless still keen (primarily perhaps for economic reasons) to allow 'the right kind of immigrant' in wherever possible. But is this 'restrictive turn' (see Joppke, 2007a) really due to pressure from the radical right inside or outside government (see Minkinberg, 2002, Schain, 2006; Williams, 2006)? Perhaps mainstream parties are responding – in more or less democratic fashion – to real problems (or at least problems that are perceived as real) by the electorate (see Bale, 2008). This is a classic conundrum for comparative politics and, indeed, political science as a whole: since an actor was present, how do we judge whether action would have been taken in their absence, and, just because they were present, does that mean that they were responsible?

Less difficult to answer is another, more substantive question related to the issue of populist parties in office; namely, does it do them any good in the long term? The answer would seem to be no, at least in the short term; however, the difficulty of converting rash promises into hard choices may not prevent them from staying in the game and maybe even making a comeback at a later date. The fate of the FPÖ in Austria, which was controversially first invited into a coalition in 1999, is a case in point (see Fallend, 2004; Heinisch, 2003; and Luther, 2003). The party fell apart and eventually split; however, unlike, say, the LPF in the Netherlands, it lived to fight another day – indeed, if the votes of the two parties that emerged from the split are put together, one can argue that the populist radical right actually gained from its second period in government (see Table 10.6). Reports of the death of the Italian LN have also been exaggerated on a number of occasions, although the crisis provoked by the severe stroke suffered by its leader, the bombastic Umberto Bossi, in 2004 (a calamity from which he eventually recovered), poses another interesting question, can it survive the passing of a dominant, charismatic leader (see Pedahzur and Brichta, 2002)? This is a dilemma, of course, for populist radical right parties all over Europe: 2006, for example, saw Carl I. Hagen finally step down after twenty-eight years at the helm of the Norwegian Progress Party, now one of the best supported parties of its kind in Europe. Whether his successor, Siv Jensen, can maintain that support will be interesting to watch.

Integrating and protecting migrants and minorities

No doubt, if many of today's immigrants did not look so different, were more widely dispersed, and did not insist on their human right to hold onto their religion and culture, things might be easier. European countries might be able to muddle through and let hypocrisy – and, of course, the immigrants themselves and those who live directly alongside them – take the strain. But the problem is, in part, one of visibility, of concentration and of an apparent 'failure' of **integration** or **assimilation** that is subjected to increasing media and political attention. Many of Europe's biggest cities (particularly in western Europe) are now multicultural. They are not, however, always 'melting-pots': different communities live alongside each other but often share little in common. To the middle-class liberal, **multiculturalism** could be a cause for celebration, bringing welcome diversity in the arts, in cuisine and in the economy. Others, whether they live in the cities and resent the changes and the differences or, instead, live outside them and see them as modern-day dens of iniquity, are less welcoming, perhaps distrustful and even downright hostile. Both as a cause and an effect of this negative reaction, Europe's ethnic minorities congregate in particular parts of particular cities. It is also obvious that newly arrived immigrants will set up where they have family and friends, and where there may be jobs. For instance, foreigners constitute, at most, 8 per cent of the population of the Netherlands, but in Rotterdam they make up around 30 per cent.

KEY POINT

European governments have begun to place more emphasis on ensuring that immigrants fit into the countries they come to rather than relying on a policy of 'live and let live'. Many have tried to balance this by stepping up anti-discrimination efforts.

Integration is about newcomers fitting peacefully and productively into a host society. **Assimilation** involves minorities and/or migrants adopting the practices, customs, language, manners and even the mores of the host country. **Multiculturalism** implies the preservation and coexistence of separate ethnicities – communities living alongside each other but not necessarily interacting or sharing much in common.

There is nothing new in this concentration, perhaps. Anyone familiar with the US will know that certain neighbourhoods in certain cities are often associated with a particular ethnic group. But in the US, the strong sense of American identity, the stress on English and the drive toward upward mobility, all reinforced by an education system that stresses citizenship and an economic system that makes such mobility possible for so many, tends to work against the establishment of ghettos from which there is no escape. At least, this is the case for people who, whatever their creed, could pass as 'white' (something that has never been true for African-Americans and, at the moment, seems difficult for Latinos and some Asians). In Europe, the state – with the exception of France (see Box 10.7) – is rather more reluctant to force the issue in schools, where minority languages are often protected by law. Welfare can also more easily become a way of life – albeit not a very comfortable one. And many immigrants (and even their children) have little hope of passing as 'white'. Therefore, reassurances that all this is 'just a phase' that has to be gone through every so often are, perhaps understandably, met with rather more scepticism and distrust.

As a response to fears about the threat to security (cultural and physical) posed by the separatism supposedly inherent in multiculturalism, many governments have put an additional premium in recent years on the integration, if not the full-blown

BOX 10.7

Determined integration or indefensible discrimination? Bans on religious dress

French public education has, for a hundred and fifty years, insisted on a secular approach: the state must be kept separate from religion. In recent years, this has caused problems with France's 4–5 million Muslims, many of whom argue that girls should be allowed to cover their heads in accordance with their religion. After a series of court rulings, French President Jacques Chirac announced in December 2003 that, in the light of a commission report, not only ostentatious and provocative but also all obvious symbols of religion would be prohibited in schools, and that he would seek a legal ban on the wearing of 'conspicuous' religious symbols by pupils. Although the ban covers all religions and seemed to have the support of around two thirds of the French public (and, according to some opinion polls, about half of all Muslim women), it was seen by some Islamic groups as deliberately targeting Muslim schoolgirls who wished to wear traditional dress. Many commentators compared what they saw as the 'over-the-top' reaction of the French with the much more relaxed attitudes to the question in other European countries. However, in June 2004, the UK High Court upheld an English school's ban on a pupil wearing the jilbab (a long flowing robe covering everything but feet and face), claiming that its already liberal, culturally-sensitive dress-code was sufficient to guarantee the girl's human rights under the European Convention on Human Rights.

assimilation, of minorities. The most obvious way to do this – at least formally – is to grant them citizenship, and it is clear from Table 10.7 that European countries are still doing this, although the rates do vary quite widely, especially if population is taken into account. Each European country allows resident foreigners to gain citizenship in different ways and at different rates, each having its own citizenship requirements based on a sometimes bewildering (and changing) combination of birth and residency requirements (see Bauböck *et al.*, 2006). But in increasing numbers of them, these requirements are now moving beyond simply birth and residence to include familiarity with the country and its language being tested before citizenship and even, in some cases, residency is granted – which could well have the (intended) knock-on effect of making immigration more difficult (see Joppke, 2007b). From March 2006, all foreigners applying for permanent residency in the Netherlands, for example, have had to pass a test on Dutch language and society – unless, that is, they are citizens of another EU country, Switzerland, the US, Japan and New Zealand, or if they are a victim of human trafficking. There are similar schemes in other European countries, among them France, Germany and the UK. In the Netherlands, you even have to pay for the privilege – around €350 for the test and €65 to prepare for it. During the first six months of the test, just under 1,500 people took it and nine out of ten passed (see *Migration News*, 14 (2), 2007).

Politicians all over Europe, then, have been calling for and putting into place measures that they claim are designed to improve the integration of immigrants, most notably language and citizenship classes. Again, this is Europeanization, but by learning and following best practice (if that is what it is) rather than driven by the EU. As to the practical results of such measures, beyond providing a measure of reassurance to 'host' populations, it may be too early to tell. Critics on both sides see such attempts as symbolic sops that will make little or no difference. To ardent multiculturalists, they represent a pointless attack on their 'live and let live' approach. To those who believe that integration should mean nothing less than complete assimilation into the culture and belief system of the receiving country (assuming for the moment that countries of several million individuals can be said to possess a uniform set of practices and values), the odd citizenship and language class cannot possibly hope to deliver what they want.

But if immigration is to be controlled and immigrants integrated, then native populations presum-

Table 10.7 The granting of citizenship, 2002–5

	Numbers granted citizenship			
	2002	**2003**	**2004**	**2005**
UK	n/a	124295	140740	161755
France	n/a	139938	168826	154827
Germany	154547	n/a	127153	117241
Spain	21805	26517	38220	42860
Sweden	37792	33222	28893	39573
Netherlands	45321	28799	26171	28488
Italy	n/a	13406	n/a	n/a
Poland	1182	1653	1937	2866
Czech Rep.	3261	2199	5020	2626

Source: Data from Eurostat, *Population and Social Conditions* (2007).

ably have to do their bit, too. Racism leading (at the very least) to discrimination, after all, is by no means a thing of the past in most European countries. Belgium, for instance, made the news all around Europe (not an easy thing to do, as we saw in Chapter 7) when couples in the town of St Niklaas cancelled their weddings when they learned they were to be married by a recently appointed black registrar. But some countries take the problem much more seriously than others – something that is neatly illustrated by a report on their progress in implementing their commitment, under the EU's Racial Equality Directive (2000), to set up systems for dealing with and sanctioning racial and ethnic discrimination (see Table 10.8).

Of course, just because a country has a system and uses it does not mean it has fewer problems with discrimination. Indeed, it might suggest it has more than most: research in France, for instance, suggests that employers routinely ignore or turn down job applications from people with Arab names or addresses in the notorious *banlieux* – the high-rise housing projects on the outskirts of cities and towns. However, lack of progress could well connote a lack of commitment to doing something about problems that do exist. A 'framework agreement' was signed in April 2007, following six years of stop-start negotiations, by the justice ministers of the twenty-seven EU states, and commits them to introducing sentences of between one and three years for anyone 'publicly inciting to violence or hatred directed against [persons] defined by reference to race, colour, religion, descent or national or ethnic

Table 10. 8 Systems addressing racial or ethnic discrimination, 2005–6

Sanctions or awards are comparably severe and/or frequent 2005–6	Sanctions or awards are not severe or frequent 2005–6	No data on effectiveness of legislation concerning racial/ethnic discrimination available 2005–6	No sanctions or awards 2005–6	Specialised body exists, but received negligible amount of complaints 2005–6	No operational specialised body 2005–6
France Ireland Hungary Romania Sweden UK	Belgium Denmark Latvia Austria	Bulgaria Poland	Greece Italy Cyprus Lithuania Netherlands Portugal Slovakia Finland	Estonia Slovenia	Czech Rep. Germany Spain Luxembourg Malta

Source: Fundamental Rights Agency (2007), *Report on Racism and Xenophobia in the Member States of the EU*.

origin'. Whether the Agreement actually results in more action being taken will be interesting to see. It is also interesting to note that hostility directed to another minority subject to vicious intolerance and discrimination, especially in Eastern Europe – namely, homosexual people – seems not to be taken so seriously (see 'Crucible of Hate', *Guardian*, 1 June 2007).

Policy responses – towards 'Fortress Europe'?

Just as there have been moves between the EU's member states to share (and, to some extent, force the pace on) 'best practice' with regard to discrimination, they have begun to co-operate more closely on immigration – or at least on those aspects of it that they find difficult to manage on their own. They have been spurred on by its salience as a domestic political issue and by the knowledge that, since Europe's internal borders have come down under the *Schengen Agreement* (see Box 10.8), it is much easier for illegal immigrants and asylum seekers to move around the continent and select the country of their choice. Realizing that it would not be enough to nag vulnerable 'gatekeepers' such as Spain and, in particular, Italy (with its 8,000 km coastline) to improve security, they began to put in place collective agreements such as the *Dublin Accord* (which insists that asylum seekers must make their claim in the first EU country they arrive in and can be returned there if necessary).

Theoretically, even for non-Schengen states, the national veto on so-called Justice and Home Affairs (JHA) issues has been eroded by bringing as many of them as possible under the first or EC pillar of the EU's three-pillar structure (see Chapter 2). On the face of it, then, migration policy is being Europeanized. But, in fact, most informed observers remain convinced that member states have pooled their resources only on those aspects of policy that they believe will support their main aim, which is to ensure they maintain national control in an area that goes to the heart of sovereignty and which their voters obviously care so much about (see Geddes, 2003 and Lahav, 2004). European states, in other words, are in effect 'contracting out' responsibility for immigration only where it would make little or no sense for them to try to do the job themselves and/or where collective action helps in the construction of a 'first line of defence'. This line began to move outward (via subsidies toward the cost of improved border protection) even before CEE states were formally admitted to the EU in 2004 and 2007.

KEY POINT

European governments have also begun to co-operate on controlling immigration, but only where it suits them (i.e. illegal immigration and asylum). Other aspects of their regimes remain distinctive and firmly under national control.

BOX 10.8

The EU's Schengen Agreement

Although signed in 1985, the provisions of this multilateral agreement designed to promote the free movement of people (primarily as consumers and labourers) first came into force in 1995. By it, EU countries (minus the UK and Ireland), along with Norway and Iceland, commit themselves to allowing citizens and those who are legally resident in the 'Schengen' countries to pass between them without needing to show a passport. The *quid pro quo* for this freedom of movement is supposed to be strengthened security at the external borders of the EU. Also important are police co-operation, information-sharing (using the computerized Schengen information system or SIS) and the establishment of a common visa policy. Non-citizens coming into the *Schengen area* as visitors are limited to a three-month stay, will almost certainly need a visa and might need to show means of support. Schengen was incorporated into the Union's *acquis communautaire* (with derogations – get-out clauses – for the UK, Ireland, and also Denmark) by the Amsterdam Treaty in 1997. The key challenge now is the entry (with the exception of Cyprus) into Schengen of the countries that joined the EU in 2004, with Slovakia, which shares a mountainous and forested border with Ukraine, a particular cause for concern.

DEBATE 10.1

SHOULD IMMIGRATION BE STOPPED?

YES

- Immigrants disturb the social balance of a nation, bringing with them cultures and religions that are fundamentally incompatible with those of the host population.
- That host population were never given a chance to vote on whether the new arrivals should have come in the first place. Now that they have, and more arrive every day, we are seeing the rise of some very nasty parties. Unless we stop immigration, they will get bigger and bigger.
- Immigrants are more likely to be unemployed, claim welfare benefits and get involved in crime. Even those who are law-abiding and get jobs to support their families place a strain on public services – healthcare and education – and the housing stock. They also hold down the wages of those who are already badly off and discourage government and employers from upskilling their native workforces and introducing technology to improve productivity. Moreover, they are only a short-term answer to an ageing population because they get old, too.
- Immigrants and their descendents represent a security threat.

NO

- It is doubtful whether individual nations and/or states ever possessed timeless and unified cultural identities. The idea that they can continue to do so in a globalized and mediatized world is ridiculous. Indeed, to operate successfully in that world, especially economically, it is essential that a country have as many points of contact with it as possible: multiculturalism is not only inevitable, it is functional.
- It was elected governments that allowed immigration to occur and there are now parties that campaign to stop it: they receive relatively little support and there is no correlation between numbers of newcomers and the success of such parties.
- The bulk of immigrants and their descendents get jobs and pay far more in taxes than they ever take out. Besides, without immigrant workers, many of Europe's basic services would collapse – not only garbage collection or street sweeping or transport (or, for that matter, the hospitality industry), but also healthcare. The evidence that they provide a cheap labour force that undercuts native workers and reduces the pressure on the state and on firms to provide training and technology is scanty. And just because they aren't *the* answer to the worker-pensioner ratio, they are a part of the answer.
- It is not immigrants but the violent ideologies that a tiny minority of people will always buy into that pose a terrorist threat.

Indeed, it can be argued that the need for secure borders was one of the drivers for enlargement. It then became one of its preconditions, with post-communist states having to make big changes (and investments) in improved border security and tighter immigration regimes – moves made not just at the behest of the EU acting collectively but also via overlapping bilateral arrangements with the immigration and labour ministries of existing member states (see Grabbe, 2006: Chapter 7 and Guiraudon and Jileva, 2006). Whether this has contributed to ensuring that CEE countries still get, for example, only around 10 per cent of the asylum applications of their western counterparts is difficult to say – there are signs that the numbers coming will rise as their economies begin to catch up. The main point is, however, that co-operation on immigration has been far more fulsome from countries with reasonable (and, in some cases, now realized) prospects of joining the EU than from those (such as Albania or Morocco) who do not, at least in the short to medium term, have a hope of joining (see Joppke, 2002: 272).

That said, European countries are trying – again, both via the EU and using bilateral agreements – to persuade states which are major sources of (or transit points for) illegal immigrants and asylum seekers to reduce the flow. Ongoing attempts are being made to bring migration issues into the dialogue the EU has with third countries under the Common Foreign and Security Policy (CFSP), as well as into negotiations on development aid, focusing in particular on North Africa and, to a lesser extent, the Middle East (see Chapter 11). There was, however, little support in 2002 for a UK government suggestion that the EU consider reducing aid to poorer countries who failed to do enough to stop their citizens emigrating. Neither was support forthcoming when, the following year, the UK (backed again by Spain) suggested that the EU consider Australian-style detention camps outside its borders to which would-be refugees could be deported and then processed. However, a watered-down (and arguably more sensible, as well as more ethical) suggestion – that the EU manage facilities in other parts of the world closer to the flashpoints which produce refugees, and co-operate more with sending and transit countries (Boswell, 2003) – was greeted more sympathetically. European countries are also having some success in getting their immigration officers located at airports and ports in developing countries, either actually checking papers or giving local staff – often airline or shipping company employees – some idea of what to look out for.

In addition, EU member states have taken collective action and built collective institutions to try to crack down on unauthorized immigration. Perhaps the most high-profile of these is *Frontex*, headquartered in Poland, which began its work in 2005. Originally intended as a training and co-ordinating body, it has since taken on more operational duties, using both its own aircraft and boats to patrol the Mediterranean routinely in the hope of heading off would-be illegals and asylum seekers heading to Europe from (and through) West Africa, most often via Spain's Canary Islands (see Box 10.3). Since the summer of 2007, Frontex patrols have also been tasked to prevent people leaving Libya and ending up in both Italy and Malta. Many, of course, get stranded in the waters between, thereby causing rows between the countries over who should pick them up, the most infamous of which occurred in June 2007 when nearly thirty Africans had to cling to tuna nets before the Italian navy was eventually prevailed upon to take responsibility. Such cases inevitably bring calls for a system of 'burden-sharing' – mostly ignored – but also for more formal arrangements with poor African countries that would allow more legal recruitment of temporary workers there in exchange for better policing on their part, along with an agreement to take back automatically any of their nationals found to be in Europe illegally.

Just as importantly, European states have also followed each other in 'contracting out' responsibility to private actors, such as airlines and shipping companies, by making them, via so-called 'carrier-sanctions', financially liable for bringing in passengers without appropriate documentation. Many of them have also introduced an expanded 'white list' of those countries from which applications for asylum will be assumed to be unfounded and added countries to their lists of countries from which visas will be required. Many have also made it tougher for asylum seekers to get state benefits. This is an example of states learning from each other – of Europeanization via best practice, if you like. But this is not full harmonization because learning and co-operation goes only so far and there is no surrender of sovereignty. There may be superficial similarities, but states are unwilling, for instance, to harmonize the way they either treat or make decisions on immigrants, citizenship and asylum – indeed, the continuing persistence of wide variations in the rate at which different member states grant refugee status to applicants from the same country (see Neumayer, 2005) is clear proof of their desire and capacity to differ. Each European country, then, continues to operate its own immigration regime with respect to non-EU nationals. These regimes have developed, in a 'path-dependent' manner (see Hansen, 2002), in response to individual states' immigration priorities, history and institutional structure (see Box 10.9).

European states, then, have preserved their competence when it comes to controlling the numbers coming into their countries. If policy fails to restrict those numbers, it will not be because states have somehow surrendered competence to the EU. Rather, it is because they themselves find it difficult to construct controls that will meet sometimes contradictory objectives simultaneously. First, a regime will have to cope with the sheer unpredictability of migrant flows. Second, states continue to want to run broadly humane asylum, family re-unification

BOX 10.9

Immigration regimes – still path dependent?

Germany's attitude to immigration and citizenship is rooted in the fact that its main postwar aim was to leave the door open for ethnic Germans who, as a result of the Second World War and the Cold War, were left stranded outside the Federal Republic. This conception of citizenship as being limited to those with blood links rather than being based on birth and residence, also meant, however, that it was very reluctant to offer German nationality (and certainly not joint nationality) to the other immigrants that its powerful economy sucked in as *gastarbeiter* (or guest-workers). As a consequence, there are currently around 7 million 'foreigners' in Germany of whom 1.5 million were born there, many of them as members of a Turkish community numbering 2.7 million. At the same time, Germany was determined to demonstrate its liberal credentials by running a relatively relaxed asylum regime, which meant, in the early 1990s, that it experienced a huge influx of refugees from the former Yugoslavia. All this left the country with a large number of people who were long-term residents but still foreigners – even if they were born in Germany and were in some ways more 'German' than new arrivals of ethnic Germans from the former Soviet bloc. These anomalies, along with concerns about integration and the recognition that Germany needs immigrants to help tackle long-term population decline (see Chapter 1), meant many politicians, especially on the left, believed the time had come for change. German policy makers, however, operate in a federal and consensual system that gives many 'veto players' a say (see Chapters 3 and 4). This arguably encourages immobilism, making it hard to make changes. Germany has therefore found it difficult to get domestic legislation on matters like citizenship and immigration past voters (whose suspicions were whipped up even by supposedly respectable opposition parties), and past legislators, state parliaments and the Federal Constitutional Court. Difficult, but not impossible: Germany eventually introduced a theoretically more liberal law on citizenship in 2000 and, in 2006, an immigration law that tried to balance the desire to attract more skilled workers from abroad with concerns about encouraging both newcomers and existing minorities to better integrate into German society. Whether this will lead to more people coming to Germany, becoming German, and becoming more German, however, remains to be seen (see Green *et al.*, 2007: Chapter 6; see also Green, 2004).

France, on the other hand, has – since the nineteenth century – had a hang-up about underpopulation. Partly as a consequence of this, and partly as a consequence of its tendency to incorporate its overseas possessions directly into the French state, it has historically made it very easy for immigrants to come to France (even *sans papiers*, i.e. illegally), as well as for foreigners to gain French citizenship. This, along with the decolonization process in North Africa and the country's relative economic strength in the postwar period, resulted in a large minority population which, even if it feels alienated, has every right to be there, whatever the arguments of the far-right *Front National* (FN). On the other hand, what is (compared to Germany, anyway) a relatively unencumbered state machine has the potential – if not complete freedom (see Hollifield, 1994) – to change direction at the behest of its politicians. President Nicolas Sarkozy already has a record of not only tough talk but also tough action on migrants and minorities (see Marthaler, 2008): on his way to winning the election in 2007, he promised to clean up the suburbs dominated by ethnic minorities, tried (controversially) to increase deportations of illegals, and endorsed the suggestion that those who didn't like France were welcome to leave; once in power he created a ministry of Immigration, Integration, National Identity and Co-development, set tougher targets for arrests and deportations, talked of expanding repatriation programmes, making newcomers pass tests on French language and values. On the other hand, Sarkozy has talked about the need for more skilled immigration, and made moves towards more explicit recognition of and dialogue with minority groups, and even talked about positive discrimination – things that traditionally were seen as impossible given France's commitment to supposedly 'colour-blind' citizenship. He also raised eyebrows among France's governing elite by appointing as his justice minister Rachida Dati, a judge but, more importantly, a self-made woman of Arab descent who grew up, along with her eleven brothers and sisters, on a tough housing estate in eastern France.

and relatively generous welfare arrangements. Third (and related), they want to insulate those arrangements from legal challenge, especially given the ever-increasing role of the courts, national and supranational, in human rights (broadly defined). Fourth, they want enough 'wiggle room' to allow them – either formally, or (especially in southern Europe), informally – to make room for migrants who add to the skills base and/or the flexibility of their domestic labour markets (see Favell and Hansen, 2002 and Geddes, 2003). In as much as 'Fortress Europe' (or Fortress Britain, Fortress Germany, Fortress France, etc.), exists, those who man its ramparts are aware that it has to have a drawbridge – not just for humanitarian and legal reasons, but in the knowledge that they can, if needs be, let it down to allow people to trip across.

In short, if there is co-operation – even Europeanization (see Faist and Ette, 2007) – that appears to involve the compromise of sovereignty, it is essentially self-interested and proceeds only cautiously, extending mainly to asylum and illegal immigration but not to citizenship or schemes to attract skilled workers (an area in which states, after all, are in competition). It is a 'guarded multilateralism' (Messina, 2007: 238) driven by the acknowledgement that the national interest is sometimes better promoted, just as it is when it comes to terrorism (see Monar, 2007), by collective rather than independent action. This collective action – whether it be operational (like the Frontex patrols) or more aspirational (like the so-called Hague Programme, which calls for the stepping up of progress towards common policies on asylum, visas and illegal immigration) – might be a response to a problem exacerbated by globalization; namely, the mass movement of people from less to more fortunate parts of the planet. But it does not mean that governments are powerless and inevitably lose their autonomy in the face of globalization: this assertion is no more valid on migration than it is with regard to welfare (see Chapter 9).

Neither, since we are making the link between the two topics, a link that is often made by populist politicians, screaming media headlines – and, indeed, many ordinary Europeans – is there much validity in the assertion that hostility to migration and multiculturalism will inevitably undermine support for the welfare state. We know that immigrants are routinely thought of as a drain on the welfare state: the disproportionate number of migrants and minorities on benefits are more visible (and pointed to) than the vast but relatively invisible army of tax-paying, wealth-creating, new entrants and their descendents, many of whom, ironically, actually work in the welfare state itself or as private carers. We also know that the welfare state relies, in part, on the political support generated by the idea that we pool our risks with people with whom we feel some mutual affinity and towards whom we feel a duty. If our support for the redistribution that the welfare state entails is eroded by the feeling that there are too many differences between those getting what they need and those giving what they can, will this end up delegitmizing the welfare state, making it easier for those who want to roll it back to do so? Research from America, which suggests quite persuasively that the historical 'underdevelopment' of the US welfare state was due in no small part to the racial and ethnic diversity that has long characterized that country, has recently been wheeled in to fuel that anxiety – one already raised in centre-left circles (Goodhart, 2004). The question is a serious one, but the answer needs to take into account the empirical reality that diversity appears to have a much weaker impact on welfare spending in Europe than it does in the US, mainly because support for it is much greater across all social groups and because social democracy (which doesn't really exist in America) is much more of a force in government (see Taylor-Gooby, 2005). In other words, as in so many other areas of socio-economic and political life, Europe will not inevitably become more like the US.

The Roma – Europe's oldest ethnic minority

Unlike other European minorities with claims to nationhood, the claim by some Roma (or Gypsies) that they constitute a nation is based not on territory but on identity. Even then, it is greeted with some scepticism. This is understandable perhaps in view of a widespread tendency among the Roma to see themselves in terms of families or possibly clans rather than a people as a whole. That they do so is not surprising in view of their origins: they came in dribs and drabs. While there is evidence to show that

KEY POINT

One of Europe's oldest minorities, the Roma, are still at the bottom of the heap.

their ancestors had begun arriving in eastern Europe from India in the eleventh century, possibly as mercenaries, there is no recorded mass influx. What we do know is that from very early on (possibly because they were associated with the non-Christian Ottoman empire) they were subject to vicious, often murderous, prejudice. This prejudice, along with restrictions on their liberty (up to and including slavery in Romania until the mid-nineteenth century), made it very difficult for them to integrate into the mainstream economy and society. Integration would not have been easy in any case, given their own desire to preserve their language and their physical separation from *gadje* – the non-Roma majority.

This separation continues to a greater or lesser extent in whichever country Europe's 4–5 million (some put the figure as high as 9 million) Roma find themselves living. As Table 10.9 shows, they are widely but not evenly distributed. Roma are concentrated in Southern and (despite Nazi attempts to exterminate them along with the Jews) in Central and Eastern Europe. Few nowadays are nomadic, but their more settled life has not meant they have caught up in socio-economic or, indeed, political terms with the majorities around them (see Baran, 2002). Living, as many do, a ghetto-style existence on the margins of society, and sometimes on the margins of legality, Roma are much more likely than others to suffer ill-health, to have bigger families and to be uneducated, unemployed, on welfare and in prison. They are also frequently the victims of racially motivated attacks. Their participation in electoral politics is at best minimal. The few political parties that have organized to represent them have found it hard going, not least because they find it difficult to overcome the fragmentation and infighting that some argue characterizes Roma culture more generally.

Table 10.9 Where most Roma live in Europe

Country	Estimated number of Roma living in the country	Roma as proportion of total population (%)
Romania	1,500,000	6.5
Spain	600,000	1.0
Hungary	482,000	4.7
Bulgaria	700,000	8.5
Slovakia	500,000	9.5
Czech Rep.	200,000	2.0

Sources: Data on CEE from Barany (2002: 160); data on Spain from Spanish government delegation working with UNHCR – see United Nations (2000).

At a transnational level, however, organization has proved somewhat more successful. In the European Parliament, there are a number of MEPs who campaign actively on their behalf, managing to pass a resolution calling for member states and the Commission to prioritize their rights. The International Romani Union (IRU) was given advisory committee status at the UN in 1993 and has now celebrated three decades of work. At its fifth World Congress in Prague in 2000, the IRU demanded the world recognize Roma as a non-territorial nation. It also declared that it would henceforth attempt to organize not just 'embassies' in other countries, but also a parliament or parliaments – something that is perhaps more possible than one might think, given the successful running of such institutions by the *Sami* people (sometimes called Lapplanders) who are spread across four countries in northern Scandinavia and Russia (see Myntti, 2002). It also attempted to progress its claims for compensation for Roma murdered in the *Porajmos* (as they call the Holocaust).

Interestingly, the sponsor of the congress was the Czech government – something which prompted considerable criticism among west European Roma. They single out that country – or, at least, its population – as being one of the worst offenders against Roma rights (see Box 10.9). Certainly, the Czech Republic seems to have started putting its house in order only as a condition of joining the EU (see Ram, 2003) and after pressure from existing member states complaining that poor treatment encouraged asylum seeking by Roma in their countries. Such cynicism might be warranted but, on the other hand, it begs the question whether one of the positive sides of EU expansion is its capacity to

BOX 10.10

Bottom of the heap – Roma in the Czech and Slovak Republics

Partly because it seems to contrast so sharply with its reputation (or, at least, the reputation of its liberal former president, Václav Havel), the Czech Republic's treatment of its small Roma population has attracted widespread attention in the European media. The new state's beginning was marred by its insistence in 1993 that some 100,000 Roma were, in fact, Slovaks, despite the majority having been born, apparently, in Czech territory. Fast forward to the present and there are still regular reports of police and officials displaying blatant discrimination towards Roma. Evidence of deliberate and persistent segregation in both education and housing is overwhelming, while the Roma unemployment rate is around 70 per cent – almost ten times the rate for the general population. Hardly surprising then, if many Czech Roma, much to the disquiet of some western Europeans (and their populist newspapers), were keen to leave the country and claim asylum elsewhere on the continent. On the other hand, things were certainly no better for the Roma of Slovakia who, owing to a fertility rate that is more than double that of other Slovaks, are predicted by some demographers to become the majority by the end of the twenty-first century. Both republics made conspicuous efforts to improve in the run-up to EU accession – especially with regard to education, health and even housing. But how effective such measures will be in the long term, let alone the short term, is hard to predict. However earnest the intentions of politicians may be, they cannot turn around centuries of popular prejudice in a few short years. And reports by European monitoring bodies (see Fundamental Rights Agency, 2007) suggest progress is very slow, although they also suggest that the Czech Republic and Slovakia are by no means the only places where discrimination against Roma is rife – and that Roma are not the only ethnic group to be badly treated.

oblige applicant states to conform to liberal democratic norms, be they in the commercial or the civil rights sphere? As long as the EU, via information provided by its own monitoring and that done by pressure groups, ensures such norms are maintained and more than cosmetic – then does it really matter that they did not originate out of the goodness of Czechs' (or Slovaks' or Hungarians' or Romanians') hearts?

While clearly the Roma receive a raw deal in the EU's new member states and current applicants, they have long been subject to serious discrimination in those western countries in which they have a presence, including most obviously Spain and (to a lesser extent) Greece. Certainly, they are rarely accorded any more respect than immigrant minorities, even though they can claim to have been in some European countries longer than many of those who now consider themselves part of the 'native' majority. Interestingly, Roma can claim to be the prototypical postmodern European citizens, scattered throughout a continent and possessing several identities – ethnic, state and European – simultaneously. Yet in other ways, they are more like sub-Saharan Africans: according to a UN development report released in January 2003 (which made the comparison) one in six of the estimated 5 million Roma in Europe goes constantly hungry, and only two-thirds even make it through primary school.

Given this, it hardly comes as a surprise to find Roma trying to migrate in order to make a better life elsewhere in Europe. Some just turn up openly looking for work and/or welfare: by the summer of 2007, Italy was seeing around 1,000 Roma (mostly from Romania) arrive every month – far in excess of those who could be offered work, let alone housing, forcing the Italian authorities to construct huge camps in order to contain them. Other Roma claim asylum but, increasingly, their claims are treated with scepticism. Indeed, it is difficult to see how it can be otherwise: the west European nations they try to get into, after all, can hardly accept that Roma face persecution in the very same countries they have just agreed to admit as functioning liberal democracies to the EU. In some ways, the Roma plight symbolizes the complex difficulties faced by Europe – or, at least, some countries in it – with regard to all minorities. According to many in their native countries, they do not belong there since they exist outside the mainstream majority of 'the nation'. If they manage to make it out to other countries, they suffer and present similar difficulties to other immigrant minorities. Hanging on to their language and their culture, refusing to 'marry out' of it, means they will retain their identity, which is perhaps essential to human happiness. The flipside, however, is their visibility – one of the things that makes it so hard for them to gain acceptance (or at least indifference) rather than hostility.

Learning Resources for Chapter 10

Further reading

Anyone interested in immigration policy in Europe should go straight to the special issue (edited by Lahav and Guiraudon) of the journal *West European Politics*, 29(2), 2006. Also very useful are the volumes edited by Cornelius *et al.* (2004), *Controlling Immigration*, and by Giugni and Passy (2006), *Dialogues on Migration Policy*, as well as a special issue of the journal *Political Quarterly*, 74 (1), 2003. Messina (2007), *The Logics and Politics of Post-WWII Migration to Western Europe* is also recommended, as is the collection edited by Messina and Lahav (2005), *The Migration Reader*. Cohen (2006), *Migration and Its Enemies*, is a stimulating general read. On patterns of migration, a must-read is the collection edited by Penninx *et al.* (2006), *The Dynamics of International Migration and Settlement in Europe*. On European co-operation on immigration and integration, see the collection edited by Faist and Ette (2007), *The Europeanization of National Policies and Politics of Immigration*, and Geddes (2008), *Immigration and European Integration*. For more on how some mainstream parties have reacted, see the collection edited by Bale (2008), *Immigration and Integration Policy in Europe*. Several specialist journals cover migration and minority issues: *The Journal of Ethnic and Migration Studies* (JEMS), *Ethnic and Racial Studies*, and *International Migration Review*. The far right receives what is probably disproportionate coverage in many political science journals. As for books, those interested should certainly read Mudde (2007), *Populist Radical Right Parties in Europe*; Norris (2005), *The Rise of the Radical Right*; and Carter (2005), *The Extreme Right in Western Europe*; and the collections edited by Rydgren (2004), *Movements of Exclusion*, and by Eatwell and Mudde (2003), *Western Democracies and the Extreme Right Challenge*. On the Roma, see Barany (2002), *The East European Gypsies*; for a more journalistic but still useful portrait, see 'Gypsies: The World's Outsiders', *National Geographic* (April 2001).

On the web

www.migrationinformation.org – wealth of information on migration

migration.ucdavis.edu – discussion and news on migration

www.compas.ox.ac.uk – links and working papers on migration

www.migrationwatchuk.org – for a sceptical view on migration

www.unhcr.org and www.ecre.org – refugees and asylum issues

fra.europa.eu – racism and discrimination in Europe

webhost.ua.ac.be/extremismanddemocracy – academic research on extremist parties

www.errc.org and romnews.com – Roma news and issues

Discussion questions

1. Why, historically, have European countries attracted migrants, be they from inside or outside Europe?
2. In recent years, where have migrants to Europe come from, why have they come, and where do they go?
3. Do you think increased immigration in and of itself satisfactorily explains the rise of the far right in Europe?
4. In your opinion, are some European countries right to be more anxious about asylum seekers than others?
5. Europe's population is ageing: can migration help solve the problem?
6. Does the EU undermine or support European countries' attempts to control immigration?
7. How are European countries trying to integrate or assimilate migrants? Is this something you think should be encouraged?
8. Does the historical and present plight of Europe's gypsies – the Roma – give us cause for optimism or pessimism?

Chapter 11

Protecting and promoting – Europe's international politics

Security and defence – the background	337
'Old' and 'New' Europe	339
Still 'the German Question'	342
Russia – Eurasia's (ex-?) superpower	344
Europe's Mediterranean 'neighbours'	348
Towards a European army?	350
Foreign policy	352
Europe in the developing countries	357
Europe and the global environment	361
Europe as a global trader	362
Lest we forget – the enlargement and domestication of international politics	365

No exploration of the politics of a continent is complete without an assessment of how the states within it handle – both jointly and severally – their relations with each other and with the rest of the world. Such an assessment is far from easy. Europe contains states of vastly different weights and sizes. Some fought wars against each other, often alongside allies (most obviously the US) that are now rivals as well as friends. Some have close geographical or colonial relationships with countries that barely even registered on the radar of other states in spite of the fact that they are now part of the same 'ever closer union'. The latter (the EU) is not a permanent member of the UN Security Council. Neither (see Laatikainen and Smith, 2006) does it have much leverage there over the two member states (France and Britain) who are, even though neither can claim the population or the economic power of Germany, which isn't. Not only does each state have more or less unique ideas (and pretentions) about its interests and its role in the world, it also goes about promoting, playing, and deciding on them in very different ways. Moreover, there are many analysts who would regard it as hopelessly old-fashioned and simplistic to talk about states as if they were unitary and potentially autonomous actors. Lastly, for all the talk of a world that is getting smaller every day, it is still rather a big place: like policy-makers, we can only focus on a few aspects of how Europeans operate, and co-operate, within it.

This chapter plunges into these deep, wide and choppy waters – fully aware that they are they are normally home to those specializing in international relations, foreign policy analysis and European integration rather than in comparative politics – by looking at security and defence. It moves on to look at foreign policy – clearly a related area but one in which European states have, on the face of it, been rather more prepared to compromise. Next, it looks at an area in which co-operation is often thought to be even more comprehensive – namely, aid to the developing countries. Finally, after a brief examination of another field apparently characterized by co-operation – the environment – it focuses on one in which European co-operation and compromise is said to have gone furthest; namely, trade. As the chapter moves progressively through the themes, it moves the focus further and further into the world; but it makes no apology for taking as its start and end point Europe itself, believing that it is all too easy to forget, particularly when it comes to security, that this is where governments have over the years concentrated most of their efforts and scored most of their achievements. The focus at all times is on the interaction between individual state concerns and instruments and the collective action of the EU.

Security and defence – the background

Long before the attacks of 11 September 2001 in New York and Washington, it was fashionable to suggest that the end of the Cold War between 1948 and 1989 (see Chapter 1), far from ushering in a 'new world order' to be overseen by 'the international community', might paradoxically have made the world a more dangerous place (see the yearly *Conflict Barometer* for plentiful evidence of the fact). As the director of the US Central Intelligence Agency (CIA) told the Senate in February 1993: 'We have slain a large dragon, but we live in a jungle filled with a bewildering variety of poisonous snakes.' These include the 'rogue states', terrorists, or WMD (weapons of mass destruction) that threaten our way of life and the raw materials on which such weapons depend, or drug and people trafficking by organized crime, or civil wars spilling thousands of refugees across vulnerable borders – all of which blur the boundaries between 'external defence' and 'internal security'.

KEY POINT

Europe has a troubled history which still affects the present, notwithstanding the new challenges presented by an ever-wider definition of what constitutes security

Yet the CIA director's warning had more than a little amnesia about it. As one analyst acerbically observed (Mueller, 1994: 358), the Cold War itself was 'a jungle filled with at least two dragons and poisonous snakes, some of whom were variously, changeably, and often quite ambiguously, in devious complicity with one or other of the dragons'. Moreover, the relatives of hundreds of people who lost their lives as a result of 1970s bombings and shootings in West Germany, Italy and the UK could have reminded him that there was nothing new about terrorism. So, too, could the survivors of the aeroplane hijackings that first became fashionable in that decade. Europe has known for a long time that, in a world where extremes of material wealth and spiritual values continue to co-exist, its democracy and its peace and prosperity cannot be taken for granted, but have to be promoted and protected, not least within the continent itself (see Box 11.1).

Security is about perception, about the absence, or at least the minimization, of unacceptable risk not just to life, but to those things that are thought to make it worthwhile or at least easier – freedom and prosperity via access to essentials like food and water and to the raw materials and friendly fellow nations that make trade possible (see Wyllie, 1997). Providing it, and providing for the defence of the realm, is one of the most fundamental functions of the state: it has a responsibility to its people and is the guarantor of its own survival. Maintaining the armed forces that are traditionally thought of as the ultimate upholders of security, and holding on to the right to deploy them, is not only one of the symbols of sovereignty, it is also a crucial part of its substance. Hardly surprising, then, that governments do not give up such things lightly, if indeed they are willing to give them up at all. They are, however, realistic. They know that they are unlikely to be able to protect their people unless they combine their own efforts with those of other states.

They also know that security in the twenty-first century has to be broader than a concern with territorial integrity and therefore inevitably involves more than the state alone (see Cottey, 2007 and Rothschild, 1995). The threat to the latter has receded, though not completely disappeared. Threats to the peaceful and relatively prosperous way of life led by Europeans have, on the other hand, multiplied, necessitating a multifaceted, more-than-military response – one that involves Europe projecting not just power but norms, values and institutions. This not only costs money and necessitates interstate and supranational co-operation. It also entails overlapping and contested responsibilities exercised by a mix of actors that are not hierarchically organized and often have different, even contradictory, interests and ways of getting things done. In short, security, like so many other policies (see Chapter 3), might still be guaranteed (if not always effectively) by govern*ments*, but it is

BOX 11.1

Europe's traditional democracy promoters – the CoE and OSCE

The Council of Europe (CoE), founded in 1949, was one of the forerunners of the EU. However, it involved the UK (which did not join the EU until the 1970s) and other countries such as Switzerland and Norway that have never joined. Also, it was always a forum for political, legal and cultural co-operation rather than economic integration. From the early 1990s, its membership swelled to encompass most of postcommunist Europe. It is governed by foreign ministers, but it also has a parliamentary assembly. It was set up to promote parliamentary democracy, human rights and the rule of law, and if possible to set pan-European standards for them. To that end, it has overseen almost 200 binding treaties and conventions, most famously the European Convention for the Protection of Human Rights and Fundamental Freedoms (known as ECHR), which most European countries (including most recently the UK) have incorporated into their domestic law. The convention is overseen by the European Court of Human Rights, a body that is completely distinct from the EU's Court of Justice (ECJ). The ECHR sits in Strasbourg and can be appealed to from member states. The CoE is now tasked, among other things, with assisting postcommunist countries to integrate human rights and the protection of minorities into their reform programmes.

The Organization for Security and Co-operation in Europe (OSCE) was finally established as a permanent body in 1949. With the end of the Cold War, the OSCE was used as a framework in which arms reduction negotiations could take place. Now with a membership of fifty-five nations that includes Europe, most of the former Soviet Union (FSU) and the US and Canada, it has its headquarters in Vienna, but, like the CoE, it is governed by member states' foreign ministers. Its main activities are election monitoring (e.g. Ukraine in 2004), and the resolution and policing of border disputes in the new democracies of Europe, the Balkans and Eurasia. Given the role played by the EU in some of these regions and activities, some observers worry that the organization is now being sidelined, despite the fact that it potentially has a useful role to play (see Biscop, 2006).

increasingly delivered via multilevel gover*nance* (see Kirchner, 2006).

In Europe, this knowledge is reinforced by often bitter historical experience. But the history of the hundred and fifty years prior to 1945 also presented Europe with something of a 'catch-22'. Clearly, maintaining some kind of 'balance of power' between various alliances of states was ultimately insufficient to prevent the outbreak of armed conflict (see Chapter 1). Yet the gap in military potential between France and Germany could not be effectively offset either by Britain (an island) or Russia (which had huge ambitions of its own), meaning that peace and some kind of stability could be achieved only with the help of an extra-European power – the US – that might one day prove unwilling to assist. The only feasible way out of this *impasse* was to enmesh the continental powers of Germany and France and their smaller allies in an indigenous institution that would effectively ensure their economic interdependence, making them realize that their best interests lay in peaceful co-operation rather than armed conflict. Whatever the criticisms of this institution – now known as the EU – few would deny that it has achieved what, beneath both the grand rhetoric and the less edifying wheeling and dealing, was always its primary purpose: to bring stability and security to a continent that otherwise seemed destined periodically to tear itself apart.

Yet the EU and its forerunners were only a necessary rather than a sufficient condition of peace in Europe after 1945. In fact, the absence of war also relied, in depressingly familiar fashion, on a balance of power – this time between the two nuclear-armed superpowers, the Russian-dominated Soviet Union and the US, with European countries as members either of the Russian-led Warsaw Pact or the US-led

NATO (see Chapter 1). To Europe's political and military leaders, concerned about a possible return of US isolationism ushering in either Soviet domination or a return to western European rivalry, NATO had three basic purposes. These were pithily summed up by its first Secretary General: to 'keep the Russians out, the Germans down, and the Americans in' (see Lundestad, 1998a, 1998b). While the definition of European security and the instruments used to strive for it have expanded in recent years, European states have, by and large, not lost sight of those three basics. And for many of the states that have 'rejoined Europe' after first Nazi and, then, Russian Soviet repression, those basics remain as relevant as they ever were for their western counterparts.

'Old' and 'New' Europe

The 2003 war in Iraq is often said to have brought into sharp relief two competing visions for European security and defence. For many, these rival visions were symbolized in the row over the public letter of support for the US signed in January 2001 by the prime ministers of Denmark, Hungary, Italy, Poland, Portugal, Spain and the UK, as well as the president of the Czech Republic. This group of countries apparently shared a perspective that during the Cold War was labelled 'Atlanticist'. This perspective holds that European states must implicitly acknowledge their limitations and therefore do nothing which endangers a security relationship with what is now the world's only superpower, the US. This is then contrasted with the perspective of what American Defense Secretary at the time, Donald Rumsfeld, dismissed as 'old Europe' – especially France and Germany. The leadership of the latter came in for particular criticism because it had, claimed Washington, allowed its desire to cosy up to antiwar voters in the general election of 2002 to override its responsibilities to the 'transatlantic alliance' and the US-led 'War on Terror'.

Rumsfeld had a point. Many postcommunist states did back the Anglo-American position on Iraq

Figure 11.1 Europeans' 'favourable' attitudes to the US (and its rivals)

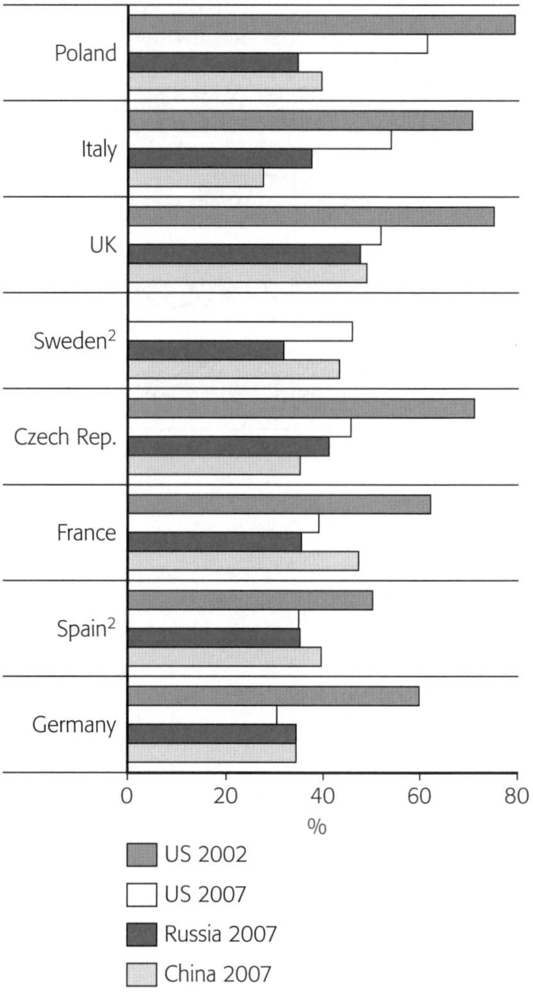

Notes: 1. Percentage of respondents saying they had a favourable attitude to the country concerned.
2. No figure for 2002 available for Sweden and Spanish figure is for 2000.
3. The Netherlands was not in the survey.

Source: Data from PewResearchCentre, *Global Attitudes Survey* (June 2007).

KEY POINT

Distinctions between 'old' and 'new' Europe are not irrelevant but, even though the transatlantic relationship has been strained by the Iraq war, they can be over-stated. So can the idea that the EU and its member states are preoccupied more with soft than hard power. The European Security Strategy sees a role for both, though military spending is comparatively low.

Figure 11.2 Europeans' favourable views on Americans, their culture and their ideas

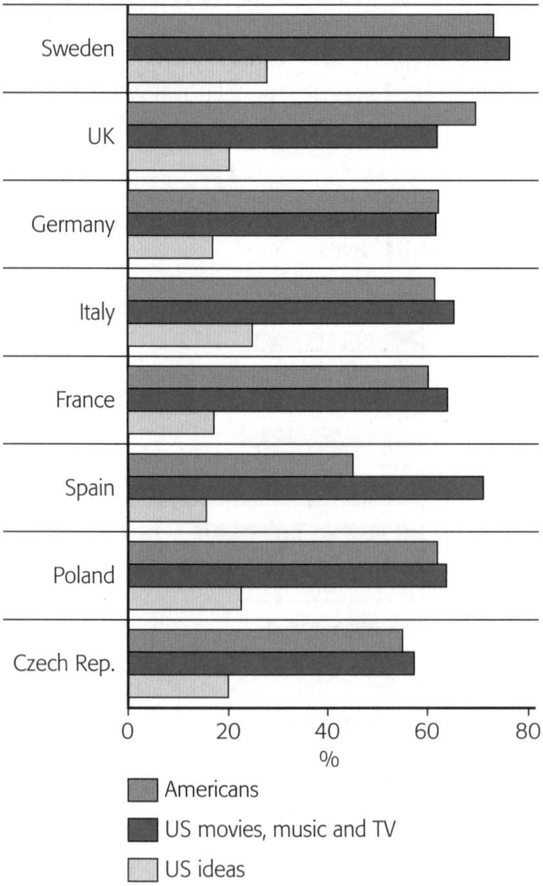

Note: Percentage of respondents saying they felt positively. The Netherlands was not in the survey.

Source: Data from PewResearchCentre, *Global Attitudes Survey* (June 2007).

for both ideological and material reasons (see Fawn, 2006). And there is an 'old Europe' perspective that holds that the continent should pursue a more independent course, especially in the light of the Iraq conflict – a debacle that has so damaged the US's reputation among ordinary Europeans that in some countries people apparently have a more favourable view of Russia and China, although they continue to like Americans and their culture, if not their country's ideas (see Figures 11.1 and 11.2). Such thinking is partly motivated by objections in principle to a 'unipolar' world dominated by a US 'hyper-power' that some Europeans have always held in cultural contempt (see Markovits, 2004, 2005). It might also have something to do with the fact that European countries cannot as yet, and might never wish to, project power to the same extent or in the same way as the Americans (see Kagan, 2002, 2004). Instead, they place more weight on the value of diplomacy and on the ideas of **soft power** and **security community.**

Soft power comprises trade and aid, cultural links and institutionalized 'political dialogue' through a web of sometimes overlapping international organizations (such as the OSCE and possibly NATO) that, at least within Europe itself, constitutes what some call a **security community** – an area characterized by such a high level of transactions and communication that conflicts are always resolved peacefully.

But some of these distinctions are too simplistic – and not only on the level of culture (see Figure 11.2). 'Old Europe' is not simply a collection of introverted pacifists and appeasers who habitually shy away from confrontation. In fact, some of those European countries most closely associated with 'old Europe', not least France, argue that both a European security community and European autonomy should be reinforced by a measure of 'hard' (i.e. military) power. And, interestingly, other countries that would escape US criticism, primarily the UK, have some sympathy with this idea. They are, though, more ambivalent about achieving it by bringing security and defence more firmly into the provenance of the EU by, for example, making available sufficient forces and instituting majority voting for the European Security and Defence Policy (ESDP) (see Howorth, 2007 and Box 11.2). This is because such a policy could complement American efforts, but it might sometimes diverge from them: theoretically, at least, Europe could decide on some issues not to stand 'shoulder to shoulder' with the US – something which the UK, keen to maintain its 'special relationship' with the Americans (see Dumbrell, 2001), still tends to do.

On the other hand, just like other Europeans, the British have to at least consider the possibility that the US might not always be there to keep the peace in Europe. This is especially true in the light of America's declared intention, after coming to Europe's aid on several occasions in the 1990s when

BOX 11.2

European Security and Defence Policy – key dates and events

1992 Maastricht Treaty makes moves towards a common foreign and security policy (CFSP).

1997 EU's Amsterdam Treaty incorporates 'Petersberg Tasks' (humanitarian search and rescue missions, peace keeping, crisis management and 'peace making' by combat forces). The new 'High Representative' appointed to oversee CFSP (ex-head of NATO, Javier Solana) would (in 1999) become the head of the West European Union (WEU), which would, in effect, be incorporated into the EU (basically confirmed by the Nice Treaty of 2000).

1998 France and the UK sign 'St Malo Declaration', outlining the need for more effort on defence by the EU countries (the UK emphasis) and greater autonomy for the EU to carry out missions without NATO (the French emphasis).

1999 EU's Cologne summit notes that 'the Union must have the capacity for autonomous action, backed up by credible military forces, the means to decide to use them, and a readiness to do so, in order to respond to international crises without prejudice to actions by NATO'. Helsinki summit sets 'headline goals' including the creation by December 2003 of an EU 'Rapid Reaction Force' (RRF) for 'Petersberg Task'-style missions. It also sets up military planning/liaison bodies in the Council. Meanwhile Poland, Hungary and the Czech Republic join NATO

2002 Despite ESDP being declared operational, EU peace-keeping force to Former Yugoslav Republic of Macedonia (FYROM) delayed because countries other than France and Belgium insist that ESDP operate on a 'Berlin-plus' basis – i.e. with the ability to call on NATO assets if needed. Delays and disputes also arise because of difficulties raised by NATO (but non-EU) member Turkey, and because of suspicions of smaller EU countries about pretensions to leadership by a *directoire* of France, the UK and Germany, who themselves are in dispute concerning the French desire to stress the autonomy of ESDP from NATO.

2003 France, UK and Germany fall out further over the Iraq war (see Schuster and Maier, 2006). France, Germany, Belgium and Luxembourg hold their own summit meeting on ESDP, hinting at closer integration on defence by core countries and a possible NATO-style 'mutual defence clause' for the EU, obliging them to come to each other's aid militarily if attacked. The US and the UK are furious, so too are other EU member states. 'Chocolate makers', as the small group of countries are dismissively labelled, back down and re-stress their commitment to NATO. Henceforth, the 'Berlin-plus' basis (see above; also Reichard, 2006) becomes the consensus. EU 'Operation Concordia', keeping the peace in FYROM, begins in April, with 250 EUFOR troops from 15 member states. June sees the start of 'Operation Artemis', keeping the peace in part of the Congo, involving 1,500 troops (most of them, as with Concordia, French) – the first EU mission outside Europe. At the end of the year, Rome summit agrees to an advanced strategic planning capability for EU, but one that will liaise closely with NATO, which announces the entry in 2004 of the former Soviet states Estonia, Latvia and Lithuania, as well as Slovenia, Slovakia, Bulgaria and Romania. 'European Security Strategy' (Council, 2003) approved.

2004–6 NATO hands responsibility for peace keeping in Bosnia to EU, which launches EUFOR-Althea operation in December 2004. EU cooperates with five ASEAN countries in 2005 to form, in Indonesia, the Aceh Monitoring Mission (AMM) – the first ever ESDP mission in Asia. EUFOR-RDCongo sent in 2006 to support and protect the UN mission overseeing, and civilians participating in, elections in the Democratic Republic of Congo.

it proved unable to end civil wars in the former Yugoslavia, to focus less US time, men and money on the defence of a continent that many in Washington believe should start looking after itself. The question for the UK, and for other European nations, is whether attempts to show that they are more willing than previously to shoulder the burden of their own defence will fuel or forestall US impatience. And could it, in the very long term, even begin to worry the US that Europe might try to match it militarily, as it is trying to match it politically, economically and diplomatically? Are we seeing the stirrings of a 'European superpower', albeit one not simply based on military might alone (McCormick, 2006; see also see Haseler, 2004; Reid, 2005 and Rifkin, 2004)?

There are some who believe, especially after the arguments over Iraq, that a European challenge to US hegemony and hyper-power is not just inevitable but also perhaps even desirable if that is what it takes to finally force people into thinking of themselves as 'European' (see the pundits cited in Markovits, 2004: 25–7). Others laugh at the idea that such a challenge is imminent, especially in the light of the failure in 2005 of the Constitutional Treaty that would have given the EU its own 'foreign minister' and legal personality. Most European countries (especially those that had to meet the strict convergence criteria for monetary union) spent the 1990s cashing in on the post-Cold War 'peace dividend' of lower defence spending. As a result, they are nowhere near matching or even approaching US defence spending (see Box 11.3). But, just as significant as spending totals, is the way armed forces are organized. The UK, and to a lesser extent, France, because they were global powers, have more mobile forces that can be deployed overseas reasonably rapidly. Most other European states, however, constructed rather static, conscript-based forces that are far less suitable for today's flexible power projection and 'crisis management' scenarios: the US has over 250 large transport planes, the EU countries put together possess fewer than fifteen! Defence analysts also argue that research and development (R&D) makes up such a low proportion of spending, and is so fragmented between countries, that European forces risk losing out to technologically superior opposition or remaining forever reliant on American hi-tech equipment that is either expensive to buy or could be denied them should the US not support their actions.

Still 'the German Question'

But it is not just the US that is crucial to the calculations of Europe's biggest defence players: France and the UK. The question of Germany is just as important as ever – perhaps even more important than it has been for decades. On the one hand, Germany had to be persuaded (and to persuade its people) that it could and should contribute more and more practically to European defence. On the other, any increased contribution must not allow it to slip the bonds that had seen it safely locked into, rather than dominating, the continent. Germany, since reunification, has been trying to come to terms with this dilemma itself. Since the 1950s, it had been used to thinking of itself as a 'civilian power' (see Haftendorn, 2006; Hyde-Price, 2003; and Maull, 1990) – a polity that, like Japan and perhaps also the EU, sought multilateral and non-military solutions to international problems – if necessary, through what critics sometimes labelled 'chequebook diplomacy'.

KEY POINT

Few seriously expect Germany to constitute a threat to European peace any longer, but it is seeking to combine its 'civilian power' tradition with a stance more in keeping with its size and weight.

Germany's re-birth as Europe's biggest (and still richest) nation in 1990, however, gave it the confidence to go against its so-called 'co-ordination reflex' (the tendency not to act without consulting and getting the consent of its EU partners) and recognize Croatia and Slovenia when they declared independence from Yugoslavia. This move was regarded with some concern on the part of other member states, especially France and Britain, who (rightly, it turned out) feared it would ignite a war in the Balkans – one in which none of them wanted to intervene. Ironically, it was this war, and the genocidal atrocities that accompanied it, that (with the

BOX 11.3

Europe's 'meagre' defence spending

The US has by far the biggest defence budget of any single state on the planet: its spending amounts to around 45 per cent of global defence spending and, if one were to take the top ten spenders, the Americans spend more than the other nine combined. This is not altogether surprising: as a continental power surrounded by vast oceans on either side, the US necessarily requires a huge navy and air force to defend itself and project its power abroad. Its high spending is also due, in part, to its desire to maintain an edge in technology and, of course, to the upkeep and development of its still-extensive nuclear arsenal. On the other hand, the US can take advantage of considerable economies of scale, both in terms of its purchasing power and its world-beating and more integrated defence industries – something Europe has decided to try and do something about by creating the European Defence Agency, which reports to the EU's council of (defence) ministers. Although, as Table 11.1 shows, there are considerable variations in the relative and absolute size of each country's armed services, Europe as a whole fields more personnel than the US. But, as the table also shows, it spends less than half of the US spend, and spending as a proportion of GDP is much lower by comparison: this is true as a whole and of individual countries, although again there are considerable differences in this respect.

Table 11.1 EU and US defence spending, 2005

	Defence spending as % of GDP (2005)	Defence spending € billion (2005)	Defence spending *per capita*, € (2005)	Defence spending as % of government spending (2005)	Military personnel, (2005 total)	Military personnel, (2005 as % of total workforce)
France	2.49	42.53	702	4.6	351,000	0.013
UK	2.47	44.20	736	5.5	205,000	0.007
Czech Rep.	1.86	1.84	180	4.3	25,000	0.005
Italy	1.90	26.96	461	3.9	325,000	0.013
Poland	1.90	4.64	122	4.5	150,000	0.009
Sweden	1.54	4.43	492	2.7	21,000	0.004
Netherlands	1.53	7.69	472	3.4	50,000	0.006
Germany	1.36	30.60	371	2.9	246,000	0.006
Spain	1.16	10.50	244	3.0	120,000	0.006
EU members	1.81	193.00	425	n/a	1,858,000	0.009
US	4.06	406.00	1363	n/a	1,400,000	0.009

Note: n/a = Not available.

Source: Data from European Defence Agency (2005) plus 2005 workforce data from European Labour Force Survey and US Department of Labor.

help of Federal Constitutional Court rulings in 1994 declaring 'out-of-area' deployment of German armed forces legal) allowed Germany's leaders to persuade enough of its people that it should henceforth play a more active, assertive and military role in world affairs. This new role was symbolized not just by peace-keeping missions in the former Yugoslavia, but also by German participation in NATO bombing raids in Kosovo in 1999 and in the removal of the *Taliban* regime in Afghanistan that had provided a safe haven for *al Quaeda*.

BOX 11.4

Europe and the aftermath of the 2006 war in Lebanon

In the aftermath of the month-long war between Israel and Hezbollah in Lebanon in the summer of 2006, the UN authorized a peacekeeping force (UNIFIL) of 15,000 troops. EU countries are providing personnel, though not in as large numbers as had been initially hoped. The UK had something of an excuse, given its continuing involvement in the Iraqi quagmire and the fact that its government had been roundly criticized (outside Washington and Tel Aviv, anyway) for supposedly being too sympathetic to Israel. But the initially niggardly response to the call for troops of France, which has long positioned itself as a friend of the Arab nations, attracted some ridicule. It began by promising just a couple of hundred soldiers, until stung into action by Italy which, under its new prime minister (and former president of the European Commission) Romano Prodi, decided it was finally time it took something of a lead in the region and offered 3,000 personnel. France then conjured up a force of 2,000 for a mission commanded by one of its one of its own military men, (the ironically rather Italian-sounding) General Pellegrini. It should be noted, however, that France took the lead to help head off a humanitarian crisis in Chad, by getting the EU in September 2007 to consider sending 3,000 mainly French EU troops to protect displaced people. Critics, however, saw even this as characteristic of France's continuing interference in its former colonies.

Indeed, the negative reaction of the German government to the invasion of Iraq has to be seen in the context of the potential of such an unpopular action to undermine its painstaking (and painful) attempt to convince a still sceptical German public that military action abroad is not inherently wrong. Meanwhile, Germany's support for ESDP has to be seen in the light of that same desire to move towards being a 'normal' country and away from being one that forswears the full range of instruments to protect and promote its considerable economic interests (see Maull, 2006). Europeanizing security and defence policy (see Miskimmon, 2007) offers Germany a way to do this at the same time as reassuring its partners that it will not seek to do anything more than return to normality, hence the country taking a lead role in the EU's contribution to the military operation safeguarding the electoral process in the Democratic Republic of Congo in 2006, its contribution to the EU effort in the Lebanon following the war in the summer of the same year (see Box 11.4), and its close co-operation with the UK and France on trying (however unsuccessfully) to talk Iran out of developing a nuclear capability as part of the so-called 'EU-3' (Germany, France and the UK).

Whether this reassurance really works, however, is another matter – especially when it comes to some CEE countries. The fear that in the long term Germany might choose to play a more assertive role closer to home – notwithstanding its leading role in facilitating their accession to the EU (see Tewes, 2001 and Thompson, 2001) – could help explain why so many of Europe's new democracies sided with the US (and the UK, Spain, and Italy) over Iraq. But their decision to do so was also prompted by concern over what was seen – especially by an understandably suspicious Poland (see Box 11.5) – as Germany's 'cosying up' to Russia under former Chancellor Gerhard Schröder.

Russia – Eurasia's (ex-?) superpower

Because of its valuable energy exports to an EU increasingly reliant on imports of oil and gas, and because of its 143 million consumers, Russia repre-

KEY POINT

A newly assertive Russia and its former empire constitute both an opportunity and something of a threat to Europe. The enlargement of the EU, its energy needs, and the European aspirations of some former Soviet states have complicated relations considerably.

sents considerable, and as yet under-realized, trade opportunities for Europe. But it also represents a considerable security threat – and, if opinion polls are accurate, continues to be regarded with suspicion by many ordinary Europeans (see Box 11.5). There might be little likelihood (certainly in the short to medium term) of Russia precipitating interstate conflict with European nations (see Mangott, 2000), but the Russian Federation contains a number of republics which would like to break away (most notoriously, Chechnya), provoking uncertainty and therefore insecurity. It also borders a number of former Soviet and now 'newly independent states' that, in addition to being geographically close and potentially economically important to the EU, contain very big Russian minorities: examples include Belarus (1 million Russians or 11 per cent of the population), the Ukraine (11 million or 22 per cent) and Kazakhstan (4.5 million or 30 per cent). A number of these states, as well as Russian republics, also harbour their own ethnic conflicts, as well as religious extremists who might respond to global faith-based terrorism. All this creates potential instability not just in Russia itself, but also in Europe's eastern 'near abroad'. It also creates problems further afield. Russia (like the UK and France, we should note) is still one of the world's biggest arms producers and sellers, and has continued to provide several Middle Eastern countries with weapons, and more besides: the nuclear technology which some fear Iran will use to develop WMD was sold to them by a Russia desperate to maintain and increase its trade.

The most obvious way in which Europe deals with this potential instability to its east is the continuation and expansion of NATO, as well as its extension into a forum for dialogue with Russia in what is called the NATO–Russia Council, established in May 2002. NATO therefore operates both as a workable military alliance and as part of a system of 'multilateral security governance' wherein institutionalized dialogue with potential adversaries can be conducted and their potential risks thereby scaled down (see Smith, 2000). In so doing, it complements European (and US) attempts to involve and enmesh Russia in the institutionalized 'international community' that have cleared the way to its membership of non-security bodies such as the G-8 meetings of the leaders of the world's industrialized countries and the World Trade Organization (WTO). On the other hand, Russian dialogue with NATO and its members does not extend to its being granted a say (or even to its being consulted) on military operations that they deem necessary, such as airstrikes in Kosovo in 1999.

The second way Europe deals with the security risk that Russia potentially presents is somewhat old-fashioned, hardly savoury, but, for all that, possibly necessary. It is to allow the Russian Federation what amounts to a 'sphere of influence' over much, though (as the dispute over Ukraine in 2004 showed) not all, of the territory formerly presided over by the Soviet Union (see Chapter 1). This policy, for example, involves the tacit acceptance (despite formal scoldings) that Russia can do what it likes in the breakaway republic of Chechnya – important to Russia not only in symbolic but also economic terms, since it is the main route for oil from Kazakhstan to Russia's big Black Sea port of Novorossiysk. This tacit acceptance of Moscow's hard-line stance risks offending Islamic extremists; but it also has the considerable advantage – especially in the wake of the massacre of schoolchildren in Beslan in September 2004 – of allowing Europe, the US and Russia to feel, rightly or wrongly, they have something in common in the 'War on Terror'.

The third way Europe has attempted to reduce the risk to its security from Russia and the other countries of the former Soviet Union is to provide substantial financial and development assistance, accompanied by political dialogue and promises of improved access to the European single market. EU funding is significant, beginning with the establishment in the early 1990s of the TACIS (Technical Assistance to the CIS) programme. But much of the assistance has been bilateral. German aid to Russia, for instance, is particularly significant – something that might also have something to do with the fact that the country is by far Russia's biggest trading partner. On a political level, the EU and Russia agreed to two summits per year and, at the 2003 St Petersburg summit, it was decided to establish a 'Permanent Partnership Council' (PPC) to promote ministerial contact between member states and Russia. In 2005, the summit came up with so-called 'road-maps' for the closer co-operation. October of the same year saw the first meeting of the EU–Russia Partnership Council on Energy.

But, so far anyway, these frameworks have not done away with genuine clashes of interests and values. Russia, now stronger and much wealthier than it was in the 1990s, is increasingly assertive about defending and promoting its interests, and remains suspicious of anything that smacks of interference in what it regards as its internal affairs or, indeed, those of states it considers as in its own backyard. It was particularly irritated by what it saw as the 'western' meddling that brought about and supported the 'Rose' and 'Orange' revolutions in former Soviet states Georgia and Ukraine in 2003 and 2004 respectively. At the same time, the EU has added members who are determined not to be pushed around by a state they clearly regard as their old nemesis and are determined to steer EU policy as far in their direction as possible. Particularly vociferous are the formerly Soviet Baltic states, in which Russian minorities are still poorly treated (and in many cases denied full citizenship), and Poland (see Box 11.5). But even one of the newest members, Romania, represents something of a threat to Russian interests by taking an interest in the fate of neighbouring Moldova, where Russia has a military presence. As if this weren't enough, Russia – which declared in 1999 that it was uninterested in ever joining the EU – is concerned (however unlikely it may sound) that the EU will eventually tempt countries that it is currently trying to organize into its own regional organizations, be they economic or military (like the Collective Security Treaty Organization, or CSTO, comprising Russia, Belarus, Kazakhstan, Kyrgyzstan, Tajikistan, Armenia and Uzbekistan). Russia is also clearly worried by US plans to site infrastructure for its proposed missile defence system not just in the UK but also in the former Soviet bloc states of Poland and the Czech Republic – a decision which, it insists, cannot help but alter the nuclear balance to the Americans' advantage.

On the other hand, argue some observers, Russia is by no means always the victim of bullying. Few believed that its decision (literally) to turn off the gas in a price dispute with the Ukraine during the winter of 2005–6 had nothing to do with geo-politics. Not only was it a sign of continuing displeasure with the regime in Kiev, it was also a reminder (and a very tangible one given the drop in gas pressure experienced in western Europe during the dispute) of Europe's heavy reliance on Russian energy. This reliance will only increase as Russian state-sponsored energy giant Gazprom expands into western Europe and into the central Asian republics that European countries once hoped they could deal with in order to bypass Russia. In fact, it would be more accurate to say 'some European countries' because their dependence on gas from the east varies enormously. According to figures compiled by the BBC during the Ukranian gas dispute in early January 2006, Germany gets around 40 per cent of its gas from Russia and this will increase; the figures for France (around a quarter) and Italy (nearly a third), however, are lower, but those for Austria (75 per cent), Greece and Lithuania (80 per cent), Bulgaria, Slovakia, Lithuania and Finland (90–100 per cent) are much higher. On the other hand Belgium, Ireland, Portugal, Spain, Sweden and the UK import little or no gas from the Russians, while Denmark (like non-EU member Norway) is self-sufficient.

It may be simplistic to suggest that states' relations with Russia are a function of their energy dependence, but the variation in that dependence will not do much to ensure that the EU pursues a consistent line. Germany's obvious reluctance to sanction concerted EU support for the UK's attempt extradite the ex-KGB agent accused of the Litvinenko poisoning is a case in point. On the other hand, not even the emollient Frau Merkel could rescue the EU–Russia summit in May 2007 from descending into acrimony, with the President of the European Commission warning Russia not to try to undermine the solidarity of the member states and Vladimir Putin accusing some of them of 'economic selfishness that does not always correspond to the EU's interests'.

Notwithstanding these spats, combined economic and political co-operation between the EU and Russia is proceeding, albeit not as smoothly or as quickly as some had hoped. It is supposedly being

BOX 11.5

Poland and Russia (and Germany)

Polish–Russian relations have been difficult for quite some time, although the idea that the Polish population is particularly ill-disposed to Russia may well be something of a myth: a PewResearchCentre poll published in June 2007 suggested that 24 per cent of Poles felt unfavourable rather than favourable to Russia, but the French (–30), Spanish and Swedish (both –28) were even more negative – indeed, only the British (who appear unaffected by the high-profile poisoning of Russian dissident Alexander Litvinenko in London in 2006) were on balance favourable. The Baltic states (particularly Estonia) can also claim to be just as much a victim of what they claim is Russian bullying as Poland,while, in 2007, the British and Swedish ambassadors in Moscow shared the dubious distinction with their Estonian counterpart of being subjected to intimidation and even assault by 'patriotic' youth movements loyal to Mr Putin. The relationship between Warsaw and Moscow, however, has been under severe strain for some time. It took its first turn for the worse when Poland backed (and persuaded the EU to back) a re-run of the Ukrainian presidential election of 2004 and then supported the eventual winner, leader of the so-called Orange Revolution, Victor Yuschenko, who has continued to press the case for his country's eventual membership of the EU.

The relationship deteriorated still further in 2005. In July, Russia made clear its continued support for the Belarussian dictator, Aleksander Lukashenko, whom Poland was accusing of mistreating the hundreds of thousands of ethnic Poles living in his country. In August, diplomats and their families were attacked in both Warsaw and Moscow. In September, Germany and Russia agreed to build a 1,200km (and €3.5 billion) gas pipeline which, by running partly under the Baltic Sea, would bypass Poland thereby raising fears that Russia may attempt to deny it access to vital energy supplies. The deal prompted the Polish Foreign Minister into an indirect but ill-judged comparison with the Molotov–Ribbentrop Pact between Nazi Germany and Soviet Russia. This understandably contributed to a worsening of relations between the two EU members, which reached its nadir during difficult negotiations on EU voting reform in 2007: the highly nationalistic government led by the Kaczynski twins had already inflamed things by suggesting that, but for Germany's aggression in the Second World War, Poland would have had a bigger population, thereby fully entitling it to the vote share that others wanted to cut; but things got even worse when the front cover of the Polish weekly *Wprost* (not a government publication, it must be said) proclaimed German Chancellor Angela Merkel the 'Stepmother of Europe' against a photo-shopped image of the twins sucking her bare breasts. More prosaically, Poland's frustration with what it regarded as a politically motivated ban on its substantial meat exports by Russia was holding up re-negotiation of the EU–Russia Partnership and Cooperation Agreement (PCA).

complemented – but also perhaps disrupted – by the announcement at the end of 2003 of the so-called 'European Neighbourhood Policy' (ENP). Reduced to its essentials, this sees a number of states bordering the EU offered the prospect not of membership but of 'a stake in the EU's internal market'. Each has an 'Action Plan' detailing the administrative and political reforms (covering things like respect for borders, markets, the rule of law and human and minority rights) it needs to make in order to qualify for aid from and market access to the EU. Russia is not strictly a part of the policy, having its own 'Strategic Partnership' with the EU, but should share in the economic benefits on offer because it has economic and other relationships with former Soviet states; namely, Moldova, Ukraine, Georgia, Armenia and Azerbaijan. On the other hand, the ENP could prove a source of friction with Russia if it turns out to be – despite the EU's best intentions – a 'waiting room' for states that are eventually allowed to join the EU, as some have said they wish to do (see Smith, 2005a).

One 'neighbour' that has repeatedly declared it does want to join, notwithstanding the EU's

Figure 11.3 Fighting terrorism – a collaborative effort

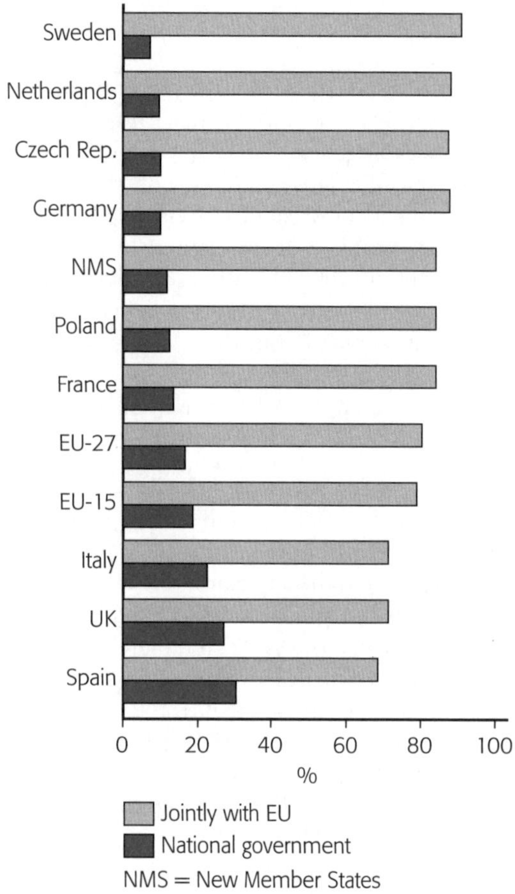

Source: *Eurobarometer*, 67 (2007): 'Decisions on fighting terrorism should be made by the government or jointly within the European Union'.

persistent refusal to listen, is Ukraine. It, at least, has the advantage of being seen by most Europeans, according to recent opinion polling (see *Special Eurobarometer* 285, 2007), as a neighbour. All the other ENP countries are clearly rejected as such, although it is clear that views vary according to location, with more (though rarely most) people in the Mediterranean member states being prepared to see the North African countries as neighbours and more people in the CEE states doing the same for their easterly 'neighbours'. Across the EU-27, however, a majority of respondents declared 'little or no interest' in what was happening in the ENP countries and did not feel they had values in common with them. Eight out of ten had never heard of the ENP and most believed any help that could be given would end up costing a great deal without many economic benefits accruing to Europe in return. Virtually everyone, however, thought it sensible to pursue good relations with Europe's neighbours, with concerns about organized crime and terrorism and reducing the risk of illegal immigration, war and conflicts in Europe very much to the fore. On the surface, at least, Europeans appear to be sceptical and rational realists. Consistent with the lack of attention paid to foreign countries in their media (see Chapter 7), Europeans don't spend much of their valuable time thinking about them, suspect that dealing with them will involve spending a lot of money that they will never see again, but realize that it may be worth it if it protects them. The latter is very much in keeping with a wider tendency to favour co-operation on issues, such as fighting terrorism, where even the most obtuse of us would have trouble arguing that 'going it alone' makes much sense (see Figure 11.3).

Europe's Mediterranean 'neighbours'

In fact, the idea of a European 'neighbourhood', and the potential economic benefits that might flow from 'neighbourly' behaviour began life as part of Europe's attempt to handle the security risks posed by countries not to its immediate east but to its south, along the Mediterranean (Map 11.1). Those affected include Morocco, Algeria and Tunisia (which historically have been intertwined with France, and to a lesser extent Spain, and which are often collectively referred to as the *Maghreb*), as well as Egypt, Israel, Jordan, Lebanon, Libya, Palestine and (possibly) Syria. Many of them are economically troubled and politically unstable. They are experi-

KEY POINT

The ENP that applies to several East European and Eurasian states also applies to the countries of the South Mediterranean: its aim of encouraging political and economic development in order to reduce instability and illegal immigration might be hard to achieve.

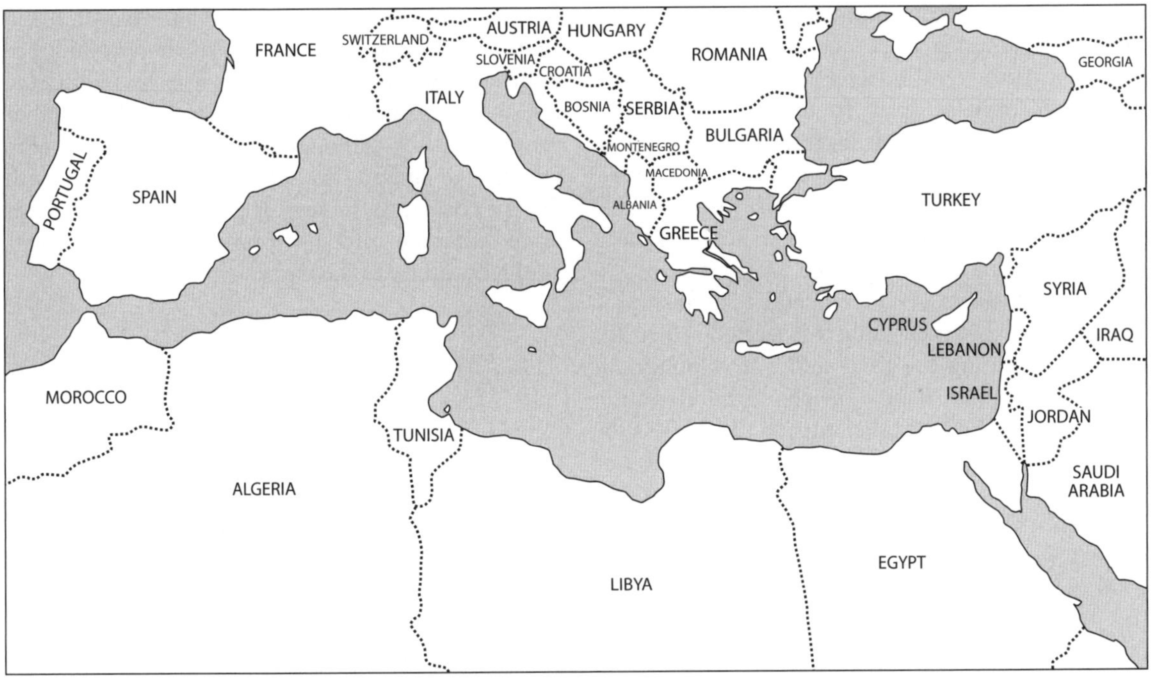

Map 11.1 Europe's Mediterranean neighbourhood

encing a population explosion in spite of the poverty that pervades the majority of them, and in many of them there is significant opposition to the governing regimes. At the same time, they are a significant source, or at least a conduit, for the energy resources on which Europe relies. Whether they be 'failed', 'rogue' states or simply troubled states, they therefore represent a fertile ground for almost everything Europe worries about (see Coulombis and Veremis, 1999): maritime pollution, illegal immigration and drug trafficking, and terrorist threats to mainland Europe or, just as seriously, to its energy supply.

Although France maintained postcolonial links with some pretty unsavoury regimes in the region (see Meyrede, 1999), there was surprisingly little collective thought about the southern Mediterranean until Spain joined the EU in 1986 (see Gillespie, 2000). Spain, like France has a complicated mesh of bilateral security and economic agreements with a number of North African states to its south, and for some time they have played a much bigger role in both its trade and its foreign policy than have states that are often (but wrongly) assumed to matter more to Spain for cultural reasons, such as those in South America (see Kennedy, 2000: 122). In the early 1990s, Spain began a concerted attempt (with the French and Italians) to draw the EU's attention to the need to 'do something' for the Mediterranean. Its efforts finally paid off in the so-called 'Barcelona Declaration' of 1995, by which the states were offered a much bigger and more comprehensive package of EU assistance – accompanied by political dialogue aimed at securing improvements in human rights.

EU development assistance to the southern Mediterranean runs into the billions. Free trade, too, is supposed to be an important part of the package on offer, although the extent to which the countries in the region actually trade with the EU varies considerably – all the way from Libya and Tunisia (which do 80 per cent of their trade with the EU), through Morocco and Algeria (70 per cent) and Syria (60 per cent) to Israel, the Lebanon and Egypt (25–30 per cent), and finally Jordan (less than 5 per cent). The ENP, then, builds on efforts already in place, but adds political conditions to the prospect of a bigger economic gain via closer integration with the EU's internal market. However, if one regards poverty as the main source of instability, then simply encouraging trade and providing development assistance (and attaching strings to both) is unlikely to prove a quick fix to the security risks posed by the southern Mediterranean. Israel's GDP *per capita* may reach 80 per cent of the EU average, but (with the exception of Lebanon, where it is 20 per cent), not one of the Southern Mediterranean countries can claim to reach even 10 per cent.

These differences – plus bilateral relationships – already mean that each country is treated rather differently, rendering the ENP more of 'a policy for neighbours rather than a neighbourhood policy' (Smith, 2005a: 771). On the other hand, the ENP, by providing off-the-shelf regulatory regimes, promoting good policy and opening up markets can potentially help each neighbour progress economically as well as politically (see Dodini and Fantini, 2006). But this will take time. Right now, the fear is that the extreme poverty of many of the countries involved will lead to ever-greater migratory pressure. This, combined with heightened concerns about Islamist terrorism, could mean that ENP ends up reinforcing the impression that, whatever the rhetoric, the EU will end up as a 'gated community' – prepared to pay to keep 'undesirables' at a safe and well-policed distance but never to welcome them inside, other than as temporary (and even then not particularly trusted) servants (see Zaiotti, 2007).

These risks are why many would argue that 'soft power' instruments such as trade and aid have, in the end, to be backed up by 'hard power' – military threats or even actual force. In fact, when it comes to the Middle East, Europeans probably need to be as much, if not more, interested in that region's oil than the nation many of them like to think of as the 'bad guy', the US. In fact, Europe consumes over three times the amount of oil it produces and is more reliant on Arab energy suppliers than the Americans. Along with the need to keep onside what in some countries is a sizable Muslim population (see Chapter 1), this is why European countries have been so keen to try to counterbalance US backing of Israel in the drawn-out Palestinian peace process (see van Dosenrode and Stubkjær, 2002). This is also why even those governments critical of America's policy in the Middle East have to help clear up the mess they believe it has created in places such as Iraq. In any case, their doing so, some wryly observe, fits nicely into the pattern created after the US interventions in the former Yugoslavia whereby 'America fights and Europe does the dishes' by providing the bulk of men and money for peacekeeping. Rather less pejoratively (though employing rather more jargon), we might talk of complementarity, with Europe bringing increasingly sophisticated, integrated civilian-military preventative and post-conflict capacity to the party.

Towards a European army?

Actually, one can question how hard and fast this putative division of labour between Europe and the US really is. True, European countries did indeed provide most of the 'stabilization force' that came in once the Americans had toppled the *Taliban* regime in Afghanistan, while the EU and its member states have provided around a third of the total international aid to the country (some €4 billion). But not all observers dismiss the initial warfighting role of French and British forces in Afghanistan as insignificant (see Menon, 2004a). Conversely, the US remains heavily involved, on the ground as well as at the diplomatic level (see US Mission to Pristina, 2007) in trying to achieve lasting peace in Kosovo, much to the chagrin of Russia and China that which fear the granting of independence (supervised by the EU) will set a worrying precedent. Moreover, even assuming the clichéd EU–US division of labour – between a US specializing in 'hard power' and a Europe that is better at 'soft power' – exists, can it go on for ever? The question raises once again the extent to which Europe is willing to both share the burden with the US (the UK emphasis) and/or assume some degree of autonomy from it (the French emphasis).

This, as we have seen, is what ESDP, at least in part, is about. Whether Europe actually needs or finds it convenient to use it in an operational as well as a symbolic sense, however, remains to be seen. For

KEY POINT

Despite developments and missions carried out under auspices of the European Security and Development Policy (ESDP), a European army, though not as much of a pipe-dream as some suggest, is still a long way off.

one thing, however much commentators talk about Sweden, Finland, Austria and Ireland supposedly moving toward 'postneutrality' in what seems to be a more dangerous world, there seems little prospect of them surrendering their neutrality soon. This means that they may pick and choose missions, preferring perhaps to contribute to the non-military side of putative European operations (see Menon, 2004a). For another, experience also suggests that the key to things working is as much political as institutional. Unless big players, big contributors and big strategic thinkers such as France, Germany and Britain form some kind of informal trilateral *directoire* (and are allowed to do so by the other member states), things just will not happen (see Crowe, 2004: 41–2; and Menon, 2004b).

Experience also suggests that – especially in times of crisis – institutions will not stop the formation of ad hoc 'coalitions-of-the-willing' making use of national rather than multinational military assets (see Duke, 2000: 29). This is true whether they involve countries outside Europe, as in Iraq, or inside, as in the little remembered Italian-led intervention in Albania in 1997, undertaken in order to prevent a breakdown in state control turning into complete anarchy (see Foster, 1998 and Silvestri, 1997). Neither will institutional membership prevent those states in Europe with global pasts and global pretensions projecting their power (albeit in ways that they think are for the best) in smaller conflicts well away from Europe. The sending of British troops to Sierra Leone to shore up a UN force in trouble is one example. The (possibly less successful) French intervention of 2002 in the Ivory Coast (where France has a permanent military base) is another.

What ESDP is certainly *not* about – at least in the foreseeable future – is establishing EU control over the defence capability of its member states, forcing them to say 'yes' to what other states want them to do or preventing them from saying 'no'. Neither, for the moment, is it trying to balance rather than complement NATO (see Cimbalo, 2004) or to swap the intergovernmental logic of the latter with the supranational logic that some see as inherent in the EU (see Ojanen, 2006). True, there now exists a *Eurocorps*, based on 900 dedicated soldiers from France, Germany, Spain, Belgium and Luxembourg, but this was set up separately from ESDP. There are also, since 2007, 'EU battlegroups' – rapid reaction forces made up from several member states which are assigned for exclusive EU use on a six-monthly rotation basis. There is also a civil-military planning cell, run by the (currently British-commanded) EU Military Staff (EUMS), which aims to improve the EU's ability to deploy such collective resources quickly. There have been complaints, too, (for example, from NATO's Secretary General in a speech in late January 2007) that co-operation between his organization and the EU remained very narrow. However, the decision-making basis for ESDP remains intergovernmental (see Chapter 2). It may now be possible for some states to go ahead with a mission should others who do not support it choose to let them to get on with it; but if they want to, they

Figure 11.4 'Should decisions on defence and foreign affairs be made by national government or jointly within the EU?'

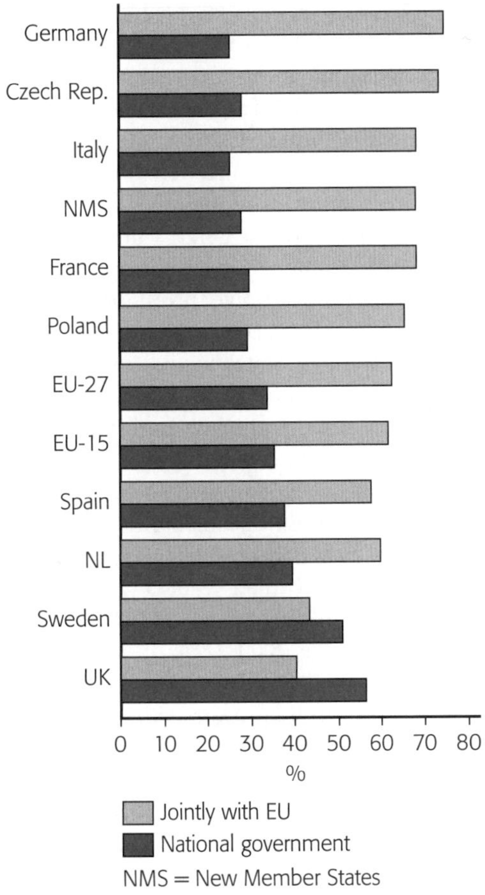

Source: Data from *Eurobarometer* (67, 2007).

can still veto any operation. Neither, we should note, does the supranational Commission, which is at least consulted on and can make suggestions in EU foreign policy, have any formal role in ESDP.

In any case, a report on ESDP approved by all heads of state and government at the EU's Nice summit in 2000 (see UK House of Lords, 17 January 2002, *Hansard*, Column 1210) made three things crystal clear. First, that 'NATO remains the basis of the collective defence of its members. Second, that '[t]he development of the ESDP will contribute to the vitality of a renewed transatlantic link'. And, third, that it 'does not involve the establishment of a European army. The commitment of national resources by Member States to [its] operations will be based on their sovereign decisions.' It is difficult to see how in the short to medium term this can be got around. Moreover, significant numbers of European people do not want it to be got around, especially in western European countries and particularly in Scandinavia and the UK (see Figure 11.4). Nor, one suspects, do their leaders, civil and military. As one US ambassador to the EU put it in the early 1990s (see Duke, 2000: 188):

> Until the major European nations, including Germany, are prepared to send their young men abroad to fight, and to die if necessary, in a European cause, under a European flag, and within a European command, no amount of planning for a European security identity will field a single battalion.

Figure 11.5 'Do you think that, fifty years from now, the EU will have its own army?'

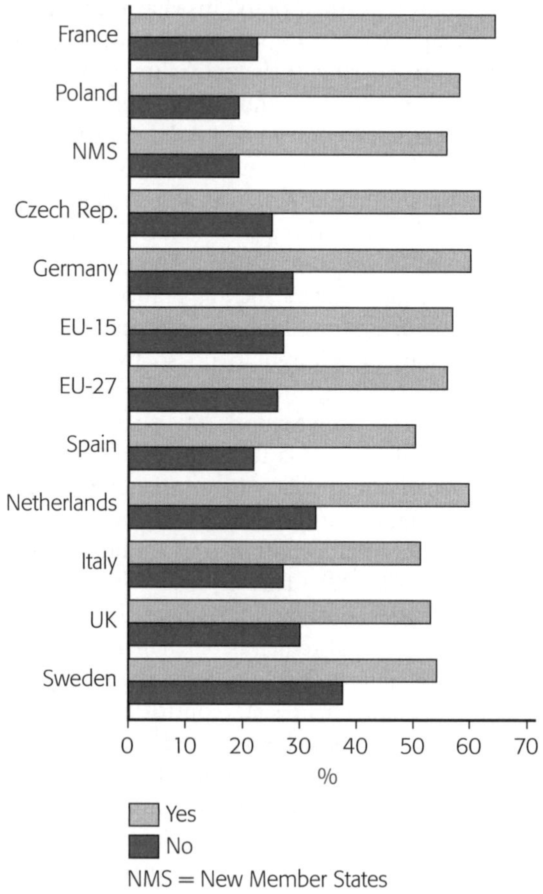

Source: *Eurobarometer* (67, 2007).

This, of course, is the ultimate test. And, strangely enough, there are signs that, even if Europeans don't appear to want it, many of them regard some kind of European army as something that will eventually come about (see Figure 11.5). But even on rather less ambitious criteria, there is precious little evidence of Europeanization when it comes to the impact of the EU on defence policy. The most recent comprehensive attempt to find it, wisely looking country-by-country, uncovered some indirect effects. The single currency may have forced member states to spend even less on defence than they might have done; there are moves towards a rationalization of European defence industries and procurement; and, most interestingly, German policy makers used the need to be good Europeans to ease their country out of its relatively passive stance. But the same study found that 'big decisions are still national' and that, for all the rhetoric about interdependence, 'the EU itself has exercised little or no direct impact over shifts in national defence policy' (see Freedman and Menon, 1997: 156ff.).

Foreign policy

The right to determine their own defence policies is clearly something European states are keen to protect. When it comes to foreign policy – often a rather less highly charged area – there is a similar concern to preserve their sovereignty. But there is also, too, more of a recognition – at a mass as well as

KEY POINT

The EU has come a long way in co-ordinating the foreign policy stances of individual states, not least because it serves their purposes and adds value. But they continue to differ when and where they believe it really counts.

an elite level (see Figure 11.6) – that co-operation with other states, particularly if they are also in the EU, can be beneficial. Even before the formal declaration in the Maastricht Treaty signed in 1992 that the EU would establish (albeit intergovernmentally rather than supranationally) a 'Common Foreign and Security Policy' (widely known as CFSP), member states were engaging in what had become known as 'European Political Co-operation' or EPC (see Nuttall, 2000).

Yet much of the potential afforded by the CFSP for common action – and for the EU to assert its 'presence' and its 'actorness' (see Allen and Smith, 1998; Bretherton and Vogler, 2005; and Hill, 1993) – remains unrealized, as various audits undertaken by academic observers, more or less ruefully note (see, for example, Holland, 2004a). There are many reasons for this. At the level of process, the insistence by EU member states on a clear distinction between the EU's foreign policy, on the one hand, and its trade and aid policies, on the other, means that many of the instruments that they themselves routinely use to support their bilateral aims cannot be brought to bear by the EU. This, plus the fact that, as yet, the EU has long lacked a constitutionally and internationally recognized 'legal personality' that would allow it to act more cohesively in global forums, also often means that it has to be content with 'declaratory diplomacy'. Yet even when it manages to go further, and (say) impose sanctions on a foreign regime abusing human rights, the hard-won consensus for that action soon frays under pressure from contradictory national interests. The relations between Europe and Zimbabwe are a case in point (see Weiland, 2004). In 2007, it was clear that most member states were prepared to tolerate the attendance of Robert Mugabe at an EU–Africa summit in Lisbon (despite the fact that he was officially the subject of an EU travel ban) if that was what it was going to take to get all the other African nations on board. To the UK, however, this was

Figure 11.6 'Are you for or against a common foreign policy among the Member States of the EU towards other countries?'

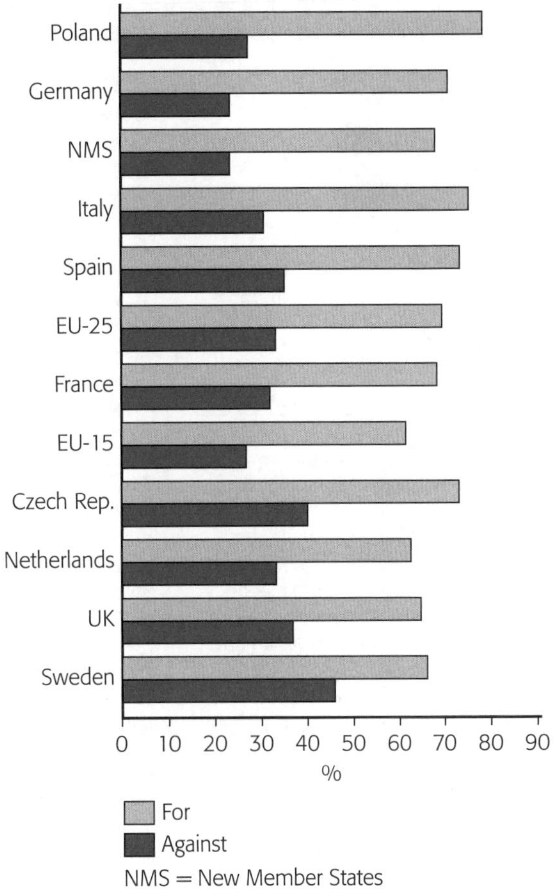

Source: *Eurobarometer* (66, 2007).

clearly unacceptable. As long as state interests remain so diverse and potentially contradictory – other 'hard cases' include Cuba and Burma (see Smith, 2006) – then no amount of institutional tinkering can compensate for the lack of political will that, ultimately, lies behind what some see as the failure of the CFSP.

That said, we should think twice before portraying the national interest vs CFSP as some sort of simple zero-sum game. Indeed, it is clear that European co-operation offers individual states or groups of states opportunities to better pursue their national interests, at least where they are perceived to coincide with those of the rest. For instance, states such as France, the UK, Portugal and Belgium can use the

COUNTRY PROFILE

Sweden (Sverige)

Area: 410,900 km^2 (9.8% of EU-27)

Population: 9.0 million (1.8% of EU-27)

Religious heritage: Protestant

GDP (2006): €282 billion (2.4% of EU-27)

GDP *per capita* as percentage of EU-27 average: 120

Female representation in parliament and cabinet (end 2007): 47% and 41%

Joined EU: 1995

Top 3 cities: Stockholm – capital city (0.8 million), Gothenburg (0.5 million); Malmö (0.3 million).

History: Sweden's early history was bound up with that of the other Nordic countries (box below). It conquered Finland in the thirteenth century, but was then subsumed into the kingdom of Denmark. It regained its independence in the early sixteenth century under a king elected by its parliament, the *Riksdag*. For the next one hundred and fifty years, it went from strength to strength, conquering territory in modern-day Estonia, Latvia, Russia, Germany and Poland, and even pushing into what is now the Czech Republic during the high point of its power, the Thirty Years War (1618–48). After this, it began to lose out to other powers, most notably Russia, to which it was forced to cede Finland in 1809. Things looked up soon after when the *Riksdag* elected a high-ranking French soldier as regent and then king, creating the line of Bernadotte, which still reigns in Sweden today. As a reward for siding with Britain and Prussia (now part of Germany) against the French dictator, Napoleon Bonaparte, Sweden was granted effective control over the kingdom of Norway – a situation that lasted until 1905 when the Norwegians peacefully regained their independence. The nineteenth century saw Sweden adopt, first, a liberal constitution, then (in the 1860s) parliamentary government and, finally, a fully fledged democracy after the First World War (1914–18).

Sweden did not take part in that conflict and likewise remained neutral in the Second World War (1939–45), managing to escape the occupation endured by its Nordic neighbours and to develop its economy by trading with the combatants. If neutrality was the first defining feature of the twentieth century for Sweden, the second was the unparalleled political hegemony of its Social Democratic Party (SAP). The SAP effectively ran Sweden from 1932 to 1976. During this period it pioneered anti-recessionary public spending and then went on to construct the third defining feature of Sweden in the twentieth century, its highly comprehensive welfare state. Even since wresting power from the SAP in the mid-1970s, the so-called 'bourgeois' parties of the centre-right, led by the conservative Moderates, have only managed to govern Sweden three times – once between 1976 and 1982, then between 1991 and 1994, and finally, after over a decade of the Social Democrats being kept in office by the smaller, more radical Left Party and the Greens, since 2006.

Economy and society: Sweden's citizens are some of the richest in Europe, with a *per capita* GDP a fifth above the EU average. Much of their income, however, is swallowed up by taxes to pay for the welfare state, although the universal nature of many of the benefits it offers (in both cash and in kind) means that support for it remains high, even amongst those who pay most. This is despite the fact that recent pension reforms will see the introduction of an element of means testing that for some goes against the fiercely egalitarian grain. Sweden can afford its welfare state because it has a very competitive international trading sector which, although privately owned, seems to benefit from the stable economic environment, industrial harmony and active labour market policies facilitated by the state. Things are not perfect, of course: there is unemployment, much of it disproportionately affecting

WHAT'S IN AN ANTHEM?

The vaguely Tolkeinesque *Du gamla, Du fria* dates back to the nineteenth century, which is partly why neither of the two official verses mentions Sweden by name but instead refers to the 'ancient . . . free . . . [and] mountainous north'. The first verse goes on to talk of the 'green meadows' of 'the most beautiful land on earth', before recalling, in the second, the great days of yore when the place was honoured throughout the world. It reinforces the stereotype of a nation no longer interested in conquest and more concerned with keeping itself clean and green.

Sweden's half a million or so immigrant population, many of whom arrived only in the 1980s–1990s from places such as the former Yugoslavia and the Middle East. Until their arrival, Sweden was unusually ethnically homogeneous – a homogeneity that also applied to religion: over nine out of ten Swedes still identify, even if only minimally, with the state Lutheran (Protestant) church which is financed through the tax system.

Governance: Sweden is a parliamentary democracy and a constitutional monarchy. Its unicameral legislature reflects the relatively consensual nature of Swedish political life. Its procedures, like policy making more generally, encourage consultation with outside interests, especially the powerful unions (to which most people belong) and employers' organizations, although the latter have cooled somewhat toward government-facilitated economic planning in recent years. Responsibility for many state functions is exercised by agencies, often at the regional or county level. Strong respect for due process has not precluded adaptation and innovation: Sweden undertook a major overhaul of its constitution as recently as the mid-1970s, and was the pioneer of the *ombudsman* system designed to help citizens redress grievances against public bodies without expensive recourse to the law – a system that has since spread to other countries.

Foreign policy: Sweden put off joining the EU until 1995. By then, the end of the Cold War had calmed concerns about membership undermining its neutral, non-aligned stance. Nevertheless, the country rejected adopting the euro in a referendum in 2003. Sweden still declines to join NATO, but is active in a non-combat role in humanitarian interventions all over the world (see box above).

A KEY CONTEMPORARY CHALLENGE
BALANCING NEUTRALITY AND THE NATO RELATIONSHIP

Sweden is not a full member of NATO, but in 1994 it joined the Partnership for Peace, which works towards interoperability between NATO and non-NATO forces that will hopefully improve any joint response in a crisis. It also promotes a security dialogue and information sharing between NATO and its partners. Recently, Sweden has requested more of this information sharing, posing something of a dilemma for NATO which, on the one hand, can see it makes sense but, on the other, has to maintain the advantages of (and the privileges that come with) membership. In fact, Swedish troops already serve under NATO command in Kosovo and Afghanistan, where 300 Swedes are stationed. NATO is also interested in having Sweden contribute to its rapid reaction force but there is debate within Sweden as to whether this would constitute too close an involvement. Defence is, anyway, a difficult issue for reasons other than geo-political and ideological: in 2007 the Swedish Defence Minister resigned when the Minister of Finance publicly announced that he would only be able to afford tax cuts if he forced through reductions in military spending. In fact, of course, the two issues – continued neutrality and financial pressures – are related: it is extremely costly for a small country, even one as relatively well-off as Sweden – to meet all its military needs when they might be better met by being part of an alliance to which some functions and capabilities could in effect be 'contracted out'.

Contemporary challenges

- Ensuring the survival of (and service-delivery to) communities in sparsely populated areas
- Deciding on the extent to which Sweden's tradition of neutrality should be maintained, particularly in view of close co-operation with NATO
- Reconciling a high-cost welfare state with an ageing population and concern about taxation;
- Meeting EU demands for liberalization of services
- Tackling what some regard as excessive labour market regulation
- Restoring the faith of the public after both politicians and civil servants have been implicated in petty tax evasion.

Learning resources: Start with Kent (2008), *A Concise History of Sweden*. After that, try Arter (2006), *Democracy in Scandinavia*, and Einhorn and Logue (2003), *Modern Welfare States*. Finally, move on to Ingebritsen (2006), *Scandinavia in World Politics*. Keep up with the news at http://www.sr.se/international/index.stm

CFSP to speak and act on African questions without necessarily drawing attention to (and fire for) supposedly 'neo-colonial' attitudes. Meanwhile, states such as Ireland, Austria, Finland and Sweden can use participation in the CFSP at least to finesse, if not necessarily to transcend, their non-aligned or neutral stances (see Manners and Whitman, 2000). The release in the summer of 2007 of six Bulgarian healthcare workers Libya had held for seven years was almost certainly accelerated by Bulgaria joining the EU at the start of that year, and perhaps by the (then) French 'first lady' Cécilia Sarkozy, who went to Libya 'as a woman, as a mother' to secure their release. Likewise, the EU's collective condemnation of attacks on Danish embassies in the wake of the cartoon crisis (see Chapter 10) almost certainly prevented the row turning into a bigger trade boycott against a small member state. Similarly, the immediate EU backing of the UK's demand that Iran release its captured sailors in the spring of 2007 was probably also useful – although the absence of any concomitant threat of sanctions unfortunately spoke volumes about the unwillingness of certain member states to sacrifice their commercial relationships with Tehran.

Neither should we think of European countries' foreign policy elites as somehow insulated from each other. Far from it: observers draw attention to the effect of Europeanization on the tendency of states in Europe to consult each other almost as a reflex and often before their traditional allies. For example, Scandinavian policy makers will tend to think 'European' rather than simply 'Nordic', while those in the UK might now think of consulting their partners across the Channel rather than going across the Atlantic first (see Manners *et al.*, 2000: 249). On the other hand, the extent to which socialization into collective habits, norms and identities has taken place is easily overdone, especially with regard to policy makers from larger member states such as France, Germany and the UK. This is irrespective of the fact that they have been in the Community as long (or in some cases longer) than some of the member states in which that socialization is more noticeable (Manners and Whitman, 2000: 251–2).

This points to a more general pattern among EU member states. States with more global interests, such as France and Britain, tend to be rather more reticent about foreign policy convergence than often (but not always smaller) states with a more exclusive European focus, such as (prototypically) Belgium or Italy. The latter realize that Europe could afford them far more say in world affairs than they could ever hope to get acting alone; the former that the less intergovernmental the process, the less likely a putative European policy is to reflect the interests of the larger member states. Located between these two extremes are three groups. First, there are the states with a more 'Atlanticist' focus but that also like to think of themselves as good Europeans (Denmark, the Netherlands, Portugal, and Spain). Second, there are states with a particular regional focus and/or a tradition of neutralism (Austria, Finland, Ireland and Sweden) or at least multilateralism (Germany). Third, there are the postcommunist states: they are concerned to be good Europeans and, to some extent, share the anxieties of other smaller states that a purely intergovernmental 'European foreign policy' will be dominated by larger states; but they are also determined to preserve the sovereignty that they have only just won back after years of Soviet domination.

It is also important to remember that Europeanization, and the variation in the extent to which it seems to have affected the foreign policy-making of EU member states (see Wong, in Hill and Smith, 2005) is by no means the only factor impacting on such policy-making. Any list would have to include the following questions (many of which are posed in Manners and Whitman, 2000: 252–61). How important is parliamentary oversight on foreign policy: practically unimportant as in France and the UK, or a potential constraint, as in the Nordic countries? To what extent do subnational governments get involved: not at all, as in most states, or increasingly often as in the federal states such as Belgium or Germany? Do parties make a difference: who would argue with the assertion that the election of a Socialist government in Spain in 2004 very swiftly reoriented Spain back to a more 'European' as opposed to 'Atlanticist' foreign policy orientation? Does this indicate that foreign policy – traditionally rather an elitist forum (a policy community rather than an issue network, to use the language of Chapter 8) – is becoming more generally politicized and even rising in salience among voters? Does this explain how the German SPD, by departing from its traditional acquiescence and criticizing the US over Iraq in the autumn of 2002, managed to stave off electoral defeat that, given difficulties on the home front, it otherwise deserved? How influential are pressure groups: do defence industry lobbies push some countries (France and Britain) in one direction, while internationalist trade unions try to push other governments (Sweden, Germany) in another? How extensive is prime ministerial (or, in the case of France, presidential) intervention in foreign policy: is the foreign minister and his department very much in charge (as in, say, the Netherlands) or do they have to work hand in hand with the head of government (as in the UK, France, Germany and, increasingly, Italy)? And what about the bureaucratic politics and foreign ministries (see Hocking and Spence, 2002): to what extent are they under pressure financially and losing exclusive competence over foreign (and especially European affairs) to a whole range of departments who find themselves consulting with their opposite numbers in other member states?

Most of these issues, of course, pertain to foreign policy makers 'at home' in Europe. There is less research on the Europeanization of those who carry out those policies 'in country' outside Europe. What work there is (see Bale, 2000, 2004) suggests a familiar pattern. By and large, diplomats from smaller states are keener on co-operation with their fellow ambassadors than those from larger states; meanwhile, all states see the multilateral approach as a more or less useful addition to, rather than as a substitute for, their primarily bilateral approaches. Material, and not merely symbolic, obstacles remain in the way of any moves toward some kind of integrated, 'European' diplomacy. It might make sense in terms of upfront cost savings, but individual European countries would lose the considerable commercial benefit of their own flag-waving public diplomacy. It would demand changes from a group of relatively insulated and privileged civil servants.

In the end, it is hard to see a European diplomatic service until there is a clear 'European' interest to represent. In as much as there is one already – on aid and trade (our next topics) – it is already well represented by the European Commission's own external service which runs over 120 diplomatic delegations throughout the world (see Bruter, 1999). That said, the proposed European External Action Service (EEAS) seems to have survived the wreck of the Constitutional Treaty, although it looks more likely to involve personnel drawn from member state diplomatic services working direct to the proposed 'European Foreign Minister' than the conversion of the Commission delegations into full blown embassies (see Allen and Smith, 2007).

None of this makes it any easier for Europe to 'speak with one voice' in or to the rest of the world, notwithstanding the appointment, following the Amsterdam Treaty, of a 'High Representative' who is supposed to do just that – a High Representative who, interestingly, was almost completely bypassed by both 'old' and 'new' Europe in the intra-European row in the run-up to the Iraq war in spite of his widely acknowledged qualities as a networker and credible mover-and-shaker (Crowe, 2004: 37). None of this means that European foreign policy is necessarily a mess, but it is necessarily messy. As the pre-eminent analyst of European foreign policy, puts it (Hill, 1998: 48–9):

> We cannot know where the European foreign policy system is heading ... What is clear, however, is the interplay taking place between the national and the collective ... This has produced a pattern of multi-level diplomacy in which the various elements sometimes, compete, sometimes reinforce each other, and sometimes merely co-exist.

Europe in the developing countries

Europe may spend less than two thirds of what the US spends on the military, but it prides itself in spending at least twice as much on development assistance. Indeed, European countries provide over half of the what governments around the world give in aid to developing countries, with the EU-15 providing some $78 billion dollars in 2005. The UN target is that donor countries should be giving 0.7 per cent of their gross national income (GNI), although Denmark, Luxembourg, the Netherlands, Norway and Sweden are the only countries in the world to meet the target. Since September 2005, the EU has had its own target for member states of 0.51 per cent by 2010, although it is not clear how any of

KEY POINT

European states, both bilaterally and through the EU, provide a massive amount of aid to the developing world, although the good they do has to be offset against their continued protectionism.

the new member states will come close to it. Much of this overseas development assistance (ODA) is still provided on a bilateral basis to particular countries, often those with colonial links (as Table 11.2 also shows), but a significant proportion now comes through the EU. It is managed on their behalf by the Commission as the 'European Development Fund' (EDF) and goes to some 650 million people living in seventy-seven African, Caribbean and Pacific nations – the so-called 'ACP countries' – under an agreement signed at Cotonou in June 2000 that came into force in April 2003 for a twenty-year period, subject to five-yearly reviews.

Table 11.2 Who spends how much on aid, and where and how they spend it

	ODA (% GNI) (2005)	ODA (US$ billion) (2005)	ODA spent bilaterally (2005) (%)	Debt relief as % of ODA (2005)	Top three recipients	ODA *per capita* (US$) (2004)
Sweden	0.94	3.362	66	2.4	Tanzania, Mozambique, Russia	302
Netherlands	0.82	5.115	72	7.0	Indonesia, India, Tanzania	258
France	0.47	10.026	72	34.7	Ivory Coast, French Polynesia, New Caledonia	137
UK	0.47	10.767	75	32.9	India, Serbia and Montenegro	131
Germany	0.36	10.082	64	34.5	Serbia and Montenegro, China, Bolivia	91
Italy	0.29	5.091	45	33.0	Mozambique, Tanzania, Eritrea	43
Spain	0.27	3.018	62	20.7	Nicaragua, El Salvador, China	56
European Commission	n/a	9.390	n/a	n/a	Turkey, Serbia and Montenegro, Morocco	n/a
USA	0.22	27.622	92	15.6	Egypt, Russia, Israel	67

Note: n/a = Not available.

Sources: Data from OECD, *Development Cooperation Report, 2006*. *Per capita* ODA from UN, *Human Development Report* (2006).

Figure 11.7 Where ODA channelled through the EU goes

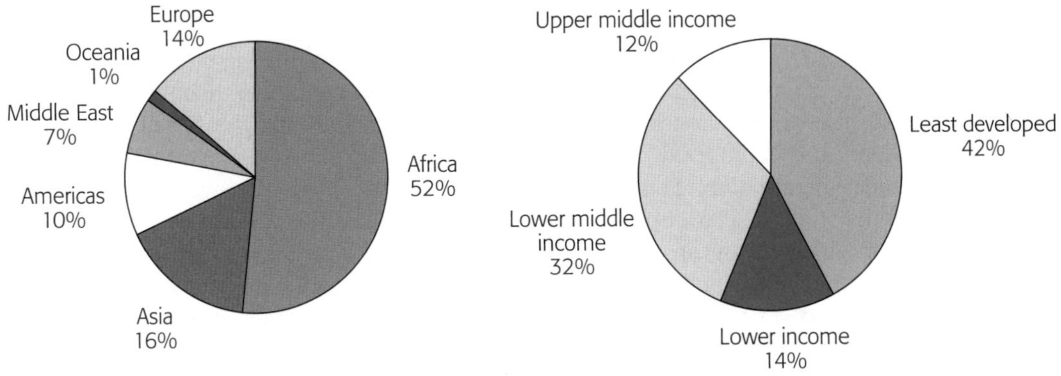

Source: 2005 data from OECD, *DAC Peer Review of the European Community* (2007).

The Cotonou Agreement is the latest in a long line of agreements under which the EU and its forerunners have provided ODA and preferential access to European markets to countries which, more often than not, are former colonies of member states. Unfortunately, while the assistance provided to the ACP should not be sniffed at, the Commission itself noted prior to Cotonou that the results were pretty meagre in terms of the overall EU development goals (namely, to reduce poverty and produce sustainable socio-economic development in the countries helped) to facilitate their integration into the world economy and to support democracy and human rights. According to European Commission figures, per capita GDP in sub-Saharan African (SSA) – where most EU help goes (see Figure 11.7) – grew on average only 0.4 per cent per year between 1960 and 1992, compared to 2.3 per cent for developing countries as a whole. Only 6 per cent of African trade is intra-African: most African nations (indeed, most ACP nations) are still exporting to and importing from Europe instead of, as it were, building indigenous (and possibly economically more rational) trade networks. And yet, ACP countries' share of the EU market was not only over-concentrated in a few commodities (60 per cent of trade was in only ten products), but between the mid-1970s and the late 1990s it actually halved.

Irrespective of outcomes, there has been considerable criticism of the way in which, over the years, Europe's development assistance has been managed. First, there is the overlap and duplication between EU programmes, the bilateral efforts of member states and the work of non-European governments, other international organizations and non-governmental organizations (NGOs). Second, there is the corruption and misspending in the developing countries themselves. These criticisms led to the establishment of *EuropeAid*, an EU agency tasked with co-ordinating and implementing the EU effort – an arrangement that appears to be improving matters considerably. Co-ordination will always be an issue, of course, but most analysts believe that a 'mixed economy' of donors is healthy, even if there is some risk of overlap. They also point to the fact that the EU has considerable advantages over bilateral providers. For instance (although this could change with an increased security and foreign policy presence), it is seen by most receiving countries as 'neutral' rather than 'neo-colonial'. In addition, the fact that the EU, via the Commission, is responsible for negotiating multilateral trade agreements (see below) means it is in a better position than single countries to ensure coherence between these agreements and aid packages. On the other hand, European countries continue to run with bilateral trade agreements and often (all too often, say critics) tie aid to a commitment on the part of the recipient to buy their goods and services. One advantage of EU action in this area is that this kind of 'tied aid' is much reduced, even if it is not yet completely eliminated.

The other big change that has come about in recent years is the increasing 'conditionality' attached to development assistance coming from European countries (see Holland, 2004a). While some of the conditions have to do with promoting economic reform, most of them are to do with good governance (transparency and accountability) and, increasingly, human rights and gender equality. This is part of an overall trend towards including a political dimension in the aid relationship. Also important, but rather less trumpeted, is the encouragement of trade liberalization. This has to happen so that most, if not all, ACP countries, and their trade relationships with European countries that are still inclined to grant them non-reciprocal, special treatment, can meet ever-stricter WTO rules. The downside of this will be that their markets will be open to the advanced industrialized countries. The upside of this is the granting to the least-developed countries (or LDCs) practically free access to European markets. The fact that free access will apply only to the poorest of the poor raises the critical question of coherence. Put bluntly, European countries give with one hand but take away with the other by continuing to protect markets – particularly agricultural markets – in which developing countries could well enjoy a comparative advantage. Whether this will change with the announcement in early 2001 that the EU would, within a decade, allow free access to its markets for around fifty of the world's LDCs – the so-called 'Everything but Arms' (EBH) proposal – is a moot point (see Holland, 2002: 225–31).

Another, recent criticism is that Europe is increasingly using aid as a tool of foreign and security policy, meaning that its 'near abroad' will get an unfair share compared with those far-away countries who need it more. Those concerned with security are, of course, right to point to the fact that, as the European Security Strategy of 2003 (see Box 11.2) put it, 'security is a precondition of development'. But many in the development community suspect that the security to be protected is less that of the developing countries than that of Europe itself. Only the naive would expect or demand no linkage between development assistance and foreign and security policy, but many would argue it would be misguided if long-term goals such as poverty reduction (which might eventually contribute to a more secure world) were made subordinate to immediate security priorities. In any case, controlling and/or reducing the flow of migrants into Europe (see Chapter 10) can also be seen as a security priority, which aid to the sending countries (especially if made conditional) might address (Boswell, 2003).

Critical voices in the development community also argue that the newer member states (whose commitment to and capacity for helping the poorest countries is probably lower than that of their richer counterparts in western Europe) should not deflect EU efforts even further away from the far-away poor to the non-EU countries of eastern Europe. This would be understandable – they have closer trading relationships and obvious security concerns – but would be a very negative consequence of enlargement. Those concerned with the far-away poor are probably also right to worry that the security focus of the EU as a whole on Islamic North Africa and the Middle East also risks diverting its attention from the ACP. On the other hand, it has long been a criticism of EU assistance policy that (at least as far as EDF financing goes, and owing in no small part to the initial influence of the French) it has been over-concentrated on the ACP, leaving out massive areas of poverty in Asia and, to a lesser extent, in Latin America.

These criticisms notwithstanding, few would begrudge the EU making the most of its aid role. Admittedly, its efforts are far from perfect and it has a nasty habit, first, of forgetting that much of 'its' spending is actually done by individual member states and, second, of making comparisons with the US only on publicly provided aid when the Americans spend almost four times as much on privately provided aid as the Europeans. Nevertheless, the EU is clearly a major player in the developing world, and it does seem to be the case that Europe's aid and development policies have been subject over the years to Europeanization. Almost every country still handles most of its ODA bilaterally (see Table 11.2). Yet increasingly, all of them try to help LDCs in a way that attempts not to cross-cut or duplicate EU efforts. This would seem not only to make sense, but also to be in keeping with the wishes of most of their citizens. A Eurobarometer poll in 2003 found that on average 70 per cent of Europeans thought decisions on humanitarian aid should be made jointly between their national government and the EU, although in Sweden (a very generous donor) a majority wanted things left to their own politicians. This does not mean, however, that individual

European countries will eventually subsume their development spending into the EU effort: as with diplomacy, there are both symbolic and bottom-line reasons for continuing to maintain a national presence in the world.

Europe and the global environment

Europe leaves a big footprint in the world. Its citizens, its industries (and its highly subsidized farm animals!) are responsible for billions of tons of sometimes toxic waste, for depleting fish stocks, eroding soil and for 15 per cent of world emissions of greenhouse gases. With the growing realization that the latter, in particular, are contributing to global warming, European countries have, in recent years, come to realize that environmental policy cannot be pursued simply at a national, nor even just a regional, EU-wide level. Of course, they still have a lot to learn and a lot to do at those levels (see McCormick, 2001), even though they have taken the opportunity offered by EU enlargement to force the relatively high standards of the northern part of the continent onto the southern and eastern parts. But the EU has also turned its attention further afield. As Bretherton and Vogler (1999: 96) note, it is 'the clear aspiration of the Commission and Member State governments to move well beyond . . . essentially regional concerns and to adopt a global leadership and [an] "agenda-setting-role"'.

Figure 11.8 Other countries' views of the EU

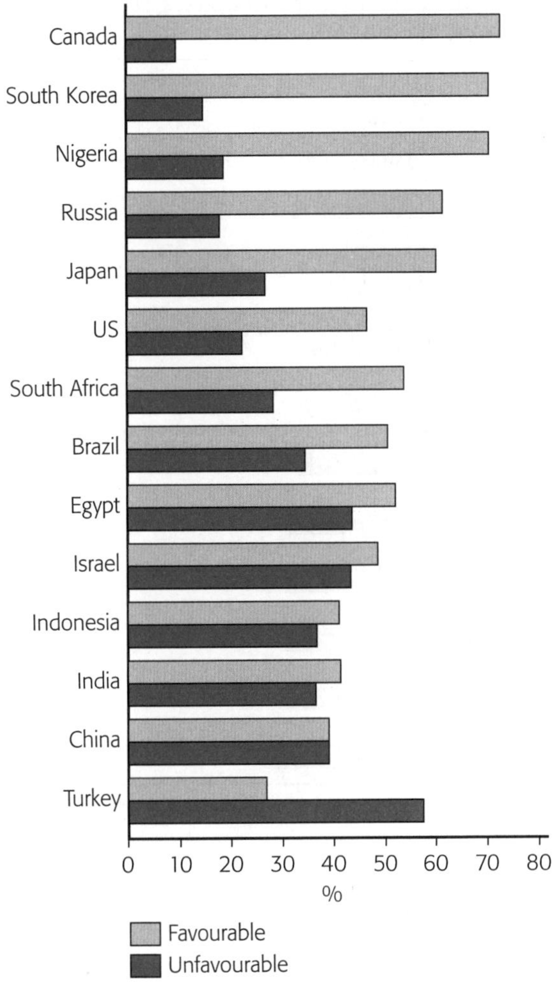

Source: PewResearchCentre, *Global Attitudes Survey* (June 2007).

KEY POINT

Environmental policy is another area where Europe takes the lead, although it is by no means perfect and continues to have trouble persuading its allies to follow that lead.

It, and they, have pursued this role in spite of manifold and manifest difficulties caused by the 'mixed competence' (between the EU and the member states) that characterizes policy and the capacity to make international agreements in this area, as well as the big inconsistencies in European countries' taxation and energy regimes (see Bretherton and Vogler, 2005). This is partly due to the seriousness of the situation, and partly due to the fact that European unity is seen as the only way of (a) governments persuading their own populations and business sectors to make sacrifices; and (b) getting foreign powers (not least the US and Japan) to agree to do so. But whatever its causes, this unity was crucial in getting the agreement to cut greenhouse gas emissions that was affirmed in the UN-based Kyoto Treaty negotiated in 1997. Along with what was widely perceived as the intransigence of the US during the negotiations, this could well have contributed at least a little to the 'presence' – or, at least, the recognition – of the EU

Figure 11.9 'Should decisions on protecting the environment be made by national government or jointly within the EU?'

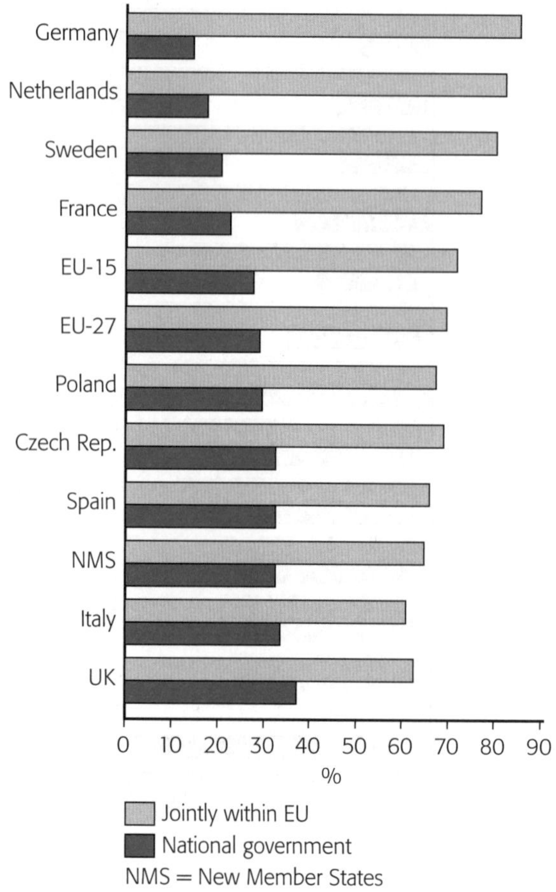

Source: *Eurobarometer* (67, 2007).

in the world, and perhaps even the generally favourable attitudes other countries' populations seem to have of it (see Figure 11.8). How much this impression is based on knowledge, however, is a moot point: a more detailed opinion survey carried out by Gallup in the US in May 2004 might have made depressing reading for the EU: 77 per cent of Americans admitted to knowing very little or nothing about it (for instance, that its population is larger than that of the US). On the other hand, although the US was rated more positively than the EU on promoting peace and economic growth, and fighting poverty and terrorism, the EU was rated by Americans as better on 'protection of the environment'.

Unfortunately, say critics, what happened to the Kyoto Treaty might have demonstrated the truth of this impression, but it has also demonstrated European weakness. Leaving aside the fact that a number of countries within Europe look set to miss their target contributions to the overall EU reduction of 8 per cent (as the US said would happen all along), the EU has been able to do nothing to prevent the US from refusing to ratify an agreement that needed ratification from states that produce 55 per cent of greenhouse gases in order – in theory, anyway – to make it binding on those states that signed but did not ratify. On the other hand, Europe's relations with other states eventually turned about to be enough to get Kyoto over the 55 per cent hurdle. By supporting its passage into the WTO, the EU helped secure Russia's ratification and the treaty came into force in February 2005. Things have moved on since then, though. US intransigence is beginning to crumble, albeit slowly, in the face of overwhelming scientific evidence that climate change is 'man-made', but the developing nations, China and India, especially remain huge obstacles to progress. The EU, in the knowledge that most of its citizens realize it has a role alongside their national governments on what is the ultimate cross-border issue (see Figure 11.9) has committed itself to cut CO_2 emissions by 20 per cent by 2020 – and even more if others follow. It has also, through the G8, apparently negotiated a deal with Japan and Canada to cut emissions by at least 50 per cent by 2050. Indeed, in the summer of 2007, it even looked as if the US might help convert that deal into a 'post-Kyoto agreement' – but only as long as China and India (whose populations are, interestingly, some of the most ambivalent about the EU) signed up, too.

Europe as a global trader

Europe is able to exert this kind of leverage (and, indeed, provide so much aid) because it is one of the wealthiest places on the planet. Europe might only contain 5 per cent of the world's population, but it produces nearly one-third of the world's economic output, accounts for about one fifth of all trade flows (indeed, nearer a half if one includes intra-EU trade), and at least one third of the world's foreign direct investment (FDI). Not only this, but trade is

KEY POINT

Europe is the biggest trade bloc in the world and increasingly acts accordingly, sometimes putting commercial interests above the foreign policy wishes of its allies.

the one area in which the EU has really got its act together. Member states – at least, in theory – allow the European Commission to act as their single negotiator (at least, when it comes to goods, if not services) in world trade forums such as the WTO. Consequently, its voice has to be listened to, even by a country such as the US, which in other areas can think and act relatively unilaterally.

If even the US has to listen, so, too, do less powerful countries. Many of these like to present themselves to their publics as doing battle with 'Fortress Europe'. This apparently protectionist behemoth seems to them determined to protect the interests of its producers (particularly, via the hated CAP, its agricultural producers), even if it means denying its consumers access to the cheap imports that third countries are dying to provide. This could be a misleading impression: even though things continue to move slowly on agriculture, the EU is (relatively speaking) no longer so bent on protection – indeed, some would say quite the opposite (see Woolcock, 2005). But it is a persistent impression. In many countries, especially, for instance, Australia and New Zealand (see Chaban *et al.*, 2003; and Murray, 2003), the EU (inasmuch as it is thought of at all) has a pretty poor reputation – in marked contrast, it should be said, to many of the member states who are happy to let the Commission do their dirty work for them.

These impressions notwithstanding, the trade and investment links between the EU and other advanced industrial and rapidly industrializing countries are highly significant. For instance, China and Europe might have public slanging matches over allegedly unequal access to their respective domestic markets (peaking in the so-called 'Bra wars' of 2005), but that is partly because they are each other's second biggest trading partners. According to European Commission merchandize figures for 2006, China made up 14.2 per cent of the EU-25's imports and was the destination for 5.4 per cent of its exports. For Japan, the figures were 5.6 per cent and 3.8 per cent, respectively, although for both countries the trade in services was much lower (China accounting for just 3.2 per cent of the EU in 2006 and Japan 4.7 per cent). In Australia, EU countries account for 13 per cent of imports and 21 per cent of exports, in New Zealand 16 and 17 per cent and in Canada 6 and 12 per cent. It is these kinds of volumes that guarantee Europe – or, at least, European countries – a significant 'presence'. So, increasingly, will the fact that many overseas financial institutions now hold currency reserves in euros, especially in the light of a weaker dollar. Indeed, it could well be the case that the € sign is as familiar to non-Europeans as the blue flag with twelve gold stars – a symbolic advantage not lost on advocates of the single currency.

Trade between the country whose currency is presently the world leader, the US, and countries belonging to the European Union is highly significant. Just as importantly, for those who worry on both sides of the Atlantic about balance of payments deficits, it is also relatively even. This in marked contrast to the dealings of both America and Europe with, say, China and Japan. Both the US and the EU countries account for around 20 per cent of each other's trade – around €1 billion per day. The US accounts for 34.8 per cent (2006) of European trade in services, and also exports significant amounts of energy to the EU countries, which in return run a balance of payment surplus with the US on machinery, and especially cars. Some 60 per cent of foreign investment in the US is from Europe, which in turn derives 50 per cent of its foreign investment from the US. Moreover, trading and investment relationships are growing as multinational companies on each continent buy into, takeover and merge with each other. European ownership of *Dunkin Donuts* and *Dr Pepper* is just the tip of a very large iceberg: the US has more invested in Germany alone than in the whole of South America (see Howorth, 2007: 417). It is not just a relationship *à deux*, either. Between them, the EU and the US are easily the world's most successful capitalist economies. As such, they go some way to determining, via the various rounds of WTO negotiations, the trading framework for the rest of the world – even if, as in 2006, they were unable to pursue the so-called Doha Development Round to a successful conclusion.

Partly because of this, and partly because of the media's preference for conflict (see Chapter 7), the very healthy trading relationship between Europe and the US can sometimes get subsumed in tales of sporadic (though sometimes long-running) disputes. Sometimes these occur at world trade talks: during the negotiation of the so-called Uruguay Round of GATT, the WTO's predecessor, which basically ran from 1986 to 1993, there were huge arguments over Europe's refusal to allow services (and particularly cultural matters) to be opened up to US firms, as well as over agriculture. These arguments saw the French emerge as the intransigent (and convenient) fall guy for all concerned – a pattern that seems to have become a persistent feature of transatlantic relations more generally. They also rather undermined the notion of the Commission as 'Europe's' sole negotiator not needing to look over its shoulder at individual countries. It was clear that many aspects had to be cleared by individual member states – some (the UK, the Nordics and the Netherlands) historically liberal, some (the Mediterranean countries) more protectionist (see Woolcock, 2005) – before the Commission could sign off on them. This requirement, which affects not only negotiations on trade but also on foreign, environmental and other policies, can be infuriating for third parties. European countries are reluctant to bargain before they have established a collective position then, once they have done so, claim they cannot enter into further discussion since that might wreck the compromise they have arrived at! This, plus genuine conflicts of interest, could explain why, outside of these multilateral trade talks, there have also been big bilateral rows between the US and Europe over steel tariffs (in 2002), GM crops and animal growth hormones (ongoing), Cuba (also ongoing), jumbo jets (likewise) and (strange, but true) bananas.

Amid these very public spats, it is easy to see why the media, and therefore citizens, lose sight of things like the 'New Transatlantic Agenda', signed by Bill Clinton and EU representatives in 1995 – an agreement designed to provide some wordy reassurance (and institutional infrastructure) to back up continued political co-operation (and, hopefully, enhanced trade co-operation) in the post-Cold War era. Things are not helped either by accusations by American commentators and policy makers that Europeans are rather keener than they should be to see 'the flag following trade' rather than using economic clout to achieve foreign policy objectives or to reward good behaviour on the part of foreign regimes.

Although these accusations might to some extent be motivated by the fact that the EU is now no pushover in international trade negotiations (see Meunier, 2007), American critics have a point. What they see as Europe's intransigence goes right back to the reluctance among European states to support Israel in the 1973 war with Arab countries, partly (though not purely) because they feared a backlash by oil-producing states. Americans were also enraged by European states' refusal to stop importing gas from the Soviet Union following its role in suppressing the 1981 liberalization of the then communist regime in Poland. Europe's determination to ignore the US boycott of Cuba, with which it has trade, tourism and (Spanish) cultural links, has also been a problem (see Byron, 2000). And, much to the irritation of some in the US, European states, both collectively and individually, continue to attempt a constructive dialogue with the Islamic regime in (oil- and gas-rich) Iran and not to allow 'local difficulties' in Tibet and Taiwan to interfere in relations with the economic powerhouse that is China. Indeed, one of the lowest points in transatlantic relations in recent years came about when, in 2005, European countries, especially those with big and increasingly pan-European defence industries (see Epstein and Gheciu, 2006: 323–8), looked as if they might lift the US-led arms embargo on China – a possibility that was only averted when the American administration (after its so-called European 'charm offensive' in early 2005 appeared to alter little more than the mood music) made it clear in no uncertain terms that it would have huge negative repercussions. Its attempt to prevent European firms trading with Iran, however, seems to have run into the sand.

But things are changing. It would be naive to think that European pragmatism is ever likely to give way to wide-eyed idealism. But European governments, particularly acting together as the EU, are beginning to realize that their collective interests (in the trade as well as the security field) could well lie in investing more political content in what previously have been very much economic relationships, perhaps via bilateral forums or perhaps via contacts with Asian regional co-operation organizations like ASEAN and ASEM (see Forster, 2000). This is especially true in East and South East Asia, (see Edmonds, 2002 and Wiessala, 2002). If anything, given heightened fears concerning migration and WMD in North Korea, collective diplomacy in those regions could well increase, as will the tendency to insist that any agreements entered into by the EU with other countries include conditions on progress toward human rights and democracy.

But we should be careful. For one thing, there is evidence that the European states' commitment to conditionality is more rhetorical than real where it clashes with their economic or strategic interests (Smith, 2005b). For another, EU specialists are bound to stress the role of collective, as opposed to bilateral, diplomacy between individual member states and the countries concerned. Similarly, it is all very well for the EU to claim that it accounts for a large chunk of world trade and therefore enjoys massive presence; but it is a little misleading. Obviously, the EU helps provide the framework for those trade flows; but it is individual member states and the companies within them that actually do the business. It is rather like UEFA (the body which regulates soccer in Europe) claiming credit for all the goals scored and wins notched up by European countries in the World Cup finals that, via its association with FIFA (the world governing body), it goes some way to helping stage every four years. Clearly, at least some of the audience will recognize the collective brand, but many more of them will be aware of the nations of which it is composed. This could change, however, as the EU, frustrated at lack of progress in the WTO, begins to look toward doing bilateral deals with single countries, including India (see Allen and Smith, 2007).

Lest we forget – the enlargement and domestication of international politics

'Europe' in the world, then, is a complex mix of individual states and the European Union of which the majority are a part. And it is about the interaction between national foreign policies, CFSP (and ESDP), and the 'external relations' of the EU when it operates in the trade (and increasingly perhaps) the aid and the environmental field (see Knodt and Princen, 2003). There is no reason to think this will change any time soon. Certainly, we should be careful not to presume that foreign policy in Europe is somehow on an inevitable evolutionary progress towards eventual integration. Doing so will only disappoint, since the gap between expectations and capability is unlikely to disappear (see Hill, 1993). As Smith (2004) argues (see also Hill, 1998), it could be that the 'part-formed foreign policy' of the EU will always be expressed as much by supposedly non-foreign policy instruments such as trade and aid, and that it is pointless, in the absence of a collective 'European interest' to expect it to take on the forms we traditionally associate with states – states that, in any case, wish to cling on to those forms even in the 'postmodern' or 'postsovereign' age.

KEY POINT

Enlargement of the EU is probably the biggest foreign policy success of the last half-century, rendering Europe more secure than it has ever been. Whether enlargement, and Europe's relative standing in the world, can continue forever is another matter.

But whatever 'Europe's' place in the wider world, the biggest success story with regard to defence, foreign policy and even development aid, has been Europe itself. Prior to the founding and development of what is now the EU, most European countries regarded their immediate neighbours as part of the rest of the world. That is no longer the case: within Europe, international politics have been substantially 'domesticated'. It is not just that European states – even those states that retain global interests and/or wish to maintain a close relationship with the US – no longer consider armed conflict between themselves as even an outside possibility. It is also that, at the very least, they reflexively think about the mutual consequences of their following their own interests and, in some, cases hesitate even to define those interests without or before consultation (Aggestam, 2000: 71). And even where those interests would appear to differ, they will often lay them

Figure 11.10 Varying attitudes on future EU enlargement

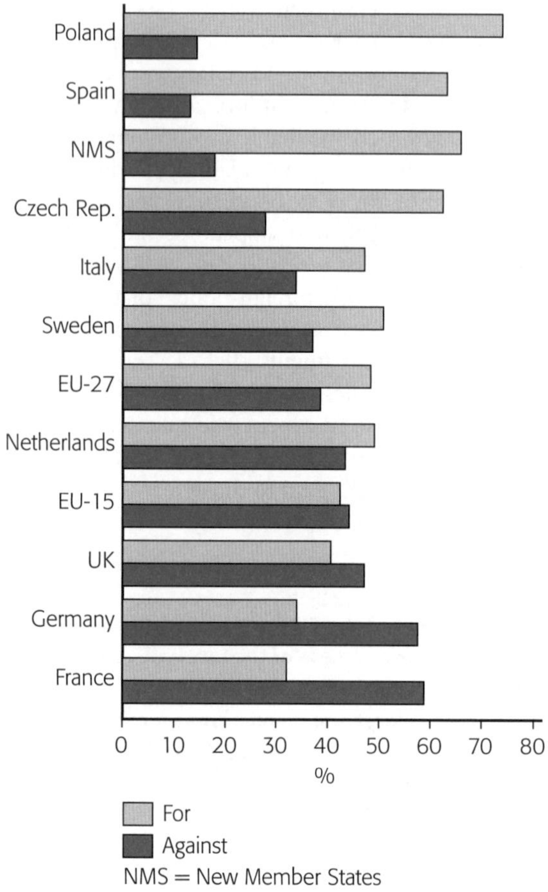

Source: *Eurobarometer* (67, 2007).

Figure 11.11 'Do you think that, fifty years from now, the EU will be a leading diplomatic power in the world?'

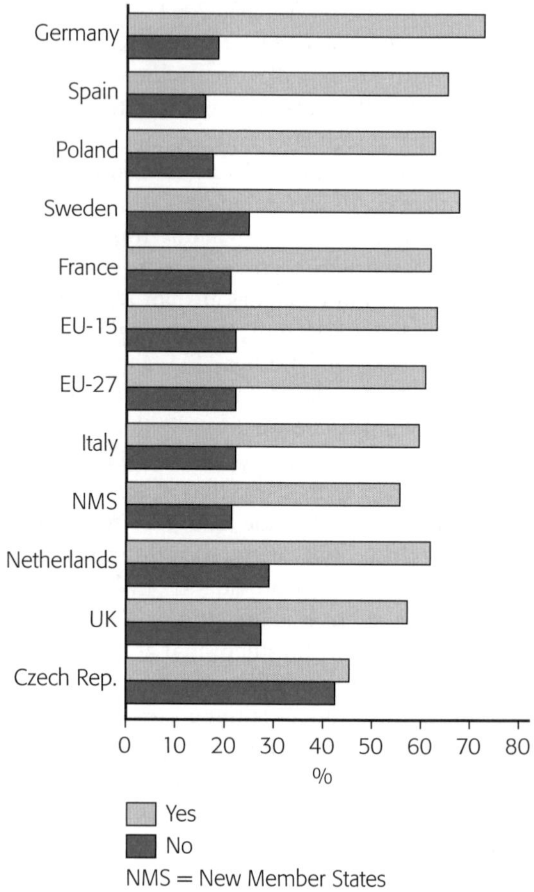

Source: *Eurobarometer*, 67 (2007).

aside for what they consider as more important in the long term; namely, a security and a prosperity that they recognize is best guaranteed collectively. The EU, probably more even than organizations such as the OSCE, contributes to a European security community.

The most obvious recent example of this, of course, is EU enlargement. This was achieved not just because of the long-term economic potential of expanding the single market. It also fitted with the even longer-term foreign policy goal – albeit not one always very consciously or consistently pursued (see Zielonka, 1998) – of 'securing' the 'near abroad' by locking-in' democracy, just as it was locked-in in Spain, Portugal and Greece in the 1980s and in the previously non-democratic states of western Europe after the Second World War. Even the prospect of membership, it seems, is enough to persuade potentially troublesome states, especially in the Balkans, to 'behave themselves' – witness the progress of Croatia, officially declared a candidate for EU membership in June 2004.

The enlargement that took place in 2004, we should also note, was achieved – particularly as accession became a reality – without the support of the majority in some of the biggest countries of what was then the EU-15 (see *Eurobarometer 61*). Hopefully, experience will show that their leaders really did 'know best'. However, they may be less able to insulate themselves against public opinion – and,

DEBATE 11.1

SHOULD TURKEY JOIN THE EU?

YES

- Turkey has played an integral part in European history and has grown closer to Europe in recent times. It is an officially secular state and an increasingly stable democracy. By denying Turkey entry, the EU would send a signal to the Islamic world that ultimately its religion is a sticking point.
- Turkey, a long-term and loyal member of NATO for half a century, would provide a buffer zone against, and a bridgehead into, potentially unstable (but also potentially lucrative) parts of the world. Turkish entry would be looked on favourably by the US.
- Incorporating Turkey into the EU would help consolidate democracy there and improve its economy, thereby reducing any potential risk to its European neighbours
- Turkey's population is much younger than that of the current EU member states and would help with the demographic crunch that is fast approaching.
- Turkey will have to meet EU-determined criteria before it can join. If and when it does join, institutional fixes and transition periods can, if necessary, be put in place.

NO

- The first obstacle is Turkey's sheer size: in under a decade its population will match Germany's, and is already bigger than the combined population of the ten states that joined the EU in 2004. This would give Turkey a big say in EU institutions.
- Turkey's poverty (its unevenly distributed *per capita* income is only around a quarter of the EU average) would see it swallow up large amounts of EU regional funding.
- Imagine Europeans' anxiety if Turks, of whom there are already millions in Germany and elsewhere, are granted free movement and the right to work in Europe? The EU's absorption capacity is not infinite; better a deal that stops short of full membership.
- Turkey's Islamic culture means that it simply does not belong in Europe, which has its roots in Christianity and a more secular enlightenment tradition of respecting the rights of the individual. And what about the danger of importing Islamic terrorism?

indeed, their own prejudices – when it comes to enlarging the EU to include a country like Turkey, whose claim to be part of 'us' rather than 'them' (see Neumann, 1998) is, for many, less persuasive (see Debate 11.1). Turkey has been formally associated with the EU since 1963 and first applied to join in 1987 (see Müftüler-Bac, 1997). After a customs union took effect in 1996, Turkey was finally accepted as a candidate country in 1999, since when it has accelerated economic and political reforms (see Hughes, 2004). Negotiations began in earnest in 2005, although in 2006 they ran into difficulty over Cyprus (see Chapter 2). The previous year, the prospect of Turkish accession appeared to have contributed to the negative result of the Dutch and especially the French referendums on the EU's Constitutional Treaty in 2005. Meanwhile, the negative rhetoric coming from some European countries, plus the realization that compromises to its sovereignty and way of life will have to be made before it can join, are beginning to dampen EU-enthusiasm among the Turkish population (see Figure 11.9). Support for further enlargement among the EU's population is questionable, especially in the larger, older member states whose politicians are insisting that the EU have regard to its so-called 'absorption capacity'.

Judging by the widespread apathy that greeted the accessions of 2004 and 2007, as well as the lack of enthusiasm in some key member states for more (see Figure 11.10), a degree of 'enlargement fatigue' is affecting European publics. The problem with responding to this by declaring an end to new accessions is that, by effectively fixing what become finite borders, the EU will lose some of its capacity – amply demonstrated in the case of CEE (see Grabbe, 2003, 2006; though see also Sedelmeier, 2005) – to exert leverage over the behaviour of aspirant states. Losing that capacity will do nothing to enhance European security, whether one defines it narrowly as territorial defence or more broadly as providing a environment in which nearly half a billion sometimes very different people can continue to pursue their personal and political aspirations in comparative safety and comfort.

Which bring us neatly to our final point. Europeans – especially those in the west – have grown accustomed to their relative wealth and the position in the world that comes with it. Many of them assume that the latter will be maintained diplomatically over the next century, whether it be by their own country or by the EU collectively (see Figure 11.11). But are they right? Or are they complacent? By the end of the century, less than one in twenty of the world's population will be European. And their wealth might not look quite so impressive in comparison to that of the populations of a resurgent Russia and of emerging economic and political powers like India and China, let alone the existing superpower, the US. Consequently, the ability of Europeans to help set the global agenda and secure and promote their values and interests could diminish, at least in relative terms. One early demonstration of this was the failure in early 2006 of either India or the US to forewarn most European governments of a nuclear technology deal between them that seemed to ignore the fact that India is not a signatory to the non-proliferation treaty. It is not immediately obvious that acting in even greater consort through the EU rather than maintaining the current combination of bi-lateral and multi-lateral action will have much more impact on these profound global shifts in influence. Politics matters in many ways (see Chapter 9), but it cannot achieve miracles.

Learning Resources for Chapter 11

Further reading

Good reads on individual countries' foreign policies and their interaction with the EU include Christiansen and Tonra (2004), *Rethinking EU Foreign Policy*; the collection edited by Carlsnaes *et al.* (2004), *Contemporary European Foreign Policy*; and the collection edited by Manners and Whitman (2000), *The Foreign Policies of European Union Member States*. The best first port of call on the issue of Europe (and the EU) in the world is Bretherton and Vogler (2005), *The European Union as a Global Actor*.

On EU foreign policy, the literature is massive: the collection edited by Casarini and Musu (2007), *European Foreign Policy in an Evolving International System*, offers an accessible starting point but the authoritative work is probably the collection edited by Hill and Smith (2005), *International Relations and the EU*. Also useful – and, of course, much shorter – is the chapter by Bicchi *et al.* in *Developments in European Politics*. The three chapters by Woolcock, Sedelmeier and Wallace in Wallace *et al.* (2005), *Policy-Making in the European Union*, provide useful overviews on the history and process of EU trade, enlargement, and foreign and security policy. The chapters on the EU's relationship with 'the wider Europe' and the rest of the world in the *JCMS Annual Review of the European Union* are a very good way of keeping up to speed.

On defence and security, see Howorth (2007), *Security and Defence Policy in the European Union*; Kirchner and Sperling (2007), *EU Security Governance*; and the collection edited by Hauser and Kernic (2006), *European Security in Transition*. Also recommended as a stimulating short read is Manners (2006), 'Normative Power Europe Reconsidered: Beyond the Crossroads', *Journal of European Public Policy*, 13(2), 182–99. On development and aid, see Holland (2002), *The European Union and the Third World*; and (2004b), 'Development Policy', in the collection edited by Green Cowles and Dinan. On trade, try the special issue on 'The European Union and the New Trade Politics' of the *Journal of European Public Policy*, 13(6), 2006. On postcommunist states' foreign policies, see the special issue on 'Ideology and National Identity in Post-Communist Foreign Policies' of the *Journal of Communist Studies and Transition Politics*, 19(3), 2003.

Those interested in Europe in particular parts of the world should consult the following texts: on the transatlantic relationship, see the collection edited by Peterson and Pollack (2003), *Europe, America, Bush*; and the wonderfully readable chapter by Howorth in the collection edited by Hay and Menon (2007), *European Politics*. On Asia in general, see Wiessala (2002), *The European Union and Asian Countries*, and on Japan in particular Ueta and Remacle (2005), *Japan and Enlarged Europe*; on the Middle East, Youngs (2006), *Europe and the Middle East*; on the Mediterranean, see Youngs (2003), 'European Approaches to Security in the Mediterranean', *Middle East Journal*, 57(3); on China, see the collection edited by Crossick and Reuter (2008), *China–EU*; on Russia, see the collection edited by Timmins and Gower (2007), *Russia and Europe in the Twenty-First Century*; on Africa, see Bagoyoko and Gibert (2007), *The European Union in Africa*, IDS Working Paper 284; and on South America, see the collection edited by Grabendorff and Seidelmann (2005), *Relations between the European Union and Latin America*.

The debate on whether the future is European, on what sort of power (civilian or super) Europe is, and on how big and autonomous a player it will become in the security field can be fruitfully pursued in McCormick (2006), *The European Superpower*; Teló (2006), *Europe*; and the collection edited by Gänzle and Sens (2007), *The Changing Politics of European Security*. Finally, for a provocative return to a 'realist', state-centred perspective on European foreign and security policy, see Hyde-Price (2007), *European Security in the Twenty-First Century*.

On the web

www.fornet.info – academic site on European foreign policy

www.iss-eu.org – commentary on foreign policy and security matters

www.oecd.org/dac/ and **ec.europa.eu/development** – development issues and statistics

ec.europa.eu/external_relations/gac – EU foreign policy

http://www.eurocorps.org – EU's military force

ec.europa.eu/trade – European trade statistics and analysis

members.tripod.com/~ForeignPolicy – foreign and security policy links

www.consilium.europa.eu/esdp – info. on ESDP missions

www.hiik.de/konfliktbarometer – monitors conflicts worldwide

Discussion questions

1. Do you think that Europe is a safer place to live in now compared with at the height of the Cold War?
2. During the Iraq crisis, some US politicians claimed there was a difference between 'Old' and 'New' Europe. What did they mean and were they right?
3. Can and should European countries act together to integrate and build up a European security and defence capability?
4. What is Europe's policy on relations with Russia? Do you think it has been successful?
5. How and why is Europe becoming more serious about its relations with the countries of the southern Mediterranean?
6. What are the arguments – and what is the evidence – for and against a Europeanization of foreign policy?
7. The EU makes a good deal of its role both in helping developing countries and on environmental issues. In your view, is it right to do so?
8. Is Europe's foreign policy really driven by its trading interests? If so, is that wrong?
9. What do you think of the argument that Europe's biggest success is that relations between the continent's countries are now no longer thought of mainly in terms of defence and foreign policy?

References

A

Aars, Jacob and Strømsnes, Kristin (2007) 'Contacting as a Channel of Political Involvement: Collectively Motivated, Invidually Enacted', *West European Politics*, 30(1), pp. 93–120.

Aarts, Kees and Semetko, Holli A. (2003) 'The Divided Electorate: Media Use and Political Involvement', *Journal of Politics*, 65(3), pp. 759–84.

Aberbach, J.D., Putnam, R.D. and Rodman, B.A. (1981) *Bureaucrats and Politicians in Western Democracies* (Cambridge: Harvard University Press).

Achterberg, Peter (2006) 'Class Voting in the New Political Culture: Economic, Cultural and Environmental Voting in 20 Countries', *International Sociology*, 21(2), pp. 237–61.

Adams, R.H. and Page, J. (2005) 'Do International Migration and Remittances Reduce Poverty in Developing Countries?', *World Development*, 33(10), pp. 1645–69.

Aelst, Peter van and Walgrave, Stefaan (2001) 'Who is that (Wo)man in the Street? From the Normalisation of Protest to the Normalisation of the Protester', *European Journal of Political Research*, 39(4), pp. 461–86.

Aggestam, Lisbeth (2000) 'Germany', in Ian Manners and Richard G. Whitman (eds), *The Foreign Policies of European Union Member States* (Manchester: Manchester University Press).

Agranoff, Robert (1996) 'Federal Evolution in Spain', *International Political Science Review*, 17(4), pp. 385–401.

al-Azmeh, Aziz and Fokas, Effie (2007) *Islam in Europe: Diversity, Identity and Influence* (Cambridge: Cambridge University Press).

Albertazzi, Daniele and McDonnell, Duncan (eds) (2007) *Twenty-First Century Populism: The Spectre of Western European Democracy* (Basingstoke: Palgrave Macmillan).

Allan, James P. and Scruggs, Lyle (2004) 'Political Partisanship and Welfare State Reform in Advanced Industrial Societies', *American Journal of Political Science*, 48(3), pp. 496–512.

Allen, David and Smith, Michael (1998) 'The EU's Security Presence: Barrier, Facilitator, or Manager?', in Carolyn Rhodes (ed) *The European Union in the World Community* (Boulder, CO: Lynne Rienner).

Allen, David and Smith, Michael (2007) 'Relations with the Rest of the World', *Journal of Common Market Studies*, 45, pp. 163–81.

Allern, Elin H. (2007) *Parties, Interest Groups and Democracy: Political Parties and their Relationship with Interest Groups in Norway* (Oslo: Unipub).

Allern, Elin H. and Pedersen, Karina (2007) 'The Impact of Party Organizational Changes on Democracy', *West European Politics*, 30(1), pp. 69–92.

Almond, Gabriel and Verba, Sidney (1963) *The Civic Culture: Political Attitudes and Democracy in Five Nations* (Princeton: Princeton University Press).

Alvarez, Michael R., Garrett, Geoffrey and Lange, Peter (1991) 'Government Partisanship, Labor Organization and Macroeconomic Performance', *American Political Science Review*, 85(2), pp. 539–56.

Amable, Bruno, Gatti, Donatella and Schumacher, Jan (2006) 'Welfare-State Retrenchment: The Partisan Effect Revisited', *Oxford Review of Economic Policy*, 22(3), pp. 426–44.

Anckar, Carsten (1997) 'Determinants of Disproportionality and Wasted Votes', *Electoral Studies*, 16(4), pp. 501–15.

Anderson, Benedict (1991) *Imagined Communities: Reflections on the Origin and Spread of Nationalism* (London: Verso).

Anderson, K.M. (2001) 'The Politics of Retrenchment in a Social Democratic Welfare State: Reform of Swedish Pensions and Unemployment Insurance', *Comparative Political Studies*, 34(9), pp. 1063–91.

Andeweg, Rudy B. (2000) 'Ministers as Double Agents? The Delegation Process Between Cabinet and Ministers', *European Journal of Political Research*, 37(3), pp. 377–95.

Andeweg, Rudy B. and Irwin, Galen A. (2005) *Governance and Politics of the Netherlands*, 2nd edn (Basingstoke and New York: Palgrave Macmillan).

Andrews, Josephine T. and Jackman, Robert W. (2005) 'Strategic Fools: Electoral Rule Choice under Extreme Uncertainty', *Electoral Studies*, 24, pp. 65–84.

Armingeon, Klaus (2007) 'Political Participation and Associational Involvement', in Jan van Deth, José Ramon Montero and Anders Westholm (eds), *Citizenship and Involvement in European Democracies* (London: Routledge).

Armingeon, Klaus and Giger, Nathalie (2006) 'The Electoral Consequences of Welfare State Retrenchment in OECD Nations', Paper presented at the Fifteenth International Conference of the Council for European Studies, Chicago, 29 March–2 April.

Art, David (2007) 'Reacting to the Radical Right: Lessons from Germany and Austria', *Party Politics*, 13(3), pp. 331–49.

Arter, David (ed.) (2001) *From Farmyard to City Square: The Electoral Adaptation of the Nordic Agrarian Parties* (Aldershot: Ashgate).

Arter, David (2006) *Democracy in Scandinavia: Consensual, Majoritarian or Mixed?* (Manchester: Manchester University Press).

Arts, Will, Hagneaars, Jacques and Halman, Loek (2004) *The Cultural Diversity of European Unity: Findings, Explanations and Reflections from the European Values Survey* (Leiden: Brill).

Asp, Kent (1983) 'The Struggle for the Agenda: Party Agenda, Media Agenda, and Voter Agenda in the 1979 Swedish Election Campaign', *Communication Research*, 10(3), pp. 333–55.

Arzheimer, Kai (2006) 'Dead Men Walking? Party Identification in Germany, 1977–2002', *Electoral Studies*, 25(4), pp. 791–807.

Arzheimer, Kai and Carter, Elisabeth (2006) 'Political Opportunity Structures and Right-Wing Extremist Party Success', *European Journal of Political Research*, 45(3), pp. 419–43.

Aspinwall, M. (2006) 'Government Preferences on European Integration', *British Journal of Political Science*, 37(1), pp. 89–1140

Astudillo Ruiz, Javier (2002) 'The Spanish Experiment: A Social Democratic Party–Union Relationship in a Competitive Union Context', Harvard Centre for European Studies, Working Paper 83.

Auer, Andreas and Bützer, Michael (eds) (2001) *Direct Democracy: The Eastern and Central European Experience* (Aldershot: Ashgate).

Avdagic, Sabina (2005) 'State–Labour Relations in East Central Europe: Explaining Variations in Union Effectiveness', *Socio-Economic Review*, 3(1), pp. 25–53.

Avdagic, Sabina and Crouch, Colin (2006) 'Organized Economic Interests: Diversity and Change in an Enlarged Europe', in Paul Heywood, Erik Jones, Martin Rhodes and Ulrich Sedelmeier (eds), *Developments in European Politics* (Basingstoke: Palgrave Macmillan).

Axford, Barrie and Huggins, Richard (eds) (2000) *New Media and Politics* (London: Sage).

Aylott, Nicholas (1999) *Swedish Social Democracy and European Integration: The People's Home on the Market* (Aldershot: Ashgate).

B

Baccaro, L. (2002) 'Negotiating the Italian Pension Reform with the Unions: Lessons for Corporatist Theory', *Industrial and Labour Relations Review*, 55(3), pp. 413–31.

Baccaro, L. (2003) 'What is Alive and What is Dead in the Theory of Corporatism?', *British Journal of Industrial Relations*, 41(4), pp. 683–706.

Bache, I. and George, S. (2006) *Politics in the European Union*, 2nd edn (Oxford: Oxford University Press).

Badescu, Gabriel and Neller, Katja (2007) 'Explaining Associational Involvement', in Jan Van Deth, José Ramon Montero and Anders Westholm (eds) *Citizenship and Involvement in European Democracies* (London: Routledge).

Badinger, Harald and Breuss, Fritz (2003) 'What has Determined the Rapid Post-war Growth of intra-EU Trade?', IEF Working Paper 48, Wirtschaftsuniversität Wien.

Bagoyoko, Niagalé and Gibert, Marie V. (2007) 'The European Union in Africa', IDS Working Paper 284, available at http://www.ids.ac.uk/ids/bookshop/wp/wp284.pdf

Bakke, Elizabeth and Sitter, Nick (2005) 'Patterns of Stability, Party Competition and Strategy in Central Europe since 1989', *Party Politics*, 11(2), pp. 243–63.

Baldassarri, Delia and Schadee, Hans (2006) 'Voter Heurustics and Political Cognition in Italy: An Empirical Typology', *Electoral Studies*, 125(3), pp. 448–66.

Bale, Tim (2000) 'Field-level CFSP: EU Diplomatic Cooperation in Third Countries', *Current Politics and Economics of Europe*, 10(2), pp. 187–212; also available at http://www.lse.ac.uk/Depts/intrel/pdfs/EFPU%20Working%20Paper%204.pdf

Bale, Tim (2003) 'Cinderella and her Ugly Sisters: The Mainstream and Extreme Right in Europe's Bipolarising Party Systems', *West European Politics*, 26(3), pp. 67–90.

Bale, Tim (2004) 'Business as Usual? Europe's Overseas Diplomacy in the Age of CFSP', in Martin Holland (ed.), *Common Foreign and Security Policy: The First Ten Years* (London: Continuum).

Bale, Tim (2006) 'Between a Soft and a Hard Place? The Conservative Party, Valence Politics, and the Need for a New "Eurorealism"', *Parliamentary Affairs*, 59(3), pp. 385–400.

Bale, Tim (2007) 'Are Bans on Political Parties Bound to Turn Out Badly? A Comparative Investigation of Three "Intolerant" Democracies: Turkey, Spain and Belgium', *Comparative European Politics*, 5(2), pp. 141–57.

Bale, Tim (ed.) (2008) *Immigration and Integration Policy in Europe: Why Politics – and the Centre-Right – Matter*, (London: Routledge).

Bale, Tim and Bergman, Torbjörn (2006) 'Captives no Longer, but Servants Still? Contract Parliamentarism and the New Minority Governance in Sweden and New Zealand', *Government and Opposition*, 41(3), pp. 422–49.

Bale, Tim and Biezen, Ingrid van (2007) 'Political Data in 2006', *European Journal of Political Research*, 46(7–8).

Bale, Tim, Green-Pedersen, Christoffer, Krouwel, André, Luther, K. Richard and Sitter, Nick (2008) 'If you Can't Beat Them, Join Them: The West European Social Democrats' Responses to the Challenge from the Populist Right', Unpublished MS.

Bale, Tim and Kopecký, Petr (1998) 'Can Young Pups Teach an Old Dog New Tricks? Legislative Lessons for Britain from Eastern Europe's New Constitutional Democracies', *Journal of Legislative Studies*, 4(2), pp. 159–78.

Bale, Tim and Szcerbiak, Aleks (2008) 'Why Is There No Christian Democracy In Poland – And Why Should We Care?', *Party Politics*, 14(4).

Bale, Tim, Webb, Paul and Taggart, Paul (2006) 'You Can't Always Get What You Want: Populism and the Power Report', *Political Quarterly*, 77 (2), pp. 195–203.

Balme, Richard, Chabanet, Didier and Wright, Vincent (eds) (2002) *L'action collective en Europe* (Paris: Presses de Sciences Po).

Barany, Zoltan (2002) *The East European Gypsies: Regime Change, Marginality, and Ethnopolitics* (Cambridge: Cambridge University Press).

Barnett, Steven (2002) 'Will a Crisis in Journalism Provoke a Crisis in Democracy?', *Political Quarterly*, 2(4), pp. 400–8.

Barrett, David B., Kurian, George T. and Johnson, Todd M. (2001) *World Christian Encyclopedia: A Comparative Survey of Churches and Religion in the Modern World*, 2nd edn (New York: Oxford University Press).

Bartolini, Stefano (2007) *Restructuring Europe: Centre Formation, System Building, and Political Structuring Between the Nation State and the European Union* (Oxford: Oxford University Press).

Batory, Agnes and Sitter, Nick (2004) 'Cleavages, Competition and Coalition-building: Agrarian Parties and the European Question in Western and East Central Europe', *European Journal of Political Research*, 43(4), pp. 523–46.

Bauböck, Rainer, Ersboll, Eva, Groenendijk, Kees and Waldrauch, Harald (2006) *Acquisition and Loss of Nationality: Policies and Trends in 15 European Countries: Comparative Analyses* (Amsterdam: Amsterdam University Press).

BBC (2006) 'Excerpts: Hungarian "lies" speech', available at http://news.bbc.co.uk/1/hi/world/europe/5359546.stm.

BBC (2007) 'Migrant Workers: What We Know', available at, http://news.bbc.co.uk/1/hi/uk/6957171.stm.

Becker, Rolf and Saalfeld, Thomas (2004) 'The Life and Times of Bills', in Herbert Döring and Mark Hallerberg (eds) *Patterns of Parliamentary Behaviour* (Aldershot: Ashgate).

Bekke, Hans A.G.M. and Meer, Frits M. van der (eds) (2000) *Civil Service Systems in Western Europe* (Cheltenham: Edward Elgar).

Bekkers, René (2005) 'Participation in Voluntary Associations: Relations with Resources, Personality, and Political Values', *Political Psychology*, 26(3), pp. 439–54.

Bell, David S. (2002) *French Politics Today* (Manchester: Manchester University Press).

Bennie, Lynne G. (1998) 'Brent Spar, Atlantic Oil and Greenpeace', *Parliamentary Affairs*, 51(3), pp. 397–410.

Bentivegna, Sara (2006) 'Rethinking Politics in the World of ICTs', *European Journal of Communication*, 21(3), pp. 331–43.

Berger, Stefan and Compston, Hugh (eds) (2002) *Policy Concertation and Social Partnership in Western Europe* (Oxford: Berghahn Books).

Bernhagen, Patrick (2007) *The Political Power of Business: Structure and Information in Public Policymaking* (London: Routledge).

Bernhagen, Patrick and Marsh, Michael (2007) 'Voting and Protesting: Explaining Citizen Participation in Old and New European Democracies', *Democratization*, 14(1), pp. 44–72.

Bevir, Mark, Rhodes, R.A.W. and Weller, Patrick (2003) 'Comparative Governance: Prospects and Lessons', *Public Administration*, 81(1), pp. 191–210.

Beyers, Jan (2002) 'Gaining and Seeking Access: The European Adaptation of Domestic Interest Associations', *European Journal of Political Research*, 41 (5), pp. 585–612.

Beyers, Jan (2004) 'Voice and Access: Political Practices of European Interest Associations', *European Union Politics*, 5(2), pp. 211–40.

Beyers, Jan and Kerremans, Bart (2004) 'Bureaucrats, Politicians, and Societal Interests: How is European Policy Making Politicized?', *Comparative Political Studies*, 37(10), pp. 1119–50.

Biezen, Ingrid van (2003) *Political Parties in New Democracies: Party Organization in Southern and East-Central Europe* (Basingstoke: Palgrave Macmillan).

Biezen, Ingrid van (2004) 'Political Parties as Public Utilities', *Party Politics*, 10 (6), pp. 701–22.

Bille, Lars (2007) 'Denmark', *European Journal of Political Research*, 46(7–8).

Billig, Michael (1995) *Banal Nationalism* (London: Sage).

Binderkrantz, Anne (2005) 'Interest Group Strategies: Navigating Between Privileged Access and Strategies of Pressure', *Political Studies*, 53, pp. 694–715.

Birch, Sarah, Millard, Frances, Popescu, Marina and Williams, Kieran (2002) *Embodying Democracy: Electoral System Design in Post-Communist Europe* (Basingstoke: Palgrave Macmillan).

Birdlife International (2007) available at http://www.birdlife.org.

Biscop, Sven (2006) 'The EU, the OSCE and the European Security Architecture: Network or Labyrinth?', *Asia Europe Journal*, 4(1), pp. 25–9.

Blair, Tony and Schröder, Gerhard (1999) *Europe: The Third Way/Die Neue Mitte*, available on numerous websites, e.g. http://www.iedm.org/library/blair_en.html

Blais, A., Blake, D. and Dion, S. (1996) 'Do Parties Make a Difference? A Reappraisal', *American Journal of Political Science*, 40(2), pp. 514–20.

Blanden, Jo, Gregg, Paul and Machin, Stephen (2005) *International Mobility in Europe and North America* (London: LSE Centre for Economic Performance).

Blom Hansen, J. (2001) 'Organized Interests and the State: A Disintegrating Relationship? Evidence from Denmark', *European Journal of Political Research*, 39(3), pp. 391–416.

Blondel, Jean and Müller-Rommel, Ferdinand (eds) (1997) *Cabinets in Western Europe* (Basingstoke: Palgrave Macmillan).

Blondel, Jean and Müller-Rommel, Ferdinand (2001) *Cabinets in Eastern Europe* (Basingstoke: Palgrave Macmillan).

Blondel, Jean, Müller-Rommel, Ferdinand and Malová, Darina (2007) *Governing New European Democracies* (Basingstoke: Palgrave Macmillan).

Blondel, Jean, Sinnott, Richard and Svensson, Palle (1998) *People and Parliament in the European Union: Participation, Democracy and Legitimacy* (Oxford: Clarendon Press).

Boix, Charles (1998) *Political Parties, Growth and Equality: Conservative and Social Democratic Economic Strategies in the World Economy* (Cambridge: Cambridge University Press).

Boix, Charles (1999) 'Setting the Rules of the Game: The Choice of Electoral Systems in Advanced Democracies', *American Political Science Review*, 93(3), pp. 609–24.

Bomberg, Elizabeth (2002) 'The Europeanisation of Green Parties: Exploring the EU's Impact', *West European Politics*, 25(3), pp. 29–50.

Bonoli, Giuliano (2004) 'Social Democratic Party Policies in Europe: Towards a Third Way?', in Giuliano Bonoli and Martin Powell (eds), *Social Democratic Party Policies in Contemporary Europe* (London: Routledge/ECPR).

Bonoli, Guiliano and Powell, Martin (eds) (2004) *Social Democratic Party Politics in Contemporary Europe* (London: Routledge).

Borraz, O. and John, P. (2004) 'The Transformation of Urban Political Leadership in Western Europe', *International Journal of Urban and Regional Research* , 28(1), pp. 107–20.

Bortolotti, Bernard and Siniscalco, Dominico (2004) *The Challenges of Privatization: An Internal Analysis* (Oxford: Oxford University Press).

Börzel, Tanja and Sedelmeier, U. (2006) 'The EU Dimension in European Politics', in Paul Heywood, Erik Jones, Martin Rhodes and Ulrich Sedelmeier (eds), *Developments in European Politics* (Basingstoke: Palgrave Macmillan).

Boswell, Christina (2003) 'The "External Dimension" of EU Immigration and Asylum Policy' *International Affairs*, 79(3), pp. 619–38.

Boucher, G. and Collins, G. (2003) 'Having One's Cake and Being Eaten Too: Irish Neo-liberal Corporatism', *Review of Economy*, 61(3), pp. 295–316.

Bouwen, Pieter (2002) 'Corporate Lobbying in the European Union: The Logic of Access', *Journal of European Public Policy*, 9(3), pp. 365–90.

Bouwen, Pieter and McCown, Margaret (2007) 'Lobbying versus Litigation: Political and Legal Strategies of Interest Representation in the European Union', *Journal of European Public Policy*, 14(3), pp. 422–43.

Bowler, Shaun, Donovan, Todd and Hanneman, Robert (2003) 'Art for Democracy's Sake? Group Membership and Political

Engagement in Europe', *Journal of Politics*, 65(4), pp. 1111–29.

Brady, David (2003) 'The Politics of Poverty: Left Political Institutions, the Welfare State, and Poverty', *Social Forces*, 82(2), pp. 557–88.

Bradley, David, Huber, Evelyne, Moller, Stephanie, Nielsen François and Stephens, John D. (2003) 'Distribution and Redistribution in Postindustrial Democracies', *World Politics*, 55(2), pp. 193–228.

Brandenburg, Heinz (2002) 'Who Follows Whom? The Impact of Parties on Media Agenda Formation in the 1997 British General Election Campaign', *Harvard International Journal of Press/Politics*, 7(3), pp. 34–54.

Brants, Kees and Siune, Karen (1998) 'Politicization in Decline', in Denis McQuail and Karen Siune (eds), *Media Policy: Convergence, Concentration and Commerce* (London: Sage).

Breen, Richard (ed.) (2004) *Social Mobility in Europe* (Oxford: Oxford University Press).

Bretherton, Charlotte and Vogler, John (1999 and 2005) *The European Union as a Global Actor* (London: Routledge).

Brettschneider, Frank (1997) 'The Press and the Polls in Germany, 1980–1994: Poll Coverage as an Essential Part of Election Campaign Reporting', *International Journal of Public Opinion Research*, 9(3), pp. 248–65.

Brettschneider, Frank, Neller, Katya and Anderson, Christopher J. (2006) 'Candidate Images in the 2005 German National Election', *German Politics*, 15(4), pp. 481–99.

Bridges, Brian (1999) *Europe and the Challenge of the Asia Pacific: Change, Continuity and Crisis* (Cheltenham: Edward Elgar).

Brighton, Paul and Foy, Dennis (2007) *News Values* (London: Sage).

Brookes, Rod, Lewis, Justin and Wahl-Jorgensen, Karin (2004) 'The Media Representation of Public Opinion: British Television News Coverage of the 2001 General Election', *Media, Culture & Society*, 26(1), pp. 63–80.

Brooks, Clem, Nieuwbeerta, Paul and Manza, Jeff (2006) 'Cleavage-Based Voting Behavior in Cross-National Perspective: Evidence from Six Postwar Democracies', *Social Science Research*, 35(1), pp. 88–128.

Broughton, David and Donovan, Mark (eds) (1999) *Changing Party Systems in Western Europe* (London: Pinter).

Broughton, David and Ten Napel, Hans-Martien (2000), *Religion and Mass Electoral Behaviour in Europe* (London: Routledge).

Brug, W. van der, Fennema, M. and Tillie, J. (2000) 'Anti-immigrant Parties in Europe: Ideological or Protest Vote?', *European Journal of Political Research*, 37(1), pp. 77–102.

Bruszt, László (2002) 'Making Markets and Eastern Enlargement: Diverging Convergence', *West European Politics*, 25(2), pp. 121–40.

Bruter, Michael (1999) 'Diplomacy without a State: The External Delegations of the European Commission', *Journal of European Public Policy*, 6(2), pp. 183–205.

Bruter, Michael (2005) *Citizens of Europe? The Emergence of a Mass European Identity* (Basingstoke: Palgrave Macmillan).

Budge, Ian, Crewe, Ivor, McKay, David and Newton, Ken (2007) *The New British Politics* (London: Longman).

Budge, Ian and Keman, Hans, (1990) 'New Concerns for Coalition Theory: Allocation of Ministries and Segmental Policy-making; A Comparative Analysis', *Acta Politica*, 90(2), pp. 151–85.

Budge, Ian and McDonald, Michael D. (2006) 'Choices Parties Define: Policy Alternatives in Representative Elections, 17 Countries 1945–1998', *Party Politics*, 12(4), pp. 451–66.

Burchell, John (2001) 'Evolving or Conforming? Assessing Organisational Reform within European Green Parties', *West European Politics*, 24(3), pp. 113–43.

Buruma, Ian (2007) *Murder in Amsterdam: The Death of Theo Van Gogh and the Limits of Tolerance* (London: Atlantic Books).

Byrnes, Timothy A. and Katzenstein, Peter J. (2006) *Religion in an Expanding Europe* (Cambridge: Cambridge University Press).

Byron, J. (2000) 'Square Dance Diplomacy: Cuba and CARIFORUM, the European Union and the United States', *European Review of Latin American and Caribbean Studies*, 68, pp. 23–45, available at http://www.cedla.uva.nl/fs_top.htm?60/60_publications 61_en_infoeurrev.htm.

C

Callaghan, Helen and Höpner, Martin (2005) 'European Integration and the Clash of Capitalisms: Political Cleavages over Takeover Liberalization', *Comparative European Politics*, 3(3), pp. 307–32.

Callaghan, John (2000) *The Retreat of Social Democracy* (Manchester: Manchester University Press).

Callinicos, Alex (2001) *Against the Third Way* (Cambridge: Polity Press).

Campbell, Rosie (2004) 'Gender, Ideology and Issue Preference: Is There Such a Thing as a Political Women's Interest in Britain?', *British Journal of Politics and International Relations*, 6, pp. 20–46.

Carlsnaes, Walter, Sjursen, Helene and White, Brian (eds) (2004) *Contemporary European Foreign Policy* (London: Sage).

Carter, Elisabeth (2005) *The Extreme Right in Western Europe* (Manchester: Manchester University Press).

Carty, R. Kenneth (2004) 'Parties as Franchise Systems: The Stratarchical Organizational Imperative', *Party Politics*, 10(1), pp. 5–24.

Casado-Díaz, M.A. (2006) 'Retiring to Spain: an Analysis of Differences among North European Nationals', *Journal of Ethnic and Migration Studies*, 32(8), pp. 1321–39.

Casarini, Nicola and Musu, Costanza (2007) *European Foreign Policy in an Evolving International System: The Road towards Convergence* (Basingstoke: Palgrave Macmillan).

Cassese, Sabino (1999) 'Italy's Senior Civil Service: An Ossified World', in Edward C. Page and Vincent Wright (eds), *Bureaucratic Elites in Western European States* (Oxford: Oxford University Press).

Castells, Manuel (2007) 'Communication, Power and Counter-power in the Network Society', *International Journal of Communication*, 1, pp. 238–66.

Castles, Francis (2004) *The Future of the Welfare State: Crisis Myths and Crisis Realities* (Oxford: Oxford University Press).

Castles, Stephen (2004) 'Why Migration Policies Fail', *Ethnic and Racial Studies*, 27(2), pp. 205–27.

Caul, Miki L. and Gray, Mark M. (2000) 'From Platform Declarations to Policy Outcomes: Changing Party Profiles and Partisan Influence over Policy', in Russell J. Dalton and Martin P. Wattenberg (eds), *Parties without Partisans: Political Change in Advanced Industrial Democracies* (Oxford: Oxford University Press), pp. 208–37.

CCS (2004) http://www.lse.ac.uk/collections/CCS/introduction.htm#generated-subheading2

Chaban, Natalia, Holland, Martin and Benson-Rea, Maureen (2003) *External Perceptions of the European Union: A Survey of New Zealanders' Perceptions and Attitudes towards the European Union*, NCRE Research Series, No. 1, University of Canterbury, New Zealand, available at http://www.europe.canterbury.ac.nz/research/nc/survey _identity_nz.pdf

Chadwick, Andrew (2006) *Internet Politics: States, Citizens, and New Communication Technologies* (Oxford: Oxford University Press).

Chalaby, Jean K. (2002) 'Transnational Television in Europe: The Role of Pan-European Channels', *European Journal of Communication*, 17(2), pp. 183–203.

Chawla, Mukesh, Bechterman, Gordon and Banerji, Arup (2007) *From Red to Grey: The 'Third Transition' of Ageing Populations in Eastern Europe and the Former Soviet Union* (Washington, DC: World Bank).

Chondroleou, Georgia (2004) 'Public Images and Private Lives: The Greek Experience', *Parliamentary Affairs*, 57(1), pp. 53–66.

Christensen, Tom and Lægreid, Per (eds) (2002) *New Public Management: the Transformation of Ideas and Practice* (Aldershot: Ashgate).

Christiansen, Thomas and Tonra, Ben (eds) (2004) *Rethinking EU Foreign Policy: Beyond the Common Foreign and Security Policy* (Manchester: Manchester University Press).

Chu, Jeff (2003) 'O Father, where art thou', *Time Magazine*, 16 June, 2003, available at *http://www.time.com/time/europe/archive/.*

Church, Clive H. (2004) *The Politics and Government of Switzerland* (Basingstoke: Palgrave Macmillan).

Cichowski, Rachel A. (2007) *The European Court and Civil Society: Litigation, Mobilization and Governance* (Cambridge: Cambridge University Press).

Cimbalo, Jeffrey L. (2004) 'Saving NATO from Europe', *Foreign Affairs*, November/December, pp. 111–21.

Clark, David (1998) 'The Modernization of the French Civil Service: Crisis, Change and Continuity', *Public Administration*, 76(1), pp. 97–116.

Clift, Ben (2001) 'The Jospin Way', *Political Quarterly*, 72(2), pp. 170–9.

Clift, Ben (2002) 'Social Democracy and Globalisation: The Case of France and the UK', *Government and Opposition*, 37(4), pp. 466–500.

Clifton, Judith, Comín, Francisco and Díaz Fuentes, Daniel (2006) 'Privatizing Public Enterprises in the European Union 1960–2002: Ideological, Pragmatic, Inevitable?', *Journal of European Public Policy*, 13(5), pp. 736–56.

Coen, David (1998) 'European Business Interests and the Nation State: Large Firm Lobbying in the European Union and Member State', *Journal of Public Policy*, 18(1), pp. 75–100.

Cohen, Robin (2006) *Migration and Its Enemies: Global Capital, Migrant Labour and the Nation-state* (Aldershot: Ashgate).

Cole, Alistair (1999) 'The *service publique* under Stress', *West European Politics*, 22(4), pp. 166–84.

Cole, Alistair and Drake, Helen (2000) 'The Europeanization of the French Polity: Continuity, Change and Adaptation', *Journal of European Public Policy*, 7(1), pp. 26–43.

Cole, Alistair and Raymond, Gina (2006) *Redefining the French Republic* (Manchester: Manchester University Press).

Cole, Alistair, Le Gales, Patrick and Levy, Jonah (2008) *Developments in French Politics 4* (Basingstoke: Palgrave Macmillan).

Coleman, Stephen (2003) *A Tale of Two Houses – The House of Commons, the Big Brother House and the People at Home* (London: Hansard Society).

Coleman, Stephen (2005) 'Blogs and the New Politics of Listening', *Political Quarterly*, 76(2), pp. 272–80.

Collins, Neil and Butler, Patrick (2004) 'Political Mediation in Ireland: Campaigning between Traditional and Tabloid Markets', *Parliamentary Affairs*, 57(1), pp. 93–107.

Colomer, Josep M. (2002) 'Spain and Portugal: Rule by Party Leadership', in Josep Colomer (ed.), *Political Institutions in Europe* (London: Routledge).

Compston, Hugh (1998) 'The End of Policy Concertation? Western Europe since the Single European Act', *Journal of European Public Policy*, 5(4), pp. 507–26.

Compston, Hugh (ed.) (2004) *Handbook of Public Policy in Europe: Britain, France and Germany* (Basingstoke: Palgrave Macmillan).

Compston, Hugh (2006) *King Trends and the Future of Public Policy* (Basingstoke: Palgrave Macmillan).

Conant, Lisa J. (2002) *Justice Contained: Law and Politics in the European Union* (Ithaca: Cornell University Press).

Conceição, Pedro, Ferreira, Pedro and Galbraith, James K. (2001) 'Inequality and Unemployment in Europe: The American Cure', in James K. Galbraith and Maureen Berner (eds), *Inequality and Industrial Change: A Global View* (Cambridge: Cambridge University Press).

Cook, Linda J. (2007a) 'Negotiating Welfare in Postcommunist States', *Journal of Comparative Politics*, 40(1), pp. 41–62.

Cook, Linda J. (2007b) *Postcommunist Welfare States: Reform Politics in Russia and Eastern Europe* (Ithaca: Cornell University Press).

Cook, Timothy E. (1998) *Governing with the News: The News Media as a Political Institution* (Chicago: University of Chicago Press).

Corbett, Richard, Jacobs, Francis and Shackleton, Michael (2003) *The European Parliament* (London: John Harper).

Cordell, Karl and Wolff, Stefan (eds) (2004) *The Ethnopolitical Encyclopaedia of Europe* (Basingstoke: Palgrave Macmillan).

Cornelius, Wayne, Tsuda, Takeyuki, Martin, Philip L. and Hollifeld, James F. (eds) (2004) *Controlling Immigration: A Global Perspective* (Stanford: Stanford University Press).

Costa Lobo, Marina (2006) 'Short-Term Voting Determinants in a Young Democracy: Leader Effects in Portugal in the 2002 Legislative Elections', *Electoral Studies*, 25(2), pp. 270–86.

Cotta, Maurizio and Verzichelli, Luca (2007) *Political Institutions in Italy* (Oxford: Oxford University Press).

Cottey, Andrew (2007) *Security in the New Europe* (Basingstoke: Palgrave Macmillan).

Coulombis, Theodore and Veremis, Thomas (1999) 'Introduction: The Mediterranean in Perspective', in Stelios Stavridis, Theodore Coulombis, Thomas Veremis and Neville Waites (eds), *Foreign Policies of the EU's Mediterranean States and Applicant Countries in the 1990s* (Basingstoke: Palgrave Macmillan).

Coulson, Andrew and Campbell, Adrian (eds) (2006) *Local Government in Central and Eastern Europe: The Rebirth of Local Democracy* (London: Routledge).

Council of the European Union (2003) *European Security Strategy*, available at http://www.consilium.europa.eu/uedocs/cmsUpload/78367.pdf

Cowles, Maria Green, Caporaso, James and Risse, Thomas (eds) (2001) *Transforming Europe: Europeanization and Domestic Change* (Ithaca: Cornell University Press).

Cowles, Maria Green and Dinan, Desmond (eds) (2004) *Developments in the European Union 2* (Basingstoke: Palgrave Macmillan).

Crossick, Stanley and Reuter, Etienne (2008) *China–EU: A Common Future* (Singapore: World Scientific Publishing).

Crouch, Colin (1999) *Social Change in Western Europe* (Oxford: Oxford University Press).

Crowe, Brian (2004) 'A Common European Foreign Policy after Iraq?', in Martin Holland (ed.), *Common Foreign and Security Policy: The First Ten Years* (London: Continuum).

Crowley, Stephen (2004) 'Explaining Labor Weakness in Post-Communist Europe: Historical Legacies in Comparative Perspective', *East European Politics and Societies*, 18(3), pp. 394–429.

Csergo, Zsuzsa and Goldgeier, James M. (2004) 'Nationalist Strategies and European Integration', *Perspectives on Politics*, 2(1), pp. 21–37.

Curran, James (2002) *Media and Power* (London: Routledge).

Curran, James and Leys, Colin (2000) 'Media and the Decline of Liberal Corporatism in Britain', in James Curran and Myung-Jin Park (eds), *De-Westernizing Media Studies* (London: Routledge).

Curzon Price, Victoria (2004) 'Industrial Policy', in Ali M. El-Agraa, (ed.), *The European Union: Economics and Policy*, 7th edn (London: Prentice-Hall/FT).

D

Dahlgren, Peter (2000) 'Communication and Democracy in Late Modernity', in Barrie Axford and Richard Huggins (eds), *New Media and Politics* (London: Sage).

Dalton, Russell J. (2000) 'The Decline of Party Identification', in Russell J. Dalton and Martin P. Wattenberg (eds), *Parties without Partisans: Political Change in Advanced Industrial Democracies* (Oxford: Oxford University Press).

Dalton, Russell J. (2002) 'Political Cleavages, Issues and Electoral Change,' in Lawrence LeDuc, Righard Niemi and Pippa Norris (eds), *Comparing Democracies*, 2nd edn (Thousand Oaks, CA: Sage Publications).

Dalton, Russell J., McAllister, Ian and Wattenberg, Martin P. (2000) 'The Consequences of Partisan Dealignment', in Russell J. Dalton and Martin P. Wattenberg (eds), *Parties without Partisans: Political Change in Advanced Industrial Democracies* (Oxford: Oxford University Press).

Dalton, Russell J., McAllister, Ian and Wattenberg, Martin P. (2002) 'The Consequences of Partisan Dealignment', in Russell J. Dalton and Martin P. Wattenberg (eds), *Parties without Partisans: Political Change in Advanced Industrial Democracies* (Oxford: Oxford University Press).

Dalton, Russell J. and Wattenberg, Martin P. (eds) (2002) *Parties without Partisans: Political Change in Advanced Industrial Democracies* (Oxford: Oxford University Press).

Dalton, Russell J. and Weldon, Steven (2005) 'Public Images of Political Parties: A Necessary Evil?', *West European Politics*, 28(5), pp. 931–51.

Damgaard, Erik and Mattson, Ingvar (2004) 'Conflict and Consensus in Committees', in Herbert Döring and Mark Hallerberg (eds), *Patterns of Parliamentary Behaviour* (Aldershot: Ashgate).

Dancygier, Rafaela and Saunders, Elizabeth M. (2006) 'A New Electorate? Comparing Preferences and Partisanship between Immigrants and Natives', *American Journal of Political Science*, 50(4), pp. 962–81.

Davies, Norman (2007) *Europe East and West* (London: Pimlico).

Dawisha, Karen and Deets, Stephen (2006) 'Political Learning in Post-Communist. Elections', *East European Politics and Society*, 20(4), pp. 691–728.

De Winter, Lieven (2004) 'Government Declarations and Law Production', in Herbert Döring and Mark Hallerberg (eds) *Patterns of Parliamentary Behavior: Passage of Legislation Across Western Europe* (Aldershot: Ashgate).

Deacon, Bob (2000) 'Social Policy in Eastern Europe: The Impact of Political Globalisation', *Journal of European Social Policy*, 10(2), pp. 146–61.

Deacon, Bob (2005) 'From "Safety Nets" back to "Universal Social Provision": Is the Global Tide Turning?', *Global Social Policy*, 5(1), pp. 19–28.

de Bens, Els and Østbye, Helge (1998) 'The European Newspaper Market', in Denis McQuail and Karen Siune (eds), *Media Policy: Convergence, Concentration and Commerce* (London: Sage).

Dekker, Paul and Broek, Andries van den (2005) 'Involvement in Voluntary Associations in North America and Western Europe: Trends and Correlates, 1981–2000', *Journal of Civil Society*, 1(1), pp. 45–59.

della Porta, Donatella and Caiani, Manuela (2007) 'Europeanization from Below? Social Movements and Europe', *Mobilization*, 12(1), pp. 1–20.

della Porta, Donatella and Diani, Mario (2005) *Social Movements: An Introduction* (Oxford: Blackwell).

della Porta, Donatella and Tarrow, Sidney (2005) *Transnational Protest and Global Activism* (Lanham: Rowman & Littlefield).

Delli Carpini, Michael X. and Williams, Bruce (1994) 'Fictional and Non-Fictional Television Celebrates Earth Day', *Cultural Studies*, 8, pp. 74–98.

Denemark, David (2002) 'Television Effects and Voter Decision Making in Australia: A Reexamination of the Converse Model', *British Journal of Political Science*, 32(4), pp. 663–90.

Denters, Bas and Rose, Lawrence (2005) *Comparing Local Governance: Trends and Developments* (Basingstoke: Palgrave Macmillan).

Deschouwer, Kris (2006) 'Political Parties as Multi-level Organizations', in Richard Katz and William Crotty (eds) *Handbook of Political Parties* (London: Sage).

Deth, Jan van and Janssen, Joseph (1994) 'Party Attachments and Political Fragmentation in Europe', *European Journal of Political Research*, 25, pp. 87–109.

Deth, Jan van, Montero, José Ramon and Westholm, Anders (eds) (2006) *Citizenship and Involvement in European Democracies* (London: Routledge).

Detterbeck, Klaus (2005) 'Cartel Parties in Western Europe?', *Party Politics*, 11(2), pp. 173–91.

de Vreese, Claes H. (2001) 'Election Coverage: New Directions for Public Broadcasting', *European Journal of Communication*, 16(2), pp. 155–80.

de Vreese, Claes H. (2005) 'The Spiral of Cynicism Reconsidered: The Mobilizing Function of News', *European Journal of Communication*, 20(3), pp. 283–301.

de Vreese, Claes H. (2007) 'A Spiral of Euroscepticism: the Media's Fault?', *Acta Politica*, 42(2–3), pp. 271–86.

de Vreese, Claes H., Banducci, S., Semetko, H.A. and Boomgaarden, Hajo G. (2006) 'The News Coverage of the 2004 European Parliamentary Election Campaign in 25 Countries', *European Union Politics*, 7(4), pp. 477–504.

de Vreese, Claes H. and Boomgaarden, Hajo, G. (2006a) 'Media Message Flows and Interpersonal Communication: The Conditional Nature of Effects on Public Opinion', *Communication Research*, 33(1), pp. 19–37.

de Vreese, Claes H. and Boomgaarden, Hajo, G. (2006b) 'Media Effects on Public Opinion about the Enlargement of the European Union', *Journal of Common Market Studies*, 44(2), pp. 419–36.

de Vreese, Claes H. and Boomgaarden, Hajo G. (2006c) 'News, Political Knowledge and Participation: the Differential Effects of News Media Exposure on Political Knowledge and Participation', *Acta Politica*, 41(4), pp. 317–41.

de Vries, Catherine E. (2007) 'Sleeping Giant: Fact or Fairytale? How European Integration Affects National Elections', *European Union Politics*, 8(3), pp. 363–85

Dewan, Torun and Dowding, Keith (2005) 'The Corrective Effect of Ministerial Resignations on Government Popularity', *American Journal of Political Science*, 49(1), pp. 46–56.

de Winter, Lieven (2004) 'Government Declarations and Law Production', in Herbert Döring and Mark Hallerberg (eds) *Patterns of Parliamentary Behaviour* (Aldershot: Ashgate).

de Winter, Lieven, Gómez-Reino, M. and Lynch, P. (eds) (2006) *Autonomist Parties in Europe: Identity Politics and the Revival of the Territorial Cleavage* (Barcelona: Institut de Ciències Polítiques i Socials).

Diani, Mario and McAdam, Doug (eds) (2003) *Social Movements and Networks: Relational Approaches to Collective Action* (Oxford: Oxford University Press).

Díez Medrano, Juan and Gutiérrez, Paula (2001) 'Nested Identities: National and European Identity in Spain', *Ethnic and Racial Studies*, 24(5), pp. 753–78.

Dimitrakopoulos, Dyonissis, G. (2001) 'Incrementalism and Path Dependence: European Integration and Institutional Change in National Parliaments', *Journal of Common Market Studies*, 39(3), pp. 405–22.

Dimitrov, Vesselin, Goetz, Klaus H. and Wollman, Hellmut (eds) (2006) *Governing after Communism: Institutions and Policy Making* (Lanham: Rowman & Littlefield).

Dodini, Michaela and Fantini, Marco (2006) 'The EU Neighbourhood Policy: Implications for Economic Growth and Stability', *Journal of Common Market Studies*, 44(3), pp. 507–32.

Dogan, Mattei (2001) 'Class, Religion, Party: Triple Decline of Electoral Cleavages in Western Europe', in Lauri Karvonen and Stein Kuhnle (eds), *Party Systems and Voter Alignments Revisited* (London: Routledge).

Donk, Wim van de, Loader, Brian, Nixon, Paul and Rucht, Dieter (eds) (2003) *Cyberprotest: New Media, Citizens and Social Movements* (London: Routledge).

Donovan, Todd and Karp, Jeffrey (2006) 'Popular Support for Direct Democracy', *Party Politics*, 12(5), pp. 671–88.

Donsbach, Wolfgang (1995) 'Lapdogs, Watchdogs and Junkyard Dogs', *Media Studies Journal*, 9(4), pp. 17–30.

Donsbach, Wolfgang and Klett, Bettina (1993) 'Subjective Objectivity: How Journalists in Four Countries Define a Key Term of their Profession', *Gazette*, 51, pp. 53–83.

Donsbach, Wolfgang and Patterson, Thomas, E. (2004) 'Political News Journalists: Partisanship, Professionalism, and Political Roles in Five Countries', in Frank Esser and Barbara Pfetsch (eds) *Comparing Political Communication: Theories, Cases, and Challenges* (Cambridge: Cambridge University Press).

Döring, Herbert (ed.) (1995) *Parliaments and Majority Rule in Western Europe* (New York: St Martin's Press).

Döring, Herbert and Hallerberg, Mark (eds) (2004) *Patterns of Parliamentary Behaviour* (Aldershot: Ashgate).

van Dosenrode, Soren and Stubkjær, Anders (2002) *The European Union and the Middle East* (London: Sheffield Academic Press/Continuum).

Dover, Caroline and Barnett, Stephen (2004) *The World on the Box* (London: 3WE).

Dowding, Keith (2005) 'Why do People Vote? Five Types of Answer and a Suggestion' *British Journal of Politics and International Relations*, 7(3), pp. 442–59.

Downs, Anthony (1972) 'Up and Down with Ecology: "The Issue Attention Cycle"', *The Public Interest*, 28, pp. 38–50, available at http://www.anthonydowns.com/ upanddown.htm

Druckman, James N. and Roberts, Andrew (2007) 'Communist Successor Parties and Coalition Formation in Eastern Europe', *Legislative Studies Quarterly*, 32(1), pp. 5–31.

Drummond, Andrew (2006) 'Electoral Volatility and Party Decline in Western Democracies: 1970–1995', *Political Studies*, 54(3), pp. 628–47.

Duch, Raymond M. and Stevenson, Randy (2006) 'Assessing the Magnitude of the Economic Vote over Time and Across Nations', *Electoral Studies*, 25(3), pp. 528–47.

Duke, Simon (2000) *The Elusive Quest for European Security: From EDC to CFSP* (Basingstoke: Palgrave Macmillan).

Dumbrell, John (2001) *A Special Relationship: Anglo-American Relations in the Cold War and After* (Basingstoke: Palgrave Macmillan).

Duncan, Fraser (2006) 'A Decade of Christian Democratic Decline: The Dilemmas of the CDU, ÖVP and CDA in the 1990s', *Government and Opposition*, 41(4), pp. 469–90.

Duncan, Fraser (2007) '"Lately, Things Just Don't Seem the Same". External Shocks, Party Change and the Adaptation of the Dutch Christian Democrats during "Purple Hague" 1994–8', *Party Politics*, 13(1), pp. 69–87.

Dunleavy, Patrick (1990) 'Mass Political Behaviour: Is There More to Learn?', *Political Studies*, 38(3), pp. 453–69.

Dunleavy, Patrick (1991) *Democracy, Bureaucracy and Public Choice: Economic Explanations in Political Science* (Hemel Hempstead: Harvester Wheatsheaf).

Dunleavy, Patrick, Gamble, Andrew, Heffernan, Richard and Peele, Gillian (2003) *Developments in British Politics 7* (Basingstoke: Palgrave Macmillan).

Dunphy, Richard (2004) *Contesting Capitalism? Left Parties and European Integration* (Manchester: Manchester University Press).

Dunphy, Richard and Bale, Tim (2007) 'Red Flag Still Flying? Explaining AKEL – Cyprus's Communist Anomaly', *Party Politics*, 13(3), pp. 287–304.

Dutta-Bergman, Mohan J. (2004) 'Complementarity in Consumption of News Types across Traditional and New Media', *Journal of Broadcasting & Electronic Media*, 48(1), pp. 41–60.

Duverger, Maurice (1954) *Political Parties: Their Organization and Activity in the Modern State* (London: Methuen).

Dyson, Kenneth and Featherstone, Kevin (1999) *The Road to Maastricht: Negotiating Economic and Monetary Union* (Oxford: Oxford University Press).

E

Earnshaw, David and Judge, David (2002) 'No Simple Dichotomies: Lobbyists and the European Parliament', *Journal of Legislative Studies*, 8(4), pp. 61–79.

Eatwell, Roger (2000). 'The Rebirth of the Extreme Right in Western Europe', *Parliamentary Affairs*, 53(3), pp. 407–25.

Eatwell, Roger and Mudde, Cas (2003) *Western Democracies and the Extreme Right Challenge* (London: Routlege).

Edmonds, Richard Louis (ed.) (2002) 'China and Europe Since 1978', Special Issue of *China Quarterly*, 169.

Eijk, C. van der and Franklin, M. (eds) (1996) *Choosing Europe? The European Electorate and National Politics in the Face of Union* (Ann Arbor: University of Michigan Press).

Einhorn, Eric S. and Logue, John (2003) *Modern Welfare States: Scandinavian Politics and Policy in the Global Age* (New York: Praeger).

Eising, Rainer and Kohler-Koch, Beate (1999) 'Introduction: Network Governance in the European Union', in Beate Kohler-Koch and Rainer Eising (eds), *The Transformation of Governance in the European Union* (London: Routledge/ECPR).

Elazar, D.J. (1997) 'Contrasting Unitary and Federal Systems', *International Political Science Review*, 18(3), pp. 237–51.

Elgie, Robert (ed.) (1999) *Semi-presidentialism in Europe* (London: Frank Cass).

Elgie, Robert and Stapleton, John (2006) 'Testing the Decline of Parliament Thesis: Ireland, 1923–2002', *Political Studies*, 54, pp. 465–85.

Elster, Jon (1986) 'Introduction', in Jon Elster (ed.), *Rational Choice* (Oxford: Blackwell).

Enyedi, Zsolt (2006) 'Party Politics in Post-Communist Transition', in Richard Katz and William Crotty (eds), *Handbook of Party Politics* (London: Sage).

Epstein, Rachel and Gheciu, Alexandra (2006) 'Beyond Territoriality: European Security after the Cold War', in Paul Heywood, Erik Jones, Martin Rhodes and Ulrich Sedelmeier (eds), *Developments in European Politics* (Basingstoke: Palgrave Macmillan).

Ericson, Richard, Baranek, Patricia and Chan, Janet B.L. (1989) *Negotiating Control: A Study of News Sources* (Toronto: University of Toronto Press).

Esping-Andersen, Gøsta (1990) *The Three Worlds of Welfare Capitalism* (Cambridge: Polity Press).

Esser, Frank (1999) '"Tabloidization" of News: A Comparative Analysis of Anglo-American and German Press Journalism', *European Journal of Communication*, 14(3), pp. 375–405.

Esser, Frank, Reinemann, Carsten and Fan, David (2000) 'Spin Doctoring in British and German Election Campaigns: How the Press is being Confronted with a New Quality of Political PR', *European Journal of Communication*, 15(2), pp. 209–39.

Esser, Frank, Reinemann, Carsten and Fan, David (2001) 'Spin Doctors in the United States, Great Britain, and Germany: Metacommunication about Media Manipulation', *Harvard International Journal of Press/Politics*, 6(1), pp. 16–45.

Esser, Frank and Pfetsch, Barbara (eds) (2004) *Comparing Political Communication: Theories, Cases, and Challenges* (Cambridge: Cambridge University Press).

EUMAP (2005) *Television Across Europe*, available at http://www.eumap.org/topics/media/television_europe

European Commission (2006) http://ec.europa.eu/employment_social/news/2006/feb/report_en.pdf

European Commission (2007) *Towards Common Principles of Flexicurity*, available at http://ec.europa.eu/employment_social/employment_strategy/flexicurity%20media/flexicurity-publication_2007_en.pdf

European Women's Professional Network (2006) *European PWN Board Women Monitor 2006*, available at www.EuropeanPWN.net

Evans, Geoffrey (1999) *The End of Class Politics?: Class Voting in Comparative Context* (Oxford: Oxford University Press).

Evans, Geoffrey (2006) 'The Social Bases of Political Divisions in Post-Communist Eastern Europe', *Annual Review of Sociology*, 32, pp. 245–70.

Evans, Jocelyn A.J. (ed.) (2002) *The French Party System* (Manchester: Manchester University Press).

Evans, Jocelyn, A.J. (2003) *Voters and Voting: An Introduction* (London: Sage).

Evans, Jocelyn A.J. (2004) 'Ideology and Party Identification: A Normalisation of French Voting Anchors?', in Michael Lewis-Beck (ed.), *The French Voter* (Basingstoke: Palgrave Macmillan).

F

Faas, T. (2003) 'To Defect or Not to Defect? National, Institutional and Party Group Pressures on MEPs and their Consequences for Party Group Cohesion in the European Parliament', *European Journal of Political Research*, 42(6), pp. 841–66.

Faas, T. and Maier, J. (2004) 'Chancellor-candidates in the 2002 Televised Debates', *German Politics*, 13(2), pp. 300–16.

Fairbrass, J. and Jordan, A. (2001) 'Protecting Biodiversity in the European Union: National Barriers and European Opportunities', *Journal of European Public Policy*, 8(4), pp. 499–518.

Faist, Thomas and Ette, Andrew (2007) *The Europeanization of National Policies and Politics of Immigration* (Basingstoke: Palgrave Macmillan).

Falkner, Gerda (2000a) 'How Pervasive are Euro-politics? Effects of EU Membership on a New Member State', *Journal of Common Market Studies*, 38(2), pp. 223–50.

Falkner, Gerda (2000b) 'The Council or the Social Partners? EC Social Policy between Diplomacy and Collective Bargaining', *Journal of European Public Policy*, 7(5), pp. 705–24.

Falkner, Gerda, Treib, Oliver, Hartlapp, Miriam and Leiber, Simone (2004) 'Non-Compliance with EU Directives in the Member States: Opposition through the Backdoor?', *West European Politics*, 27(3), pp. 452–73.

Fallend, Franz (2004) 'Are Right-Wing Populism and Government Participation Incompatible? The Case of the Freedom Party of Austria', *Representation*, 40(2), pp. 1156–30.

Farrell, David M. (2001) *Electoral Systems: A Competitive Introduction* (Basingstoke and New York: Palgrave Macmillan).

Farrell, David M. and Schmitt-Beck, Rüdiger (2002) *Do Political Campaigns Matter? Campaign Effects in Elections and Referendums* (London: Routledge).

Farrell, David M. and Webb, Paul (2002) 'Political Parties as Campaign Organisations', in Russell J. Dalton and Martin P. Wattenberg (eds), *Parties without Partisans: Political Change in Advanced Industrial Democracies.* (Oxford: Oxford University Press).

Favell A. and Hansen R. (2002) 'Markets against Politics: Migration, EU Enlargement and the Idea of Europe', *Journal of Ethnic and Migration Studies*, 28(4), pp. 581–601.

Fawn, Rick (2000) *The Czech Republic: A Nation of Velvet* (London: Routledge).

Fawn, Rick (ed.) (2003) 'Ideology and National Identity in Post-communist Foreign Policies', Special Issue of the *Journal of Communist Studies and Transition Politics*, 19(3).

Fawn, Rick (2006) 'Alliance Behaviour, the Absentee Liberator and the Influence of Soft Power: Post-communist State Positions over the Iraq War in 2003', *Cambridge Review of International Affairs*, 19(3), pp. 465–80.

Feigenbaum, Harvey, Henig, Jeffrey and Hamnett, Chris (1998) *Shrinking the State: The Political Underpinnings of Privatization* (Cambridge: Cambridge University Press).

Ferge, Zsuzsa (2001) 'Welfare and "Ill-fare" Systems in Central and Eastern Europe', in Robert Sykes, Bruno Palier and Pauline M. Prior (eds), *Globalization and European Welfare States: Challenges and Change* (Basingstoke: Palgrave Macmillan).

Ferguson, Ross and Howell, Milica (2004) *Political Blogs – Craze or Convention?* (London: Hansard Society), available at http://www.hansardsociety.org.uk/assets/Final_Blog _Report_.pdf

Fink-Hafner, Danica (2007) 'Slovenia', *European Journal of Political Research*, 46(7–8), pp. 1107–13.

Fletcher, John (2006) 'Dominique Baudis and the Alègre affair in Toulouse', *Journal of European Studies*, 36(2), pp. 201–08.

Forster, Anthony (2000) 'Evaluating the EU–ASEM Relationship: A Negotiated Order Approach', *Journal of Public Polity*, 17(5), pp. 787–805.

Foster, Edward (1998) 'Ad hoc in Albania: Did Europe Fail?, *Security Dialogue*, 29(2), pp. 213–18.

Franklin, Mark N. (2001a) 'How Structural Factors Cause Turnout Variations at European Parliament Elections', *European Union Politics*, 3(2), pp. 309–28.

Franklin, Mark N. (2001b) 'European Elections and the European Voter', in Jeremy Richardson (ed.), *European Union: Power and Policy-making*, 2nd edn (London: Longman).

Franklin, Mark (2002) 'The Dynamics of Electoral Participation', in Lawrence LeDuc, Richard Niemi and Pippa Norris (eds), *Elections and Voting in Global Perspective 2* (Thousand Oaks, CA: Sage).

Franklin, Mark N. (2004) *Voter Turnout and the Dynamics of Electoral Competition in Established Democracies since 1945* (New York: Cambridge University Press).

Franklin, Mark N., MacNie, Thomas and Valen, Henry (eds) (1992) *Electoral Change: Responses to Evolving Social and Attitudinal Structures in Western Countries* (Cambridge: Cambridge University Press).

Franks, Suzanne (2006) 'Lacking a Clear Narrative: Foreign Reporting after the Cold War', in John Lloyd and Jean Seaton (eds), *What Can be Done? Making the Media and Politics Better* (Oxford: Blackwell).

Freedman, Lawrence and Menon, Anand (1997) 'Conclusion: Defence, States and Integration', in Joylon Howorth and Anand Menon (eds), *The European Union and National Defence Policy* (London: Routledge).

Friedman, Jeffrey (ed.) (1996) *The Rational Choice Controversy: Economic Models of Politics Reconsidered* (New Haven, CT: Yale University Press).

Fuchs, Dieter and Klingemann, Hans-Dieter (2002) 'Eastward Enlargement of the European Union and the Identity of Europe', *West European Politics*, 25(2), pp. 19–54.

FRA (Fundamental Rights Agency) (2007) *Report on Racism and Xenophobia in the Member States of the EU*, available online at http://fra.europa. eu/fra/material/pub/racism/report_racism_0807_en.pdf

Furusawa, Katsuto (2006) 'Participation and Protest in the European Union and "Outsider States"', *Contemporary Politics*, 12(2), 207–23.

G

Gabel, Matthew J. (2000) 'European Integration, Voters and National Politics', *West European Politics*, 23(4), pp. 52–72.

Gabel, Matthew J. and Anderson, Christopher J. (2002) 'The Structure of Citizen Attitudes and the European Political Space', *Comparative Political Studies*, 35(8), pp. 893–913.

Gaddis, John Lewis (2007) *The Cold War* (London: Penguin)

Gaffney, John (ed.) (1996) *Political Parties and the European Union* (London: Routledge).

Gains, Francesca (2003) 'Executive Agencies in Government: The Impact of Bureaucratic Networks on Policy Outcomes', *Journal of Public Policy*, 23(1), pp. 55–79.

Gallagher, Michael (2008) Electoral systems website, http://www.tcd.ie/PoliticalScience/Staff/MichaelGallagher/ElSystems/

Gallagher, Michael, Laver, Michael and Mair, Peter (2006) *Representative Government in Modern Europe* (New York: McGraw-Hill).

Gallagher, Michael and Mitchell, Paul (eds) (2005) *The Politics of Electoral Systems* (Oxford: Oxford University Press).

Gamson, William A. (2004) 'Bystanders, Public Opinion, and the Media', in David A. Snow, Sarah Soule and Hanspeter Kriesi (eds) (2004), *The Blackwell Companion to Social Movements* (Oxford: Blackwell).

Ganghof, Steffen (2006) *The Politics of Income Taxation: A Comparative Analysis of Advanced Industrial Countries* (Colchester: ECPR Press).

Gänzle, Stefan and Sens, Allen G. (2007) *The Changing Politics of European Security* (Basingstoke: Palgrave Macmillan).

Garbaye, Romain (2005) *Getting Into Local Power: The Politics of Ethnic Minorities in British and French Cities* (Oxford: Blackwell).

Garrett, Geoffrey (1998a) *Partisan Politics in the Global Economy* (Cambridge: Cambridge University Press).

Garrett, Geoffrey (1998b) 'Global Markets and National Politics: Collision Course or Virtuous Circle', *International Organization*, 52(4), pp. 787–824.

Gavin, Neil and Sanders, David (2003) 'The Press and its

Influence on British Political Attitudes under New Labour', *Political Studies*, 51(3), pp. 573–91.
Geddes, Andrew (2003) *The Politics of Migration and Immigration in Europe* (London: Sage).
Geddes, Andrew (2008) *Immigration and European Integration: Beyond Fortress Europe?* (Manchester: Manchester University Press).
Genschel, Philipp (2004) 'Globalization and the Welfare State: a Retrospective', *Journal of European Public Policy*, 11(4), pp. 613–36.
Gertner, Jon (2004) 'The Very, Very Personal is the Political', *New York Times Magazine*, 15 February.
Geys, Benny (2006) 'Explaining Voter Turnout: a Review of Aggregate-Level Research', *Electoral Studies*, 25(4), pp. 637–63.
Gibson, Rachel and Harmel, Robert (1998) 'Party Families and Democratic Performance: Extraparliamentary vs Parliamentary Group Power', *Political Studies*, 46(3), pp. 633–50.
Gibson, Rachel, Nixon, Paul and Ward, Stephen (eds) (2003) *Political Parties and the Internet: Net Gain?* (London: Routledge).
Gibson, Rachel K. and Römmele, Andrea (2005) 'Truth and Consequence in Web Campaigning: Is there an Academic Digital Divide?', *European Political Science*, 4, pp. 273–87.
Gibson, Rachel, Römmele, Andrea and Ward, Stephen (2003) 'German Parties and Internet Campaigning in the 2002 Federal Election', *German Politics*, 12(1), pp. 79–108.
Giddens, Anthony (1990) *The Consequences of Modernity* (Stanford: Stanford University Press).
Gijsberts, Mérova and Nieuwbeerta, Paul (2000) 'Class Cleavages in Party Preferences in the New Democracies in Eastern Europe: A Comparison with Western Democracies', *European Societies*, 2(4), pp. 397–430.
Gillespie, Richard (2000) *Spain and the Mediterranean: Developing a European Policy towards the South* (Basingstoke: Palgrave Macmillan).
Gilson, Julie (2000) *Japan and the European Union: A Partnership for the Twenty-First Century* (Basingstoke: Palgrave Macmillan).
Ginsborg, Paul (2003) *Italy and Its Discontents 1980–2001: Family, Civil Society, State* (London: Penguin).
Ginsborg, Paul (2004) *Silvio Berlusconi: Television, Power and Patrimony* (London: Verso).
Giugni, Marco and Passy, Florence (eds) (2006) *Dialogues on Migration Policy* (Lanham: Lexington Books).
Givens, Terri and Luedtke, Adam (2005) 'European Imigration Policies in Comparative Perspective: Issue Salience, Partisanship and Immigrant Rights', *Comparative European Politics*, 3, pp. 1–22.
Glyn, Andrew (2001) *Social Democracy in Neoliberal Times* (Oxford: Oxford University Press).
Goerres, Achim (2007) 'Why are Older People More Likely to Vote? The Impact of Ageing on Electoral Turnout in Europe', *British Journal of Politics and International Relations*, 9(1), pp. 90–1.
Goetz, Klaus (2001) 'Making Sense of Post-Communist Central Administration: Modernization, Europeanization or Latinization', *Journal of European Public Policy*, 8(6), pp. 1032–51.
Goetz, Klaus H. (2006) 'Power at the Centre: the Organization of Democratic Systems', in Paul Heywood, Erik Jones, Martin Rhodes and Ulrich Sedelmeier (eds) (2006) *Developments in European Politics* (Basingstoke: Palgrave Macmillan).
Goetz, Klaus and Zubek, Radoslav (2007) 'Government, Parliament and Lawmaking in Poland 1997–2001', *Journal of Legislative Studies*, 13(4), pp. 517–38.
Golder, Sona N. (2005) 'Pre-electoral Coalitions in Comparative Perspective: a Test of Existing Hypotheses', *Electoral Studies*, 24, pp. 643–63.
Goodheart, David (2004) 'Too Diverse', *Prospect*, February.
Goodin, Robert, Headey, Bruce, Muffels, Ruud and Dirven, Henk-Jan (1999) *The Real Worlds of Welfare Capitalism* (Cambridge: Cambridge University Press).
Goodwin, Jeff, Jasper, James M. and Polleta, Francesca (eds) (2001) *Passionate Politics: Emotions and Social Movements* (Chicago: University of Chicago Press).
Górny, Agata and Ruspini, Paolo (eds) (2004) *Migration in the New Europe: East–West Revisited* (Basingstoke: Palgrave Macmillan).
Grabbe, Heather (2003) 'Europeanization Goes East: Power and Uncertainty in the EU Accession Process', in Kevin Featherstone and Claudio Radaelli (eds), *The Politics of Europeanization* (Oxford: Oxford University Press).
Grabbe, Heather (2006) *The EU's Transformative Power: Europeanization through Conditionality in Central and Eastern Europe* (Basingstoke: Palgrave Macmillan).
Grabendorff, Wolf and Seidelmann, Reimund (2005) *Relations between the European Union and Latin America* (Baden-Baden: Nomos Verlag).
Gray, Pat and t'Hart, Paul (eds) (1998) *Public Policy Disasters in Western Europe* (London: Routledge).
Graziano, Paolo and Vink, Maarten (eds) (2006) *Europeanization: New Research Agendas* (Basingstoke: Palgrave Macmillan).
Green, Donald P. and Paterson, William E. (eds) (2005) *Governance in Contemporary Germany: The Semisovereign State Revisited* (Cambridge: Cambridge University Press).
Green, Donald P. and Shapiro, Ian (1994) *Pathologies of Rational Choice Theory: A Critique of Applications in Political Science* (New Haven: Yale University Press).
Green, Jane (2007) 'When Voters and Parties Agree: Valence Issues and Party Competition', *Political Studies*, 55(3), pp. 629–55.
Green, Simon (2004) *The Politics of Exclusion: Institutions and Immigration Policy in Contemporary Germany* (Manchester: Manchester University Press).
Green, Simon, Hough, Dan, Miskimmon, Alister, Timmins, Graham (2007) *The Politics of the New Germany* (London: Routledge)
Green-Pedersen, Christoffer (1999) 'The Danish Welfare State under Bourgeois Reign', *Scandinavian Political Studies*, 22(3), pp. 243–60.
Green-Pedersen, Christoffer (2001) 'Welfare-state Retrenchment in Denmark and the Netherlands, 1982–1998: The Role of Party Competition and Party Consensus', *Comparative Political Studies*, 34(9), pp. 963–85.
Green-Pedersen, Christoffer, Kersbergen Kees van and Hemerijck, Anton (2001) 'Neo-liberalism, the "Third Way" or What? Recent Social Democratic Welfare Policies in Denmark and the Netherlands', *Journal of European Public Policy*, 8(2), pp. 307–25.

Green-Pedersen, Christoffer and Odmalm, Pontus (2008) 'Going Different Ways? Right-wing Parties and the Immigrant Issue in Denmark and Sweden', *Journal of European Public Policy*, 15(3).

Greenwood, Justin (2007) *Interest Representation in the European Union* (Basingstoke: Palgrave Macmillan).

Greer, Scott L. (2007) *Nationalism and Self-government* (Albany: SUNY Press)

Greskovits, Béla (1998) *The Political Economy of Protest and Patience* (Budapest: Central European University Press).

Gros, Daniel (2002) 'Health not Wealth: Enlarging the EU', *West European Politics*, 25(2), pp. 141–51.

Gross, Peter (2004) 'Between Reality and Dream: Eastern European Media Transition, Transformation, Consolidation, and Integration', *East European Politics and Societies*, 18(1), pp. 110–31.

Grzymala-Busse, Anna and Innes, Abby (2003) 'Great Expectations: The EU and Domestic Political Competition in East Central Europe', *East European Politics and Societies*, 17(1), pp. 64–73.

Guarnieri, Carlo and Pederzoli, Patrizia (2002) *The Power of Judges: A Comparative Study of Courts and Democracy* (Oxford: Oxford University Press).

Guibernau, Montserrat (1999) *Nations Without States* (Oxford: Blackwell).

Guild, Elspeth and van Selm, Joanne (eds) (2005) *International Migration and Security: Opportunities and Challenges* (London: Routledge).

Guillén, Mauro F. and Suárez, Sandra L. (2005) 'Explaining the Global Digital Divide: Economic, Political and Sociological Drivers of Cross-National Internet Use', *Social Forces*, 84(2), pp. 681–708.

Guiraudon, Virginie and Jileva, Elena (2006) 'Immigration and Asylum', in Paul Heywood *et al.* (eds) (2006) *Developments in European Politics* (Basingstoke: Palgrave Macmillan).

Gulyás, Agnes (2003) 'Print Media in Post-Communist East Central Europe', *European Journal of Communication*, 18(1), pp. 81–106.

Gulyás, Agnes (2004) 'Public Images and Private Lives: The Case of Hungary', *Parliamentary Affairs*, 57(1), pp. 67–79.

Gunther, Richard, Montero, José Ramón, and Wert, José Ignacio (2000) 'The Media and Politics in Spain: from Dictatorship to Democracy', in Richard Gunther and Anthony Mughan (eds) *Democracy and the Media: A Comparative Perspective* (Cambridge: Cambridge University Press).

Gunther, Richard, Montero, José Ramón and Botella, Joan (2004) *Democracy in Modern Spain* (New Haven: Yale University Press).

Gunther, Richard, Montero, José Raman and Linz, Juan J. (2002) *Political Parties: Old Concepts and New Challenges* (Oxford: Oxford University Press).

Gunther, Richard and Mughan, Anthony (eds) (2000) *Democracy and the Media: A Comparative Perspective* (Cambridge: Cambridge University Press).

Gustavsson, Sverker and Lewin, Lerf (1996) *The Future of the Nation State* (London: Routledge).

Guyomarch, Alain, Machin, Howard, Hall, Peter A. and Hayward, Jack (2001) *Developments in French Politics 2* (Basingstoke: Palgrave Macmillan).

H

Habermas, Jürgen (1989) *The Structural Transformation of the Public Sphere* (Cambridge: Polity).

Haftendorn, Helga (2006) *Coming of Age: German Foreign Policy Since 1945* (Lanham: Rowman & Littlefield).

Hall, Peter A. and Soskice, David (2001) 'An Introduction to Varieties of Capitalism', in Peter A. Hall and David Soskice (eds), *Varieties of Capitalism: The Institutional Foundation of Comparative Economic Advantage* (Oxford: Oxford University Press).

Hallin, Daniel C. and Mancini, Paolo (2004) *Comparing Media Systems: Three Models of Media and Politics* (Cambridge: Cambridge University Press).

Halman, Loek and Riis, Ole (2002) *Religion in a Secularizing Society: The Europeans' Religion at the end of the 20th Century* (Leiden and Boston: Brill).

Hamman, Kerstin and Kelly, John (2007) 'Party Politics and the Re-emergence of Social Pacts in Western Europe', Comparative Political Studies, 40(8), pp. 971–94.

Hancock, M. Donald (2003) 'Sweden', in M. Donald Hancock *et al., Politics in Europe* (Basingstoke: Palgrave Macmillan).

Hanley, David (ed.) (1994) *Christian Democracy in Europe: A Comparative Perspective* (London: Pinter).

Hanley, Sean (2006) *The New Right in the New Europe* (London: Routledge).

Hansen, R. (2002) 'Globalization, Embedded Realism and Path Dependence: The Other Immigrants to Europe', *Comparative Political Studies*, 35(3), pp. 259–83.

Hantrais, Linda (2007) 'Welfare Policies', in Colin Hay and Anand Menon, *European Politics* (Oxford: Oxford University Press).

Harcourt, Alison J. (2003) 'Europeanization as Convergence: The Regulation of Media Markets in the European Union', in Kevin Featherstone and Claudio Radaelli (eds), *The Politics of Europeanization* (Oxford: Oxford University Press).

Harcourt, Alison J. (2005) *The European Union and the Regulation of Media Markets* (Manchester: Manchester University Press).

Hardt, Michael and Negri, Antonio (2000) *Empire* (Cambridge, MA: Harvard University Press).

Hargreaves Heap, Shaun, Hollis, Martin, Lyons, Bruce, Sugden, Robert and Weale, Albert (1992) *The Theory of Choice: A Critical Guide* (Oxford: Blackwell, 1992).

Harjes, Thomas (2007) 'Globalization and Income Inequality: a European Perspective', IMF Working Paper 07/169, available at www.imf.org/external/pubs/ft/wp/2007/wp07169.pdf

Harrison, J.L. and Woods, L.M. (2001) 'Defining European Public Service Broadcasting', *European Journal of Communication*, 16(4), pp. 477–504.

Haseler, Stephen (2004) *Super State: The New Europe and its Challenge to America* (London: I.B. Tauris).

Haupt, Andrea B. (2007) 'What is Right for the Right? Austrian and German Catch-All Parties' Responses to Globalization', Unpublished MS, available at http://psweb.sbs.ohio-state.edu/faculty/haupt/right.pdf

Hauser, Gunther and Kernic, Franz (2006) *European Security in Transition* (Aldershot: Ashgate).

Hay, Colin (2000) 'Contemporary Capitalism, Globalization, Regionalization and the Persistance of National Variation', *Review of International Studies*, 26(4), pp. 509–31.

Hay, Colin and Menon, Anand (eds) (2007) *European Politics* (Oxford: Oxford University Press).

Hayward, Jack (1982) 'Mobilising Private Interests in the Service of Public Ambitions: The Salient Element in the Dual French Policy Style', in Jeremy J. Richardson (ed.), *Policy Styles in Western Europe* (London: George Allen & Unwin).

Hecke, Steven van and Gerard, Emmanuel (eds) (2004) *Christian Democratic Parties in Europe since the End of the Cold War* (Leuven: Leuven University Press).

Heidar, Knut and Koole, Ruud (2000) *Parliamentary Party Groups in European Democracies: Political Parties Behind Closed Doors* (London: Routledge).

Heinderyckx, F. (1993) 'TV News Programmes in Western Europe', *European Journal of Communication*, 8(4), pp. 425–50.

Heinisch, Richard (2003) 'Success in Opposition – Failure in Government: Exploring the Performance of the Austrian Freedom Party and other European Right-wing Populist Parties in Public Office', *West European Politics*, 26(3), pp. 91–130.

Heipertz, Martin and Verdun, Amy (2003) *Ruling Europe: Theory and Politics of the Stability and Growth Pact, Draft Report* (Cologne: Max Planck Institute), available at http://www.mpifg-koeln.mpg.de/people/hz/Dokumente/hz-av_gesamt.pdf

Held, David (1987) *Models of Democracy* (Stanford: Stanford University Press).

Held, David, McGrew, Anthony, Goldblatt, David and Perraton, Jonathan (1999) *Global Transformations: Politics, Economics and Culture* (Cambridge: Polity Press).

Helms, Ludger (2005) *Presidents, Prime Ministers and Chancellors: Executive Leadership in Western Democracies* (Basingstoke: Palgrave Macmillan).

Helms, Ludger (2006) 'The Changing Parameters of Political Control in Western Europe', *Parliamentary Affairs*, 59(1), pp. 78–97.

Hemerijck, Anton, Keune, Maarten and Rhodes, Martin (2006) 'European Welfare States: Diversity, Challenges and Reforms' in Paul Heywood, Erik Jones, Martin Rhodes and Ulrich Sedelmeier (eds), *Developments in European Politics* (Basingstoke: Palgrave Macmillan).

Hemerijck, Anton and Visser, Jelle (2001) 'Dutch Lessons in Social Pragmatism', in Stuart White (ed.), *New Labour: The Progressive Future?* (Basingstoke: Palgrave Macmillan).

Henderson, Ailsa and White, Linda A. (2004) 'Shrinking Welfare States? Comparing Maternity Leave Benefits and Child Care Programs in European Union and North American Welfare States, 1985–2000', *Journal of European Public Policy*, 11(3), pp. 497–519.

Hendy, David (2000) *Radio in the Global Age* (Cambridge: Polity Press).

Hennessy, Peter (2005) 'Rulers and Servants of the State: the Blair Style of Government 1997–2004', *Parliamentary Affairs*, 58(1), pp. 6–16.

Héritier, Adrienne, Kerwer, Dieter, Knill, Christopher, Lehmkuhl, Dirk, Teutsch, Michael and Douillet, Anne-Cécile (2001) *Differential Europe: The European Union Impact on National Policy Making* (Lanham: Rowman & Littlefield).

Heyns, Barbara (2005) 'Emerging Inequalities in Central and Eastern Europe', *Annual Review of Sociology*, 31: 163–97.

Heywood, Paul, Jones, Erik, Rhodes, Martin and Sedelmeier, Ulrich (eds) (2006) *Developments in European Politics* (Basingstoke: Palgrave Macmillan).

Hick, Steven and McNutt, John G. (2002) *Advocacy, Activism and the Internet: Community Organnization and Social Policy* (Chicago: Lyceum Books).

Hicks, Alexander (1999) *Social Democracy and Welfare Capitalism: A Century of Income Security Politics* (Ithaca: Cornell University Press).

Hill, Christopher (1993) 'The Capability–Expectations Gap, or Conceptualising Europe's Global Role', *Journal of Common Market Studies*, 31(3), pp. 305–28.

Hill, Christopher (1998) 'Convergence, Divergence and Dialectics: National Foreign Policies and the CFSP', in Jan Zielonka (ed.), *Paradoxes of European Foreign Polity* (London: Kluwer).

Hill, Christopher and Smith, Michael (eds) (2005) *International Relations and the EU* (Oxford: Oxford University Press).

Hill, Kevin A. and Hughes, John E. (1998) *Cyberpolitics: Citizen Activism in the Age of the Internet* (Lanham: Rowman & Littlefield).

Hilson, C. (2002) 'New Social Movements: The Role of Legal Opportunity', *Journal of European Public Policy*, 9(2), pp. 238–55.

Hirschl, Ran (2004) *Toward Juristocracy: The Origins and Consequences of the New Constitutionalism* (Cambridge: Harvard University Press).

Hirst, Paul and Thompson, Grahame (1999) *Globalization in Question: The International Economy and the Possibilities of Governance*, 2nd edn (Cambridge: Polity Press).

Hix, S. (2002) 'Parliamentary Behavior with Two Principals: Preferences, Parties, and Voting in the European Parliament', *American Journal of Political Science*, 46(3), pp. 688–98.

Hix, Simon (2005) *The Political System of the European Union*, 2nd edn (Basingstoke: Palgrave Macmillan).

Hix, Simon and Goetz, Klaus (2000) *Europeanized Politics? European Integration and National Political Systems* (London: Frank Cass).

Hix, Simon, Kreppel, Amy and Noury, Abdul (2003) 'The Party System in the European Parliament: Collusive or Competitive?', *Journal of Common Market Studies*, 41(2), pp. 309–31.

Hix, Simon, Noury, Abdul G., and Roland, Gérard (2007) *Democratic Politics in the European Parliament* (Cambridge: Cambridge University Press).

Hobolt, Sara (2006) 'Direct Democracy and European Integration', *Journal of European Public Policy*, 13(1), pp. 153–66.

Hocking, Brian and Spence, David (2002) *Foreign Ministries in the European Union* (Basingstoke: Palgrave Macmillan).

Holbrook, Andrew and Hill, Timothy G. (2005) 'Agenda-Setting and Priming in Prime Time Television: Crime Dramas as Political Cues', *Political Communication*, 22(3), pp. 277–95.

Holland, Martin (2002) *The European Union and the Third World* (Basingstoke: Palgrave Macmillan).

Holland, Martin (2004a) 'When is Foreign Policy not Foreign Policy? Cotonou, CFSP and External Relations with the Developing World', in Martin Holland (ed.), *Common Foreign and Security Policy: The First Ten Years* (London: Continuum).

Holland, Martin (2004b) 'Development Policy: Paradigm Shifts and the "Normalization" of a Privileged Partnership', in Maria Green Cowles and Desmond Dinan (eds), *Developments in the European Union 2* (Basingstoke: Palgrave Macmillan).

Hollifield, James F. (1994) 'Immigration and Republicanism in France: The Hidden Consensus', in Wayne A. Cornelius, Philip L. Martin and James F. Hollifield (eds), *Controlling Immigration: A Global Perspective* (Stanford: Stanford University Press).

Holtz-Bacha, Christina (2004) 'Germany: How the Private Life of Politicians got into the Media', *Parliamentary Affairs*, 57(1), pp. 41–52.

Holzhacker, R. (2002) 'National Parliamentary Scrutiny over EU Issues: Comparing the Goals and Methods of Governing and Opposition Parties', *European Union Politics*, 3(4), pp. 459–80.

Hooghe, Liesbet (2007) 'What Drives Euroskepticism? Party-Public Cueing, Ideology and Strategic Opportunity', *European Union Politics*, 8, pp. 5–12.

Hooghe, Liesbet and Marks, Gary (2001) *Multi-level Governance and European Integration* (Lanham: Rowman & Littlefield).

Hooghe, Liesbet and Marks, Gary (eds) (2007) 'Understanding Euroscepticism', *Acta Politica*, Special issue, 42(2–3).

Hooghe, Liesbet, Marks, Gary and Wilson, Carole J. (2002) 'Does Left/Right Structure Party Positions in European Integration?', *Comparative Political Studies*, 35(8), pp. 965–89.

Hooghe, Marc (2002) 'Watching Television and Civic Engagements: Disentangling the Effects of Time, Programs, and Stations', *Harvard International Journal of Press/Politics*, 7(2), pp. 84–104.

Hooghe, Marc, Maddens, B. and Noppe, J. (2006) 'Why Parties Adapt: Electoral Reform, Party Finance and Party Strategy in Belgium', *Electoral Studies*, 25(2), pp. 351–68.

Hooghe, Marc and Stolle, Dietland (2003) *Generating Social Capital: Civil Society and Institutions in Comparative Perspective* (Basingstoke: Palgrave Macmillan).

Hooper, John (2006) *The New Spaniards* (London: Penguin).

Hopkin, Jonathan (1999) *Party Formation and Democratic Transition in Spain: The Creation and Collapse of the Union of Democratic Centre* (Basingstoke: Palgrave Macmillan).

Hopkin, Jonathan (2003) 'Political Decentralization, Electoral Change and Party Organizational Adaptation: A Framework for Analysis', *European Urban and Regional Studies*, 10(3), pp. 227–37.

Hopkin, Jonathan and Paolucci, Caterina (1999) 'The Business Firm Model of Party Organisation: Cases from Spain and Italy', *European Journal of Political Research*, 35(3), pp. 307–38.

Hopkins, Thomas D. (1998) 'The Czech Republic's Privatization Experience', in Demetrius S. Iatridis and June Gary Hopps (eds), *Privatization in Central and Eastern Europe: Perspectives and Approaches* (London: Praeger).

Hough, Dan (2005) 'Third Ways or New Ways? The Social Democratic Left in East Central Europe', *Political Quarterly*, 76(2), pp. 253–63.

Hough, Dan, Koß, M. and Olsen, J. (2007) *The Left Party in Contemporary German Politics* (Basingstoke: Palgrave Macmillan).

Howard, Marc Morjé (2003) *The Weakness of Civil Society in Post-Communist Europe* (Cambridge: Cambridge University Press).

Howard, Philip N. (2005) 'Deep Democracy, Thin Citizenship: The Impact of Digital Media in Political Campaign Strategy', *Annals of the American Academy of Political and Social Science*, 597, pp. 153–70.

Howarth, David (ed.) (2004) 'The Stability and Growth Pact', *Journal of European Public Policy*, Special issue, 11(5).

Howorth, Joylon (2007) *Security and Defence Policy in the European Union* (Basingstoke: Palgrave Macmillan).

Huber, Evelyne and Stephens, John D. (2001) *Development and Crisis of the Welfare State: Parties and Policies in Global Markets* (Chicago: University of Chicago Press).

Hug, Simon (2002) *Voices of Europe: Citizens, Referendums, and European Integration* (Lanham: Rowman & Littlefield).

Hughes, James, Sasse, Gwendolyn and Gordon, Claire (2004) *Europeanization and Regionalization in the EU's Enlargement to Central and Eastern Europe: The Myth of Conditionality* (Basingstoke: Palgrave Macmillan).

Hughes, Kirsty (2004) *Turkey and the European Union: Just Another Enlargement? Exploring the Implications of Turkish Accession* (Brussels: Friends of Europe Working Papers), June, available at http://www.friendsofeurope.org

Huysmans, Jef (2006) *The Politics of Insecurity: Fear, Migration and Asylum in the EU* (London: Routledge).

Hyde-Price, Adrian (2003) 'Defence and Security Policy', in Stephen Padgett, William E. Paterson and Gordon Smith (eds), *Developments in German Politics 3* (Basingstoke: Palgrave Macmillan).

Hyde-Price, Adrian (2007) *European Security in the Twenty-First Century: The Challenge of Multipolarity* (London: Routledge).

I

Iankova, Elena A. (2002) *Eastern European Capitalism in the Making* (Cambridge: Cambridge University Press).

Iatridis, Demetrius S. and Hopps, June Gary (eds) (1998) *Privatization in Central and Eastern Europe: Perspectives and Approaches* (London: Praeger).

IDEA (2003) *Funding of Political Parties and Election Campaigns* (Stockholm: IDEA).

IDEA (2007) Voter Turnout Website, http://www.idea.int/vt/index.cfm

Ignazi, Piero (2003) *Extreme Right Parties in Western Europe* (Oxford: Oxford University Press).

Imbeau, L. M., Pétry, F. and Lamari, M. (2001) 'Left–right Party Ideology and Government Policies: A Meta Analysis', *European Journal of Political Research*, 40(1), pp. 1–29.

Imig, Doug (2002) 'Contestation in the Streets: European Protests and the Emerging Euro-polity', *Comparative Political Studies*, 35(8), pp. 914–33.

Imig, Doug and Tarrow, Sidney (1999) 'The Europeanisation of movements? Contentious Politics and the European Union', in Donatella della Porta, Hanspeter Kriesi and Dieter Rucht (eds), *Social Movements in a Globalizing World* (Basingstoke: Palgrave Macmillan).

Imig, Doug and Tarrow, Sidney (2001) *Contentious Europeans: Protest and Politics in an Integrating Europe* (Lanham: Rowman & Littlefield).

Ingebritsen, Christine (2006) *Scandinavia in World Politics* (Lanham: Rowman & Littlefield).

Inglehart, Ronald and Catterberg, Gabriela (2002) 'Trends in Political Action: the Developmental Trend and the Post-Honeymoon Decline', *International Journal of Comparative Sociology*, 43(3–5), pp. 300–16.

Inglehart, Ronald and Norris, Pippa (2000) 'The Development Theory of the Gender Gap: Women's and Men's Voting in Global Perspective', *International Political Science Review*, 21(4), pp. 441–63.

Inglehart, Ronald and Rabier, Jacques-René (1986) 'Political Realignment in Advanced Industrial Society: From Class-based Politics to Quality of Life Politics', *Government and Opposition*, 21, pp. 456–79.

Internet World Stats (2007) http://www.internetworldstats.com

Iversen, Torben and Soskice, David (2006) 'Electoral Institutions and the Politics of Coalitions: Why Some Democracies Redistribute More Than Others', *American Political Science Review*, 100 (2), pp. 165–81.

J

Jagers, Jan and Walgrave, Stefaan (2007) 'Populism as Political Communication Style: An Empirical Study of Political Parties' Discourse in Belgium', *European Journal of Political Research*, 46(3), pp. 319–45.

Jakubowicz, Karol (2004) 'Ideas in Our Heads. Introduction of PSB as Part of Media System Change in Central and Eastern Europe', *European Journal of Communication*, 19(1), pp. 53–74.

Jasiewicz, Krzysztof (2007) 'Parties and Party System in Poland', in Paul Webb and Stephen White, (eds), *Party Politics in New Democracies* (Oxford: Oxford University Press).

Jeffries, Stuart (2002) 'How the French Lost their Cleavage', *Guardian*, 15 April 2004.

Johansson, Karl Magnus and Zervakis A. Peter (eds) (2002) *European Political Parties between Cooperation and Integration 2002* (Baden-Baden: Nomos Verlag).

Johns, Robert and Shephard, Mark (2007) 'Gender, Candidate Image and Electoral Preference', *British Journal of Politics and International Relations*, 9(3), pp. 434–60.

Jones, Erik (2002) *The Politics of Economic and Monetary Union: Integration and Idiosyncrasy* (Lanham: Rowman & Littlefield).

Jones, Erik (2007) *The Dark Heart of Italy* (London: Faber).

Jones, Erik and Verdun, Amy (eds) (2004) *The Political Economy of European Integration: Arguments and Analysis* (London: Routledge).

Joppke, Christian (2002) 'European Immigration Policies at the Crossroads', in Paul Heywood, Erik Jones and Martin Rhodes (eds), *Developments in West European Politics* (Basingstoke: Palgrave Macmillan).

Joppke, Christian (2007a) 'Beyond National Models: Civic Integration Policies for Immigrants in Western Europe', *West European Politics*, 30 (1): 1–22.

Joppke, Christian (2007b) 'Transformation of Immigrant Integration: Civic Integration and Antidiscrimination in the Netherlands, France and Germany', *World Politics*, 59, pp. 243–73.

Jordan, Andrew (ed.) (2001) *Environmental Policy in the European Union: Actors, Institutions and Processes* (London: Earthscan).

Jordan, Grant and Maloney, William (1997) *Protest Businesses? Mobilising Campaigning Groups* (Manchester: Manchester University Press).

Jordan, Grant and Maloney, William (2006) '"Letting George Do It": Does Olson Explain Low Levels of Participation?', *Journal of Elections, Public Opinion and Parties*, 16(2), pp. 115–39.

Jorgensen Knud Erik, Pollack, Mark and Rosamond, Ben J. (eds) (2007) *The Sage Handbook of European Union Politics* (London: Sage)

Judt, Tony (2007) *Postwar: A History of Europe Since 1945* (London: Pimlico).

Jungerstam-Mulders, Susanne (ed.) (2006) *Post-Communist EU Member States: Parties and Party Systems* (Aldershot: Ashgate).

K

Kagan, Robert (2002) 'Power and Weakness', Policy Review (Hoover Institution), 113, available at http://www.policyreview.org/JUN02/kagan.html

Kagan, Robert (2004) *Paradise and Power: America and Europe in the New World Order* (New York: Atlantic Books).

Kaid, Lynda and Holz-Bacha, Christina (2006) *The Sage Handbook of Political Advertising* (London: Sage).

Kalogeropoulou, Efthalia (1989) 'Election Promises and Government Performance in Greece: PASOK's Fulfilment of its 1981 Election Pledges', *European Journal of Political Research*, 17(3), pp. 289–311.

Karvonnen, Lauri (2004) 'Preferential Voting: Incidence and Effects', *International Political Science Review*, 25(2), pp. 203–26.

Karyotis, Georgios (2007) 'European Migration Policy in the Aftermath of September 11: The Security–Migration Nexus, *Innovation*, 20(1), pp. 1–17.

Katz, Richard and Crotty, William (eds) (2006) *Handbook of Party Politics* (London: Sage).

Katz, Richard and Mair, Peter (1995) 'Changing Models of Party Organization and Party Democracy: The Emergence of the Cartel Party', *Party Politics*, 1(1), pp. 8–28.

Kaufman, Bruno and Waters, M. Dane (2004) *Direct Democracy in Europe: A Comprehensive Reference Guide to the Initiative and Referendum Process in Europe* (Durham, NC: Carolina Academic Press).

Keating, Michael (2000) *The New Regionalism in Western Europe: Territorial Restructuring and Political Change* (Aldershot: Edward Elgar).

Keating, Michael (2001) *Nations Against the State: The New Politics of Nationalism in Quebec, Catalonia and Scotland* (Basingstoke: Palgrave Macmillan).

Keating, Michael (2006) 'Territorial Politics in Europe', in Paul Heywood, Erik Jones, Martin Rhodes and Ulrich Sedelmeier (eds), *Developments in European Politics* (Basingstoke: Palgrave Macmillan).

Keating, Michael and Hooghe, Liesbet (1996) 'By-passing the Nation State? Regions and the EU Policy Process', in Jeremy Richardson (ed.), *European Union: Power and Policy Making* (London: Routledge), pp. 216–29.

Keating, Michael, Loughlin, John and Deschouwer, Kris (2005) *Culture, Institutions and Economic Development* (Aldershot: Edward Elgar).

Kelley, Judith (2004) 'International Actors on the Domestic

Scene: Membership Conditionality and Socialization by International Institutions', *International Organization*, 58, pp. 425–57.

Keman, Hans (2002a) 'The Low Countries: Confrontation and Coalition in Segmented Societies', in Josep M. Colomer (ed.), *Political Institutions in Europe* (London: Routledge).

Keman, Hans (2002b) *Comparative Democratic Politics* (Oxford: Oxford University Press)

Keman, Hans (2003) 'Explaining Miracles: Third Ways and Work and Welfare', *West European Politics*, 26(2), pp. 115–35.

Kennedy, Paul (2000) 'Spain', in Ian Manners and Richard G. Whitman (eds), *The Foreign Policies of European Union Member States* (Manchester: Manchester University Press).

Kent, Neil (2008) *A Concise History of Sweden* (Cambridge: Cambridge University Press).

Kenworthy, Lane (2004) *Egalitarian Capitalism: Jobs, Incomes and Growth in Affluent Countries* (New York: Russell Sage Foundation).

Kenworthy, Lane and Pontusson, Jonas (2005) 'Rising Inequality and the Politics of Redistribution in Affluent Countries', *Perspectives on Politics*, 3(3), pp. 449–71.

Kepplinger, Hans Mathias (2007) 'Reciprocal Effects: Towards a Theory of Mass Media Effects on Decision Makers', *Harvard Journal of Press/Politics*, 12(2), pp. 3–23.

Ker-Lindsay, James (2006) 'Presidential Power and Authority in the Republic of Cyprus', *Mediterranean Politics*, 11(1), pp. 21–37.

Kersbergen, Kees van (1995) *Social Capitalism: A Study of Christian Democracy and the Welfare State* (London: Routledge).

Kersbergen, Kees van (2003) 'The Politics and Political Economy of Social Democracy', *Acta Politica*, 38(3), pp. 255–73.

Kersbergen, Kees van (2000) 'The Declining Resistance of Welfare States to Change?', in Stein Kuhnle (ed.), *Survival of the European Welfare State* (London: Routledge/ECPR).

Kersbergen, Kees van, Hemerijck, Anton and Manow, Philip (2000) 'Welfare without Work? Divergent Experiences of Reform in Germany and the Netherlands', in Stein Kuhnle (ed.), *The Survival of the European Welfare State* (London: Routledge).

Kersbergen, Kees van and Krouwel, André (2008) 'A Double-Edged Sword! The Dutch Centre-Right and the "Foreigners Issue"', in Tim Bale (ed.), *Immigration and Integration Policy in Europe: Why Politics – and the Centre-Right – Matter* (London: Routledge).

Keune, Maarten (2006) 'The European Social Model and Enlargement', in M. Jepsen and A. Serrano (eds), *Unwrapping the European Social Model* (Bristol: Policy Press).

Kevin, Deirdre (2003) *Europe in the Media: A Comparison of Reporting: Representation and Rhetoric in National Media Systems* (Mahwah: Lawrence Erlbaum & Associates).

King, Anthony (1975) 'Overload: Problems of Governing in the 1970s', *Political Studies*, 23(2–3), pp. 284–96.

King, Anthony (1976) 'Modes of Executive–Legislative Relations: Great Britain, France and West Germany', *Legislative Studies Quarterly*, 1(1), pp. 11–36.

King, Anthony (1994) '"Chief Executives" in Western Europe', in Ian Budge and David McKay (eds), *Developing Democracy: Comparative Research in Honour of J.F.P. Blondel* (London: Sage).

King, Anthony (ed.) (2002) *Leaders' Personalities and the Outcomes of Democratic Elections* (Oxford: Oxford University Press).

Kirchheimer, Otto (1966) 'The Transformation of the Western European Party System', in Joseph La Palombara and Myrah Weiner (eds), *Political Parties and Political Development* (Princeton: Princeton University Press).

Kirchner, Emil J. (2006) 'The Challenge of European Security Governance', *Journal of Common Market Studies*, 44(5), pp. 947–68.

Kirchner, Emil J. and Sperling, James (2007) *EU Security Governance* (Manchester: Manchester University Press).

Kiss, Csilla (2002) 'From Liberalism to Conservatism: The Federation of Young Democrats in Post-Communist Hungary', *East European Politics and Societies*, 16(3), pp. 739–63.

Kitschelt, Herbert (1994) *The Transformation of European Social Democracy* (Cambridge: Cambridge University Press).

Kitschelt, Herbert (2000) 'Citizens, Politicians, and Party Cartellization: Political Representation and State Failure in Post Industrial Democracies', *European Journal of Political Research*, 37, pp. 149–79.

Kitschelt, Herbert, (2007) 'Growth and Persistence of the Radical Right in Postindustrial Democracies: Advances and Challenges in Comparative Research', *West European Politics*, 30(5), pp. 1176–206

Kittel, Bernhard and Obinger, Herbert (2003) 'Political Parties, Institutions, and the Dynamics of Social Expenditure in Times of Austerity', *Journal of European Public Policy*, 10(1), pp. 20–45.

Kittilson, Miki Caul (2006) *Challenging Parties, Changing Parliaments: Women and Elected Office in Contemporary Western Europe* (Columbus: Ohio State University Press).

Klausen, Jytte (2005) *The Islamic Challenge: Politics and Religion in Western Europe* (Oxford: Oxford University Press).

Kleinnijenhuis, Jan, Maurer, Marcus, Kepplinger, Hans Mathias and Oegema, Dirk (2001) 'Issues and Personalities in German and Dutch Television News: Patterns and Effects', *European Journal of Communication*, 16(3), pp. 337–59.

Klich, Jacek (1998) 'The Concept of Mass Privatization in Poland: Theoretical and Practical Considerations', in Demetrius S. Iatridis and June Gary Hopps (eds), *Privitization in Central and Eastern Europe: Perspectives and Approaches* (London: Praeger).

Klitgaard, Michael B. (2007) 'Why are They Doing It? Social Democracy and Market-Oriented Welfare State Reforms', *West European Politics*, 30(1), pp. 172–94.

Knapp, Andrew and Wright, Vincent (2006) *Government and Politics of France* (London: Routledge).

Knodt, Michèle and Princen, Sebastiaan (2003) *Understanding the European Union's External Relations* (London: Routledge).

Knutsen, Oddbjørn (2004) 'Religious Denomination and Party Choice in Western Europe: A Comparative Longitudinal Study from Eight Countries, 1970–97', *International Political Science Review*, 25(1), pp. 97–128.

Knutsen, Oddbjørn (2005) 'The Impact of Sector Employment on Party Choice: A Comparative Study of Eight West European Countries', *European Journal of Political Research*, 44(4), pp. 593–621.

Knutsen, Oddbjørn (2006) *Class Voting in Western Europe: A Comparative Longitudinal Study* (Lanham: Lexington Books).

Knutsen, Oddbjørn and Scarbrough, Elinor (1995), 'Cleavage Politics', in Jan W. van Deth and Elinor Scarbrough (eds), *The Impact of Values* (Oxford: Oxford University Press).

Koopmans, Ruud (2004) 'Integrated Report: Cross-National, Cross-Issue, Cross-Time', Project report for the EU-funded project *The Transformation of Political Mobilisation and Communication in European Public Spheres*, available at http://europub.wz-berlin.de/project%20reports.en.htm

Koopmans, Ruud and Erbe, Jessica (2004) 'Towards a European Public Sphere?', *Innovation: The European Journal of Social Sciences*, 17(2), pp. 97–118.

Kopecký, Petr (2007) 'Structures of Representation', in Stephen White, Paul G. Lewis and Judy Batt (eds) *Developments in Central and East European Politics* (Basingstoke: Palgrave Macmillan).

Kopecký, Petr and Mudde, Cas (2002) *Uncivil Society: Contentious Politics in Post-communist Europe* (London: Routledge).

Korpi, Walter and Palme, Joakim (2003) 'New Politics and Class Politics in the Context of Austerity and Globalization: Welfare State Regress in 18 Countries, 1975–95', *American Political Science Review*, 97(3), pp. 425–46.

Korupp, Sylvia E. and Szydlik, Marc (2005) *European Sociological Review*, 21(4), pp. 409–22.

Kostadinova, Tatiana (2003) 'Voter Turnout Dynamics in Post-communist Europe', *European Journal of Political Research*, 42(6), pp. 741–60.

Kovács, János Mátyás (2002) 'Approaching the EU and Reaching the US? Rival Narratives on Transforming Welfare Regimes in East-Central Europe', *West European Politics*, 25(2), pp. 175–204.

Kreidel, Miroslav and Vlachová, Klára (2003) 'Rise and Decline of Right-Wing Extremism in the Czech Republic in the 1990s', *Czech Sociological Review*, 8(1), pp. 69–910.

Kreppel, A. (2000) 'Rules, Ideology and Coalition Formation in the European Parliament: Past, Present and Future', *European Union Politics*, 1(3), pp. 340–62.

Kreppel, A. (2002) *The European Parliament and Supranational Party System* (Cambridge: Cambridge University Press).

Kriesi, Hanspeter (1998) 'The Transformation of Cleavage Politics', *European Journal of Political Research*, 33, pp. 165–85.

Kriesi, Hanspeter (2007) 'The Role of European Integration in National Election Campaigns' *European Union Politics*, 8(1), pp. 83–108.

Kriesi, Hanspeter, Armingeon, Klaus, Siegrist, Hannes and Wimmer, Andreas (eds) (2003) *Nation and National Identity: The European Experience in Perspective* (West Lafayette: Purdue University Press).

Kriesi, Hanspeter, Koopmans, Ruud, Duyvendak, Jan Willem and Giugni, Marco G. (1995) *New Social Movements in Western Europe: A Comparative Analysis* (London: UCL Press).

Krönig, Jürgen (2006) 'Hotting it up', in John Lloyd and Jean Seaton (eds), *What Can be Done? Making the Media and Politics Better* (Oxford: Oxford Blackwell).

Krouwel, André (2006) 'Party Models', in Richard Katz and William Crotty (eds) (2006) *Handbook of Party Politics* (London: Sage).

Krupavicius, Algis (2007) 'Lithuania', *European Journal of Political Research*, 46(7–8).

Kselman, Thomas and Buttigieg, Joseph A. (eds) (2003) *European Christian Democracy: Historical Legacies and Comparative Perspectives* (Notre Dame: University of Notre Dame Press).

Kuhn, Raymond (2004) '"Vive la différence"? The Mediation of Politicians' Public Images and Private Lives in France', *Parliamentary Affairs*, 57(1), pp. 24–40.

L

Laatikainen, Katie and Smith, Karen E. (2006) *The European Union at the United Nations* (Basingstoke; Palgrave Macmillan).

Ladrech, Robert (2000) *Social Democracy and the Challenge of European Union* (Boulder: Lynne Rienner).

Ladrech, Robert (2002) 'Europeanization and Political Parties: Towards a Framework for Analysis', *Party Politics*, 8(4), pp. 389–403.

Lahav, Gallya (2004) *Immigration and Politics in the New Europe: Reinventing Borders* (Cambridge: Cambridge University Press).

Lahav, Gallya and Guiraudon, Virginie (eds) (2006) *West European Politics*, 29(2).

Lahusen, Christian (2004) 'Joining the Cocktail Circuit: Social Movement Organizations at the European Union', *Mobilization*, 9(1), pp. 55–71.

Laitin, David D. (2002) 'Culture and National Identity: "The East" and European Integration', *West European Politics*, 25(2), pp. 55–80.

Lang, Sabine (2004) 'Local Political Communication: Media and Local Publics in the Age of Globalization', in Frank Esser and Barbara Pfetsch (eds) *Comparing Political Communication: Theories, Cases, and Challenges* (Cambridge: Cambridge University Press).

Lange, Sarah L. de (2007) 'A New Winning Formula? The Programmatic Appeal of the Radical Right', *Party Politics*, 13(4), pp. 411–35.

Lauf, Edmund (2001) 'The Vanishing Young Reader: Socio-demographic Determinants of Newspaper Use as a Source of Political Information in Europe, 1980–1998', *European Journal of Communication*, 16(2), pp. 233–43.

Lawson, Kay and Merkl, Peter (2007) *When Political Parties Prosper: The Uses of Electoral Success* (Boulder: Lynne Rienner)

LeDuc, Lawrence (2003) *The Politics of Direct Democracy: Referendums in Global Perspective* (Toronto: Broadview Press).

Lelieveldt, Herman and Caiani, Manuela (2007) 'The Political Role of Associations', in William A. Maloney and Sigrid Roßteutscher (eds), *Social Capital and Associations in European Democracies: A Comparative Analysis* (London: Routledge).

Levy, Jonah (1999) 'Vice into Virtue? Progressive Politics and Welfare Reform in Continental Europe', *Politics and Society*, 27(2), pp. 239–74.

Levy, Jonah (ed.) (2006) *The State After Statism: New State Activities in the Age of Liberalization* (Cambridge: Harvard University Press).

Levy, Mark R. (1981) 'Disdaining the News', *Journal of Communication*, 31(3), pp. 24–31.

Lewanski, Rudolf (1999) 'Italian Administration in Transition', *South European Society and Politics*, 4(1), pp. 97–131.

Lewanski, Rudolf (2000) 'The Development and Current Features of the Italian Civil Service System', in Hans A.G.M.

Bekke and Frits M. van der Meer (eds), *Civil Service Systems in Western Europe* (Cheltenham: Edward Elgar).

Lewis, Paul G. (2006) 'Party Systems in Post-communist Central Europe: Patterns of Stability and Consolidation', *Democratization*, 13(4), pp. 562–83.

Lewis, Paul G. and Mansfeldova, Zdenka (eds) (2007) *The European Union and Party Politics in Central and Eastern Europe* (Basingstoke: Palgrave Macmillan).

Lightfoot, Simon (2005) *Europeanizing Social Democracy? The Rise of the Party of European Socialists* (London: Routledge).

Lindblom, Charles (1977) *Politics and Markets* (New York: Basic Books).

Lijphart, Arend (1999) *Patterns of Democracy: Government Forms and Performance in Thirty-six Countries* (New Haven, CT: Yale University Press).

Lindbom, Anders (2006) 'The Swedish Conservative Party and the Welfare State. Institutional Change and Adapting Preferences', available at http://www.framtidsstudier.se/file-bank/
files/20061219$150744$fil$WzVdt44BrN9HJWw03jVb.pdf

Lipset, Seymour Martin and Rokkan, Stein (1967) 'Cleavage Structures, Party Systems and Voter Alignments: An Introduction', in Seymour Martin Lipset and Stein Rokkan (eds), *Party Systems and Voter Alignments: Cross-National Perspectives* (New York: Free Press).

Lloyd, John (2004) *What the Media are Doing to Our Politics* (London: Constable).

Lloyd, John (2005) 'The Epiphany of Joe Trippi', *Political Quarterly*, 76, pp. 33–45.

Lord, Christopher (2004) *A Democratic Audit of the European Union* (Basingstoke: Palgrave Macmillan).

Louw, Eric (2005) *The Media and Political Process* (London: Sage).

Lubbers, Marcel, Gijsberts, Merove and Scheepers, Peer (2002) 'Extreme Right-wing Voting in Europe,' *European Journal of Political Research*, 41(3), pp. 345–78.

Lucassen, L. (2006) *The Immigrant Threat: the Integration of Old and New Migrants in Western Europe since 1850* (Chicago: University of Illinois Press).

Lukowski, Jerzy and Zawadzki, Hubert (2006) *A Concise History of Poland* (Cambridge: Cambridge University Press).

Lundell, Krister (2004) 'Determinants of Candidate Selection: The Degree of Centralization in Comparative Perspective', *Party Politics*, 10(1), pp. 25–47.

Lundestad, Geir (1998a) *Empire by Integration: The United States and European Integration, 1945–1997* (Oxford: Oxford University Press).

Lundestad, Geir (1998b) *No End to Alliance. The United States and Western Europe: Past, Present and Future* (Basingstoke: Palgrave Macmillan).

Luther, Kurt Richard (2003) 'The Self-Destruction of a Right-Wing Populist Party? The Austrian Parliamentary Election of 2002', *West European Politics*, 26(3), pp. 91–130.

Luther, Kurt Richard and Müller-Rommel, Ferdinand (eds) (2002) *Political Parties in the New Europe: Political and Analytical Challenges* (Oxford: Oxford University Press).

M

MacInnes, John (2006) 'Work–Life Balance in Europe: A Response to the Baby Bust or Reward for the Baby Boomers?', *European Societies*, 8(2), pp. 223–49.

Machill, Marcel, Beiler, Markus and Fischer, Corinna (2006) 'Europe-Topics in Europe's Media. The Debate about the European Public Sphere: A Meta-Analysis of Media Content Analyses', *European Journal of Communication*, 21(1), pp. 57–88.

Magalhães, Pedro C. (2007) 'What Are (Semi)Presidential Elections About? A Case Study of the Portuguese 2006 Elections', *Journal of Elections, Public Opinion and Parties*, 17(3), pp. 263–91.

Magone, José M. (2007) 'Portugal', *European Journal of Political Research*, 46(7–8).

Magone, José M. (2008) *Contemporary Spanish Politics* (London: Routledge).

Mahler, Vincent A. (2004) 'Economic Globalization, Domestic Politics, and Income Inequality in the Developed Countries: A Cross-National Study', *Comparative Politics*, 37(9), pp. 1025–53.

Mailand, Mikkel and Due, Jesper (2004) 'Social Dialogue in Central and Eastern Europe: Present State and Future Development', *European Journal of Industrial Relations*, 10 (2), pp. 179–97.

Mainwaring, Scott and Zoco, Edurne (2007) 'Political Sequences and the Stabilization of Interparty Competition Electoral Volatility in Old and New Democracies', *Party Politics*, 13(2), pp. 155–78.

Mair, Peter (1996) 'Party Systems and Structures of Competition', in Lawrence le Dine, Richard G. Niemi and Pippa Norris (eds), *Comparing Democracies: Elections and Voting in Comparative Perspective* (London: Sage).

Mair, Peter (2000) 'The Limited Impact of Europe on National Party Systems', *West European Politics*, 23 (4), pp. 27–51.

Mair, Peter (2001) 'The Green Challenge and Political Competition: How Typical is the German Experience?', *German Politics*, 10(2), pp. 99–116.

Mair, Peter (2002) 'In the Aggregate: Mass Electoral Behaviour in Western Europe, 1950–2000', in Hans Keman (ed.), *Comparative Democratic Politics: A Guide to Contemporary Theory and Research* (London: Sage).

Mair, Peter (2006a) 'Political Parties and Party Systems', in Paolo Graziano and Maarten Vink, (eds), *Europeanization: New Research Agendas* (Basingstoke: Palgrave Macmillan).

Mair, Peter (2006b) 'Ruling the Void: The Hollowing of Western Democracy', *New Left Review*, 42, pp. 25–52.

Mair, Peter and Biezen, Ingrid van (2001) 'Party Membership in Europe, 1980–2000', *Party Politics*, 7(1), pp. 5–21.

Mair, Peter and Mudde, Cas (1998) 'The Party Family and its Study', *Annual Review of Political Science*, 1, pp. 211–29.

Mair, Peter, Müller, Wolfgang and Plasser, Fritz (eds) (2004) *Political Parties and Electoral Change* (London: Sage).

Majone, Giandomenico (1996) *Regulating Europe* (London: Routledge).

Malgin, Artem (2002) 'The Commonwealth of Independent States: Summary of a Decade', *Russian Politics and Law*, 40(5), pp. 43–54.

Maloney, William A. and Roßteutscher, Sigrid (eds) (2007a)

Social Capital and Associations in European Democracies: A Comparative Analysis (London: Routledge).

Maloney, William A. and Roßteutscher, Sigrid (2007b) 'Associations, Participation and Democracy', in William A. Maloney and Sigrid Roßteutscher (eds), *Social Capital and Associations in European Democracies: A Comparative Analysis* (London: Routledge).

Mangott, Gerhard (2000) 'Farewell to Russia: The Decline of a Global Power', in Heinz Gartner, Adrian Hyde-Price and Erich Reiter (eds), *Europe's New Security Challenges* (Boulder: Lynne Rienner).

Mann, Michael (1997) 'Has Globalization Ended the Rise and Rise of the Nation State?', *Review of International Political Economy*, 4(3), pp. 472–96.

Manners, Ian and Whitman, Richard G. (eds) (2000) *The Foreign Policies of European Union Member States* (Manchester: Manchester University Press).

Manow, Philip, Schäfer, Armin and Zorn, Hendrik (2008) 'Europe's Party Political Centre of Gravity, 1957–2003' *Journal of European Public Policy*, 15(1), pp. 20–39.

Markovits, Andrei (2004) 'European Anti-Americanism (and Anti-Semitism): Ever Present though always Denied', Harvard Centre for European Studies Working Paper 108, available at http://www.ces.fas.harvard.edu/working_papers/Markovits.pdf

Markovits, Andrei (2005) *European Anti-Americanism and Anti-Semitism in a Changing Transatlantic Relationship* (Princeton: Princeton University Press).

Marks, Gary and Steenbergen, Marco R. (eds) (2004) *European Integration and Political Conflict* (Cambridge: Cambridge University Press).

Marsh, Michael (2007) 'Candidates or Parties? Objects of Electoral Choice in Ireland', *Party Politics*, 13(4), pp. 500–27.

Martell, Luke (2001) 'Capitalism, Globalization and Democracy: Does Social Democracy have a Role?' in Luke Martell (ed.), *Social Democracy: Global and National Perspectives* (Basingstoke: Palgrave Macmillan).

Marthaler, Sally (2008) 'Nicolas Sarkozy and the Politics of French Immigration Policy', *Journal of European Public Policy*, 15(3).

Martin, Andrew and Ross, George (eds) (2004) *Euros and Europeans: Monetary Integration and the European Model of Society* (Cambridge: Cambridge University Press).

Martinez-Herrera, Enric (2002) 'From Nation Building to Building Identification with Political Communities: Consequences of Political Decentralisation in Spain, the Basque Country, Catalonia and Galicia, 1978–2001', *European Journal of Political Research*, 41, pp. 421–53.

Massetti, Emanuele (2006) 'Electoral Reform in Italy: From PR to Mixed System and (Almost) Back Again', *Representation*, 42(3), pp. 261–9.

Mateju, P. and Vlachová, K. (1998) 'Values and Electoral Decisions in the Czech Republic', *Communist and Post-Communist Studies*, 31(3), pp. 249–69.

Mateo Diaz, Mercedes (2005) *Representing Women? Female Legislators in West European Parliaments* (Colchester: ECPR Press).

Matland, Richard E. and Studlar, Donley T. (2004) 'Determinants of Legislative Turnover: A Cross-National Analysis', *British Journal of Political Science*, 34, pp. 87–108.

Mattson, Ingvar and Strøm, Kaare (2004) 'Committee Effects on Legislation', in Herbert Döring and Mark Hallerberg (eds), *Patterns of Parliamentary Behaviour* (Aldershot: Ashgate).

Maull, Hanns W. (1990) 'Germany and Japan: The New Civilian Powers', *Foreign Affairs*, 69(5), pp. 91–106.

Maull, Hanns, W. (ed.) (2006) *Germany's Uncertain Power: Foreign Policy of the Berlin Republic* (Basingstoke: Palgrave Macmillan).

Maurer, Andreas, Mittag, Jürgen and Wessels, Wolfgang (2003) 'National Systems' Adaptation to the EU System: Trends, Offers, and Constraints', in Beate Kohler-Koch (ed.), *Linking EU and National Governance* (Oxford: Oxford University Press).

Maurer, Andreas and Wessels, Wolfgang (2001) *National Parliaments on their Ways to Europe: Losers or Latecomers?* (Baden-Baden: Nomos).

Mazower, Mark (1998) *Dark Continent: Europe's Twentieth Century* (London: Allen Lane).

Mazzoleni, Gianpietro (1987) 'Media Logic and Parry Logic in Campaign Coverage: The Italian General Election of 1983', *European Journal of Communication*, 2(1), pp. 81–103.

Mazzoleni, Gianpietro, Stewart, Julianne and Horsfield, Bruce (eds) (2003) *The Media and Neo Populism: A Contemporary Comparative Analysis* (London: Praeger).

McAdam, Doug, McCarthy, John D. and Zald, Mayer N. (eds) (1996) *Comparative Perspectives on Social Movements: Political Opportunities, Mobilizing Structures, and Cultural Framings* (NewYork: Cambridge University Press).

McAllister, Ian and White, Stephen (2007) 'Political Parties and Democratic Consolidation in Post-Communist Societies', *Party Politics*, 13(2), pp. 197–216.

McCarthy, John D. and Zald, Mayer N. (1977) 'Resource Mobilization and Social Movements: A Partial Theory', *American Journal of Sociology*, 8(6), pp. 1212–41.

McCormick, John (2001) *Environmental Policy in the European Union* (Basingstoke: Palgrave Macmillan).

McCormick, John (2006) *The European Superpower* (Basingstoke: Palgrave Macmillan).

McCormick, John (2007) *Contemporary Britain*, 2nd edn (Basingstoke: Palgrave Macmillan).

McCormick, John (2008) *Understanding the European Union*, 4th edn (Basingstoke: Palgrave Macmillan).

McGarry, John and Keating, Michael (eds) (2006) *European Integration and the Nationalities Question* (London: Routledge).

McGowan, Francis (2001) 'Social Democracy and the European Union: Who's Changing Whom?', in Luke Martell (ed.), *Social Democracy: Global and Local Perspectives* (Basingstoke: Palgrave Macmillan).

McMenamin, Iain (2002) 'Polish Business Associations: Flattened Civil Society or Super Lobbies?', *Business and Politics*, 4, pp. 299–315.

McNair, Brian (2007) *An Introduction to Political Communication* (London: Routledge).

McNair, Brian, Hibberd, Matthew and Schlesinger, Philip (2002) 'Public Access Broadcasting and Democratic Participation in the Age of Mediated Politics', *Journalism Review*, 3(3), pp. 407–22.

McQuail, Denis (1998) 'Commercialization and Beyond', in Denis

McQuail and Karen Siune (eds), *Media Policy: Convergence, Concentration and Commerce* (London: Sage).
McQuail, Denis (2001) 'The Media in Europe', in Montserrat Guibernau (ed.), *Governing European Diversity* (London: Sage).
Meehan, Elizabeth (1993) 'Citizenship and the European Community', *Political Quarterly*, 64(2), pp. 172–86.
Meguid, Bonnie (2005) 'Competition between Unequals: The Role of Mainstream Party Strategy in Niche Party Success', *American Political Science Review*, 99(3), pp. 347–59.
Menon, Anand (2004a) 'The Foreign and Security Policies of the European Union', in Maria Green Cowles and Desmond Dinan (eds), *Developments in the European Union 2* (Basingstoke: Palgrave Macmillan).
Menon, Anand (2004b) 'From Crisis to Catharsis: ESDP after Iraq', *International Affairs*, 80(4), pp. 631–49.
Mény Yves and Surel, Yves (eds) (2002) *Democracies and the Populist Challenge* (Basingstoke: Palgrave Macmillan).
Merkel, Wolfgang (1992) 'After the Golden Age', in Christiane Lemke and Gary Marks (eds) *The Crisis of Socialism in Europe* (Durham, NC: Duke University Press.)
Messina, Anthony M. (2007) *The Logics and Politics of Post-WWII Migration to Western Europe* (Cambridge: Cambridge University Press).
Messina, Anthony M. and Lahav, Gallya (2005) *The Migration Reader: Exploring Politics and Policies* (Boulder: Lynne Rienner).
Messmer, William B. (2003) 'Taming Labour's MEPs', *Party Politics*, 9(2), pp. 201–18.
Meunier, Sophie (2007) *Trading Voices: The European Union in International Commercial Negotiations* (Princeton: Princeton University Press).
Meunier, Sophie and McNamara, Kathleen R. (eds) (2007) *Making History: European Integration and Institutional Change at Fifty* (Oxford: Oxford University Press).
Meyer, Philip (2004) *The Vanishing Newspaper: Saving Journalism in the Information Age* (Columbia: University of Missouri Press).
Meyer-Sahling, Jan-Hinrik (2004) 'Civil Service Reforms in Post-Communist Europe', *West European Politics*, 27(1), pp. 71–103.
Meyrede, Laurant (1999) 'France's Foreign Policy in the Mediterranean', in Stelios Stavridis, Theodore Couloumbis, Thanos Veremis and Neville Waites (eds), *Foreign Policies of the EU's Mediterranean States and Applicant Countries in the 1990s* (Basingstoke: Palgrave Macmillan).
Michels, Robert (1962) *Political Parties: A Sociological Study of the Oligarchical Tendencies of Modern Democracy* (New York: Free Press), also available at http://religionanddemocracy.lib.virginia.edu/library/tocs/MichPoli.html
Miley, Thomas Jeffrey (2007) 'Against the Thesis of the "Civic Nation": The Case of Catalonia in Contemporary Spain', *Nationalism and Ethnic Politics*, 13(1), pp. 1–37.
Millard, Frances (2004) *Elections, Parties and Representation in Post-Communist Europe* (Basingstoke: Palgrave Macmillan).
Milner, Henry (2002) *Civic Literacy: How Informed Citizens Make Democracy Work* (London: Tufts University Press).
Minkinberg, M. (2002) 'The New Radical Right in the Political Process: Interaction Effects in France and Germany', in M. Schain, A. Zolberg and P. Hossay (eds), *Shadows Over Europe: The Development and Impact of the Extreme Right Wing in Western Europe* (Basingstoke: Palgrave Macmillan).
Miskimmon, Alister (2007) *Germany and the Common Foreign and Security Policy of the European Union: Between Europeanization and National Adaptation* (Basingstoke: Palgrave Macmillan).
Mitchell, Paul (2005) 'United Kingdom: Plurality Rule Under Siege', in Michael Gallagher and Paul Mitchell (eds), *The Politics of Electoral Systems* (Oxford: Oxford University Press).
Molina, Oscar and Rhodes, Martin (2002) 'Corporatism: The Past, Present and Future of a Concept', *Annual Review of Political Science*, 5, pp. 305–31.
Molle, Willem (2001) *The Economics of European Integration: Theory, Practice, Policy* (Aldershot: Ashgate).
Monar, Jörg (2007) 'Common Threat and Common Response? The European Union's Counter-Terrorism Strategy and its Problems', *Government and Opposition*, 42(3), pp. 292–313.
Morales, Laura and Geurts, Peter (2006) 'Associational Involvement' in Jan van Deth, José Ramón Montero and Anders Westholm (eds), *Citizenship and Involvement in European Democracies: A Comparative Analysis* (London: Routledge).
Moran, Michael (2005) *Politics and Governance in the UK* (Basingstoke: Palgrave Macmillan).
Moran, Michael, Rein, Martin and Goodin, Robert E. (2006) *The Oxford Handbook of Public Policy* (Oxford: Oxford University Press).
Moravcsik, Andrew (2001) *The Choice for Europe: Social Purpose and State Power from Messina to Maastricht* (Ithaca: Cornell University Press).
Mudde, Cas (2004) 'The Populist Zeitgeist', *Government and Opposition*, 39(3), pp. 541–63.
Mudde, Cas (2007) *Populist Radical Right Parties in Europe* (Cambridge: Cambridge University Press).
Mueller, J. (1994) 'The Catastrophe Quota', *Journal of Conflict Resolution*, 38(3), pp. 355–75.
Müftüler-Bac, Meltem (1997) *Turkey's Relations with a Changing Europe* (Manchester: Manchester University Press).
Mughan, Anthony (2000) *Media and the Presidentialization of Parliamentary Elections* (Basingstoke: Palgrave Macmillan).
Müller, Wolfgang C. and Saalfield, Thomas (eds) (1997) *Members of Parliament in Western Europe: Roles and Behaviour* (London: Frank Cass).
Müller, Wolfgang C. and Strøm, K. (eds) (2000) *Coalition Governments in Western Europe* (Oxford: Oxford University Press).
Murray, Philomena (2003) 'An Asia Pacific Response to the European Union: Australian Elite Perceptions', *Asia-Europe Journal*, 1, pp. 103–19.
Murray, Rainbow (2007) 'How Parties Evaluate Compulsory Quotas: A Study of the Implementation of the "Parity" Law in France', *Parliamentary Affairs*, 60(4), pp. 568–84.
Murschetz, P. (1998) 'State Support for the Daily Press in Europe: A Critical Appraisal', *European Journal of Communication*, 13(3), pp. 291–313.
Myant, Martin, Slocock, Brian and Smith, Simon (2000) 'Tripartism in the Czech and Slovak Republics', *Europe Asia Studies*, 52(4), pp. 723–40.
Myntti, Kristian (2002) 'The Sami Cultural Autonomies in the

Nordic Countries', in Kinga Gál (ed.), *Minority Governance in Europe* (Budapest: Local Government and Public Service Reform Initiative/Open Society Institute).

N

NEC Estonia (2007) www.vvk.ee.engindex.html

Negrine, Ralph (1998) *Parliament and the Media: A Study of Britain, Germany and France* (London: Pinter).

Negrine, Ralph and Lilleker, Darren (2002) 'The Professionalization of Political Communication: Continuities and Change in Media Practices', *European Journal of Communication*, 17(3), pp. 305–23.

Negrine, Ralph and Stanyer, James (2006) *The Political Communication Reader* (London: Routledge).

Neumayer, Eric (2004) 'Asylum Destination Choice. What Makes Some West European Countries More Attractive than Others?' *European Union Politics*, 5(2). pp. 155–80.

Neumayer, Eric (2005) 'Asylum Recognition Rates in Western Europe: Their Determinants, Variation, and Lack of Convergence', *Journal of Conflict Resolution*, 49(1), pp. 43–66.

Neumann, Iver B. (1998) *Uses of the Other: 'The East' in European Identity Formation* (Minneapolis: University of Minnesota Press).

Newell, James (2000) *Parties and Democracy in Italy* (Aldershot: Dartmouth).

Newell, James and Bull, Martin (2005) *Italian Politics: Adjustment Under Duress* (Cambridge: Polity).

Newton, Kenneth (2006) 'May the Weak Force Be With You: The Power of the Mass Media in Modern Politics', *European Journal of Political Research*, 45, pp. 209–34.

Newton, Kenneth and Artingstall, Nigel (1994) 'Government and Private Censorship in Nine Western Democracies', in Ian Budge and David McKay (eds), *Developing Democracy: Comparative Research in Honour of J.F.P. Blondel* (London: Sage).

Newton, Kenneth and Brynin, Malcolm (2001) 'The National Press and Party Voting in the UK', *Political Studies*, 49(2), pp. 265–85.

Neyer, Jürgen and Wolf, Dieter (2003) 'Horizontal Enforcement in the EU: The BSE Crisis and the Case of State Aid Control', in Beate Kohler-Koch (ed.), *Linking EU and National Governance* (Oxford: Oxford University Press).

Nguyen, A. and Western, M. (2006) 'The Complementary Relationship between the Internet and Traditional Mass Media: The Case of Online News and Information', *Information Research*, 11(3) Paper 259, available at http://InformationR.net/ir/11-3/paper259.html

Nieuwbeerta, Paul and De Graaf, Nan Dirk (1999) 'Traditional Class Voting in 20 Postwar Societies', in Geoffrey Evans, *The End of Class Politics?: Class Voting in Comparative Context* (Oxford: Oxford University Press).

Nikolenyi, Csaba (2004) 'Cabinet Stability in Post-Communist Central Europe', *Party Politics*, 10(2), pp. 123–50.

Nord, Lars (2006) 'Still the Middle Way: A Study of Political Communication Practices in Swedish Election Campaigns', *Harvard International Journal of Press/Politics*, 11(1), pp. 64–76.

Norris, Pippa (2000) *A Virtuous Circle: Political Communication in Postindustrial Societies* (Cambridge: Cambridge University Press).

Norris, Pippa (2001) *Digital Divide: Civic Engagement, Information Poverty and the Internet Worldwide* (Cambridge: Cambridge University Press).

Norris, Pippa (2002) *Democratic Phoenix: Reinventing Political Activism* (Cambridge: Cambridge University Press).

Norris, Pippa (2004a) 'Global Political Communication: Good Governance, Human Development, and Mass Communication', in Frank Esser and Barbara Pfetsch (eds), *Comparing Political Communication: Theories, Cases, and Challenges* (Cambridge University Press).

Norris, Pippa (2004b) *Electoral Engineering: Voting Rules and Political Behaviour* (Cambridge: Cambridge University Press.

Norris, Pippa (2005) *The Rise of the Radical Right* (Cambridge: Cambridge University Press).

Norris, Pippa (2006) 'Recruitment', in Richard Katz and William Crotty (eds) *Handbook of Party Politics* (London: Sage).

Norris, Pippa and Inglehart, Ronald (2004) *Sacred and Secular: Religion and Politics Worldwide* (Cambridge: Cambridge University Press).

Norton, Philip (ed.) (1999) *Parliaments and Governments in Western Europe* (London: Frank Cass).

Núñez, Xosé-Manoel (2001) 'What is Spanish Nationalism Today? From Legitimacy Crisis to Unfulfilled Renovation (1975–2000)', *Ethnic and Racial Studies*, 24(5), pp. 719–52.

Nuttall, Simon J. (2000) *European Foreign Policy* (Oxford: Oxford University Press).

Nygård, Mikael (2006) 'Welfare–Ideological Change in Scandinavia: A Comparative Analysis of Partisan Welfare State Positions in Four Nordic Countries, 1970–2003' *Scandinavian Political Studies*, 29(4), pp. 356–85.

O

O'Donnell, R. (2001) 'Towards Post-corporatist Concertation in Europe', in Helen Wallace (ed.), *Interlocking Dimensions of European Integration* (London: Pinter).

O'Dwyer, Conor (2006) *Runaway State-Building: Patronage Politics and Democratic Development* (Baltimore: Johns Hopkins University Press).

O'Neil, Patrick H. (ed.) (1997) *Post-Communism and the Media in Eastern Europe* (London: Frank Cass).

OECD (2005) *Modernising Government: The Way Forward* (Paris: OECD).

OECD (2007) DAC Peer Review of the European Community, 2007, available at http://www.oecd.org/dataoecd/57/6/38965119.pdf

Ofcom (2007) The Communications Market, http://www.ofcom.org.uk/research/cm/cmr07/

Ohmae, Kenichi (1996) *The End of the Nation State: The Rise of Regional Economies* (London: HarperCollins).

Ojanen, Hanna (2006) 'The EU and Nato: Two Competing Models for a Common Defence Policy', *Journal of Common Market Studies*, 44(1), pp. 57–76.

Olcott, Martha Brill, Åslund, Anders and Garnett, Sherman W. (2000) *Getting It Wrong: Regional Cooperation and the Commonwealth of Independent States* (Washington, DC: Carnegie Endowment for International Peace).

Olson, Mancur (1982) *The Rise and Decline of Nations: Economic Growth, Stagflation, and Social Rigidities* (New Haven, CT: Yale University Press).

Ootschot, Wim van and Uunk, Wilfred (2007) 'Welfare Spending and the Public's Concern for Immigrants: Multilateral Evidence for Eighteen European Countries,' *Journal of Comparative Politics*, 40(1), pp. 63–82.

Ost, David (2000) 'Illusory Corporatism in Eastern Europe: Neoliberal Tripartism and Postcommunist Class Identities', *Politics and Society*, 28(4), pp. 503–30.

P

Pacek, Alexander C., Grigore Pop-Eleches and Joshua A. Tucker (2007) 'Disenchanted or Discerning: Voter Turnout in Post-Communist Countries', Unpublished MS, available at http://homepages.nyu.edu/~jat7/Turnout_PPT_2006.pdf

Padgett, Stephen (2000) *Organizing Democracy in Eastern Germany: Interest Groups in Post-Communist Society* (Cambridge: Cambridge University Press).

Padgett, Stephen, Paterson, William E. and Smith, Gordon (2003) *Developments in German Politics 3* (Basingstoke: Palgrave Macmillan).

Pagden, Anthony (ed.) (2002) *The Idea of Europe: From Antiquity to the European Union* (Cambridge: Cambridge University Press).

Page, Edward C. and Wouters, Linda (1995) 'The Europeanisation of the National Bureaucracies', in Jon Pierre (ed.), *Bureaucracy in the Modern State: An Introduction to Comparative Public Administration* (Aldershot: Edward Elgar).

Page, Edward C. and Wright, Vincent (1999) *Bureaucratic Elites in Western European States: A Comparative Analysis of Top Officials* (Oxford: Oxford University Press).

Page, Edward and Wright, Vincent (eds) (2006) *From the Active to the Enabling State: The Changing Role of Top Officials in European Nations* (Basingstoke: Palgrave Macmillan).

Palmer, Jerry (2002) 'News Production: News Values', in Adam Briggs and Paul Cobley (eds), *The Media: An Introduction* (London: Longman).

Panayi, Panikos (2000) *An Ethnic History of Europe since 1945: Nations, States and Minorities* (London: Longman Pearson).

Panebianco, Angelo (1988) *Political Parties: Organisation and Power* (Cambridge: Cambridge University Press).

Papadopoulos, Yannis (2001) 'How Does Direct Democracy Matter? The Impact of Referendum Votes upon Politics and Policy-Making', *West European Politics*, 24(2), pp. 35–58.

Papathanassopoulos, S. (2001) 'The Decline of Newspapers: The Case of the Greek Press', *Journalism Studies*, 2(1), pp. 109–23.

Papatheodorou, E. and Machin, D. (2003) 'The Umbilical Cord that was Never Cut: The Post-dictatorial Intimacy Between the Political Elite and the Mass Media in Greece and Spain', *European Journal of Communication*, 18(1), pp. 31–54.

Parker, David (ed.) (1998) *Privatisation in the European Union: Theory and Policy Perspectives* (London: Routledge).

Parsons, Craig A. and Smeeding, Timothy M. (eds) (2006) *Immigration and the Transformation of Europe* (Cambridge: Cambridge University Press).

Paul, T.V., Ikenberry, John and Hall, John (2003) *The Nation State in Question* (Princeton: Princeton University Press).

Pedahzur, Ami and Brichta, Avraham (2002) 'The Institutionalization of Extreme Right-Wing Charismatic Parties: A Paradox?', *Party Politics*, 8(1), pp. 31–49.

Pedersen, Karina and Saglie, Jo (2005) 'Technology in Ageing Parties: Internet Use in Danish and Norwegian Parties', *Party Politics*, 11(3) 3, 359–77.

Penninx, R., Berger, M. and Kraal, K. (eds) (2006) *The Dynamics of International Migration and Settlement in Europe* (Amsterdam: Amsterdam University Press).

Pérez-Solórzano Borragán, Nieves (2006) 'Post-Communist Interest Politics: A Research Agenda', *Perspectives on European Politics and Society*, 7(2), pp. 134–54.

Péteri, György (2000) 'Between Empire and Nation-state: Comments on the Pathology of State Formation during the "Short Twentieth Century"', *Contemporary European History*, 9(3), pp. 367–84.

Peters, B. Guy (2001) *The Politics of Bureaucracy* (London: Routledge).

Peters, B. Guy (2007) 'Executives', in Colin Hay and Anand Menon (eds) *European Politics* (Oxford: Oxford University Press).

Peters, B. Guy and Pierre, Jon (2000) *Governance, Politics and the State* (Basingstoke: Palgrave Macmillan).

Peters, B. Guy and Pierre, Jon (eds) (2004) *The Politicization of the Civil Service in Comparative Perspective: A Quest for Control* (London: Routledge).

Peters, B. Guy and Wright, Vincent (2000) *Administering the Summit: Administration of the Core Executive in Developed Countries* (Basingstoke: Palgrave Macmillan).

Peterson, John and Pollack, Mark (2003) *Europe, America, Bush: Transatlantic Relations After 2000* (London: Routledge).

Petersson, Olof, Djerf-Pierre, Monika, Holmberg, Sören, Strömbäck, Jesper and Weibull, Lennart (2006) 'Media and Elections in Sweden' (SNS Förlag), available at www.sns.se/document/dr_2006_english_web.pdf

PewResearchCenter, available at http://pewglobal.org/reports/pdf/256.pdf

Pfetsch, B. (1996) 'Convergence through Privatization? Changing Media Environments and Televised Politics in Germany', *European Journal of Communication*, 11(4), pp. 427–51.

Pierre, Jon (ed.) (1995) *Bureaucracy in the Modern State: An Introduction to Comparative Public Administration* (Aldershot: Edward Elgar).

Pierson, Christopher (2001) *Hard Choices: Social Democracy in the Twenty-First Century* (Cambridge: Polity Press).

Pierson, Paul (1996) 'The New Politics of the Welfare State', *World Politics*, 48 (2), pp. 143–79.

Pinto-Duschinsky, Michael (2002) 'Financing Politics: A Global View', *Journal of Democracy*, 13(4), pp. 69–86.

Pissarides, Christopher, Garibaldi, Pietro, Olivetti, Claudia, Petrongolo, Barbara and Wasmer, Etienne (2004) 'Women in the Labour Force: How Well is Europe Doing?', in Tito Boeri, Daniela Del Boca and Christopher Pissarides (eds), *Women at Work: An Economic Perspective. A Report for the Fondazione Rodolfo Debenedetti* (Oxford: Oxford University Press).

Plasser, Fritz and Plasser, Gunda (2002) *Global Political Campaigning: A Worldwide Analysis of Campaign Professionals and their Practices* (Westport: Greenwood/Praeger).

Poguntke, Thomas, Aylott, Nicholas, Carter, Elisabeth, Ladrech,

Robert and Luther, Kurt Richard (eds) (2006) *The Europeanization of National Political Parties: Power and Organizational Adaptation* (London: Routledge).

Poguntke, Thomas and Webb, Paul (eds) (2004) *The Presidentialization of Politics: A Comparative Study of Modern Democracies* (Oxford: Oxford University Press).

Poitras, Guy E. (2003) 'Resisting Globalization: The Politics of Protest in the Global Political Economy', *International Politics*, 40(3), pp. 409–24.

Pollitt, Christopher and Bouckaert, Geert (2000) *Public Management Reform: A Comparative Analysis* (Oxford: Oxford University Press).

Pollitt, Christopher, Talbot, Colin, Caulfield, Janice and Smullen, Amanda (2007) *Agencies: How Governments Do Things Through Semi-Autonomous Organizations* (Basingstoke: Palgrave Macmillan).

Pollitt, Christopher, Thiel, Sandra van and V.M.F. Homburg (eds) (2007) *The New Public Management in Europe: Adaptation and Alternatives* (Basingstoke: Palgrave Macmillan).

Pontusson, Jonas (2005) *Inequality and Prosperity: Social Europe vs. Liberal America* (Ithaca: Cornell University Press).

Poppe, Christian and Kjærnes, Unni (2003) *Trust in Food in Europe: A Comparative Analysis* (Oslo: National Institute for Consumer Research).

Procházka, Radoslav (2002) *Mission Accomplished: On Founding Constitutional Adjudication in Central Europe* (Budapest: Central European University Press).

Przeworski, Adam and Wallerstein, Michael (1988) 'Structural Dependence of the State on Capital', *American Political Science Review*, 82: 11–29.

Putnam, Robert D. (1988) 'Diplomacy and Domestic Politics: The Logic of Two Level Games', *International Organization*, 42(3), pp. 427–60.

Putnam, Robert D. (2000) *Bowling Alone: The Collapse and Revival of American Community* (New York: Simon & Schuster).

Putnam, Robert, D., Leonardi, Robert and Nanetti, Raffaella, Y. (2000) *Making Democracy Work: Civic Traditions in Modern Italy* (Princeton: Princeton University Press).

Q

QAA (2000) *Politics and International Relations Subject Benchmark Statement* (Gloucester: Quality Assurance Agency for Higher Education), available at http://www.qaa.ac.uk/crntwork/benchmark/politics.pdf

Qvortrup, Mads (2002, 2005) *A Comparative Study of Referendums: Government by the People* (Manchester: Manchester University Press).

Qvortrup, Mads (2007) *The Politics of Participation* (Manchester: Manchester University Press).

R

Radaelli, Claudio (1997) 'How Does Europeanization Produce Domestic Policy Change?', *Comparative Political Studies*, 30(5), pp. 553–75.

Radaelli, Claudio (2004) 'The Puzzle of Regulatory Competition', *Journal of Public Policy*, 24(1), pp. 1–23.

Rahat, Gideon (2007) 'Candidate Selection: The Choice Before the Choice', *Journal of Democracy*, 18(1), pp. 157–70.

Rallings, Colin (1987) 'The Influence of Election Programmes: Britain and Canada, 1945–79', in Ian Budge, David Robertson and Derek Hearl (eds), *Ideology, Strategy and Party Changes: Spatial Analysis of Post-War Election Programmes in 19 Democracies* (Cambridge: Cambridge University Press).

Ram, M. (2003) 'Democratization through European Integration: The Case of Minority Rights in the Czech Republic and Romania', *Studies in Comparative International Development*, 38(2), pp. 28–56.

Raunio, Tapio and Hix, Simon (2000) 'Backbenchers Learn to Fight Back: European Integration and Parliamentary Government', *West European Politics*, 23(4), pp. 142–68.

Rawcliffe, Peter (1998) *Environmental Pressure Groups in Transition* (Manchester: Manchester University Press).

Reeves, Minou (2003) *Muhammad in Europe: A Thousand Years of Western Myth-Making* (New York University Press).

Reichard, Michael (2006) *The EU–NATO Relationship: A Legal and Political Perspective* (Aldershot: Ashgate).

Reid, T.R. (2005) *United States of Europe: The Superpower No-One Talks About* (London: Penguin).

Rhodes, R.A.W. (1997) *Understanding Governance: Policy Networks, Governance, Reflexivity and Accountability* (Buckingham: Open University Press).

Rhodes, R.A.W. (2002) 'Globalization, EMU and Welfare State Futures', in Erik Jones, Paul Hayward and Martin Rhodes (eds), *Developments in West European Politics* (Basingstoke: Palgrave Macmillan).

Rhodes, R.A.W. and Weller, P. (eds) (2001) *The Changing World of Top Officials: Mandarins or Valets?* (Buckingham: Open University Press).

Richardson, Jeremy (2001) 'Policy-making in the EU: Familiar Ambitions in Unfamiliar Settings', in Anand Menon and Vincent Wright (eds), *From the Nation State to Europe?* (Oxford: Oxford University Press).

Richardson, Jeremy, Gustafsson, Gunnel and Jordan, Grant (1982) 'The Concept of Policy Style', in Jeremy Richardson (ed.), *Policy Styles in Western Europe* (London: George Allen & Unwin).

Richardson, Kay and Meinhof, Ulrike H. (1999) *Worlds in Common? Television Discourse in a Changing Europe* (London: Routledge).

Riddell, Peter (2006) 'The Rise of the Ranters: Saving Political Journalism', in John Lloyd and Jean Seaton (eds), *What Can Be Done? Making the Media and Politics Better* (Oxford: Blackwell).

Rifkin, Jeremy (2004) *The European Dream: How Europe's Vision of the Future is Quietly Eclipsing the American Dream* (Cambridge: Polity Press).

Rihoux, B. and Rüdig, Wolfgang (eds) (2006) 'The Greens in Power', *European Journal of Political Research*, Special issue, 45.

Rodgers, Jayne (2003) *Spatializing International Politics: Analysing Activism on the Internet* (London: Routledge).

Roller, Elisa (2004) 'Conflict and Cooperation in EU Policy making: The Case of Catalonia', *Perspectives on European Politics and Society*, 5(1), pp. 81–102.

Roncarolo, Franca (2004) 'Mediation of Italian Politics and the Marketing of Leaders' Private Lives', *Parliamentary Affairs*, 57(1), pp. 108–17.

Rootes, Christopher (2004) 'Is There a European Environmental Movement?', in Brian Baxter, John Barry and Richard Dunphy (eds), *Europe, Globalisation and Sustainable Development* (London: Routledge).

Rose, Richard (2004) *Learning Lessons in Comparative Public Policy* (London: Routledge).

Ross, Fiona (2000) '"Beyond Left and Right": The New Partisan Politics of Welfare', *Governance*, 13(2), pp. 155–83.

Ross, George, Hoffman, Stanley and Malzacher, Sonja (1987) *The Mitterrand Experiment* (Cambridge: Polity Press).

Ross, Karen (2004) 'Political Talk Radio and Democratic Participation: Caller Perspectives on Election Call', *Media Culture and Society*, 26(6), pp. 785–801.

Rössler, Patrick (2004) 'Political Communication Messages: Pictures of Our World on International Television News', in Frank Esser and Barbara Pfetsch (eds) *Comparing Political Communication: Theories, Cases, and Challenges* (Cambridge: Cambridge University Press).

Rössler, Patrick (2006) 'Political Communication Messages: Pictures of our World on International Television News', in Frank Esser and Barbara Petsch (eds), *Comparing Political Communication: Theories, Cases and Challenges* (Cambridge: Cambridge University Press).

Rothschild, Emma (1995) 'What Is Security?', *Daedalus*, 124(3), pp. 53–98.

Rouban, Luc (1995) 'Public Administration at the Crossroads: The End of French Exceptionalism', in Jon Pierre (ed.), *Bureaucracy in the Modern State: An Introduction to Comparative Public Administration* (Aldershot: Edward Elgar).

Rucht, Dieter (2003) 'The Changing Role of Political Protest Movements', in *West European Politics*, 26(4), pp. 153–78.

Ruzza, Carlo (2004) *Europe and Civil Society: Movement Coalitions and European Governance* (Manchester: Manchester University Press).

Ryan, Johnny (2007) *Countering Militant Islamist Radicalization on the Internet* (Dublin: Institute of European Affairs).

Ryan, Rosalind (2008) 'How the Muhammad Cartoon Row Escalated', *Guardian*, 12 February 2008.

Rydgren, Jens (ed.) (2004) *Movements of Exclusion. Radical Right-wing Populism in the Western World* (Hauppauge: Nova Science).

S

Saalfeld, Thomas (2006) 'Conflict and Consensus in Germany's Bi-cameral System: A Case Study of the Passage of the '*Agenda 2010*', *Debatte*, 14(3), pp. 247–69.

Sadurski, Wojciech (2005) *Rights Before Courts: A Study of Constitutional Courts in Postcommunist States of Central and Eastern Europe* (Amsterdam: Kluwer).

Saggar, Shamit (2000) *Race and Electoral Politics in Britain* (London: UCL Press).

Sanders, Karen with Canel, Maria José (2004) 'Spanish Politicians and the Media: Controlled Visibility and Soap Opera Politics', *Parliamentary Affairs*, 57(1), pp. 196–208.

Sanford, George (2002) *Democratic Government in Poland: Constitutional Politics Since 1989* (Basingstoke: Palgrave Macmillan).

Sartori, Giovanni (1997) *Comparative Constitutional Engineering: An Inquiry into Structures, Incentives and Outcomes* (Basingstoke: Palgrave Macmillan).

Sassoon, Donald (1997) *One Hundred Years of Socialism: The West European Left in the Twentieth Century* (London: Fontana).

Scarrow, Susan E. (1994) 'The "Paradox of Enrolment": Assessing the Costs and Benefits of Party Membership', *European Journal of Political Research*, 25(1), pp. 41–60.

Scarrow, Susan E. and Kittilson, Miki Caul (2003) 'Political Parties and the Rhetoric and Realities of Democratization', in Russell Dalton, Bruce Cain and Susan Scarrow (eds), *Democracy Transformed? Expanding Citizen Access in Advanced Industrial Democracies* (Oxford: Oxford University Press).

Schain, Martin (2006) 'The Extreme-right and Immigration Policy-making: Measuring Direct and Indirect Effects', *West European Politics*, 29(2), pp. 270–89

Scharpf, Fritz (1998) 'Negative and Positive Integration in the Political Economy of European Welfare States', in Martin Rhodes and Yves Mény (eds), *The Future of European Welfare: A New Social Contract* (Basingstoke: Palgrave Macmillan).

Schlesinger, Philip (1993) 'Wishful Thinking: Cultural Politics, Media and Collective Identities in Europe', *Journal of Communication*, 43(2), pp. 6–17.

Schlesinger, Philip and Kevin, Deirdre (2000) 'Can the European Union become a Sphere of Publics?', in Erik Oddvar Eriksen and John Erik Fossum (eds), *Democracy in the European Union: Integration through Deliberation?* (London: Routledge).

Schludi, Martin (2005) *The Reform of Bismarkian Pension Systems: A Comparison of Pension Politics in Austria, France, Italy, and Sweden* (Amsterdam: Amsterdam University Press).

Schmidt, Manfred G. (1996) 'When Parties Matter: A Review of the Possibilities and Limits of Partisan Influence on Public Policy', *European Journal of Political Research*, 30(2), pp. 155–83.

Schmidt, Manfred G. (2002) 'The Impact of Political Parties, Constitutional Structures and Veto Players in Public Policy', in Hans Keman (ed.), *Comparative Democratic Politics* (London: Sage).

Schmidt, Vivien A. (1999) 'National Patterns of Governance under Seige: The Impact of European Integration', in Beate Kohler Koch and Rainer Eising (eds), *The Transformation of Governance in the European Union* (London: Routledge/ECPR).

Schmidtke, Oliver (2002) *The Third Way Transformation of Social Democracy* (London Ashgate).

Schmidt, Vivien A. (2001) 'The Politics of Adjustment in France and Britain: When Does Discourse Matter?', *Journal of European Public Policy*, 8(2), pp. 247–64.

Schmitt, Hermann and Holmberg, Sören (1995) 'Political Parties in Decline?', in Hans-Dieter Klingemann and Dieter Fuchs (eds), *Citizens and the State* (Oxford: Oxford University Press).

Schmitt, Vivien A. (2006) *Democracy in Europe: The EU and National Politics* (Oxford: Oxford University Press).

Schmitt-Beck, Rüdiger (2004) 'Personal Communication Effects: the Impact of Mass Media and Personal Conversations on Voting', in Frank Esser and Barbara Pfetsch (eds), *Comparing Political Communication: Theories, Cases, and Challenges* (Cambridge: Cambridge University Press).

Schneider, Volker and Häge, Frank M. (2008) 'Europianization

and the Retreat of the State', *European Journal of Public Policy*, 15(1), pp. 1–19.
Schoen, Harald (2007) 'Campaigns, Candidate Evaluations, and Vote Choice: Evidence from German Federal Election Campaigns, 1980–2002', *Electoral Studies*, 26(2), pp. 324–37.
Scholte, Jan Aart (2001) *Globalization: A Critical Introduction* (Basingstoke: Palgrave Macmillan).
Schöpflin, George (1995) 'Nationalism and Ethnicity in Europe, East and West', in Charles A. Kupchan (ed.), *Nationalism and Nationalities in the New Europe* (Ithaca: Cornell University Press).
Schudson, Michael (2002) 'The News Media as Political Institutions', *Annual Review of Political Science*, 5, pp. 249–269.
Shudson, Michael (2003) *The Sociology of News* (New York: W. W. Norton).
Schudson, Michael (2005) 'The Virtues of an Unlovable Press', *Political Quarterly*, 76, pp. 23–32.
Schulz, Winfried (2004) 'Reconstructing Mediatization as an Analytical Concept', *European Journal of Communication*, 19(1), pp. 87–101.
Schulz, Winfried, Zeh, Reimar and Quiring, Oliver (2005) 'Voters in a Changing Media Environment: A Data-Based Retrospective on Consequences of Media Change in Germany', *European Journal of Communication*, 20(1), pp. 55–88.
Schuster, Jürgen and Maier, Herbert (2006) 'The Rift: Explaining Europe's Divergent Iraq Policies in the Run-Up to the American-Led War on Iraq', *Foreign Policy Analysis*, 2(3), pp. 223–44.
Schwindt-Bayer, Leslie A. (2005) 'The Incumbency Disadvantage and Women's Election to Legislative Office', *Electoral Studies*, 24, pp. 227–44.
Sciarini, Pascal, Fischer, Alex and Nicolet, Sarah (2004) 'How Europe Hits Home: Evidence from the Swiss Case', *Journal of European Public Policy*, 11(3), pp. 353–78.
Scott, James Wesley (2006) *EU Enlargement, Region Building and Shifting Borders of Inclusion and Exclusion* (Aldershot: Ashgate).
Scruggs, Lyle and Allan, James P. (2006a) 'Welfare-state Decommodification in 18 OECD Countries: A Replication and Revision', *Journal of European Social Policy*, 16(1), pp. 55–72.
Scruggs, Lyle and Allan, James P. (2006b) 'The Material Consequences of Welfare States: Benefit Generosity and Absolute Poverty in 16 OECD Countries', *Comparative Political Studies*, 39(7), pp. 880–904.
Sedelmeier, Ulrich (2005) *Constructing the Path to Eastern Enlargement: The Uneven Policy Impact of EU Identity* (Manchester: Manchester University Press).
Semetko, Holli A. (2000) 'Great Britain: The End of News at Ten and the Changing News Environment', in Richard Gunther and Anthony Mughan (eds), *Democracy and the Media: A Comparative Perspective* (Cambridge: Cambridge University Press).
Semetko, Holli A., Vreese, Claes H. de and Peter, Jochen (2000) 'Europeanised Politics – Europeanised Media? European Integration and Political Communication', *West European Politics*, 23(4), pp. 121–41.
Setälä, Maija (1999) *Referendums and Democratic Government: Normative Theory and the Analysis of Institutions* (Basingstoke: Palgrave Macmillan).
Sides, John and Citrin, Jack (2007) 'European Opinion about Immigration: The Role of Identities, Interests and Information', *British Journal of Political Science*, 37, pp. 477–504.
Silvestri, Stefano (1997) 'The Albanian Test Case', *International Spectator*, 32(3–4), pp. 87–98.
Sitter, Nick (2003) 'Cleavages, Party Strategy and Party System Change in Europe, East and West', in Paul Lewis and Paul Webb (eds), *Pan European Perspectives on Party Politics* (Leiden: Brill).
Siune, Karen, Svensson, Palle and Tongsgaard, Ole (1994) 'The European Union: The Danes Said "No" in 1992 but "Yes" in 1993: How and Why?', *Electoral Studies*, 13(2), pp. 107–16.
Skenderovic, Damir (2007) 'Immigration and the Radical Right in Switzerland: Ideology, Discourse and Opportunities', *Patterns of Prejudice*, 41(2), pp. 155–76.
Sklair, L. (2000) 'The Transnational Capitalist Class and the Discourse of Globalisation', *Cambridge Review of International Affairs*, 14(1), pp. 67–85.
Sklair, Leslie (2002) *Globalization: Capitalism and its Alternatives*, 3rd edn (Oxford: Oxford University Press).
Smith, Anthony D. (1991) *National Identity* (London: Penguin).
Smith, Anthony D. (1992) 'National Identity and the Idea of European Unity', *International Affairs*, 68(1), pp. 55–76.
Smith, Karen E. (2005b) *Engagement and Conditionality: Incompatible or Mutually Reinforcing?* (London: Foreign Policy Centre).
Smith, Karen E. (2006) 'The Limits of "Proactive Cosmopolitanism": EU Policy towards Burma, Cuba and Zimbabwe', in Ole Elgstrom and Michael Smith (eds), *The European Union's Roles in International Politics: Concepts and Analysis* (London: Routledge).
Smith, Mark (2000) 'Nato Enlargement and European Security', in Lisbeth Aggestam and Adrian Hyde-Price (eds) *Security and Indentity in Europe: Exploring the New Agenda* (Basingstoke: Palgrave Macmillan).
Smith, Martin J. (1993) *Pressure, Power and Policy: State Autonomy and Policy Networks in Britain and the United States* (New York: Harvester Wheatsheaf).
Smith, Michael (2004) 'CFSP and ESDP: From Idea to Institution to Policy', in Martin Holland (ed.), *Common Foreign and Security Policy: The First Ten Years* (London: Continuum).
Smith, Karen E. (2005a) 'The Outsiders: the European Neighbourhood Policy', *International Affairs*, 81(4), pp. 757–73.
Sniderman, Paul M. and Hagendoorn, Paul (2007) *When Ways of Life Collide: Multiculturism and its Discontents in the Netherlands* (Princeton: Princeton University Press).
Snow, David A., Soule, Sarah and Kriesi, Hanspeter (eds) (2004) *The Blackwell Companion to Social Movements* (Oxford: Blackwell).
Snyder, James M. and Ting, Michael M. (2002) 'An Informational Rationale for Political Parties', *American Journal of Political Science*, 46(1), pp. 90–110.
Sotiropoulos, Dimitri A. (2004) 'Southern European Public Bureacracies in Comparative Perspective', *West European Politics*, 27(3), pp. 405–22.
Sparks, Colin (1997) Post-communist Media in Transition', in John Corner, Philip Schlesinger and Roger Silverstone (eds),

International Media Research: A Critical Survey (London: Routledge).

Sparks, Colin (2000) 'Media Theory after the Fall of European Communism: Why the Old Models from East and West Won't Do Anymore', in James Curran and Myung-Jin Park (eds), *De-Westernizing Media Studies* (London: Routledge).

Spirova, Maria (2007) 'Bulgaria', *European Journal of Political Research*, 46(7–8).

Spohn, Willfried and Triandafyllidou, Anna (eds) (2002) *Europeanisation, National Identities and Migration: Changes in Boundary Constructions between Western and Eastern Europe* (London: Routledge).

Stammers, Neil (2001) 'Social Democracy and Global Governance', in Luke Martell (ed.), *Social Democracy: Global and National Perspectives* (Basingstoke: Palgrave Macmillan).

Stanyer, James and Wring, Dominic (eds) (2004) *Public Image, Private Lives: The Mediation of Politicians Around the Globe*, *Parliamentary Affairs*, Special issue, 57(1).

Starke, Peter (2006) 'The Politics of Welfare State Retrenchment: A Literature Review', *Social Policy and Administration*, 40(1), pp. 104–20.

Starke, Peter (2007) *Radical Welfare State Retrenchment* (Basingstoke: Palgrave Macmillan).

Steeg, Marianne van de (2006) 'Does a Public Sphere Exist in the European Union? An Analysis of the Content of the Debate on the Haider Case', *European Journal of Political Research*, 45, pp. 609–34.

Stephens, J.D., Huber, E. and Ray, L. (1999) 'The Welfare State in Hard Times', in Herbert Kitschelt, Peter Lange, Gary Marks and John D. Stephens (eds), *Continuity and Change in Contemporary Capitalism* (Cambridge: Cambridge University Press).

Stille, Alexander (2007) *The Sack of Rome: Media + Money + Celebrity = Power = Silvio Berlusconi* (London: Penguin).

Stolle, Deitlind and Hooghe, Marc (2005) 'Shifting Inequalities? Patterns of Exclusion and Inclusion in Emerging Forms of Political Participation', APSA Annual Meeting paper.

Stolle, Dietlind, Hooghe, Marc and Micheletti, Michele (2005) 'Politics in the Supermarket: Political Consumerism as a Form of Political Participation', *International Political Science Review*, 26(3), pp. 245–69.

Stone Sweet, Alec (2000) *Governing with Judges: Constitutional Politics in Europe* (Oxford: Oxford University Press).

Stone Sweet, Alec (2004) *The Judicial Construction of Europe* (Oxford: Oxford University Press).

Strange, Gerard (2002) 'British Trade Unions and European Integration in the 1990s: Politics versus Political Economy', *Political Studies*, 50(2), pp. 332–53.

Stråth, Bo (ed.) (2001) *Europe and the Other and Europe as the Other* (Brussels: Peter Lang).

Strøm, Kaare (1990) *Minority Government and Majority Rule* (Cambridge: Cambridge University Press).

Strøm, Kaare, Budge, I. and Laver, M. (1994) 'Constraints on Cabinet Formation in Parliamentary Democracies', *American Journal of Political Science*, 38(2), pp. 303–35.

Sturm, Roland and Dieringer, Jürgen (2005) 'The Europeanization of Regions in Eastern and Western Europe: Theoretical Perspectives', *Regional and Federal Studies*, 15(3), pp. 279–94.

Sunstein, Cass R. (2007) *Republic.com 2.0* (Princeton: Princeton University Press).

Swank, Duane (2005) 'Globalisation, Domestic Politics, and Welfare State Retrenchment in Capitalist Democracies', *Social Policy and Society*, 4(2), pp. 183–95.

Szczerbiak, Aleks (2000) *Poland within the EU: The New Awkward Partner* (London: Routledge).

Szczerbiak, Aleks (2002) *Poles Together? The Emergence and Development of Political Parties in Postcommunist Poland* (Budapest: Central European University Press).

Szczerbiak, Aleks (2003) 'Old and New Divisions in Polish Politics: Polish Parties' Electoral Strategies and Bases of Support', *Europe-Asia Studies*, 55(5), pp. 729–46.

Szczerbiak, Aleks and Taggart, Paul (2004) 'The Politics of European Referendum Outcomes and Turnout: Two Models', *West European Politics*, 27(4), pp. 557–83.

Szczerbiak, Aleks and Taggart, Paul (2008) *Opposing Europe: The Comparative Party Politics of Euroscepticism, Volumes I and II* (Oxford: Oxford University Press).

Szukala, Andrea (2003) 'France: The European Transformation of the French Model', in Wolfgang Wessels, Andreas Maurer and Jürgen Mittag (eds), *Fifteen into One? The European Union and its Member States*, 2nd edn (Manchester: Manchester University Press).

T

Taggart, Paul (2000) *Populism* (Buckingham: Open University Press).

Tarrow, Sidney G. (2005) *The New Transnational Activism* (Cambridge: Cambridge University Press).

Tavits, Margit (2005) 'The Development of Stable Party Support: Electoral Dynamics in Post-Communist Europe', *American Journal of Political Science*, 49(2), pp. 283–98.

Tavits, Margit (2006) 'Party System Change: Testing a Model of New Party Entry', *Party Politics*, 12(1), pp. 99–119.

Tavits, Margit and Annus, Taavi (2006) 'Learning to Make Votes Count: The Role of Democratic Experience', *Electoral Studies*, 25(1), pp. 72–90.

Taylor-Gooby, Peter (ed.) (2004) *New Risks, New Welfare: The Transformation of the European Welfare State* (Oxford: Oxford University Press).

Taylor-Gooby, Peter (2005) 'Is the Future American? Or, Can Left Politics Preserve European Welfare States through Growing "Racial" Diversity', *Journal of Social Policy*, 34(4), pp. 661–72.

Teague, Paul and Donaghey, James (2003) 'European Economic Government and the Corporatist quid pro quo', *Industrial Relations Journal*, 34(2), pp. 104–18.

Teló, Mario (2006) *Europe: A Civilian Power? European Union, Global Governance, World Order* (Basingstoke: Palgrave Macmillan).

Tesser, L. (2003) 'The Geopolitics of Tolerance: Minority Rights under EU Expansion in East-Central Europe', *East European Politics and Societies*, 17(3), pp. 483–532.

Tewes, Henning (2001) *Germany, Civilian Power and the New Europe* (Basingstoke: Palgrave Macmillan).

Thomassen, Jacques (2005) *The European Voter: A Comparative Study of Modern Democracies* (Oxford: Oxford University Press).

Thompson, Mark (2006) 'Television in Europe', *Political Quarterly*, 77(1), pp. 124–7.

Thompson, W.C. (2001) 'Germany and the East', *Europe Asia Studies*, 53(6), pp. 921–52.

Thomson, Robert (2001) 'The Programme to Policy Linkage: The Fulfillment of Election Pledges on Socio-economic Policy in the Netherlands, 1986–1998', *European Journal of Political Research*, 40(2), pp. 171–97.

Thomson, Robert, Stokman, Francis, Achen, Christopher and König, Thomas (eds) (2000) *The European Union Reader* (Cambridge; Cambridge University Press).

Thomson, Robert, Stokman, Francis, Achen, Christopher and König, Thomas (eds) (2006) *The European Union Decides: Political Economy of Institutions and Decisions* (Cambridge: Cambridge University Press).

Thomson, Stuart (2000) *The Social Democratic Dilemma: Ideology, Governance and Globalization* (Basingstoke: Palgrave Macmillan).

Thorisdottir, Hulda, Jost, John T., Liviatan, I. and Shrout, Patrick E. (2007) 'Psychological Needs and Values Underlying Left–Right Political Orientation: Cross-National Evidence from Eastern and Western Europe', *Public Opinion Quarterly*, 71(2), pp. 175–203.

Threlfall, Monica (2007) 'Explaining Gender Party Representation in Spain: The Internal Dynamics of Parties', *West European Politics*, 30(5), pp. 1008–95.

Tilly, Charles (1975) 'Reflecting on the History of European State-making', in Charles Tilly (ed.), *The Formation of the National State in Western Europe* (Princeton: Princeton University Press).

Tilly, Charles (1993) *Coercion, Capital and European States, AD 990–1992* (Oxford: Blackwell).

Tilly, Charles (2004) *Social Movements, 1768–2004* (London: Paradigm).

Timmins, Graham and Gower, Jackie (2007) *Russia and Europe in the Twenty-first Century* (London: Anthem Press).

Timonen, Virpi (2003) *Restructuring the Welfare State: Globalization and Social Policy Reform in Finland and Sweden* (Cheltenham: Edward Elgar).

Tóka, Gábor (2006) Elections and Representation' in Paul Heywood, Erik Jones, Martin Rhodes and Ulrich Sedelmeier (eds), *Developments in European Politics* (Basingstoke: Palgrave Macmillan).

Trappel, Josef and Meier, Werner A. (1998) 'Media Concentration: Options for Policy', in Denis McQuail and Karen Siune (eds), *Media Policy: Convergence, Concentration and Commerce* (London: Sage).

Tremlett, Giles (2007) *Ghosts of Spain* (London: Faber & Faber).

Triandafyllidou, Anna (2003) 'The Launch of the Euro in the Italian Media', *European Journal of Communication*, 18(2), pp. 255–63.

Tridimas, Takis (2008) *The European Court of Justice and the EU Constitutional Order* (Oxford: Hart).

Tsebelis, George, Jensen, Christian B., Kalandrakis, Anastassios and Kreppel, Amie (2001) 'Legislative Procedures in the European Union: An Empirical Analysis', *British Journal of Political Science*, 31(4), pp. 573–99.

Turner, Barry (2007) *Statesman's Yearbook 2008: The Politics, Cultures and Economies of the World* (Basingstoke: Palgrave Macmillan).

U

Ueta, Takako and Remacle, Eric (eds) (2005) *Japan and Enlarged Europe: Partners in Global Governance* (Frankfurt: Peter Lang).

UK Government Petitions (2007) http://petitions.pm.gov.uk/

United Nations (2000) http://www.unhchr.ch/huricane/huricane.nsf/view01/59FCECC36567F2DA802568A20061B8AA?opendocument

US Mission to Pristina (2007) http://pristina.usmission.gov

V

van Cuilenburg, Jan and McQuail, Dennis (2003) 'Media Policy Paradigm Shifts: Towards a New Communications Policy Paradigm', *European Journal of Communication*, 18(2), pp. 181–207.

Vatta, A. (2001) 'Concertation and Employers' Organizations in Italy: The Case of Confindustria', *South European Society and Politics*, 6(3), pp. 103–22.

Verheijen, Tony (ed.) (1999) *Civil Service Systems in Central and Eastern Europe* (Cheltenham: Edward Elgar).

Verhulst, Joris and Walgrave, Stefaan (2007) 'Protest and Protesters in Advanced Industrial Democracies: The Case of the 15th February Global Anti-war Demonstrations', in Derrick A. Purdue (ed.), *Civil Societies and Social Movements: Potentials and Problems* (London: Routledge).

Visser, Jelle (1998) 'Learning to Play: The Europeanization of Trade Unions', in Patrick Pasture and Johan Verberckmoes (eds), *Working Class Internationalism and the Appeal of National Identity: Historical Debates and Current Perspectives* (Oxford: Berg).

Visser, Jelle (2006) 'Union Membership Statistics in 24 Countries', *Monthly Labor Review*, January.

Vlachová, Mira (2001) 'Party Identification in the Czech Republic: Inter-party Hostility and Party Preference', *Communist and Post-Communist Studies*, 34(4), pp. 479–99.

Volden, Craig and Carrubba, Clifford J. (2004) 'The Formation of Oversized Coalitions in Parliamentary Democracies', *American Journal of Political Science*, 48(3), pp. 521–37.

Volkens, Andrea (2004) 'Policy Changes of European Social Democrats, 1945–1998', in Guiliano Bonoli and Martin Powell (eds), *Social Democratic Party Policies in Contemporary Europe* (London: Routledge).

Volkens, Andrea and Klingemann, Hans-Dieter, (2002) 'Parties, Ideologies, and Issues. Stability and Change in Fifteen European Party Systems 1945–1998', in Kurt Richard Luther and Ferdinand Müller-Rommel, (eds) *Political Parties in the New Europe: Political and Analytical Challenges*, (Oxford University Press, Oxford).

W

Wagener, Hans-Jürgen (2002) 'The Welfare State in Transition Economies and Accession to the EU', *West European Politics*, 25(2), pp. 152–74.

Walgrave, Stefaan and Van Aelst, Peter (2006) 'The Contingency of

the Mass Media's Political Agenda Setting Power: Toward a Preliminary Agenda', *Journal of Communication*, 56, pp. 88–109.
Wallace, Helen (2000) 'Europeanization and Globalization: Complementary or Contradictory Trends', *New Political Economy*, 5(3), pp. 369–82.
Wallace, Helen, Wallace, William and Pollack, Mark (eds) (2005) *Policy-Making in the European Union* (Oxford: Oxford University Press).
Waller, M. and Myant, M. (1994) *Parties, Trade Unions and Society in East-Central Europe* (London: Frank Cass).
Ward, Stephen and Lusoli, Wainer (2003) 'Dinosaurs in Cyberspace?: British Trade Unions and the Internet', *European Journal of Communication*, 18(2), pp. 147–79.
Ware, Alan (1996) *Political Parties and Party Systems* (Oxford: Oxford University Press).
Waters, Malcolm (2001) *Globalization* (London: Routledge).
Wattenberg, Martin P. (2007) *Is Voting for Young People?* (London: Longman).
Weaver, D.H. (1998) 'Journalists around the World: Commonalities and Differences', in D.H. Weaver (ed.), *The Global Journalist: News People around the World* (Cresskill: Hampton Press).
Webb, Paul, Farrell, David M. and Holliday, Ian (eds) (2002) *Political Parties in Advanced Industrial Democracies* (Oxford: Oxford University Press).
Webb, Paul and Kolodny, Robin (2006) 'Professional Staff in Political Parties' in Richard Katz and William Crotty (eds), *Handbook of Party Politics* (London: Sage).
Webb, Paul and White, Stephen (2007) *Party Politics in New Democracies* (Oxford: Oxford University Press).
Wehner, Joachim (2006) 'Assessing the Power of the Purse: an Index of Legislative Budget Institutions', *Political Studies*, 54(4), pp. 767–85.
Weiland, Heribert (2004) 'EU Sanctions against Zimbabwe: A Predictable Own Goal?', in Martin Holland (ed.), *Common Foreign and Security Policy: The First Ten Years* (London: Continuum).
Weiss, Linda (1998) *The Myth of the Powerless State: Governing the Economy in a Global Era* (Cambridge: Polity).
Weldon, Steven A. (2006) 'Downsize My Polity? Impacts of Size on Party Membership and Member Activism', *Party Politics*, 12(4), pp. 467–81.
Weller, Patrick, Barkis, Herman and Rhodes, R.A.W. (eds) (1997) *The Hollow Crown: Countervailing Trends in Core Executives* (Basingstoke: Palgrave Macmillan).
Welzel, Christian, Inglehart, Ronald and Deutsch, Franziska (2005) 'Social Capital, Voluntary Associations and Collective Action: Which Aspects of Social Capital Have the Greatest "Civic" Payoff?', *Journal of Civil Society*, 1(2), pp. 121–46.
Wessels, Wolfgang, Maurer, Andreas and Mittag, Jürgen (eds) (2003) *Fifteen into One? The European Union and its Member States*, 2nd edn (Manchester: Manchester University Press).
Wheeler, Mark (2004) 'Supranational Regulation: Television and the European Union', *European Journal of Communication*, 19(3), pp. 349–69.
White, Stephen, Lewis, Paul G. and Batt, Judy (eds) (2007) *Developments in Central and East European Politics* (Basingstoke: Palgrave Macmillan).
Whitefield, Stephen (2002) 'Political Cleavages and Post-communist Politics', *Annual Review of Political Science*, 5, pp. 181–200.
Wiessala, Georg (2002) *The European Union and Asian Countries* (London: Sheffield Academic Press/Continuum).
Wilensky, Harold (2002) *Rich Democracies: Political Economy, Public Policy, and Performance* (Berkeley: University of California Press).
Wilke, Jürgen and Reinemann, Carsten (2001) 'Do the Candidates Matter? Long Term Trends of Campaign Coverage – A Study of the German Press Since 1949', *European Journal of Communication*, 16(3), pp. 291–314.
Williams, Garrath (2005) 'Monomaniacs or Schizophrenics?: Responsible Governance and the EU's Independent Agencies', *Political Studies*, 53(1), pp. 82–99.
Williams, Michelle Hale (2006) *The Impact of Radical Right-Wing Parties in Western Democracies* (New York: Palgrave Macmillan).
Wilson, David and Game, Chris (2006) *Local Government in the United Kingdom*, 2nd edn (Basingstoke: Palgrave Macmillan).
Wincott, Daniel (2003) 'Beyond Social Regulation? New Instruments and/or a New Agenda for Social Policy at Lisbon?', *Public Administration*, 81(3), pp. 533–53.
Wolczuk, Kataryna (2007) 'Constitution-Making and Semi-Presidentialism in Central and Eastern Europe' in Stephen White, Paul G. Lewis and Judy Batt (eds) *Developments in Central and East European Politics* (Basingstoke: Palgrave Macmillan).
Wolinetz, Stephen (ed.) (1997) *Party Systems* (Aldershot: Ashgate).
Wolinetz, Stephen (ed.) (1998) *Political Parties* (Aldershot: Dartmouth).
Woolcock, Stephen (2005) 'Trade Policy', in Helen Wallace, William Wallace and Mark Pollack (eds), *Policy-Making in the European Union* (Oxford: Oxford University Press).
Wright, Vincent and Hayward, Jack (2000) 'Governing from the Centre: Policy Co-ordination in Six European Core Executives', in R.A.W. Rhodes (ed.), *Transforming British Government, 2: Changing Roles and Relationships* (Basingstoke: Palgrave Macmillan).
Wurff, Richard van der (2004) 'Supplying and Viewing Diversity: The Role of Competition and Viewer Choice in Dutch Broadcasting', *European Journal of Communication*, 19(2), pp. 215–37.
Wyllie, James H. (1997) *European Security in the New Political Environment* (London: Longman).

X, Y, Z

Yanai, Nathan (1999) 'Why do Political Parties Survive? An Analytical Discussion', *Party Politics*, 5(1), pp. 5–18.
Young, Alisdair and Wallace, Helen (2000) *Regulatory Politics in the Enlarging European Union: Weighing Civic and Producer Interests* (Manchester: Manchester University Press).
Youngs, Richard (2003), 'European Approaches to Security in the Mediterranean', *Middle East Journal* 57(3), pp. 414–31.
Youngs, Richard (2006) *Europe and the Middle East: In the Shadow of September 11* (Boulder: Lynne Rienner).
Zaiotti, Ruben (2007) 'Of Friends and Fences: Europe's

Neighbourhood Policy and the "Gated Community Syndrome"', *Journal of European Integration*, 29(2), pp. 143–62.

Zaslove, Andrej (2004) 'The Dark Side of European Politics: Unmasking the Radical Right,' *Journal of European Integration*, 26(1), pp. 61–81.

Zeff, Eleanor E. and Pirro, Ellen B. (2001) *The European Union and the Member States: Cooperation, Coordination and Compromise* (Boulder: Lynne Rienner).

Zeidenitz, S. and Barkow, B. (1999) *The Xenophobe's Guide to the Germans* (London: Oval).

Zielinksi, Jakub (2002) 'Translating Social Cleavages into Party Systems: The Significance of New Democracies', *World Politics*, 54(2), pp. 184–211.

Zielinski, Jakub, Slomczynski, Kazimierz, M. and Shabad, Goldie (2005) 'Electoral Control in New Democracies: The Perverse Incentives of Fluid Party Systems', *World Politics*, 57(3), pp. 365–95.

Zielonka, Jan (ed.) (1998) *Paradoxes of European Foreign Policy* (London: Kluwer Law International).

Ziller, Jacques (2001) 'European Models of Government: Towards a Patchwork with Missing Pieces', *Parliamentary Affairs*, 54, pp. 102–19.

Zittel, Thomas (2004) 'Political Communication and Electronic Democracy: American Exceptionalism or Global Trend?', in Frank Esser and Barbara Pfetsch (eds), *Comparing Political Communication: Theories, Cases, and Challenges* (Cambridge: Cambridge University Press).

Zmerli, Sonja, Newton, Kenneth and Montero, José Ramón (2007) 'Trust in People, Confidence in Political Institutions and Satisfaction with Democracy', in Jan van Deth, José Ramón Montero, and Anders Westholm (eds), *Citizenship and Involvement in European Democracies: A Comparative Analysis* (London: Routledge).

Zohlnhöfer, Reimut and Obinger, Herbert (2006) 'Selling Off the "Family Silver": The Politics of Privatization,' *World Political Science Review*, 2(1), article 2, available at http://www.bepress.com/wpsr/vol2/iss1/art2

Zolo, Danilo (2007) *Globalisation: An Overview* (Colchester: ECPR Press).

Zoonen, Liesbet van (2006) 'The Personal, the Political and the Popular: A Woman's Guide to Celebrity Politics', *European Journal of Cultural Studies*, 9(3), pp. 287–301.

Zubek, Radoslaw (2006) 'Poland: a Core Ascendent?', in Vesselin Dimitrov, Klaus H. Goetz and Helmut Wollman (2006), *Governing after Communism: Institutions and Policy Making* (Lanham: Rowman & Littlefield).

Zürn, M. and Joerges, C. (eds) (2005) *Law and Governance in Postnational Europe* (Cambridge: Cambridge University Press).

Index

acquis communautaire 56, 58
administrative reform *see* new public management
Africa 304–5
ageing population 26, 32, 281, 294
agrarian parties *see* centre parties
aid 349, 357–61, 365
Albania 35, 327, 351
America *see* USA
Amsterdam, Treaty of *see under* European Union, treaties
Anglo-Saxon capitalism 271
anti-Americanism 339–40
anti-discrimination agencies 325
anti-war demo 243
army, European, 350–2
assimilation **323**
asylum 306, 310–14, 318, 322
asymmetrical federalism *see under* Spain
atheism 33
Australia 304, 363
Austria 11, 13, 24, 26, 32, 35, 41, 44, 60, 72, 75, 82, 91, 101, 110, 123, 138, 142, 145–7, 152, 157, 169, 174, 178, 180, 182, 185, 193–4, 211, 227, 232–4, 273, 278, 281, 300, 314–15, 317–19, 322, 325, 346, 351, 356

balance of power 12, 338
Basque country 46–9
Belgium 12, 15–16, 20, 26, 32–3, 35–6, 41–6, 57, 66–7, 72, 75, 82, 101, 107, 109–10, 114–15, 120, 142, 143, 145, 149–50, 157, 167, 170, 178, 182, 185, 194, 196, 207, 213, 232–3, 243, 250, 256, 296, 305, 309, 311, 315, 317, 325, 341, 346, 353, 356
bicameralism 115–18
bipolarization (two-bloc politics) 136, 156, 299
birth rate 26, 31, 309–10
blogging 228
Bosnia 43, 341
Britain *see* United Kingdom
Bulgaria 12–14, 18, 22, 33, 36, 66, 101, 115, 146, 150, 178, 194, 284, 314, 317, 319, 325, 331, 341, 346, 356
bureaucracy *see* civil service
business interests and organisations 254–5
'buycotts' 243

cabinet 87, **100**, 101, 104, 114–15
cabinet 83
Canada 363
capitalism 16, 22, 271–2, 274
cartel party 133
Catalunya (Catalonia) 49, 52, 141, 149, 155, 218–9
catch-all party 133, 190
centre parties, 150
China 22, 43, 68, 305, 340, 358, 361–4, 368
Christian democratic parties 142–3, 185–6, 207, 277
church attendance 33
citizenship 325
civil service 77–81
civil society **239**, 254, 256
class 26–8, 182–4
see also under elections, voting behaviour
cleavages **8**, 137–8, 150, 182–3
centre–periphery 137, 150
church–state 137, 143, 184–5
class (owner–worker) 26–8, 148, 182–4
democracy–totalitarianism 137
materialist–postmaterialist 137, 144, 149
multiculturalism–homogeneity 137
revolution–gradualism 137
rural–urban (land–industry) 137, 140, 151
voting behaviour 140, 153–5, 180, 184–5
CO_2 emissions 21
coalitions *see* government
coalition agreements 119
cohabitation 79
Cold War 7, 15, 148, 337–8, 342, 364
collective responsibility 114
Committee of Permanent Representatives (COREPER) *see under* European Union
Committee of Regions (COR) *see under* European Union
committees, parliamentary 121
common agricultural policy (CAP) *see* European Union, agriculture
Common Foreign and Security Policy (CFSP) *see* European Union, foreign policy

Commonwealth of Independent States 17
communism 13, 16–17, 146–8, 298
communist and left parties *see* left parties
compulsory voting *see* elections
confidence votes 107, 110, 117–18
consensus democracies 119
conservative parties 140–1, 277–9
constitutional courts 91–3
contract parliamentarism 107–8
core executive 72, 77–84
corporatism **240**, 247–8, 253–4, 261, 266–7, 290
Corsica 36, 53–4, 88
Cotonou Agreement 358–9
Council of Europe (CoE) 338
Council of Ministers *see under* European Union
Croatia 13, 43, 342, 366
Cuba 353, 364
curvilinear disparity 132
Cyprus 36, 55, 66–7, 69, 90, 101–2, 148, 157, 170, 251, 305, 307–8, 312–13, 325–6, 367
Czech Republic *see throughout* and country profile, 320–1

dealignment **153**, 155–7, 182, 185
decentralization 71–2, 76–7
decolonization 305
defence 336–43, 360
see also under EU, ESDP
democratic deficit 123–4, 266
democratization 167
Denmark 14, 30, 33, 35, 55, 62, 64, 65, 66, 72, 80, 101, 107–8, 114, 122, 145–6, 149, 155, 157, 173, 178, 180, 182–3, 194, 196–7, 233–4, 240, 250, 276, 281, 290, 300, 313–7, 320, 322, 326, 340, 346, 356, 358.
development assistance *see* aid
devolution 42, 45, 51, 52, 72
digital divide **229**
direct action 257, 260
direct democracy 167, 192–7
direct mail 230
domestic work 31

economy 16, 17–23, 55–6, 271ff
economic nationalism 287–8

education 8, 15, 26–30, 36, 45, 47, 49, 52, 61, 66, 74, 87, 89, 113, 118, 181, 183, 196, 201–2, 241, 246, 256, 259, 273, 279–80, 288, 298, 299, 307, 315, 321, 323–4, 332
  see also welfare
elections
  compulsory voting, 177, 179
  dealignment 153, 182
  electoral volatility 153, 179–80
  electronic voting 168
  European Parliament elections 191–2
  timing 168
  turnout 175–9, 191–2
  voting age 167
  voting behaviour 180–90
    class 182–4; ethnicity and race 188–90; gender 189; 'issue voting' 189–90; leaders 189–90; media *see* media, effect on voting; party identification 180–1; values 18
electoral systems
  district magnitude 171
  'electoral engineering' 172
  electoral formulas 173
  impact on party systems 152, 173–5
  plurality/majority (first past the post/FPP) **168–9**
  proportional systems 168–73; (list PR 170; mixed 170–1; single transferable vote (STV) 171
  thresholds 171
empires
  Austro-Hungarian 12, 41
  British 12
  Holy Roman 10
  Macedonian 9
  Ottoman 11–12
  Roman 9
Russian 12
  Soviet 7–13
  Spanish 10
energy 346, 350
England *see* United Kingdom
environment 361–2
Estonia 13, 17, 20, 22, 36, 42, 101, 168, 170, 178, 194, 241, 325, 341, 347
ethnicity 35, 303
ethnic parties *see* regional and ethnic parties
ethnonationalism *see* minority nationalism
euro *see* European union, single currency
Eurocorps 351, 370
European Central Bank (ECB) *see under* European Union
European Convention on/European Court of Human Rights (ECHR) 91, 96, 265, 338, 324
European Council *see under* European Union
European Environmental Agency (EEA) 265
European Free Trade Association (EFTA) 56
European identity 35–7
European Parliament *see under* European Union
European Trade Union Confederation (ETUC) 267–9
European Union
  Africa 358–60
  agriculture 20, 55–9, 63, 87, 233, 249, 263, 292, 307, 360, 363–4
  aid 357–61
  Asia 364–5
  budget 59, 63, 297
  CFSP *see* foreign policy
  Charter of Fundamental Rights 65
  China 364
  Committee of the Regions (CoR) 55
  common external tariff (CET) 55–6
  constitution (constitutional treaty) 64–6, 192
  COREPER 62, 114
  Council of Ministers (Council of the European Union) 62
  corporatism 267
  decision-making process 63, 65, 124
  directives **58**
  domestic political competition, effect on 192
  Dublin Accord 326
  Economic and Monetary Union (EMU) *see* single currency
  enlargement 17, 57, 83, 197, 365–8
  environmental policy 21, 265, 361–2
  European Central Bank (ECB) 59, 64
  European Coal and Steel Community (ECSC) 14,55
  European Commission 55, 58, 65, 74, 263, 266, 286–9, 291–3, 346, 357, 359, 363
  European Council 62, 65, 124, 162, 260
  European Court of Justice (ECJ) 56, 58, 63–6, 90, 95–6, 98, 207–8, 211, 265, 287, 292–3, 338
  European Economic Community (EEC) 14
European Neighbourhood Policy (ENP) 347–50
  European Parliament 59, 63, 65, 123–6, 162–3, 169, 191–2, 232, 265, 331
European Security and Defence Policy (ESDP) 340–1, 350–1, 356–7
  foreign perceptions of 361
  foreign policy (CFSP) 63, 65, 351–3, 356–7
  history 14, 15, 17
  immigration 326–30
  intergovernmentalism and supranationalism 56
  justice and home affairs (JHA) 63
  Lisbon process 286
  media 207–8, 230–3
  neo-liberalism 290–3
  pillars 63–5
  pressure groups 263–8
  pros and cons of membership 68
  qualified majority voting (QMV) 58–9
  referendums 65, 197
  regional aid 293
  regionalism 75
  regulations 58
  Russia 344–8
  Schengen Agreement 326
  services directive 265, 293
  single currency 63–4, 290ff.
  Single European Act of 1987 (SEA) 56, 95, 263
  single/internal market 55–6, 58, 63, 95, 207, 263, 265, 290–2, 345, 347, 349, 366
  social chapter and social policy 267, 281
  Stability and Growth Pact (SGP) 290–1
  structural funds 6, 68, 75
  trade 23, 362–5
  terrorism 348
  Treaties: Amsterdam 63, 65, 123, 207–8, 326, 341, 357; Lisbon 64–6 Maastricht (Treaty on European Union – TEU) 62–3, 65, 74, 92, 267, 341, 353; Nice 59, 65, 197, 341, 352; Rome 55, 65
  Transatlantic relations 362, 364
  Turkey 361, 367
  United Nations (UN) 336
Europeanization 5, 8, 22–3, 64, 75, 83–5, 87–90, 94–5, 153, 162–4, 201, 208, 230–3, 263–8, 271, 289–93, 324, 326, 328, 330, 344, 352, 356–7, 360
eurozone 22

farming lobby 248–50
far right 146, 157, 299–300, 317–19, 321–3
fascism 14
Federal Republic of Germany *see* Germany

federal states **44**, 72
federal and unitary government 72–3
Finance Ministers 104
Finland 14, 17, 26, 33, 36, 66, 101, 107, 109, 119, 134, 145, 148, 150, 155, 157, 169–70, 178, 182, 194, 250, 276, 294, 315, 326, 346, 351, 354, 356
First World War 13
foreign direct investment (FDI) 22, 265, 362
foreign policy 328
fortress Europe 330
France *see throughout and* country profile, 88–9
Franco-German axis 61
freezing hypothesis *see under* party systems

Georgia 7, 13, 17, 346–7
gender inequality 29–32, 127
Germany *see throughout* and country profile 60–1
Gibraltar 48
glasnost 16
globalization 3, 8, 22–3,8, 190, 234, 241, 257, 271–2, 274, 276–7, 283–4, 290, 295, 299–300, 330
Gorbachev, Mikhail 16
governance 5, 61, 68, 71–99, 113, 123, 128, 158, 162, 186–7, 200–1, 210, 219, 247–8, 259, 264, 297, 321, 338, 345, 355, 360
government
  duration and stability 110
  formation 105–11
  portfolio allocation 110–11
  types of 105–11
grand coalition 109–10
Greece 9, 14, 16, 20, 24, 26, 28, 32–3, 75, 82, 87, 91, 101, 105, 119–20, 138, 140, 145, 157, 167, 170, 173, 178, 188, 194, 207, 209, 211, 251, 256, 273, 278, 292, 313, 315, 317, 325, 332, 346, 366
gross domestic product (GDP) 17–18
green parties 143–6, 157
gypsies *see* Roma

head of state (monarchs and presidents) 101–2
health *see* welfare
Holocaust 14, 34, 60, 147, 258, 305, 331
Hungary 11–14, 20, 22, 27, 33, 36, 41, 43, 66, 102, 107–8, 110, 112, 140, 142, 150, 157, 171, 178, 193–4, 201, 206–7, 251, 253, 281–2, 293, 325, 331–2, 339, 341

Iceland 56, 178, 326
immigration *see* migration
income distribution *see* inequality
India 68, 358, 361–2, 365, 368
industrialization 12–13, 19–21, 183
inequality 26–30
inflation 16, 18–19, 22, 64, 248, 253, 271, 273–4, 279, 281, 290
integration (of immigrants) 234
interest groups *see* pressure groups
International Monetary Fund (IMF) 24
Internet *see* media
investiture vote 107
Iraq 69, 81, 113, 187, 219, 234, 243, 273, 311–12, 229–342, 344, 350–1, 357
Ireland, Republic of 18, 24, 27, 32–3, 41, 50–1, 55, 90, 94, 101–2, 105, 107, 119–20, 145, 155, 157, 168, 171, 174, 176, 178, 182–3, 193–4, 196–7, 211–12, 230, 233, 246, 252–3, 256, 273, 314–15, 325–6, 346, 356
Irish peace process 50–1
Irish Republican Army (IRA) 50–1
Iron law of oligarchy 134
irredentism 41
Islam 34–5
Islamophobia 316
Israel 344, 348–50, 358, 361, 364
issue networks **84**, 248, 356
issue voting *see* elections, voting behaviour
issue ownership 189
Italy *see throughout* and country profile 186–7

Japan 12–14, 18, 21, 26, 56, 60, 324, 342, 361–3, 369
Jews 32, 34–5
joined-up government 82
judicial review **94**
judicialization 90–6
judiciary 90–6
juristocracy 90

Keynesian economics 18–19, 208
Kosovo 35, 43, 61, 344–5, 350–1, 355
Kyoto 361–2

labour force 29–30
Latvia 13, 17, 22, 36, 42, 110, 143, 178, 194, 241, 251, 252, 341, 354
Lebanon 344
Left parties 146–9, 157, 295–6
legislation/law-making 118–19
legislature *see* parliaments
Liechtenstein 56
Liberal parties 142–3
Lisbon Treaty *see* EU, treaties
Lithuania 13, 17, 22, 42, 101–2, 108, 110, 122, 143, 152, 168, 171, 178, 195, 241, 251, 325, 341, 346
local government 72–3, 78
Luxembourg 55, 58, 178, 208, 315, 325, 341, 351, 357

Maastricht Treaty *see under* European Union, treaties
majoritarian versus consensual systems 119
Malta 33, 55, 90, 105, 140, 168–9, 171, 174, 178, 251, 308, 312–13, 325, 328
Marshall Plan 14
manifestos 272–3, 275
mayors 78
media
  attack dog journalism 217, 220
  Berlusconi 222, 230
  censorship 200, 209–10
  effect on voting, 221–6
  Europeanization and EU 207–8, 230–3
  'fourth estate' 200
  Internet 228–9
  mediatization 200
  news values 203
  newspapers 201–7
  ownership 205–7
  political bias 221
  political coverage: advertising and debates 214–15; aggressive 217, 220; fragmentation 212–13; commercial media logic 213–14; personalization 216–17
  political interference 206, 211
  pressure groups 226–7
  public broadcasting 208–10
  radio 204
  soundbites 216
  structure and regulation 204–8
  systems 155, 201, 210–12
  television 201–3, 204–10, 212–16, 220–2, 224–7 231–2, 234
  trust 224
  usage variations in 201–2
Mediterranean 349
members of parliament, representativeness of 127
Mezzogiorno *see under* Italy
migration
  assimilation 323
  asylum 297, 304, 306–7, 310–14, 317–18, 322, 326–33
  demographics of migrants 307–8
  employment of migrants 309
  EU 326–330
  EU-A8 314–15
  foreign population 307
  historical flows 304–7
  integration 323–6
  multiculturalism 323

migration – *continued*
national regimes, persistence of 326–30
numbers coming to Europe 303
perceptions (negative) of 310–16
pros and cons 327
stereotypes of migrants 309, 315
types of 306
welfare 330
see also immigration
military *see* defence
minimal connected winning coalition 106
minimal winning coalition 105–6
minority governments 49, 103, 105–6, 107, 108, 110, 122, 126, 155, 256, 273
minority nationalism 36, 40–54, 66–7
ministers 103–5, 113–15
resignations, 78
mixed economy 23
MMP *see* electoral systems, proportional systems, mixed
mobile phones 229–30
moderate multipartism 107–8
modernization thesis 181
monarchy *see under* head of state
multiculturalism 323
multilevel governance 5, 68, 72, 75, 84, 162, 231, 258, 261–2, 264, 266, 268, 338, 357
see also governance
Muslims *see* Islam

nation state 40, 65–8
nationalism 12, 36, 42, 66–8, 140–1, 146, 188
negative parliamentarism 107
neo-liberalism 271, 272, 278–9, 290–1
Netherlands *see throughout* and country profile 296–7
new public management (NPM) 77–81, 245
new social movements 241, 255–7, 260–3
New Zealand 16, 363
news values 203, 213–4, 225, 227
Nice, Treaty of *see under* European Union, treaties
North Atlantic Treaty Organization (NATO) 141, 345, 339, 341, 344, 352, 355
Northern Ireland 50–51
Norway 7, 14, 17–18, 26, 29–30, 56, 68, 101, 105, 107, 109–10, 116, 118, 143, 145, 149, 152, 157, 168, 178, 180, 182, 194, 209, 214, 234, 240, 247, 276, 287, 300, 317, 319, 322–3, 326, 338, 346, 351, 357
'old' Europe 339–40

Organisation for Economic Co-operation and Development (OECD) 79, 83, 286
Organization on Security and Co-operation in Europe (OSCE) 338
overseas development assistance (ODA) 358
oversized majority coalitions 109–110

Padania 44
Parliament 115–28
participation
unconventional as conventional 241
geographically skewed 243–4
socially skewed 241–2
elite-challenging behaviour, rise of 242
intensity of, high and low 241–2, 244
group membership 245
transnational activism 260
parties 131
families 136–50, 156
candidate selection 134–5
Europeanization 162–4
funding 159
freezing hypothesis 136, 153
members 132–3, 158
organization 132–5
parliamentary parties 126–8
party discipline 126
party identification 180–1
party system 131, 135–8, 150–3
party system change 153–8
roles/functions 132
survival of 158–62
transnational 129–31
trust in 132
pay gap 31
pensions and pensioners 25, 87, 89, 93, 95, 155, 187, 219, 231, 252–4, 279–82, 289, 294, 321, 327, 354
perestroika 14
pluralism 247
plurality/majority *see under* electoral systems
Poland *see throughout and* country profile 259–60
policy communities 84, 248–9, 261, 356
policy influence differential 108
policy-making 84–7
policy networks 84, 247–8
policy style 84, 85–7
population decline 26
political opportunity structure 246
'politics matters' 273
politicization of the bureaucracy, 81–3
populism 146, 197, 227, 249, 300, 315
populist radical right parties *see* far right

Portugal 10, 13–15, 18, 20, 24, 28, 32–3, 87, 91, 101–2, 107, 120, 138, 145, 169, 173, 178, 182, 194, 196, 211, 232, 240, 251, 256, 284, 292, 305–6, 308, 315, 325, 339, 346, 353, 356, 367
position issues 189
post-industrialism 20–1, 183
postmaterialism 183
postwar boom 16
poverty 27
presidents *see* head of state
pressure groups
asymmetry of interests 249, 255
business associations 254–5
campaign/cause group functions 261
collective action problem 255
and democracy 262
Europeanization 263–8
farming lobby 248–50
insider–outsider distinction 245–6, 260–1
and parliament 246
and parties 247
protest businesses 260–1
trade unions 250–4
presidentialization 104
prime minister 102–5
private members' bills 118–19
privatization 21–2, 77, 283–8
proportional representation (PR) *see under* electoral systems

qualified majority voting (QMV) *see under* European Union

race 303
radio 204
rational choice 256
referendums 192–7, 152–5, 240
see also under European Union
regional and ethnic parties 150
regional aid *see under* European Union
regional government 73–6
regional variations (in economy) 19–20
regionalism *see under* European Union
religion 32–5, 41, 81, 109, 114–5, 137–8, 143, 146, 153, 184–8, 190, 246, 316, 324, 345, 367
representative democracy 167, 192, 272
Roma 14, 330–3
Roman law 90–1
Romania 12, 14, 17–18, 20, 22, 33, 36, 41, 66, 101–2, 105, 110, 116, 150, 171, 178, 187, 194, 240, 284, 314, 319, 325, 331–2, 341, 346
Rome, Treaty of *see under* European Union, treaties

Russia 7, 12–14, 22, 28, 42–3, 258–9, 311, 339, 344–8, 350, 358, 361–2, 368
see also Soviet Union

Schengen Agreement *see under* European Union
Scotland 42, 51–2
Second World War 7, 13–14
security 337
secularization 43, 81, 136, 185
security community 340
semi-presidentialism 101–2
separation of powers 71–72, 100
Serbia 12–13, 35, 41, 43, 311, 358
single currency *see under* European Union
Single European Act of 1987 *see under* European Union
single transferable vote (STV) *see under* electoral systems
Slovakia 17, 20, 22, 36, 41–2, 45–6, 66, 101, 105, 145–6, 150, 172, 178, 194, 257, 317, 320, 325, 326, 331, 341, 346
Slovenia 13, 20, 22, 26, 43, 64, 66, 101–2, 105, 142–3, 146, 178, 194, 240, 251, 324, 341–2
social capital 239, 244
social democracy 271, 274–7, 288–9, 295, 298–9, 319
socialism 12, 14, 138–9, 267, 274, 283, 298
see also social democracy
socialist and social democratic parties 138–40
soft power 340, 350
sovereignty 40, 64–5, 67
Soviet Union 13, 14–15, 40–1, 338–9
Spain *see throughout* and country profile 218–19
stability and growth pact *see under* European Union
state aid 95, 208, 288
supply-side policies 288–90, 292
support party 107–8
surplus majority coalitions 109–10
Sweden *see throughout and* country profile 354–5
Switzerland 7, 13, 18, 26, 32, 35–6, 44, 56, 68, 72–4, 116, 120, 124, 143, 145–6, 167, 170, 177–8, 182, 192–7, 208, 211, 234, 240, 273, 284, 310–13, 317–18, 324, 338

tax 25–6, 29, 47, 49, 51–2, 56, 64, 72–3, 76, 130, 139–41, 144, 146, 148, 183, 190, 206, 233, 246, 248, 254, 257, 274, 277–95, 306, 327, 330, 354–5, 361
television *see* media, television
terrorism 34,47, 50, 53, 68, 91, 113, 115, 141, 218–19, 222, 234, 315, 319, 330, 337, 345, 348, 350, 363, 367
'Third Way' 271, 274–5, 285, 288
trade 23, 362–5
trade unions 19, 24, 61, 89, 115, 138–140, 142–3, 150, 185, 228, 240, 247–8, 250–4, 257, 265–7, 273, 278–9, 280–1, 285, 289, 283, 300, 314, 321, 357
transition from communism 21–2
transnational party federations 162–3
Trianon, Treaty of 13
trust, in politicians, judges and the media 96, 224
Turkey 7, 11, 13, 18, 21, 35, 67, 311, 341, 358, 361, 367

Ukraine 7, 13, 17, 57, 326, 338, 345–8
Ulster *see* Northern Ireland
unemployment 16, 19, 22, 28, 30, 112, 252, 271, 273, 277, 279, 285, 288–9, 300, 309, 315, 332
unitary government *see* federal and unitary government
unitary states 40, **44**, 47, 54, 66, 72–3, 116
see also federal and unitary government
United Kingdom *see throughout* and country profile 112–13
United Nations 13, 67, 331, 336, 342, 344, 351, 357, 362
United States of America 13–15, 18, 21–4, 44, 50, 56, 72, 74, 83–4, 90–1, 94, 101, 103,105, 115, 118, 120, 122, 125–7, 135, 140, 176, 182, 188, 193, 202, 209, 212, 214, 217, 220, 227–31, 233–4, 323, 330, 337–46, 350–1, 358, 361–5
USSR *see* Soviet Union

'velvet divorce' 45–6
Versailles, Treaty of 13
voting *see* elections

Wales 51–2
Wallonia (Wallonie) 44–6
Warsaw Pact 15, 41, 339
welfare state (includes spending and reform 8, 15, 23–6, 28–30, 32, 61–2, 80, 87, 89, 113, 140–4, 146, 148–51, 164, 180, 183, 188–90, 211, 217, 275–84, 298–300, 305, 319–21, 323, 328, 330–1, 354–5
Western European Union (WEU) 341
women
- employment 29–32, 61, 222, 289
- fertility 26, 31
- media use 202
- muslims 316, 324
- parliament 127, 176
- participation 243
- party leaders in the media 215
- voting 167, 189

working class 13, 14, 27–9, 35, 127, 139–40, 146, 150, 170, 182–3, 185, 299, 319
World Bank 24, 258, 279, 287, 294, 307
World Trade Organization (WTO) 58, 208, 345, 360, 362–5
World Wars 1, 6–7
see also First World War, Second World War

xenophobia 44, 146, 186, 196, 271, 317, 319–20, 325

Yugoslavia (and former) 7, 13, 42–3, 311, 329, 341–2, 344, 350, 355